Politics, Protest, and Empowerment in Digital Spaces

Yasmin Ibrahim
Queen Mary, University of London, UK

A volume in the Advances in Electronic Government, Digital Divide, and Regional Development (AEGDDRD) Book Series

IGI GLOBAL
DISSEMINATOR OF KNOWLEDGE

www.igi-global.com

Published in the United States of America by
IGI Global
Information Science Reference (an imprint of IGI Global)
701 E. Chocolate Avenue
Hershey PA, USA 17033
Tel: 717-533-8845
Fax: 717-533-8661
E-mail: cust@igi-global.com
Web site: http://www.igi-global.com

Library of Congress Cataloging-in-Publication Data

CIP Data Pending

ISBN: 978-1-5225-1862-4
eISBN: 978-1-5225-1863-1

This book is published in the IGI Global book series Advances in Electronic Government, Digital Divide, and Regional Development (AEGDDRD) (ISSN: 2326-9103; eISSN: 2326-9111)

British Cataloguing in Publication Data
A Cataloguing in Publication record for this book is available from the British Library.

For electronic access to this publication, please contact: eresources@igi-global.com.

Advances in Electronic Government, Digital Divide, and Regional Development (AEGDDRD) Book Series

Zaigham Mahmood
University of Derby, UK & North West University, South Africa

ISSN:2326-9103
EISSN:2326-9111

Mission

The successful use of digital technologies (including social media and mobile technologies) to provide public services and foster economic development has become an objective for governments around the world. The development towards electronic government (or e-government) not only affects the efficiency and effectiveness of public services, but also has the potential to transform the nature of government interactions with its citizens. Current research and practice on the adoption of electronic/digital government and the implementation in organizations around the world aims to emphasize the extensiveness of this growing field.

The Advances in Electronic Government, Digital Divide & Regional Development (AEGDDRD) book series aims to publish authored, edited and case books encompassing the current and innovative research and practice discussing all aspects of electronic government development, implementation and adoption as well the effective use of the emerging technologies (including social media and mobile technologies) for a more effective electronic governance (or e-governance).

Coverage

- Social Media, Web 2.0, and Mobile Technologies in E-Government
- ICT Infrastructure and Adoption for E-Government Provision
- Knowledge Divide, Digital Divide
- E-Citizenship, Inclusive Government, Connected Government
- Public Information Management, Regional Planning, Rural Development
- ICT within Government and Public Sectors
- Frameworks and Methodologies for E-Government Development
- E-Governance and Use of Technology for Effective Government
- Issues and Challenges in E-Government Adoption
- Online Government, E-Government, M-Government

IGI Global is currently accepting manuscripts for publication within this series. To submit a proposal for a volume in this series, please contact our Acquisition Editors at Acquisitions@igi-global.com or visit: http://www.igi-global.com/publish/.

The Advances in Electronic Government, Digital Divide, and Regional Development (AEGDDRD) Book Series (ISSN 2326-9103) is published by IGI Global, 701 E. Chocolate Avenue, Hershey, PA 17033-1240, USA, www.igi-global.com. This series is composed of titles available for purchase individually; each title is edited to be contextually exclusive from any other title within the series. For pricing and ordering information please visit http://www.igi-global.com/book-series/advances-electronic-government-digital-divide/37153. Postmaster: Send all address changes to above address.

Titles in this Series

For a list of additional titles in this series, please visit: www.igi-global.com

Population Growth and Rapid Urbanization in the Developing World
Umar G. Benna (Ahmadu Bello University, Nigeria) and Shaibu Bala Garba (Qatar University, Qatar)
Information Science Reference • copyright 2016 • 358pp • H/C (ISBN: 9781522501879) • US $205.00 (our price)

Political Discourse in Emergent, Fragile, and Failed Democracies
Daniel Ochieng Orwenjo (Technical University of Kenya, Kenya) Omondi Oketch (Technical University of Kenya, Kenya) and Asiru Hameed Tunde (Umaru Musa Yar'adua University, Nigeria)
Information Science Reference • copyright 2016 • 412pp • H/C (ISBN: 9781522500810) • US $185.00 (our price)

International Perspectives on Socio-Economic Development in the Era of Globalization
Saurabh Sen (Sunbeam College for Women, India) Anshuman Bhattacharya (Sunbeam College for Women, India) and Ruchi Sen (Sunbeam College for Women, India)
Business Science Reference • copyright 2016 • 288pp • H/C (ISBN: 9781466699083) • US $175.00 (our price)

Comparative Political and Economic Perspectives on the MENA Region
M. Mustafa Erdoğdu (Marmara University, Turkey) and Bryan Christiansen (PryMarke, LLC, USA)
Information Science Reference • copyright 2016 • 386pp • H/C (ISBN: 9781466696013) • US $205.00 (our price)

Handbook of Research on Entrepreneurial Success and its Impact on Regional Development
Luísa Carvalho (Universidade Aberta, Portugal & CEFAGE, Universidade de Évora, Portugal)
Information Science Reference • copyright 2016 • 878pp • H/C (ISBN: 9781466695672) • US $430.00 (our price)

Trends, Prospects, and Challenges in Asian E-Governance
Inderjeet Singh Sodhi (St. Wilfred's P.G. College, India)
Information Science Reference • copyright 2016 • 410pp • H/C (ISBN: 9781466695368) • US $190.00 (our price)

Handbook of Research on Comparative Approaches to the Digital Age Revolution in Europe and the Americas
Brasilina Passarelli (School of Communications and Arts, University of São Paulo, Brazil) Joseph Straubhaar (The University of Texas at Austin, USA) and Aurora Cuevas-Cerveró (Complutense University of Madrid, Spain)
Information Science Reference • copyright 2016 • 530pp • H/C (ISBN: 9781466687400) • US $325.00 (our price)

Cloud Computing Technologies for Connected Government
Zaigham Mahmood (University of Derby, UK & North West University, South Africa)
Information Science Reference • copyright 2016 • 416pp • H/C (ISBN: 9781466686298) • US $195.00 (our price)

To Vappa and the children who are forced to leave behind their homelands for a better life.

Table of Contents

Detailed Table of Contents

The self is performed through the banal of the everyday on social media. The banality of the everyday constitutes an integral part of our communication on digital platforms. Taking this as part of our performative lives in the digital economy, the paper looks at ways in which we co-produce the self through the banality of the everyday as well as a wider imagination and engagement with the world. These wider engagements are termed as 'fictive' not because they are unreal but through a conceptual notion of how the self is performed and imagined through wider world events in digital platforms and screen cultures where convergence of technologies allow us to be constantly consumed through the screen as we live out our daily lives. The narration of our lives through the banal and the fictive constantly co-produces the self through a situated domesticity of the everyday and equally through the eventful. In the process it reveals our ongoing relationship with the screen as an orifice for the production of self and the construction of a social reality beyond our immediate domesticity.

Widely influential low-carb high fat diet (LCHF) promoters have been using social media to marshal support when contesting the nutritional recommendations provided by the National Swedish Food Agency (NFA). Political events led to an increased public awareness of the LCHF diet, which in turn provided the advocates with vital opportunities to contest the established nutritional authorities. This study explored how three of the leading promoters transact their criticisms of nutrition authorities, and how they use social media for this purpose. A longitudinal thematic analysis of the diet promoters' social media presence demonstrates that they made full use of media convergence to form opinion and attain their goals. The LCHF promoters utilized a rhetorical arsenal based in science popularization to appeal to the public and social media allowed for the spread of anecdotal evidence of individual dieters. Interestingly, social media also facilitated the advocates to network their expertise and to start science initiatives evolving from merely anecdotal methods to conventional approaches.

This chapter discusses the impact of transmedia campaigns aimed at achieving a certain level of government policy change. Transmedia campaigns comprise a series of coordinated activities and organized efforts designed to achieve a social, political, or commercial goal by means of multiple media platforms. The Great British Property Scandal and Food, Inc. transmedia campaigns are considered to introduce the argument that this kind of multiplatform campaigning can actually produce concrete results in the political sphere. Moreover, this chapter focuses on the in-depth analysis of the transmedia strategies of the Fish Fight campaign to demonstrate how exactly transmedia strategies collaborate to influence policy change. The research findings point to the effective role of transmedia storytelling strategies in raising awareness in the political sphere through public participation in supporting relevant issues, influencing policy change.

In this chapter, we expand the idea that conflict avoidance (CA) inhibits online political participation. We specifically propose that CA has a direct negative link with traditional online political participation and online political expression, and an indirect negative link with these two forms of participation when mediated by political interest and internal political efficacy. We test our propositions through analyzing data from a survey of young adult college students residing in a battleground state in the U.S. Midwest conducted during the weeks prior to the 2012 U.S. presidential election. Our results showed that CA has a direct negative association with both traditional online political participation and online political expression. CA also has a negative relationship with political interest and internal political efficacy, which in turn, are positively linked with traditional online political participation and online political expression. We discussed implications.

Political messaging is adapting to new digital spaces. However, the power of citizens through the use of this digital spaces is still unknown. Many citizens criticize political candidates using Facebook or Twitter, others build networks in Snapchat and some others try to collaborate with candidates using Periscope or WhatsApp. This research is focused in understanding this adaptation of political message on this platforms, analyzing the case of the presidential candidate Enrique Peña Nieto (PRI) in Mexico who won the presidency with a large participation but without the support of Twitter users. After two online protests against this presidential candidate - #IamnotProletariat and #Iam132 – political image could have been undermined and voters could have thought differently. But this was not the case and despite of this, the candidate won. The challenge to understand this online protest and its link to the political message is addressed in this paper.

Within Western democracies there has been a growing demand to use ICT to enable citizens to get more involved with local political issues. Western local governments have claimed that ICT can empower citizens and strengthen local democracy. This chapter will focus on one aspect of this and examine the provision of online direct democracy and whether citizens do indeed have the opportunity to vote more in local policy decision making. Using Michel Foucault's concepts of power and domination this research will explore if local governments and their citizens, through strategies of power, use one type of ICT, online forums, to change local representative democracy. In order to examine whether online forums can increase direct democracy for citizens, a quantitative data collection method was implemented in this study which produced a data set of 138 online forums. This article argues that online forums do not increase direct democracy, because citizens along with local governments use ICT to maintain the political status quo online?

This study focuses on the political strategies that are utilized in the context of eLearning. The starting point for this paper is the eLearning Political Strategies (ELPoS) model. The model is based on two dimensions: 1) the direction of the political strategy (upward or downward), and 2) the scope of the political strategy (individual or group based). The interaction between the above dimensions defines four types of eLearning political strategies, which result in different political outcomes. The presentation of the model is followed by four mini case studies that demonstrate the political strategies that the model outlines. The discussion and conclusion sections integrate the findings from the case studies and elaborate on the rules that govern the application of political strategies in different eLearning contexts.

Austerity food blogs have come to the fore with the emergence of a neoliberal ideology of austerity, which in Britain has seen cuts to welfare benefits legitimized through individual failure explanations of poverty and the stigmatizing of benefit claimants. The consequence has been to distance ministers from food poverty and de-politicize it. Austerity food blogs, written by those forced to live hand-to-mouth, are a hybrid form of digital culture that merge narratives of lived experience, food practices and political commentary in ways that challenge the dominant views on poverty so re-politicize it. A Girl Called Jack did this by breaking the silence that the stigma of poverty imposes, by personalizing hunger through Jack Monroe's narratives of her lived experience of it and inviting the pity of the reader. Monroe also challenged austerity through practices derived during the struggle to survive and eat healthily on £10-a-week food budget. Her blog resonated powerfully but also revealed a British society deeply uneasy and polarized over modern poverty.

In our digital world, our notions of intimacy, communion and sharing are increasingly enacted through new media technologies and social practices which emerge around them. These technologies with the ability to upload, download and disseminate content to select audiences or to a wider public provide opportunities for the creation of new forms of rituals which authenticate and diarise everyday experiences. Our consumption cultures in many ways celebrate the notion of the exhibit and the spectacle, inviting gaze, through everyday objects and rituals. Food as a vital part of culture, identity, belonging, and meaning making celebrates both the everyday and the invitation to renew connections through food as a universal subject of appeal.

Internet trolling describe the posting of any content on the Internet which is provocative or offensive, which is different from the original meaning online in the 1990s, referring to the posting of messages for humourous effect. Those systems operators (sysops) who run online communities are being targeted because of abuse posted on their platforms. Political discussion groups are some of the most prone to trolling, whether consensual or unwanted. Many such websites ara open for anyone to join, meaning when some members post messages they know are offensive but legal, others might find grossly offensive, meaning these messages could be illegal. This paper develops a questionnaire called the This Is Why We Can't Have Nice Things Scale (TIWWCHNT-20), which aims to help sysops better plan the development of online communities to take account of different users' capacity to be offended, and for users to self-assess whether they will be suited to an online community. The scale is discussed in relation to different Internet posting techniques where different users will act differently.

The use of negative ads in traditional election campaigns has been well-documented, but we know little about the use of Twitter to "go negative." We content analyze candidate tweets from four different gubernatorial elections in 2011 to understand how candidates are using Twitter. We coded 849 tweets to explain the determinants of "going negative" on Twitter. Our results show that while tweets are overwhelmingly positive, candidates go negative by tweeting about policy. We believe this supports the innovation hypothesis and argue that Twitter is a conducive social media forum for policy-based messages due to its highly partisan nature. However, other determinants of negative campaigning such as competitiveness of the race and campaign funding were consistent with the normalization hypothesis. Our mixed results are consistent with other studies on social media and suggest there is still much to be learned from this tool.

Numerous researchers have found a correlation between citizens' use of social networking sites (SNS) like Facebook and their likelihood for eParticipation. However, SNS use does not have the same effect on all citizens' political engagement. In authoritarian countries, Facebook offers a platform for citizens to challenge the power of the state, provide alternative narratives and mobilise for political change. This chapter examines how using Facebook affects the participative behaviours of Ugandans and concludes that in low internet use, authoritarian contexts, the Civic Voluntarism Model's postulation of the factors that explain political participation, and the benefits Facebook brings to participation in Western democracies, are upended. Overwhelming detachment from politics, low belief in citizens' online actions influencing change and fear of reprisals for criticising an authoritarian president in power for 30 years, severely dulled the appetite for eParticipation. Hence, Facebook was growing citizens' civic skills but hardly increasing online participation.

This chapter covers the pressing issues of online free expression at the time of global telecommunication services and social media. What once was the domain of the state has become the prerogative of private global companies – it is their terms of service and sense of social responsibility that have replaced local perceptions of morality and set limits to individual personal rights. Whether protecting privacy or defending against defamation, it is the Internet Service Provider who can offer tools far more effective and prompt than any national court and law enforcement agency. And even though the right to free expression is firmly rotted in the global standard of article 19 UDHR, nowhere than online are the differences in its interpretation, originated by history, morality and religion, more palpable. The paper aims to discuss each of the three composite rights of free expression (the right to hold, impart and receive information and ideas) and identify the actual limitations originated by national laws. The author emphasizes states' positive obligation to take active measures aimed at protecting free expression, ensuring that all human rights are "protected, respected and remedied". This obligation makes the interrelationship between national lawmakers and international telecommunication service providers complex as the latter serve as the actual gate keepers of free expression in the information society. The paper covers a discussion on how different countries deal with this challenge through various approaches to ISP liability, including the notice-and-take down procedure as well as content filtering (preventive censorship). The author goes on to criticize those mechanisms as enabling ISPs too much freedom in deciding upon the shape and scope of individuals' right to impart and receive information.

Delegated transferable voting (DTV) refers to an approach to counting votes in elections that extends non-preferential voting systems like First Past The Post (FPTP) to include a transferable element similar to Single Transferable Voting (STV) but instead of voters indicating who they wish their votes to go to on an individual level they entrust that decision in the candidate they vote for, who could be from a small political party that might otherwise be deemed a "wasted vote" under first-past-the-post systems where the candidate they least want could win by having the most votes but still have less than 50% of the popular vote. This chapter discusses how DTV might work in practice through an auto-ethnographic approach in which the authors play an active part in elections in order to test the approach. The elections contested in the UK included to local council level in the Pontypridd area and national elections to the UK Parliament and Welsh Assembly. The potential impact of DTV on these election and method of campaigning used at some of these elections might have had on the voting outcome are discussed.

This chapter employs irony as a tool to make clearer the workings of one form of the e-politics of food, namely, the structural food oppression linked to the weight and shape of the female body. The authors argue that the e-politics of the weight and shape of the female body is one of the most important incarnations of the e-politics of food and one of the most vigorously contested. This chapter examines many forms of public discourse and e-politics, from Bing to Tumblr, from Huffington Post to the Mirror (UK), from TV news in Lacrosse, Wisconsin to The Times of India, from the documentary film Killing Us Softly to the book You Are What You Eat, and from WebMD to Twitter, in the end, with a central focus on Rachel Frederickson on the TV show, The Biggest Loser. The critical rhetorical analysis finds some support for the Women Can't Win thesis. Women are in a Catch-22 situation, trapped between fat-shaming and skinny-shaming.

In the context of the new media environment, several social, political and economic divides are being produced. As the effects of those changes are not neutral, because of gender inequality, the status of women's human rights in the digital age are precarious. To what extent does the new media environment promote women's human and communication rights or contribute to sustaining the oppression of women in society? Based on the feminist political economy perspective, the aim of this paper is to analyze some of the critical issues on gender equality and ICTs in Latin America.

In today's screen saturated culture, perceptions of food are overwhelmingly formed by images circulated via the internet and mobile. The Facebook game FarmVille is the subject of Kheti Badi (Shah, 2015), a photographic artwork reflexively engaging with the contemporary scenario of 'post-photography'. The work comprises not of photographs taken with a traditional camera but of screenshots of a farm and its holdings as displayed in Farmville; the highly compressed jpegs cropped and resized to the point of destabilizing visual coherence are depictions not of pastoral landscapes but of computer vision and the programmable character of photography. While photography remains an instrument for recording material realities, its power extends toward feeding back into the very processes through which science and technology modify food production. This chapter explores how Kheti Badi, through a series of hyper artificial and un-photographic images, shows the constructed nature of both what we put our hands on in the supermarket and see in advertising's dreamscapes.

The starting point for this paper is the eLearning Political Strategies (ELPoS) model. The model is based on two dimensions: 1) the direction of the political strategy (upward or downward), and 2) the scope of the political strategy (individual or group based). The interaction between the above dimensions defines four different types of eLearning political strategies, which result in different political outcomes. The model is accompanied with one case study that is divided into four parts ("acts"). Each of the acts provides an example of one of the four strategies in the model. The discussion and conclusions sections integrate the findings from the case study, outline the rules that govern the application of political strategies in the context of eLearning, and list some of the theoretical and practical implications from a better understating of the politics of eLearning.

Preface

The internet has many faces. It is many things to many people. Today, it is a platform which situates a multitude of activities, performing to and for a large range of actors and interlocutors spanning and entwining the virtual with vast geographical physical terrains where it is intrinsically moulded by indigenous politics and social norms and behaviour on the ground. The internet is a space of culture and cultural manifestations as we incorporate it into our daily lives, inscribing expectations and our social and political agendas into it. It is an entity completely disrupted by humans and their offline environments while being malleable to its own technical architecture; amenable to different the forms of control, regulation and power which cross it invariably making it a contested and ambivalent entity. With the age of technical and technological convergence, the internet speaks to static and mobile platforms making uploads and downloads, and our ability to join in conversations seamless and to be part of worlds beyond us. Its appropriation as a social, political or artistic tool presents human civilizations and societies with a range of opportunities for empowering our lives but equally for presenting us with distinct and disparate challenges (Ibrahim, 2010) from the use of drones as part of state warfare, robots which can augment human labour force to the cumulative transgressions of what we may deem as our private spaces. Technology remains far from neutral constantly entering realms of work and leisure and spaces in between. It invites us into new possibilities, to connect and imagine our worlds where the screen as part of wearable technologies mediates our sense of sociality and social reality ubiquitously. The self and our surrounds, the familiar and the dissonant are reframed through these mediated platforms and in the process we become implicated with these technologies implicitly in our everyday lives and the formation of the self. The internet is about the everyday while expanding into our immediate and distant futures through trajectories of innovation and corporeal embedding which make these technologies intimate and part of our sensory worlds.

This diverse collection of essays explores a range of possibilities presented by new media technologies and their convergence in enabling social and political agency. They reflect the ways in which we use interactive and mobile platforms as social and political tools from political campaigning, storytelling, elearning to its use as aesthetic platforms to thwart mainstream and hegemonic representations ranging from poverty to consumer culture. Ubiquitous computing and imaging can be lodged in the everyday and can be intimately implicated in our notions of self and self-identity (Ibrahim, 2015). Equally they can disrupt the ways in which we make connections between images as referential objects, invoking a critical gaze into political and social issues. Both the political and social are bound within the spaces of internet through human interactions and communication patterns where our values systems and norms can be reiterated by the virtual environment and equally thwarted. The internet as a social and political tool presents us with innumerous ways to engage with our political and social environments. The architecture of immediacy, interactivity and ubiquity seek to conjoin individual with collective agency and to re-engage with distant political and social environments with the 'reach' new media technologies offer. As such the internet is imagined through ideals of democracy and agora, imbuing it with our fertile expectations and hopes. On the other hand, it is imagined as corroding our public spheres with the trivial and inane and depleting conversations and political deliberations, collapsing them into images and emoticons. The polarizing of the internet in our fervent imagination between humanistic ideals and through its deep dark abyss of the sinister cannot negate the domains of grey where cultural, social and the political of human agency interplay with the webbed interactivity of the internet and its global reach. The essays here capture this in-between spaces while at times sustaining the normative values we continually underpin to the internet as a formidable social and political force.

The collection acknowledges the internet as a multifaceted site in enacting the political and social. In *Self and the Relationship with the Screen*, the performance of the self through its daily interactions as well as extraordinary events, are explored. It acknowledges that the banality of the everyday constitutes an integral part of our communication on digital platforms. It argues that new media technologies are implicated in the production of self-identity. In the process it reveals our ongoing relationship with the screen as an orifice for the production of self and the construction of a social reality beyond our immediate domesticity. The notion of identity and the internet is also explored through dietary habits and food preferences. Christian Holmberg in his article, *Using the Blogosphere to Promote Disputed Diets*, argues the digital revolution has permanently reformed the way we approach food, and our food culture has become digitized. As such the level of public discourse about diets and health is more sophisticated than it was years ago. Food is a realm of political contestations and means to enact our value systems and beliefs about how we treat our environment and our recurrent worries about its depletion.

In this vein, Gambarato and Medvedev in *Transmedia Storytelling Impact on Government Policy Change*, examine the notion of storytelling as a potent form of activism to lobby policy changes in the fishing sector. Their in-depth transmedia analysis of the '*Fish Fight*' campaign demonstrates how transmedia storytelling contributed to raising public awareness of the wasteful discarding of healthy fish at sea under the EU fishing quotas, and in reviewing and amending EU fishing policies. From transmedia storytelling as a positive force, Dalisay, Kushin and Yamamoto in *The Demobilizing Potential of Conflict for Web and Mobile Political Participation* review the notion of conflict avoidance and how this can impact and inhibit online political participation. They test this link through a survey of young adult college student in the US Midwest within the context of the 2012 US presidential election. Their findings reveal a causal link between conflict avoidance and political participation and political expression online.

Similarly, the sustained interest in new media technologies particularly social networking sites and their increased use in political campaigns becomes the core emphasis for Rodrigo Sandoval-Almazan in *Political Messaging in Digital Spaces*. The challenges of using messaging technologies are explored through the case study of the presidential candidate Enrique Peña Nieto (PRI) in Mexico who won the presidency with a large participation but without the support of Twitter users. The study underscores the ambiguity of these new digital spaces as political platforms for campaigning. The question of the democratic nature of the internet remains a much debated issue. This libertarian and idealized notion of the internet as a platform to realize and enact democracy is explored by Kerill Dunne in *ICTs as Ancillary Tools for Indirect Democracy?* Using Michel Foucault's concepts of power and domination, the chapter explores whether online platforms are used for political participation or to maintain the existing status quo. The dialectical interplay of power and political participation becomes the main thrust in this analysis. This leads to the exploration of the internet as a learning platform where active political strategies are relevant to enable successful outcomes. Romm-Livermore, Rippa, and Raisinghani explore this terrain in *Towards a Political Theory of eLearning* with their Elearning Political Strategies paradigm or the ELPOS model to discern how the outcomes can be influenced through top-down or bottom-up interventions and/or whether these are initiated in collective or individual modes. Their model is augmented by four mini case studies to illuminate the distinct characteristics of their proposed model.

Reframing the official representations of poverty is explored by Anita Howarth in *Challenging the Repoliticization of Food Poverty* through her case study of austerity food blogs. Blogs as archives of people's narratives to humanise poverty while presenting a counter site to government's representation of hungry bodies as failed entities are offered as cogent political tools in this chapter. Food as a site of the social imaginary is also extended in the next chapter. Food images as a form of constant connection as well as a form of leaving our cultural imagination online is explored in *Ubiquitous Food Imaging: Food images as Digital Spectacle.* Food images in many ways celebrate the notion of the exhibit and the spectacle inviting gaze through everyday objects and rituals. The chapter argues that food imagery as a form of transacted materiality online offers familiarity, comfort, co-presence but above all a common elemental literacy where food transcends cultural barriers, offering a universal pull towards a commodity which is ephemeral yet preserved through the click economy.

From the multitude of phenomena which bring communion online, Jonathan Bishop probes a more dark and insidious activity in *Dealing with Internet Trolling in Political Online Communities*. Bishop contends that political discussion groups are prone to trolling as these are often open platforms where anyone can join in. An innovative scale is developed and proposed to better understand the phenomenon of trolling in the chapter. The negative side of Twitter in political advertising is explored by Marija Bekafigo and Allison Clark Pingley in *Do Campaigns "Go Negative" on Twitter*? In their content analysis of tweets from four different gubernatorial elections in 2011, they argue that while tweets are overwhelmingly positive, candidates 'go negative' by tweeting about policy and that twitter may be a conducive social media forum for policy-based messages due to its highly partisan characteristic.

Sustaining the thrust and relationship between social media and campaigning, Wairagala Wakabi probes the use of Facebook in authoritarian countries in his chapter, *When Citizens in Authoritarian States Use Facebook for Social Ties but not Political Participation*. The chapter examines how Facebook affects the participative behaviours of Ugandans. E-participation in repressive environments is seen to be curtailed through a detachment from politics, low belief in citizens' online actions influencing change and fear of reprisals. From Big Brother watching to the dominance of corporations controlling the internet, Joanna Kulesza covers the pressing issues of *Online Free Expression and its Gatekeepers*. In examining free expression online she argues what once was the domain of the state has become the prerogative of private global companies. She contends it is their terms of service and sense of social responsibility that have replaced local perceptions of morality and set limits to individual personal rights. From freedom of expression to voting, Jonathon Bishop and Mark Beech test the concept of the Delegated Transferable Voting or DTV in practice and determine its workability through an auto-ethnograpic approach in local and national level elections.

Again the limits of morality are explored by Bruner, Valine and Ceja in *Women Can't Win: Gender Irony and the E-Politics of The Biggest Loser* through notion of body shaming in the disembodied environment of the internet. They interrogate what they term as 'the structural food oppression linked to the weight and shape of the female body', arguing that the female body becomes an incarnation of the e-politics of food and one of the most vigorously contested entities online. Its entrapment between fat-shaming and skinny-shaming online reveal the ways in which it is narrated through discourses of deviance and acceptability in society. In congruence with the contentiousness of the female form and her denigration online, Aimée Vega Montiel dicusses the difficult issue of the status of women's human rights in the digital age in *Critical Issues on Gender Equality and ICTs in Latin America.* She questions the ethical strands of the online environment by asking to what extent does the new media environment promote women's human and communication rights or contribute to sustaining the oppression of women in society. By employing feminist political economy perspectives she analyses the critical issues of ICTs and gender issues in Latin America.

Aileen Blaney in *Food Photography, Pixelated Produce and Cameraless Images* confronts contemporary screen-saturated culture filled with images and the aesthetic and political roles these can enact as interlopers. Through the case study of a photographic artwork, Blaney shows the disruptions between food and hyper-reality and the dissonance produced between what we consume in the supermarket and in advertising dreamscapes. The last chapter in this book, *eLearning Political Strategies-A Four Act Play*, further expands on the elearing political Strategies (ELPOS) model discussed in chapter 7 through one case study divided into four parts to test the four strategies which are conceived in the elearning model to outline the rules that govern the application of political strategies in the context of eLearning, and to list some of the theoretical and practical implications for a better understanding and mediation of the internet as a learning environment.

Yasmin Ibrahim
Queen Mary, University of London, UK

REFERENCES

Ibrahim, Y. (2010). The regulation of gaze and capture: New media and the image economy. *International Journal of Technoethics*, 40–63.

Ibrahim, Y. (2015). Instagramming life: Banal imaging and the poetics of the everyday. *Journal of Media Practice*.

Chapter 1
Self and the Relationship with the Screen:
Interrogating the Fictive and Banal in Self Production

Yasmin Ibrahim
Queen Mary, University of London, UK

ABSTRACT

The self is performed through the banal of the everyday on social media. The banality of the everyday constitutes an integral part of our communication on digital platforms. Taking this as part of our performative lives in the digital economy, the paper looks at ways in which we co-produce the self through the banality of the everyday as well as a wider imagination and engagement with the world. These wider engagements are termed as 'fictive' not because they are unreal but through a conceptual notion of how the self is performed and imagined through wider world events in digital platforms and screen cultures where convergence of technologies allow us to be constantly consumed through the screen as we live out our daily lives. The narration of our lives through the banal and the fictive constantly co-produces the self through a situated domesticity of the everyday and equally through the eventful. In the process it reveals our ongoing relationship with the screen as an orifice for the production of self and the construction of a social reality beyond our immediate domesticity.

INTRODUCTION

The notions of identity and the performative are tightly entwined in our digital lives. Our daily interactions and engagements online contribute to identity creation. The banal and the perfunctory as they migrate to online spaces of communication, everyday life becomes performed online and these mediated rituals of communicating the mundane and ritualistic can be therapeutic while enabling the self to be consumed by others. Both the ways in which we perceive ourselves through our daily rituals and the ways in which others consume us are important to the notion of presence in digital culture. The communication of the daily rituals also inscribes a sense of space demarcating certain spaces with a sense of familiarity

DOI: 10.4018/978-1-5225-1862-4.ch001

and resonance online. As such the self is constantly produced and renewed through the everyday. The diarisation of our lives and equally the exhibitionistic qualities along with the performative means the self is produced and consumed contemperously in online spaces as we go about our daily routines in our physical environments. Beyond the routine and perfunctory of the everyday, self-production online entails interaction with a wider world. These wider worlds of conversations, political events, popular imagination and fantasy equally conjoin with the everyday. The self is then co-produced through the banal and the fictive as we conceive them in our everyday imagination.

This paper explores the notion of self-production online through the categories of the banal representing the everyday and the notion of entwining the self with the wider world events which I term as the 'fictive'. The fictive of the wider world is an important part of inserting the self into a social reality beyond personal lived experiences and the routines of the everyday life, where the political and aesthetic self emerges and interacts with a world imagined, experienced and performed through digital platforms and experienced through the screen.

The Banal and the Fictive

The project of self-construction online has entailed the sharing of our intimate and private moments with a perceived sense of audience eager to consume the self, crafted through its everyday experiences. We have as such made the representation of the everyday a vital content for consumption in online spaces (Ibrahim 2015). The banal and routine is experienced both in the material world and equally experienced through its projection, narration and exhibition online. Engagement and consumption through the screen has experiential properties as the screen offers us a means to produce our disembodied selves which we can equally consume in real time while living out our daily lives. This duality is part of digital living where the corporeal experiences and lived experiences become conjoined. As bodies become domesticated through mobile technologies, life experiences become conjoined through the screen with the convergence of technologies and our ability to produce ourselves as content on the move. The production of the self through the everyday is a necessary part of our sense of sociality and engagement with a community. But importantly it asserts the sense of presence in the digital environment by enacting the familiar and the perfunctory through the routines of the everyday. The digital age and our obsession with the self is also seen as a 'narcissistic turn' where we can produce and curate ourselves online (See Ibrahim 2009).

The projection of the everyday onto the screen for sharing affords a resonance with fellow human beings. While much has been written about the domestication of technology in our domestic environments, we need to reconsider how we have inscribed domesticity onto the screen as a means to communicate our presence on the screen and to equally live through the screen. Screen living has domesticated the banal and perfunctory as a form of resonant code of communication that engenders familiarity and solidarity with fellow humans. It forms the basis of not just presence but an essential element of sharing and sociality online. The sociality of the everyday by showcasing the intimate happenings of domesticity and the banal produces highly personal moments online and is part of our semantics of bonding with others in our everyday engagements online. This screen living assumes a degree of 'publicness' in enacting ones' daily routines and in communicating the everyday.

The communication of the everyday whether it be Snapchats of your breakfast or pet, or sharing the aggravation of your delayed train encode an implicit intimacy as these are resonant depictions of the everyday and the familiar of our social settings. The banal of the everyday renders a therapeutic element to digital communication underpinning implicit codes of familiarity which others can identify with. As such the 'banal of the everyday' stands in contrast with an attention economy where the unexpected and salacious events punctuate our routine lives with breaking news of explosion and disruption in the age of anxiety. The communication of the everyday whether through text or images provide a therapeutic value in this 'age of anxiety' where we are constantly distracted by the next big event. The interplay of people's intimate and everyday routines communicated and consumed through a screen which can equally call us to bear witness to other worlds and events beyond our control asserts the therapeutic value in consuming the familiar and inscribing the perfunctory of the everyday into social media platforms. The banal of the everyday has social value. As the 'non-event' of the banal saturates our image landscape with objects of domesticity, it lends an important role in asserting and sustaining normalcy and in enabling a communion with an intimate and imagined audiences on social media platforms. Our notions of sociality are also constantly reconfigured through these public displays but equally in how others consume us. The reciprocity of offering our banal lives for others and an expectation that we are consumed through our daily routines becomes a means to pattern therapeutic communications online. The banal in the age of anxiety seeks to retain the routine and patterns and indeed the normalcy of our everyday lives as these become disrupted through unexpected events which are constantly thrust into our lives without warning.

If the banal reinserts the time and space of the everyday, the self is also constantly co-produced through a wider world of events and interactions beyond the banal of the everyday. The wider world of the political, popular culture, consumerism, national conversations and voyeurism of the digital world is what I term the 'fictive'. The fictive does not imply the real is not encoded in the wider happenings of the world. The fictive here is defined as what is represented through a digital environment and landscape where we can gain proximity and intimacy which may not be afforded in the real world. The fictive of the digital world allows the layperson to be part of wider political debates, to partake in world events and popular culture without being materially present in these events and happenings in offline spaces. This possibility to insert the self into a wide array of events ranging from the popular to the political is enabled through the interactivity and mobility of the internet where social conversations can signpost events and enable engagements with distant events both in terms of consumption of these online and to partake in them through conversations and discussions. The convergence of technologies and the architecture of web 2.0 presents the possibility to archive and curate images even when we don't produce or own them and as such to create an intimacy through our engagements and modes of consumption of the fictive. It presents us with unlimited possibilities to veer into virtual image galleries and video platforms and to curate images from a wide repertoire of offerings from professional to amateur productions. The immense digital landscape allows one to negotiate the sense of time and space and equally to re-position notions of intimacy and proximity with the wider world represented through the digital terrain. It allows us to tag, to like, to follow the stranger and the celebrity while showcasing these wider engagements through the projection of the self online. As such our imagination of the world is co-produced though these wider engagements while centring the self as an interlocutor between the fictive and the banal.

The Screen Self and Self-Commodification

The passing of the terrestrial age into a digital one brought an immense and renewed awe with technology. The digital age in contrast to the terrestrial age of broadcasting is one which allows us to be inserted inside the screen. The age of broadcasting produced both a fascination with the screen and its ability to re-produce and project the world into our intimate social settings. It provided a means to represent a wider world and mediate it through a screen culture of consuming what was out there through the confines of the home. The screen domesticated through the hearth and home provided an intimacy to distant and remote world events (Williams, 1974). The screen over time acquired a social status of being a filter to the outside world. Unlike radio or print, the screen could fill ones' senses with sights and sounds supplanting imagination while offering ways to consume the world. Screen as receptacle of the popular culture, political events and a platform for marking national processions and sharing the traumatic produced an incestuous bind with the screen over time, reifying it as a cultural and communal artefact that provided connections with the wider world through everyday consumption habits.

While the age of broadcasting, the domestication of the television and its centrality as a cultural artefact where it provided communion with an imagined community became underpinning factors which sustained the screen as a space of cultural veneration. The screen provided a means to gaze at others and to be mobile even in the private spaces of the home. The intimate relationship with television as a central technology in the home crafted the screen as an edifice for escape but equally for forms of sociality and in patterning our sense of time and space through broadcast schedules and the act of watching. The watching of television produced an imagined sense of solidarity with the unknown other. The screen produced this implicit social bond while asserting its dominance in the privacy of our homes. The screen as such was bound with domesticity and consumed through the pace and rhythm of domestic life. The screen prevailed as a filter for viewing another world, signifying a place of make believe and escape. The screen's association with make believe and its ability to showcase the powerful and the deviant, or celebrity or the suffering of the unknown expanded our field of vision beyond the immediate surrounds to encompass another world of staging events and productions. The screen provided the technical orifice for entering another world and hence the screen symbolised not just the expansion of vision and our ability to see beyond our immediate surrounds but also the possibility of immersing ourselves into alternate realities far removed from our own. The screen acquired a prominence in modernity where it was the source of entertainment, information and mass communication in society. This doubling of our field of vision through the screen made the screen an intimate part of reality construction in modernity.

The emergence of various forms of mobile gadgets again valorised the screen but also introduced the possibilities for solitary pleasure. The advent of the internet age and the incorporation of the PCs and laptops in work environments as well as the home, enabled us to think about the screen where we could control, produce and mediate content directly. We could capture ourselves and others through the convergence of technologies and through mobile gadgets. It enabled an obsession to image ourselves and others non-stop and in the process in produced different forms of gaze enable through existing power relationship and as well as through the subversion of prevailing norms (See Ibrahim, 2011).

The screen became much more malleable beyond watching one's favourite movies through the video recorder or the DVD. With the World Wide Web and the possibilities to browse disparate content, to communicate synchronously and asynchronously, the screen transcended into a much more personal artifice truncating it from its earlier social role as the immobile centre piece in the living room. As the screen became more personalised through PCs and laptops, it came to signify much more intimate and private engagements while mediating a wider world through it. The convergence of technologies, the advent of web 2.0, better bandwidth along with the refinements in handheld smart technologies which targetted the corporeal body rather than the physical space of the home, the screen entered a new era of social relevance. The body as a site for embedding smart communication technologies produced the self as constantly mediated through both its physical space and the virtual one enabled through the screen. If the screen acquired social resonance and dominance in the age of broadcasting, it acquired a bodily intimacy in the age of the digital media, becoming an extension of the body where it was possible to ubiquitously consume the world as well as our selves online while simultaneously offering ourselves to others for consumption.

Beyond the 'intimatisation' of the screen, the transcendence from the broadcasting age to the social media age was marked through our ability to see ourselves inside the screen. The screen no longer belonged to the powerful or the celebrity, it became a space in which one could view oneself and offer the self to others as an object and subject. The self-became part of content production online and became a means to fill the spaces of social media platforms becoming part content and part data where these can be transacted with and without human consent. The inserting of the self into the screens, our ability to consume and narrate ourselves and equally to make ourselves content for consumption of friends and strangers extended the social importance of the screen in the digital age. The screen belonged to us and we started to belong to the screen.

With reality television, the loss of scripting and the demise of production values were critiqued. Nevertheless, reality television made confessional television and consuming ordinary people part of the fabric of television and consumption. The changing political economy of broadcasting particularly the shift from terrestrial broadcasting to the satellite and cable television, banished issues with spectrum scarcity enabling a whole array of niche lifestyle and reality programmes to saturate television broadcasting. It led to criticisms about the loss of quality and the demise of the public sphere and public service broadasting with less funding routed to public information and education programmes. The incorporation of reality television and the re-fashioning of public gaze to view the ordinary and intimate details of people's everyday lives became a precursor in enabling the perfunctory and the everyday to become part of media content. The unscripted watching of people and leveraging on people performing for the camera or 'acting up' constituted a new era of watching others but equally envisioning the screen as part of the expose. Equally it re-inscribed the banal and domestic routines of peoples' uneventful lives and the ordinariness of existence to become viable subjects. Television veering beyond the valued principles of education, information and communication entered a phase of perverse and pervasive people watching which the digital age sort to expand infinitum. However, it went a step further where people could watch themselves and also offer themselves for others to watch. Self gaze became an intrinsic component of watching in the digital era and hence it created the asetheticization of the self, evident in rise and rise of selfies and a whole repository of advice and technical proficiency in presenting and curating the self aesthetically online.

With social media, the self-became commodified as content and data – as a commodity for exchange and transaction. It provided a means for people to insert themselves into the screen. This self-commodification again reconfigured the relationship with the screen and equally the narration of the routine and banal as content online. Prior to the digital age e we domesticated technologies such as the television and other domestic appliances into our private realm, in the digital age the technologically embodied body co-opted the banal and the routine in our private domains as content for social media and new media platforms. The corporeal embedding of technology meant it entered a much more intimate realm then the age of television. While television as a technology projected content from outside, the technologically embodied self-projected the domestic and banal or what may been deemed as private onto to the outer world. Technology's conquest of the body also meant an increasing loss of inhibition and increasing blurring of boundaries on what can be deemed public or private. As technologies became part of the body and extended vision, memory and sensory perceptions and to live our lives through the screen, the banal and the everyday became genre of content others could find communion and resonance with. Digital age in essence made the banal an intrinsic part of sociality and in gaining intimacy with others.

While mobile gadgets privatised the screen by decoupling it from the domestic environment, social media inverted the screen into a mirror where people could watch themselves forging an intense intimacy through the everyday and in terms of transforming the self into a disembodied entity online. The screen was no longer just private or solitary space and but one which recorded 'the daily and the everyday' and projected it to others updating on the movements and experiences of the self.

While reality television enabled us to insert ordinary people into the screen and consume them, social media enabled the self to be part of the content of the screen enabling visibility to a wider audience and equally propelling the self into a public arena. This duality of the self where life is experienced through ones' physical environment and equally through how it is experienced and narrated online, meant that the screen acquired a projective quality of extending the real into the virtual. The public quality of social media platforms enabled the self to become a performative entity and to exist through the consumption and the endorsement of an imagined public.

With the proliferation of new channels and programmes with cable and satellite broadcasting, social media conceived the hoi polloi as content. While imparting notions of its democratic potential as a people's communication tool, social media leveraged on people as content and data to drive these platforms and to create value (See Bonsu & Darmody, 2008; Terranova, 2000). It extracted people and their daily lives as content. The digital platforms enticed people to share stories, direct gaze, to endorse people, products and services to signpost information but most importantly to sign up to an economy where these creative enterprises whether these be in the form of text, videos or images did not foreclose of people revealing the personal and the intimate and courting public gaze. While the empowering qualities of the internet and social media platforms were constructed through issues of access, connectivity and the ability to transform people into public entities, it laid claims to the commodification of self and creating value through the public transaction of the self. It in many ways symbolised the ultimate triumph of capitalism where the self could be monetised and transacted as content and data in online platforms while creating value for advertisers and social media sites by conjoining them to products and services. The lure of the screen and our awe with it also meant the increasing loss of inhibition where we are willing to be intimate and public on the screen. The monetisation of the self-meant that we as digital tribes became complicit in the digital economy of exchange and value creation. Equally, we became complicit in wanting to share our lives online and hence became part of complicit risk economy (Ibrahim, 2008a).

As social media commodified the self, it also became a place to share the banal and the perfunctory of everyday life. Social media eager to fill empty spaces on digital platforms, offered the self as commodity for transaction and consumption in a mediated world. The domesticity of the everyday, our everyday routines and the perfunctory became means to narrate our lives and to offer them as content for others to consume. In the process we consumed ourselves and equally sought to see how others consumed us through page visits and endorsements such as likes, reposting and re-tweeting. The ubiquity of mobile technologies, its co-location on the corporeal body and the emergence of a sociality through the everyday made the banal a resonant part of human communication and communion.

'Je Sui World'

The participatory elements in new media technologies, the ability to partake in public conversations and democratic potential to be a producer of content online, enabled the self to be narrated beyond the banal or the perfunctory. The self and its engagement with the world and the public nature of these engagements sought to narrate the self through wider events of the world and the market place. The self through its instagram or twitter accounts could be part of the conversations and as such it enabled the self to be re-fashioned from purely as narcissistic production modes to one in which it interacted with world events. The self as a reactive and expressive entity to the wider world composed through the screen is also an important part of identity creation today. Thus beyond our composition through the everyday, the wider world and its happenings co-construct the self. While broadcasting sought to reconfigure our notions of space and time through the screen, social media age intensified this. By mediating the virtual world through the screen, time and space are not only reconfigured but a distinct proximity is created through our engagements with the fictive world as represented on the screen. The convergence of technologies means that we not only gaze but consume and communicate ubiquitously expecting an instant gratification from our activities online afforded through synchronous communication such as chat facilities and people reading posts in real time and endorsing these.

In contrast to the broadcast age, the screen does only double the vision into an alternate reality but also enables the self to be re-cast with world events through the ability to partake in them through discussions, signposting, re-tweeting, blogs, image curation, etc. The self can perform solidarity with renunciations of atrocity or commune with trauma where these occur. The self has become a means to stand in solidarity and to co-produce it as a symbol of protest during times of crisis. The rise of 'solidarity selfies' revealed the entity of the self as an active agent in terms of political engagement. The re-fashioning of the self as part of another person's trauma or misfortune not only communicated the solidarity in these enactments but equally the potency of employing the self as a political tool to express disaffect, citizenship, protest and communion with the dispossessed. The rise of solidarity selfies doesn't necessarily decentre the self but provides a means to locate politics through its disembodied representation online while using it as a form of political expression. In numerous political contexts and situations of social dissent, the selfie has become a hybrid form of social protest; of standing in consensus with the crowd yet employing the individual self to be part of the collective. Hence the 'fictive' of the wider world becomes renegotiated through the sense of self online both through its political orientations and the self as an entity for public and symbolic protest. The new media screen allows the individual to delve into the virtual and to be mobile within its offering and to exercise choice and agency. While television was about mobile privatisation, new media allowed one to go beyond and to add to the content creation online. Thus images could be re-hashed and real events can be satirised through memes and mashups. Where real world events can be narrated through user-generated content and personal commentary to reconfigure the sacred and puerile in the virtual world. Where people in elongate event creation by partaking in both celebrations and tragedies online through the projection of the self onto the screen. As such digital platforms have become spaces to enact new rituals of mourning and celebration and to create social norms where the self is never completely de-centred.

If television allowed us to witness tragedies and be part of national mourning and celebration through the notion of mass audience and consumption, the mobile screen of tablets and smart phones personalised our engagements with the wider world. It allowed us to be selective with what we let into our screen while being enticed into a whole array of content online through cookies and algorithms which track your preference and seek attention constantly. Today watching communally then entails also the phenomenon of 'second screening' where people interact about content while they consume it. It conjoins a connection with a wider audience where it was previously imagined through the nation state in the age of broadcasting (See Anderson, 1991). If the age of broadcasting prior to the notion of 'television on demand' sought to order time and space through broadcasting schedules and to impose the notion of an imagined community through broadcasting in a nation-state, the personal screen of today has made it a reality for us to speak to this 'imagined' community while consuming and watching, relating our comments in real time. Our public spheres forming through text and images exchanged in real time.

The digital age is an age of distraction, where advertising content and alerts add layers to the screen vision, seeking to distract and divert the self elsewhere. While the screen of the mass consumption as conceived through the television sought to deliver mass mediated world, the small screen signified by the personalised gadget fractured and personalised the virtual arena, seeking to impress the self as an individual with its own preferences and agency. While the proliferation of multiple channels on the television screen stood for choice and leisure. The small screen of fracture is a screen that conjoins several platforms including television programmes and user-generated content. It stands for a distraction economy where the engagement of the self in terms of content can leave a data trail while creating a browser history unique to it (Ibrahim, 2008b). Hence the self is constantly narrated through its data trail where it can be coded as part of the big data and equally through its unique preferences and settings. If the screen stood for communion in the age of broadcasting, in the digital age the screen is a fluid space that requires the self to be both performed and coded through its consumption and preferences. The digital screen requires a more active engagement seeking to build private spaces through logins and passwords while seeking to render one a subject of wider invisible processes of turning everything into data.

CONCLUSION

The paper reviewed the notions of banal and fictive mainly as a means to interrogate how the self is performed through the everyday and through world events where these provide a theatre to narrate the self and its engagements. The banal is part of self-objectification where our ability to insert ourselves into the screen enable us to perform the self through the everyday routines and rituals. This exposition of the banal is a therapeutic element of communion and sociality today. The objectification of the self also devised a more intense relationship with the screen where notions of privacy and intimacy and equally of being connected became reconfigured. The intense relationship with the screen and the transformation of the self as an object of consumption through its daily rituals provide a means to fill a vast abyss of the digital terrain with content. The self is both content and data online where it is both consumed and transacted through algorithms creating value for advertisers and organisations. In the contrast to the banal, the self is also narrated through a wider world of events where the self is imagined by inserting it into trauma, celebrations, rituals of mourning and protest. The engagement with the fictive allows the self to be more than just a voyeur in the new media economy. It can partake and elongate event creation without decentring the self while sustaining itself as a form of commodity for others to consume. The fictive of the wider world can be owned, curated and co-produced through the self in this digital screen culture.

REFERENCES

Anderson, B. (1991). *Imagined communities: reflections on the origins and spread of nationalism.* London: Verson.

Bonsu, S. K., & Darmody, A. (2008). Co-creating Second Life: Market-Consumer Cooperation in Contemporary Economy. *Journal of Macromarketing*, *24*(4), 355–368. doi:10.1177/0276146708325396

Ibrahim, Y. (2008a). The New Risk Communities: Social Networking Sites and Risk. *International Journal of Media and Cultural Politics*, *4*(2), 245–253. doi:10.1386/macp.4.2.245_3

Ibrahim, Y. (2008b). The Co-opted Body and Counter-Surveillance: The Body as Data and Surveillance. *International Journal of the Humanities*, *5*(12), 1–8.

Ibrahim, Y. (2009). Social Networking Sites (SNS) and the 'Narcissistic Turn'. In Collaborative Technologies and Applications for Interactive Information Design: Emerging Trends in User Experiences. Academic Press.

Ibrahim, Y. (2011). The non-stop capture: The politics of looking in postmodernity. *The Poster*, *1*(2), 167–185. doi:10.1386/post.1.2.167_1

Ibrahim, Y. (2012). The Politics of Watching: Visuality and the New Media Economy. *International Journal of E-Politics*, *3*(1), 1–11. doi:10.4018/jep.2012010101

Ibrahim, Y. (2015). Instagramming life: Banal imaging and the poetics of the everyday. *Journal of Media Practice*, *16*(1), 42–54. doi:10.1080/14682753.2015.1015800

Terranova, T. (2000). Free Labour: Producing Culture for the Digital Economy. *Social Text*, *18*(2), 33–58. doi:10.1215/01642472-18-2_63-33

Williams, R. (1974) Television: Technology and Cultural Form. London: Fontana. doi:10.4324/9780203426647

Chapter 2
Using the Blogosphere to Promote Disputed Diets:
The Swedish Low-Carb High-Fat Movement

Christopher Holmberg
University of Gothenburg, Sweden

ABSTRACT

Widely influential low-carb high fat diet (LCHF) promoters have been using social media to marshal support when contesting the nutritional recommendations provided by the National Swedish Food Agency (NFA). Political events led to an increased public awareness of the LCHF diet, which in turn provided the advocates with vital opportunities to contest the established nutritional authorities. This study explored how three of the leading promoters transact their criticisms of nutrition authorities, and how they use social media for this purpose. A longitudinal thematic analysis of the diet promoters' social media presence demonstrates that they made full use of media convergence to form opinion and attain their goals. The LCHF promoters utilized a rhetorical arsenal based in science popularization to appeal to the public and social media allowed for the spread of anecdotal evidence of individual dieters. Interestingly, social media also facilitated the advocates to network their expertise and to start science initiatives evolving from merely anecdotal methods to conventional approaches.

INTRODUCTION

Dietary habits and food preferences bear political and sociocultural implications as our dietary practices are a part of who we are—individually, collectively, and even nationally (Cwiertka, 2006; Kaplan, 2012). The politicization of food concerns the consumption of food, as well as the production, inspection, regulation, and marketing. As cookbooks are chart toppers and cooking shows abundant, the level of public discourse about diets and health is more sophisticated than it was years ago; the public is more knowledgeable about food politics than ever (Counihan & Van Esterik, 2013; Kaplan, 2012). One explanation for this is the pace and magnitude of information regarding food and diets and how they are transmitted in this connected day and age (Wansink, Tal, & Brumberg, 2014). The digital revolution

DOI: 10.4018/978-1-5225-1862-4.ch002

has permanently reformed the way we approach food, and our food culture has become digitized. With the emergence of the interactive Web, or Web 2.0 (Freeman & Chapman, 2008), individuals can create and share user-generated content (UGC) in applications and platforms known as social media, e.g., Web logs (blogs), Facebook, Instagram, and YouTube (Holmberg, Chaplin, Hillman, & Berg, 2016; Lenhart, Smith, Anderson, Duggan, & Perrin, 2015).

A specific feature of social media is the way it can attract advocates of certain ideals and stances, such as diets (Rousseau, 2012). These proponents have increasing influence as conventional expert knowledge regarding food and nutrition faces mounting criticism in a wide range of contexts (Närvänen, Kartastenpää, & Kuusela, 2013; Pellizzoni, 2003). Healthy eating is a continually salient topic in public discussions, for which the issues of knowledge and understanding are essential but commonly disputed. In the public domain, recourse to nutrition science is no guarantee of dietetic credibility. According to Shapin (2007), scientific claims need to be carefully constructed to appear as epistemically credible as possible in a cultural climate where various actors compete for their understanding of healthy eating to be recognized as the most convincing. What constitutes healthy eating is thus experiencing ongoing public debate, and this debate is increasingly taking place online. One arena where this has been noticed is in the ever-growing blogosphere (Bonetta, 2007). The disputes around online activists' pseudoscience trials of conventional and regulatory expertise are expected to become increasingly polarized and substantial over the next few years. Citizens' trust in institutions such as national health organizations is decreasing, due to amongst other things, heightened cultural awareness of the risks related to technological and scientific development (Edelman Trust Barometer, 2012). Hence, according to Thompson (2005), different peer groups and networks that criticize and offer alternatives to the official expert systems play a significant role in guiding consumers.

This chapter will focus on how three influential promoters of the low-carb high-fat (LCHF) diet— Dr. Dahlqvist, Diet Doctor and Fernholm—have utilized social media, such as blogs, as means to undermine the expert authority of the Swedish National Food Agency (NFA). These three promoters all possess certain scientific credentials but function as non-mainstream experts since they do not abide by the state-sanctioned dietary recommendations. Sweden has a long tradition of national nutrition policies, and the first recorded governmental dietary guidelines were set in Sweden, Finland, and Norway in 1968 (Kjaernes, 2003; Lang & Heasman, 2004). The three LCHF promoters have challenged the established nutritional community through social media by using science popularization as an instrument against established scientists (Gunnarsson & Elam, 2012), all while gaining international attention (Mann & Nye, 2009).

Disputed Low-Carbohydrate Diets

Low-carbohydrate diets have moved through stages of popularity since the nineteenth century (cf. Banting, 1863), with increases in the late 1920s and 1970s (cf. Atkins, 1972; Lieb, 1929). Of late, low-carbohydrate diets arose in popularity in English-speaking high-income countries and the Nordic countries, during the late 1990s and early 2000s (Gunnarsson & Elam, 2012; Knight, 2011). These food regimes consist of diets such as the South Beach Diet and the Montignac method (Agatston, 2003), but the best-known low-carbohydrate diet is probably the Atkins diet, proposed by the American cardiologist Robert Atkins (1972). Dismissing traditional dietary recommendations, the Atkins diet asks dieters to lose weight by avoiding carbohydrates while continuing to eat proteins and fats. Losing weight and gaining better health by consuming more lavishly is the tempting message.

Considering the popularity of the diets and its variants, advocates of low-carb diets are often in open and highly public disagreement with nutritional authorities and establishment. The dieters and proponents of these diets draw from different theoretical and epistemological perspectives in doing so. In a recent publication by Knight (2015), she argues that the popular low-carbohydrate literature exhibits a strong discourse of "nutritional primitivism". This is a discursive approach and a quest of allegedly simpler, more natural and genuine ways of eating, as part of a general mission for health. When the proponents ask their dieters to avoid sugars and other fast-acting carbohydrates, Knight notes that they place their rhetoric in nutritional primitivism as they embrace evolutionary explanations for obesity and type 2 Diabetes, and utilize arguments based on nutritional anthropology.

Some recent studies have also noted that the low-carb dieters draw from personal experiences and engage with dieters individually unlike the established nutrition authorities. Huovila and Saikkonen (2015) explored how popular Finnish nutrition counselling bloggers construct dietetic credibility and understanding by analyzing the bloggers rhetorical discourse. The researchers compared their argumentation to that of academic experts contributing to the blog of the National Institute for Health and Welfare. Huovila and Saikkonen (2015) found that academic nutritional science bloggers talked about human bodies as populations, while the mainstream dietetic literature acknowledges that people usually consider themselves to be unique individuals and addressed them as such. The bloggers stylistically thus created a more individualistic understanding of healthy eating in their argumentation in opposition to the universalistic and population-based understanding projected by members of the nutritional establishment.

This demonstrates that proponents of disputed and alternative diets often place themselves in particular and unique communicative positions. Bearing in mind the contrasting argumentation and the differing framing of ideas, the low-carb diet promoters are often in public dispute with nutritional establishments. The latest public clash in Sweden took place a few years ago when a specific version of the low-carb diet family, the low-carb high fat diet (LCHF) movement, received widespread media attention (Gunnarsson & Elam, 2012).

A Swedish Food War: The Contested LCHF Diet

Unlike the Atkins diet, the current widespread version of the LCHF diet in Sweden generally involves a more drastic restriction of total carbohydrate intake (normally less than 12% of energy intake) and large unrestricted intakes of foods rich in saturated fat (Mann, McLean, Skeaff, & Morenga, 2014). The regime has been the source of public conflict and debate between various supporters of the diet and representatives from the Swedish NFA since 2004 (Mann & Nye, 2009). The LCHF diet has become increasingly popular; its cookbooks have been on the bestseller lists (Bokus, 2015) and the media has reported on grocery stores running out of butter due to widespread use in the food regime (Martin, 2011). A similar food consumption trend related to the low-carb high fat diet was also manifested in Finland at the time, with a steep decrease in the consumption of bread (Jauho, 2016).

Representatives from the NFA has been concerned because the diet goes against the advice of the Nordic Nutrition Recommendations (Nordic council of ministers, 2014) on which the agency bases its nutritional recommendations. In one of Sweden's leading newspapers, representatives from the agency published a statement arguing against the diet's proposed health benefits (GP, 2012). It is primarily the replacement of carbohydrates with saturated fats that attracts criticism. Agency officials generally refer to a large Swedish study when arguing against LCHF promoters. In the study, participants decreased their reported fat intake in the first seven years (1986–1992), but after 2004, fat intake—especially saturated fat—increased drastically, corresponding with the introduction of positive media support for the LCHF diet. The decline and subsequent upsurge in cholesterol levels occurred in line with the trends over time in food selection. The authors of the study concluded that these changes in risk factors could have significant effects on the prevention of cardiovascular disease (Johansson et al., 2012). Besides representatives from the NFA, noted professors in epidemiology also warned the Swedish public against the LCHF diet when they published an article in one of Sweden's major newspapers (DN, 2013). The epidemiologists claimed that the unusual increase in the incidences of stroke and myocardial infarction, which has been noted among young men and women (The National Board of Health and Welfare, 2013), could be partly explained by the increased popularity of the LCHF diet.

Evidently, there is a polarization between LCHF promoters, and representatives from the NFA, as well as acknowledged academics, regarding the nutritional qualities of the diet. Rather than focus on the nutritional qualities of the particular diet, this chapter will focus on the political game that played out. When analyzing the Swedish discourse concerning the LCHF movement, it is noticeable that the battle is fought in different channels. While established nutritional researchers mostly undertook their argumentation in mass media channels (e.g., print newspapers), the three LCHF promoters have gained wide success by utilizing social media channels. This was also recently highlighted by two prominent professors in nutrition, as they published a debate article in the Journal of the Swedish Medical Association (Cederholm & Rothenberg, 2016). The authors argue that social media played an incremental role in promoting the controversial diet, as it allowed the personal opinions dismissed on the promoters' blogs to gain widespread attention also in traditional mass media.

The aim of this study is to investigate how three influential Swedish promoters and non-conventional experts of the LCHF movement transact their criticisms of current nutrition authorities, and how they utilize social media for this purpose. The three promoters are Andreas Eenfelt, a medical doctor and owner of the blog Diet Doctor; Annika Dahlqvist, also a medical doctor and owner of the blog Dr. Dahlqvist; and finally, Ann Fernholm, a published author who holds a PhD in molecular biotechnology. The study examines how these three promoters utilize specific features of social media to further their cause. The postmodern medical paradigm, the theory of science popularization, and spreadability theory will serve as theoretical reference frames.

CONCEPTUAL AND THEORETICAL FRAMEWORK

Social media can facilitate dietary and health communication as individuals engage and inform others by sharing health-related stories, such as treatment achievements and disappointments (Eckler, Worsowicz, & Rayburn, 2010; Norman, 2012). These features are linked to the present medical paradigm, that of postmodernism (Laugharne, 1999). The postmodern paradigm has established new and additional responsibilities for health professionals, highlighting morals, evidence, a concern about hazards over benefits, and the rise of the informed patient (Gray, 1999). While nutritional and medical knowledge was previously bound to textbooks and scientific journals, the Internet permits entrance to the school of lay medicine (Kata, 2012). This has also reformed the way in which science, as an activity and authority, is credited. The postmodern characteristics of disenchantment and suspicion toward science and the notion of expertise have contributed to a decreased trust in expert systems (Giddens, 1990).

This postmodern medical paradigm questions the legitimacy of science and authority, emphasizing the need for the public to gain more power. One interesting aspect of this paradigm is its implication for science popularization. Science popularization is normally recognized as having political implications and for reinforcing the epistemic authority of the institutions of science in society (Myers, 2003). Dividing the work of producing new knowledge from its dissemination, popularization stimulates public understanding and the appreciation of science situated outside public reach and influence. Still, merely by insisting upon such a dissection, popularization remains susceptible to seizure by capable and resourceful communicators intent on turning it against the conventional authority of scientists (Gunnarsson & Elam, 2012).

Unconventional scientists habitually publish in the public domain, and even conventional scientists who have been unsuccessful in publishing in the peer-reviewed literature may look to popular media as a channel for their work (Gregory & Miller, 2000). Scientists' calculated use of media to circumvent peer scrutiny and resolve in-house conflicts has been described earlier (e.g. Bucchi, 1998). With today's media convergence—i.e. the movement of content across multiple media platforms (Jenkins, 2008)—more and more scientists turn to social media to spread their views (Bonetta, 2007). While media convergence inspires participation and collective intelligence (Jenkins, 2008), the possibility of linking people together also brings together those who were previously considered to be peripheral members of disregarded groups (e.g., anti-vaccine promoters), as they can effortlessly and uncritically interact with similar-minded people online (Gerstenfeld, Grant, & Chiang, 2003). And as Jenkins, Ford, & Green (2013) argue, spreadable media constructs a system which pays more attention to the public interest—defined not through elite organizations but by the public itself—by its acts of assessment and transmission. This also has consequences, as judiciously crafted evidence can be placed next to the thoughts of activists and pseudoscientists, conceivably weakening communications from qualified expertise (Wilson & Keelan, 2009).

Another implication is that social media has advanced postmodern models by modifying the notion of truth (Keen, 2007). The endless individualized truths presented online are each rendered as legitimate. This is fortified by the postmodern conception of relativism—that there are no objective facts, but rather a multitude of meanings and ways of knowing (Gray, 1999). When a wealth of information regarding food and nutrition is available in a range of platforms, it is difficult to evaluate which source is reliable. The polemic around the LCHF-diet also demonstrates how issues of expertise and scientific knowledge progressively take place in the arena of personal wellbeing. In the postmodern medical paradigm, a cultural climate infiltrated by 'healthism' (Crawford, 1980), and the imperative of personal health care responsibilities and risk management generates active health identities, that do not all obey to conventional forms of expertise. Unconventional dietary regimes contest the authority of mainstream medicine and nutritional science. According to Davison et al. (1991), these dietary regimes typically include a lay epidemiology which may draw from medical concepts but also media discourses and observations rising from individual experiences.

The more information we have about food, the greater uncertainty there is about what constitutes the right diet (Brunel & Pichon, 2004; Järvelä, Mäkelä, & Piiroinen, 2006). Individuals then tend to cluster together in networks constituting believers of the same dietary practice. This is encouraged in the spreadability paradigms, as it refers to the potential, both practical and political, for groups to share content for their own devotion (Jenkins et al., 2013). As argued by Latour (1987) this collaboration is crucial for similar-minded scientists as they need to network themselves into deciding bodies and organs all while communicating intensively, to build up supporters for the facts they wish to establish. Thus, the making of facts, and the resources necessary to make them, depends to a certain extent on gathering allies. Forming communities through blogs belonging to influential proponents of diets is one way of doing just that, which is why it is necessary to study the political use of social media as a networked practice (Jenkins, 2008).

METHOD

Data Collection and Analysis

The substantial social media presence of the LCHF movement was explored, with particular focus on three popular blogs linked to leading spokespersons of the movement. These also constitute public arenas for individual testimonies of different LCHF dieters. According to the largest Swedish blog aggregator Bloggportalen (Twingly, 2015), Diet Doctor and Dr. Annika Dahlqvist's blogs are recurrently among the top ten most-visited blogs in the category for health-related blogs, with Diet Doctor being the continuous number one. A third blog by Ann Fernholm, a supporter to the LCHF community, who holds a PhD in molecular biotechnology, was included in the analysis as she is an influential published author (e.g. Fernholm, 2012) and was named scientific journalist of the year in 2010 (Scientific journalists, 2015). Most of the materials analyzed are written or published in Swedish, although Diet Doctor also has a small English version. The texts make extensive reference to international debate regarding dietary content, but they are intelligible to those with an understanding of the Swedish language.

Data were generated using theoretical sampling (Närvänen et al., 2013). Because of the high number of posts, it was not feasible to analyze the entirety of the blogs. In order to obtain a complete overview the blogs were read in their entirety however. The analysis covered materials published on the blogs between 2004 and 2015. Information on the blogs corresponding to the research objectives was included in the analysis. This included presentation texts (e.g., "About" sections) and blog postings (including comments from users). A theory-driven qualitative thematic analysis was performed on the material following guidelines from Braun and Clarke (2006). The theoretical framework guided the analysis in order to ascertain, analyze, and report patterns identified in the material. Thematic analysis has been used in other studies analyzing materials in social media (e.g. De Brun, McCarthy, McKenzie, & McGloin, 2014; Shepherd, Sanders, Doyle, & Shaw, 2015).

To ascertain the official view of Swedish food and nutrition regulators, reports authored by the Swedish national food agency (NFA, 2011, 2013a, 2013b), including statements regarding the LCHF diet were examined. Publications from established academics (DN, 2013) and the Swedish Council on Health Technology Assessment (Aftonbladet, 2013; SCHTA, 2010) were also investigated. Using the Swedish media archive Retriever (2015) and Google Trends (Google Inc., 2015), impactful press coverage of the LCHF movement was explored to gain an understanding of the phenomena in a public and mass media context (e.g. Eriksson, 2009; Expressen, 2014; Stahl, 2013; Winbladh, 2011).

RESULTS

This section is outlined as follows: first, events on the national level which have led to an increased public awareness of the LCHF diet will be explained. These events have provided the LCHF promoters with an invaluable opportunity to criticize the established nutritional community. Next, features of social media which enable the sharing of anecdotal evidence as a way to increase the diet's acceptability will be illustrated. Lastly, examples of how leading LCHF promoters work to proliferate their scientific authority will be presented.

National Events Leading to Increased Alleged Credibility of the LCHF Diet

The first example illustrates how medical authorities and experts are unable to agree, leading to a decreased trust in expert systems that is typical to the postmodern paradigm of medicine (Giddens, 1990). Scientific uncertainty, whether real or perceived, can seriously undermine the centrality of scientific expertise (Pellizzoni, 2003). And these events opened up public criticism of established Swedish governmental nutritional expertise, while acting as entry tickets for the LCHF promoters in the debate that followed.

As noted by Mann and Nye (2009) in their *Lancet* commentary, controversy stirred following Dahlqvist's recommendation of the LCHF diet to patients with diabetes early in 2005. Two dieticians accused Dahlqvist of practicing against scientific and evidence-based medicine when she recommended the diet in her capacity as a physician; this is why she was investigated by the National Board of Health and Welfare. Dahlqvist was exonerated, but the report leading to her exculpation was full of caveats as they took into account LCHF studies with limited study periods (Närlid, 2008). The trial generated massive media attention, and interest in what had previously been a relatively low-key investigation escalated rapidly. It was reported that Dahlqvist was exonerated so headlines proclaimed a turnaround by the board. The decision to exonerate Dahlqvist also made an impact online, highlighted by Dr. Eenfeldt: "The decision implies that physicians now can offer these types of [dietary] recommendations to patients…. Congratulations Annika! Hopefully more and more people will now take the step from thinking to acting." (Diet Doctor, 2008; my translation). Siding with Dahlqvist, Dr. Eenfeldt showed his support early on signaling a potential alliance with the fellow medical doctor.

Besides having stirred up considerable attention in the LCHF diet by the general public with Dahlqvist's hearing, the board committed another error. As the board was about to disseminate a report on nutritional recommendations for individuals with diabetes, two of the members working on generating guidelines in the expert group were removed. Allegedly, the director-general thought that they might be perceived to have a conflict of interest, as they were associated with the food industry by the nature of their relationship with the Swedish Nutrition Foundation (SNF). Like similar foundations worldwide, the SNF obtains food industry backing but offers independent scientific advice to the industry. The two researchers who were removed were both internationally renowned scientists. The media reports framed the sequence of events as another example of experts being unable to agree, and this became justification enough for patients and the public at large to conclude that the LCHF diet was on par with nutritional guidelines.

Inherent Features of Social Media Generates Opportunities for Alternative Nutritional Ideals

Free Dissemination of Information while Converging the Media

As Loader and Mercea (2012) have reasoned, there is usually an assumption that "the widespread use of the Internet for social networking, blogging, video-sharing and tweeting has an elective affinity with participatory democracy" (p. x). This has indeed been noticed within the LCHF community. Unlike scientific articles—which are restricted to pricey subscriptions and copyright protections—LCHF promoters utilize the free and egalitarian dissemination of information in various social media channels. This online participation is highly encouraged by leading promoters: "Comment on blogs, discussion forums, and in papers, start a blog yourself, prepare a lecture, talk to your doctor. Feel free to spread the link to dietdoctor.com and the talk on YouTube above. You may also use anything you find on this page in whatever way you like" (Diet Doctor, 2015a). As featured in the spreadability paradigm, Dr. Eenfeldt emphasizes producing content in easy-to-share formats (Jenkins et al., 2013). Taking advantage of the media convergence, Eenfeldt uses various media platforms and services to appeal to different sectors of his blog readers by catering to their differing inclinations.

Due to the commercialization and introduction of new electronic media, the public realm is no longer the sole center of debate. Consequently, civic activities are now progressively being practiced from the safety and comfort of the private domain (Papacharissi, 2010). This is reflected in a multitude of platforms used by the LCHF promoters. When it was determined that the NFA was losing credibility among the Swedish people, Eenfeldt (Diet Doctor, 2013) started a Facebook group to gather supporters who wanted to close down the NFA.

The National Food Agency's old recommendations for fat-free light products are losing credibility among the Swedish people (and among professors). There is a new Facebook group titled "We who want to close down the National Food Agency. Is this a group for you?" (Diet Doctor, 2013; my translation)

Lewenstein (1995) argues that the role of the media should be an exploration of the complexity of interaction among all media. And in addition to these blogs, various online forums and Facebook groups exist dealing with the evidence put forward by LCHF promoters (e.g. Diet Doctor, 2012). These examples reflect the notion of the democratization of individual voices through online networks (Doyle, 2012). Promoters of the diet use various free online services to disseminate information standing in opposition to established dietary beliefs. Social media is thus a tool for individual members of society to gain power and make their voices heard. Emphasis is on the role of the online promoters as the driver of democratic organization through the self-actualized networking of citizens committed in dietary lifestyle politics (Dahlgren, 2009; Loader & Mercea, 2012).

Construction and Dissemination of Anecdotal Evidence

A characteristic feature of social media is the ability to share user-generated content (UCG) (Wofford, 2012). This enables personal testimonies and stories to be quickly uploaded, shared, and spread in the online milieu. When it comes to the LCHF diet, both Diet Doctor and Dahlqvist use their personal experiences as successful examples when promoting the food regime.

In the fall of 2004 I discovered how the low-carb diet helped me to combat overweight and ill-health. I had suffered from irritable bowel syndrome, gastritis, and esophagitis.... All these illnesses and disease disappeared rather rapidly as I decreased intake of carbohydrates while increasing the consumption of natural fats. (Dahlqvist, 2015; my translation).

Some high-profile individuals within the LCHF community who had been overweight have now lost weight. They usually advocate dissemination of anecdotal evidence and using social media to form communities and share personal success stories. These subjective and emotional stories further perpetuate the diet's believability. This also emphasizes the key feature of social media—enabling people to communicate with and influence each other as a networked practice (Jenkins et al., 2013). An identified online practice in this regard is that of seeking information and feedback from other members of the online community (Närvänen et al., 2013). For example, Dr. Eenfeldt urges those with success stories to share them, along with pictures, on his blog (Diet Doctor, 2014b).

This way, accumulated evidence of scientific research can be contrasted with the immediate experiences of individual dieters. These may be exclusive and impossible for others to experience in the same way, but their presence demonstrates how an LCHF diet is working for a steadily increasing number of individuals. The individual truths presented on the blogs are each rendered as valid and this is enhanced by the postmodern notion of relativism—that there are numerous meanings and ways of knowing (Gray, 1999). Attributable to their affiliation with primary health care, general practitioners such as Dr. Eenfeldt and Dahlqvist can side with those who are eager to openly disclose the benefits they have derived from an LCHF diet. With these newfound confidants, Dahlqvist and Diet Doctor can then launch renewed criticism against a detached and isolated establishment in the citadel of science (Martin, 1998), which seeks to reject and demean the relief experienced by so many beneficiaries of an LCHF regimen.

A particular interesting piece of anecdotal evidence was provided by Diet Doctor—he showcased his blood tests spanning the eight years he has been on the diet. By employing an objective medical method while using himself as an example, he provides a complex yet individual piece of information. Self-experimentation has a long history in nutritional research (Widdowson, 1993). Research by self-experiment involves changing the conditions by, for example, taking what is regarded as too little or too much of a nutrient and studying the consequences. The investigator may use himself as the subject of the investigation and he may work alone or take part as the leader of a group.

The naïve rumors on how LCHF is detrimental longitudinally did now show in my blood samples. After eight years on the LCHF diet my values are exemplary, just as when I started the regime.... In conclusion, all the parameters associated with metabolic syndrome and type 2 diabetes has improved with LCHF. (Diet Doctor, 2014a; my translation).

In this case, Eenfeldt took part as the leader of a group, namely the proponents of the LCHF diet that follow his blog. When utilizing his expertise as a medical doctor to draw the blood samples from himself, he corroborates his personal beliefs with scientific evidence. Besides the main writers on the blogs, the readers that comment on the blog posts usually testify to the diet's plausibility, reaffirming the sense of a larger LCHF community and validating the examples illustrated on the blogs. Drawing parallels to the work of Jenkins et al. (2013), the individuals reading and commenting act more like a public than an audience. While publics are held to be collectives more than the sum of their parts, audiences are considered purely aggregates of individuals. The blog has formed a community of other LCHF supporters supporting each other, which acts more like an intertwined network with a clear intention towards agenda formation.

Strategies Used by LCHF Promoters to Gain Scientific Credibility

Within the dominant view of science popularization (Hilgartner, 1990), it is presumed that expert and lay audiences are separated by a wide gulf. This would certainly seem to be true, when as scholars we browse in any section of the library apart from our own, or when we see how issues from our own specialist subjects appear in the media. It is not easy to critique established scientific institutions, and not everyone can get away with it. By highlighting attributes associated with trustworthiness, all three LCHF promoters make extensive use of professional titles and university degrees on their blogs when presenting themselves to the public: Eenfeldt is a Swedish medical doctor specializing in family medicine (Diet Doctor, 2015a); Dahlqvist is a medical doctor who specializes in family medicine (Dahlqvist, 2015); and Fernholm has worked as a science journalist since 2001 when she completed her PhD in molecular biotechnology (Fernholm, 2015).

In order to question conventional science, the promoters need to construct their own authority. With credentials accepted in the two worlds, they are also able to act as mediators between established science institutions and laymen, or between science and popularized science (Gregory & Miller, 2000). Similarly, both Diet Doctor and Dahlqvist wear doctor's coats and stethoscopes on their blog profile pictures. Similar to another medical doctor and promoter of a controversial diet, Robert Atkins (1972), this attire is also reflected on their book covers. By wearing this symbolic attire and making references to their official credentials, they can be seen as belonging to the legitimate scientific community. However—paraphrasing Martin (1998)—by no longer preaching according to established convention, they have escaped from the citadel of dietary science, and now act as truth-tellers on behalf of the common man. The truth-teller approach is most evident with Fernholm:

My goal as a journalist is to scrutinize the scientific community in the same way as politicians are being investigated. Researchers and scientists have power over our health and wellbeing. My time in the research community has taught me that many draw far-fetched conclusions based on less robust science. This has among other things lead to the fat controversy which we see today. (Fernholm, 2015; my translation).

Many LCHF promoters believe the sugar industry to be responsible for the obesity epidemic, and that this industry is sponsoring the established nutrition committees. Thus, the researchers at the NFA are not to be trusted because they are receiving industry funding. On her blog, Dr. Dahlqvist states that "it is extremely insulting to blame all individuals who are overweight on their lack of physical activity. It is the sugar industry's strategy to promote their sugary products" (Dahlqvist, 2014; my translation). With these types of statements, the online promoters want to raise public skepticism over the alleged expert control of physical processes (Gregory & Miller, 2000). The non-mainstream diet experts also situate themselves as a freedom fighter against traditional health promotion institutions. Huovila and Saikkonen (2015) called this 'cultural struggle' and showed that nutrition counselling bloggers often positioned themselves as agents of cultural change against established authorities. It highlights the power structures that are associated and exercised in the context of healthy eating.

Meanwhile, the success of the LCHF diet suggests for many that archaic dietary advice is influenced by economical and market interests and the drastic prevalence of obesity and diabetes may be attributed to misleading official dietary recommendations. Researchers at the NFA usually have PhDs and use evidence-based recommendations. The three influential profiles in social media promoting LCHF also possess qualifications by being medical doctors or published researchers. Hence, they are asserting the fact that they are not merely "self-proclaimed experts" that use social media to promote their own opinions, but people with educational merits similar to researchers at national institutions. The difference they wish to highlight however is that they are not corrupted by industry.

It is interesting to note however that the most successful of these blogs is himself affiliated with industry. Diet Doctor is the most-visited health related blog in Sweden. Once he attained wide-ranging credibility and influence he was not slow to commercialize the newly acquired success. Dr. Eenfeldt sells vitamin supplements and blood pressure monitors on his blog (Diet Doctor, 2015c). When ordered through his website, a percentage of the sales are used to finance his commercial site. Thus, as argued by Jenkins (2008), Diet Doctor can be seen acting as a grassroots intermediary between the dieters reading his blog and the franchise wanting to capitalize from it. Dr. Eenfeldt has broadened his scope from focusing solely on the LCHF diet to including more health-related products and goods. As suggested by Jenkins (2008), brand messages gain greater credibility if shared by someone the audience already knows and trust. For that reason, companies have sought to identify and bolster their strongest online supporters, giving them what they need to help spread the word through the various networks to which they belong.

Moving from Subjective to Objective Evidence Formation

As LCHF promoters have mainly been criticized for using subjective evidence and personal stories, new online scientific initiatives have been started. Crowdfunding is an alternate source of funding, allowing entrepreneurs to raise funds through an open call on the Internet, usually within online social networks or blogs (Belleflamme, Lambert, & Schwienbacher, 2014). Instead of raising money from a small group of special investors, crowdfunding enables money to come from large audiences, where each person provides a small amount. As the LCHF community has grown more expansive during recent years, this strategy follows an intuitive logic. Both Fernholm and Eenfeldt are board members of a crowdfunding enterprise and make reference to the organization on their blogs. The Diet Fund was initiated in June 2014 (Diet Fund, 2014a), and as two of the five board members are high-profile LCHF promoters, it is difficult to see how this would not be reflected in the organization's work. The articulated objective with the fund is to sponsor well-designed nutrition studies to accumulate evidence that would reinforce individual testimonies and anecdotal evidence with credible research.

Medical treatments cannot be based on biomedical hypothesis or anecdotal stories. For a physician to recommend a certain diet, well-designed studies are needed that prove the effects and consider potential side effects. This is where the Diet Fund comes in, as it was started to finance high-quality studies. (Diet Fund, 2014b; my translation).

In addition to raising capital to conduct scientific studies, profiles within the LCHF community adapt similar organizational schemes as the conventional scientific establishment. One illustration is the well-regarded scientific conference (Hessel, 2015). The conference is an important arena for scholars to disseminate and recommence present trends in science. In 2015, one of the world's largest conferences of the LCHF diet was held—the Old Mutual Health Convention (2015). The event was widely promoted in social media and was sponsored by international renowned experts in the field of LCHF such as Professor Tim Noakes and his movement, the Real Meal Revolution (2014; 2015). There were around 650 people in the audience, mostly medical professionals, and there are already tentative plans for a similar conference next year in Europe, according to Eenfeldt (Diet Doctor, 2015b). The conference can be seen as a physical manifestation of the persuasive online networking conducted by these promoters. Thus, as put argued by Latour (1987), the online environment has enabled these advocates and non-mainstream scientists to connect with each other forming supporting coalitions aligning with traditional scientific traditions. Also, using functions qualified by larger online networks such as crowdfunding, LCHF promoters intend to gather resources to amass scientific evidence supporting their personal beliefs. If successful, this can be the last step toward gaining official recognition by the establishment, and in the long run, a modification of official dietary guidelines.

DISCUSSION AND CONCLUSION

This chapter has explored how well-timed events, such as the controversial trial with Dahlqvist and her subsequent vindication, paved the way for widespread LCHF opinion formation in social media. Social media channels, particularly different blog platforms, were then used as way to offer anecdotal evidence supporting the claims. As illustrated in this study, the potential to share user-generated content qualifies anecdotal evidence as a way of increasing the diet's believability. As Jenkins et al. (2013) argues, looking at consumers in social media as active rather than passive, they function as translators between information's contexts of production and reception. The people offering anecdotal evidence on the blogs act as 'multipliers' who attach new meaning to existing properties, as appraisers who evaluate the worth of different bids on our attention. Thus, under the spreadability model, information is often tailored and localized for certain audiences, by other members of the community. The members of the network evangelize for dietary information and experiences they want other community members to appreciate (Jenkins et al., 2013).

The constructions of anecdotal evidence constitute a benchmark for expert opinion of the permissibility of scientific knowledge and lay contestation of the margins of this knowledge. Moore and Stilgoe (2009) argues that in modern democratic societies, expertise must be both convincing and trustworthy when public engagement is no longer elective. At a certain point therefore, experts and decision makers must manage the claims made by non-scientists in public disputes. As Nisbet puts it (cited in Bonetta, 2007, p. 444),

In the digital age, information is found based on availability rather than accuracy. If different interest groups start blogs that attack peer-reviewed science, and the scientific community does not engage in similar communication mode, they will miss an important opportunity to educate the public.

The promotion of anecdotal evidence and self-experimentation however is typically scientifically inadequate due to lack of proper controls and sufficient subjects to generate meaningful results (Davis, 2003). Anecdotal evidence is a term whose denotation and dominion has mainly been delineated in contrast to expertise. Lay knowledge arguments from narrative traditions of social sciences refine the discrepancy between scientific and lay understandings of healthy nutrition (Gunnarsson & Elam, 2012; Moore & Stilgoe, 2009). Rhetorical and communicative approaches are usually outlined differently, depending on the underlying purpose. Huovila and Saikkonen (2015) showed that popular Finnish nutrition counselling bloggers favored personal, practical, and moral knowledge. This differed compared to the Finish National Institute for Health and Welfare (NIHW) bloggers that typically used less relatable, population-based means and causalities in their argumentation. However, both the nutrition counselling bloggers and the NIHW bloggers sought to create a connection with their respective audiences in order to express identification for typical challenges relating to healthy dieting. The primary objective between the bloggers diverged however; for the nutrition counselling bloggers, this was also an epistemic stance, as personal experiences of what kind of dietary regime that works were constructed as epistemically valid. On the contrary, for the NIHW bloggers, this sort of personal appealing simply functioned as a communicative tactic, and personal experiences were separated from knowledge claims about healthy eating.

An Evolution from Anecdotal to Evidence-Based Tactics

Interestingly the longitudinal analysis demonstrated how the LCHF promoters have started to primarily move from using anecdotal initiatives, to also enabling the accumulation of conventional scientific evidence. By using online initiatives such as crowdsourcing, the promoters aim to finance reliable scientific studies. Thus, these promoters try to capitalize on the network formation through social media by coming together and turning to idea formation. Overall, these findings partly contradict Latour (1987), since certain members of the public who challenge scientific claims can in fact gain a similar sort of authority as scientific experts. By attributing themselves with authority, such as highlighting their medical degrees, and using various forms of social media platforms, e.g., blogs and online social networks, they can marshal networks of support for their claims. In fact, social media permits the promoter of a scientific claim to disseminate scientific claims in action, to network opinion, and promptly dismiss scientific claims proclaimed by opponents.

This goes in line with Jauho (2016), who found that low-carbohydrate high-fat proponents in Finland are neither ignorant about scientific facts nor anti-science. Instead, Jauho showed that the proponents express multifaceted viewpoints about the nature of science, the place of individual experience in nutritional recommendations, and the reliability and trustworthiness of expert knowledge. Jauho (2016) further argues that the advocates of the diet engage in what he labels the social construction of competence because they present their positions as grounded in science and portray themselves as lay experts. Similarly, Knight (2015) showed that the low-carbohydrate dieters that she interviewed consisted of a mixed group in terms of how they perceived the science underling the particular diet. While some dieters wholeheartedly believed in nutritionist primitivism others were more skeptical. The dieters that were more skeptical emphasized a more intricate and complex reasoning of the primitive past, human evolutionary development and cross-cultural discrepancies in health and body weight.

This prove that the online diet proponents fill many and varied functions depending on the needs of the individual dieters following them. In the study by Setälä and Väliverronen (2014) the authors demonstrated that nutritional field experts were not sources of information when compared to scientific experts. Instead, the field experts functioned as authorized users of nutritional knowledge and information. They could provide advice and give practical and feasible recommendations to the dieters. Setälä and Väliverronen (2014) showed that the nutritional field experts also acted as what they label mediators of biological citizenship, as they encouraged their followers to claim a greater responsibility for their health. The informal experts thus complemented, rather than opposed, conventional nutritional experts.

Spreadable Media Facilitates Networked Alternative Expertise

In all, the promotion of the LCHF diet as an online phenomenon could be generalizable to a wider array of movements utilizing social media to provide an alternative to existing health-related standards and guidelines. It is a controversial topic wherein supporters use spreadable media to gain momentum and promote their cause against national agencies. Parallels can thus be drawn with other controversial topics such as anti-vaccine advocates working against national health ministries (Kata, 2012). The online environment provides easy access to information regarding nutrition and diets. Through the reframing of expertise and the notion of relativism, postmodernism allows for that information to be interpreted in various ways. Instead of a construal being wrong, it can be redefined as an alternate path to knowledge. With this paradigm in place, it is not difficult to see how online users attending the University of Google may be induced by what they might discover and how they can be cajoled by online promoters.

A communication network model should consider the borders of science not as hedges between isolated areas of intellectually activity, but as confines of open territories which could overlap with other domains, and which are themselves superposed on unabridged culture. These territories contain networks that define themselves by communication (Jenkins et al., 2013; Lewenstein, 1995). Thus, a network is defined by communication between its members, and membership in the community is conditioned on the act of communication. In this conceptual model, the popular and scientific becomes part of the same communication system, and the communicators involved become part of a single community. In line with ideas from the sociology of science, a communication network model permits popularization to be examined not as something marginal to scientific activity, or as aberrant or pathological, but as a vital function of regular scientific life (Gregory & Miller, 2000; Lewenstein, 1995).

Still, some researchers point out that the non-scientist public should not have the same kind of authority since their claims have not been exposed to the kind of challenges that claims endure in traditional scientific protocol (Bazerman, 1988). If a scientific claim that appears in the public domain has not first been published in peer-reviewed literature, the scientist has then broken with an important professional tradition (Gregory & Miller, 2000). However, members of the public have their own influential features because they can relate the abstractions of scientific knowledge to lived experience, and public debates provide their own sort of encounters with arguments. While it is important to recognize and correct inconsistent arguments, a strategy that goes beyond providing mere facts is probably necessary. With the LCHF promoters embracing the postmodern paradigm, which essentially questions an authoritative approach, facts may be reinterpreted as yet another opinion. This matter is as much about the perceived context around science, notions of risk, and trust in expertise as it is about the diet itself.

REFERENCES

Aftonbladet. (2013). *No, we did not claim that LCHF is necessarily the best diet* [my translation]. Retrieved February 2, 2015, from http://www.aftonbladet.se/debatt/article17631151.ab

Agatston, A. (2003). *The South Beach Diet*. London: Headline.

Atkins, C. R. (1972). Dr. Atkins' Diet Revolution: The High Calorie Way to Stay Thin Forever. D. McKay Co.

Banting, W. (1863). *Letter on Corpulence, Addressed to the public*. London: Harrison and Sons.

Bazerman, C. (1988). *Shaping Written Knowledge: The Genre and Activity of the Experimental Article in Science*. Madison, WI: University of Wisconsin Press.

Belleflamme, P., Lambert, T., & Schwienbacher, A. (2014). Crowdfunding: Tapping the Right Crowd. *Journal of Business Venturing*, *29*(5), 585–609. doi:10.1016/j.jbusvent.2013.07.003

Bokus. (2015). *Bestseller list - Medical literature* [my translation]. Retrieved February 5, 2015, from www.bokus.com/topplistor/medicin

Bonetta, L. (2007). Scientists Enter the Blogosphere. *Cell*, *129*(3), 443–445. doi:10.1016/j.cell.2007.04.032 PMID:17482534

Braun, V., & Clarke, V. (2006). Using thematic analysis in psychology. *Qualitative Research in Psychology*, *3*(2), 77–101. doi:10.1191/1478088706qp063oa

Brunel, O., & Pichon, P.-E. (2004). Food-related risk-reduction strategies: Purchasing and consumption processes. *Journal of Consumer Behaviour*, *3*(4), 360–374. doi:10.1002/cb.148

Bucchi, M. (1998). *Science and the Media: Alternative routes in scientific communication*. London: Routledge. doi:10.4324/9780203263839

Cederholm, T., & Rothenberg, E. (2016). Krypskytte mot vetenskapen äventyrar folkhälsosatsningar[Sniper attacks against science jeopardize public health investments]. *Lakartidningen*, *113*(16).

Counihan, C., & Van Esterik, P. (2013). *Food and Culture: A Reader* (Vol. 3). New York: Routledge.

Crawford, R. (1980). Healthism and the medicalization of everyday life. *International Journal of Health Services*, *10*(3), 365–388. doi:10.2190/3H2H-3XJN-3KAY-G9NY PMID:7419309

Cwiertka, J. K. (2006). *Modern Japanese cuisine: food, power and national identity*. London: Reaktion Books.

Dahlgren, P. (2009). *Media and Political Engagement: Citizens, Communication and Democracy*. Cambridge: Cambridge University Press.

Dahlqvist, A. (2014). Mai-Lis Hellenius: Sedentary disease [my translation]. *Dr Dahlqvist's blog concerning food and health.* Retrieved January 18, 2015, from http://annikadahlqvist.com/2014/07/06/mai-lis-hellenius-sittsjukan/

Dahlqvist, A. (2015). About Dr Annika Dahlqvist [my translation]. *Dr Annika Dahlqvist's weblog about food and health.* Retrieved January 21, 2015, from http://annikadahlqvist.com/om-dr-annika-dahlqvist/

Davis, J. K. (2003). Self-Experimentation. *Accountability in Research*, *10*(3), 175–187. doi:10.1080/714906095 PMID:14979319

Davison, C., Smith, G. D., & Frankel, S. (1991). Lay epidemiology and the prevention paradox: The implications of coronary candidacy for health education. *Sociology of Health & Illness*, *13*(1), 1–19. doi:10.1111/1467-9566.ep11340301

De Brun, A., McCarthy, M., McKenzie, K., & McGloin, A. (2014). Weight stigma and narrative resistance evident in online discussions of obesity. *Appetite*, *72*, 73–81. doi:10.1016/j.appet.2013.09.022 PMID:24096083

Diet Fund. (2014a). *About the diet fund* [my translation]. Retrieved January 27, 2015, from http://www.kostfonden.se/om-kostfonden/

Diet Fund. (2014b). *Our vision: more people should lead a healthier life* [my translation]. Retrieved January 3, 2015, from http://www.kostfonden.se/var-vision-fler-manniskor-ska-leva-ett-friskare-liv/

DN. (2013). *The popular high fat diets are a threat to public health* [my translation]. Retrieved January 8, 2015, from http://www.dn.se/debatt/de-populara-fettdieterna-ar-ett-hot-mot-folkhalsan/

Doctor, D. (2008). *The National Board of Health and Welfare approves of low carb diet* [my translation]. Retrieved January 18, 2015, from http://www.kostdoktorn.se/socialstyrelsen-godkanner-lagkolhydratskost

Doctor, D. (2012). *Food revolution: consume real food and eat your way to a better health* [my translation]. Retrieved February 4, 2015, from https://www.youtube.com/watch?v=9Hy737EuL-o

Doctor, D. (2013). *We who want to close down the National food agency* [my translation]. Retrieved January 12, 2015, from http://www.kostdoktorn.se/vi-som-vill-avveckla-livsmedelsverket

Doctor, D. (2014a). *My blood values after eight years of following the LCHF diet* [my translation]. Retrieved January 17, 2015, from http://www.kostdoktorn.se/mina-halsovarden-efter-atta-ar-pa-lchf

Doctor, D. (2014b). *Overall, I Now Have a Completely New Life*. Retrieved February 3, 2015, from http://www.dietdoctor.com/overall-now-completely-new-life

Doctor, D. (2015a). *About Diet Doctor*. Retrieved January 2, 2015, from http://www.dietdoctor.com/about

Doctor, D. (2015b). *The Launch of the Amazing LCHF Conference*. Retrieved February 27, 2015, from http://www.dietdoctor.com/the-launch-of-the-lchf-conference

Doctor, D. (2015c). *Reliable health products* [my translation]. Retrieved January 23, 2015, from http://www.kostdoktorn.se/rekommenderade-halsoprodukter

Doyle, J. (2012). New media and democratisation. *Irish Studies in International Affairs, 23*, 1-4. doi:10.3318/ISIA.2012.23.1

Eckler, P., Worsowicz, G., & Rayburn, J. W. (2010). Social Media and Health Care: An Overview. *PM & R*, *2*(11), 1046–1050. doi:10.1016/j.pmrj.2010.09.005 PMID:21093840

Edelman Trust Barometer. (2012). Retrieved 12 April, 2015, from http://trust.edelman.com/trust-download/global-results/

Eriksson, N. (2009). *Stupidly fat? The Doctor's solution to disease stirs debate* [my translation]. Retrieved February 1, 2015, from http://www.aftonbladet.se/nyheter/svininfluensan/article11978275.ab

Expressen. (2014). *Mats Lindgren, 61: LCHF cured me* [my translation]. Retrieved 8 February, 2015, from http://www.expressen.se/halsoliv/halsovikt/mats-lindgren-61-lchf-gjorde-mig-frisk/

Fernholm, A. (2012). *A sweeter blood: consequences on our health of living with a century of sugar* [my translation]. Stockholm: Natur & kultur.

Fernholm, A. (2015). Om Ann Fernholm [About Ann Fernholm]. *A sweeter life* [my translation]. Retrieved January 24, 2015, from http://ettsotareblod.se/ann-fernholm/

Freeman, B., & Chapman, S. (2008). Gone viral? Heard the buzz? A guide for public health practitioners and researchers on how Web 2.0 can subvert advertising restrictions and spread health information. *J Epidemiol Commun H*, *62*(9), 778–782. doi:10.1136/jech.2008.073759 PMID:18701726

Gerstenfeld, P. B., Grant, D. R., & Chiang, C.-P. (2003). Hate Online: A Content Analysis of Extremist Internet Sites. *Analyses of Social Issues and Public Policy (ASAP)*, *3*(1), 29–44. doi:10.1111/j.1530-2415.2003.00013.x

Giddens, A. (1990). *The consequences of modernity*. Cambridge, UK: Polity Press.

Google Inc. (2015). *Google trends*. Retrieved February 8, 2015, from http://www.google.se/trends/

GP. (2012). *Real meals are best for the health* [my translation]. Retrieved January 8, 2015, from http://www.gp.se/nyheter/debatt/1.901957-riktig-mat-ar-bast-for-halsan

Gray, J. A. (1999). Postmodern medicine. *Lancet*, *354*(9189), 1550–1553. doi:10.1016/S0140-6736(98)08482-7 PMID:10551517

Gregory, J., & Miller, S. (2000). Science. In *Public: Communication, Culture, And Credibility*. Cambridge, MA: Perseus Publishing.

Gunnarsson, A., & Elam, M. (2012). Food Fight! The Swedish Low-Carb/High Fat (LCHF) Movement and the Turning of Science Popularisation Against the Scientists. *Science as Culture*, *21*(3), 315–334. doi:10.1080/09505431.2011.632000

Hessel, V. (2015). Conferences are scientific market places. *Green Processing and Synthesis*, *4*(1), 1–2. doi:10.1515/gps-2014-0106

Hilgartner, S. (1990). The Dominant View of Popularization: Conceptual Problems, Political Uses. *Social Studies of Science*, *20*(3), 519–539. doi:10.1177/030631290020003006

Holmberg, C., Chaplin, E. J., Hillman, T., & Berg, C. (2016). Adolescents presentation of food in social media: An explorative study. *Appetite*, *99*, 121–129. doi:10.1016/j.appet.2016.01.009 PMID:26792765

Huovila, J., & Saikkonen, S. (2015). Establishing credibility, constructing understanding: The epistemic struggle over healthy eating in the Finnish dietetic blogosphere. *Health*. doi:10.1177/1363459315595849 PMID:26220062

Järvelä, K., Mäkelä, J., & Piiroinen, S. (2006). Consumers everyday food choice strategies in Finland. *International Journal of Consumer Studies*, *30*(4), 309–317. doi:10.1111/j.1470-6431.2006.00516.x

Jauho, M. (2016). The social construction of competence: Conceptions of science and expertise among proponents of the low-carbohydrate high-fat diet in Finland. *Public Understanding of Science (Bristol, England)*, *25*(3), 332–345. doi:10.1177/0963662514558167 PMID:25415233

Jenkins, H. (2008). *Convergence Culture: Where Old and New Media Collide*. New York: NYU Press.

Jenkins, H., Ford, S., & Green, G. (2013). *Spreadable Media: Creating Value and Meaning in a Networked Culture*. New York: NYU Press.

Johansson, I., Nilsson, L., Stegmayr, B., Boman, K., Hallmans, G., & Winkvist, A. (2012). Associations among 25-year trends in diet, cholesterol and BMI from 140,000 observations in men and women in Northern Sweden. *Nutrition Journal*, *11*(1), 40. doi:10.1186/1475-2891-11-40 PMID:22686621

Kaplan, M. D. (2012). *The Philosophy of Food*. University of California Press.

Kata, A. (2012). Anti-vaccine activists, Web 2.0, and the postmodern paradigm – An overview of tactics and tropes used online by the anti-vaccination movement. *Vaccine*, *30*(25), 3778–3789. doi:10.1016/j.vaccine.2011.11.112 PMID:22172504

Keen, A. (2007). *The cult of the amateur: How today's Internet is killing our culture* (1st ed.). New York: Doubleday.

Kjaernes, U. (2003). Food and nutrition policies of Nordic countries: How have they been developed and what evidence substantiates the development of these policies? *The Proceedings of the Nutrition Society*, *62*(2), 563–570. doi:10.1079/PNS2003269 PMID:14506905

Knight, C. (2011). If Youre Not Allowed to Have Rice, What Do You Have with Your Curry?: Nostalgia and Tradition in Low-Carbohydrate Diet Discourse and Practice. *Sociological Research Online*, *16*(2), 8. doi:10.5153/sro.2342

Knight, C. (2015). We Can't Go Back a Hundred Million Years. *Food, Culture & Society*, *18*(3), 441–461. doi:10.1080/15528014.2015.1043107

Lang, T., & Heasman, M. (2004). *Food Wars: The Global Battle for Mouths, Minds and Markets*. London: Earthscan Publications.

Latour, B. (1987). *Science in Action: How to Follow Scientists and Engineers through Society*. Milton Keynes, UK: Open University Press.

Laugharne, R. (1999). Evidence-based medicine, user involvement and the post-modern paradigm. *Psychiatric Bulletin*, *23*(11), 641–643. doi:10.1192/pb.23.11.641

Lenhart, A., Smith, A., Anderson, M., Duggan, M., & Perrin, A. (2015). *Teens, Technology and Friendships: Video Games, Social Media and Mobile Phones Play an Integral Role in How Teens Meet and Interact With Friends*. Retrieved August 10, 2015, from http://www.pewinternet.org/files/2015/08/Teens-and-Friendships-FINAL2.pdf

Lewenstein, B. V. (1995). From Fax to Facts: Communication in the Cold Fusion Saga. *Social Studies of Science*, *25*(3), 403–436. doi:10.1177/030631295025003001

Lieb, C. W. (1929). The effects on human beings of a twelve months exclusive meat diet: Based on intensive clinical and laboratory studies on two arctic explorers living under average conditions in a new york climate. *Journal of the American Medical Association*, *93*(1), 20–22. doi:10.1001/jama.1929.02710010026005

Loader, B. D., & Mercea, D. (2012). *Social Media and Democracy: Innovations in Participatory Politics*. London: Routledge.

Mann, J., McLean, R., Skeaff, M., & Morenga, L. T. (2014). Low carbohydrate diets: Going against the grain. *Lancet*, *384*(9953), 1479–1480. doi:10.1016/S0140-6736(14)61413-6 PMID:25390561

Mann, J., & Nye, E. R. (2009). Fad diets in Sweden, of all places. *Lancet*, *374*(9692), 767–769. doi:10.1016/S0140-6736(09)61575-0 PMID:19733769

Martin, E. (1998). Anthropology and the Cultural Study of Science. *Science, Technology & Human Values*, *23*(1), 24–44. doi:10.1177/016224399802300102

Martin, R. (2011). *Sweden battles national butter shortage*. Retrieved January 17, 2015, from www.thelocal.se/20110928/36412

Moore, A., & Stilgoe, J. (2009). Experts and Anecdotes: The Role of Anecdotal Evidence in Public Scientific Controversies. *Science, Technology & Human Values*, *34*(5), 654–677. doi:10.1177/0162243908329382

Myers, G. (2003). Discourse Studies of Scientific Popularization: Questioning the Boundaries. *Discourse Studies*, *5*(2), 265–279. doi:10.1177/1461445603005002006

Närlid, M. (2008). The National Board of Health and Welfare exonerate Annika Dahlqvist, but does not address the dietary recommendations [my translation]. *Journal of the Swedish Medical Association* [my translation]. Retrieved February 9, 2015, from http://www.lakartidningen.se/OldWebArticlePdf/8/8643/LKT0804s191_193.pdf

Närvänen, E., Kartastenpää, E., & Kuusela, H. (2013). Online lifestyle consumption community dynamics: A practice-based analysis. *Journal of Consumer Behaviour*, *12*(5), 358–369. doi:10.1002/cb.1433

NFA. (2011). *Annual report - 2010* [my translation]. Retrieved January 8, 2015, from http://tinyurl.com/ldlx2lx

NFA. (2013a). *Annual report - 2012* [my translation]. Retrieved January 8, 2015, from http://tinyurl.com/k7d3la4

NFA. (2013b). *Good school meals: Guidelines for primary schools, secondary schools and youth recreation centres*. Retrieved January 8, 2015, from http://tinyurl.com/lue3maa

Noakes, T. (2014). *The Noakes Foundation*. Retrieved February 26, 2015, from http://thenoakesfoundation.org/

Nordic Council of Ministers. (2014). *Nordic Nutrition Recommendations 2012* (5th ed.). Author.

Norman, C. (2012). Social media and health promotion. *Global Health Promotion and Education*, *19*(4), 3–6. doi:10.1177/1757975912464593 PMID:24803437

Old Mutual Health Convention. (2015). *The Old Mutual Health Convention 2015 Cape Town*. Retrieved February 19, 2015, from https://www.youtube.com/watch?v=x4XgqJjfLqs

Papacharissi, A. Z. (2010). *A Private Sphere: Democracy in a Digital Age*. Malden, MA: Polity.

Pellizzoni, L. (2003). Knowledge, Uncertainty and the Transformation of the Public Sphere. *European Journal of Social Theory*, *6*(3), 327–355. doi:10.1177/13684310030063004

Real Meal Revolution. (2015). *The Real Meal Revolution*. Retrieved February 14, 2015, from http://realmealrevolution.com/

Retriever. (2015). Retrieved January 3, 2015, from http://www.retriever-info.com/en/category/news-archive/

Rousseau, S. (2012). *Food and Social Media: You Are What You Tweet*. Lanham, MD: AltaMira Press.

SCHTA. (2010). *Food when you have Diabetes: A systematic literature review* [my translation]. Retrieved January 19, 2015, from http://www.sbu.se/contentassets/923855c431bc4f668746920cfb49d590/mat_vid_diabetes_fulltext.pdf

Scientific Journalists. (2015). *The scientific journalists* [my translation]. Retrieved January 8, 2015, from http://www.vetenskapsjournalisterna.se/index.php?page=english

Setälä, V., & Väliverronen, E. (2014). Fighting Fat: The Role of Field Experts in Mediating Science and Biological Citizenship. *Science as Culture*, *23*(4), 517–536. doi:10.1080/09505431.2014.905526

Shapin, S. (Ed.). (2007). *Expertise, common sense, and the Atkins diet*. Toronto, Canada: University of Toronto Press. doi:10.3138/9781442684720-012

Shepherd, A., Sanders, C., Doyle, M., & Shaw, J. (2015). Using social media for support and feedback by mental health service users: Thematic analysis of a twitter conversation. *BMC Psychiatry*, *15*(1), 29. doi:10.1186/s12888-015-0408-y PMID:25881089

Stahl, A. B. (2013). *Lchf less militant* [my translation]. Retrieved February 12, 2015, from http://www.svd.se/mat-och-vin/lchf-mindre-militant_8053806.svd

The National Board of Health and Welfare. (2013). *The National Public Health Report 2013* [my translation]. Retrieved January 9, 2015, from http://www.socialstyrelsen.se/Lists/Artikelkatalog/Attachments/19032/2013-3-26.pdf

Thompson, C. J. (2005). Consumer Risk Perceptions in a Community of Reflexive Doubt. *The Journal of Consumer Research*, *32*(2), 235–248. doi:10.1086/432233

Twingly. (2015). *The Blog portal* [my translation]. Retrieved January 3, 2015, from http://www.bloggportalen.se/BlogPortal/view/Home

Wansink, B., Tal, A., & Brumberg, A. (2014). Ingredient-based food fears and avoidance: Antecedents and antidotes. *Food Quality and Preference*, *38*(0), 40–48. doi:10.1016/j.foodqual.2014.05.015

Widdowson, E. M. (1993). Self-Experimentation in Nutrition Research. *Nutrition Research Reviews*, *6*(01), 1–17. doi:10.1079/NRR19930004 PMID:19094300

Wilson, K., & Keelan, J. (2009). Coping with public health 2.0. *CMAJ: Canadian Medical Association Journal*, *180*(10), 1080–1080. doi:10.1503/cmaj.090696 PMID:19433834

Winbladh, L. F. (2011). *LCHF: A fat food philosophy* [my translation]. Retrieved February 13, 2015, from http://www.sydsvenskan.se/mat--dryck/lchf-en-fet-matfilosofi/

Wofford, J. (2012). User-generated content. *New Media & Society*, *14*(7), 1236–1239. doi:10.1177/1461444812453563

KEY TERMS AND DEFINITIONS

Anecdotal Evidence: The use of one or more personal accounts to either support or refute a (scientific) claim.

Blogs: A discussion or informational platform published online consisting of entries (i.e. blog posts) commonly presented in reverse chronological order.

Fad Diets: A diet that promises specific health benefits such as weight loss or longer life, with questionable evidence supporting it. The diets are characterized by decidedly restrictive or unusual food choices and normally follow nutrition trends.

Media Convergence: The integration of mass communication channels such as print, television, and the Internet, along with mobile and interactive technologies through digital media platforms.

Online Social Networks: Online services that allows individuals to construct a public or semi-public profile within a network, and specify other users with whom they share a connection.

Postmodern Medical Paradigm: Contemporary movement and paradigm asserting that patients are informed and actively involved in their health care by questioning traditional medical authorities.

Science Popularization: Traditionally refers to a two-stage approach whereby scientists first produce the genuine scientific knowledge that popularizers consequently distribute through simplified accounts.

Social Media: Umbrella term for online platforms and applications that allow its users to create individual personal profiles, generate and access searchable online content (e.g., videos, photos), construct online connections with other users, and view these social connections.

Chapter 3
Transmedia Storytelling Impact on Government Policy Change

Renira Rampazzo Gambarato
National Research University Higher School of Economics, Russia

Sergei Andreevich Medvedev
Dublin Institute of Technology, Ireland

ABSTRACT

This chapter discusses the impact of transmedia campaigns aimed at achieving a certain level of government policy change. Transmedia campaigns comprise a series of coordinated activities and organized efforts designed to achieve a social, political, or commercial goal by means of multiple media platforms. The Great British Property Scandal and Food, Inc. transmedia campaigns are considered to introduce the argument that this kind of multiplatform campaigning can actually produce concrete results in the political sphere. Moreover, this chapter focuses on the in-depth analysis of the transmedia strategies of the Fish Fight campaign to demonstrate how exactly transmedia strategies collaborate to influence policy change. The research findings point to the effective role of transmedia storytelling strategies in raising awareness in the political sphere through public participation in supporting relevant issues, influencing policy change.

INTRODUCTION

Transmedia storytelling involves the unfolding of a storyworld (Jenkins, 2006) in which installments of the narrative are spread across multiple media platforms to engage the audience and offer a more meaningful experience. More specifically, a transmedia campaign comprises a series of coordinated activities and organized efforts designed to achieve a social, political, or commercial goal by means of multiple media platforms (Francoli, 2014). This chapter discusses the impact of transmedia campaigns aimed at achieving a certain level of government policy change. *The Great British Property Scandal* and *Food, Inc*. transmedia campaigns are considered to introduce the argument that this kind of multiplatform campaigning can actually produce concrete results in the political sphere. Moreover, this chapter focuses on the analysis of the transmedia strategies of the *Fish Fight* campaign. This campaign, initiated in 2010,

DOI: 10.4018/978-1-5225-1862-4.ch003

was produced by the public service broadcaster Channel 4 in the United Kingdom (UK) and hosted by British chef Hugh Fearnley-Whittingstall. The transmedia campaign was designed to:

1. Draw the public's attention to the reckless discarding of caught fish because of the quota system intended to conserve fish stocks in the domain of the European Union (EU); and to
2. Pressure the authorities to change the EU Common Fisheries Policy (CFP).

The in-depth transmedia analysis of *Fish Fight* demonstrate how transmedia storytelling contributed to:

1. Make the public aware of the wasteful discarding of healthy fish at sea under the EU fishing quotas; and
2. To amend EU fishing policies.

The theoretical framework contemplates the conceptualization of transmedia storytelling (Gambarato, 2013; Jenkins, 2003, 2006; Pratten, 2011; von Stackelberg & Jones, 2014) in the scope of participatory theory (Arnstein, 1969; Carpentier, 2011, 2015, 2016; Carpentier & Dahlgren, 2014). The methodological approach of the fully developed case study is based on the transmedia analytical model by Gambarato (2013) and applied to *Fish Fight* to depict, in great detail, how exactly transmedia strategies collaborate to influence policy change. The research findings point to the effective role of transmedia storytelling strategies in raising awareness in the political sphere throughout public participation in supporting relevant issues, culminating in policy amendment. It is not surprising that storytelling has become an important tool in facilitating change in society (Maas, 2012; Semetko, 2004) because the human species is addicted to story, and stories touch every aspect of our lives, even saturating it (Gottschall, 2013).

Today's complex media environment is changing audience expectations of how, when, and where information is consumed. Media convergence is driving the development of new forms of storytelling in which integrated narratives are presented across multiple media. Participatory engagement of audiences through games, remixing content, and original user-created content is increasingly common. (von Stackelberg & Jones, 2014, p. 58)

This is the scenario in which transmedia storytelling is inserted. Although transmedia storytelling remains under construction, there are solid indications of its conceptualization. The advent of convergence culture made people's daily contact with media more complex from the viewpoint of the media platforms involved in the process as well as the blurring boundaries between audience consumption and production. Convergence as "the flow of content across multiple media platforms, the cooperation between multiple media industries, and the migratory behavior of media audiences who will go almost anywhere in search of the kinds of entertainment experiences they want" (Jenkins, 2006, p. 2) is closely associated with the idea of transmedia storytelling. "Thus, if convergence culture involves a multitude of mediums to provide the consumer with numerous ways of gathering communication and to enhance the participation and enjoyment of the audience, the use of TS [transmedia storytelling] seems the natural way to fulfill these expectations" (Gambarato & Alzamora, 2012, pp. 53–54). In this context, transmedia storytelling contributes to the increasing need for media projects that conform to the new multiscreen and multiplatform modes, content expansion, and audience participation. The transmedia approach provides the audience the opportunity to stay within the scope of a single story universe, while accessing unfolded content through various media channels. The term transmedia storytelling was coined by Henry Jenkins (2003, 2006) and defined as the art of building a storyworld, in which each extension makes a distinctive and valuable contribution to the overall story. Transmedia storytelling is not about repurposing the same content across different platforms but about the meaningful experience that the audience can have by engaging with the content extension of a story spread throughout multiple media channels. Pratten (2011, p. 1) emphasizes the importance of participatory elements inherently incorporated into transmedia narratives: "transmedia storytelling is telling a story across multiple media … with a degree of audience participation, interaction or collaboration." Hancox (2014) discusses transmedia strategies applied to social change and concludes that this kind of approach highlights "the dignity of the subjects and strives to convey the complexities of the lives and issues by taking advantage of the technology available to challenge audiences to enter, experience and interact with the stories in new ways." Gaming elements and participatory features, often present in transmedia projects, help transmedia producers interest audiences in various topics unrelated to the entertainment industry.

In this chapter, the in-depth analysis is focused on how the non-fictional *Fish Fight* campaign took advantage of transmedia storytelling strategies to engage the public and encourage them to take purposeful political action. The structure of the article includes:

1. The participation theory framework outlined in the realm of transmedia storytelling;
2. A brief description of the methodological approach;
3. The *Fish Fight* transmedia analysis;
4. The repercussion of the *Fish Fight* case; and
5. The conclusion, in which the key research findings are summarized.

PARTICIPATORY THEORY

In the midst of convergence and participatory cultures (Jenkins, 2006; Jenkins, Ford, & Green, 2013; Jenkins, Ito, & Boyd, 2015), or more precisely participatory theory (Carpentier, 2011, 2015, 2016; Carpentier & Dahlgren, 2014), participation is the key concept. From Arnstein's (1969, p. 216) definition of participation as "the redistribution of power that enables the have-not citizens, presently excluded from the political and economic process, to be deliberately included in the future," to Carpentier and Dahlgren's (2014, p. 45) statement that "participation captures a specific set of social practices that deal with the decision-making practices of actors," participation is intertwined with other concepts, such as empowerment, involvement, engagement, and so forth. Carpentier (2015) differentiates participation from access and interaction in the context of media production/reception. In relation to media content, Carpentier (2015) considers access as the presence of previously produced content, interaction as the selection and interpretation of content, and participation as the co-decision between producers and consumers on/with content. Moreover, the author highlights that, "Despite its conceptual contingency, participation is still very much defined by the concept of power" (Carpentier, 2015, p. 19) and "Participation then becomes defined as the equalisation of power relations between privileged and non-privileged actors in formal or informal decision-making processes" (Carpentier, 2016, p. 72). Jenkins et al. (2013, p. 156) also tackle the power issue and discuss meaningful participation, acknowledging the struggle between *corporate conception of participation (which includes within it a promise of making companies more responsive to the needs and desires of their "consumers") and a political conception of participation (which focuses on the desire for us all to exercise greater power over the decisions which impact the quality of our everyday lives as citizens).*

Jenkins et al. (2013, p. 163) emphasize that political participation reflects "a world where more media power rests in the hands of citizens and audience members, even if the mass media holds a privileged voice in the flow of information." This kind of participation in association with digital technologies leads to participatory political acts, such as being part of online communities, posting and sharing content in the realm of politics on social media networks, voting, and signing petitions online, for instance. According to Cohen, Kahne, Bowyer, Middaugh, and Rogowski (2012), participatory politics can attain large audiences and mobilize networks, support political agendas and provide feedback to politicians, and help circulate political information and produce original user-generated content. Benkler (2006, p. 11) debates the network topology and how the Internet improves the structure of the public sphere. In this sense, he depicts how mechanisms, such as mailing lists, websites, and mobility, are embedded in the social system and become a platform for politically relevant information. These mechanisms

enable anyone, anywhere, to go through his or her practical life, observing the social environment through new eyes—the eyes of someone who could actually inject a thought, a criticism, or a concern into the public debate. Individuals become less passive, and thus more engaged observers of social spaces that could potentially become subjects for political conversation; they become more engaged participants in the debates about their observations.

Carpentier and Dahlgren (2014, p.44) also "say that participation implies the involvement with the political, regardless of the character or scope of the context." Brough and Shresthova (2012) emphasize that younger generations "have become civically and politically engaged in new and different ways, related less to electoral politics or government or civic organizations and more to personal interests, social networks, and cultural or commodity activism." In this context, *Fish Fight* transmedia strategies establish the role of professional producers as facilitators, who engage the public across multiple media platforms aiming at generating awareness of the fish discard cause and serving as a call to political action. Media producers stimulate the audience's contribution to achieve their goal, changing the CFP. *Fish Fight* exemplifies grassroots circulation practices in which "a media text becomes material that drives active community discussion and debate at the intersection between popular culture and civic discourse—conversations that might lead to community activism or social change" (Jenkins et al., 2013, p. 168). Kligler-Vilenchik, McVeigh-Schultz, Weitbrecht and Tokuhama (2012), in their study of fan activism—that "brings together elements from fandom with elements that have traditionally been attributed to volunteerism and activism," stress that "shared media experiences, a sense of community, and the wish to help" emerged as characteristics that may unite fandom and the aspiration for social and political change.

The key to transmedia social impact campaigns is to harness the power of media narratives to activate audience's passion to act for the benefit of social and civic good. The power of media in this equation lies in its ability to raise awareness, deepen understanding, and stimulate participatory culture. (Zeiser, 2015, p. 357)

However, what motivates people to participate and take action, and embrace transmedia campaigns, such as *The Great British Property Scandal*, *Food, Inc.*, and *Fish Fight*? Drawing on Bradham's (2013, p. 122) list of motivations, individuals, in these cases, would like:

1. To challenge themselves to solve a tough problem;
2. To contribute to a large project of common interest;
3. To share with others;
4. To collaborate on environmental issues;
5. To protect food safety and animal welfare; and
6. To make a difference in society.

Nanì (2013, p. 20) adds "publics participate and get engaged because of the rise of a new culture that enhances the co-creation of 'spreadable' texts." Among the series of models of engagement, such as the *dragonfly effect* by Aaker and Smith (2010), the equation proposed by Nanì (2013, p. 36) seems to clearly describe the major focuses that should be involved in the development of transmedia projects for social (political) change in the scope of participatory culture: "Civic engagement = specific proposition + design to call attention + publics' empowerment."

Following the equation, *a specific proposition* refers to offering the public concrete goals. "Goals that are not specific are usually vague, risking, therefore, not being meaningful … and most likely unclear, ergo lacking engaging power" (Nanì, 2013, p. 36). *Design to call attention* concerns the use of text and audiovisual features across multiple media platforms to attract people's attention to the project and, consequently, to the cause behind it. *Publics' empowerment* is about "the synergy between producers and publics in the co-production of meaningful texts" (Nanì, 2013, p. 37). In the case of *Fish Fight*, which will be deeply analyzed later, its specific proposition is the goal to change the CFP because 50% of the fish caught in the North Sea are thrown back dead (*Fish Fight*, 2014). The design of the Channel 4 project calls attention with a contemporary clean layout, the good technical quality of the audiovisual content, and the leadership of a celebrity chef. The public empowerment of *Fish Fight* gives people the opportunity to demonstrate their support by signing an online petition to end fish discarding. More than 870,000 signatures to the petition accompanied by 225,000 emails and 220,000 tweets to members of the European Parliament (MEPs) (*Fish Fight*, 2014) secured discussion of the issue and kept the pressure on the discard ban high. As a result, in 2013, the parliament voted to ban the wasteful practice of throwing away healthy fish at sea. "After significant opposition to the changes from the powerful industrial fishing lobby, and multiple attempts to scupper the process, the final vote was won by an emphatic 502 votes to 137" (Harvey, 2013a).

The Case of *The Great British Property Scandal* and *Food, Inc.*

The Great British Property Scandal is a transmedia experience aiming to offer an alternative solution to the long-standing housing-crisis in the UK. In 2011, Channel 4 created the project together with architect George Clarke, who started a personal crusade against the British housing problem after realizing the fact that there are two million families in need of a home and one million empty houses in the UK (Syndicut, n.d.). The project is focused on not wasting empty properties as a result of the difficulties faced by private owners to bring them back into use. Therefore, the main goal is to force the issue on the government agenda, fighting for effective policy amendment and, consequently, promoting the revitalization of abandoned properties.

The project has as its specific propositions the goal to report empty homes to the authorities and establish a low-cost loan fund to support empty homes owners, who want to refurbish their properties and put them back into the market. The design of the Channel 4 project calls attention with an updated layout, the good technical quality of the audiovisual content, and the leadership of Clarke, a well-known host. The publics' empowerment of *The Great British Property Scandal* gives the audience the opportunity to demonstrate their support by reporting empty homes via mobile application and by signing an online petition to pressure the government to launch a low-cost loan fund in favor of the renovation of empty properties. The transmedia project revolves around two TV series and Channel 4 broadcasted simultaneously two other TV programs integrated into *The Great British Property Scandal* storyworld: *Phil's Empty Homes Giveaway* and *Kevin's Grand Design*. The single episode of *Phil's Empty Homes Giveaway* is dedicated to the homeless issue and the two episodes of *Kevin's Grand Design* discuss the building of affordable and sustainable homes. In addition, the project's website (Channel 4, n.d.b) serves as a hub to redirect the audience to the other transmedia extensions and, above all, is the platform for the online petition. Facebook and Twitter accounts promote the project and become an important source of information about parallel initiatives related to the housing-crisis. The YouTube channel helped to spread the trailer of the project that went viral and helped to call people's attention to the housing issue. The iOS mobile application *Empty Homes Spotter* enables the audience to make photos of empty properties and report them to the authorities.

The achievements of *The Great British Property Scandal* demonstrate that the project was able to inspire the audience to take action regarding the deep-rooted housing issue in the UK and to promote concrete policy change. According to Channel 4 (n.d.a), *The Great British Property Scandal* results are:

1. Over 118,200 petition signatures,
2. 10,000 empty homes were reported,
3. £17 million allocated for the new low-cost loan fund in the UK, and
4. George Clarke was appointed Independent Empty Home Advisor to the Government.

In spite of all the positive results connected to this project, the endemic housing-crisis in the UK is far from a complete resolution.

In 2009, the feature-length documentary *Food, Inc.*, directed by Robert Kenner, shocked audiences worldwide. The film exposes the dubious practices of corporate farming in the United States (US) and its close relationship with the government, concluding that the agribusiness produces unhealthy and environmentally harmful food. In addition, the documentary depicts the abusive treatment dispensed by farmers to both animals and corporate employees. Milner (2010) argues that "Food, Inc. is not a documentary, it is a shockumentary. Its sole purpose is to make the viewer so outraged at the content that they react." *Food, Inc.* storyworld expanded in transmedial directions, especially focusing on social actions regarding the food industry, such as *Take Part* (dealing with school lunch policy change) and *Fix Food* (fighting to reduce the amount of antibiotics given to animals).

The production company Participant Media, one of the film co-producers, took the lead on the film's outreach campaign: "its goals are to reform food policies and empower individuals to influence corporations through their consumer choices" (Golding, 2009).

Through strategic partnerships with nonprofits and corporations, Participant [Media] is working to get the film into diverse communities as well as organizing screenings for policy gatekeepers. They recently brought Food, Inc. to Washington, DC, where the film was shown to some very high level administrators including Congress and cabinet members, as well as figures at major regulatory agencies. (Golding, 2009)

Take Part (n.d.) campaign, connected to *Food, Inc.*, provides a space where the general public can learn more about food issues and support legislation to exclude junk food from schools in the US. Participant Media, which is behind this initiative, hosted a petition that garnered 250,000 signatures (Nelson, 2012) to change national school lunch policy and the campaign succeeded: "Thanks in part to action by our *Food, Inc.* community, the Child Nutrition Reauthorization act passed in 2010. And today, (…) ambitious new nutrition guidelines for school meals were unveiled. It's a move that will significantly impact our nation's youth" (Nelson, 2012). The new policy specifies larger amounts of fruit, vegetable, and whole grains intake in schools and less sodium and trans fat. Notwithstanding, the new lunch standards for school children do not end the American battle against obesity and unhealthy industrial food system.

TRANSMEDIA ANALYSIS OF *FISH FIGHT*

With the purpose to go deeper into the impact of transmedia storytelling on government policy change, the *Fish Fight* case study is analyzed applying Gambarato's (2013) transmedia project design analytical model. The model aims at outlining the essential features of the campaign, which depicts how multiplatform production, audience participation, and digital technology concretely contribute to policy change. The analytical model is structured according to 10 distinguishable topics guided by a series of practicable questions. A concise description of the analytical model is provided in Table 1.

The Case of *Fish Fight*

Premise and Purpose

For centuries, discarded fish has been an inevitable consequence of the fishing industry, which is justified by numerous economic, political, biological, and technological reasons. European fisheries look for ways to reduce expenses, and landing the whole catch would impose extra costs on the economic sector. Discarding fish allows fisheries to land only the species considered valuable by the final consumers. Undersized or unsellable species are often thrown back into the sea dead, but through this process, final consumers can purchase fish and other marine products they want at more affordable prices. Fishing fleets are also subject to the European CFP, which sets quotas for how much of each species can be caught in a specific area. European fisheries operate under individual quota shares, which, sometimes, do not allow fishing companies to land certain non-target species. In some cases, this bycatch may be reduced by improving gear technology used by fishing vessels. However, common fishing technologies do not completely avoid bycatch, since some fish species swim together.

The current European environmental discourse, which proclaims that society is responsible for protecting nature, was a fertile ground for the *Fish Fight* grassroots campaign and was its fundamental premise. The sustainable fishing campaign developed by Fearnley-Whittingstall benefited from and effectively incorporated the discourse supported by Europeans. The petition launched by the campaign and signed

Table 1. Concise description of the transmedia project design analytical model

Topic	Practicable Questions
1. Premise and purpose State clearly what the project is about and why it exists.	What is the project about? Is it a fiction, nonfiction, or mixed project? What is its fundamental purpose? Is it to entertain, to teach, or to inform? Is it to market a product?
2. Narrative It is the structure that storyworlds evoke in the transmedia milieu.	What are the narrative elements of the project? What is the summary of its storyline? What is the time frame of the story? What are the strategies for expanding the narrative? Are negative capability and migratory cues included? Is it possible to identify intermedial texts in the story?
3. Worldbuilding A storyworld or story universe should be robust enough to support expansions, going beyond a single story.	When does the story occur? Which is the central world where the project is set? Is it a fictional world, the real world, or a mixture of both? How is it presented geographically? Is the storyworld large enough to support expansions?
4. Characters The features of the characters and how they appear across all the platforms should be consistent.	Who are the primary and secondary characters of the story? Does the project have any spinoffs? Can the storyworld be considered a primary character on its own? Can the audience be considered a character as well?
5. Extensions Transmedia storytelling involves multiple media in which the storyworld will unfold and be experienced.	How many extensions does the project have? Are the extensions adaptations or expansions of the narrative through various media? Is each extension canonical? Does it enrich the story? Are the extensions able to spread the content and provide the possibility to explore the narrative in-depth?
6. Media platforms and genres A transmedia project necessarily involves more than one medium and can also embrace more than one genre (science fiction, action, comedy, etc.).	What kind of media platforms (film, book, comics, games, etc.) are involved in the project? Which devices (computer, game console, tablet, mobile phone, etc.) are required by the project? How does each platform participate and contribute to the whole project? What are their functions in the project? Is each medium really relevant to the project? What is the rollout strategy to release the platforms? Which genres (action, adventure, detective, science fiction, fantasy, etc.) are present in the project?
7. Audience and market Scoping the audience is fundamental for a more appropriate delivery of the transmedia experience. The TS involves some level of audience engagement.	Who is the target audience of the project? What kind of "viewers" (real-time, reflective, and navigational) does the project attract? Do similar projects exist? Do they succeed in achieving their purpose? What is the project's business model? Was the project successful revenue-wise? Why?
8. Engagement All the dimensions of a transmedia project, at a lower or higher level, are drawn into the experience of people when engaging with the story.	Through what point of view (PoV) does the audience experience this world: first person, second person, third person, or a mixture of them? What role does the audience play in this project? What are the mechanisms of interaction in this project? Is there any participation involved in the project? Does the project work as a cultural attractor/activator? Is there UGC related to the story (parodies, recaps, mash-ups, fan communities, etc.)? Does the project offer the audience the possibility of immersion into the storyworld? Does the project offer the audience the possibility to take elements of the story and incorporate them into everyday life? Is there a system of rewards and penalties?
9. Structure The organization of a transmedia project, the arrangement of its constituent elements, and how they interrelate can offer concrete elements for analysis.	When did the transmediation begin? Is it a proactive or retroactive project? Is this project closer to a transmedia franchise, a portmanteau transmedia story, or a complex transmedia experience? Can each extension work as an independent entry point to the story? What are/were possible endpoints of the project? How is the project structured?
10. Aesthetics The visual and audio elements of a transmedia project should also contribute to the overall atmosphere and enhance the experience spread throughout multiple media platforms.	What kinds of visuals are used (animation, video, graphics, a mix) in the project? Is the overall appearance realistic or a fantasy environment? Is it possible to identify specific design styles in the project? How does audio work in this project? Are there ambient sounds (rain, wind, traffic noises, etc.), sound effects, music, and so forth?

(Gambarato, 2014, pp. 96–97)

by 870,000 people was intended to demonstrate people's concern about existing discarding practices and current European regulations for the fishing industry (*Fish Fight*, 2014). As declared by *Fish Fight* creators, the specific propositions of the campaign were to stop "environmental crime" and eliminate the practice of the "waste of good food" (*Hugh's Fish Fight*, 2010) by reforming the CFP. The project is non-fictional. It was designed to affect the real lives of millions of people, who are involved with the fishing industry as either producers or consumers, by changing industry regulations and practices as well as people's consumer habits.

Narrative

The narrative of the project began in November 2010, when the campaign's website (*Fish Fight*, 2014) was launched and the first video was uploaded on the official *Fish Fight* YouTube channel. The video quickly went viral, and therefore, the discard topic entered the agenda. Further developments of the campaign demonstrated how *Fish Fight* was intended to tackle the two purposes of the campaign, as the narrative clearly unfolded in two directions. First, the sustainable fishing campaign tried to popularize bycatch species among consumers. For instance, the *Fish Fight* iOS mobile application included a menu composed exclusively of dishes that contained unpopular, unsellable fish species. Second, *Fish Fight* actively supported the idea of banning discarding practices, which finally resulted in a historical decision made by the European Commission in 2013 (*Fish Fight*, 2014). The narrative also incorporated gaming elements. About 42,000 people took the *Fish Fight* quiz designed to educate consumers about fish (Peters, 2011). The key factor that led to the positive result was the signed petition along with tweets and emails sent by *Fish Fight* enthusiasts to the members of the European Parliament. The campaign succeeded in its primary goal, but the fight is not over.

Worldbuilding

The *Fish Fight* story developed between 2010 and 2013. The campaign started as a local British project; it soon extended beyond the British borders as thousands of people all over the world participated in the actions generated by *Fish Fight* (*Fish Fight*, 2014). Jenkins et al. (2013, p. 133) stress that "the licensing and coproduction arrangements sustaining transmedia practices have evolved over several decades, and so has audience appreciation of 'world building.'" Regarding the key stakeholders, which felt an impact from the *Fish Fight* activities, the sustainable fishing campaign was designed to embrace everyone involved in the marine product production to consumption process, that is, final consumers, supermarkets, fish suppliers, fisheries, and the European Commission, which sets the CFP. In particular, as part of the strategy encouraging people to eat a more diverse range of fish, *Fish Fight* initially persuaded about 450 fish and chips shops in the UK to start selling the Mac "Mackerel" Baps. An interactive Mac Map available on the website (*Fish Fight*, 2014) shows that currently 6,000 additional fish and chips shops consume the undervalued mackerel, promoted by the campaign (*Fish Fight*, 2014). Even more importantly, because of the campaign, major UK supermarket chains finally agreed to change their fish sourcing policies (*Fish Fight*, 2014). The world of *Fish Fight* is robust enough to support extensions. Initially targeted at British society, the campaign influenced the fishing industry throughout the whole EU. The Channel 4 *Fish Fight* TV series was filmed in Thailand, the Philippines, and Antarctica, which expanded the campaign's borders (Richardson, 2012).

Characters

The celebrity chef, food writer, and television host Hugh Fearnley-Whittingstall is the face of *Fish Fight*. He focused on the topic long before the beginning of the campaign discussed in this paper. He received controversial publicity as the host of *River Cottage*, a Channel 4 documentary TV series which portrayed him downsizing to a small English town to create and live on a subsistence farm. As the *Fish Fight* campaign gained momentum, Fearnley-Whittingstall became a symbol of the fight to ban fish discards. However, the audience of *Fish Fight* is a primary character of the project, since people played a crucial role in campaigning. Without the support demonstrated by hundreds of thousands, the campaign would not have succeeded in pressuring the European Parliament. Tens of celebrities, among them Prince Charles, openly supported the sustainable fishing campaign and shared the *Fish Fight* message among millions of their followers on social media. More precisely, the celebrity supporters "carried the message to an online audience of over 16,000,000" (*Fish Fight*, 2014). One of the most influential supporters was the internationally acclaimed British chef, TV host, and restaurateur Gordon Ramsay. He stated:

It just doesn't make any sense that in this day and age, when we are so aware of the depletion of our fish stocks, thousands of tonnes of dead fish are being thrown back into the sea. Something has to be done and by supporting this campaign, we are one step closer to bringing about reform. (Fish Fight, 2014)

Some of the campaign extensions—such as the *Fish Fight* quiz and the Mac Bap campaign—focus on mackerel, emphasizing this specific undervalued species. In addition, *Fish Fight* has spinoffs, such as the *What Are Your Prawns Eating?* campaign and *Hugh's Fish Fight: Save Our Seas*, which extend the boundaries of the project and exploit a wider range of topics related to the current European environmental discourse.

Extensions

The *Fish Fight* campaign, as a transmedia project, has multiple extensions throughout different media platforms. Distinctive and valuable units of content are distributed to provide the audience with the opportunity to explore the narrative in depth and change food policy. *Fish Fight* includes the following extensions (*Fish Fight*, 2014) (see Table 2).

The projects' narrative is consistent along all the extensions, and each one, including the spinoffs, is canonical. The audience is encouraged to spread the content since the extensions, to a greater or lesser extent, are connected to social media networks. Most importantly, the majority of the extensions are designed to enable the audience to express their opinion and make an impact on relevant environmental issues by signing the petition and flooding officials with emails and tweets.

Media Platforms and Genres

The media involved in *Fish Fight* encompass the Web, television, DVD, mobile, print, and social media. The rollout strategy started with the release of the viral video *Hugh's Fish Fight: Join the Fish Fight* on YouTube, in 2010. The video exposes shocking facts about the fish discard in the North Sea, such as the amount of healthy fish thrown back dead because of the CFP regulations. The video boosted audience interest, directed them to seek more information in the campaign's website, and encouraged further

Table 2. The Fish Fight extensions

Extension	Media Platform	Date of Launch	Commentary
Hugh's Fish Fight: Join the Fish Fight YouTube video	Web (Hugh's Fish Fight: Join the Fish Fight, 2010)	Nov 2010	Video with more than 356,000 views
Fish Fight website	Web (Fish Fight, 2014)	Nov 2010	The petition and the mailing and tweeting campaigns are available in the website
Facebook page	Social media (Hugh's Fish Fight, n.d.)	Nov 2010	245,000 fans in May 2016
Twitter account	Social media @hughsfishfight	Nov 2010	50,400 followers in May 2016
Hugh's Fish Fight television series	Television	Season 1 = Jan 2011 Season 2 = Feb 2013	Two seasons aired on Channel 4
Fish Fight quiz	Web (Peters, 2011)	Jan 2011	42,000 players
Mac Bap campaign	Print and Web	Jan 2011	
Fish Fight iOS mobile application	Mobile	Aug 2011	Free app (105,000 downloads)
Full-page newspaper advertisements	Print	June 2012	Ads in four European newspapers targeting key ministers of fisheries
DVDs of *Fish Fight*	DVD	Autumn 2012	DVDs were sent to hundreds of MEPs across Europe
Hugh's Fish Fight: Save Our Seas campaign	Television and Web	Feb 2013	24,000 emails to the government
What Are Your Prawns Eating? campaign	Television and Web	Feb 2013	About 50,000 tweets to supermarkets

discussions and sharing on social networks. The campaign was followed by the broadcast of the two seasons of *Fish Fight* on Channel 4. The successful television series—the first season with four episodes and the second with three—had a considerable impact on a broader audience and participatory actions. The television series attracted more than 3 million viewers, were re-broadcasted in 28 other countries, and were screened at 11 international film festivals (*Fish Fight*, 2014). During the broadcast of the first series, the petition signatures increased from 30,000 to 500,000 within three days (*Fish Fight*, 2014). In one advertisement break alone, 40,000 people signed the petition, and the website had 12 million page views during the airing of the television series' first season (*Fish Fight*, 2014).

The launch of the iOS mobile application also helped increase audience engagement. The aim of the application was to encourage users to consume sustainable fish by displaying valuable information about a number of fish species, offering 50 recipes with sustainable fish choices, and revealing a guide of restaurants committed to sustainability. "The app proved popular and became Channel 4's second most downloaded app. In addition to this, the app went on to be included in the App Store Rewind 2011—'The Best of the Year', within the Lifestyle section" ("Fish Fight included in App Store Rewind," 2011). Although the application was available only to iOS users, *Fish Fight* made a downloadable .pdf version accessible to everyone. Concerning devices, a computer is required to gain access to the online extensions of the project, a television set in the case of the Channel 4 broadcasting and a smartphone or tablet to better benefit from the mobile application. Documentary is the genre that most appropriately describes the *Fish Fight* approach, uniting old and new media to shape food policy change. The purpose of embracing different media platforms to develop the storyworld is to intensify audience engagement, although an era of transmedia extensions might be criticized by the "decline of any type of storytelling that doesn't lend itself well to a webisode series, co-creation with the audience, or 'user-generated content'" (Jenkins et al., 2013, p. 140).

Audience and Market

The project, although primarily focused on the UK audience, easily reached international audiences mainly because of the direct involvement of the EU in the discard issue, Channel 4 penetration, and the spreadable potentiality of social media networks. Thus, *Fish Fight* turned into a global call-to-action in the public and private spheres. For instance, people in 195 countries supported the campaign's online petition (*Fish Fight*, 2014). "In a world where audiences now regularly use Twitter, Facebook, blogs, and video-sharing sites to react to mass-media offerings, media producers and marketers increasingly recognize and respect the influence of these grassroots intermediaries" (Jenkins et al., 2013, p. 142). *Fish Fight* not only recognized the influence of grassroots intermediaries but also invested in the public's participation to pressure the political authorities and legitimately change fishery policy.

In this context, the actual audience of *Fish Fight* goes beyond a particular demographic group and incorporates savvy online users as well as offline crowds. The objective, clear, and direct specific proposition of *Fish Fight* and the audience's free access to the campaign collaborated to hook different prospective audiences. Within the story universe of the campaign, as Jenkins et al. (2013, p. 148) stated, "producers envision the transmedia space as offering different appeals to different niche audiences: the people playing the games may not be the same people reading the webcomics." Fearnley-Whittingstall's project inspired several other campaigns regarding similar issues, such as ocean conservation. For instance, non-profit organizations (NGOs) like Greenpeace, Marine Conservation Society, World Wild Fund for Nature (WWF), and Client Earth are actively fighting for marine causes. In 2011, the cross-party Fish for the Future (2013) group was established within the European Parliament to combat overfishing. More recently, Oceana's global campaign *Save the Oceans: Feed the World* was launched with the support of 20 of the top chefs worldwide, including Ferran Adrià and Joan Roca (Embiricos, 2015). Furthermore, Germany, Spain, France, and Poland launched their own fish fights (*Fish Fight*, 2014). In Germany, for instance, chef Tim Mälzer joined the cause and launched *Tims Fish Fight* (Mälzer, 2012) in April 2012, in front of the parliament in Berlin. "German politicians have shown strong support for ending discards and overfishing in the new CFP" (*Fish Fight*, 2014). Concomitantly, in Poland, chef Robert Makłowicz (2012) launched *Ryba za Burta!* (Fish Overboard!) in front of the parliament in Warsaw.

The focus on the wasteful practice of discarding was tabled by the European Commission already under the previous Commissioner for Maritime Affairs & Fisheries, Joe Borg. Since then the issue has been influenced by the Fish Fight campaign, which has helped the current Commissioner, Maria Damanaki, highlight the problem of discarding among the general public across Europe. ("Fish Fight campaign launch in Poland," 2012)

In addition, Greenpeace played an important role in *Fish Fight*: "Greenpeace has been proud to fight the good fish fight with Hugh and we have been collaborating with him on a number of issues"

(Mackenzie, 2011). For instance, the research by Greenpeace concerning fishing methods was used by the campaign (Bravo, n.d.), as well as the NGO's expertise in dealing with environmental issues and videos and other materials they produce. The organization's international network amplified the *Fish Fight* message. Greenpeace acknowledges that

by championing the need for real reform of European fishing laws—something Greenpeace and other groups are working on—and exposing the wasteful reality of discards, Hugh has helped raise awareness at the highest levels in Europe. It now seems that real action to end discarding fish might actually happen. (Mackenzie, 2011)

Engagement

The project turned hundreds of thousands of ordinary people into campaign supporters by informing them about the issue, as seen from the viewpoint of the project's authors, and then turned supporters into activists by supplying them with mechanisms for influencing government decisions related to the issue. *Fish Fight* effectively utilized the campaign's enthusiasts as its driving force and empowered the public. In addition to the call-to-action to sign the petition, in December 2011, when the new CFP was being discussed in the European Parliament, the *Fish Fight* webpage offered the public the opportunity of easily sending thousands of emails to MEPs and, consequently, directly influence the CFP. In March 2012, when the future of the discard ban was threatened by countries such as Spain and France, which did not support the new CFP, and the major fish suppliers in the EU, *Fish Fight* developed "an online tool allowing Fish Fighters to tweet every fisheries minister across Europe in their own language. Over 135,000 tweets were sent" (*Fish Fight*, 2014). Jenkins et al. (2013, p. 136) discussed the dominant appointment model (dependence on the broadcast schedule) versus the emergent engagement model and stated that "the engagement model suggests that having something to do also gives fans something to talk about and encourages them to spread the word to other potential audience members." In addition, Jenkins et al. (2013, p. 140) urge us to "think of 'engagement' as the emotional connections between viewers and desired content." The *Fish Fight* storyworld, experienced in the second and third person, emotionally connects the audience to the relevant environmental, political, and economic issues of discard.

Fish Fight operates in participation *in* the media and participation *via* the media levels. The first implies using media and engaging in the creation (or co-creation) of content, specially facilitated by digital technologies. The latter involves the context and the issues to which the media connect the audience. Participation via the media surpasses the media and focuses on mediatized social domains (Carpentier & Dahlgren, 2014, p. 44). This is an inherent characteristic of transmedia storytelling. Jenkins et al. (2013, p. 148) have emphasized how "transmedia practices, for example, are designed to give viewers something to do and something to talk about in relation to media content."

Structure

Fish Fight was designed to embrace multiplatform media production from the beginning in 2010 (the pro-active transmedia project). The transmedia strategy involved launching the website and the viral video on YouTube first, in anticipation of the premiere of the Channel 4 television series, in January 2011. Along with the preparation for the airing of the first episode of the television series, the campaign's website was updated and re-launched. The success of *Fish Fight* lead to the release of the iOS mobile application and the second season on Channel 4. All the social media channels have been available since 2010 and concretely contributed to the effectiveness of the public participation. The different extensions of *Fish Fight* functioned as independent entry points, welcoming the audience to be immersed in the storyworld. The audience could choose their own path throughout the multiple media platforms incorporated in the campaign, without necessarily accessing all of them. The reward in migrating from one extension to another is the enrichment of the overall transmedia experience. Although the campaign officially ended, it is still running online and attracting participation despite the positive results the campaign has already achieved.

Aesthetics

The overall design of the project reflects its documentary nature and its digital appeal. The Channel 4 television series, on the one hand, attracted attention with a high-quality production of audiovisual content (documentary style), and the well-known host Hugh Fearnley-Whittingstall as well as other celebrity chefs such as Jamie Oliver and Gordon Ramsay. In addition, the design of the multiple digital extensions, especially the campaign's website, attracts attention by the profuse use of information graphics—infographics. The combination of data visualization and design to increase engagement and memorability, popularized infographics in recent years. Harrison, Reinecke, and Chang (2015, p. 1187) stress that the infographics'

goal is to provide readers with an overview of a particular topic through data and other available information. Infographics are an effective means for telling stories about data, as they capture a reader's attention by structuring these data stories with principles of graphic design.

Harrison et al.'s (2015, p. 1190) experiment on the aesthetic appeal of infographics indicates that "the first impression of appeal is based on how colorful and visually complex an infographic is." In addition, in order to optimize the design of infographics to make a good first impression, "designers should aim for a low to medium complexity (e.g., by choosing a limited number of image and text areas), and a medium to high colorfulness (e.g., by increasing the saturation and contrast between colors)." The series of *Fish Fight* infographics operate with low complexity, focusing on a simple, clean, and clear layout, which follows the research results by Harrison et al. (2015). However, regarding the colorfulness, *Fish Fight* infographics mostly rely on blue palettes, and the monotone choice, although coherent to the campaign's topic, does not necessarily take full advantage of color contrast. Notwithstanding this, the design of *Fish Fight* functions as a tool of engagement, disseminating the relevant information around discard issues and calling people to participate actively. The campaign's rhetorical style is persuasive, strong and quite assertive. Expressions such as "crazy EU laws," "senseless waste," and "insane waste" (*Fish Fight*, 2014) describe the issue in the infographics, for instance, and collaborate to sensitize both the general audience and the politicians. Overall, the ample usage of infographics across the digital channels of the campaign is an efficacious measure for engaging the public.

FISH FIGHT REPERCUSSIONS

The *Fish Fight* campaign motivated people to oppose fish discards as conservation practice. The acclaimed production won several prizes ("Hugh's Fish Fight shortlisted again," 2012), among them the 2011 BAFTA for best program in the features category and the 2013 Maritime Media Award. The fact that the campaign was backed by Channel 4, a significant public service broadcaster, and celebrities such as Stephen Fry, Jamie Oliver, and Gordon Ramsay, definitely contributed to its achievements. Parenthetically, Channel 4, as a pioneer in multiplatform production, made a "significant economic investment" in multiplatform commissioning with "considerable economic and cultural rewards" (Bennett, Strange, Kerr & Medrado, 2012, p. 6) and became a "world leader in multiplatform production" (Bennett et al., 2012, p.18). "The value of multiplatform is connected to the ability of online platforms to provide greater depth of information and opportunities for participation, which at their best, can empower citizens to 'make a difference'" (Bennett et al., 2012, p. 18). In a research report concerning British multiplatforming public service broadcasting, Bennett et al. (2012, p. 14) conclude that the new characteristics of the sector are connected to "its potential to inspire, empower and engage; and an emphasis on innovation in digital production." In the context of *Fish Fight*, as stressed by Blake (2011), "officials are bowing to pressure for reform of Europe's fishing industry after more than 650,000 [870,000 in 2014] people signed a petition calling for 'discards' to be banned following a series of programs publicizing the issue on Channel 4." Although the EU quota system could be considered "bizarre" (Blake, 2011), the ban of this conservation practice advocated by *Fish Fight* was far from unanimous.

On the one hand, the enormous waste of fish because of the CFP is undeniably pernicious. Chivers (2014) stated that, "in one of the European Union's more ludicrous and inexcusable laws, fishermen have to throw away huge amounts of perfectly good fish, because of badly designed and frankly idiotic quota rules." One main reason behind the overfishing and consequent discard is that "in mixed fisheries, it can be impossible for fishermen to control the species that they catch in their nets" (Blake, 2011). Therefore, when they have exceeded their quota or do not have quota for certain species they have caught, the discard occurs. "Discarding … has been the most striking example of the failures of a common fisheries policy that green groups have said is 'broken' and encourages overfishing instead of protecting dwindling stocks" (Harvey, 2013a). The result is that "about half of the fish in the North Sea alone [is] being thrown back dead, even though they are edible and healthy" (Harvey, 2013b). In addition, the majority of discarded fish are already dead. The Food and Agriculture Organization of the United Nations estimated that "1.3 million tons of fish and other marine animals are thrown back every year" (Blake, 2011).

On the other hand, the Scottish Fishing Federation (SFF), for instance, opposed the proposals spearheaded by Hugh Fearnley-Whittingstall, saying that it "would do more harm than good and represent a threat to coastal communities across the country" (Johnson, 2011). Spain and France also opposed the policy change because "the reforms could mean fishermen would have to stop fishing when they have reached their quota for a particular species to avoid catching it accidentally" (Blake, 2011). Moreover, there was concern about the enforcement measures. The EU's fishing lobby heavily opposed the changes, particularly the operators of industrial-size vessels, because if they "are forced to land all the fish they net, they could end up with catches of lower value species, or lower quality specimens, so being able to select the highest value fish can help them maximize their profits" (Harvey, 2013a).

Notwithstanding this, Maria Damanaki, the EU fisheries commissioner, proposed changes in the CFP. Her proposal suggested that "all catches should be landed and counted against quota" (Blake, 2011). The commissioner praised the work of the *Fish Fight* campaigners in bringing the subject to wider attention and mobilizing citizens to sign the online petition (Harvey, 2013b). Meanwhile, Hugh Fearnley-Whittingstall renewed the campaign in 2013 (Roberts, 2013). The new Channel 4 series *Hugh's Fish Fight: Save Our Seas* highlights the destruction of the seabed:

The dredging of seabeds with nets weighted with huge metal ploughs, tearing up all life, rocks and seaweeds and leaving a barren environment is one of the most destructive ways of gathering seafood, but is legally used to gather scallops and other bottom-dwelling species. (Harvey, 2013b)

The fight now is to persuade EU ministers to define a broader network of marine conservation zones, where fishing would be regulated to preserve stocks and the seabed. In addition, the campaign intends to pressure supermarkets to not commercialize seafood caught with destructive methods such as dredging. The goal is to ban destructive fishing methods (*Fish Fight*, 2014). In anticipation of consumer reaction, at least one retailer, Booths, has stopped selling dredged scallops (Harvey, 2013b). The new campaign also received criticism. Once more, the SFF is against *Fish Fight* arguing that "scallop dredging had been portrayed in a way that was 'inaccurate and negative'" (Harvey, 2013b).

Bertie Armstrong, SFF chief executive, insisted that scalloping affects a very small part of the seabed, with vessels continuously fishing in the very same area for decades; therefore, it would be disproportionate to imply that scalloping causes major damage (Harvey, 2013b). Despite criticism, *Fish Fight* exceeded its original goal. EU fish discard ban was adopted by the Fisheries Council of Ministers in February 2013. British Prime Minister David Cameron concluded that "the current regime of discarding fish that are perfectly heathy is not acceptable and needs to change" (*Fish Fight*, 2014).

The ban is being introduced in phases to help fishermen adapt to a landing obligation. The pelagic discard ban came into force on 1 January 2015. It prohibits the dumping of species like mackerel and herring, which Hugh's *Fish Fight* campaign had a focus on from the beginning. The demersal discard ban took effect in January 2016, covering the discard of seabed species such as haddock. In addition, the reformed CFP increased quotas for European fisheries and included funding for new and more sustainable fishing gear. As agreed by EU officials, "a complete ban on the discarding of all quota species will be in place by 2019" ("Department for Environment, Food & Rural Affairs," 2016).

CONCLUSION

The Great British Property Scandal, Food, Inc., and especially *Fish Fight* demonstrate how multiplatform media production could raise public awareness and influence policy change with political participation. The synergy between various media platforms resulted in varied options for the audience to access the campaigns and motivated them to join the fight to reform rules and regulations for social good. "Transmedia approaches yield more meaningful entertainment experiences" (Jenkins et al., 2013, p. 137). Although Jenkins et al. (2013) stressed the entertainment facet of transmedia storytelling, it certainly goes beyond entertainment, as the purposeful experience of these campaigns confirms.

Carpentier and Dahlgren (2014, p.43) acknowledge that "we see many citizens engaging politically, but outside the electoral system" and justify that it happens "often propelled by frustrations that the established parties are insufficiently responsive." That is what happened in all the transmedia campaigns mentioned in the chapter. In the case of *Fish Fight*, citizens were absorbed by the debate about the fishing industry, the market prices, the government quota system, the need to secure fish stocks, and alternative sustainability, and consequently were compelled to act politically. Hugh Fearnley-Whittingstall concluded that "when people take action…. Politicians have to listen" (*Fish Fight*, 2014), and they did. Carpentier (2011, p. 17) proposes minimalist and maximalist kinds of participation, and *The Great British Property Scandal, Food, Inc.* and *Fish Fight* exemplify the maximalist version, which goes beyond the selection of representatives by voting (minimalist) and offers a more extensive form of participation by influencing policymaking. Participation focuses "on the distribution of power within society" (Carpentier & Dahlgren, 2014, p. 47) and these transmedia campaigns represent the viability to achieve it.

Taken together, the phenomena of collective intelligence and participatory culture require media to set the audience into motion. Media projects, which can unite people with common interests and provide them with practical tools to express themselves, were defined by Jenkins (2006, p. 95) as cultural attractors and cultural activators. *The Great British Property Scandal, Food, Inc.*, and *Fish Fight* functioned as cultural attractors and activators. In the case of *Fish Fight*, the campaign dealt with an issue relevant to the contemporary European environmental agenda and, therefore, amassed a huge audience interested in the problem and enthusiastic about participating in the problem-solving actions. *Fish Fight* effectively exploited the spectrum of environmental and food issues that people are concerned about and embraced further problems related to the campaign's initial purpose.

REFERENCES

Aaker, J., & Smith, A. (2010). *The dragonfly effect: Quick, effective, and powerful ways to use social media to drive social change*. San Francisco, CA: Jossey-Bass.

Arnstein, S. R. (1969). A ladder of citizen participation. *Journal of the American Planning Association, 35*(4), 216–224.

Benkler, Y. (2006). *The wealth of networks: How social production transforms markets and freedom*. New Haven, CT: Yale University Press.

Bennett, J., Strange, N., Kerr, P., & Medrado, A. (2012). *Multiplatforming public service broadcasting: The economic and cultural role of UK digital and TV independents*. London: Royal Holloway and University of London. Retrieved from http://eprints.bournemouth.ac.uk/21021/1/bennett-strange-kerr-medrado-2012-multiplatforming-psb-industry-report.pdf

Blake, H. (2011, February 28). Hugh Fearnley-Whittingstall wins his Fish Fight: Discarding dead fish may be banned. *The Telegraph*. Retrieved from http://www.telegraph.co.uk/news/worldnews/europe/8350443/Hugh-Fearnley-Whittingstall-wins-his-Fish-Fight-discarding-dead-fish-may-be-banned.html

Bradham, D. (2013). Crowdsourcing: A model for leveraging online communities. In A. Delwiche & J. Henderson (Eds.), *The participatory culture handbook* (pp. 120–129). New York, NY: Routledge.

Bravo, L. (n.d.). Fish labels debunked. *Channel 4*. Retrieved from http://www.channel4.com/programmes/hughs-fish-fight/articles/all/fish-labels-debunked

Brough, M. M., & Shresthova, S. (2012). Fandom meets activism: Rethinking civic and political participation. *Transformative Works and Cultures, 10*. doi:10.3983/twc.2012.0303

Carpentier, N. (2011). *Media and participation: A site of ideological–democratic struggle*. Bristol, UK: Intellect.

Carpentier, N. (2015). Differentiating between access, interaction and participation. *Conjunctions: Transdisciplinary Journal of Cultural Participation*, *2*(2), 7–28. doi:10.7146/tjcp.v2i2.22915

Carpentier, N. (2016). Beyond the ladder of participation: An analytical toolkit for the critical analysis of participatory media processes. *Javnost. The Public*, *23*(1), 70–88.

Carpentier, N., & Dahlgren, P. (2014). The social relevance of participatory theory. In G. Patriarche, H. Bilandzic, N. Carpentier, C. Ponte, K. C. Schrøder, & F. Zeller (Eds.), Building bridges: Pathways to a greater societal significance for audience research (pp. 37–52). Brussels, Belgium: COST Action ISO906.

Channel 4. (n.d.a). *Campaign results*. Retrieved from http://www.channel4.com/programmes/the-great-british-property-scandal/articles/all/campaign-results

Channel 4. (n.d.b). *The Great British Property Scandal*. Retrieved from http://www.channel4.com/programmes/the-great-british-property-scandal

Chivers, T. (2014, March 2). Hugh's Fish Fight, Channel 4, review. *The Telegraph*. Retrieved from http://www.telegraph.co.uk/culture/tvandradio/tv-and-radio-reviews/10669329/Hughs-Fish-Fight-Channel-4-review.html

Cohen, C., Kahne, J., Bowyer, B., Middaugh, E., & Rogowski, J. (2012). *Participatory politics: New media and youth political action*. Oakland, CA: Mills College School of Education.

Department for Environment, Food & Rural Affairs. (2016). *UK fishermen see next phase of the discard ban take effect* [Press release]. Retrieved from https://www.gov.uk/government/news/uk-fishermen-see-next-phase-of-the-discard-ban-take-effect

Embiricos, G. (2015, February 10). 20 of the world's top chefs are gathering for a cause: To save the oceans. *Food Republic*. Retrieved from http://www.foodrepublic.com/2015/02/10/20-worlds-top-chefs-are-gathering-cause-save-ocean

Fish Fight. (2014). Retrieved from http://www.fishfight.net/

Fish Fight campaign launch in Poland. (2012, March 15). *The Fisheries Secretariat*. Retrieved from http://www.fishsec.org/2012/03/15/fish-fight-campaign-launch-in-poland/

Fish Fight included in app store rewind 2011. (2011, December 20). *Clusta*. Retrieved from http://www.clusta.com/blog/fish-fight-included-in-app-store-rewind-2011

Fish for the Future. (2013). Retrieve from https://fishforthefutureeu.wordpress.com/

Francoli, M. (2014). Exploring the concept of "social media campaign.". In J. Bishop (Ed.), *Transforming politics and policy in the digital age* (pp. 133–144). Hershey, PA: IGI Global. doi:10.4018/978-1-4666-6038-0.ch009

Gambarato, R. R. (2013). Transmedia project design: Theoretical and analytical considerations. *Baltic Screen Media Review*, *1*, 80–100.

Gambarato, R. R. (2014). Transmedia storytelling in analysis: The case of Final Punishment. *Journal of Print and Media Technology Research*, *3*(2), 95–106.

Gambarato, R. R. & Alzamora, G. (2012). Transmedia storytelling initiatives in Brazilian media. *Medien Journal – Zeitschrift für Kommunikationskultur*, *4*, 51–62.

Golding, S. (2009). *Change: It's what's for dinner: 'Food, Inc.' takes on agribusiness*. International Documentary Association. Retrieved from http://www.documentary.org/content/change-its-whats-dinner-food-inc-takes-agribusiness

Gottschall, J. (2013). *The storytelling animal: How stories make us human*. New York, NY: Houghton Mifflin Harcourt.

Hancox, D. (2014, January 10). Amplified activism: Transmedia storytelling and social change. *The Writing Platform*. Retrieved from http://www.thewritingplatform.com/2014/01/amplified-activism-transmedia-storytelling-and-social-change/

Harrison, L., Reinecke, K., & Chang, R. (2015). Infographic aesthetics: Designing for the first impression. In *Proceedings of the SIGCHI Conference on Human Factors in Computing Systems* (pp. 1187–1190). New York, NY: ACM. doi:10.1145/2702123.2702545

Harvey, F. (2013a, February 6). MEPs vote to ban discards in historic reform of fishing policy. *The Guardian*. Retrieved from http://www.theguardian.com/environment/2013/feb/06/meps-back-fishing-policy-reform

Harvey, F. (2013b, February 14). Fish Fight renews campaign to protect the seabed. *The Guardian*. Retrieved from http://www.theguardian.com/environment/2013/feb/14/fish-fight-campaign-marine-life

Hugh's Fish Fight. (n.d.). In *Facebook* [Page type]. Retrieved from https://www.facebook.com/hughs-fishfight

Hugh's Fish Fight: Join the Fish Fight. (2010, November 17). Retrieved from http://www.youtube.com/watch?v=L2fZcmjbqpA

Hugh's Fish Fight shortlisted again. (2012, February 21). *KEO films*. Retrieved from http://www.keo-films.com/news/hughs-fish-fight-shortlisted-again/

Jenkins, H. (2003, January 15). Transmedia storytelling. *Technology Review*. Retrieved from http://www.technologyreview.com/news/401760/transmedia-storytelling/

Jenkins, H. (2006). *Convergence culture: Where old and new media collide*. New York, NY: New York University Press.

Jenkins, H., Ford, S., & Green, J. (2013). *Spreadable media: Creating value and meaning in a networked culture*. New York, NY: New York University Press.

Jenkins, H., Ito, M., & Boyd, D. (2015). *Participatory culture in a networked era: A conversation on youth, learning, commerce, and politics*. Malden, MA: Polity Press.

Johnson, S. (2011, March 1). Fishermen attack "superficial TV" discards ban. *The Telegraph*. Retrieved from http://www.telegraph.co.uk/news/uknews/scotland/8354266/Fishermen-attack-superficial-TV-discards-ban.html

Kligler-Vilenchik, N., McVeigh-Schultz, J., Weitbrecht, C., & Tokuhama, C. (2012). Experiencing fan activism: Understanding the power of fan activist organizations through members' narratives. *Transformative Works and Cultures*, *10*. doi:10.3983/twc.2012.0322

Maas, A. (2012). Living storytelling as an impetus for organizational change: Towards connective observing and writing. *Narrative Works: Issues, Investigations, and Interventions*, *2*(1), 150–169.

Mackenzie, W. (2011, August 4). Hug brings his Fish Fight for one last round. *Greenpeace*. Retrieved from http://www.greenpeace.org.uk/blog/oceans/hugh-fearnley-whittingstall-brings-back-fish-fight-one-last-round-20110804

Makłowicz, R. (2012). *Ryba za Burta!* [Fish Overboard!]. Retrieved from http://www.maklowicz.pl/o-mnie/robert-maklowicz/akcje

Mälzer, T. (2012). *Tims Fish Fight*. Retrieved from http://www.tim-maelzer.info/tag/wwwfishfightde/

Milner, J. (2010, April 20). Documentary review: Food, Inc. *My Literary Quest*. Retrieved from https://myliteraryquest.wordpress.com/2010/04/20/documentary-review-food-inc/

Nanì, A. (2013). *Crossmedia practices for the enhancement of civic engagement* (Unpublished master's thesis). Tallinn University Baltic Film and Media School, Tallinn, Estonia.

Nelson, N. (2012, January 25). 'Food, Inc.' fans helped changed national school lunch policy. *Take Part*. Retrieved from http://www.takepart.com/article/2012/01/25/lunch-looking-new-federal-guidelines-mandate-more-fruits-and-veggies-school-kids

Peters, R. (2011, January 11). Quiz: do you know your sea fish? *The Guardian*. Retrieved from http://www.theguardian.com/lifeandstyle/quiz/2011/jan/11/sea-fish-quiz

Pratten, R. (2011). *Getting started in transmedia storytelling: A practical guide for beginners*. Seattle, WA: CreateSpace.

Richardson, C. (2012, July 23). River Cottage's Hugh Fearnley-Whittingstall is coming to town. *Mercury*. Retrieved from http://www.thewestonmercury.co.uk/what-s-on/latest-films-reviews/river_cottage_s_hugh_fearnley_whittingstall_is_coming_to_town_1_1455913

Roberts, C. (2013, February 15). Why Hugh Fearnley-Whittingstall's Fish Fight is still necessary. *The Guardian*. Retrieved from http://www.theguardian.com/commentisfree/2013/feb/15/hugh-fearnley-whittingstall-fish-fight-necessary

Semetko, H. A. (2004). Media, public opinion, and political action. In J. Downing (Ed.), *Handbook of media studies* (pp. 351–374). Thousand Oaks, CA: Sage. doi:10.4135/9781412976077.n18

Syndicut. (n.d.). *The Great British Property Scandal*. Retrieved from http://www.syndicut.com/Posts/Channel-4/Great-British-Property-Scandal

Take Part. (n.d.). *Food, Inc*. Retrieved from http://www.takepart.com/foodinc/

von Stackelberg, P., & Jones, R. E. (2014). Tales of our tomorrows: Transmedia storytelling and communicating about the future. *Journal of Futures Studies*, *18*(3), 57–76.

Zeiser, A. (2015). *Transmedia marketing: From film and TV to games and digital media*. Burlington, MA: Focal Press.

KEY TERMS AND DEFINITIONS

Bycatch: The incidental capture of non-target species during fishing.

Common Fisheries Policy (CFP): A set of rules and regulations supporting sustainable fishing practices in EU countries.

Demersal Fish: Fish species living on or near the bottom of seas or lakes.

Grassroots: Pertaining to ordinary people, especially contrasted with an elite.

Pelagic Fish: Fish species inhabiting open water away from the bottom.

Proactive Transmedia Project: A project planned to be transmedia from the beginning.

Spinoff: A narrative work that focuses on a particular topic, character, or event of an already existing work.

Viral Video: The video that becomes popular through a rapid process of Internet sharing, especially through social media networks.

Chapter 4

The Demobilizing Potential of Conflict for Web and Mobile Political Participation

Francis Dalisay
University of Guam, Guam

Matthew J. Kushin
Shepherd University, USA

Masahiro Yamamoto
University at Albany, State University of New York, USA

ABSTRACT

In this chapter, we expand the idea that conflict avoidance (CA) inhibits online political participation. We specifically propose that CA has a direct negative link with traditional online political participation and online political expression, and an indirect negative link with these two forms of participation when mediated by political interest and internal political efficacy. We test our propositions through analyzing data from a survey of young adult college students residing in a battleground state in the U.S. Midwest conducted during the weeks prior to the 2012 U.S. presidential election. Our results showed that CA has a direct negative association with both traditional online political participation and online political expression. CA also has a negative relationship with political interest and internal political efficacy, which in turn, are positively linked with traditional online political participation and online political expression. We discussed implications.

INTRODUCTION

Conflict is ubiquitous in American politics (Jamieson, 1992). During the run up to the 2016 presidential election, for instance, it was not uncommon to see candidates and their supporters attacking their opponents (Jaffe, 2016; Chozik, 2016). American media also tend to cover politics as a conflict between political actors or groups (Cappella & Jamieson, 1997; Herbst, 2010). Viewers of American television are also constantly exposed to conflict-laden news coverage on 24-hour news cycle cable channels such as CNN, Fox, and MSNBC that often portray heated exchanges between political commentators (For-

DOI: 10.4018/978-1-5225-1862-4.ch004

gette & Morris, 2006; Jamieson & Cappella, 2009; Mutz, 2015; Sobieraj & Berry, 2011). Furthermore, political arguments have been commonplace in U.S. online forums and social network sites (Coe, Kenski, & Rains, 2014; Hmielowski, Hutchens, & Cicchirillo, 2014; Papacharissi, 2004; Sobieraj & Berry, 2011). In a recent study of more than 400,000 tweets posted by more than 140,000 individual Twitter users during the 2012 election, Vargo and Hopf (in press) found a prevalence of incivility on the social media platform.

The ever-present nature of conflict in American politics and public affairs media coincides with a scholarly interest in the potential that such conflicts might alienate citizens from the political process (e.g., McClurg, 2006). Research particularly suggests that conflict avoidance (CA) could be inhibiting offline political participation, political interest, and internal political efficacy (Ulbig & Funk, 1999). However, in light of today's world of ubiquitous Internet connectivity, this line of research remains narrow in two important ways. First, there is limited understanding about the potential that CA might also decrease online political participation. With a few exceptions (e.g., Vraga, Thorson, Kligler-Vilencik, & Gee, 2015), few studies have examined whether CA is inversely related with online forms of political participation more common in today's Internet landscape, including online forms of politically expressive acts performed via social media and mobile devices (Pew Research Center, 2014; Smith, 2009, 2011; Yamamoto, Kushin, & Dalisay, 2015). Second, while research shows political interest and internal political efficacy are two key psychological antecedents of offline political participation (e.g., McLeod, Scheufele, & Moy, 1999; Moeller, de Vreese, Esser, & Kunz, 2014; Verba, Schlozman, & Brady, 1995), a question not satisfactorily investigated by empirical studies is whether CA may also undermine online political participation by first inhibiting efficacy and political interest. That is, CA may be linked to lower online political participation because it may dampen one's interest in, and perceived competence to be part of, the political process.

To address the two above noted voids in the research, the present study's purpose is two-fold. First, we examine whether CA has a direct negative relationship with traditional online political participation and online political expression. Second, we test a mediation model whereby CA is posited to be indirectly related to online political participation and online political expression via its negative links with political interest and internal political efficacy. Using data from a survey of young adult college students conducted during the weeks prior to the 2012 presidential election, and in a battle ground state in the U.S., the present study examines the potential direct and indirect negative relationship of conflict avoidance with traditional online political participation and online political expression. A state in the U.S. Midwest, where campaign battles were heated leading up to the election, serves as a proper context for the present research. We examine the demobilizing role of CA in online participation among young adults because these persons are known to use digital and social media more frequently than other age groups (e.g., Pew Research Center, 2014; Smith, 2009, 2011). Empirical investigation along these lines is important and timely, given that research suggests that conflict, as manifested in both civil and uncivil discourse, is pervasive in online public affairs discussions (Coe et al., 2014; Papcharissi, 2004).

BACKGROUND

Conflict Avoidance

Interpersonal conflict refers to a disagreement or difference between two or more individuals (Putnam & Poole, 1987). Conflict occurs when a party perceives and/or actually experiences an "incompatibility of values, expectations, processes or outcomes" with another party (Ting-Toomey, 1994, p. 360). Conflicts are inherent in human interactions. As such, people adopt particular styles to resolve or manage them. Defined broadly, a conflict management style is a patterned response to interpersonal conflict that is a product of socialization (Lim, 2009). Scholars have generally studied five types of conflict management styles: avoiding, obliging, compromising, dominating, and integrating (Rahim, 1983). Avoidance, in particular, is the style categorized as the refusal to recognize a conflict and engage in any action toward its resolution. Individuals tending to resolve conflict with this style evade directly addressing disagreements through suppressing their opinions, withdrawing, or failing to act (Rahim, 1983). Conflict avoidance is known to make one reluctant to join interpersonal discussions (e.g., Conrad, 1991). Further, individuals who evade conflict tend to refrain from conflict-related communication in an attempt to maintain harmonious relationships (Lim, 2009).

Forms of Online Political Participation

The general will of the people of a political state is dependent on the willingness of individual citizens to participate in policy making processes (Friend, 2015). This idea of citizen engagement, expressed long ago by Rousseau, remains central in a modern democracy. Verba et al. (1995) define political participation as citizen acts that have the potential to influence public policies or the election of policymakers, including but not limited to voting, working for political campaigns, signing petitions, and attending political rallies. Political participation, thus, is the mechanism through which citizens voice their interests, concerns, and preferences, and engage in democratic governance.

In today's digitally networked society, political participation is not limited to offline, face-to-face settings. The growth of the Internet and social media enables citizens to partake in politics in new ways. Citizens can visit a candidate's Website to make campaign contributions, watch videos of political rallies live-streamed by a campaign, and sign up online to volunteer for a campaign, encourage others to vote, among others (Gil de Zúñiga, Molyneux, & Zheng, 2014; Yang & DeHart, 2016). Beyond these conventional types of political participation, citizens also use interactive online media, such as blogs, Facebook, and Twitter to express political opinions such as through posting political views, sharing news, and creating political videos and photos (Gil de Zúñiga et al., 2014; Rainie, Smith, Schlozman, Brady, & Verba, 2012; Yamamoto et al., 2015).

While online political participation is common among older adults (Towner &Muñoz, 2016), reports suggest that this activity is especially popular among young adults (Rainie, 2012; Rainie et al., 2012). Given varied forms of political participation enabled by online media, Bennett, Wells, and Freelon (2011) proposed two styles of participation among the young in today's digital era. The dutiful style of online participation concerns one-way input by young citizens directed at government and formal public institutions (e.g., sending emails to public officials and news media outlets, singing online petitions, making campaign contributions online). The actualizing style of online participation focuses on self-expression, with civic input covering various action contexts (e.g., government, activism). This style of participation stresses communal interaction where citizens are both creators and consumers of collective intelligence. Interactive online platforms have been shown to promote this actualizing style of online political engagement (Shehata, Ekström & Olsson, 2015).

Political expression via mobile devices is another avenue for an actualizing form of online political participation. Communication enabled by mobile phones has multiple unique characteristics such as portability, mobility, and immediacy. As Campbell (2013) notes, mobile media can foster "mediated social connectivity while the user is in physical motion" (p. 9), thus enabling continuous human interaction without interruption caused by device size and distances in physical space. Mobile phones are now widely adopted among young Americans (Anderson, 2015; Smith, 2015), and increasingly used for political purposes (Martin, 2015; Yamamoto et al., 2015; Rainie et al., 2012). In the 2016 presidential election primaries, campaigns actively use text messages and apps to send updates to supporters and recruit volunteers. Supporters also can use mobile phones to engage in various expressive activates such as posting photos or videos of campaign rallies and telling others that they are at political events on social networking sites.

As citizens increasingly engage in politics online, researchers have re-conceptualized political participation in online contexts and examined what drives online political participation (e.g., Gil de Zúñiga et al., 2014; Kushin, 2009; Towner, 2013; Yang & DeHart, 2016). This line of inquiry recognizes differences in skills and resources required for offline and online political participation. For example, Best and Krueger (2005) reported that civic skills, such as making a group decision at a meeting and planning a meeting, were positively linked with offline political participation, but not online political participation. In contrast, Internet skills predicted online, but not offline, political participation. Hargittai and Shaw (2013) similarly showed that Internet skills were positively associated with online political information consumption and expression. Also, online media can reduce one's inhibition because of such factors as perceived anonymity and a lack of social cues (Suler, 2004), which allows one to engage in political activities that he/she might otherwise not do offline.

Considering the different nature of offline and online political participation, it is important to examine the two forms of participation separately with a further differentiation between dutiful and actualizing styles of participation. However, prior research has focused mainly on CA as an inhibitor of offline political participation, leaving unexplored the possibility that CA might also inhibit one's willingness to engage in politics online. Understanding the role of CA in online political participation among young adults offers useful insights, as online forms of participation are especially popular for this age cohort (Towner, 2013).

MAIN FOCUS OF THE CHAPTER

The Demobilizing Potential of Conflict Avoidance for Online Political Participation

Conflict is integral in politics, where the expression of differences, disagreements, and grievances is commonplace (McClurg, 2006; Mutz, 2002). The participatory nature of politics in the U.S., particularly, necessitates the ability to make informed decisions through the civil exchange of differing opinions (Cappella & Jamieson, 1997). Yet the U.S. party system additionally creates an adversarial political environment that may intensify disagreements between opposing parties (Jamieson, 1992; Kagan, 1991), which may foster incivility (Herbst, 2010; Vargo & Hopf, in press).

The online political environment is no different, as both civil and uncivil political disagreements occur in Internet discussions (e.g., Coe et al., 2014; Rowe, 2015; Sobieraj & Berry, 2011). Indeed, Papacharissi (2004) argued that civil forms of online political discussions are not always polite, and such often-heated and passionate civil discussions may involve poor manners. Papacharissi thus believed that impolite online political discourses do not necessarily undermine the democratic process. Guided by Papacharissi's ideas, Rowe (2015) analyzed a sample of user comments posted to articles on the Washington Post Website and its Facebook page and found that overall the comments posted on the newspaper's Website and the Facebook page contained a similar amount of impoliteness.

On the other hand, online political discourse may also involve uncivil political disagreements and arguments. To Papacharissi (2004), uncivil online political discourses "demonstrate offensive behavior toward social groups that their behavior becomes undemocratic" (p. 267). Several studies have demonstrated the prevalence of incivility across various interactive online platforms. For example, as noted above, Vargo and Hopf (in press) analyzed more than 400,000 tweets posted by more than 140,000 individual Twitter users during the 2012 election, and found a prevalence of incivility on the platform. Further, Sobieraj and Berry (2011) found that about 83% of political blogs sampled included at least one incident of outrage language. Coe et al.'s (2014) content analysis of comments posted to newspaper articles showed that 22% included incivility elements and about 50% of commenters wrote at least one uncivil comment.

Lampe, Zube, Lee, Park, and Johnston (2014) described the nature of uncivil online discussions, noting that "there are angry 'flame' messages, designed to lash out at participants; 'troll' messages that offer falsely polemic positions to elicit anger from other users" (p. 1). A study conducted by Hmielowski, Hutchens, and Cicchirillo (2014) suggests that engagement in online political discussion leads citizens to perceive flaming as an acceptable type of behavior, and consequently, this increases their intent to flame. Hmielowski et al. also found that individuals with high levels of aggression are also more likely to flame. In another study, Buckels, Trapnell, and Paulhaus (2014) found that having a personality tendency toward sadism is positively linked with trolling. Whereas, others have explored the effect of such messages on the consumer. Research shows that it only takes exposure to one uncivil online comment to increase hostile cognitions among the reader (Rösner, Winter, & Krämer, 2016). Such emotional reactions would likely be uncomfortable for the conflict avoidant.

Yet digital and social media also enable multiple forms of exposure to politics. Dunne (2009), for instance, concluded that local online political forums can foster cross-cutting political discussions, or discussions that expose individuals to views that are in opposition to their own. Kim (2011) similarly showed that use of social network sites is positively associated with exposure to cross-cutting political views. Indeed, some research suggests online media may foster selective exposure whereby individuals seek out pro-attitudinal news sources and engage in political exchanges with like-minded individuals (e.g., Lee & Myers, 2016; Smith, 2009), users can be incidentally exposed to political content through their online personal networks (Kim, Chen, & Gil de Zúñiga, 2013), such as when friends share news, express opinions, and engage in discussions. Due to the heterogeneity of online networks lending to a tendency for persons to be exposed to a plurality of political viewpoints (Kim et al., 2013; Vraga et al., 2015), conflict-avoidant persons are not fully insulated from exposure to the disagreements and argumentative nature of politics in the world of online politics.

Furthermore, given that political activities frequently occur in conflict-laden situations (e.g., Jamieson, 1992), those apt to avoid volatile situations may choose not to participate through self-censorship (Hayes et al., 2006). Research indicates that conflict avoidance decreases interpersonal political discussion and expression (e.g., Ulbig & Funk, 1999). Citizens likely to avoid conflict tend not to express opinions on controversial political topics in both informal-private (e.g., backyard barbecues) and formal-public settings (e.g., community meetings) (Dalisay, 2012). However, as boyd (2010) suggests, online expression is unique in its aim at an imagined audience; it is uncertain who in a social network or among the online public will receive a posted message. In this "collapsed context" online, determining the appropriateness of, or predicting reactions to one's posts adds risk and uncertainty that can cause discomfort (boyd, 2010).

When one considers the pervasiveness of disagreements and arguments in both civil and uncivil online political discourse (Coe et al., 2014; Papacharissi, 2004; Vargo & Hopf, in press), it is plausible to expect conflict-averse persons to avoid online political participation. Limited research in this area has tested this expectation, however. One exception is the work of Vraga et al. (2015), which found conflict avoidance was negatively associated with the perception that political expression on Facebook produced negativity and that Facebook was not an appropriate place for politics. The study also reported that conflict avoidance was marginally negatively related to sharing political content. To extend the current understanding of the role of CA in online political participation, we propose the following hypothesis:

Hypothesis 1: *Conflict avoidance will be inversely associated with a) traditional online political participation and b) online political expression.*

The Mediating Role of Political Interest and Internal Political Efficacy

In addition to the direct negative link, CA also may have an indirectly effect by dampening mediators that motivate online political participation. We consider two such mediators, political interest and internal political efficacy (IPE). The mediation model we advance here is guided by three lines of research. The first line suggests that CA could inhibit political interest and IPE (Ulbig & Funk, 1999). The second line indicates that political interest and IPE are key psychological factors that foster political participation (McLeod et al., 1999; Jung, Kim, & Gil de Zúñiga, 2011; Verba et al., 1995). Based on H1, the third line suggests that CA is negatively related to online forms of political participation (Vraga et al., 2015). In sum, we propose that CA would be linked to lower political interest and IPE, which in turn, would lead to a reduction in online political participation.

Existing literature conventionally distinguishes political efficacy into internal and external aspects. Internal political efficacy refers to one's perceived ability to understand and effectively participate in politics. External political efficacy concerns one's perception of how responsive government is to public will (Niemi, Craig, & Mattei, 1991). In the present study, we focus on internal political efficacy (IPE) as a possible mediating mechanism, because it is a personal characteristic of citizens, whereas external political efficacy is outwardly oriented. The goal of the current study is to examine how individual traits affect online political participation. Furthermore, evidence suggests that IPE is key to political participation among young adults in particular (Glassford, 2008; Moeller et al., 2013). In fact, IPE is known to be associated with online political expression among young adults, a behavior analyzed in this study (Kushin & Yamamoto, 2010: Moeller et al., 2013).

Evidence suggests that attention to political news on traditional online sources (e.g., news websites) is related to IPE (Kushin & Yamamoto, 2010; Moeller, de Vreese, Esser, & Kunz, 2013). However, as noted above, conflict-avoidant persons are likely to evade political news content online given the conflict nature of politics. They thus may not develop the sense of efficacy that might help stimulate online political participation. However, incidental exposure to political postings and discussions on social media is common (Kim, Chen, & Gil de Zúñiga, 2013), and such exposure may have negative cognitive implications. Experimental evidence indicates that when exposed to uncivil political messages, conflict avoidant persons tend to experience decreases in trust in government whereas the same was not true for those who were not conflict avoidant (Mutz & Reeves, 2005). Other research suggests trust is associated with efficacy (Craig, 1979). Similarly, when individuals witness high levels of disagreement on Facebook, they are less likely to believe in the appropriateness of Facebook for politics (Vraga et al., 2015). Further, research shows that witnessing political information on social media is unrelated to internal efficacy (Kushin & Yamamoto, 2010) but is related to cynicism and apathy, two known antecedents of political interest (Yamamoto & Kushin, 2014). Taken together, we can surmise that when one is incidentally exposed to vitriolic, partisan political content on social media, this may have politically demobilizing implications on political interest and internal political efficacy, which may then encourage abstinence from participating online or expressing oneself politically on social media. In other words, CA may have an indirect negative relationship with online forms of political participation through its negative association with political interest and internal political efficacy. To test this mediation model, we propose the following hypotheses:

Hypothesis 2a: *CA will have an indirect negative association with traditional online political participation through its negative association with political interest and internal political efficacy.*

Hypothesis 2b: *CA will have an indirect negative association with online political expression through its negative association with political interest and internal political efficacy.*

METHOD

We conducted an Internet survey of college students at a mid-sized university in the Upper Midwest over the three-weeks before the 2012 election. The university is located in a battle ground state where campaign battles were heated leading to the election, providing a proper research context involving the presence of heightened political conflict. A researcher obtained a probability-based sample of the student body from the university registrar. Students were contacted via their university-assigned email address. In total, 839 students responded to the survey. Two-hundred-thirty-nine responses were removed due to failure to finish the majority of the survey, resulting in a final sample of 600 respondents with a final response rate of 12.0%. These respondents completed all or nearly all of the survey. Although admittedly low, this response rate is typical for Internet surveys (Shih & Fan, 2008). Because this study focuses on young adults (ages 18-29), 49 respondents who did not provide their age or were above 29 years old were removed from the analysis.

Measures

Independent Variable

Conflict avoidance was measured by four items with a focus on non-contextual relationships per the DUTCH conflict instrument format (Daly et al., 2010): two items modified from previous research ("I try to avoid open discussions of differences with others" and "I try to avoid unpleasant exchanges with others") (Daly et al., 2010; Oetzel, 1998; Ting-Toomey et al., 2000) and two original items ("I keep disagreements with others to myself in order to prevent disrupting my relationships with them" and "I generally try to avoid conflict situations with others"). Each item was measured using a 7-point Likert type scale (1 = *strongly disagree*, 7 = *strongly agree*) and averaged to form one index (M = 4.75, SD = 1.25, α = .88).

Mediators

Political interest was measured by asking respondents how interested they were in politics (1 = *not interested*; 7 = *absolutely interested*) (M = 3.63, SD = 1.77).

Internal political efficacy was measured with the following items adapted from Craig, Niemi, and Silver (1990) (1 = strongly disagree, 7 = strongly agree): 1) I consider myself to be well-qualified to participate in politics, 2) I think I am as well-informed about politics and government as most people, 3) I feel that I could do as good a job in public office as most other people, and 4) I feel I have a pretty good understanding of the important political issues facing our country. We combined and averaged these items to form a single index (M = 4.06, SD = 1.37, α = .83).

Dependent Variables

Traditional online political participation was measured with four items listed in Table 1, which mimic measures of traditional online political participation used in prior studies (e.g., Gil de Zúñiga, Veestra, Vraga, & Shah, 2010). Respondents were asked, on a 7-point Likert-type scale (1 = *not at all*, 7 = *very often*), how often they used the Internet to engage in activities online. Responses were averaged to form an index of traditional online political participation (M = 1.61, SD = .70, α = .70).

Online political expression was measured with eight items adapted from previous studies (e.g., Kushin & Yamamoto, 2010). A 7-point Likert-type scale was used to ask respondents how often they engaged in online and mobile politically expressive activities. The items are listed in Table 1. Responses were averaged to form an index of online political expression (M = 1.42, SD = .70, α = .90).

Because our study distinguishes traditional online political from online political expression, we employed a principle component analysis using varimax rotation on the online political participation items to examine whether they represented separate constructs. Results of the PCA showed that two factors emerged with eigenvalues greater than 1, and explained more than 60% of the variance. As Table 1 shows, the items intended to measure traditional online political participation loaded along one factor. The items intended to measure online political expression loaded on the second factor.

Control Variables

To counteract potential misspecification errors, several variables were included as statistical controls. Age was measured in an open-ended format (M = 20.13, SD = 1.78). Sex was measured with females as the high value and men as the low value (M = .76, SD = .43). Race was measured with Caucasians as the high value and all other groups as the low value (M = .91, SD = .28). Political ideology was measured by a single item on a 5-point scale (1 = *very conservative*; 5 = *very liberal*) (M = 3.22, SD = .94).

In addition, external political efficacy was measured by three 7-point Likert scale items used in the study of Gastil and Xenos (2010) (e.g., people like me don't have any say about what the government does). The items were combined and averaged to form a single 7-point scale, with higher scores indicating higher external political efficacy (M = 4.15, SD = 1.05, α = .59, inter-item correlations = .32). We also controlled for newspaper use, television news use, government/candidate website use, online news

Table 1. Results of a principle components analysis for items measuring traditional online political participation and online political expression

	Factor 1: Traditional Online Political Participation	Factor 2: Online Political Expression
Use E-mail to contact a politician	**.82**	.10
Send an email to an editor of a newspaper/magazine	**.74**	.00
Sign an online petition	**.68**	.28
Make a campaign contribution online	**.46**	.37
Write posts on online social networks about the election, candidates, and political issues (e.g., Facebook, Twitter, Google+, etc.)	.11	**.85**
Use a smart phone to post comments about political events or items (e.g., candidate speeches, political rallies, campaign bumper stickers, campaign billboard signs, etc.) on social networks sites (e.g., Facebook, Twitter, Foursquare)	.16	**.83**
Use a smart phone to post photos or videos of political events or items (e.g., candidate speeches, political rallies, campaign bumper stickers, campaign billboard signs, etc.) on social networks sites (e.g., Facebook, Twitter, Foursquare)	.16	**.80**
Exchange opinions about candidates, the election, or political issues online (e.g., blogs, Facebook, Twitter, Google+, etc.).	.15	**.80**
Use a smart phone to tell others on social network sites (e.g., Facebook, Twitter, Foursquare) that I am at a political event (e.g., candidate speeches, political rallies, campaign headquarters, etc.).	.14	**.77**
Share political news, video clips, photos, computer artwork, or others' blog posts online.	.29	**.72**
Create and post online audio, video, animation, photos or computer artwork to express political views.	.05	**.60**
Write blog posts on the election, candidates, and political issues.	.22	**.57**
Eigenvalue	1.5	5.32
% of Variance	12.7%	44.3%

Note: For column 3, $p < .05$, ** $p < .01$, *** $p < .001$.

use, and social media news use to separate out the potential impact that these other sources of political information may have on traditional and online political participation. *Newspaper use* was measured by a 7-point scale item asking respondents how much attention they paid to print newspapers to learn about the election ($M = 3.03$, $SD = 1.81$). *Television news use* was measured by two 7-point items asking respondents how much attention they paid to network television and cable television to learn about the election. These items were combined and averaged to construct a single 7-point scale ($M = 3.72$, $SD = 1.72$, $r = .66$). *Government/candidate website use* was measured by two 7-point scale items asking respondents how much attention they paid to government and candidate websites to learn about the election. The two items were averaged ($M = 2.34$, $SD = 1.48$, $r = .59$). *Online news use* was measured by four 7-point scale items asking respondents how much attention they paid to television news websites, online newspapers, radio news websites, and news portal websites to learn about the election. The four items were averaged ($M = 3.11$, $SD = 1.39$, $\alpha = .74$). *Social media news use* was measured by three 7-point scale items asking respondents how much attention do you pay to each of the following to learn about the election: video-sharing websites (e.g., YouTube, etc.), Twitter, social networking websites (e.g. Facebook, Google+, etc.) ($M = 2.99$, $SD = 1.62$, $\alpha = .73$).

Analysis

To test the hypotheses, ordinary least squares (OLS) regression models were estimated with traditional online political participation and online political expression respectively regressed on the control variables (age, sex, race, political ideology, external political efficacy, newspaper use, TV news use, online news use, government/candidate website use, social media news use) for model 1, the controls and mediators (political interest, internal political efficacy) for model 2, and the controls, mediators, and CA for model 3.

In addition, to test for indirect effects, we used Hayes' SPSS PROCESS macro (2013), which estimated the indirect effects of CA on traditional political participation and online political expression through political interest and internal political efficacy. We employed bootstrap methods with 5,000 bootstrap samples and 95% bias-corrected confidence intervals to infer indirect effects.

Results

Before testing our hypotheses, we examined the zero-order correlations for the relationships between conflict avoidance and each of the items measuring online political participation. Our results indicated that conflict avoidance was inversely associated with all of the single items used to measure these forms of traditional online participation (e.g., used email to contact a politician) and all of the items for online political expression (e.g., wrote posts on online social networks about the election, candidates, and political issues) except "create and post online audio, video, animation, photos or computer artwork to express political views."

In addition, we examined the zero-order correlations between conflict avoidance and the key variables in our regression models. We found that conflict avoidance was negatively associated with political interest ($r = -.30, p < .001$) and internal political efficacy ($r = -.32, p < .001$). These results were confirmed in regression analyses with the control variables and CA entered as predictors of political interest and IPE. The regression findings showed CA negatively predicts political interest ($\beta = -.15, p < .001$) and IPE ($\beta = -.14, p < .001$). The zero order correlations also revealed that being conflict avoidant was positively associated with being female ($r = .18, p < .001$), yet negatively associated with newspaper

H1 proposed that conflict avoidance will be inversely associated with a) traditional online political participation and online political expression. As shown in Table 2, after all other variables in the model were simultaneously taken into account, conflict avoidance predicted less traditional online political participation ($\beta = -.09, p < .05$) and less online political expression ($\beta = -.12, p < .01$). H1 was supported.

The second hypothesis proposed that CA will have an indirect negative association with traditional online political participation (**H2a**) and online political expression (**H2b**) through its negative association with political interest and internal political efficacy. Results support H2. CA had a significant and negative indirect effect on traditional political participation through political interest (point estimate = -.016, 95% CI [-.039 to -.006]) and internal political efficacy (point estimate = -.018, 95% CI [-.033 to -.004]). CA also had a significant and negative indirect effect on online political expression through political interest (point estimate = -.211, 95% CI [-.348 to -.110]) and internal political efficacy (point estimate = -.094, 95% CI [-.188 to -.027]).

Table 2. Regression results for conflict avoidance as a predictor of traditional online political participation and online political expression

	Traditional Online Political Participation			Online Political Expression		
	Model 1	Model 2	Model 3	Model 1	Model 2	Model 3
Age	.02	.00	.00	-.10*	-.12**	-.12**
Sex (female)	-.05	.02	.03	-.08+	.00	.02
Race (Caucasian)	-.12**	-.13**	-.13**	-.03	-.04	-.04
Political ideology	.22***	.20***	.20***	.13**	.10**	.10*
External political efficacy	.08*	.06	.05	-.00	-.03	-.04
Print newspaper use	-.05	-.09	-.09	-.05	-.09	-.10+
TV news use	-.03	-.04	-.04	.07	.05	.05
Government/candidate websites use	.16**	.10+	.09+	.20***	.11*	-.10*
Online news use	.29***	.24**	.24**	.21**	.14+	.15*
Social media news use	.05	.05	.05	.30***	.29***	.29***
Total R^2 (%)	24.3%***	--	--	31%***	--	--
Political interest	--	.12*	.11+	--	.23***	.21***
Internal political efficacy	--	.15**	.14*	--	.13*	.11*
Total R^2 (%)	--	27.9%***	--	--	36.9%***	--
Conflict avoidance	--	--	-.09*	--	--	-.12**
Total R^2 (%)	--	--	28.5%*	--	--	38.1%**

Note: Table presents standardized regression coefficients. + $p < .10$ * $p < .05$, ** $p < .01$, *** $p < .001$.

news use ($r = -.12$, $p < .001$), government/candidate websites use ($r = -.19$, $p < .001$), and online news use ($r = -.16$, $p < .001$). No significant correlations were found between conflict avoidance and age, race, political ideology, social media news use, and TV news use.

SOLUTIONS AND RECOMMENDATIONS

The salience of conflict in American politics has stimulated scholarly interest in the potential that such conflicts could demobilize young adults from participating in the political process (e.g., McClurg, 2006; Mutz, 2002; Wojcieszak, 2009). To examine the politically demobilizing role of conflict avoidance for young adults, we analyzed conflict avoidance's impact on online political participation during the 2012 U.S. presidential election. While past research has focused on the demobilizing role of conflict avoidance on offline forms of political participation (e.g., Mutz, 2002), limited research has examined whether conflict avoidance could inhibit online forms of political participation. Our findings thus contribute to the current literature in a number of ways.

First, we examined traditional online participation, *a la* the dutiful style of politics focused on the one-way input of citizens to government and formal public institutions (Bennett et al., 2011). Our findings reveal that the conflict avoidance tendency can inhibit traditional online political behaviors, such as sending an email to politicians and signing online petitions. The conflict avoidant person may be associating the disagreeing and argumentative nature of politics with conflict. As such, those holding a tendency toward CA may feel uncomfortable from participating in the aforementioned traditional political acts.

Second, today's social Web is open to a wide range of expressive political behaviors (Rainie et al., 2012; Smith & Duggan, 2012a, 2012c). As such, our study also analyzed online political expression, a form of online engagement popular among young adults today. Our study showed that conflict avoidance is inversely associated with online political expression. Due to context collapse, posting online exposes one's opinions to a wide and diverse audience resulting in uncertainty about who will receive the message and how they will react (boyd, 2010). With impolite language, arguments, and rants salient to the end user (Vraga et al., 2015), the social Web may appear ripe for conflict and thus be demobilizing for conflict-avoidant persons. Our results support limited research in this area by Vraga et al. (2015).

Interestingly, the results of our study indicate the relationship between CA and traditional online participation was weaker than the relationship between CA and online political expression. We speculate that the political acts we used as measures for online political expression (e.g., exchanging opinions about candidates, the election, or political issues online) may be perceived as being more adversarial than the items used to measure traditional online political participation. Indeed, as we noted above, politics requires one to be able to exchange opinions in environments and situations that are often heated and not always polite (Cappella & Jamieson, 1997). The adversarial political environment, in addition, may be intensifying differences and disagreements between individuals and groups who hold different political views (Kagan, 1991). The idea of whether the negative impact of CA on online political participation differs depending on whether the form of participation is more or less adversarial, should thus be examined by future research.

Third, our results expand prior findings by identifying individual characteristics that may contribute to the inverse relationship between conflict avoidance and online participation, as explained below. Our study also revealed that CA had a negative association with traditional online participation and online political expression indirectly through its negative relationship with political interest and internal political efficacy. These findings indicate two pathways whereby CA inhibits young adults' political participation. These results imply CA may not only directly affect behavioral decisions to evade political acts, but also demoralize psychological engagement with politics. Some young adults choose not to participate in politics not only because they are not willing to directly face conflict that may occur in the political process, but also because such conflict avoidant traits make them less interested in politics and they do not feel competent enough to be part of it. Political decision-making is a complex process involving motivations, psychological states, and mental processes that scholars have long worked to uncover. Our findings support prior research on the psychological implications for conflict avoidant persons as a result of experiencing conflict-laden politics (Mutz & Reeves, 2005; Vraga et al., 2015). Future research should further investigate characteristics and psychological factors contributing to lowered participation among the conflict averse.

There has been speculation that the Web may equalize the political field by offering engagement opportunities to those otherwise unlikely to participate (e.g., Castells, 2007; Xenos, Vromen, & Loader, 2014). The Web has unique characteristics such as affordances of anonymity or the sense of safety not present in engagement with politics offline, which may put individuals at ease in engaging in political acts or expressing political opinions online (e.g., Rowe, 2015). Yet it appears that for the conflict avoidant young adults in our study, this was not the case. The common thread of conflict (Mutz, 2002) appears to permeate both offline and mediated politics. Online interaction often contains interpersonal attacks and other conflict-laden communication (Davis, 1999, 2005). The risk in posting one's opinions to a diverse online audience and the unpredictability of how that audience will react (boyd, 2010) may discourage participation. We found no indication that the Web offers affordances for the conflict averse to overcome the demobilizing role of conflict in politics. However, with the ever-changing Internet landscape, and the growing trend of posting photos and videos online in apps such as Instagram, future research should consider exploring whether conflict avoidance hinders a wider range of online politically expressive behaviors.

On the other hand, our findings also help reinforce previous empirical studies that have suggested exposure to cross-cutting discussions, or online interactions that expose individuals to views opposing their own, has the potential of inhibiting political participation (Mutz, 2006). For example, Lee & Meyers (2016) found that those who were exposed to cross-cutting political views on an issue, but who did not engage in cross-cutting discussion, were not more involved in the political issue and may remain ambivalent. On the other hand, other researchers such as Dunne (2009) have argued for the reverse—that online discussions that are more cross-cutting are also more politically active than online discussions that are less cross-cutting. In this case, exposure to cross-cutting discussions may actually induce rather than inhibit political participation. Such argument aligns with other studies that have suggested larger networks are able to facilitate a higher frequency of political discussion than smaller networks (e.g., McLeod, Scheufele, & Moy, 1999). Thus, it is plausible that the characteristics of online social networks, such as their size, may impact the extent to which conflict avoidance may inhibit participation. For example, the strength of inverse link between CA and political participation may be moderated by network size.

FUTURE RESEARCH DIRECTIONS

We outline a few limitations that should be acknowledged with the purpose of making recommendations for future research. First, our sample was restrained to college students enrolled at a mid-sized university in the U.S. Therefore, the generalizability of the present findings is limited. In particular, the preference to manage conflict through avoidance may be linked to cultural values and norms. It is possible that one's tendency to avoid conflict is a learned behavior shaped by one's cultural environment (Cai & Fink, 2002). In addition, at the social structural level, a long line of research suggests that media of small and homogeneous communities would emphasize consensus and avoid conflict when reporting about public affairs (Tichenor, Donohue, & Olien, 1980). Given these potential differences in managing conflict, the observed findings might be unique to the current sample, and is worthwhile investigating from a multilevel perspective. For instance, cross-cultural samples may be used, with participants drawn from different clusters such as states, countries, and regions to capture cultural variations in conflict management styles and examine how such variations are linked to political participation and disaffection.

Second, the cross-sectional nature of the data used in this study does not permit establishing a causal relationship between conflict avoidance and the outcome variables of interest. It is likely, for instance, that unpleasant and negative political experiences via Internet and mobile use to participate in politics or express political opinions increase levels of conflict avoidance. Therefore, we recommend that experiments or panel studies be conducted to allow for rigorous tests of causality of the relationship between conflict avoidance and the indicators of online political mobilization under investigation.

Third, the reliability of the measures of online political participation was marginally acceptable, suggesting that the measures may not have reliably measured the same underlying online political participation behavior. Although the items came from previous work, future research should consider refining the measurement scheme of this variable. Fourth, there might be other useful indicators of a politically vibrant citizenry that are related to conflict avoidance. For instance, Mutz and Reeves (2005) showed that exposure to incivility, or highly contentious television programs, decreased levels of political trust. Their experiments also indicated that the inverse relationship between exposure to conflict-laden programs and political trust was a function of individual differences in conflict avoidance. Specifically, for those who scored higher on conflict avoidance, exposure to a conflict-laden program resulted in lower levels of political trust than exposure to a non-conflict-laden program. Further research can test the potential that conflict avoidance reduces levels of political trust.

Fifth, the means for the measure of online political expression are admittedly low. This may be a result of the relative newness of mobile devices, and their relatively high cost for the phone and service. As adoption has continued, however, trends in the 2014 midterm election indicate that interaction with politics via mobile Internet has grown in popularity since the 2012 election when data for the present study was gathered (Smith, 2014). Continued research is thus needed of the mobile landscape as it continues to grow and change in order to assess its relationship with conflict management styles and politics.

Sixth, as we noted above, it is plausible that the characteristics of online social networks (e.g., their size) may impact the extent to which conflict avoidance may inhibit participation. However, because our study did not examine online social network characteristics, future research could investigate their role in explaining the link between CA and political participation.

Finally, in the first section of this chapter, we discussed the run up to the 2016 presidential election, a political context when it was not uncommon to see candidates attacking their opponents (Jaffe, 2016; Chozik, 2016). Some have particularly argued that attacks made by presidential candidate Donald Trump have had the potential to encourage political activism among those who have been most civically disengaged, disaffected and disconnected (Appelbaum, 2016). Such a phenomenon, however, is not unique to the U.S. Indeed, in the run up to the Philippines' 2016 presidential election, the then anti-establishment candidate Rodrigo Duterte, commonly used uncivil discourse and various vulgarities during speeches and political rallies (e.g., Rothwell, 2016). Such incivility had been previously uncommon in past presidential elections in the Philippines. Duterte, however, was able to rally close to 16 million Filipinos and eventually win the presidency. On balance, the Trump and Duterte examples imply the potential that incivility may have the potential to engage voters who may have a high level of apathy toward the political establishment. It could be that those high in apathy may gravitate toward less conventional types of political acts, such as uncivil forms of political expression. However, because our study did not incorporate political apathy, we could not examine its relationship with conflict avoidance, and as such, we recommend that future research explore this link.

CONCLUSION

The current study has shown evidence in support of the politically demobilizing role of conflict avoidance. Digital and social media are commonly viewed as an equalizing platform that can bring individuals into the political process by lowering barriers and opening opportunities for opinion expression, engagement with political actors, and action intended to affect political outcomes. Our findings suggest, however, that conflict avoidance may be a barrier that inhibits online political participation and expression. If digital and social media do not necessarily foster entrance into politics among conflict-avoidant persons, it is important to examine what features of online politics serve as roadblocks to conflict avoidant citizens and what steps can be taken to encourage their participation in politics.

REFERENCES

Abramowitz, A. L., & Saunders, K. L. (2008). Is polarization a myth? *The Journal of Politics*, *70*(2), 542–555. doi:10.1017/S0022381608080493

Anderson, A. A., Brossard, D., Scheufele, D. A., Xenos, M. A., & Ladwig, P. (2014). The nasty effect: Online incivility and risk perceptions of emerging technologies. *Journal of Computer-Mediated Communication*, *19*(3), 373–387. doi:10.1111/jcc4.12009

Anderson, M. (2015, October 29). Technology device ownership: 2015. *Pew Research Center Internet, Science & Tech*. Retrieved from http://www.pewinternet.org/2015/10/29/technology-device-ownership-2015/

Applebaum, Y. (2016, April 7). Why Donald Trump voters are civically disengaged—a fact that may cost him the nomination. *The Atlantic*. Retrieved May 16, 2016, from http://www.theatlantic.com/politics/archive/2016/04/voting-alone/477270/

Bennett, W. L., Wells, C., & Freelon, D. (2011). Communicating civic engagement: Contrasting models of citizenship in the youth web sphere. *Journal of Communication*, *61*(5), 835–856. doi:10.1111/j.1460-2466.2011.01588.x

Best, S., & Krueger, B. S. (2005). Analyzing the representativeness of Internet political participation. *Political Behavior*, *27*(2), 183–216. doi:10.1007/s11109-005-3242-y

boyd, D. (2010). Social network sites as networked publics: Affordances, dynaicms, and implications. In Z. Papacharissi (Ed.), *Networked self: Identity, community, and culture on social network sites* (pp. 39-58). New York, NY: Routledge.

Buckels, E. E., Trapnell, P. D., & Paulhaus, D. L. (2014). Trolls just want to have fun. *Personality and Individual Differences*, *67*, 97–102. doi:10.1016/j.paid.2014.01.016

Cai, D. A., & Fink, E. L. (2002). Conflict style differences between individualists and collectivists. *Communication Monographs*, *69*(1), 67–87. doi:10.1080/03637750216536

Campbell, S. W. (2013). Mobile media and communication: A new field, or just a new journal? *Mobile Media & Communication*, *1*(1), 8–13. doi:10.1177/2050157912459495

Cappella, J. N., & Jamieson, K. H. (1997). *Spiral of cynicism*. New York: Oxford University Press.

Castells, M. (2007). Communication, power and counter-power in the network society. *International Journal of Communication*, *1*, 238–266.

Chozik, A. (2016, May). Hillary Clinton targets republicans turned off by Donald Trump. *New York Times*. Retrieved May 9, 2016, from http://www.nytimes.com/2016/05/07/us/politics/hillary-clinton-republican-party.html

Coe, K., Kenski, K., & Rains, S. A. (2014). Online and uncivil? Patterns and determinants of incivility in newspaper website comments. *Journal of Communication*, *64*(4), 659–679. doi:10.1111/jcom.12104

Conrad, C. (1991). Communication in conflict: Style-strategy relationships. *Communication Monographs*, *58*(2), 135–151. doi:10.1080/03637759109376219

Craig, S. C. (1979). Efficacy, trust, and political behavior. *American Politics Research*, *7*(2), 225–239. doi:10.1177/1532673X7900700207

Craig, S. C., Niemi, R. G., & Silver, G. E. (1990). Political efficacy and trust: A report on the NES pilot study items. *Political Behavior*, *12*(3), 289–314. doi:10.1007/BF00992337

Dalisay, F. (2012). The spiral of silence and conflict avoidance: Examining antecedents of opinion expression concerning the U.S. military buildup in the Pacific Island of Guam. *Communication Quarterly*, *60*(4), 481–503. doi:10.1080/01463373.2012.704567

Daly, T. M., Lee, J. A., Soutar, G. N., & Rasmi, S. (2010). Conflict-handling style measurement: A best-worst scaling application. *The International Journal of Conflict Management*, *21*(3), 281–308. doi:10.1108/10444061011063180

Davis, R. (1999). *The web of politics: The Internet's impact on the American political system*. New York: Oxford University.

Davis, R. (2005). *Politics online: Blogs, chatrooms, and discussion groups in American democracy*. New York: Routledge.

Dunne, K. (2009). Cross cutting discussion: A form of online discussion discovered within local political online forums. *Information Polity*, *14*, 219.

Ellison, N., & Hardey, M. (2014). Social media and local government: Citizenship, consumption and democracy. *Local Government Studies*, *40*(1), 21–40. doi:10.1080/03003930.2013.799066

File, T. (2014). *Young-adult voting: An analysis of presidential elections, 1964–2012*. U.S. Department of Commerce. Retrieved from http://www.census.gov/prod/2014pubs/p20-573.pdf

Forgette, R., & Morris, J. S. (2006). High-conflict television news and public opinion. *Political Research Quarterly*, *59*(3), 447–456. doi:10.1177/106591290605900312

Friend, C. (2015). *Social contract theory. The Internet encyclopedia of philosophy: A peer-reviewed academic resource*. Retrieved from http://www.iep.utm.edu/soc-cont/#SH2c

Gil de Zúñiga, H., Copeland, L., & Bimber, B. (2014). Political consumerism: Civic engagement and the social media connection. *New Media & Society*, *16*(3), 488–506. doi:10.1177/1461444813487960

Gil de Zúñiga, H., Puig-I-Abril, E., & Rojas, H. (2009). Weblogs traditional sources online & political participation: An assessment of how the Internet is changing the political environment. *New Media & Society*, *11*(4), 553–574. doi:10.1177/1461444809102960

Gil de Zúñiga, H., Veenstra, A., Vraga, E., & Shah, D. (2010). Digital democracy: Reimagining pathways to political participation. *Journal of Information Technology & Politics*, *7*(1), 36–51. doi:10.1080/19331680903316742

Hargittai, E., & Shaw, A. (2013). Digitally savvy citizenship: The role of Internet skills and engagement in young adults political participation around the 2008 presidential election. *Journal of Broadcasting & Electronic Media*, *57*(2), 115–134. doi:10.1080/08838151.2013.787079

Harvard Institute of Politics. (2014, August 29). *Survey of young Americans' attitudes toward politics and public service* (25th ed.). Retrieved from http://www.iop.harvard.edu/Spring-2014-HarvardIOP-Survey

Hayes, A. F. (2013). *Introduction to mediation, moderation, and conditional process analysis: A regression-based approach*. New York: Guilford Press.

Hayes, A. F., Scheufele, D. A., & Huge, M. E. (2006). Nonparticipation as self-censorship: Publicly observable political activity in a polarized opinion climate. *Political Behavior*, *28*(3), 259–283. doi:10.1007/s11109-006-9008-3

Herbst, S. (2010). *Rude democracy: Civility and incivility in American politics*. Philadelphia, PA: Temple University Press.

Himelboim, I., Lariscy, R. W., Tinkham, S. F., & Sweetser, K. D. (2012). Social Media and Online Political Communication: The Role of Interpersonal Informational Trust and Openness. *Journal of Broadcasting & Electronic Media*, *56*(1), 92–115. doi:10.1080/08838151.2011.648682

Hmielowski, J. D., Hutchens, M. J., & Cicchirillo, V. J. (2014). Living in an age of online incivility: Examining the conditional indirect effects of online discussion on political flaming. *Information Communication and Society*, *17*(10), 1196–1211. doi:10.1080/1369118X.2014.899609

Jaffe, A. (2016, May 7). Trump slams Hillary Clinton as 'nasty, mean enabler,' of husband's affairs. *NBC News*. Retrieved May 9, 2016, from http://www.nbcnews.com/politics/2016-election/trump-slams-hillary-clinton-nasty-mean-enabler-husband-s-affairs-n569791

Jamieson, K. H. (1992). *Dirty politics: Deception, distraction, and democracy*. New York: Oxford University Press.

Jamieson, K. H., & Cappella, J. N. (2009). *Echo chamber: Rush Limbaugh and the conservative media establishment*. New York, NY: Oxford University Press.

Jung, N., Kim, Y., & Gil de Zúñiga, H. (2011). The mediating role of knowledge and efficacy in the effects of communication on political participation. *Mass Communication & Society*, *14*(4), 407–430. doi:10.1080/15205436.2010.496135

Kagan, R. A. (1991). Adversarial legalism and American government. *Journal of Policy Analysis and Management*, *10*(3), 369–406. doi:10.2307/3325322

Kushin, M. J. (2009). How young adults and social media are challenging traditional perspectives of civic life. *Rocky Mountain Communication Review*, *6*, 26–31.

Kushin, M. J., & Yamamoto, M. (2010). Did social media really matter? College students use of online media and political decision making in the 2008 election. *Mass Communication & Society*, *13*(5), 608–630. doi:10.1080/15205436.2010.516863

Lampe, C., Zube, P., Lee, J., Park, C.-H., & Johnston, E. (2014). Crowdsourcing civility: A natural experiment examining the effects of distributed moderation in online forums. *Government Information Quarterly, 31,* 317-326. http://dx/doi.org/10.1016/j.giq.2013.11.005

Lee, J., & Myers, T. A. (2016). Can social media change your mind? SNS use, cross-cutting exposure and discussion, and political view change. *Social Media Studies*, *2*, 87–97. doi:10.15340/2147336622992

Lim, L. L. (2009). The influences of harmony motives and implicit beliefs on conflict styles of the collectivist. *International Journal of Psychology*, *44*(6), 401–409. doi:10.1080/00207590802512765 PMID:22029658

Martin, J. A. (2015). Mobile news use and participation in elections: A bridge for the democratic divide? *Mobile Media & Communication*, *3*(2), 230–249. doi:10.1177/2050157914550664

Matz, D. C., & Wood, W. (2005). Cognitive dissonance in groups: The consequences of disagreement. *Journal of Personality and Social Psychology*, *88*(1), 22–37. doi:10.1037/0022-3514.88.1.22 PMID:15631572

McClurg, S. (2006). Political disagreement in context: The conditional effect of neighborhood context, disagreement and political talk on electoral participation. *Political Behavior*, *28*(4), 349–366. doi:10.1007/s11109-006-9015-4

Mcleod, J. M., Scheufele, D., & Moy, P. (1999). Community, communication, and participation: The role of mass media and interpersonal discussion in local political participation. *Political Communication*, *16*(3), 315–336. doi:10.1080/105846099198659

Moeller, J., de Vreese, C., Esser, F., & Kunz, R. (2014). Pathway to political participation: The influence of online and offline news media on internal efficacy and turnout of first-time voters. *The American Behavioral Scientist*, *58*(5), 689–700. doi:10.1177/0002764213515220

Mutz, D. (2006). *Hearing the other side: Deliberative versus participatory democracy*. Cambridge, MA: Cambridge University Press. doi:10.1017/CBO9780511617201

Mutz, D. C. (2002). The consequences of cross-cutting networks for political participation. *American Journal of Political Science*, *46*(4), 838–855. doi:10.2307/3088437

Mutz, D. C. (2015). *In-your-face politics: The consequences of uncivil media*. Princeton, NJ: Princeton University Press. doi:10.1515/9781400865871

Mutz, D. C., & Reeves, B. (2005). The new videomalaise: Effects of televised incivility on political trust. *The American Political Science Review*, *99*(01), 1–16. doi:10.1017/S0003055405051452

Niemi, R. G., Craig, S. C., & Mattei, F. (1991). Measuring internal political efficacy in the 1988 National Election Study. *The American Political Science Review*, *85*(4), 1407. doi:10.2307/1963953

Oetzel, J. G. (1998). The effects of self-construals and ethnicity on self-reported conflict styles. *Communication Reports*, *11*(2), 133–144. doi:10.1080/08934219809367695

Papacharissi, Z. (2004). Democracy online: Civility, politeness, and the democratic potential of online political discussion groups. *New Media & Society*, *6*(2), 259–283. doi:10.1177/1461444804041444

Putnam, L. L., & Poole, S. M. (1987). Conflict and negotiation. In F. M. Jablin, L. L. Putnam, K. H. Roberts, & L. W. Porter (Eds.), Handbook of organizational communication: An interdisciplinary perspective (pp. 549-599). Thousand Oaks, CA: Sage.

Rahim, M. A. (1983). A measure of styles of handling interpersonal conflict. *Academy of Management Journal*, *26*(2), 368–376. doi:10.2307/255985 PMID:10263067

Rainie, L., Smith, A., Schlozman, K. L., Brady, H., & Verba, S. (2012). Social media and political engagement. *Pew Internet & American Life Project*. Retrieved from http://pewinternet.org/~/media//Files/Reports/2012/PIP_SocialMediaAndPoliticalEngagement_PDF.pdf

Rösner, L., Winter, S., & Krämer, N. C. (2016). Dangerous minds? Effects of uncivil online comments on aggressive cognitions, emotions, and behavior. *Computers in Human Behavior*, *58*, 461–470. doi:10.1016/j.chb.2016.01.022

Rowe, I. (2015). Civility 2.0: A comparative analysis of incivility in online political discussion. *Information Communication and Society*, *18*(2), 121–138. doi:10.1080/1369118X.2014.940365

Shehata, A., Ekström, M., & Olsson, T. (2015). Developing Self-Actualizing and Dutiful Citizens Testing the AC-DC Model Using Panel Data Among Adolescents. *Communication Research*, 0093650215619988.

Shih, T., & Fan, X. (2008). Comparing response rates from web and mail surveys: A meta-analysis. *Field Methods*, *20*(3), 249–271. doi:10.1177/1525822X08317085

Smith, A. (2014). Cell phones, social media and campaign 2014. *Pew Internet & American Life Project*. Retrieved from http://www.pewinternet.org/2014/11/03/cell-phones-social-media-and-campaign-2014/

Smith, A. (2015, April 1). U.S. smartphone use in 2015. *Pew Research Center Internet, Science & Tech*. Retrieved from http://www.pewinternet.org/2015/04/01/us-smartphone-use-in-2015/

Smith, A., & Duggan, M. (2012a). Online political videos and campaign 2012. *Pew Internet & American Life Project*. Retrieved from http://pewinternet.org/Reports/2012/Election-2012-Video.aspx

Smith, A., & Duggan, M. (2012b). Presidential campaign donations in the digital age. *Pew Internet & American Life Project*. Retrieved from http://pewinternet.org/~/media//Files/ Reports/2012/PIP_State_of_the_2012_race_donations.pdf

Smith, A., & Duggan, M. (2012c). The state of the 2012 election – Mobile politics. *Pew Internet & American Life Project*. Retrieved from http://pewinternet.org/Reports/2012/Election-2012-Mobile.aspx

Sobieraj, S., & Berry, J. M. (2011). From incivility to outrage: Political discourse in blogs, talk radio, and cable news. *Political Communication*, *28*(1), 19–41. doi:10.1080/10584609.2010.542360

Suler, J. (2004). The online disinhibition effect. *Cyberpsychology & Behavior*, *7*(3), 321–326. doi:10.1089/1094931041291295 PMID:15257832

Tichenor, P., Donohue, G. A., & Olien, C. N. (1980). *Community conflict and the press*. Thousand Oaks, CA: Sage.

Ting-Toomey, S. (1994). Managing interpersonal conflict effectively. In L. Samovar & R. Porter (Eds.), *Intercultural communication: A reader* (7th ed.; pp. 360–372). Belmont, CA: Wadsworth.

Ting-Toomey, S., Yee-Jung, K. K., Shapiro, R. B., Garcia, W., Wright, T. J., & Oetzel, J. G. (2000). Ethnic/cultural identity salience and conflict styles in four US ethnic groups. *International Journal of Intercultural Relations*, *24*(1), 47–81. doi:10.1016/S0147-1767(99)00023-1

Towner, T. (2013). All political participation is socially networked? New media and the 2012 election. *Social Science Computer Review*, *31*(5), 527–541. doi:10.1177/0894439313489656

Towner, T. L., & Dulio, D. A. (2011). An experiment of campaign effects during the YouTube election. *New Media & Society*, *13*(4), 626–644. doi:10.1177/1461444810377917

Towner, T. L., & Muñoz, C. L. (2016). Baby Boom or Bust?: The New Media Effect on Political Participation. *Journal of Political Marketing* (forthcoming).

Ulbig, S. G., & Funk, C. L. (1999). Conflict avoidance and political participation. *Political Behavior*, *21*(3), 265–282. doi:10.1023/A:1022087617514

Vargo, C. J., & Hopp, T. (in press). Socioeconomic status, social capital, and partisan polarity as predictors of political incivility on Twitter: A congressional district-level analysis. *Social Science Computer Review*. doi:10.1177/0894439315602858

Verba, S., Schlozman, K. L., & Brady, H. E. (1995). *Voice and equality: Civic voluntarism in American politics*. Cambridge, MA: Harvard University Press.

Vraga, E. K., Thorson, K., Kligler-Vilenchik, N., & Gee, E. (2015). How individual sensitivities to disagreement shape youth political expression on Facebook. *Computers in Human Behavior*, *45*, 281–289. doi:10.1016/j.chb.2014.12.025

Wojcieszak, M. (2009). Carrying online participation offline: Mobilization by radical online groups and politically dissimilar offline ties. *Journal of Communication*, *59*(3), 564–586. doi:10.1111/j.1460-2466.2009.01436.x

Xenos, M., Vromen, A., & Loader, B. D. (2014). The great equalizer? Patterns of social media use and youth political engagement in three advanced democracies. *Information Communication and Society*, *17*(2), 151–167. doi:10.1080/1369118X.2013.871318

Yamamoto, M., & Kushin, M. J. (2014). More harm than good? Online media use and political disaffection among college students in the 2008 election. *Journal of Computer-Mediated Communication*, *19*(3), 430–445. doi:10.1111/jcc4.12046

Yamamoto, M., Kushin, M. J., & Dalisay, F. (2015). Social media and mobiles as political mobilization forces for young adults: Examining the moderating role of online political expression in political participation. *New Media & Society*, *17*(6), 880–898. doi:10.1177/1461444813518390

Yang, H., & DeHart, J. L. (2016). Social media use and online political participation among college students during the US election 2012. *Social Media + Society, 2*, 1-18. doi:10.1177/2056305115623802

Chapter 5
Political Messaging in Digital Spaces:
The Case of Twitter in Mexico's Presidential Campaign

Rodrigo Sandoval-Almazan
Autonomous University of the State of Mexico, Mexico

ABSTRACT

Political messaging is adapting to new digital spaces. However, the power of citizens through the use of this digital spaces is still unknown. Many citizens criticize political candidates using Facebook or Twitter, others build networks in Snapchat and some others try to collaborate with candidates using Periscope or WhatsApp. This research is focused in understanding this adaptation of political message on this platforms, analyzing the case of the presidential candidate Enrique Peña Nieto (PRI) in Mexico who won the presidency with a large participation but without the support of Twitter users. After two online protests against this presidential candidate - #IamnotProletariat and #Iam132 – political image could have been undermined and voters could have thought differently. But this was not the case and despite of this, the candidate won. The challenge to understand this online protest and its link to the political message is addressed in this paper.

INTRODUCTION

The use of computers to predict voters behavior is not new (Farrell, 2012; Jon B., 1998; Macintosh, Malina, & Farrell, 2002). Although, the use of technology to interact with voters and expand the political message is more recent and expands very fast (Best, Krueger, & Ladewig, 2007).

Nowadays the spread of the use of internet and web 2.0 technologies are changing the way politicians conduct their political campaigns using websites, forums and chats to deliver their message and interactions with citizens (Baldwin-Philippi, 2013; Bimber & Copeland, 2013).

The use of digital spaces through different platforms such as videoblogs (vine) online chats (snapchat, What'sApp) YouTube, Twitter and Facebook became a new trend for political strategies (Fox & Ramos, 2012). The Obama campaign is the stepping stone of the novel use of social media communications

DOI: 10.4018/978-1-5225-1862-4.ch005

inside a successful political campaign (Harfoush, 2009; Karlsen, 2013; Katz, Barris, & Jain, 2013) The Trump vs Clinton presidential campaign in the U.S. has not being and exemption. Otherwise increase the use of this digital spaces to continue the debate and expand the ideas of this two candidates.

Several scholars have followed the Obama campaign replications in different countries such as the German election in 2009 (Jungherr, Jürgens, & Schoen, 2011), and the debate about the use of the Twitter platform to forecast electoral results (Tumasjan, Sprenger, Sandner, & Welpe, 2011b). This intrusion of technological participation using Twitter and Facebook has change the organization and structure of political campaigns, adding new elements to the complex system of attracting and convincing voters (Mashable, 2012; Towner, 2012).

A different path in the political field is the use of technology for social protests. The most studied examples are the Arab Spring revolts in Egypt, Tunisia and Iran (Anderson, 2011; Andrea Kavanaugh, Yang Seungwon, & Edward Fox, 2011; Gilad, Erhardt, Mike, Devin, & Ian, 2011). The introduction of the technological element as a new communication channel, different from the traditional media, has empowered citizen's capabilities of organization, information sharing and collaboration to reach collective goals. However, these social protests also have the cyberactivism component that starts its own transformation (Khamis & Vaughn, 2012; Michael D. yers & Maccaughey, 2003; Sandoval-Almazan & Gil- Garcia, 2013).

Mexico has not been excluded from the influence of technology in politics and social protests. The oldest example is the use of emails by the Zapatista army in 1995 (Cleaver, 1998) to expand their influence using a combination of new technologies – email – and the traditional media, the worldwide newspapers that received letters and provided coverage to the indigenous uprising (Garrido & Halavais, 2003).

In 2009 when the Mexican Senate had to consider a large group of citizens who gathered on the Twitter's social network, managing to stop an Internet tax which had been approved by the House and the senators stopped just on time (Riva-Palacio, 2009). After having gathered more than a hundred thousand messages through this network, the Mexican Twitters put on so much pressure that senators had to attend the claimers. The Senate had to stop the tax on Internet. This way, Twitters activists achieved their objective using information technology (Sandoval-Almazan and Alonzo, 2011).

The Senate's case is a clear example of the Morozov's (2011) idea of the perils to open government debates into public and the use of technology to pressure government or citizens. The case of the city of Veracruz shows Morozov's idea of net delusion clearer when the government used technologies to make authoritarian behaviors and control internet ideas in order to maintain peace and security (Sandoval-Almazan & Gil-Garcia, 2012).

Most recently, the Ayotzinapa scandal in which 43 students remain lost or hijacked in Mexico is an ongoing trend on twitter in Mexican politics. Every day at 10 pm many journalists, NGOs related to human rights start sending images and the names of the 43. In order to claim for justice or actions from the Federal Government (Fernández-Poncela (2015).

The use of Twitter to make and state official postures about facts and the use of law to entrench citizens freedoms are examples of this clear condition of internet control (Morozov, 2011).

Previous cases in Mexico and the Arab Spring present the long lasting friction between citizens and governments. Both try to control each other, putting pressure, neutralizing, promoting, establishing boundaries and limiting actions. The main difference is that information technologies are in the middle of the friction. Some citizens' groups are using it more efficiently than governments. In other cases the governments are more clever and powerful. But the statement is clear, web 2.0 technology is the middleware of this battle (Bannister & Wilson, 2011; Dutton & Peltu, 2007; Evans & Ulbig, 2012).

The fact is that information technologies have become the intermediary in many political campaigns expanding its role and influence. More recently, research has confirmed that there are significant positive relationships between the use of digital media and web 2.0 technologies and political participation and knowledge (Boulianne, 2009; Dalrymple & Scheufele, 2007; Dimitrova, Shehata, Strömbäck, & Nord, 2014; Kiousis & Dimitrova, 2006; Tolbert & Mcneal, 2003).. However, the Mexican presidential race presented a different case when presidential candidate Peña Nieto had against the opinion of Twitter and Facebook users but won the presidency. He won just 38% of the votes and his margin of victory was half the double-digit spread most polls had predicted. The PRD's candidate Andrés Manuel López Obrador, took second with 32%, while the PAN's candidate Josefina Vázquez Mota topped 25% at a distant third place (Padgett, 2012).

The purpose of this chapter is to understand how the Mexican candidate of the Institutional Revolutionary Party (PRI) has been affected by the digital spaces used as platforms for sending political messages and undermines its social media presence as a result of two online protests. The first one during his precampaign – #IamnotProletariat – and the second one during his political campaign - #Iam132 – but won the general election. In order to achieve this goal, this research was designed in two steps: 1. The precampaing stage and, 2. The political campaign. Th evidence that supported this research was monitored Twitter and Facebook accounts of presidential candidates from 2011 until July 2nd of 2012. The remainder of this chapter is organized as follows. This introductory section which states the problem. The second section is a literature review of Twitter use on elections, social media, elections and web 2.0 components as a main overview of social media. A third section describes Mexican background and electoral context. The fourth section is a methodological section. The final section will discuss conclusions for the election and its impact on politics.

LITERATURE REVIEW

Nowadays social networks have been pointed out with the use of Twitter and Facebook (Aleman-Meza et al., 2008). Twitter had over 1.3 billion registered users in 2015 and 310 million people uses twitter, 100 million uses it everyday but 550 million of register users have ever sent a tweet (Smith 2016). This web application was developed by Jack Dorsey, Evan Williams and Biz Stone who have been online since 2006 and have gained popularity worldwide. The main difference between Twitter and other social networks is that the messages called "tweets" are limited to 140 characters and have the function to send URLs that are linked to audio, video or images. Twitter has also the function to send direct messages person to person or to send them to a general public of subscribers and this messages can then be resent - re-tweeted to their own network of subscribers (Swamynathan, Wilson, Boe, Almeroth, & Zhao, 2008).

Research over digital spaces and political message could started with Castells (2009) and the use of communication to create new networks of power along the information society. Several scholars has made related research, for example Bastos et. Al (2013) has done research of gatekeeping twitter message diffusion. The PEW report (2013) of Civic Engagement in the Digital Age found that well -educated and well-off are more likely than other to participate in civic life online. Political activity in social networking spaces shows a somewhat more moderate versión. Jungherr (2015) research based on these mediating factors it seems plausible that Twitter data might serve as an indicator of Twitter users' attention shifts with regard to political information but hold little information on public opinion at large. And most recently, McLean et. al (2016) research over the Facebook group "destroy the Joint" with feminism and misogyny found different perspectives because they map and a survey profiles and people to understand their effects.

One part of this research of digital spaces is the use of Twitter and Facebook to communicate political message. The use of this two platforms has exploded since 2008 Obama's presidential campaign. At least two seminal books collected research trends on this area (Fox & Ramos, 2012; Romm-Livermore, 2012). This literature review is build for three main theoretical fields of research to organize contributions on this area: 1) Social media and political participation analysis; 2) Social media contribution to political campaigns; and 3) Social media effects on politics.

The first theoretical field related to social media and political participation started with Bimber's contributions on the Internet impact in communication and interaction of citizens and politics (Bimber & Copeland, 2013; Bimber, Stohl, & Flanagin, 2009; Bimber, 1998, 1999). The contribution for this field was the analysis of integrated social media efforts that consider Facebook, YouTube and Twitter as a combined strategy in different political fields like political party communities (Effing, Hillegersberg, & Huibers, 2012) or local politics (Effing, Hillegersberg, & Huibers, 2013). This integrated analysis of social media by Effing and colleagues have a seminal work that analyses the impact of these social media tools on political systems (Effing, van Hillegersberg, & Huibers, 2011). Wojcieszak & Mutz (2009) after studied 1000 U.S. citizens participation in chat rooms or message boards found that deliberation occurs when politics comes up incidentally but is not the central purpose of the discussion space. More recently, Shah (2016) analyzes the psychological implications of political expression and creative production via Information Communication Technologies (ICT), the evidence indicates that political conversation drives to participatory engagement usingi this technologies.

Research on social media for political campaigns can be divided accordingly to the different platforms: blogs, Facebook and Twitter. For the case of the blog analysis, Wallsten researched prior and after Obama's campaign and it is a starting point on this topic. (Wallsten, 2008, 2010). Later on, using the construct expressive or consumptive to determine the engagement on political activity research was done by Zúñiga, Bachmann, Hsu, & Brundidge, (2013). Similar research about blog use was made by Nahon & Hemsley,(2011) to determine how volatile the content on political blogs is.

Regarding Facebook, Robertson, Vatrapu, & Medina (2009) examined two years of posts on Facebook walls of the three major contenders for the U.S. Presidency in 2008, analyzing participation patterns of usage along dimensions of breadth and frequency, and interpreting them in terms of the concept of the "public sphere" (Robertson, Vatrapu, & Medina, 2010). Recent research from Robertson et al., (2012) based on posts from two candidates for US Congress found that political dialogue on social networks is always more positive than negative and the content analysis reveals that expressions of support are the most frequent, followed by questions and suggestions. Other scholars have been following the same path, focusing on political behavior (Bode, 2012), political engagement (Conroy, Feezell, & Guerrero, 2012) and political participation (Tang & Lee, 2013). More recently, Theocharis and Lowe (2015) has provide evidence that points Facebook use to increase political participation, at least in a some aspects under certain conditions.

Research on Twitter is more recent than Facebook. A first notice about the impact of this web 2.0 tool was the research done by Lassen and Brown (2011) analyzing the electoral connection using Twitter, followed by the research from Gainous & Wagner, (2013) and research of how political candidates use Twitter by Kruikemeier (2014) and Gruzd and Roy, (2014) whose research on political polarization in Canada through Twitter determined a new path to be followed. A controversial research was made by

Tumasjan, Sprenger, Sandner, & Welpe, (2011) when they revealed the positive impact of Twitter on elections, but was later on contradicted by another research (Daniel Gayo-Avello & Panagiotis, 2011) studying congress election on the US in 2010.

For the second theoretical research field, after the Obama's Presidential Campaign in 2008, many studies have been conducted on national and local elections (Baumgartner y Morris 2010) (Gibson y McAllister 2011). Andersen and Medaglia's (2009) research about the national campaign of the Danish Parliament suggests that candidates and voters were influenced by the use of Facebook. Feezell, Conroy, and Guerrero (2009) surveyed 455 undergraduate students and found that participation in online political groups strongly predicted offline political participation by engaging members online.

Kavanaugh et.al (2013) analyze the use of media during Mexican elections her results suggest that "in conditions of relative uncertainty and imperfect information, social media and alternative (online) news sources about political events are essential to sustaining an informed public" specially in the case of Mexico. Toledo et.al (2013) found that 1. the intense activity of individuals with relatively few connections is capable of generating highly replicated messages that contributed to Trending Topics without relying on the activity of user hubs. 2. The results support the thesis of social consensus through the influence of committed minorities, which states that a prevailing majority opinion in a population can be rapidly reversed by a small fraction of randomly distributed committed agents. After a comparison of elections on the U.S. and U.K. Aldrich et. al (2016) found that social media In terms of impact, while offline forms remain most effective in mobilizing turnout, online messages are important for campaign participation, particularly among younger citizens when they are mediated through social networks

Other cases such as social media campaign on Spanish mayor elections (Criado, Martínez-Fuentes, & Silván, 2012) confirmed this posture as well as the popularity analysis on US Midterm elections (Vaccari & Nielsen, 2013) and influence of opinion leaders in elections (Dubois & Gaffney, 2014). Another example of the usefulness of these tools is the research of Wandhoefer, Thamm, and Joshi (2011) on the German Parliament using social media tools.

Finally the third theoretical field focuses on the effects of social media on politics. There is research over different reactions on digital media technologies used accordingly in different countries, considering culture or education (Rhue & Sundararajan, 2014). Vaughn (2015) has state that "the new innovations of social media create a "marketplace of ideas" but "also promise to make the nature of political discourse more democratic and less filtered" (p 2) This leads to the question: Who controls the political message in social media platforms? Discussion over this question has attract the attention of serveral scholars, Mattoni y Treré (2014) provide a conceptual framework to investigate social movements and the media: media practices, mediation and mediatization.

Adi et.al (2014) has analyze tweets from an specific group, the Labour Party in the House of Lords on the UK, founding interaction and influence from this groups. Park (2013) supported this findings with his research also with opinion leaders that motivate users to engage and become political information seekers.

The influence of the source is also supported by different attitudes, credibility and salience on the link between politics and technology (Kiousis & Dimitrova, 2006). However, the contribution that is important for this research considers two concepts: the political knowledge and the political participation in electoral campaigns influenced by social media. Research on both topics have been made by Dimitrova (Dimitrova & Bystrom, 2013; Dimitrova et al., 2014) in order to understand the friction between citizens and politicians during campaigns.

CONTEXT: INTERNET IN MEXICO AND PEÑA NIETO'S BACKGROUND

Internet use has grown quickly in recent years in Mexico. According to the latest study of AMIPCI (2016) there are 65 million Internet users in the country. The 35% of Internet users in Mexico is in the range of 25 to 44 years. During 2016 the average daily time connection for Mexican surfers was 7 hours and 14 minutes.

INEGI (2015) reported that in terms of connectivity, 12.8 million Mexican households have internet access which represents 39.2% of the total in Mexico. This means an increase of 4.8% compared to 2014. There are 14.6 million households equipped with computers which represent 44.9% of households in the country and an increase of 6.6% in relation to last year and 50,4% with cell phone.

The study of the World Internet Project (WIP) (2013), a national survey carried out two thousand interviews, with a confidence interval of 95%, indicating that there are 59.2 million internet users in Mexico. The analysis of this study indicates that 91% of users access social networks, showing an increase of 5% in comparison with 2012. It also shows that in 2012 87% of users check their emails accounts but in 2013 there was a decrease of this activity since 85% of the people used social networks.

The Mexican Internet Association (AMIPCI) revealed in its 9th study on habits of Internet users in Mexico (2016) Mexicans accessing to social networks is the first activity online with 79% of users followed by send/receive e-mails which became the second most important activity with 70% and send/receive instant messages became the third activity for online Mexican Internet users with 68%

Enrique Peña Nieto was the former governor of the State of Mexico. He belongs to the ancient ruling party Revolutionary Party (PRI) that has ruled Mexico for 70 years. He suddenly became the first runner on the presidential campaign in Mexico, followed by Josefina Vazquez Mota, from the National Action Party (PAN), that hold the presidency for the last 12 years and the left wing candidate Andres Manuel Lopez Obrador from the Revolutionary Democratic Party (PRD).

The presidential race in Mexico started officially in May 2012 and continued till July 2, the day of the election. However, the three candidates started their campaigns at the beginning of 2012, using internet as a potential communication channel, not limited by law. One of these actions was the use of Internet to make campaign and gather followers. The purpose of this research was to follow the Twitter account of Enrique Peña Nieto (@EPN) prior the official electoral campaign and specifically to analyze a political scandal on Twitter.

Peña Nieto started his Facebook (facebook.com/EnriquePN) account four years before elections. On the early 2012 he had 1,373,912 friends that followed his activities. The Twitter account (Twitter.com/epn) started in October 2011, with an amazing response; the numbers of followers grew instantly in about one month to get 349,231 followers. Peña Nieto used his Twitter account to provide information of his political activities, and some thoughts about actual issues or political trends.

Pre-Campaign Online Protest: #IamProletariat

On December 4th 2011, the Mexican presidential candidate presented his own book at the International Book Fair in Guadalajara. During the press conference he hold on this regard, some journalist asked him about 3 books that had marked his life and political career. Unfortunately, the candidate was not able to respond. He also managed to mix the names of the authors of two well know books.

In the following hours the Twitter response to this mistake was intense. The hashtag #libreriaPeñaNieto (#PeñaNietoBookstore) became a trending topic and the Twitter followers started mocking at the candidate. Some of them created Photoshop images from a popular Mexican bookstore named Gandhi, introducing Peña's mistake and circulated it through the Twitter platform during the weekend without any response from the political team of the candidate.

Even worse, the breaking point was on Saturday night, when Paulina Peña, the candidates' daughter, made a re-tweet from her boyfriend cellphone where she insulted Mexican citizens calling them "proletariat" in a clear discriminatory way – assuring that Peña Nieto was criticized because people envied him. The word "proletariat" caused a lot of anger among the Twitter users and escaladed the press, TV and online news. Immediately a new hashtag was launched (#I am proletariat) making fun out of the candidate's daughter tweet and her father. The first response from the campaign team was to close Paulina's Twitter account and they also decided not to reply to the message. The universe of Twitter messages on that black Monday for Peña Nieto reached more than 100 thousand tweets and became another trending topic on that day.

Electronic editions of all Mexican newspapers, radio and TV news reproduced the Twitter protest and made fun of the PRI candidate during the whole day. In the afternoon the candidate posted a new tweet message from his Twitter account: "Sorry for Paulina`s mistake, I will talk to her about this…" and Paulina's account came suddenly to life again. Twitter followers answered Peña Nieto's statement but not as furious as before.

Campaign Online Protest: #Iam132

On May 11, 2012, Peña Nieto was invited to a conference at a catholic university, named Universidad Iberoamericana, in one of the wealthiest neighborhoods of Mexico City. During his lecture, he was strongly questioned about several matters related to his term as the governor of the State of Mexico. At the end he was confronted by a massive protest of students that waited for him, shouting things like "coward," "murderer," and the "Ibero University does not like you" (The economist, 2012).

After encountering a barrier on his way out, the candidate could not use the front door and had to leave the University using another exit. He was interviewed by the media and he stated that he presumed that the protesters were not students from the university, but were instead supporters of the other candidate. Later on, the president of the PRI party was also interviewed on television and radio stations where he mentioned that these were not students, but provokers, and regardless they did not represent the whole university. On May 14, students from this university organized themselves to record a video in which they show their student ID cards, saying their names, and making a small declaration against the PRI candidate. In the 11-minute video, 131 students claim for a more open and fair access to information through the electronic media and complained about the protest coverage of the two main TV broadcast stations- Televisa and TV Azteca. No one could say that these activists were not students or deny the originality of their claim. This homemade video, named "#131 Ibero Students Respond," received more than one million views in one week(Milenio, 2012; Villamil, 2012).

A few days later, students from other universities made more videos like this one, with the hashtag "#I`m number 132." This hashtag was mentioned more than 769,000 times in four days and exceeded the number of mentions about the presidential candidates, as shown at the bottom of the chart. The number of online protest increased and led to street protests in a couple of days. The shadow of #Iam132 will chase Peña Nieto during the rest of his political campaign online and offline.

METHODOLOGY

The online research has become the best way to collect, compare and analyze data for Web 2.0 tools such as Twitter and Facebook. However, very few methodologies and research models have been developed for this purpose. This situation creates confusion and difficulty about the validity and trust in research findings that collect data online (Galliers, F, & Myers M, 2002). The e-research does not only make tasks easier or automates them, it raises a whole range of methodological and epistemic issues (Estalella and Ardevol, 2011). Even though, using innovative data collection strategies does not compromise the validity of the findings. Gallupe (2007) mentions that current research on information systems (IS) seem more concerned with "how" the research is conducted more than "which" research is conducted and "why". Hewson (2008) developed the concept of Internet-Mediated Research (IMR): "Internet-Mediated Research involves the gathering of novel, original data to be subjected to analysis in order to provide new evidence in relation to a particular research question" (p. 58).

This research was divided into two main steps. Step 1 - The pre-campaign analysis and Step 2 - Campaign Analysis. For the first step, the most relevant event for the purpose of this research was the #IamProletariat online protest where the main activities were:

1. **Data Collection and Validation:** For this stage, the Twitter account of the presidential candidate was validated – some other fake accounts were released – then 2,816 tweets were downloaded using the Twitter app that allows this purpose. A sample of 314 tweets randomly selected were analyzed.
2. **Data Classification:** This stage was divided into two steps. A research assistant identified and selected 314 messages with the hashtag #Iamproletariat.. In the second stage, in order to obtain keywords from the most repeated messages, we analyzed their meaning and content using the program Textfitter (now DiscoverText.com). This is a cloud-based, collaborative text analytics solution with dozens of powerful text mining features within the same program.
3. **Analysis:** As the result of the previous analysis – human and machine – messages were organized accordingly into four main categories:
    a. Criticism;
    b. Candidate's support;
    c. Mockery of the candidate;
    d. Vote preferences.

To identify these categories we made keyword definitions and analyzed them using Table 1.

For the second step, during official political campaign in Mexico, the most relevant event was the #Iam132 protest, activities for analyzing were the following:

1. **Collection of Quantitative Data from Twitter, Facebook and YouTube Accounts:** During this activity data were retrieved directly from each social media account and compared with statistics of the Electoral Observatory from the UNAM University.
2. **Data was Organized and Classified for each Presidential Candidate:** Data was added every month and compared among each other. Data from sentiment analysis was retrieved from Aristegui, (2012).
3. **Data Analysis and Trends:** The analysis of the quantitative data was compiled and charted.

Table 1. Categories and keywords for the social media analysis: #Iamproletariat case

Category	Description	Keywords
Criticism	Comments or post criticism about the candidate's mistake with arguments or ideas about the conference and his daughter's behavior	Read, learn to read, government wages, support candidates, support politics, country, proud, deceptive
Candidate's Support	Comments supporting and agreeing with the candidate's arguments	Support, courage, enough, high aspiration, high, understand, great candidate
Mockery of the Candidate	Complains, jokes and references to the candidate's mistake	Ruin, father, daughter reputation, discrimination, mad to read
Voter Preferences	Bringing up vote preferences against and in favor of	Remember, election day, no vote, vote against, PRI
* Note: the words were chosen in Spanish and translated for the purpose of this paper.		

FINDINGS AND DISCUSSION

The first event that undermined Peña Nieto`s political image was the online protest: #I am not a proletariat – it was a pre-campaign event. Most of the Twitter users made fun (83.76%) of the candidate's mistake instead of criticizing him (10.51%). Only a very small group provided an argument to support him (0.96%) (See Figure 1).

Mocking at political candidates could be the first action to start using Twitter for political purposes. Literature indicates that the use of digital media and specifically Twitter has a positive impact on electoral campaigns (Jungherr, 2015; Dimitrova, 2014). Mocking means no political commitment or intrusion to

Figure 1. Results of #Iamproletariat

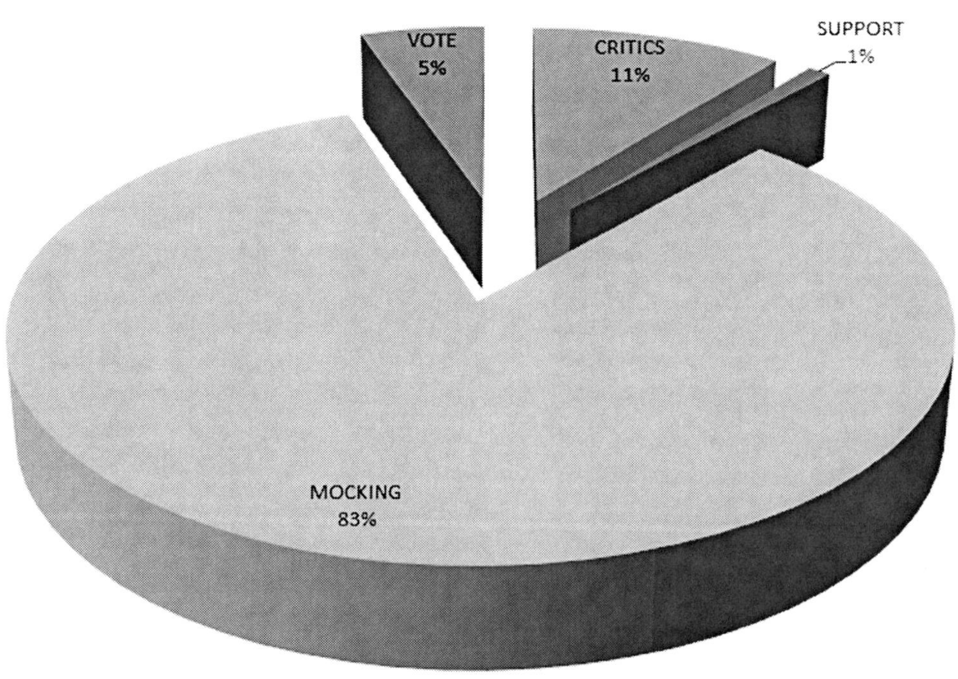

political ideas. It is a fun comment and a reason for gossiping or rumoring. This can also spread the viral effect through the Internet. Previous research mentions different directions; for example, Robertson, et. al. (2012) mentions that supporters of candidates online – in this case Facebook – send positive messages instead a negative ones, as in the case of the Mexican candidate. On the other side, research of Small (2011) describes the use of Twitter only as a communication channel to send updates on elections and candidates. In the Mexican case, the citizens' engagement for using this digital space was to diminish the popularity of the candidate of the PRI.

The viral influence of these messages contaminated the public opinion during several days, because traditional media replicated them, as Kavanaugh et.al (2013) refers mexicans seeks for political information on TV and some of use of social media. The viral influence provided users with a new tool to criticize or to talk about candidates (Aldrich et. al (2016). There were only 11% of critiques, which provided arguments, the rest were only reactions or re-tweets from other sources. According to related literature (Sha, 2016; Wallsten, 2010; Boynton, 2009), this citizens' behavior and the use of Twitter can be understood as a way of making a message viral and "interact" with the information.

The second event was the uprising of the movement #Iam132 on May 2012. This social movement was initially against the presidential candidate of the PRI; even though the discourse considered developing more democracy and opening mass media. However, references and critiques focused mostly on Peña Nieto. This movement transformed cyberactivism actions, agenda and behavior through the Mexican students that took part in this online protest through several months (Sandoval-Almazan & Gil- Garcia, 2013). This is consistent with Shah (2016) in which citizens create and thrive online conversations to promote democracy using digital spaces. This appropriation of the digital space of Twitter through debates using its characteristics, besides the online ciberactivism of #Iam132 create new behaviors and detonate new actions for the online movements. The results from the data collection of Twitter, Facebook and YouTube on the political campaign revealed several things (see Table 2). The Peña Nieto online campaign was successful only on YouTube; the number of YouTube video reproductions was above 13 million, despite the constant decrease of Twitter followers, which dropped from 19% on April-May to 11% on May-June, and the relative increase of tweets send 27% April-May and 19% May June. An important factor is the sentiment analysis of the tweets during the campaign, positive mentions on this platform continue dropping until 25% for the last month of the campaign and negative mentions 60% remain constant on two consecutive months, without any increase of neutral mentions that could balance between positive or negative tweet messages sent by the candidate. However these data show that the main strategy was focused on video productions and diffusion through YouTube rather than changing the opinion of the Twitter users.

Although the candidate increased the number of friends over his Facebook account every month during the campaign, very few of them got in contact or interact with his campaign – using the "like function" – this social media platform was only useful for information purposes rather than maintaining interaction, creating a political knowledge and developing a network of supporters as other scholars refer to (Andersen & Medaglia, 2009; Tang & Lee, 2013).

Peña Nieto's support on Facebook was strong because his account was four years old but it seems there was no electoral strategy to take advantage of all these members supporting and encouraging them to convince others and developing more engagement or even considering a vote for him (Conroy et al., 2012).

The combination of these three platforms – YouTube, Facebook and Twitter – create a digital space for Mexican political candidates, although data presented different strategies for each social media tool,

Table 2. Mexican election 2012, Presidential candidate Enrique Peña Nieto (PRI)

	Enrique Peña Nieto		
	April	**May**	**June**
Facebook friends	2,468,494	2,935,468	3,333,609
Talk about him on Facebook	245,756	335,722	488,093
Twitter followers	599,493	742,848	837,419
Tweets	682	942	1,173
Following (Twitter)	82	82	85
Average positive mentions (Twitter)	38%	28%	25%
Average negative mentions (Twitter)	46%	60%	60%
Average neutral mentions (Twitter)	16%	12%	15%
YouTube subscriptions	5,379	7,346	9,494
YouTube video reproductions	3,497,114	9,549,580	13,835,201

the virtual space for interaction is the same; citizens could post on Facebook and simultaneously on Twitter at the same time watch a video on You Tube and publish and opinion of it.

This conversations among platforms of the digital space, is not following an strategy to use social media as an interactive communications channel that allows citizens to share ideas and debates with candidates or followers, it was only conceived as a communication channel. On the other hand the political knowledge through social media tools could increase with these two events - #IamProletariat and #Iam132 – that merge on the public opinion and engage citizens on their favorite candidate.

CONCLUSION

The purpose of this research was to understand the influence of digital spaces in which took place two events using social media platforms during the Mexican presidential race in 2012. The tweet analysis of #Iamproletariat and the consequences of the emergence of #Iam132 seem not to impact on the political knowledge of Mexicans except on their political participation.

Mexican electoral participation increased after #Iam132 to reach more than 60% of Mexicans that went to the polls. Maybe the synergy created through new media and traditional media rose this participation, especially young people. But this could be an interesting research path for the future.

However the main contribution of this paper contradicts previous research that indicates a positive impact on candidates who use social media tools on campaigns (Boulianne, 2009; Dalrymple & Scheufele, 2007; Dimitrova, Shehata, Strömbäck, & Nord, 2014; Kiousis & Dimitrova, 2006; Tolbert & Mcneal, 2003). Peña Nieto won against the opinion of Twitter users and Facebook lack of activity.

Another contribution is the analysis of social media created events on political campaigns that affects – positive or negatively – candidates' public image. This research also presents quantitative data to analyze impact of political campaigns. There a no previous research on social media events that affects political campaign, this research is an starting point on this topic.

The case of #Iamproletariat is the starting point of Enrique Peña undermined presence on Twitter, but it shows the weakness of the candidate through all the electoral campaign and remained until the election day. This blind side of the campaign was hit by #Iam132.

The PRI candidate that appears unbeatable and leading the polls was debilitated using social media after May 11, 2012 conference in the Iberoamericana university. The main weapon was a combined strategy of social media: the intelligent use of YouTube - with a video of 131 students - and the viral use of the tools of Twitter and Facebook to impact on traditional media and call the attention of the general public to make their claim clear and hard into the Mexican political system.

Another indirect contribution is the digital spaces in which this events took place. The Twitter events converge using this platform but detonates on the other platform such as You Tube and Facebook to create a social movement. The digital space becomes an ecosystem for political participation that has in common the use of technology but also the lack of barriers, regulations that allows freedom of use and creation for a democratic dialogue.

The limitations of this research in terms on validaty are important. This is just one case to be analyzed, more cases like Peña Nieto must be needed in order to contradict previous research. However it is worth to mention that social media needs more research on political campaigns. Another limitation is the lack of content analysis on the electoral campaign, specially the #Iam132 case. I only present a content analysis of the #Iamproletariat on precampaign. Also both events can be debated because are in two different political stages – preCampaign and official campaign – however this distinction do not apply to social media tools. But it is clear that there is an impact through social media in politics when candidates, media and citizens use it to participate, debate and share information through these technological platforms.

More research has to be done on the social media and elections impact. This research analyzed one case of this phenomenon; it is important to analyze the rest of the hashtags, video content or posts during the campaign. This content analysis is an unexplored field of research on Twitter and Facebook's impact on political campaigns.

Another path for future research is still open which provides evidence that supports the impact of social media on political knowledge and participation. This research provides a small contribution about political engagement through Twitter with the cases of #Iamproletariat and #Iam132, but there is still a long way to understand how citizens and politicians are going to use digital spaces in the future to improve our democratic life.

REFERENCES

Adi, A., Erickson, K., & Lilleker, D. G. (2014). Elite Tweets: Analyzing the Twitter Communication Patterns of Labour Party Peers in the House of Lords. *Policy & Internet*, *6*(1), 1–27. doi:10.1002/1944-2866.POI350

Aldrich, J. H., Gibson, R. K., Cantijoch, M., & Konitzer, T. (2015). Getting out the vote in the social media era: Are digital tools changing the extent, nature and impact of party contacting in elections? *Party Politics*, *22*(2), 165–178. doi:10.1177/1354068815605304

Aleman-Meza, B., Nagarajan, M., Ding, L., Sheth, A., Arpinar, I. B., Joshi, A., & Finin, T. (2008). Scalable semantic analytics on social networks for addressing the problem of conflict of interest detection. *ACM Trans. Web, 2*(1), 1–29. Retrieved from http://portal.acm.org/citation.cfm?id=1135777.1135838#

AMIPCI. (2016). *12º Estudio sobre los Hábitos de los Usuarios de Internet en México 2016*. Asociación Mexicana de Internet. Retrieved from https://www.amipci.org.mx/images/Estudio_Habitosdel_Usuario_2016.pdf

Andersen, K., & Medaglia, R. (2009). *The Use of Facebook in National Election Campaigns: Politics as Usual?* Springer Berlin / Heidelberg. Retrieved from http://www.springerlink.com/content/b74507487472jv24/abstract/

Anderson, L. (2011, May/June). Demystifying the Arab Spring. *Foreign Affairs*. Retrieved from http://www.foreignaffairs.com/articles/67693/lisa-anderson/demystifying-the-arab-spring

Aristegui, C. (2012, March 15). *Metodología de monitoreo político en redes sociales - Aristegui Noticias*. Retrieved July 5, 2014, from http://aristeguinoticias.com/1503/post-elecciones/metodologia-de-monitoreo-politico-de-redes-sociales/

Ayers, & Maccaughey. (2003). *Cyberactivism: Online Activism in Theory and Practice* (1st ed.). New York: Routledge. Retrieved from http://www.powells.com/biblio/61-9780415943208-1

Baldwin-Philippi, J. (2013). Constructing Skeptical Citizens: How Campaign Microsites Foster New Ways of Engaging Political Information and Understanding Citizenship. *Journal of Information Technology & Politics*, *10*(3), 245–260. doi:10.1080/19331681.2013.771295

Bannister, F., & Wilson, D. (2011). O(ver)-Government? Emerging technology, citizen autonomy and the regulatory state. *Information Polity*, *16*(1), 63–79.

Best, S. J., Krueger, B. S., & Ladewig, J. (2007). The Effect of Risk Perceptions on Online Political Participatory Decisions. *Journal of Information Technology & Politics*, *4*(1), 5–17. doi:10.1300/J516v04n01_02

Bimber, B. (1998). The Internet and Political Transformation: Populism, Community, and Accelerated Pluralism. *Polity*, *31*(1), 133–160. doi:10.2307/3235370

Bimber, B. (1999). The Internet and Citizen Communication With Government: Does the Medium Matter? *Political Communication*, *16*(4), 409–428. doi:10.1080/105846099198569

Bimber, B., & Copeland, L. (2013). Digital Media and Traditional Political Participation Over Time in the U.S. *Journal of Information Technology & Politics*, *10*(2), 125–137. doi:10.1080/19331681.2013.769925

Bimber, B., Stohl, C., & Flanagin, A. J. (2009). Technological Change and the Shifting Nature of Political Organization. In A. Chadwick & P. N. Howard (Eds.), *Routledge Handbook of Internet Politics* (pp. 72–85). London: Routledge.

Bode, L. (2012). Facebooking It to the Polls: A Study in Online Social Networking and Political Behavior. *Journal of Information Technology & Politics*, *9*(4), 352–369. doi:10.1080/19331681.2012.709045

Bonchek, M. S. (1995). *Grassroots in Cyberspace: Using Computer Networks to Facilitate Political Participation*. Presented at the Midwest Political Science Association, 53rd Annual Meeting, Chicago, IL.

Boulianne, S. (2009). Does Internet Use Affect Engagement? A Meta-Analysis of Research. *Political Communication*, *26*(2), 193–211. doi:10.1080/10584600902854363

Boynton, B. (2009). Going Viral: The Dynamics of Attention. In S. Shulman & M. Xenos (Eds.), 1st Annual Journal of Information Technology & Politics Conference, YouTube and the 2008 Election Cycle in the United States (pp. 11–39). University of Massachusetts.

Castells, M., & Díaz, M. H. (2009). *Comunicación y Poder*. Madrid, España: Alianza Editorial.

Cleaver, H. (1998). The Zapatista Effect: The Internet and the Rise of an Alternative Political Fabric. *Journal of International Affairs*, *51*(2), 621–640.

Conroy, M., Feezell, J. T., & Guerrero, M. (2012). Facebook and political engagement: A study of online political group membership and offline political engagement. *Computers in Human Behavior*, *28*(5), 1535–1546. doi:10.1016/j.chb.2012.03.012

Criado, J., Martínez-Fuentes, G., & Silván, A. (2012). Social Media for Political Campaigning. The Use of Twitter by Spanish Mayors in 2011 Local Elections. In C. G. Reddick & S. K. Aikins (Eds.), *Web 2.0 Technologies and Democratic Governance* (Vol. 1, pp. 219–232). Springer New York. doi:10.1007/978-1-4614-1448-3_14

Dalrymple, K. E., & Scheufele, D. A. (2007). Finally Informing the Electorate? How the Internet Got People Thinking about Presidential Politics in 2004. *The Harvard International Journal of Press/Politics*, *12*(3), 96–111. doi:10.1177/1081180X07302881

Dang-Xuan, L., Stieglitz, S., Wladarsch, J., & Neuberger, C. (2013). An Investigation of Influentials and the Role of Sentiment in Political Communication on Twitter During Election Periods. *Information Communication and Society*, *16*(5), 795–825. doi:10.1080/1369118X.2013.783608

de Zúñiga, H. G., Bachmann, I., Hsu, S.-H., & Brundidge, J. (2013). Expressive Versus Consumptive Blog Use: Implications for Interpersonal Discussion and Political Participation. *International Journal of Communication*, *7*(0), 22.

Dimitrova, D. V., & Bystrom, D. (2013). The Effects of Social Media on Political Participation and Candidate Image Evaluations in the 2012 Iowa Caucuses. *The American Behavioral Scientist*, *57*(11), 1568–1583. doi:10.1177/0002764213489011

Dimitrova, D. V., Shehata, A., Strömbäck, J., & Nord, L. W. (2014). The Effects of Digital Media on Political Knowledge and Participation in Election Campaigns Evidence From Panel Data. *Communication Research*, *41*(1), 95–118. doi:10.1177/0093650211426004

Dubois, E., & Gaffney, D. (2014). The Multiple Facets of Influence: Identifying Political Influentials and Opinion Leaders on Twitter. *The American Behavioral Scientist*, *58*(10), 1260–1277. doi:10.1177/0002764214527088

Dutton, W. H., & Peltu, M. (2007). Reconfiguring Government-Public Engagements: Enhancing the Communicative Power of Citizens 2007. Oxford Internet Institute.

Effing, R., Hillegersberg, J., & Huibers, T. W. C. (2012). Measuring the Effects of Social Media Participation on Political Party Communities. In C. G. Reddick & S. K. Aikins (Eds.), *Web 2.0 Technologies and Democratic Governance* (Vol. 1, pp. 201–217). Springer New York. doi:10.1007/978-1-4614-1448-3_13

Effing, R., Hillegersberg, J. van, & Huibers, T. W. C. (2013). *Social Media Participation and Local Politics: A Case Study*. Enschede Council in the Netherlands.

Effing, R., van Hillegersberg, J., & Huibers, T. (2011). *Social Media and Political Participation: Are Facebook, Twitter and YouTube Democratizing Our Political Systems?* Springer Berlin / Heidelberg. Retrieved from http://www.springerlink.com/content/yg70206q2p648001/abstract/

Evans, H. K., & Ulbig, S. (2012). Social Butterflies and Politics: Exploring the Link between Sociability and Political Engagement, Online and Off. *Journal of Information Technology &amp. Politics*, *9*(4), 402–414. doi:10.1080/19331681.2012.691039

Farrell, H. (2012). The Consequences of the Internet for Politics. *Annual Review of Political Science*, *15*(1), 35–52. doi:10.1146/annurev-polisci-030810-110815

Fernandez-Poncela, A.-M. (2015). Ayotzinapa, Protestas, Solidaridades y movimientos juveniles en México. *Sapiens Research*, *5*(2), 61–65.

Fox, R. L., & Ramos, J. (2012). iPolitics: Citizens, elections, and governing in the new media era. New York: Cambridge University Press.

Gainous, J., & Wagner, K. M. (2013). *Tweeting to Power: The Social Media Revolution in American Politics*. Oxford University Press. doi:10.1093/acprof:oso/9780199965076.001.0001

Galliers, R. F. L., & Myers, M. A. D. (2002). Choosing Appropriate Information Systems Research Methodologies. In M. D. Myers & D. Avison (Eds.), Qualitative Research in Information Systems (pp. 13–16). SAGE Publications. doi:10.4135/9781849209687.n2

Garrido, M., & Halavais, A. (2003). Mapping networks of support for the Zapatista movement: applying social-network analysis to study contemporary social movements. In M. Mccaughey & M. D. Ayers (Eds.), *Cyberactivism: online activism in theory and practice* (pp. 165–184). New York: Routledge.

Gayo-Avello, and Takis Metaxas Panagiotis. (2011). Limits of Electoral Predictions Using Twitter. *Proceedings from the Fifth International AAAI Conference on Weblogs and Social Media*. Retrieved from http://www.aaai.org/ocs/index.php/ICWSM/ICWSM11/paper/view/2862

Gayo-Avello, D., & Panagiotis, T. M. (2011). *Limits of Electoral Predictions Using Twitter*. Presented at the Fifth International AAAI Conference on Weblogs and Social Media, Barcelona, España. Retrieved from http://www.aaai.org/ocs/index.php/ICWSM/ICWSM11/paper/view/2862

Gilad, L., Erhardt, G., Mike, A., Devin, G., & Ian, P. (2011). The Arab Spring| The Revolutions Were Tweeted: Information Flows during the 2011 Tunisian and Egyptian Revolutions. *International Journal of Communication*, *5*. Retrieved from http://www.ijoc.org/ojs/index.php/ijoc/article/viewArticle/1246

Gruzd, A., & Roy, J. (2014). Investigating Political Polarization on Twitter: A Canadian Perspective. *Policy & Internet*, *6*(1), 28–45. doi:10.1002/1944-2866.POI354

Harfoush, R. (2009). *Yes We Did! An inside look at how social media built the Obama brand* (1st ed.). New Riders Press.

INEGI. (2016). *Encuesta Nacional sobre Disponibilidad y Uso de Tecnologías de la Información en los Hogares (ENDUTIH) 2015*. Instituto Nacional de Estadística y Geografía. Retrieved from http://www3.inegi.org.mx/sistemas/tabuladosbasicos/tabniveles.aspx?c=33734

Jon, B. A. (1998). New Media, New Politics? From Satellite Television to the Internet in the Arab World. The Washington Institute.

Juarez, G. (2011). *Se dicta auto de formal prisión a los dos "tuiteros" veracruzanos*. Alt1040. Retrieved from http://alt1040.com/2011/09/alarmasocial-dictan-auto-de-formal-prision-a-dos-tuiteros-veracruzanos

Jungherr, A. (2015). *Twitter as Political Communication Space: Publics, Prominent Users, and Politicians*. Springer International Publishing; doi:10.1007/978-3-319-20319-5_4

Jungherr, A., Jürgens, P., & Schoen, H. (2011). Why the Pirate Party Won the German Election of 2009 or The Trouble With Predictions: A Response to Tumasjan, A., Sprenger, T. O., Sander, P. G., & Welpe, I. M. "Predicting Elections With Twitter: What 140 Characters Reveal About Political Sentiment". *Social Science Computer Review*. doi:10.1177/0894439311404119

Karlsen, R. (2013). Obamas Online Success and European Party Organizations: Adoption and Adaptation of U.S. Online Practices in the Norwegian Labor Party. *Journal of Information Technology & Politics*, *10*(2), 158–170. doi:10.1080/19331681.2012.749822

Katz, J. E., Barris, M., & Jain, A. (2013). *The Social Media President: Barack Obama and the Politics of Digital Engagement*. Palgrave Macmillan. doi:10.1057/9781137378354

Kavanaugh, A., Seungwon, Y., & Fox, E. (2011). *Between a Rock and a Cell Phone: Social Media Use during Mass Protests in Iran, Tunisia and Egypt* (No. 1149). Virginia Tech. Retrieved from http://eprints.cs.vt.edu/archive/00001149/

Kavanaugh, A. L., Sheetz, S. D., Sandoval-Almazan, R., Tedesco, J. C., & Fox, E. A. (2014, November 23). Media Use During Conflicts: Information Seeking Gratifications & Efficacy During 2012 Mexican Elections. *Proceedings of the 15th Annual International Conference on Digital Government Research (Dg.o 2014)*. http://doi.org/ doi:10.1145/2612733.2612738

Khamis, S., & Vaughn, K. (2012). We Are All Khaled Said: The potentials and limitations of cyberactivism in triggering public mobilization and promoting political change. *Journal of Arab & Muslim Media Research*, *4*(2-3), 145–163. doi:10.1386/jammr.4.2-3.145_1

Kiousis, S., & Dimitrova, D. V. (2006). Differential impact of Web site content: Exploring the influence of source (public relations versus news), modality, and participation on college students perceptions. *Public Relations Review*, *32*(2), 177–179. doi:10.1016/j.pubrev.2006.02.013

Kruikemeier, S. (2014). How political candidates use Twitter and the impact on votes. *Computers in Human Behavior*, *34*, 131–139. doi:10.1016/j.chb.2014.01.025

Lassen, D. S., & Brown, A. R. (2011). Twitter The Electoral Connection? *Social Science Computer Review*, *29*(4), 419–436. doi:10.1177/0894439310382749

Macintosh, A., Malina, A., & Farrell, S. (2002). Digital Democracy through Electronic Petitioning. In W. J. McIver & A. K. Elmagarmid (Eds.), *Advances in Digital Government. Technology, Human Factors, and Policy* (pp. 137–148). Norwell, MA: Kluwer Academic Publishers. doi:10.1007/0-306-47374-7_8

Martinez, R. (2011). *Liberan a cibernautas acusados de terrorismo y sabotaje*. Proceso.

Mashable. (2012). *Politics Transformed: The High Tech Battle for Your Vote*. Mashable, Inc.

McLean, J., & Maalsen, S. (2015). *From# destroythejoint to far reaching digital activism: Feminist revitalisation stemming from social media and reaching beyond*. Civic Media Project.

Milenio. (2012, May 14). *Responden en video 131 alumnos de la Ibero: "No somos acarreados"*. Retrieved June 2, 2012, from http://www.milenio.com/cdb/doc/noticias2011/1db22ab7d4f97d7491d79e46da38c215

Morozov, E. (2011). Whither Internet Control? *Journal of Democracy*, *22*(2), 62–74. doi:10.1353/jod.2011.0022

Nahon, K., & Hemsley, J. (2011). Democracy.com: A Tale of Political Blogs and Content. In *Proceedings of the 44th Annual Hawaii International Conference on System Sciences (HICSS 2011)* (pp. 1–10). Kauai, HI: IEEE Computer Society Conference Publishing Services. doi:10.1109/HICSS.2011.140

Padgett, T. (2012, July 2). How Enrique Peña Nieto Won Himself and His Party the Mexican Presidency. *Time*. Retrieved from http://world.time.com/2012/07/02/mexico-election-how-enrique-pena-nieto-won-himself-and-his-party-the-presidency/

Papacharissi, Z. (2009). The Virtual Sphere 2.0: The Internet, the Public Sphere and Beyond. In *Routledge Handbook of Internet Politics* (pp. 230–245). London: Routledge.

Park, C. S. (2013). Does Twitter Motivate Involvement in Politics? Tweeting, Opinion Leadership, and Political Engagement. *Computers in Human Behavior, 29*(4). doi:.10.1016/j.chb.2013.01.044

Parkinson, J. R. (2012). *Democracy and public space: The physical sites of democratic performance*. Oxford, UK: Oxford University Press. doi:10.1093/acprof:osobl/9780199214563.001.0001

Rhue, L., & Sundararajan, A. (2014). Digital access, political networks and the diffusion of democracy. *Social Networks*, *36*, 40–53. doi:10.1016/j.socnet.2012.06.007

Robertson, S. P., Vatrapu, R. K., & Medina, R. (2009). The social life of social networks: Facebook linkage patterns in the 2008 U.S. presidential election. In *Proceedings of the 10th Annual International Conference on Digital Government Research: Social Networks: Making Connections between Citizens, Data and Government (dg.o 2009)* (pp. 6–15). Puebla, Mexico: Digital Government Society of North America.

Robertson, S. P., Vatrapu, R. K., & Medina, R. (2010). Off the wall political discourse: Facebook use in the 2008 U.S. presidential election. *Information Polity*, *15*(1), 11–31. doi:10.3233/IP-2010-0196

Robertson, Douglas, Maruyama, & Chen. (2012). Political Dialog Evolution in a Social Network. In *Proceedings of the 13th Annual International Conference on Digital Government Research* (pp. 40–48). ACM.

Romm-Livermore, C. (2012). *E-politics and organizational implications of the internet: Power, influence, and social change*. Hershey, PA: IGI Global. doi:10.4018/978-1-4666-0966-2

Sandoval-Almazan, R., & Gil-Garcia, J. R. (2012). Government–Citizen Interactions Using Web 2.0 Tools: The Case of Twitter in Mexico. In C. G. Reddick & S. K. Aikins (Eds.), *Web 2.0 Technologies and Democratic Governance* (Vol. 1, pp. 233–248). Springer New York. doi:10.1007/978-1-4614-1448-3_15

Sandoval-Almazan, R., & Gil-Garcia, R. (2013). Cyberactivism through Social Media: Twitter, YouTube, and the Mexican Political Movement "I'm Number 132". In *Proceedings of the 46th Annual Hawaii International Conference on System Sciences* (Vol. 1, pp. 1704–1713). Manoa, HI: IEEE. Retrieved from http://www.cide.edu/publicaciones/status/dts/DTAP%20273.pdf

Shah, D. V., McLeod, J. M., & Lee, N. (2016). Conversation is the soul of democracy: Expression effects, communication mediation, and digital media. *Communication and the Public*, *26*(1), 12–18. doi:10.1177/2057047316628310

Small, T. A. (2011). What the hashtag? A content analysis of Canadian politics on Twitter. *Information Communication and Society*, *14*(6), 872–895. doi:10.1080/1369118X.2011.554572

Smith, C. (2016). *By the numbers: 170 + Amazing Twitter Statistics*. Retrieved from http://tinyurl.com/mbkv9t6

Swamynathan, G., Wilson, C., Boe, B., Almeroth, K., & Zhao, B. Y. (2008). Do social networks improve e-commerce?: a study on social marketplaces. In *Proceedings of the first workshop on Online social networks* (pp. 1–6). Seattle, WA: ACM. doi:10.1145/1397735.1397737

Tang, G., & Lee, F. L. F. (2013). Facebook Use and Political Participation: The Impact of Exposure to Shared Political Information, Connections With Public Political Actors, and Network Structural Heterogeneity. *Social Science Computer Review*, *31*(6), 763–773. doi:10.1177/0894439313490625

The Economist. (2012). Mexico election diary: The students are revolting. *The Economist*. Retrieved from http://www.economist.com/blogs/americasview/2012/05/mexico-election-diary

Theocharis, Y., & Lowe, W. (2015). Does Facebook Increase Political Participation? Evidence from a Field Experiment. *Information Communication and Society*, *4462*(March). doi:10.1080/1369118X.2015.1119871

Tolbert, C. J., & Mcneal, R. S. (2003). Unraveling the Effects of the Internet on Political Participation? *Political Research Quarterly*, *56*(2), 175–185. doi:10.1177/106591290305600206

Toledo-Bastos, M., Galdini-Raimundo, R. L., & Travitzki, R. (2013). Gatekeeping Twitter: Message diffusion in political hashtags. *Media Culture & Society*, *35*(2), 260–270. doi:10.1177/0163443712467594

Towner, T. L. (2012). Campaigns and Elections in a Web 2.0 World: Uses, Effects, and Implications for Democracy. In C. G. Reddick & S. K. Aikins (Eds.), *Web 2.0 Technologies and Democratic Governance* (Vol. 1, pp. 185–199). Springer New York. doi:10.1007/978-1-4614-1448-3_12

Tumasjan, A., Sprenger, T. O., Sandner, P. G., & Welpe, I. M. (2011a). Election Forecasts With Twitter. *Social Science Computer Review*, *29*(4), 402–418. doi:10.1177/0894439310386557

Tumasjan, A., Sprenger, T. O., Sandner, P. G., & Welpe, I. M. (2011b). Election Forecasts With Twitter How 140 Characters Reflect the Political Landscape. *Social Science Computer Review*, *29*(4), 402–418. doi:10.1177/0894439310386557

Vaccari, C., & Nielsen, R. K. (2013). What Drives Politicians Online Popularity? An Analysis of the 2010 U.S. Midterm Elections. *Journal of Information Technology & Politics*, *10*(2), 208–222. doi:10.1080/19331681.2012.758072

Vaughn, J. S. (2015). *Controlling the Message: New Media in American Political Campaigns*. NYU Press.

Villamil, J. (2012, May 22). Televisa y la Primavera Mexicana. *Homozapping*. Retrieved from http://homozapping.com.mx/2012/05/televisa-y-la-primavera-mexicana/

Wallsten, K. (2008). Political Blogs: Transmission Belts, Soapboxes, Mobilizers, or Conversation Starters? *Journal of Information Technology & Politics*, *4*(3), 19–40. doi:10.1080/19331680801915033

Wallsten, K. (2010). Yes We Can: How Online Viewership, Blog Discussion, Campaign Statements, and Mainstream Media Coverage Produced a Viral Video Phenomenon. *Journal of Information Technology & Politics*, *7*(2-3), 163–181. doi:10.1080/19331681003749030

WIP. (2013). *Estudio 2013 de hábitos y percepciones de los mexicanos sobre Internet y diversas tecnologías asociadas*. World Internet Project. Retrieved from http://www.wip.mx/estudios_wip.html

Chapter 6
ICTs:
Ancillary Tools for Indirect Democracy?

Kerill Dunne
Independent Researcher, Ireland

ABSTRACT

Within Western democracies there has been a growing demand to use ICT to enable citizens to get more involved with local political issues. Western local governments have claimed that ICT can empower citizens and strengthen local democracy. This chapter will focus on one aspect of this and examine the provision of online direct democracy and whether citizens do indeed have the opportunity to vote more in local policy decision making. Using Michel Foucault's concepts of power and domination this research will explore if local governments and their citizens, through strategies of power, use one type of ICT, online forums, to change local representative democracy. In order to examine whether online forums can increase direct democracy for citizens, a quantitative data collection method was implemented in this study which produced a data set of 138 online forums. This article argues that online forums do not increase direct democracy, because citizens along with local governments use ICT to maintain the political status quo online?

INTRODUCTION

In 21st century Britain there is an expectation of openness, a need for flexibility and a greater understanding that people, the "consumers of democracy", use and do not use modern technology in a manner that suits them. (Bercow, 2014).

Apart from saying that citizens consume democracy, I think that the above quote highlights one important fact about people in the West – they use technology to engage with democracy and political institutions at a level and in a manner that suits them. In other words, citizens determine their own level of online political participation.

Political participation is a mechanism by which citizens express their political attitudes, beliefs, opinions; and by using it, citizens attempt to influence goals or implement policies (Clarke et al., 2004). In attempting to influence decision making, participation can take many forms – voting, referendum,

DOI: 10.4018/978-1-5225-1862-4.ch006

demonstrating, canvassing, and engagement in community activities. Even online, citizens via a plethora of online engagement tools (rooted in representative democracy) can affect local decision making processes by influencing democratic representatives. Representative democracy is distinguished here as any democratic mechanism where citizens' representatives take decision on their behalf as opposed to citizens voting directly on the political decisions to be taken. Pateman's (1970) seminal work provides us with an applied categorization of political participation according to its impact on decision making processes. Using the latter, this chapter defines direct democracy as: a group of individuals where each member of the decision making body has equal power to determine the outcomes of decisions. Such a group is unsupervised and is self-regulating. Here, citizens must have the necessary information on which they can base their decision. This model can be summed up as:

In a participatory democracy, decision-making is the process whereby people propose, discuss, plan, and implement those decisions that affect their lives. This requires that the decision making process be continuous and significant, direct rather than through representatives, and organized around issues instead of personalities (Benello & Roussopoulos, 2005, p.6).

The decline in voter turnout within the majority of EU States signals a general weakening in democracy (Aichholzer, 2016). There have been calls for more political participation (online / offline) to resolve this problem, for example, the European Citizens' Initiative (ECI) aims to increase direct democracy by allowing citizens to participate directly in the development of EU policy.

In the early days of E-Democracy many spoke of the revolutionary impact ICT (Information Communication Technologies) would have on Western democracy and levels of citizens political participation within democratic processes. By all accounts this has been a slow revolution (Wright, 2012). If this is the case and levels of online political participation are very low then who is too blame: local governments, wider national political institutions, or citizens?

This chapter will firstly examine if the introduction of ICT on Western local government websites has brought about an increase in direct democracy? On the basis of the result of this, the chapter will then explore the theoretical causes of such a situation. There are many ICT tools available to use to provide a platform for E-Participation, and this research has chosen one of these to study - a local political online forum, defined here as: a web based forum that has a threaded asynchronous platform for discussion open to all individuals within a local area to discuss local political issues from a non-consensual position. Local political online forums were chosen because they are one of the best forms of E-Democracy for encouraging deliberation in contrast to Online blogs, Listserves, Webcasting, E-consultations and E-Petitions. Data collection was conducted at a time before social media was established as a mainstream form of online political engagement. In order to conduct this research, an international sample of 138 online forums from around the world was collected and entered into a data set for analysis. Even though a quantitative data collection method was employed, this chapter is mainly conceptual and does not employ content analysis of the discussions within the online forums, but instead focuses on the method of voting employed within online forums.

LITERATURE REVIEW

Within the West, local governments and certain E-Participation advocates have claimed that ICT can empower citizens and strengthen local democracy. I want to examine if this is the case and more specifically whether citizens have the opportunity to participate more in local politics i.e. is there an increase in local direct democracy. Using Michel Foucault's concepts of power and domination, I will explore if local governments and their citizens, through strategies of power, use online forums to change the traditional political power structures, or maintain representative democracy, local decision making mechanisms and indeed citizens' level of democratic participation. This review is broken into two sections. First, I will detail what Foucault has to say with regards to power; and second, I will examine what the E-Participation literature has to say on increasing political participation through online forums.

Foucault

Where there is power, there is resistance, and yet, or rather consequently, this resistance is never in a position or exteriority in relation to power. Should it be said that one is always inside "power", there is no "escaping" it, there is no absolute outside where it is concerned, because one is subject to the law in any case? Or that, history being the ruse of reason, power is the ruse of reason, always emerging the winner. (Foucault, 1978, P95)

In the quote above Foucault (1978) argues that power is productive, fluid and intertwined with human discourses. The latter within this chapter refers to forms of communication that create social meaning. In The History of Sexuality vol 1, Foucault shows how sexual practice and sexual discourse have changed throughout history. In order show how sex became to be repressed in the West, he identifies the relationship between sex and power and notes that citizens along with governments, the church and the educational systems all played their part in affirming this repression. Foucault (1997) notes that for power to operate in society there is a certain amount of freedom required. In other words there must be the possibility to resist power otherwise its just a state of domination.

Power relations are extremely widespread in human relations. Now, this means not that political power is everywhere, but that there is in human relationships a whole range of power relations that may come into play among individuals, within families, in pedagogical relationships, political life, and so on.... one sometimes encounters what may be called situations or states of domination in which the power relations, instead of being mobile allowing the various participants to adopt strategies modifying them, remain blocked, frozen. (Foucault, 1997, p283)

Foucault (1978) argues that within catholic countries in the 17th century, sex for the first time was transformed into a discourse when people began speaking about it in confessional booths. After this, in the 18th century Foucault argues that censoring discussions on sex led, firstly, to indecent speech, but it also led to new discourses in science to hear about it. Such censorship produced a great discourse on sex i.e. Psychoanalysis. Within the 18th century sex was tightly regulated for rational / useful purposes i.e. sex became a public issue. During this period medicine and psychiatry determined what was normal sexual behavior. But as Foucault notes, power is productive and by turning sex into a discourse and regulating sexual behavior it gave rise to multiple forms of perversions, unorthodox sexuality, and capitalist pornography. Power does not just repress but it is a producer that runs through the whole of society (Foucault, 2000). Because sex was brought into the field of rationality, Foucault argues that any attempt to tell the truth about sex is a will to power which produces a discourse.

Power is everywhere; not because it embraces everything, but because it comes from everywhere. And "Power," insofar as it is permanent, repetitious, inert, and self-reproducing, is simply the over-all effect that emerges from all these mobilities, the concatenation that rests on each of them and seeks in turn to arrest their movement. One needs to be nominalistic, no doubt: power is not an institution, and not a structure; neither is it a certain strength we are endowed with; it is the name that one attributes to a complex strategical situation in a particular society. (Foucault, 1978, P92)

As the previous quote details, there is no escaping power because it represses, excludes and always produces new discourses – power is never static but is strategical. One is always within power, it is interwoven into everything from sex to politics. Thus, power does not have one central location e.g. government, on the contrary power emanates and resists through many networked societal points (citizens, families, schools, etc.) and in Western countries there is no domination i.e. a state of affairs were individuals do not have the freedom to resist government or state institutions (Foucault, 2000).

E-Participation and Online Forums

This section will explore whether online forums have the potential to increase political participation. As noted above, this chapter marks a fundamental difference between representative democracy and direct democracy. Whether citizens can merely influence decision making processes online via representatives, or play a direct role in online voting is central to the debate on whether online engagement actually constitutes political participation. It is argued in this chapter that direct democracy (with or without deliberation) is a form of political participation. However, it is acknowledged here that voting with a period of deliberation is a far stronger form of democracy than voting without it, or voting indirectly for representatives to take decisions on one's behalf.

The existence of representative institutions at national level is not sufficient for democracy; for maximum participation by all the people at that level of socialization, or "social training", for democracy must take place in other spheres in order that the necessary individual attitudes and psychological qualities can be developed. This development takes place through the process of participation itself (Pateman, 1970, p. 42).

As the quote above shows, Pateman (1970) argues that political participation has a psychological impact on participants. Within her argument, participation is seen to educate citizens to be more democratic, encourage voting for the common good and it increases citizens' political efficacy. Thus, increased local participation has clear benefits for citizens and for increasing political participation at national / federal levels. With this in mind it must be acknowledged here that national voter turnout in certain Western countries such as Australia has remained relatively stable, albeit voting in Australia is compulsory with fines for non-participation. On the other hand, Clarke et al (2004) notes that voter turnout in Britain has gradually declined since reaching a high of 84% in the 1950s. Coleman (2005) quotes the Electoral Commission Report (2004) which found that only 14% of people in 2003 identified with any political party in Britain; and 70% of the population said they didn't trust politicians. He argues that citizen disengagement is stemming from a break in the connection between citizens and representatives. His 2005 survey found that 72% of British people felt disconnected from parliament. The survey also found that people did not feel in touch with their local MP, with only 11% feeling connected. Riley et al (2003) suggest that ICT including forums could contribute to a renewed faith in government and democracy by the creation of interactive government rooted in deliberation with the citizenry; they argue that such ICT could take Western democracies into new interactive democracies. Many argue that citizens want increased political participate within policy decision making (Coleman and Gotze, 2001, Coleman, 2005), although, this rests on the fact that other factors need to be present (Lowndes, Pratchett and Stoker, 2006). Coleman (2014a) also lists the many things local councils need to do to adapt themselves to make participation work for citizens.

Even if there is a desire among citizens for participation that does not mean it will necessarily be a straight forward process. The reason for this is that citizens' distrust of representatives is on the rise (Gouscos et al, 2012). Coleman (2014b) says that it's not the case that citizens can't be reached by local government, it's rather they don't trust their local governments to listen to them. Coleman (2005) using statistics from the Electoral Commission Report (2004) shows that 75% of UK people want to have a say in how the country is run, in 2011 this statistic dropped to 54% (Hansard Society, 2011), however, the latter statistics must be considered cautiously because:

people may like the idea rather than the reality of participating. (Lowndes, Pratchett, & Stoker, 2001, p450).

This is because other factors need to be present that encourage participation. Lowndes, Pratchett and Stoker (2006) developed a diagnostic tool for assessing initiatives aimed at encouraging political participation among citizens. The diagnostic tool (a theoretical model) was based on factors (that the authors considered) that promoted political participation. The model argues that individuals participate when they: have the resources and knowledge to do so; have strong community ties; are enabled to participate through strong civic groups and networks; and their inputs are responded to by decision makers.

However, there is a growing body of theorists such as Margolis and Resnick (2000), who argue that the advent of ICT has produced "politics as usual" and not brought forth new forms of participatory democracy to representative systems but instead has normalised the political process online. Margolis and Resnick (2000) point out that the web is dominated by commercial interests not information exchange, and reinforces current political patterns of representative democracy. Politics on the net is conducted by familiar parties where candidates and interest groups still dominate and the general citizenry still have little interest in participating in political and civic affairs. This normalization theory holds that elite groups and the traditional politically engaged will continue to dominate political engagement online, and bring with them all of the existing biases of the current political system to the detriment of "pluralistic democracy" online (Gibson et al, 2003). Indeed, Gibson et al (2002), and Jensen et al (2002) provide empirical evidence which highlights the characteristics of online politically active individuals as those that are traditionally engaged in politics offline; well educated; from higher socio-economic status; middle aged males; IT literate and are IT enabled.

Moreover, it must be noted here that the digital divide {"the patterns of unequal access to information technology based on income, race, ethnicity, gender, age, and geography"(Mossberger, Tolbert, and Stansbury 2003, P1)} may have an impact on the ability of local political online forums to support political participation. The digital divide does not only mean certain groups have no access to the internet, but lack of IT knowledge, cost of IT and technophobia all play a part. The digital divide affects many groups such as the elderly, those with a disability and those from a disadvantaged socioeconomic background.

The digital divide is understood as a multidimensional phenomenon encompassing three distinct aspects. The global divide refers to the divergence of Internet access between industrialized and developed societies. The social divide concerns the gap between information rich and poor in each nation. And finally within the online community, the democratic divide signifies the difference between those who do, and do not, use the panoply of digital resources to engage, mobilize, and participate in public life (Norris, 2001, p4).

Finally, with regards to social media and E-Participation, Gouscos et al, (2012) say that citizens real involvement within policy and decision-making processes face many barriers. Lowndes, Pratchett and Stoker's (2006) research on participatory activities within six English localities shows that while community ties (social capital) and the socio-economic position of citizens within communities shapes levels of political engagement they do not determine them. They argue that the way institutions of local government work, and how their members and officials view participation mechanisms also affects whether people participate or not.

Levels of participation are 'found to be related to the openness of the political system, [and] the presence of a public value orientation among local government managers (Lowndes, Pratchett & Stoker, 2006 b, p539) .

Pratchett, Wingfield, and Karakaya-Polat (2006) argue that tackling barriers such as;

1. The limited conceptual understanding local government members / officers have of local democracy; And
2. Practical problems such as lack of finance, closed political system; And
3. Conceptual problems such as the lack of will among members / officers to promote E-Democracy within local government, will go a long way to encouraging online participation.

The E-Participation literature above has noted many barriers that need to be resolved to encourage online political participation. These include: citizens lack of trust, the digital divide, the affects of normalization theory, the internal & external governmental barriers to increased citizens democratic participation and lack of political efficacy (citizens' familiarity with democratic procedures and their democratic skills). However, even if it were possible to put aside all of these barriers would citizens be encouraged towards online political participation? The statistic below does not bode well for such a position and the E-Participation literature, in its rush to advocate increased online participation, has not researched, in any great depth, if citizens have the opportunity to vote online, and indeed if they want increased direct democracy via local political online forums. The methodological approach by which this chapter aims to address this question will be answered is detailed in the next section.

Half of the public (52%) do not want to be involved in what Parliament does or are not really interested in it. (Hansard Society,2011, p9)

METHODOLOGY

In order to examine whether online forums can increase direct democracy a quantitative methodology was implemented in this study. This section will focus on detailing the process by which a sample of 138 local political online forums from around the world was selected. Below the criteria devised and the sampling/collection processes used will be spelt out.

Criteria

Two sets of criteria were used to select a sample of local political online forums from the Internet. Firstly, the online forum criteria will be shown. The sample included local political online forums located outside the UK because a large enough sample could not be gathered of just UK-based forums. The sample was limited to English speaking forums. This limitation biases the sample towards Western democracies; however, certain countries within this category have political disengagement issues and are of more interest to this study. Moreover, this bias could not be helped, due to time and money constraints, the researcher could not search all language types of forums and translate them. Furthermore, to save on time, only local political online forums which did not require registration were examined. The researcher does not expect that such limitation biased the study because, in the course of collecting sample forums, only three forums requiring registration were identified. Forums were also selected that allowed anyone to join (non-exclusionary) and allowed anyone to run them. Finally, moderated and un-moderated forums were chosen, however, only forums which had a rules-based framework (a set of rules within a forum that posters had to abide by) were selected. This latter criterion was included because consensus exists within the E-Democracy literature that forums without a set of rules have little chance of providing a platform for deliberation and tend to be anarchic.

Secondly, forums focusing on local political issues were selected. The political selection criteria used were developed using Barber's (1984) basic theoretical conditions that give rise to politics. Table 1 provides the selection criteria by which local political online forums were chosen for the sample list. Although the two sets of criteria are presented side by side in Table 1, there is no correlation between them. These criteria were used to capture a sample of relevant political online forums.

Sampling Strategy

Data collection began by requesting practitioners in field of E-Participation to email the researcher any online forum population lists they had, upon which samples could be drawn. These practitioners said no such databases existed. As there was no population list from which to draw a sample of local political forums it was decided to create a sample of forums from the Internet.

The sampling strategy began with the development of five search phrases (see table 2). These search phrases were used within the search engine Google to locate relevant forums. The search phrases were used individually across the Internet as a whole and not searched through geographically specific areas. Google's most relevant search result pages (results which incorporate popular sites) were only examined; Google's omitted results pages were not. Google's omitted results feature incorporates less relevant Web links in the search results and produces duplicative and irrelevant results (please see the next section for how Google searches and ranks pages). All pages and forums which appeared in the search result pages were examined and selected if they fell within the selection criteria (Table 1). Four other sampling

Table 1. Criteria used to select forums

	Political criteria	Online forums criteria
1	Necessary public action required	Situated on the English speaking World Wide Web.
2	There has to be public choice on local issues.	Did not require registration to read posts
3	Absence of independent ground i.e. conflicting viewpoints	The general layout was not that of a blog or a listserv or email list (unless list has archived threads). There had to be (the potential for) more than one contributor, each providing distinct, signed input, which remained on a message / discussion / bulletin threaded board.
4	Issues which affect all participants	Moderated or un-moderated
5	Forums which are exclusionary i.e. the republicans' forum were not collected. Nor were forums which were set up for one single issue e.g. environmentalism.	A rules based framework
6	Forums had to have a thread dedicated to a village, town or city; and not just threads for province, state or international issues. However, forums which were set up exclusively for local issues could contain some wider issues.	In the most general sense forum provided a format for citizens to participate in local / national decision making or input into policy formation
7		All citizens, private organisations and government officials had to be allowed to participate within forum.
8		Forum could be independently, privately or governmentally run.

strategies were also tried and tested, but they were considered inferior to the one described above. For example, in one strategy, the search phrases were used across specific geographic regions in Google and a random sample was taken across all regions; however, at the end of this process the sample of forums was too small to analyze.

Data Collection Procedure

Before the sampling strategy proper began, a sub-sample of sites was examined to identify common keywords. A selection of meta-tags (the Web site keywords used by Web developers for search engines) from political online forums were examined. On the bases of this exercise, five search phrases were de-

Table 2. Search phrases and the number of forums examined

	Phrase	Number of forums examined	Number of Google pages
1	Online political discussion forum	814	82
2	Local politics discussion forum	440	44
3	Community online discussion forum	859	86
4	Local government council online forum	780	78
5	Local politics message board	500	50
	Total	**3393**	**340**

veloped. All the search phrases and the amount of Web sites and forums explored during data collection are represented in Table 2. After the completion of search phrases one and two, a total of 51 forums had been selected, the majority of which came from search phrase two; after the completion of search phrases three and four a total of 113 forums had been captured. The sample itself at the end of the data-collection process contained 138 forums. This sample enveloped a third of forums from the previous geographic regions sample, and it enveloped a third of forums from another of the failed sampling strategies. There was nothing notably different about the forums selected earlier or later in the data collection process. This data-collection process took five months to complete.

Data entry took two months to complete; in total data collection and data entry took seven arduous months to be completed; because I was the principle data collector, the process was very repetitive and boring. Data entry consisted of examining each of the 138 forums and categorizing them across variables within SPSS. Direct democracy was determined on the basis that participants had an equal vote on a matter being discussed within the forum examined. The discussion within forums ranged from the local to the international. A complete content analysis of discussions within the forum is beyond this chapter.

Once data entry was completed a quality assurance (QA) exercise was carried out on 10% of the forums to make sure the data was correct. Within 10% of the forums there were only two erroneous entries within 196 entries, which is a 4% discrepancy. In terms of replication, if another researcher took the exact same forums for their sample as was used in this research, their results may vary slightly to what is here. The reason for this is that some forums may change over time and become active or be shut down. This has implications for the measurement of online forums' ability to support forms of political participation. In other words, researchers who examine the Internet need to be aware that online data is variable:

The Internet is so fluid as to be rendered meaningless as a storage medium; it is never constant, never fixed no matter that the textual traces left there seem to give it some form (Jones, 1999, p.12).

Table 3. Coding of variables

Variable	Codes
Moderated	Whether forum had a moderator or not
Inactive	If a forum had no posts registered within it for a month it was noted as inactive. However, a forum was also noted as inactive if it had a recent post and the main body of its other posts were more than a month old. Forums were also noted as inactive if the forum had a recent post situated in a forum with no other posts.
Who commissioned a forum	Forums were coded in terms of who set them up (media organization, community, or local government).
What software was used	The software that was used to build each forum was coded.
Direct democracy	Direct democracy is categorized by local government decision making processes being placed in the hands of citizens within a forum.
Location variable	Coded the geographic region of forums.
Posts, threads and users	Details were captured on the number of posts, threads and users within forums.

Furthermore, by using the search engine Google the data and results here are slightly unrepresentative. When the data collection procedure was conducted, in 2008, Google ranked search pages based on its own PageRank™ .

PageRank™ software relies on the uniquely democratic nature of the web by using its vast link structure as an indicator of an individual page's value. In essence, Google interprets a link from page A to page B as a vote, by page A, for page B. But, Google looks at considerably more than the sheer volume of votes, or links a page receives; for example, it also analyzes the page that casts the vote. Votes cast by pages that are themselves "important" weigh more heavily and help to make other pages "important." Using these and other factors, Google provides its views on pages' relative importance...Google combines PageRank with sophisticated text-matching techniques to find pages that are both important and relevant to your search. Google goes far beyond the number of times a term appears on a page and examines dozens of aspects of the page's content (and the content of the pages linking to it) to determine if it's a good match for your query. (Google, 2008)

Thus in 2008, Google's complex automated structure made external tampering on search results extremely difficult. However, forums with fewer links to them had a weaker chance of being selected by the search engine. In terms of this research, this does not bias the results of this study to any great extent because the research was more concerned with popular and active forums rather than inactive unpopular forums. However, it is acknowledged that this sampling strategy has an under representation of sites with few links to them. Furthermore, others have noted concerns over Google's position in democracy as well as its role as a search engine:

Google engages in surveillance and privacy intrusion of citizens in the gathering of consumer related data, while at the same time denying transparency in regard to, for example, its PageRank algorithm and Google Scholar search process. With its complex system for ranking search results, it matches advertisements to search parameters. (Dahlgren, 2013, P3)

FINDINGS

Before the data analysis, a summary of the basic features of the forums within the sample of 138 forums will be given. Within the sample of forums, the average number of posts within a forum was 3,333, the average number of threads was 385, and the average number of registered users was 1,400. In terms of geographic location, 62% were based in the US, while 30% were based in the UK. No clear reason was established as to why so few forums from other English speaking countries (Canada, New Zealand, Republic of Ireland, and Australia) were present in the sample except that these counties have lower populations than that of the US and the UK. Twenty-nine percent of forums were supported by small independent software companies; twenty two percent were supported by PhpBB, an open source software forum builder.

42% of forums were commissioned by independent communities or individuals, 30% by media organizations, and 22% by local government. Sixty one percent of sites had a majority of relevant debate occurring within them (focused on local political issues); and 62% of forums had a thread debating political participation, public representatives, or voting. Finally, 77% of forums were moderated, and the majority of these were run by independent communities.

In spite of all the innovations, there are still many fears over internet voting systems:

As of today, there is no technical solution available which would guarantee transparency, accessibility, resistance to intimidation and vote selling and, last but not least, resistance to fraud or errors. (Goos, Beckert & Lindner 2016, P136)

Such fears probably played a role in why no forums within this research's sample supported direct democracy. Furthermore, it is unlikely that online forums (due to their lack of connection to local government decision making processes) will be able to support direct democracy in the near future. On the other hand, they are able to support other forms of political participation which can influence / inform local representatives and their policy making mechanisms.

Just under half of the forums (43%) within the sample were inactive. Only 10% of forums were found to have a formal influence on local government, that is to say they were used as part of a government consultation, but 86% of them were found to be inactive. Twelve percent of forums were present on a government Web site and fifty three percent of these were inactive. Seventy eight percent of forums were not connected at all to a government site, and the majority of these are active. Put another way, 71% of forums commissioned by media organizations were active; 64% of forums commissioned by independent communities/individuals were active; and only 31% of local government forums were active. This research notes that online forums do not increase direct democracy for citizens.

These results must be considered carefully, even though no online forums were found to support direct democracy that does not mean that they do not exist. This international sample was quite small; thus a large scale survey should be conducted on all Western local governments' websites to examine levels of voting by citizens on local government issues. Other limitations within this chapter include generalizing its findings, which are taken from online forums predominantly based within the US and UK, and applying them to all Western democracies. Furthermore, this chapter has used the term local government in a very broad sense when in fact local government has different structures and different levels of voter engagement depending on its geographical location.

CONCLUSION

Western local governments have claimed that ICT can empower citizens and strengthen local democracy by giving citizens the opportunity to participate more in local policy decision making. This chapter argues that online forums do not increase direct democracy. Of all the forums examined not one supported a voting mechanism. More worryingly (Goos, Beckert & Lindner 2016) found there is no indication that internet voting contributes to increased voter turnout. Why is this the case and who is to blame? The quote below hints at the answer.

Revolts belong to history. But, in a certain way, they escape from it. The impulse by which a single individual, a group, a minority, or an entire people says, "I will no longer obey," and throws the risk of their life in the face of an authority they consider unjust seems to me to be something irreducible. Because no authority is capable of making it utterly impossible: Warsaw will always have its ghetto in revolt and its sewers crowded with rebels. And because the man who rebels is finally inexplicable; it takes a wrenching away that interrupts the flow of history, and its long chains of reasons, for a man to be able, "really," to prefer the risk of death to the certainty of having to obey (Foucault,2000, P448).

Why is it that online forums do not increase direct democracy for citizens? This research is aware that the barriers (unconscious and conscious) erected by certain local representatives / officials, and wider national institutions do maintain existing representative power structures and stand in the way of greater online participation. Moreover, the many other barriers mentioned above (Lack of trust, diminished efficacy, the digital divide, security concerns and the normalisation theory), also play a large role in preventing an increase in local online participatory democracy. It also must be acknowledged, that maybe there is a slow E-Participation revolution occurring and we just need to wait for the big democratic changes to take place (Wright, 2012).

These barriers all play a role in preventing online direct democracy, however, it is the contention of this chapter that the main reason as to why there is no increase in direct democracy via ICT rests with citizens themselves? As we have seen in places like Egypt and Tunisia during the Arab Spring, when citizens want change they take to the streets and force it. During the Arab Spring, social media did play a role in helping spread democratic ideals and assisted people organise protests (Howard, et al, 2011); Second, ICT also allowed pro-democratic groups / individuals to distribute information outside of traditional, government controlled media channels (Wilson M and Corey K, 2012); And third, during the Arab Spring ICT facilitated disparate group cohesion (Breuer, 2012).

The Egyptian revolution, therefore, demonstrates the opportunities offered by social media for large-scale mobilization and the organization and implementation of social movements...Social media introduced speed and interactivity that were not possible through the reliance on traditional mobilization resources such as brochures, faxes, and telephones. (Eltantawy & Wiest, 2011, P1218)

However, it must be noted:

The mobilizing effect of new information and social media networks as catalysts of broad sociopolitical protest will vary significantly from region to region and from one political context to another. The presence of multiple underlying causes for sociopolitical protest will not suffice for new information and communication networks to become a major catalyst (Stepanova, 2011,P3).

The real the driving force behind the demand for democratic change during the Arab Spring was people on the streets. As of yet, this has not produced a democracy in places like Egypt, however the desire for democracy in itself put feet on the streets in Cairo; where ICTs were merely used as a tool for the offline (Alexander & Aouragh, 2011). The majority of citizens in certain Western countries, due to time restraints, lack of interest, and apathy, simply don't want an increase in online / offline direct democracy, because if they really did want it, they would simply force it as was done during the Arab Spring by getting on the streets and protesting.

Whilst the Internet and social media may have theoretically made organization cheaper, they have not necessarily made it easier. Interestingly, this paper reveals that it was the Egyptian protesters' focus on traditional methods of organization, rather than relying on the Internet, that was largely to thank for the success of their movement. (Tusa, 2009, p17)

The E-Participation literature has not examined in any great detail the role that Western citizens play in propping up the representative democratic model online which restrains direct democracy? If according to Foucault power is not fixed and does not have one central location then we can argue that citizens are active players that not only have their democratic suffrage curtailed by local government barriers, but citizens also play an active-role in propping up a representative system which restrains direct democracy? Thus, it is argued here that local governments and citizens in certain Western countries use ICT to maintain the political status quo online. This argument does not in any way distract from the ability of ICT to spread democratic change more conveniently and proficiently than word of mouth / pamphlets as was seen during the Arab Spring.

However, as power is productive (Foucault), there is sure to be examples of how citizens in the West resist the political status quo power structures by producing alternative power strategies. Gonzalez-Bailon (2014) provides a description of how social movements operate outside traditional democratic structures by using ICTs to create more decentralized forms of horizontal participation. Indeed Gerbaudo (2012) argues that the use of social media in social movements 'harvests' the individual frustration of many citizens who do not feel represented by representative government or civil society. Because of a distrust of traditional governmental mechanisms, Gerbaudo (2012) argues that certain social movements (such as the Spanish 15-M and the Occupy movements) strive for horizontalism, direct action and direct democracy.

Social media have been chiefly responsible for the construction of a choreography of assembly as a process of symbolic construction of public space which facilitates and guides the physical assembling of a highly dispersed and individualised constituency…My key contention is that the introduction of social media in social movements does not simply result in a situation of absolute spontaneity and unrestrained participation. On the contrary, influential Facebook admins and activist tweeps become 'soft leaders' or choreographers, involved in setting the scene, and constructing an emotional space within which collective action can unfold. (Gerbaudo, 2012, P5)

Whether this type of resistance, which is disconnected from Western democratic institutions, can bring about policy changes (a form of indirect democracy) and thus be labeled E-Democracy is beyond the scope of this chapter. It is recommended that such research is carried out before studies begin examining the ability of social media (connected to policy decision-making mechanisms) to increase direct democracy.

REFERENCES

Aichholzer, G. (2016). Citizen Participation in Climate Governance. In G. Aichholzer, H. Kubicek, & L. Torres (Eds.), *Evaluating e-Participation. Frameworks, Practice, Evidence* (pp. 47–62). London: Springer. doi:10.1007/978-3-319-25403-6_3

Alexander, A., & Aouragh, M. (2011). The Egyptian Experience:Sense and Nonsense of the Internet Revolution. *International Journal of Communication*, (5): 1344–1358.

Barber, B. (1984). *Strong Democracy. Participatory Politics for a New Age*. Los Angeles, CA: University of California Press.

Bercow, J. (2014). *Why the future of democracy is digital*. Retrieved from http://www.theguardian.com/public-leaders-network/2014/jun/16/john-bercow-digital-democracy-parliamentutm_content=buffera4aaf&utm_medium=social&utm_source=facebook.com&utm_campaign=buffer

Breuer, A. (2012). *The Role of Social Media in Mobilizing Political Protest*. Bonn: D.I.E.

Clarke, H., Sanders, D., Stewart, M., & Whiteley, P. (2004). Theories and Models of Turnout. In Political Choice in Britain. Oxford, UK: Oxford University Press.

Coleman, S. (2005). Direct Representation. Towards A Conversational Democracy. London: The Institute for Public Policy Research (IPPR).

Coleman, S., & Blumer, J. (2001). *Realising Democracy Online: A civic commons in cyberspace*. London: IPPR.

Coleman, S., & Firmstone, J. (2014a). *Contested Meanings of Public Engagement: Exploring Discourse and Practice within a British City Council*. Media, Culture and Society.

Coleman, S., & Firmstone, J. (2014b). *Public engagement in local government: The voice and influence of citizens in online communicative spaces*. London: *IPPR*.

Coleman, S., & Gotze, J. (2001). *Bowling together: Online Public Engagement in Policy Deliberation*. London: Hansard Society.

Dahlgren, P. (2013). Do social media enhance democratic participation? – The importance and difficulty of being realistic. Policy Paper No. 4/2013. Academic Press.

Electoral Commission. (2004). *An Audit of Democratic Engagement*. London: Electoral Commission / Hansard Society.

Eltantawy, N., & Wiest, J. (2011). Social Media in the Egyptian Revolution:Reconsidering Resource Mobilization Theory. *International Journal of Communication*, (5): 1207–1224.

Foucault, M. (1978). *The History of sexuality* (Vol. 1). New York: Pantheon Books.

Foucault, M. (1997). Ethics: Essential works of Michel Foucault 1954-1984. Penguin.

Foucault, M. (2000). Power. The Essential Works of Michel Foucault, 1954-1984. Penguin.

Gerbaudo, P. (2012). *Tweets and the Streets. Social Media & Contemporary Action*. London: Pluto Press.

Gibson, R., Lusoli, W., & Ward, S. (2002). UK political participation. The public response. A survey of citizens' political activity via the internet. Salford: ESRC.

Gibson, R., Lusoli, W., & Ward, S. (2003). Online Participation and mobilisation in Britain: Hype, Hope and reality. *Parliamentary Affairs*, *56*(4), 652–668. doi:10.1093/pa/gsg108

Gonzalez-Bailon, S. (2014). Online Social Networks and Bottom-up Politics. In H. Dutton & M. Graham (Eds.), *Society and the internet: How Networks of Information and Communication are Changing Our Lives* (p. 209). Oxford, UK: Oxford University Press. doi:10.1093/acprof:oso/9780199661992.003.0014

Google. (2008). *Google Technology*. Retrieved from http://www.google.com/technology/

Goos, K., Beckert, B., & Lindner, R. (2016). Electronic, Internet-Based Voting. In R. Lindner, G. Aichholzer, & L. Hennen (Eds.), *Electronic Democracy in Europe. Prospects and Challenges of E-Publics, E-Participation and E-Voting* (pp. 135–184). London: Springer.

Hansard Society. (2011). *Connecting Citizens to Parliament*. London: Hansard Society.

Howard, P., Hussain, M., Mari, W., Mazaid, M., Freelon, D., & Duffy, A. (2011). Opening Closed Regimes: What Was the Role of Social Media During the Arab Spring? The Project on Information Technology and Political Islam, University of Washington.

Jensen J. (2003). Public Spheres on the Internet: Anarchic or Government-Sponsored – A Comparison. *Scandinavian Political Studies, 26*(4).

Jensen, M. (2014). *Social Media and Australian Local Government*. Canberra: ANZSIG / ACELG.

Jones, S. (1999). Studying the Net: Intricacies and Issues. In Doing Internet Research -Critical Issues and Methods for Examining the Net. Thousand Oaks, CA: Sage Publications.

Lowndes, L. P., & Stoker, G. (2006). Diagnosing and remedying the failings of official participation schemes: the CLEAR framework. Social Policy and Society, 5(2), 281-91.

Lowndes, L. P., & Stoker, G. (2001). Trends in Public Participation: Part 2 – Citizens Perspectives. *Public Administration, 79*(2), 445–455. doi:10.1111/1467-9299.00264

Margolis, M., & Resnick, D. (2000). *Politics as Usual: The Cyberspace Revolution*. London: Sage.

Mossberger, K., Tolbert, C., & Stansbury, M. (2003). *Virtual Inequality - Beyond the Digital Divide*. Washington, DC: Georgetown University Press.

Norris, P. (2001). *Digital Divide. Civic Engagement, Information Poverty, and the Internet Worldwide*. Cambridge, UK: Cambridge University Press. doi:10.1017/CBO9781139164887

Papaloi, A., Staiou, E.-R., & Gouscos, D. (2012). Blending social media with parliamentary websites: just a trend, or a promising approach to eparticipation? In C. Reddick & S. Aikins (Eds.), *Web 2.0 Technologies and Democratic Governance: Political, Policy and Management Implications*. Springer. doi:10.1007/978-1-4614-1448-3_17

Papaloi & Gouscos. (2012). An Overview of E-Parliament Services: Designing for Citizen Awareness and Participation. In E-Parliament and ICT Based Legislation: Concept, Experiences and Lessons. IGI Global.

Pateman, C. (1970). *Participation and Democratic Theory*. Cambridge, UK: Cambridge University Press. doi:10.1017/CBO9780511720444

Pratchett, L. (2006). Making local e-democracy work? In M. Virapatirin & T. Peixoto (Eds.), *e-AGORA, Le Livre Blanc de la e-démocratie locale: Réflexions et Perspectives* (pp. 319–331). Paris: Ville d'Issy-les-Moulineaux.

Pratchett, L., Wingfield, M., & Karakaya-Polat, R. (2005). *Barriers to e-Democracy: Local government experiences and responses*. London: Local e-Democracy National Project.

Riley, T., & Riley, C. (2003). International Tracking Survey Report '03 Number Five. *Egovernance to E-Democracy: Examining the Evolution.* Ottawa, Canada: Commonwealth Centre for E-Governance, Prepared under the auspices of the Commonwealth Secretariat And Co-sponsored Telecommunications and Informatics Program, Public Works and Government Services Canada.

Roussopoulos, R., & Benello, G. (2005). Components of New Society: Introduction. In R. Roussopoulos & G. Benello (Eds.), *Participatory Democracy - Prospects for Democratizing Democracy* (2nd ed.; pp. 3–11). Montreal: Black Rose Books.

Stepanova, E. (2011). *The Role of Information Communication Technologies in the "Arab Spring"*. PONARS Eurasia Policy Memo No. 159.

Tusa, F. (2009). How Social Media Can Shape a Protest Movement: The Cases of Egypt in 2011 and Iran in 2009. *Arab Media and Society, 17.*

Wilson, M., & Corey, K. (2012). The Role of ICT In the Arab Spring. *Networks and Communication Studies, 26*(3-4), 343-356.

Wright, S. (2012). Politics as Usual? Revolution, normalization and a new agenda for online deliberation. *New Media & Society*, *14*(2), 244–261. doi:10.1177/1461444811410679

Chapter 7
Towards a Political Theory of eLearning

Celia Romm-Livermore
Wayne State University, USA

Pierluigi Rippa
University of Napoli Federico II, Italy

Mahesh Raisinghani
Texas Woman's University, USA

ABSTRACT

This study focuses on the political strategies that are utilized in the context of eLearning. The starting point for this paper is the eLearning Political Strategies (ELPoS) model. The model is based on two dimensions: 1) the direction of the political strategy (upward or downward), and 2) the scope of the political strategy (individual or group based). The interaction between the above dimensions defines four types of eLearning political strategies, which result in different political outcomes. The presentation of the model is followed by four mini case studies that demonstrate the political strategies that the model outlines. The discussion and conclusion sections integrate the findings from the case studies and elaborate on the rules that govern the application of political strategies in different eLearning contexts.

INTRODUCTION

The proliferation of eLearning in the past few decades has resulted in a significant body of research on the attributes of this phenomenon. As the literature review in the following sections demonstrates, while many studies focuses on the technical and strategic aspects of eLearning, not enough attention has been paid to the social and political aspects of this phenomenon. This paper addresses this gap in the literature by focusing on the politics of eLearning.

This paper addresses the politics of eLearning in a number of ways. First, it introduces the eLearning Political Strategies (ELPoS) model, placing it in the context of previous literature on politics. Second, the paper demonstrates that eLearning is not the "neutral" phenomenon that most previous research assumed it to be, but rather an arena where political struggles take place at a number of different levels.

DOI: 10.4018/978-1-5225-1862-4.ch007

Third, by presenting the findings from a case based investigation, the major components of the model are demonstrated. Finally, by integrating the findings from the case studies in the discussion and conclusion sections, the underlying principles of eLearning are elucidated and directions for future research on the rules that govern the politics of eLearning are proposed.

THE DEFINION OF ELEARNING

An important area of contemplation in the literature on eLearning focuses on the definition of this process. Cross (2004) is considered the person who coined the term eLearning. Since then, a range of definitions have been offered by other researchers. The first type of definitions focuses on the fact that eLearning is based on the Internet. For example, Rossett (2001) defined ELearning as: "Web-based training (WBT)", Adrich (2004) defined eLearning as: "a broad combination of processes, content, and infrastructure to use computers and networks to scale and/or improve one or more significant parts of a learning value chain, including management and delivery", and Rosenberg (2001) defined eLearning as: "the use of internet technologies to deliver a broad array of solutions that enhance knowledge and performance.

Other, much broader definitions of the term eLearning, expanded it beyond the use of the Internet to include just about any type of interaction or experience that can take place in educational or other types of organizations. For example, Manville (2003) defined eLearning as: "Not only Internet-published courseware, but also the tools for managing, modularizing and handling: different kinds of content and learning objects (including both electronic and non-electronic forms, and even traditional classroom instruction), just-in-time and asynchronous learning, such as virtual labs, virtual classrooms and collaborative work spaces, simulations, document repositories and publishing programs, tools for prescribing learning, managing development pathways and goals and handling e-commerce and financial transactions related to learning, and the utilities and capabilities for supporting informal learning, mentoring, communities of practice and other non-training interventions". In other words, according to this definition, eLearning can encompass almost everything that happens in the corporate world.

Other definitions of eLearning seem to go even further. For example, Jeurissen (quoted by Moeng, 2004) defined eLearning as: "the use of innovative technologies and learning models to transform the way individuals and organizations acquire new skills and access knowledge", while Drucker (2000) defined eLearning as: "Just-in-time education that integrates high velocity value chains".

We in this paper define eLearning as both electronically based and related to teaching and learning. However, this does not mean that we restrict eLearning to activities that occur in a classroom (including an on-line classroom) or that we consider eLearning a process that takes place during the delivery of content. Quite the contrary, our definition encompasses activities that may take place outside a classroom (on-line or otherwise) and that may involve students, instructors, and administrators, within an organization that engages in teaching and learning (such as a university).

MAJOR THEMES IN THE LITERATURE ON ELEARNING

There are a number of central themes in the literature on eLearning that are directly related to our study. First, is the discussion of factors that predict attitudes to eLearning. Previous research indicated that the list of factors affecting attitudes to eLearning includes, age: gender, personality, and computer experience (e.g., Miller & Varma,1994; Taylor & Todd, 1995; Sanchez et al., 2006). Thus, it has been found that users who are younger, male, with a higher risk tolerance and more experienced with computers, are more inclined to have positive views of eLearning than users who are not.

Another theme that has attracted much research work in the area of eLearning is the study of factors that determine the effectiveness of eLearning programs. Resrach focusing on this issue identified three sets of factors that impact the effectiveness of eLearning programs: (1) technology factors (Masie, 2001; Brown, 2002); (2) psychological factors (Henning, 2003); and (3) organizational factors (Guest, 1998; Herriot et al., 1998; Martin et al.,1998; Capelli, 1998; Martin & Beaumont, 2003).

As indicated by Mital (2011), the technology factors include issues such as whether employees have access to the requisite infrastructure, whether they are trained to use the technology, and whether they are satisfied with the training provided to them. The psychological factors include issues such as whether the employees are motivated to undergo eLearning, whether they are confident of their technology skills and whether eLearning fits their personal learning style. Finally, the organizational factors include issues such as whether the organization values learning and knowledge acquisition and whether the culture in the organization encourages personal enhancement and self development.

Applying the above framework, Mital (2011) found that learner perceptions of the characteristics of learning technology can explain acceptance behavior, particularly in relation to the inclination to uptake eLearning technologies. Learner perceptions also explain the effectiveness of utilizing eLearning technologies in the long term. Most importantly, according to Mital (2011), acceptance behavior correlates with learner's expectations of the technology in terms of the suitability of the learning to the task, the applicability of the technology to the learner's needs, and the availability of the right incentives to motivate learners to use the technology.

Another theme that has attracted significant research in the area of eLearning is the comparison of face-to-face and on-line teaching and learning. In this context the concept of "interactivity" has been suggested as central. Interactivity has been defined as "the silent, critical, creative conversation within the learner's mind that is spurred and supported by the learning environment" (Markwood & Johnstone, 1994).

The interactivity of the learning experience is central for assessing the "value" of learning because research has determined that the more interactive a learning experience is, the more students benefit from it both cognitively (performance) and emotionally (satisfaction). As a result, interactivity can be used to compare the effectiveness of different learning situations, including the face-to-face, on-line, and the blended or "hybrid" approaches to learning (Bodomo, 2011).

Based on the above, Bodomo (2011) proposed a typology of interactivity that is useful for comparing different modes of delivery in the context of eLearning. The typology consists of three types of interactions:

- **Instructor-Learner Interaction:** Involves either physical face-to-face interaction through lectures, tutorials, demonstrations, and consultations, or digital information and communication technologies, such as email, bulletin boards, and possibly chat rooms, or a mixture of both.
- **Learner-Learner Interaction:** Students communicate with each other in the classroom and out of the classroom, on bulletin boards, in chat rooms, through email or through synchronous eLearning platforms that combine texting, and audio and video interface.
- **Learner-Resource Interaction:** Learners use textbooks, hard-copy hand-outs, and information and communication resources such as online lectures, CD-ROMs, calendar, quizzes, and links to other resources that do not involve exchanges with other people.

As can be deduced from the Bodomo (2011) typology, while face-to-face and on-line eLearning technologies differ from each other in significant ways, the social interactions that they support are similar. Both environments offer opportunities for students to interact with resources, with each other, and with the instructor and/or the organization outside of the class.

How Can We Distinguish Between Political Behaviors and Strategies?

Before we consider what makes some eLearning behaviors and strategies political, it is important to explain how they differ and what they are. In the context of this study behaviors are defined as "observable actions" while strategies are defined as "sets of behaviors intended to achieve a goal". Thus, "asking a question" is an example of a behavior, while "sending a letter of complaint about a professor to his/her supervisor" is a strategy. As can be deduced from these examples strategies are more complex than behaviors, are not necessarily completely observable, they imply an element of decision making or planning on the part of the initiator and may include several different behaviors.

How Do We Know that a Given Behavior or Strategy is Political?

The literature on organizational politics is replete with definitions of this political behavior. However, as indicated by Drory and Romm (1991), there is little consensus among researchers on what political behavior really is. Beyond the relatively wide consensus that political behavior involves "influence attempts", there are considerable variations among writers as to the means and circumstances that distinguish political from non-political behavior.

Building on the body of literature on Organization Politics Drory and Romm (1991) created a conceptual framework or a "map" of the range of behaviors that should be considered political. Their framework considers organizational politics as a combination of three types of elements:

1. **Necessary Elements** (e.g., "influence attempts" and "informal means"),
2. **Defining Elements** (e.g., whether the actor is an individual or a group and whether the political behavior is directed upward, downward or laterally), and
3. **Circumstantial Elements** (e.g., "the existence of a state of conflict", "working against one's organization", "power attainment", and "concealment of motive").

In two more recent publications (Romm & Pliskin, 1997a; Romm, 1999), the authors used the above framework as a basis for conceptualizing political behavior in virtual communities. Building on the Drory and Romm (1991) framework, they suggested that virtual politics can be categorized based on two major dimensions:

1. Whether the behavior is exhibited by an individual or a group, and
2. Whether the behavior is directed upward, downward, or laterally.

Based on this conceptualization, Romm (1999) outlined nine different styles of political behavior in virtual communities, depending on the number of actors involved in the political behavior and the direction of the political behavior. This conceptualization was applied to a range of empirical studies that explored its manifestations in different contexts, including: industrial relations (Pliskin, Romm and

Markey, 1997), gender relations (Romm and Pliskin, 1997b), group dynamics (Romm and Pliskin, 1998), group development (Pliskin and Romm, 1997), and leadership (Romm and Pliskin, 1999).

As for more recent studies of organizational politics in the on-line arena, some researchers have looked at the politics of blogging services and how bloggers use their blogs to influence other members of their communities (Su, Wang, & Mark, 2005). Other researchers studied the manner in which social networking communities self regulate and control their members' behavior (Barzilai-Nahon and Neumann, 2005).

Applied to our study of the politics of eLearning, there are a number of conclusions that can be drawn from the above research. First, the literature seems to support the assertion that social capital (the power that individuals have within their community) and history (the length of time and the role that individuals play while they are members of a virtual community) impact the degree to which members are capable of playing political roles within their communities. This would entail resolving conflicts with other members, exerting control over other members' behavior, and influencing other members to change their stand on issues.

It is this premise, namely that actors who are more powerful are more likely to manipulate others politically that has immediate implications to the eLearning environment. It stands to reason that in eLearning environments too, the more powerful will exert power over others and that they will do it by using political strategies. In the following sections of this paper we explore how this can be done.

THE ELEARNING POLITICAL STRATEGIES MODEL

The eLearning Political Strategies (ELPoS) model is based on several sources, including the definition of organizational politics, as "influence attempts" offered by Drory and Romm (1991), and the political strategies model proposed by Romm (1999).

The following sections explain the origins of the model and its major assumptions.

1. **Political Behavior in the eLearning Context Involves "Influence Attempts":** In line with the Drory and Romm (1991) political behavior framework, the ELPos model defines political behavior as "influence attempts". This implies that sets of behaviors or strategies such as "convincing", "selling", "negotiating", "manipulating", "coercing", etc are seen as political strategies.
2. **eLearning Political Strategies are Affected by the Identity of the Initiator of the Political Activity:** In line with the Romm (1999) political strategies model, the ELPoS model assumes that the identity of the initiator of the political activity (whether an individual or a group) will affect the type of political eLearning strategy utilized.
3. **eLearning Political Strategies are Affected by the Direction of the Political Strategy and Moderated by Demographic and Situational Variables:** In line with the Romm (1999) political strategies model, the ELPoS model assumes that political strategies are shaped by their direction (whether upward or downward).
4. **eLearning Political Strategies are Moderated by Demographic and Situational Variables:** In line with the literature on eLearning (Miller & Varma,1994; Taylor & Todd, 1995; Sanchez et al.,) the ELPoS model assumes that demographic variables (e.g., age, gender, ethnicity, experience, etc.) and situational variables (specific events within or outside the classroom) will affect the eLearning strategies utilized by actors.

Figure 1 shows the major variables in the model and the relationships between them. As indicated in the figure, the ELPoS model consists of three sets of variables. The independent or causing variables are Identity (of the political actor) and direction (of the political strategy). The political strategy is seen as the independent or outcome of the interaction between them. The demographic variables (gender, ethnicity, age, experience and situation) are seen as moderating the relationship between the independent and dependent variables.

Note that for the purpose of this investigation, not all the variables and the relationships in the model are explored. As this research is based on case studies, its focus is the independent variables only, namely, the identity of the political actor (one individual versus a group) and the direction of the political strategy (downward or upward). Table 1 below shows the interaction between the two variables and the four eLearning political strategies that result from this interaction.

Figure 1.

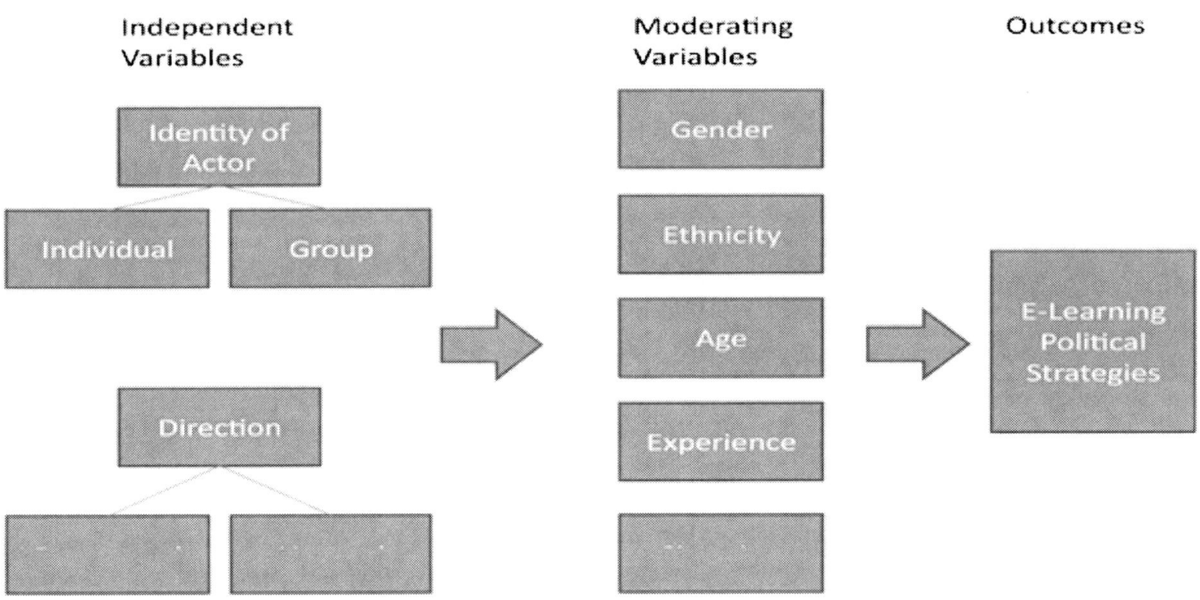

Table 1. The four elearning political strategies that result from the interaction between "identity" and "direction"

	Individual	Group
Downward	Superior attacking subordinate	A group that may consist of superior attacking subordinate
Upward	Subordinate attacking superior	A group of subordinates attacking a superior

METHODOLOGY

The objective of the study that is reported in the following sections was to develop rather than to test hypotheses. As such, this research should be seen as fitting the categories of "exploratory", "inductive", and "qualitative". In line with this methodological philosophy, the main source of data for the study was open-ended, un-structured, in-depth interviews.

To make sure that interviewees were ready to discuss issues pertaining to the politics of eLearning, they were not asked for their names and no information that could identify their organizational affiliation was documented in the interview notes.

The Interviews

Twenty interviews were conducted for this investigation. The interviews were held with instructors from a number of universities. All the instructors were involved in eLearning. The interviews focused on the interviewees' experience with the politics of eLearning. Once the interviewee identified an incident that could be described as political, the rest of the interview focused on that incident.

The interviews followed the chronological order of the events that formed the incident, with special emphasis on who initiated the political acts, who was the object of these acts, how the acts were executed, who benefited from the political acts, and how they impacted the community as a whole. Please see the interview schedule in Appendix 1. for more details about the topics that were explored during the interviews.

The Interviewees

Potential interviewees were be identified by one of the authors through her professional network. Preliminary conversations with the potential interviewees determined their suitability and once found suitable, arrangements were made with them as to the time and place of the interviews. Most interviews were held on-line through Skype. However, some interviews took place face-to-face or by phone. No interviews were held on the premises of any of the universities that the interviewees worked for to protect their privacy.

Consent

If the interview was held on-line or through the telephone, interviewees were sent information about the interview by e-mail and were asked to confirm receipt. At the beginning of the interview they were asked if they read the information and their confirmation that they read it was noted in the interview notes. If the interview was held face-to-face, interviewees were presented with the Interview Information Sheet at the beginning of the interview and the fact that they read it was noted in the interview notes too. Reading the Interview Information Sheet was considered implicit consent to participate in the interview.

Confidentiality

Given the sensitivity of the events described during the interviews, total confidentiality of the process was maintained. The notes for each interview were labeled after the fact based on the content of the incident described. For example, if the incident was about bullying, it was labeled "the Bully" with no further information about the identity of the interviewee or the identity of the group that he/she was a member of at the time that the incident took place. At no time were the names of the interviewees and/or their organizational affiliation recorded in the interview notes.

CASE STUDIES

The discussion in the following sections uses a set of mini-case studies to demonstrate the major tenets of the model. The case studies were drawn from the interviews and represent a sample of the incidents mentioned by the interviewees. The case studies are not intended to "prove" the model but to demonstrate its major components and serve as examples of how the model could manifest in the eLearning environment. To help the reader, the case studies are presented first in terms of how they fit the cells in the model (Table 2) and then each cell is discussed through an individual eLearning mini-case study.

Case #1: Punishing the Teammate - One Actor (Student Leader) the Direction is Downward

The political actor in this case was John (a fictitious name), a leader of a student team in a course in which much of the work was team based. Early in the semester, John noticed that Adel (also a fictitious name) was not contributing to the team effort. He alerted the team to the fact that Adel has not responded to messages from him for a few weeks.

In response, Adel informed John (but not the rest of the team) that his father in Libya was very sick and that he had to travel to Libya to take care of his father. Because of the war that was raging in his city, it was impossible for him to access the Internet during his visit and, so, at least for a few weeks while he was in Libya, he was not able to contribute to the group effort. Adel assured John that he was going away for a just a few weeks and that upon his return, he would compensate for his absence by investing extra effort in his team's work. Indeed, as soon as he was back from his trip, he contacted John and asked to participate in the team's last assignment. John did not respond to his message and Adel concluded from his silence that John was angry at him and not interested in his contribution.

John did not report this exchange to the other members of the team. At the end of the semester when the professor teaching the course asked for peer and leader evaluation of the team members' performance, John reported that Adel did not contribute adequately and should have his mark reduced in line with the content of the syllabus.

As soon as Adel heard about the team's decision to recommend that his mark should be reduced, he contacted the professor to explain what happened, forwarding all the correspondence that he exchanged with the John. It was clear from the messages that he sent to John that he had a convincing explanation

Table 2. The case studies as examples of political behavior in each cell

	Individual	Group
Downward	Case #1 – Punishing the teammate	Case #3 – Students and professor punishing the team leader
Upward	Case #2 – Attacking the Professor	Case #4 – Failing the team leader

for his absence and that he did try to contribute to the team's effort upon his return from Libya but was prevented from doing so by John.

The professor advised Adel to discuss the situation with his leader and with the rest of the team. Her suggestion was that he should send a message to the members of his team with a copy to her, enlightening them on the events that transpired and asking them to reconsider their decision.

John was adamant that no matter what Adel said, he did not contribute and should be punished. In line with the syllabus, the Professor had no choice but to reduce Adel's mark as punishment for his lack of contribution to the team's effort.

Interpretation

Even though the case consists of more than one type of abuse, the main political manipulation was initiated by the leader of the team (an individual) and was directed downward at a member of his team. As such this is a good example of the first cell in the model which focuses on political strategies that are individual and directed downward. Note that the case was facilitated by the fact that the incident occurred within an on-line class where the members of the team did not talk to each other than by e-mail. It was this situation that enabled John to conceal important information from the team members about Adel and it was also this situation that made it possible for him to eventually turn the team against Adel.

Case #2: Attacking the Professor- One Actor (Student) the Direction is Upward

The incident in this case started when a newly appointed non-tenured professor informed her students that she wanted to meet with them on the week before Thanksgiving even though the university's calendar indicated that no classes were to be held on that date. The professor explained that if the class agreed to meet on that date, it would be possible to have the exam earlier, giving everybody a longer Christmas holiday.

The professor informed the class of fifteen students of her suggestion by e-mail, indicating that no one will be penalized for not attending the lecture and if anyone had any problem with the change, she would accommodate him or her in every way.

Shortly after the message was sent to the class, the professor received a message from Jack (a fictitious name). He stated that he was unable to attend the class on the time that the professor mentioned and said that it would be unfair for him to miss the class as it might have an impact on his final grade for the course. The professor explained to him, also on e-mail, that attendance on this particular date was not required and that he would not be panelized for his absence in any way.

Jack responded to the professor within a few minutes with a copy to the Dean, indicating that the professor's insistence on holding the class on that specific date was illegal and discriminatory to him. He insisted that the Dean should instruct the professor to cancel the lecture immediately.

As soon as the professor received the message from Jack, she sent a message to the class stating that her proposal was off because it was inconvenient to Jack. She also wrote to the Dean, informing him that in view of the situation, she canceled the class and that, as a result, the problem that Jack raised no longer existed.

A few minutes after the professor sent her message to the class, she received a message from the Dean informing her that Jack contacted the Dean again. In his second message to the Dean, Jack claimed that because the professor used his *name* in her message to the class, he received a number of abusive messages from his class-mates. He insisted that the professor should apologize to him for her attack on him and for causing him to be attacked by his class mates. Furthermore, he threatened that if the university did not act on this matter promptly, he would sue the university.

The professor was informed by her Dean that she had to write a letter of apology to Jack and that the letter had to be approved by the Dean. After submitting a number of versions of the letter that the Dean did not approve, the professor was finally able to complete her letter of apology to the satisfaction of the Dean. She was then required to send the letter by e-mail to the class and also read it aloud when all the students, including Jack, were present. She was also instructed that Jack's final exam in the course was to be marked (at his request) by another professor and that his grade had to be an A. The professor was given to understand that if she did not comply, she would be fired.

Interpretation

Even though the case consists of different types of political manipulation, the main political actor was Jack, the student who took his attack on the professor to the Dean. As such, this case is a good example of cell #2 in the model because it represents political manipulation by an individual directed upward. Note that here too, the political manipulation was facilitated by the fact that the course was conducted at least in part on-line. It was the on-line message sent by the professor to the class that Jack interpreted as an attack on him and it was the alleged messages from the students in the class to him that were used by him as the basis for the attack on the professor.

Case #3: Punishing the Team Leader- A Professor and Students – The Direction is Downward

The incident on which this case focuses started when a team of students decided to recommend Steve (a fictitious name), their leader for "individual reward" for leadership. The recommendation was submitted by the deadline and was confirmed by the professor. Shortly after Steve received his reward, the team found out that their final assignment for the semester received a lower than expected mark. This was followed by angry accusations within the team, including the suggestion that Steve was not effective in his coordination of the team effort.

Steve responded to the accusations from the team members by stating that it was not his coordination skills but the stupidity of the team members that led to the unexpected low mark. Indeed, he sent the members of the team a series of abusive messages listing their mistakes over the whole semester and claiming that at least some of them should not have been accepted to the program at all and that the fact that they were accepted proves how bad the program was.

In response to the attack several students from Steve's team forwarded his messages to the professor, demanding that the reward for leadership that Steve initially received should be withdrawn. The professor complied with the request. This resulted in Steve's mark changing from an A to an A-.

As soon as the professor reported the change to the team, Steve sent her a message indicating that he intended to appeal her decision because it "went against the syllabus". The professor responded to Steve that the syllabus indicated that the final decision on this matter was the students' and that based on the syllabus, she had no choice but to comply with their decision.

Within a day, the professor received a copy of the message that Steve sent to the department chair and when his appeal was denied, she received a copy of his message to the Dean. It was only after the Dean considered the matter and rejected the appeal again, that the story was concluded. \

Interpretation

Even though the case contains more than one type of political manipulation, the focus here is on the professor, the students, and, eventually, the Department Chair and the Dean of the School, working together to punish the abusive leader of the team. As such, the case is an example of cell #3 because it involves a group of using downward political manipulation. Note, again, that many aspects of this case were made possible because it took place within the context of eLearning. As the team was communicating exclusively on-line, the members of the team were able to forward the messages posted by Steve to the all the people who eventually took action against him. It was these e-mail messages that made the professor, the Department Chair, and the Dean "bend" the syllabus to punish Steve. If it weren't for this evidence, he would probably be able to win his appeal because the recommendation from the team was submitted by the deadline and there was no indication in the syllabus that the mark could be changed after the deadline.

Case #4: Failing the Team Leader– A Group of Actors (Students and Others) - Direction is Upward

The incident on which this case is based started after James (a fictitious name), a leader of a student team, requested that Jill's mark (a member of the team) should be reduced because she did not contribute adequately to the team's effort.

The professor agreed that based on the evidence provided by James, Jill's mark should, indeed, be reduced. However, the professor advised the team that based on the syllabus, the maximum number of points that can be deducted from Jill's mark for this assessment item was 10 points and that this would result in the offending student's mark changing from an A to a B.

In response to the professor's message, James sent a message to Jill with a copy to the team and to the professor stating that "you, lucky devil, how did you manage to select the one and only course in the school, where you can do nothing and yet get a B?". Even though the team was in agreement about the decision to reduce Jill's mark, they were stunned by James' hostility toward Jill. Two members of the team responded by indicating that reducing Jill's grade by 10 points was enough of a punishment and that there was no need for further abuse, including bad mouthing of the professor.

James responded to the messages from his team members with another round of abuse, this time against all the members of the team, who he accused of having "no standards".

The professor learned about the continuation of the debate when a member of the team forwarded the correspondence to her, asking that she take action against the James. The member of the team reminded the professor of a netiquette clause in the syllabus which indicated that the university will take action against any student who uses the university system to abuse his or her fellow students.

Upon further investigation, the professor found out James did, indeed, use the university e-mail system for his correspondence with his team members. After making its way through the various levels of the School, the matter eventually reached the university IT Department. The head of the department relied on the university's e-mail code of practice to take action against James. Even though James finished the class with an A, his grade was overturned and he ended up failing the course.

Interpretation

Even though the case contains more than one type of political action, the focus is on the group of students who fought back a leader that was abusing them and mobilized support for their campaign from four different levels of management within the organization, the professor, the department Chair, the Dean and the Head of the IT Department. As all of these people ended up joining the punitive actions against the student, one can consider this case as an example of a group of actors (students and others) acting upwardly. Note that this case too was made possible because the case took place within an eLearning environment. The case started when the leader posted an abusive e-mail message against a member of the team, it unfolded through e-mail and it was concluded because of the university's e-mail code of practice.

DISCUSSION AND CONCLUSION

The goal of this paper was to present the eLearning Political Strategies model and use case study data to demonstrate how it manifests in educational settings. The case studies presented in the previous sections can teach us a number of lessons about the politics of eLearning:

1. **Groups Versus Individuals:** Political activities within the context of eLearning are more effective when undertaken by groups than by individuals. While each of the three cases has winners and losers, the last case, where a team of students leveraged the support of four levels of management within the university (the professor, the Department Chair, the Dean and the Head of IT) were able to accomplish the most significant victory – to punish an abusive team leader who otherwise was un-touchable.
2. **Downward Versus Upward Political Manipulation:** Downward political manipulation is more effective than upward political manipulation, particularly when the manipulation is undertaken by a group. The first and third cases describe downward political manipulation. In both cases, the final outcome was a success in that the goals of the initiator of the political act were accomplished. In case #1 (the leader who succeeded in "punishing" a team member), the leader managed to punish the student despite an attempt by the professor to stop him from doing it, and in case #3 (the team who succeeded in punishing a leader), the team managed to have the leader's mark reduced even though it was not in line with the syllabus.
3. **Breaking the Law:** Political actors who work as individuals are successful only when they have the law on their side. In case #2, a student managed to have a professor punished because the professor broke the law (by publishing the student's name on-line), in case #4, a team of students who acted together with four other levels of management above them were able to accomplish the unthinkable – to fail a student who otherwise would get an A. The reason was because the student broke the law by using the university system to abuse his fellow students.

Obviously, four case studies cannot chart the whole arena of politics of eLearning. More research is necessary to establish whether the patterns that this research reveals are generalizable to larger samples of eLearning case studies. Behavioral studies are necessary to discern the building blocks of political behavior in various eLearning settings (within classrooms, within the educational organization as a whole), and experimental research may help uncover the underlying mechanisms and rationale for the political strategies described here.

REFERENCES

Adrich, C. (2004). Simulations and the Future of Learning (p. 240). San Francisco: Pfeiffer. Retrieved from http://www.amazon.com/Simulations-FutureLearning-Innovative-Revolutionary/dp/0787969621/bigdogsbowlofbis

Barzilai-Nahon, K., & Neumann, S. (2005). *Bounded in cyberspace: An empirical model of self-regulation in virtual communities.* Paper presented at the 38th Annual Hawaii International Conference on System Sciences (HICSS), Hawaii, HI. doi:10.1109/HICSS.2005.124

Bodomo, A. (2011). Strategies for Enhancing and Evaluating Interactivity in Web-Based Learning and Teaching. In Evaluating the Impact of Technology on Learning, Teaching, and Designing Curriculum: Emerging Trends. Hershey, PA: IGI Global.

Brown, K. G. (2002). *Influence of job characteristics and perceived learning support on eLearning activity.* Paper presented in seventeenth Annual Meeting of the Society of Industrial and Organizational Psychology, Toronto, Canada.

Cappelli, P. (1998). *The New Deal at Work: Managing the Market-driven Workforce*. Boston: Harvard University School Press.

Cross, J. (2004). An Informal History of eLearning. *On the Horizon, 12*(3), 103-110.

Drory, A., & Romm, C. T. (1991). The definition of organizational politics: A review. *Human Relations, 43*(11), 1133–1154. doi:10.1177/001872679004301106

Drucker, P. (2000). *Need to Know: Integrating e- Learning with High Velocity Value Chains.* A Delphi Group White Paper.

Guest, D. E. (1998). Is the psychological contract worth taking seriously? *Journal of Organizational Behavior, 19*(S1), 649–664. doi:10.1002/(SICI)1099-1379(1998)19:1+<649::AID-JOB970>3.0.CO;2-T

Henning, E. (2003). I click, therefore I am (not): Is cognition distributed or is it contained in borderless eLearning programs? *International Journal of Training and Development, 7*(4), 303–316. doi:10.1046/j.1360-3736.2003.00188.x

Herriot, P., Hirsch, W., & Reilly, P. (1998). *Trust and Transition: Managing Today's Employment Relationship*. Chichester, UK: John Wiley.

Manville, B. (2003). *Organizing Enterprise-Wide eLearning and Human Capital Management*. Chief Learning Officer.

Markwood, R., & Johnstone, S. (1994). *New Pathways to a degree: Technology opens the college*. Boulder, CO: Western Cooperative for Educational Telecommunications, Western Interstate Commission for Higher Education.

Martin, G., & Beaumont, P. B. (2003). *What's in a Name? Building the Relationship between Branding and People Management*. Wimbledon, UK: Chartered Institute of Personnel and Development.

Martin, G., Beaumont, P. B., & Staines, H. (1998). Determinants of Management Development–Evidence from Scotland. *The International Journal of Organizational Analysis*, *6*(2), 132–145. doi:10.1108/eb028881

Masie, E. (2001). *If we build it, will they come?* Retrieved from http://www.astd.org/virtual_community/research/pdf/844-6110pdf.pdf

Miller, F., & Varma, N. (1994). The Effects of Psychosocial Factors on Indian Childrens Attitudes toward Computers. *Journal of Educational Computing Research*, *10*(3), 223–238. doi:10.2190/BMT6-WPJY-FXAR-VU06

Mital, M. (2011). Does Technology Uptake Convert to Effectiveness: Re-Evaluating ELearning Effectiveness. In E. M. W. Ng, N. Karacapilidis, & M. R. Raisinghani (Eds.), *Evaluating the Impact of Technology on Learning, Teaching, and Designing Curriculum: Emerging Trends*. Hershey, PA: IGI Global.

Moeng, B. (2004). *IBM tackles learning in the workplace*. Retrieved from http://www.itweb.co.za/sections/business/2004/0411081222.asp?A=BED&S=Business%20Education%20and%20Training&O=FPIN

Pliskin, N., & Romm, C. T. (1997). The impact of e-mail on the evolution of a virtual community during a strike. *Information & Management*, *32*(5), 245–254. doi:10.1016/S0378-7206(97)00027-X

Pliskin, N., Romm, C. T., & Markey, R. (1997). E-mail as a weapon in an industrial dispute. *New Technology, Work and Employment*, *12*(1), 3–12. doi:10.1111/1468-005X.00018

Romm, C. T. (1999). *Virtual Politicking*. Cresskill, NJ: Hampton Press.

Romm, C. T., & Pliskin, N. (1997a). Toward a virtual politicking model. *Communications of the ACM*, *40*(11), 95–102. doi:10.1145/265684.265696

Romm, C. T., & Pliskin, N. (1997b). Battle of the sexes on e-mail- or is it? *The Information Society*, *13*(3), 207–225. doi:10.1080/019722497129106

Romm, C. T., & Pliskin, N. (1998). Electronic mail as a coalition-building information technology. *ACM Transactions on Information Systems*, *16*(1), 82–100. doi:10.1145/267954.267958

Romm, C. T., & Pliskin, N. (1999). The role of charismatic leadership in diffusion and implementation of e-mail. *The Journal of Management Development*, *17*(1), 273-290.

Romm-Livermore, C., & Rippa, P. (2010). The Politics of Implementing ERP – A Cross-Cultural Comparison. In *Proceedings of the Tenth Global Information Technology Management World Conference (GITM)*.

Rosenberg, M. (2001). *eLearning: Strategies for Delivering Knowledge in the Digital Age*. Retrieved from http://www.amazon.com/ELearning-Strategies-Delivering-Knowledge-Digital/dp/0071362681/bigdogsbowlofbis

Rossett, A., & Sheldon, K. (2001). *Beyond The Podium: Delivering Training and Performance to a Digital World*. Retrieved from http://www.amazon.com/exec/obidos/tg/detail/-/0787955264/bigdogsbowlofbis

Sanchez, R. J., Bauer, T. N., & Paronto, M. E. (2006). Peer-Mentoring Freshmen: Implications for Satisfaction, Commitment, and Retention to Graduation. *Academy of Management Learning & Education*, *5*(1), 25–37. doi:10.5465/AMLE.2006.20388382

Su, N. M., Wang, Y., & Mark, G. (2005). *Politics as usual in the blogosphere*. Paper presented at the 4th International Workshop on Social Intelligence Design (SID).

Taylor, S., & Todd, P. (1995). Assessing IT Uptake: The Role of Prior Experience. *Management Information Systems Quarterly*, *19*(4), 561–570. doi:10.2307/249633

APPENDIX 1: INTERVIEW SCHEDULE

Politics of eLearning: Open Ended Interview Schedule

Think back of an incident that you would consider "political" that took place in your face-to-face or on-line class. Such an incident would involve someone trying to influence, manipulate or control another person or a group of people. Once you remember such an incident, please tell me about it chronologically. This means that for *each chronological step* in the history of this incident, we will be discussing the following issues:

Table 3.

When	When (exact date) did this step happen?
The initiator	Who initiated the political act? What do you know about the person who initiated the act? Was there a previous history that may explain the motive for the actor's behavior? Why did he/she initiate the political act at that time?
The target/s	Who was the target of the political act? What do you know about the person/s who was the target? Was there previous history that explains why this person (or persons) was selected as the target?
What	What did the political act consist of? Did it consist of overt behavior, such as a message (or messages) on the discussion board? Did it consist of other public exchanges in class? Did it consist of "behind the scenes" communication between students or between the instructor and the students?
How	What strategies were used by the various actors to accomplish their goals? How did each of the actors react to the activities by others? Did any of the actors modify their behavior in response to acts by others? What role did the observers play? What did the observers do or say? Did the observers modify their behavior as this step unfolded?
Outcome	What was the final outcome of this step? What was the final outcome of the incident as a whole? How did the incident change the power distribution in the class? What was the outcome for the individuals involved in the event? What was the final outcome for the observers?
Lessons for the future	What was the major lesson that you took with you from this experience? What lessons do you think the actor, target, and observers took from this incident? How did this incident affect the social dynamics of the class and/or the organization following the incident

Chapter 8
Challenging the De-Politicization of Food Poverty:
Austerity Food Blogs

Anita Howarth
Brunel University, UK

ABSTRACT

Austerity food blogs have come to the fore with the emergence of a neoliberal ideology of austerity, which in Britain has seen cuts to welfare benefits legitimized through individual failure explanations of poverty and the stigmatizing of benefit claimants. The consequence has been to distance ministers from food poverty and de-politicize it. Austerity food blogs, written by those forced to live hand-to-mouth, are a hybrid form of digital culture that merge narratives of lived experience, food practices and political commentary in ways that challenge the dominant views on poverty so re-politicize it. A Girl Called Jack did this by breaking the silence that the stigma of poverty imposes, by personalizing hunger through Jack Monroe's narratives of her lived experience of it and inviting the pity of the reader. Monroe also challenged austerity through practices derived during the struggle to survive and eat healthily on £10-a-week food budget. Her blog resonated powerfully but also revealed a British society deeply uneasy and polarized over modern poverty.

INTRODUCTION

The eponymous blog *A Girl Called Jack* told the story of an unemployed single mother's rapid descent into and rise out of food poverty in austerity Britain. When faced with escalating poverty Jack Monroe sold nearly everything she owned or had been given, moved with her son into a single room in a house share, started feeding the two of them on a shoestring budget using recipes she concocted or adapted and blogged about her experiences. Monroe was unusual in that her budget recipes were initially created from free emergency relief parcels from her local food bank supplemented with supermarket "value" or "basic" packs bought as part of her £10-a-week food shop because that was all she could afford. *Jack* not only included recipes, it also recounted Monroe's daily struggles to survive and after her intensely

DOI: 10.4018/978-1-5225-1862-4.ch008

personal account of the pain of poverty went viral, she attracted local, national and international media attention to her blog. Her writing expanded onto other platforms and included a weekly recipe column in a national newspaper, political commentaries in a range of broadcast and online news media as well as two books based on her blog recipes. Monroe also won awards for "revolutionizing" budget cooking and rejected an offer to sell her life rights for the making of a Hollywood film.

At one level, this was an archetypical narrative of individual triumph over adversity albeit with a social media angle. At another level, *Jack* challenged the ideology of austerity that became dominant after the 2010 election of a Conservative-led government in Britain, which valorized cuts to welfare benefits, ascribed the causes of poverty to individual failure, stigmatized benefit claimants and legitimized food banks thus de-politicized food poverty. Monroe's experiences of the direct effects of benefit cuts and poverty politicized her (Monroe cited in Godwin, 2013). As her financial situation improved with income from writing, Monroe reinvented herself as an anti-poverty campaigner, drawing on her lived experience, a natural eloquence and the platform that her media profile and sizable social media following gave her. Monroe has also used these platforms to engage very openly in transgender debates. As she reinvented herself post-poverty, Monroe renamed her blog, *Cooking on a Bootstrap,* by Jack Monroe, "Author of 'A Girl Called Jack'" thus linking her past and present while omitting the essay-type posts of the original blog that had brought her to the public attention.

The focus in this chapter is on *Jack* as an example of a type of blog that narrates the lived experiences of poverty so challenges the de-politicization of suffering. *Jack* is located within the wider context of 30 years of the rise of "mass poverty" in Britain in which a growing number of people, like Monroe, report missing meals so they can feed their children or because they cannot afford to buy food (see Caraher & Coveney, 2016; Dowler & Lambie-Mumford, 2015a; Lansley & Mack, 2015; Oxfam UK, 2012). This upward trend is due to a wide-range of factors including long-term structural changes to the job markets and systemic changes to welfare benefits. Britain's post-war welfare system was based on a normative belief in the role of the State in ameliorating poverty through an inclusive welfare system available to everybody at the point of need from "cradle to grave" (Field, 2011). The rise in mass poverty coincides with a 30 year "re-imagining and re-constructing" of this conception of welfare (see Clarke, Gewirtz, & McLaughlin, 2000, p. 2) most notably when the 1997 Labour government re-constituted welfare as "workfare", restricted benefit payments and made them contingent on "evidence" that claimants were seeking employment. The 2010 Conservative-led government drew on a new ideological and moral mantle of austerity with its emphasis on reducing the public deficit to expand workfare, legitimize "the most radical reshaping of welfare policy since 1945" (Hamnett, 2014, p. 490) and further cut benefits. Charities and churches are openly critical of the government doing so at a time of financial crisis (Perry, Williams, Sefton, & Haddad, 2014) and medical experts warn that the government's austerity agenda has reversed 60 years of progress made against food poverty and that an impending public health crisis is brewing (Ashton, Middleton, & Lang, 2014). While the poorest in society, particularly the unemployed, have been disproportionately affected by these changes (Lansley & Mack, 2015), more generally, household budgets across the country have been constrained by rising global food prices and falling or stagnating incomes. It is in this context, that food banks also proliferated as a form of charity in which free food is distributed to those deemed to be most in need. Moreover, it is also in this context that austerity-related blogs and budget cooking television programs focused on the practices of making cheap, healthy meals have proliferated.

The concern here is with austerity food blogs written by those who due to force of circumstance live hand-to-mouth (Wren, 2013). Austerity food blogs are a hybrid form of digital culture that combines narratives of lived experience of poverty, practices developed to survive it and political commentary. Thus, the blogs provide a bottom-up social history of food poverty at a critical juncture when welfare reform, the age of austerity and the rise of food banks have converged. More generally, blogs facilitate this type of history by providing platforms for people to circulate their narratives of lived experiences, recount daily practices and comment on wider social developments. Austerity food blogs are distinctive in that they are organized around a central motif of food poverty and surviving it. Furthermore, their vantage point of the lived experience of poverty potentially offers alternative views to much political discourse and popular culture which stigmatize and de-politicize food poverty. *Jack,* an exemplar of austerity food blogs, resonated powerfully as Monroe made her private trauma public so disrupted the stigmas and shame imposed on the impoverished. In making visible the vulnerabilities of a mother unable adequately to feed her child, she personalized poverty and invited the pity of readers and their proximity to her subjectivities. In describing the shame of queuing at a food banks and detailing practices she developed to survive, Monroe resisted the stigmatizing of benefit claimants as work-shy, irresponsible and self-indulgent by ministers in discourses that sought to legitimize austerity policies. Monroe grounded these practices in the grinding banality of a daily struggle to survive yet also provided a creative response to poverty in the form of budget recipes circumscribed by the financial realities of a £10-a-week food shop and fluctuating food prices yet still offered a way to prepare healthy meals. Ultimately, Monroe challenged the ideology of austerity by personalizing the effects of government policies on an individual life and reasserting the role structural change and systematic failures play in acute poverty. As *Jack* moved from relative obscurity on the margins of the blogosphere to center stage, Monroe's ideas and discourses found a broad-based platform from which to mount this challenge.

Food Banks, The Age of Austerity, and Stigmatizing the Poor

Critical to Monroe's survival was her referral to charity-run food banks (Monroe, 2012) that distribute short-term emergency food relief to ameliorate acute hunger among the poorest in society. Unlike the early American and Australian variants, British food banks distribute food directly to those referred by a doctor, care worker or school to take away and cook (Downing, et.al, 2014). Ten years ago, Britain did not have any food banks but by 2014, the largest operator was running over 400 and opening two a week (Perry, et.al, 2014). Prior to 2012, there was relatively little media coverage of food banks but thereafter they became a site of increasingly heated public and political debate as media framing of the phenomenon shifted from something "novel" or "exotic" to either a taken-for-granted or contested presence in Britain (see Wells & Caraher, 2014).

Food aid is an ancient practice with roots in the food tithes in early Judeo-Christian societies (Caraher & Cavacchi, 2014), alms for the poor in the Middle Ages and the soup kitchens of the industrial revolution and 1930s Depression. During the 20th century this fragmented provision was unified into a welfare system based on normative assumptions about the moral responsibility of the state and the practical application of this in benefit payments for housing, food and health (see Vernon, 2009). However, by the end of the 20th century these normative assumptions had eroded as a neo-liberal agenda came to dominate and governments legitimized the shrinkage of the welfare state on the grounds that it was no longer affordable. By the early part of the 21st century new forms of charitable provision had emerged in the form of food banks, which filled the void left by the retreating welfare state in dealing with food poverty. A recent government-commissioned report highlighted how falling incomes combined with rising food prices to make food 20% less affordable for those on the lowest incomes (Lambie-Mumford,

Crossley & Jensen, 2014). Ministers have argued that there is no statistical evidence of a link between growing use of food banks and their austerity policies. However, charities and churches counter that the single biggest reason cited for recourse to food aid are systemic failures in particular delays, cuts or non-payment of benefits (Downing et al., 2014). The perception of a link is highly sensitive as can be seen in the initial reluctance of parliament to debate the role of food banks (Sedgwick, 2013) and in their prominence in the 2015 general election debates (BBC News, 2014; SNP, 2015).

Food banks have become a contested symbol in the global north and central to an increasingly polarised debate about poverty (Riches & Silvasti, 2014; Ronson & Caraher, 2016). Proponents of the Conservative ideology of "Big Society", which aims to encourage voluntarism and a healthy civil society, argue that food banks are manifestations of this (Caplan, 2016). Critics counter that food is a human right, that government has a responsibility to ensure citizens are adequately fed and that the proliferation of food banks signify the institutionalization of food charity. The "gift" of food in the form of aid or charity, it is argued, is replacing the entitlement to it in wealthy societies and the presence of food banks focuses attention on the symptoms of the problem rather than the causes (Ronson & Caraher, 2016). Perhaps, more significantly, food charity in countries such as Britain has become a moral safety valve that de-politicizes issues of food poverty by deflecting attention away from its causes and government responsibilities to the vulnerable in society (Poppendieck, 1998; see also O'Connell, Knight, and Brannen, 2015). More recently, the "pivotal voter" has felt able to support what they see as the "logic" of austerity policies provided that no-one is left unable to feed themselves and something is still being done for the most vulnerable in society (Ronson & Caraher, 2016). Food banks have created the impression that something is being done to prevent people starving, appeasing those members of the public that might otherwise be appalled at starving families so depoliticized food poverty and enabled welfare reform to continue. The position of the Conservative government has been paradoxical in denying that austerity policies are exacerbating acute poverty or belittling users while at the same time lauding food banks as "evidence" of a "Big Society" manifest in growing voluntarism (Caplan, 2016). When Monroe blogged about her personal experience of food poverty and food banks, she became a key voice in exposing these contradictions in political discourse and in challenging those who would de-politicize food poverty and insulate government's austerity policies from being linked to it.

The escalation of food poverty in Britain after 2008 coincides with the emergence of a "default" response across the EU to the debt crisis. This response is rooted in a neo-liberal ideology of austerity based on the normative premise of rebalancing the economy to improve competitiveness and doing so by reducing the state's budget, debts and deficits through the raising taxes, cutting spending or both (Blyth, 2013a, 2013b). Mark Blyth argues austerity is based on a "narrative fiction" that reduces the cause of the debt crisis to an "orgy of state spending" so privileges cutting public spending in response to the economic crisis (Blyth 2013a, pp. 738–9). Notwithstanding the damage caused to the economy and individual lives, the ideology persists, he argues, because of an "intuitive" or common sense appeal that the public can relate to making it easier for politicians to sell benefit cuts, that is, "you do not spend more than you have" and that "you can't cure debt with more debt" (Blyth, 2013b, p. 2). The variant of austerity adopted by the Conservative-led government after the 2010 election has privileged benefit cuts over tax rises in ways that chimed with the party's historic ideological commitment to shrinking the welfare state (see, Thompson, 2013). Minsters have legitimized these cuts not only through appeals to common sense but also through a moralistic argument that responsible government is prudent and encourages individual responsibility and self-reliance (see Thompson 2013). They present austerity policies aimed at "capping welfare" and "getting people back to work" as a manifestation of government rectitude premised on the belief that the cause of poverty is individual failure rather than structural change so the individual is responsible for addressing their own poverty (see BBC News, 2013; Thompson, 2013).

The individual failure view of poverty assumes that most benefit claimants, of which Monroe was one, are out of work because of their own fault, have not done enough to find work or do not want to work. This stigmatization also assumes that the welfare system rather than serving as an emergency safety net has created a dependency culture that incentivizes indolence and expects the taxpayer to fund a lifestyle through benefit payments (see Lansley & Mack, 2015). Food banks are seen as a variant of this culture rather than a manifestation of genuine need (Morris, 2013; Morse, 2013; BBC News, 2013). Ministers have used these stigmas to legitimize benefit cuts not only in instrumental terms of forcing people back into work but also in moralistic terms of acting in the individual's best interest by weaning them off dependency and encouraging self-reliance. British popular culture reinforces this stereotyping by presenting benefit claimants as unable to manage their own finances and enjoying a self-indulgent lifestyle of large televisions, tattoos and unhealthy diet of cheese, chips and takeaways paid for by the taxpayer (Deans, 2013; Hollows & Jones, 2010; Littlejohn, 2013). Right-wing newspapers further accentuate the polarisation of society by distinguishing between the work-shy "skivers" living off benefit and the hard-working "strivers" whose taxes pay for benefits (Littlejohn, 2013; Williams, 2013). Recent research has suggested that public attitudes have begun to shift 'into line' with political rhetoric and popular culture in privileging an individual failure explanation of poverty and scepticism about benefits as a "solution" to poverty (Clery & Lee, 2013). Thus, the moralistic meanings of austerity juxtapose the valorizing of individual prudence or thrift, self-reliance and hard work against a set of stigmas that view poverty in terms of individual failure, dependency, indolence and self-indulgence. Monroe's blog challenges this individual failure explanation, moralizing and stigmatizing of the poor.

Ideology, Blogs, and Food

This article is based on the premise that the politics of food poverty is rooted in an ideological struggle, where popular culture is a key site of engagement and mainstream media have historically played a central role in circulating and legitimizing or de-legitimizing certain ideas and "realities" over others (Bates, 2001; Block, 2013; Fiske, 1992). Convergence culture highlights the emergence of a more fragmented and diverse media landscape since the 1990s and a multiplicity of different opportunities for content creation that reinforce or challenge existing hegemonies and flow between different platforms (Jenkins & Deuze, 2008; Jenkins, 2006). Personal blogs narrate the lived experiences of ordinary people, chronicling everyday happenings in the blogger's life and capturing their thoughts and emotions on how wider events impact their personal lives (see Tremayne, 2007b). Some narratives open "families, feelings and intimate relations to public politics" in which private trauma and pity made public become "cultivated ways of knowing" that sit alongside reason rather than supplant or displace it (Jolly, 2011, p. vi). Such narratives offer catharsis for the individual blogger (Nardi, Schiano, Gumbrecht, & Swartz, 2004) or as Monroe expressed it, "blogging about £10 a week food shop helped me cope with life" (Monroe, 2013d) and they invite strangers to share in the lived experiences and subjectivities of the blogger. Campaigning blogs, which *Jack* became, are often premised on the belief that extending and accepting such invitations has the potential to "serve as vehicles of social and political transformation" (Lénárt-Cheng & Walker, 2011, 141). This belief in the transformative power of lived narratives dates back to the Enlightenment, however, what is new is a greater willingness and ability to share these lived narratives, an awareness of the "power of intimacy in individual life stories" and a "belief in the potential communal effects" of making the private public (Lénárt-Cheng & Walker, 2011, 141). Monroe echoed some of this when she wrote that in attempting to "explain again and again" that people "can starve on benefits … [I] find myself a stuck record, plastering my personal circumstances across the media in an effort to make people understand" (Monroe, 2013f).

However, for blogs to resonate they need to be widely circulated. Consumers now actively search out new information and, as *Jack* demonstrated, can find it in a multiplicity of ways by reading recipes/articles on mainstream media or accidentally via a Google search, hypertext links from other blogs or hearing about bloggers on the radio or television. Social media interact with rather than replace traditional media with the latter still playing a critical role in raising the profile of bloggers such as Monroe and bringing their content to the attention to a wider audience (Tremayne, 2007a). However, most personal blogs remain relatively obscure with a limited circulation read by only a handful of friends and family (see Tremayne, 2007). The exception is food blogs some of which have become "online sensations turned print bestsellers" with mainstream media constructing celebrities out of previously obscure bloggers (see Denveater, 2009).

That food is able to attract such attention highlights its unique centrality in our lives and the potential for food-related issues to resonate. Food combines biological necessity, commodity, artefact and social relations but each of these and the interactions between them are encoded with meanings that signify and that can evoke powerful emotions that resonate so reinforce or disrupt existing ideas and beliefs. That is, food is both material and symbolic but it is also ideological, political and contested. It is not only about buying and selling, creating and consuming the material. Food as artefact is a "highly condensed social fact" (Appadurai, 1988, p. 494) that "sums" up the individual situation, societal context and the power relations in which it is produced and consumed, in this case of food poverty. In signifying, food serves as "vehicles" through which the political and cultural ideologies such as austerity are circulated, imposed and resisted (see LeBesco & Naccarato, 2008, p. 1). Decoding food thus draws attention to the hidden meanings and ideologies embedded in artefacts, practices and processes as well as the systems of domination and resistance.

A Girl Called Jack was concerned with a particular set of meanings used to make sense of food poverty and the constantly re-negotiated tension between food as political and ideological construct rather than just commodity. Humans must eat to survive yet as omnivores they have discretion over what to eat as well as the creativity and technology to transform selected raw materials into cultural artefacts to be consumed, shared and enjoyed or captured in the written format of recipes and circulated (see Fischler, 1988). However, food as commodity draws attention to the ideological, political and market relations that circumscribe what individuals such as Monroe can afford, what choices are available to them, so what they can create and, in extreme cases, whether they face a threat to survival. As Amartya Sen notes, food poverty is not only about supply in that "people [can] starve in front of shop windows full of food" (1983 cited in Douglas, 2003, p. 31) or as Monroe put it, "we went hungry in the world's seventh richest nation" (2013i). Food poverty, sometimes called food insecurity,[1] refers to an individual's inability to or uncertainty about consuming an "adequate quality or sufficient quantity" of food to meet what a society deems to be the nutritional needs and norms of an adequate or healthy diet (see Dowler & O'Connor, 2012, p. 4). There are no official figures in Britain but studies estimate that as many as one in five Britons have gone to bed hungry (Lansley & Mack, 2015; Oxfam UK, 2012), meaning the majority have little experience of food poverty. The power in Monroe's blogging lay in her narrations of the realities of her struggle to survive in ways that readers could relate to, bringing a proximity to the experience of food poverty. Monroe's personal blog thus provided a platform for connecting at a human level and, thereby, challenges the de-personalizing of the poor accentuated in Britain's age of austerity.

A GIRL CALLED JACK: DISRUPTING STIGMAS, CHALLENGING AUSTERITY

Austerity food blogs emerged out of conditions of austerity and take as their *raison d'etre* opposition to a neo-liberal ideology of welfare cuts legitimized through an intuitive appeal about affordable spending and the stigmatizing of poverty. The emotional valence of stigmas lies in shame, a co-construction of "internally felt inadequacies and externally inflicted judgements" (Chase & Bantebya-Kyomuhendo, 2014, p. 5) that reside at the '"irreducible absolutist core"' of the idea of poverty (Sen, 1983, p. 159).[2] External shame in Britain is imposed on the impoverished through norms surrounding work in which people are defined by and valued in terms of their job title and material possessions (see Monroe, 2012) and conversely, those out of work are often blamed for their own condition of poverty. Individual failure explanations then stigmatize benefit claimants as "scroungers" or "skivers" sponging off the hard-working and thrifty. Social shame is also "internalized and experienced as a powerful negative emotion that results in social withdrawal and a sense of powerlessness" (Walker, 2014, p. 2). The "dynamic interaction" in the co-construction of shame serves to silence the voice of the impoverished (Chase & Bantebya-Kyomuhendo, 2014, p. 5) with internalized social shame often maintaining an outward façade of normality (Walker, 2014). The façade hides what in the age of austerity is an "epidemic of private despair ... with no public spectacle to observe" (Chakrabortty, 2015). *Jack* disrupted the co-construction by making Monroe's internalized shame of poverty public, breaking the silence that confines it in private spaces.

Monroe's narratives included the physical experience of missing meals and going hungry, being cold and wet but it is in the relating of the trauma of poverty in particular the pervading emotions of shame and fear that her blog resonated, inviting pity through the affective. For instance, Monroe recounted her initial reluctance to let family and friends know "how bad things" were, preferring instead to maintain the appearance of normality (Monroe, 2013f). Of "wanting to sink into the ground" when recognized at a food bank and of the embarrassment in meeting someone's eye when they know "you are desperate and not coping" (Monroe, 2013l). Of having to "introduce" her son to the pawn shop (Monroe, 2012) and the "gut-wrenching" fear and humiliation of "failing as a parent" because she was not able to feed him (Monroe, 2014). While the particularities of her situation may be unfamiliar to most readers, the affective dimensions are not in that the emotion of shame in relation to poverty is universal (Walker, 2014) and it is through evoking familiar emotions that Monroe invited proximity. The anecdotes of personal shame and fear became the vehicle through which the reader can identify with and understand the "core" of poverty that Sen identified and enabled *Jack* to disrupt the co-construction of shame and Monroe to challenge the individual failure accounts of poverty.

The challenge is problematic. In resigning from a £27,000 a year job, Monroe was complicit in her impoverishment, a point her critics have seized upon (see Littlejohn, 2013; Selby, 2014). However, Monroe's narrative of the interweaving of mutually reinforcing factors in her rapid descent into poverty highlighted the reductionism in these criticisms and individual failure explanations. Her counter-explanation of resigning because she could not get childcare cover for her night-shifts (Monroe, 2012) drew attention to the changing nature of households and the lack of support for single mothers. In describing 300 job applications that were rejected because she was '"too old" at 23 ...[and] 16-year olds were cheaper to hire'" (Monroe, 2012, 2015a), Monroe drew attention to the structural changes in the job market that are contributing to a 30-year rise in poverty. In detailing the impact of "administrative backlogs" and an 11-week wait for housing benefit on her spiraling debt and going to bed hungry (Monroe, 2012, 2013f, 2015a), Monroe drew attention to the material consequences of the systemic chaos that has followed from the austerity reforms. Monroe's challenge therefore was to reductionist explanations of poverty that decontextualize unemployment, assume people are unemployed because they choose not to work and remain silent on the adverse consequences of austerity policies for those struggling to find a job.

Monroe's most vehement challenge was to the state's inaction on and indifference to poverty and stigmatizing of food bank users to justify this. So, when ministers claimed that food bank use is due to "financial mismanagement" of household budgets (BBC News, 2013), Monroe counter-claimed with a narrative of how delayed benefits payments meant those on very marginal budgets face the consequences in spiraling debt from arrears, charges and fees (Monroe, 2015a). When they claimed child poverty was due to irresponsible parenting, she counter-claimed that "in cutting welfare lifelines" it was the state that is irresponsible in "sending its children to school, to bed, to work hungry" (Monroe, 2013e). When senior politicians claimed that food bank users were undeserving of "sympathy" because they were "just rational opportunists" and growing demand was due to the availability of "free food" (Edwina Currie cited Monroe, 2013e), she highlighted factual inaccuracies in their comments and counter-claimed this demonstrated "a disconnect from reality" (Monroe, 2013h). When MPs voted for a "bedroom tax" which effectively reduced housing benefit by £16, she drew attention to their "£66,000 a year-plus expenses salary" and accused them of "hypocrisy" (Monroe, 2013k). Monroe constructed the government "casting around to blame anyone else while" ignoring the cold face of true poverty in the UK, as irresponsible and neglectful. She thus inverted the moralizing and stigmatizing of government used to legitimize austerity, accusing them of financial imprudence, irresponsibility, self-indulgence and neglect. Similarly, she inverted the social shame imposed on the impoverished turning it on MPs by asking why they were "not ashamed" when constituents could not afford to feed themselves (Monroe, 2013g) and why a society is not ashamed when people take back food bank parcels because they cannot afford to heat them (Monroe, 2013i). However, the rolling back of the welfare state by successive governments has seen a re-thinking of the normative assumption that the state would be the primary provider of welfare so the apparent lack of public shame is unsurprising because the social norms are shifting. At a practical level, the accelerated shrinkage of state welfare at a time of austerity has left an unfulfilled need that food banks only partly fill because their remit is short-term emergency relief not the addressing of long-term chronic poverty. The popularity of *Jack* was not only due to Monroe's vivid and moving writing; it is also due to her detailing the practices she developed to survive.

Grounded Practices: New Forms of Survival Techniques, Creative Resistance

Austerity food blogs are more than narratives of lived experiences and political commentaries censuring austerity policies. They also capture, archive and circulate a particular grounded-practice type of knowledge derived from the grinding banality of the blogger's daily struggles to survive poverty on very tight household budgets and built iteratively and reflexively around routines of grocery shopping and cooking. The knowledge distilled from these changes become new forms of survival techniques, captured and circulated online.

The need for survival techniques has arisen from major social changes since the 1970s. At the same time as a reshaping of welfare, there has been a reshaping of British households and the social norms of eating in the home. The growth in single parent families, working mothers, busier lives and the loss of stigma attached to convenience food has seen a dramatic increase in ready-meals (Craven, 2013; Purves, 2013) to the extent that "'as a society we have lost our ability to cook'" (Baroness Anne Jenkin cited in Elgot, 2014). A cross-party parliamentary inquiry into "feeding Britain" concluded that across the demographic spectrum there has been a loss of basic skills in how to shop on a tight budget and how to prepare and make a "meal from scratch" leaving many households ill-equipped to survive financial crisis (All-Party Parliamentary Inquiry, 2014). Monroe's transformation from cheap processed ready meals and little fruit and vegetables followed from her reflections on how their diet of had "led to poor sleep patterns, a constantly hungry child and ... spots [on her face]" (Monroe, 2013a). She decided to "cook meals from scratch" based on her £10-a-week food shop because that was all she could afford.

The starting point of the transformation in diet was Monroe's £10-a-week food shop and her recipes written in that period of her life detailed a range of different techniques developed to maximise the benefits of what she could afford. The weekly shop became a carefully planned operation of stocktaking, online pricing of the cheapest and healthiest products (Monroe, 2015b) and a set of survival techniques for living on very small margins that also drew attention to the grinding banality of decision-making where a rise of 6p in the price of jar of jam made it unaffordable. Monroe's shopping practices were also consistent with the intuitive appeal of austerity, that is, that people do not spend more than they have but in coming from a benefit claimant. It subverted the political ideology and challenged the assumption that certain beliefs about prudence are Conservative rather than more common ones.

Monroe started by collecting the ingredients off the back of a Lloyd Grossman sauce jar and from there created her own distinctive cuisine based on supermarket "value" packs of vegetables and beans, chickpeas and lentils as staples. Her internet research identified kale and spinach as particularly high in nutrition relative to cost so feature in many of her recipes. They also captured the very tight margins where Monroe was working on an average price-per-portion of 50p and, unusually, many of the recipes include price-per-portion making it easier for readers to substitute ingredients based on their own budgets. What she found to her surprise was that "my £10 a week budget extends to home baked breads ... wholesome protein-packed soups, winter warming casseroles and curries ... piles of fruit and vegetables" and she "fell in love with home-cooked food again" (Monroe, 2013a). The recipes on *Jack* were thus the antithesis of the unhealthy "chips and cheese" diet of the poor stereotyped in popular culture and the antithesis of associations with austere Victorian gruel. Monroe also tapped into the wider green food and environmental movement out of necessity, shopping at her local supermarket because she could walk there and, mindful of cooking on more expensive metered electricity, her recipes were fuel-efficient taking under 15 minutes to cook. She started to grows the herbs in pots in her kitchen and in some of her interactions with readers of her blog Monroe explored the feasibility of growing her own courgettes, tomatoes or peppers in a pot (see Monroe, 2013a). All her recipes could be made on the one-ring cooker or microwave predominate in cheap rented accommodation (All-Party Parliamentary Inquiry, 2014) so were the antithesis of the celebrity chef budget cooking shows which tend to be fuel inefficient and dependent on ingredients and equipment that are more expensive that what Monroe used. Thus, the recipes that emerged out of Monroe's lived experiences outlined new forms of survival techniques shaped by the particular conditions of modern poverty and became a form of creative resistance that "revolutionised" budget cooking in austerity Britain. Not only were printed copies of her recipes handed out at food banks, they were also included in some of the free cooking classes the operators run (All-Party Parliamentary Inquiry, 2014) and led to Monroe winning a number of prestigious awards (Norton, 2015), bringing an institutional validation to her grounded practices if not to her resistance.

She resisted stereotypes of benefit claimants as indolent and self-indulgent by detailing practices she developed to cope based on prudence rather than profligacy and self-indulgence, individual responsibility rather "scrounging", and tight financial management of household budgets rather than the mismanagement that ministers assume to be behind the need for food banks. The grounded practices detailed both capture the grinding banality of a daily struggle to survive yet also constituted a creative response to her situation. What *Jack* did was capture a range of survival techniques honed through personal knowledge and experience.

Resonating Narratives, Conflicted Symbol

The narratives on *Jack* resonated with many readers because they invited pity and offered a way to identify with Monroe's subjectivities, while the recipes offered grounded practices and techniques to survive on very low budgets (see Adams, 2014; Butler, 2013; Clay, 2013). The power of Monroe's grounded practices lay not only in the institutional validation afforded through awards, but also in their popular validation as widening circulation shifted the blog from relative obscurity on the margins of the blogosphere to center stage. Alerts about Monroe's latest recipes included some of the "Guardian's most viewed" tweets, her social media following expanded from ten in 2012 to over 60,000 on Twitter before she shut it down, 3300 on Instagram, over 47,000 "likes" on Facebook and 3000 email subscribers. Journalists labelled her a "fledgling social media celebrity "Britain's austerity celebrity" (Altman, 2014; Bennhold, 2014; Clay, 2013) and the "face of modern poverty in Britain" (Butler, 2013), a representative or the impoverished or symbol of resistance to government policies of cutting benefits but what does this mean?

In disrupting the silence that the stigma of poverty imposes and in making her vulnerabilities public and visible, Monroe became a conflicted symbol. Supporters and sympathisers constructed her as providing valuable insights into realities of modern poverty, a voice for those who had similar experiences to Monroe but lacked the eloquence or platform she has, or someone who could '"be anybody's daughter"' (Bennhold, 2014). Sceptics questioned whether someone whose experience of poverty, albeit acute, was limited to two years could speak for the long term unemployed and impoverished (see Hinsliffe, 2014). Critics on the left viewed her as a "hero" of the middle classes not the poor' representing the "unholy trinity of modern leftist values – thrift, subsistence and health" rather than benefit claimants (Slater, 2014). While critics on the right reiterated the individual failure argument suggesting Monroe brought poverty on herself by giving up her job and saw her as emblematic of benefit culture in which hard-working taxpayers are "forced to subsidise those for whom claiming benefits is a 'lifestyle' choice" and which government is trying to dismantle" (Littlejohn, 2013). They too saw her as distant from "ordinary people" not because she is articulate, but because her recipes included kale, which is "too posh", and red wine which was too extravagant for someone who is genuinely struggling (Hartley-Parkinson, 2014; Littlejohn, 2013; Monroe, 2013c, 2013j). Thus as much as Monroe's narratives and grounded practices resonated, resisting and disrupting the stereotypes they also exposed quite profound deep ideological divides in Britain. As much as she was "loved" by many, she was "loathed" by some (Adams, 2014) but that says more about the toxic politics of food poverty in Britain than it says Monroe herself.

CONCLUSION

This article has used *Jack* to explore a new type of hybrid blog that merges narratives, practices and political commentary in the particular context of the convergence of a shrinking welfare state and a dominant ideology of austerity, rising levels of food poverty, the emergence of new forms of food aid to provide emergency food relief and generally tighter household budgets generally. The preoccupation with how to survive austerity has seen a proliferation of new cultural forms on mainstream and social media that privilege thrift and budget cooking. Austerity food blogs are distinctive, written by those who forced to live hand to mouth and take as their dominant motif food poverty. Such blogs can therefore provide valuable insights into the subjectivities of Britain modern poor and in so doing disrupt and challenge the dominant ideology of austerity and dominant explanations that view poverty in moral terms of individual failure. Monroe disrupted these hegemonies by breaking the silence that external stigma and internal shame impose on the individual. In making public her private trauma she personalized poverty, inviting the pity of the reader and proximity to her subjectivities. Her personal narratives challenged the reductionism in dominant explanations by suggesting multiple factors contributing to spiralling poverty and her recipes derived from grounded practices of learning to live healthily on very tight budget offer a new range of survival techniques and a creative resistance that defies stereotypes of what poor people eat. The response to *Jack* has been phenomenal in terms of her mainstream and social media profile generally as well as in the opportunities given her to rise out of poverty, forging a new career, one she never anticipated when she started blogging. For researchers, austerity food blogs are a rich source of material. The narratives of living with food poverty, the practices developed to survive it and the wider public response to the blog offer social insights into the subjectivities of those experiencing food poverty. *Jack* resonated powerfully, challenging the taken-for-granted assumptions in austerity policies and the de-politicisation of poverty. Yet, the polarization of views about the blog also highlighted a fragmented public conversation about what the austerity food blogs symbolize as well as more fundamental questions as to who are the modern poor and what is modern poverty.

REFERENCES

Adams, T. (2014, February 16). Jack Monroe — Loathed by the Daily Mail, loved by almost everyone else. *Observer Food Monthly*. Retrieved from http://www.theguardian.com/lifeandstyle/2014/feb/16/jack-monroe-cook-girl-called-jack-interview

All-Party Parliamentary Inquiry. (2014). *Feeding Britain*. http://doi.org/<ALIGNMENT.qj></ALIGNMENT>10.1136/bmj.1.4348.621-a

Altman, A. (2014, February 19). No-budget recipes. *The New Yorker*. Retrieved from http://www.newyorker.com/culture/culture-desk/no-budget-recipes

Appadurai, A. (1988). How to make a national cuisine: Cookbooks in contemporary India. *Comparative Studies in Society and History*, *30*(1), 3–24. doi:10.1017/S0010417500015024

Ashton, J. R., Middleton, J., & Lang, T. (2014). Open letter to Prime Minister David Cameron on food poverty in the UK. *Lancet*, *383*(9929), 1631. doi:10.1016/S0140-6736(14)60536-5 PMID:24794817

Bates, T. (2001). Gramsci and the theory of hegemony. *Journal of the History of Ideas*, *36*(2), 351–366. doi:10.2307/2708933

BBC News. (2013, September 10). *Michael Gove "insulted" food bank users, says Labour*. Retrieved from http://www.bbc.co.uk/news/uk-politics-24042446

BBC News. (2014, August 11). *Food poverty in Scotland "not acceptable" says Sturgeon*. Retrieved from http://www.bbc.co.uk/news/uk-scotland-scotland-politics-28731402

Bennhold, K. (2014, January 14). From hunger to fame, with a shoestring budget: Jack Monroe has become Britain's austerity celebrity. *New York Times (Europe)*. Retrieved from http://www.nytimes.com/2014/01/15/world/europe/jack-monroe-has-become-britains-austerity-celebrity.html?_r=0

Block, E. (2013). A culturalist approach to the concept of the mediatization of politics: The age of media hegemony. *Communication Theory*, *23*(3), 259–278. doi:10.1111/comt.12016

Blyth, M. (2013a). Austerity as ideology: A reply to my critics. *Comparative European Politics*, *11*(6), 737–751. doi:10.1057/cep.2013.25

Blyth, M. (2013b). The austerity delusion: Why a bad idea won over the West. *Foreign Affairs*, (May/June): 1–11.

Butler, P. (2013, July 23). Jack Monroe: The face of modern poverty. *The Guardian*. Retrieved from http://www.theguardian.com/society/2013/jul/23/jack-monroe-face-modern-poverty

Caplan, P. (2016). Big society or broken society? *Anthropology Today*, *32*(1), 5–9. doi:10.1111/1467-8322.12223

Caraher, M., & Cavacchi, A. (2014). Old crises on new plates or old plates for a new crises? Food banks and food insecurity. *British Food Journal*, *116*(9), 1426–1445.

Caraher, M., & Coveney, J. (2016). Food poverty and insecurity: The poor in a world of global austerity. In M. Caraher & J. Coveney (Eds.), *Food poverty and insecurity: International food inequalities* (pp. 1–8). Heidelberg, Germany: Springer. doi:10.1007/978-3-319-23859-3_1

Chakrabortty, A. (2015, February 3). Britain's epidemic of private despair makes this an economic crisis like no other. There is no public spectacle to observe. But behind closed doors an everyday wretchedness blights lives. *The Guardian*. Retrieved from http://www.theguardian.com/commentisfree/2015/feb/03/britain-economic-crisis-public

Chase, E., & Bantebya-Kyomuhendo, G. (2014). *Poverty and shame: Global experiences*. Oxford, UK: Oxford University Press.

Clarke, J., Gewirtz, S., & McLaughlin, E. (2000). Reinventing the welfare state. In *New managerialism, new welfare* (pp. 1–26). London, UK: Sage. Retrieved from https://books.google.co.uk/books?hl=en&lr=&id=1nLeXq_V4HQC&oi=fnd&pg=PA1&dq=(reinventing+the+welfare+state)&ots=l4cFFd7Frg&sig=doEzKzgxZFXnKBieZQMAwpc80fQ#v=onepage&q=(reinventing the welfare state)&f=false

Clay, X. (2013, March 4). My 49p lunch with a girl called Jack. *The Telegraph*. Retrieved from http://www.telegraph.co.uk/foodanddrink/9900773/My-49p-lunch-with-a-girl-called-Jack.html

Clery, L., & Lee, L. (2013, April). Public attitudes to poverty and welfare 1983–2011. *Joseph Rowntree Foundation Report*. Retrieved from http://www.natcen.ac.uk/our-research/research/public-attitudes-to-poverty-and-welfare-1983-2011/

Craven, N. (2013, February 16). Horsemeat scandal: We eat as many ready meals as the rest of Europe combined—Britain's passion for the cheapest food. *Financial Mail on Sunday*. Retrieved from http://www.dailymail.co.uk/money/news/article-2279664/Chilling-truth-horsemeat-scandal-ALL-blame.html#ixzz2Lf4RYofE

Deans, J. (2013, August 27). Jamie Oliver bemoans chips, cheese and giant TVs of modern-day poverty. *The Guardian*. Retrieved from http://www.theguardian.com/lifeandstyle/2013/aug/27/jamie-oliver-chips-cheese-modern-day-poverty

Denveater. (2009). The virtual roundtable: Food blogging as citizen journalism. *World Literature Today, 83*(1), 42–46.

Douglas, M. (2003). *Food in the social order: Studies of food and festivities in three American communities*. London, UK: Routledge.

Dowler, E., & Lambie-Mumford, H. (2015a). How can households eat in austerity? Challenges for social policy in the UK. *Social Policy and Society*, *14*(3), 417–428. doi:10.1017/S1474746415000032

Dowler, E., & Lambie-Mumford, H. (2015b). Introduction: Hunger, food and social policy in austerity. *Social Policy and Society*, *14*(3), 411–415. doi:10.1017/S1474746415000159

Dowler, E., & OConnor, D. (2012). Rights-based approaches to addressing food poverty. *Social Science & Medicine*, *74*(1), 44–71. doi:10.1016/j.socscimed.2011.08.036 PMID:22000764

Downing, E., Kennedy, S., & Fell, M. (2014). *Food banks and food poverty*. London, UK: House of Commons. Retrieved from http://www.parliament.uk/briefing-papers/SN06657/food-banks-and-food-poverty

Elgot, J. (2014, December 9). Feeding Britain: Poor people don't know how to cook, says Tory Baroness Jenkin. *Huffington Post (UK)*. Retrieved from http://www.huffingtonpost.co.uk/2014/12/08/feeding-britain-tory-cook_n_6287454.html

Field, F. (2011, October 3). The welfare state—Never ending reform. *BBC*. Retrieved from http://www.bbc.co.uk/history/british/modern/field_01.shtml

Fischler, C. (1988). Food, self and identity. *Social Sciences Information. Information Sur les Sciences Sociales*, *27*(2), 275–292. doi:10.1177/053901888027002005

Fiske, J. (1992). British cultural studies and television. In R. C. Allen (Ed.), *Channels of discourse, reassembled: Television and contemporary criticism* (pp. 214–246). Chapel Hill, NC: University of North Carolina Press.

Godwin, R. (2013). Austerity's poster girl Jack Monroe, and a storm over her very middle class recipe for kale pesto. *Evening Standard*. Retrieved from http://www.standard.co.uk/lifestyle/london-life/austeritys-poster-girl-jack-monroe-and-a-storm-over-her-very-middle-class-recipe-for-kale-pesto-8932248.html

Habermas, T., & Kober, C. (2014). Autobiographical reasoning is constitutive for narrative identity: The role of the life story for personal continuity. In K. McLean & M. Syed (Eds.), *The Oxford handbook of identity development* (p. 149). Oxford, UK: Oxford University Press. doi:10.1093/oxfordhb/9780199936564.013.010

Hamnett, C. (2014). Shrinking the welfare state: The structure, geography and impact of British government benefit cuts. *Transactions of the Institute of British Geographers*, *39*(4), 490–503. doi:10.1111/tran.12049

Hartley-Parkinson, R. (2014, February 4). Benefits row live: Jack Monroe hits back at Edwina Currie in open letter after "revolting" TV debate attack. *Mirror*. Retrieved from http://www.mirror.co.uk/news/uk-news/benefits-row-live-jack-monroe-3111253

Hinsliffe, G. (2014, February 14). No sneering. Talking for other people is allowed. *The Times*. Retrieved from http://www.thetimes.co.uk/tto/opinion/columnists/article4005134.ece

Hollows, J., & Jones, S. (2010). At least hes doing something: Moral entrepreneurship and individual responsibility in Jamies Ministry of Food. *European Journal of Cultural Studies*, *13*(3), 307–322. doi:10.1177/1367549410363197

Jenkins, H. (2006). *Convergence culture: Where old and new media collide*. New York: New York University Press; doi:10.4206/rev.austral.cienc.soc.2011.n20-09

Jenkins, H., & Deuze, M. (2008). Editorial: Convergence culture. *Convergence (London)*, *14*(D), 5–12. doi:10.1177/1354856507084415

Jo, Y. N. (2013). Psycho-social dimensions of poverty: When poverty becomes shameful. *Critical Social Policy*, *33*(3), 514–531. doi:10.1177/0261018313479008

Jolly, M. (2011). Life writing as intimate publics. *Biography*, *34*(1), v–xi. doi:10.1353/bio.2011.0007

Lambie-Mumford, H., Crossley, D., & Jensen, E. (2014). *Household food security in the UK: A review of food aid final report*. Retrieved from https://www.gov.uk/government/uploads/system/uploads/attachment_data/file/283071/household-food-security-uk-140219.pdf

Lambie-Mumford, H., & Dowler, E. (2014). Rising use of food aid in the United Kingdom. *British Food Journal*, *116*(9), 1418–1425. doi:10.1108/BFJ-06-2014-0207

Lansley, S., & Mack, J. (2015). *Breadline Britain: The rise of mass poverty*. London: Oneworld Publications.

LeBesco, K., & Naccarato, P. (2008). *Edible ideologies: Representing food and meaning*. New York: State University of New York.

Lénárt-Cheng, H., & Walker, D. (2011). Recent trends in using life stories for social and political activism. *Biography*, *34*(1), 141–179. doi:10.1353/bio.2011.0005

Littlejohn, R. (2013, November 8). Ah, Pesto! These poverty poster girls of Welfare Britain want the gravy too ... without having to pay for it. *Daily Mail*. Retrieved from http://www.dailymail.co.uk/debate/article-2482111/RICHARD-LITTLEJOHN-Ah-Pesto-Meet-poverty-poster-girls.html

Monroe, J. (2012, July 30). *Hunger hurts* [Blog post]. Retrieved from http://agirlcalledjack.com/2012/07/30/hunger-hurts/

Monroe, J. (2013a, January 31). Chef for less. *Echo and Gazette (Southend)*. Retrieved from http://agirlcalledjack.com/2013/01/31/taste-echo-gazette-31st-jan/

Monroe, J. (2013b, February 2). *Courgette & Mint Fritters* [Blog post]. Retrieved from http://agirlcalledjack.com/2013/02/02/quick-courgette-mint-fritters-18p/

Monroe, J. (2013c, July 20). How blogging about £10 a week food shop helped me cope with life. *The Guardian*. Retrieved from http://www.theguardian.com/lifeandstyle/2013/jul/20/10-pound-food-shop-blog

Monroe, J. (2013d, September 10). The government are feckless, neglectful and abusive. *HuffPost (UK)*. Retrieved from http://www.huffingtonpost.co.uk/jack-monroe/government-are-feckless-neglectful-abusive_b_3900933.html

Monroe, J. (2013e, September 18). Austerity bites: You can starve on benefits in this country. *The Guardian*. Retrieved from https://www.theguardian.com/society/2013/sep/18/jack-monroe-starve-benefits-england

Monroe, J. (2013f, October 16). Food banks are testimony to the Tories' massacre of hope and dignity. *The Guardian*. Retrieved from http://www.theguardian.com/society/2013/oct/16/food-banks-tories-policies

Monroe, J. (2013g, October 16). *We need an inquiry into food banks: My column in today's Guardian* [Blog post]. Retrieved from http://agirlcalledjack.com/2013/10/16/we-need-an-inquiry-into-food-banks-my-column-in-todays-guardian/

Monroe, J. (2013h, October 29). Some British people can't afford to heat their food. Aren't we ashamed? *The Guardian. Comment Is Free* [Blog post]. Retrieved from http://www.theguardian.com/commentisfree/2013/oct/29/british-cant-afford-heat-food-big-six-energy-jack-monroe

Monroe, J. (2013i, November 1). Dear Richard Littlejohn—Here's some polish for that turd. *HuffPost (UK)*. Retrieved from http://www.huffingtonpost.co.uk/jack-monroe/richard-littlejohn-polish-for-that-turd_b_4191747.html

Monroe, J. (2013j, November 19). MPs' bedroom tax hypocrisy—a sensible solution, at last. *The Guardian*. Retrieved from http://www.theguardian.com/society/2013/nov/19/mps-bedroom-tax-hypocrisy-block-of-flats

Monroe, J. (2013k, December 3). We went hungry in world' s seventh-richest nation—It has to stop. *Mirror*. Retrieved from http://www.mirror.co.uk/news/real-life-stories/jack-monroe-food-poverty-went-2877510

Monroe, J. (2014, February 18). *Poverty can happen to anyone* [Blog post]. Retrieved from http://agirlcalledjack.com/2014/02/18/poverty-can-happen-to-anyone-guardian-column-feb-2013/

Monroe, J. (2015a, February 19). *I can't even answer my own front door* [Blog post]. Retrieved from http://agirlcalledjack.com/2015/02/19/i-cant-even-open-my-own-front-door/

Monroe, J. (2015b, April 27). *Live below the line: My £5 shop, crying in the supermarket, and the dreaded mushy peas* [Blog post]. Retrieved from http://agirlcalledjack.com/2015/04/27/live-below-the-line-my-5-shop-crying-in-the-supermarket-and-the-dreaded-mushy-peas/

Morris, N. (2013, July 2). Demand for food banks has nothing to do with benefits squeeze, says Work Minister Lord Freud. *The Independent*. Retrieved from http://www.independent.co.uk/news/uk/politics/demand-for-food-banks-has-nothing-to-do-with-benefits-squeeze-says-work-minister-lord-freud-8684005.html

Morse, F. (2013, October 3). Tory MP Paul Maynard suggests food banks could become a "habit" for people in poverty. *The Independent*. Retrieved from http://www.independent.co.uk/news/uk/tory-mp-paul-maynard-suggests-food-banks-could-become-a-habit-for-people-in-poverty-8855762.html

Nardi, B., Schiano, D., Gumbrecht, M., & Swartz, L. (2004). Why we blog. *Communications of the ACM*, *47*(12), 41–46. doi:10.1145/1035134.1035163

Norton, S. (2015, January 20). How a Girl Called Jack revolutionised budget cooking. *The Independent*. Retrieved from http://www.independent.co.uk/life-style/health-and-families/features/a-girl-called-jack-how-jack-monroe-revolutionised-budget-cooking-9989853.html?origin=internalSearch

O'Connell, R., Knight, A., & Brannen, J. (2015). Food austerity from an historical perspective. *Discover Society*, (16). Retrieved from http://discoversociety.org/2015/01/03/food-austerity-from-an-historical-perspective-making-sense-of-1950s-mass-observation-data-in-the-contemporary-era/

Oxfam, U. K. (2012). *The perfect storm: Economic stagnation, the rising cost of living, public spending cuts and the impact on UK poverty*. Retrieved from http://policy-practice.oxfam.org.uk/publications/the-perfect-storm-economic-stagnation-the-rising-cost-of-living-public-spending-228591

Perry, J., Williams, M., Sefton, T., & Haddad, M. (2014, November). *Emergency use only: Understanding and reducing the use of food banks in the UK*. Child Poverty Action Group, the Church of England, Oxfam and the Trussell Trust. Retrieved from http://www.cpag.org.uk/sites/default/files/FoodbankReport_web.pdf

Poppendieck, J. (1998). *Sweet charity: Emergency food and the end of entitlement*. Harmondsworth, UK: Viking Penguin.

Purdam, K., & Garratt, E. A. (2015). Hungry? Food insecurity, social stigma and embarrassment in the UK. *Sociology*, 1–17. doi:10.1177/0038038515594092

Purves, L. (2013, February 18). Do stop shuddering you poncey gourmands. *The Times*. Retrieved from http://www.thetimes.co.uk/tto/opinion/columnists/libbypurves/article3691099.ece

Riches, G., & Silvasti, T. (2014). Hunger in the rich world: Food aid and right to food perspectives. In G. Riches (Ed.), *First world hunger* (pp. 1–14). Basingstoke, UK: Palgrave Macmillan. doi:10.1057/9781137298737_1

Ronson, D., & Caraher, M. (2016). Food banks: Big society or shunting yards? Successful failures. In M. Caraher & J. Coveney (Eds.), *Food poverty and insecurity: International food inequalities* (pp. 79–88). Heidelberg, Germany: Springer. doi:10.1007/978-3-319-23859-3_8

Scottish National Party (SNP). (2015). *Stronger for Scotland: Election Manifesto*. Retrieved from http://votesnp.com/docs/manifesto.pdf

Sedgwick, M. (2013, May 30). What is it like to rely on food banks? *BBC News Magazine*. Retrieved from http://www.bbc.co.uk/news/uk-22715458

Selby, J. (2014, November 25). Sarah Vine criticizes lesbian mother Jack Monroe. *The Independent*. Retrieved from http://www.independent.co.uk/news/people/sarah-vine-on-jack-monroe-being-a-lesbian-mother-if-she-was-unsure-about-her-sexuality-she-should-have-taken-greater-precautions-9882054.html?origin=internalSearch

Sen, A. (1983). Poor, relatively speaking. *Oxford Economic Papers*, *35*(2), 153–169.

Slater, T. (2014, February 7). "Recessionista" Jack Monroe is a hero of the thrift-obsessed middle classes, not the poor. *Spiked*. Retrieved from http://www.spiked-online.com/newsite/article/jack-monroe-pleb-lite-for-guardianistas/14622

Thompson, H. (2013). Austerity as ideology: The bait and switch of the banking crisis. *Comparative European Politics*, *11*(6), 729–736. doi:10.1057/cep.2013.24

Tremayne, M. (2007a). *Blogging, citizenship and the future of media*. London, UK: Routledge.

Tremayne, M. (2007b). Introduction: Examining the blog–media relationship. In *Blogging, citizenship and the future of media*. London, UK: Routledge.

Vernon, J. (2009). *Hunger: A modern history*. Cambridge, MA: Harvard University Press; doi:10.1080/03071020902778634

Walker, R. (2014). *The shame of poverty*. Oxford, UK: Oxford University Press. doi:10.1093/acprof:oso/9780199684823.001.0001

Wells, R., & Caraher, M. (2014). UK print media coverage of the food bank phenomenon: From food welfare to food charity? *British Food Journal*, *116*(9), 1426–1445. doi:10.1108/BFJ-03-2014-0123

Williams, Z. (2013, January 9). Skivers v strivers: The argument that pollutes people's minds. *The Guardian. Comment Is Free* [Blog post]. Retrieved from http://www.theguardian.com/politics/2013/jan/09/skivers-v-strivers-argument-pollutes

Wren, A. (2013, July 7). The rise and rise of austerity blogs. *The Guardian*. Retrieved from http://www.theguardian.com/media/shortcuts/2013/jul/07/rise-and-rise-of-austerity-blog#comments

KEY TERMS AND DEFINITIONS

Austerity: A neoliberal ideology premised on the normative belief that states (and individuals) should not spend more than they earn and a causal assumption that the debt crisis was due to excessive state spending. Economic recovery is thus seen as dependent on reducing the public deficit and the British variant privileges cutting government spending by cutting welfare benefits. Cuts to welfare are legitimized through individual-failure explanations of poverty.

Austerity Food Blogs: Written by those who due to force of circumstance live hand-to-mouth, are a distinctive form of blog in that they are organized around a central motif of food poverty and surviving it. The blogs are a hybrid form of digital culture that combine narratives of the lived experience of poverty, practices developed to survive it, and political commentary; thus they provide a bottom-up social history of food poverty.

The "Big Society": A political ideology that proposes to integrate the free market with a social solidarity rooted in voluntarism. The idea became a flagship policy in the Conservative Party's 2010 election manifesto and formed part of the legislative agenda of the coalition government. The stated aim was to build a "Big Society" in which power would be devolved away from politicians to local communities and people who would be encouraged to address social issues, for example, the running of food banks that might previously have been the responsibility of government.

Food Banks: Run by charities, distribute short-term emergency food aid to ameliorate acute hunger among the poorest in society. In Britain, unlike in America and Australia, food banks distribute food directly to those referred by a doctor, care worker or school to take away and cook.

Food Poverty: Primarily a matter of access to healthy and affordable food of sufficient quality and quantity. Civil society organizations tend to use the term food poverty but it lacks an agreed definition and the meaning changes depending on whether it is being used to refer to starving millions who in the Global South are victims of famine or war or to those in the Global North who, unable to feed their families, are dependent on food charity. In policy circles, the term food security tends to be used instead but this is not a terminology found in common parlance of blogs and media articles.

ENDNOTES

1. Civil society organisations increasingly use the term 'food poverty' but it lacks a consistent and agreed definition despite established definitions in research literature. The term 'food security' while employed in policy circles has yet to translate into public discourse (Lambie-Mumford & Dowler, 2014, p. (p1421).
2. Credit is due here to the editor of IJEP, Dr Yasmin Ibrahim, for drawing my attention to this point about shame, the silencing effect it has and its significance therefore for austerity food blogs.

Chapter 9
Ubiquitous Food Imaging:
Food Images as Digital Spectacle

Yasmin Ibrahim
Queen Mary, University of London, UK

ABSTRACT

In our digital world, our notions of intimacy, communion and sharing are increasingly enacted through new media technologies and social practices which emerge around them. These technologies with the ability to upload, download and disseminate content to select audiences or to a wider public provide opportunities for the creation of new forms of rituals which authenticate and diarise everyday experiences. Our consumption cultures in many ways celebrate the notion of the exhibit and the spectacle, inviting gaze, through everyday objects and rituals. Food as a vital part of culture, identity, belonging, and meaning making celebrates both the everyday and the invitation to renew connections through food as a universal subject of appeal.

INTRODUCTION

What is this pervasive act of capturing our meals via our mobile and smart phones and sharing it with wider audiences through personal networks and messaging services? Why are we making a moment of the ordinary? This pervasive food sharing through mobile images is part of our digital literacy today. As an inimical part of digital culture, food images dominate as a universal symbol of social sharing and social gaze, and above all, human solidarity. Food as a subject of digital capture carries social resonance and sociability. As new behavioural and social conventions convene around the production and dissemination of food images online, food as a material yet ephemeral object ingested by the body, amenable to edible iterations as well as decomposition, has become a major subject of material objectification signifying new ways to connect, frame social relations and to negotiate our private and public realms. Food once transformed into a digital image online is often offered for public consumption, transaction and dissemination inviting the gaze of family, friends and strangers. This paper explores the notion of food porn with relevance to new media technologies and contemporary digital culture. It posits the notion that the sociality around producing and sharing food in the user generated content (UGC) economy

DOI: 10.4018/978-1-5225-1862-4.ch009

in many ways re-negotiates the unattainable quality that food porn signifies in the mainstream media. Amateur interpretations of food porn not only democratise it as a social activity but imbue new social conventions around the capture and sharing of these images.

The term 'food porn' is increasingly used to describe the act of styling and capturing food on mobile gadgets, eliciting an invitation to gaze and vicariously consume, and to tag images of food through digital platforms. The mundane and ordinary food is attributed a spectacle in this economy premising food as the message and the medium. The term 'food porn' of course predates these ubiquitous practices of capture today. Used synonymously with 'gastro porn,' it alludes to the fetishisation of food and its coalescence with desire by styling culinary offerings through the vantage point of the camera lens to be consumed by hungry publics. This food is meant to be consumed by sight and other senses (well removed from just ingesting it), evoking our hidden desires while highlighting its unattainability. Its pornographic quality removes food from the mundane and ordinary, elevating it to the level of the pornographic. This paper specifically addresses the imaging of food through new mobile technologies whilst acknowledging the wider ecology of media and marketing phenomena which have socialised us into accepting food images and the practices of imaging food as a resonant part of digital culture in our contemporary reality.

Food throughout history has been a symbol of sharing and sociality, envy and avarice, decadence and depravity, pride and repugnance and equally a resource of commonality as well as difference. Food has an elemental quality of tapping into our emotional reservoir, our nostalgic memories and inner psyche to elicit comfort, familiarity, aversion, desire, greed, degrees of pleasure and displeasure. Food has the ability to trigger forms of affect and ubiquitous food imaging through digital platforms transforms food into a digital commodity, bringing with it a plethora of social and symbolic meanings through the acts of image capture, upload, dissemination as well as archiving. But 'food is extraordinary in its ordinariness, exceptional in the extent to which we treat it as mundane, and outstanding as a focus for the study of consumption' (Marshall 2005: 69). Food serves to confirm membership as well as to set people apart. Food is connected to rituals, symbols and belief systems. It is associated with myth; the sacred and taboos. Food functions in social relationships; in terms of ethnicity, race, nationality, class, individuality and gender.

With increasing appropriation of technologies into our daily lives we don't often stop to question new forms of behaviours, conventions and habits which emerge with mediated communication. As we adopt new rituals and integrate these into our daily lives, we often struggle to completely comprehend why these new rituals become habitual and unquestioning moments of life's patterns and rhythms in contemporary culture. Imaging food and serving these to others via images is a widely accepted phenomenon today. The home photography situated the everyday through imagery. Richard Chalfen (1987) in writing about the 'home mode' and Kodak Culture highlighted the important role of photography in domestic life, where social practices involving family norms, traditions and values can be expressed and sustained. The everyday and its material practices became a site to enact and construct culture. This Kodak culture, which domesticated the everyday through imagery and food, is part of this visual literacy. With the convergence of technologies and the incorporation of recording features on the mobile phone, food becomes a site for multiple iterations from autobiography and memory making to self-representation.

In restaurants, homes and in the streets, food as a commodity is captured, shared and archived, providing a medium for human connection, communication; public and private interactions while contributing to a repository of food images on image sharing platforms online. The domestication of food images through the smartphone and the ability to consume food through screen cultures marks a shift in production values of food porn produced by expert stylists and photographers for the cultivated audience and those produced by the smartphone flaneurs, marking the division between production and consumption in the traditional media economy compared with the prosumer economy. The amateur prosumer equipped with her mobile technology can style and capture food through her sense of aesthetics and disseminate it to a potentially global audience. This smartphone food porn democratises imaging practices around food as a cultural artefact, while domesticating food imagery through pervasive technology as form of social exchange. The distance between the amateur and the professional is not obliterated but enables a mainstreaming of food photography in our cultural practices through the smartphone and mobile gadgets. With the late twentieth century's explosion of imaging and visualising technologies, everyday life has become visual culture (Lister and Wells). In this arena of hypermedia and multimedia age of visuality, 'seeing is much more than believing. It is not just a part of everyday life, it is everyday life' (Mizroeff 1999: 1).

There is a vast cultural economy around food online. From food blogging, recipe sharing, gastro tourism narratives, and food reviews to cataloguing 365 days of meals. Food imagery and meals can mediate the temporal and spatial, thus occupying a primacy in our cultural imagination and interactivity. Images are a primary form of content creation today. But what does it mean to capture something for our personal repository and image archive before we consume it? What is this urge to offer these images of food for vicarious consumption? What is it about food images which offer shared moments of communion between friends and strangers? The explanations reside at many levels and the deconstruction of these offer insights into the therapeutic nature of both food images as a cultural bridge but also social media platform as a means for sharing the banal and the mundane, and how these interactions display social relations as well as one's negotiation of self and life in the private and public realms (Ibrahim 2015). Functioning at the level of spiritual and emotional connection, ubiquitous food imaging and sharing remain an intrinsic part of digital culture today.

Food as Part of our Everyday Construction

Food is more than just a fuel for bodies. It is a site of consumption, pleasure, morality and renewed aesthetics. As Krishnendu Ray (2007) asserts the very visibility of something that was mundane, trivial, and habitual is somewhat embarrassing but the source of discomfort for some may be the dissolution of boundary between the life world and the art world. Kerry Chamberlain (2004: 468) concurs that food permeates our relationships, infiltrating our language, our images, and that metaphors of food surround us. Food is entwined with popular culture, saturating our visual and sensory modes through television, magazines, newspapers, specialist food blogs and recipe sharing cites (Chamberlain 2004; Lupton, 1996). These provide voyeuristic escapes into food and cuisines where money or calories are of no consequence (O'Neill 2003). The re-fashioning of food or gasto porn then refers to the ways in which TV-programs and cookbooks often portray food as perfect, using pornographic features and visual effects (Zukin & Maguire, 2004). Richard Magee (2007) contends that food pornography takes the form of glossily lush photographs of voluptuous and sinfully rich desserts, or of fantasy recipes and lifestyle images that are 'so removed from real life that they cannot be used except as vicarious experience'. The concept of food porn then describes a movement away from motifs of aesthetics and trespasses some kind of threshold towards the obscene and unattainable; rupturing a gap and breaching the lucidity in judging what is *real* and *illusion*.

The term *food porn* is thus not just about the *content* or *way* food is represented, but rather addresses a much more complex construct of human experience (Mitchell 2014). The term gastro porn may be attributed to Alexander Cockburn's 1977 New York Review of Books when he criticised the pornographic character of the unattainable and picture perfect dishes in connection to the insatiable desires these elicited (Cockburn, 1977). McBride (2010) suggests that the term first appeared in 1979 when Michael Jacobson as the co-found for the Centre for Science in the Public Interest used food porn to refer to unhealthy foods in the Center's newsletter. According to Jacobson he "coined the term to connote a food that was so sensationally out of bounds of what a food should be that it deserved to be considered 'pornographic' (cf. Mcbride 2010). Mcbride (2010) employs the term food porn to denote 'watching others cook on television or gazing at unattainable dishes in glossy magazines without actually cooking oneself'. Signe Rousseau (2013) contends that food porn occupies a contested space between constructions of 'legitimate' and 'illegitimate' desires when it comes to eating.

Frederick Kaufman, in likening sex porn to gastro porn observes that 'like sex porn, gastro porn addresses the most basic human needs and functions, idealizing and degrading them at the same time' (cf. Ray 2007). The sex and food corollary is reiterated in Foucault's writing. Michel Foucault (1983) observed that food in the early Christian history was an issue of primacy, just like sex has become in the modern era, where its significance is created through a complex set of restrictions and discursive practices. Food has dominated as a subject of major preoccupation throughout history. Roland Barthes (1972: 22) in discussing the relationship between food, national identity and imperialism was conscious of the centrality of food to other forms of social behaviour;

Today we might say all of them: activity, works, sports, effort, leisure, celebration – every one of these situations is expressed through food. We might almost say that this 'polysemia' of food characterizes modernity. (Barthes 1972: 25)

The fetishisation of food as well as the cultural practices convening around the visual consumption of food have become important in locating the everyday. Raymond Williams (1993) decried that 'culture is ordinary,' in attempting to locate culture as something lived in and common place rather than a work of art removed from social and material practices. Williams (1993: 11) in defining culture as a set of expressive practices implicated not just print, cinema and television, but also employed it to cover a range of new material entities which emerged in post-war Britain including canned foods, contraceptives, aspirin and baby Austins. Culture is then reproduced in multiple sites. Michel de Certeau *et al.*'s *Practice of Everyday Life living and cooking* (De Certeau *et al.*, 1998:3) assert that 'culinary virtuosities' establish 'multiple relationships between enjoyment and manipulation'. In terms of food visuality, food is not just consumed orally and ingested, but consumed through other senses and a sense of play and desire.

Food, when dislodged from the kitchen and devoid of its nutritive or taste qualities enters a realm of the performative; valorising the visual above all else and situating it within the performative (Magee 2007). Barbara Kirshenblatt-Gimblett (1999) argues that food that is dissociated from eating bypasses the nose and mouth. Such food may well be subjected to extreme visual, and for that matter tactile and verbal, elaboration. Our eyes let us 'taste' food at a distance by activating the sense memories of taste and smell. Television shows and cookbooks invite us to eat with our eyes without either cooking or eating oneself. Kirshenblatt-Gimblett reminds us that the wondrous confectionery presented at the conclusion of Renaissance banquets, while technically edible, might never be eaten, though it might be enthusiastically applauded. She contends that these monumental events cultivate the visuality and appearance rather than the flavour, hence situating appearance as enduring compared to the eating of food, which can be ephemeral. The dominance of visuality or appearance is deliberate, for it emphasises a legible (edible) visual language of emblems and signs. Here the visual is the performative. Similarly, Barbara Wheaton in *Savoring the Past* notes that, in the edible allegorical tableaus that were medieval banquets, visual effects, rarity of ingredients, opulence, and sequence of events were more important than the dishes, ingredients, preparation techniques, or flavours. Richard Magee points out that both food pornography and sexual pornography are primarily focused on food or sex as a performance, and, like all performance, are designed as a voyeuristic exercise.

While considerable attention has been accorded to food as image or symbol, food studies is somewhat muted on the topic of food as a performance medium. Allen Weiss (2002) in drawing attention to a minority stance within Western aesthetics that allows for the definition of food as art contends that the Enlightenment concord has been thwarted to expand the boundaries of form and taste. The new postmodern aesthetic premises 'the disappearance of the boundaries between the arts, disrupting the border between art and craft, repositioning classic hierarchies of form and taste.' Weiss challenges with the question; 'if fashion can become a fine art today, why not cooking?'

This variant of food porn through the smartphone invariably offers a performance medium. In digital cultures the performative and visual elements of food porn enter a complex arrangement where it is conjoined with the creation of self-identity, community, invitation to gaze, memory making, and as a form of social capital to transact and exchange. In the digital economy, the unattainable quality of food porn is mediated and made mainstream for the amateur food flaneur. Amateur food images, rather than emphasising its unattainability, hinge on the individual aesthetics and exchange of image as a form of social capital to elicit validation and to seek attention and bring moment to the everyday. The imaging of food elongates the performative, making food inedible and imbuing it with non-perishable qualities. Imaging food accords performance to the everyday while transforming the mundane into commodities for sharing. Imaging food via smartphones and mobile gadgets enables the formation of ownership to an image and intimacy which food porn of the glossy magazines and television may not engender. In so doing they don't eradicate desire or the notion of the unattainable, where one man's food is offered to another for vicarious consumption but it mediates distance and closeness to this porn through a sense of ownership. With image sharing sites allowing for dissemination, display and curation of images, the processes of creation and ownership online allows for the perception of 'this porn is mine'. The flaneur gaze of the Internet means that images can be culled from the wider web and displayed in what one might consider a personalised space online, while sustaining vicarious consumption. Desire is still a manifest part of the food porn but it can reside in the personalised spaces which we curate and publish online.

Rituals of the Internet

The Internet as a virtual space is not disembedded or dichotomised from the real world. It is mediated through social and cultural norms of our lived world. But it is equally a space that can produce cultures in its own right (Hine 2000). Our ability to enact new forms of rituals online and to seek communion, validation, therapy or to commemorate and preserve memories through image sharing and uploads has been well documented (Ibrahim 2011; 2015). The emergence of converged mobile technologies which enable publishing and social sharing while diarising the everyday has given rise to a whole host of cultural activities around image sharing and new media visualities online. Imaging the everyday by capturing our daily routines including meals has become an important part of new media rituals and validation of the self. According to a report by Pew entitled 'Photo and Video Sharing Grow Online' (Duggan 2013), 54% of adult users post original photos and videos online that they themselves have created. Another 47% of adult Internet users take videos or photos they found online and repost them on sites designed for sharing images with many people. According to Webstagram which ranks Instagram images by popularity, food images retain popular resonance through multiple tags including 'foodporn', 'yummy', 'yumgasm' and 'dessert'. For instance #food figured as number 25 in the top 100 tags on Instagram in 2014.

Marking life's everydayness and paces of routine through images, communicating these everyday images and inviting the gaze of others authenticates everyday life experiences; capturing the ephemerality of life while archiving and displaying the banal and the unusual. Food and meal times as symbolic imagery of our everyday (or the temporality of life) provide a means of communication and social sharing of a familiarity. They also serve as spatial and temporal devices to create a sense of space and a notion of lifetime online. This image literacy and reciprocity of exchange is part of digital culture. Food has a universal quality of resonance and food images carry this aura of desire, familiarity, comfort, spirituality as well as a sense of offering and a moment of display. The glimpse into one's private moment inevitably conveys an intimacy, but with social media platforms the intimate and public moments occupy a hybrid space where the private and public can co-exist. Food imagery provides an acceptable space of social and cultural exchange where the private and public can merge, forming hybrid spaces of material consumption, exchange and co-presence. These new rituals enacted through new mobile technologies and social media provide a means for shared and collective meaning making while renewing social connections.

The rich sociological literature on rituals confirms its symbolic, functional and therapeutic elements for humanity and society. Durkheimian interpretation of ritual emphasise the creation of social order and strengthening of group solidarity. Emile Durkheim (1976) accorded rituals a seminal role in enacting and sustaining the 'sacred' and in constructing a communally-shared social reality. Victor Turner (1969) conceptualised rituals as being both creative and equally subversive attributing it with 'social drama,' which can challenge social hierarchies. In contrast, Irving Goffman (1967) stresses rituals' ability to capture interactions and the performative aspects of everyday life. Rituals subsumes both the institutional and formal but also the informal and personal, providing a means for collective meaning making accounting for shared experiences as well as individual identity (Helland 2013:26; Rook 1985). Defying static manifestations to embrace the movements of time and space, rituals can reflect the changing patterns of society. As 'repeated and patterned forms of communication, rituals enable us to attach ourselves to 'our surrounding media-related world' (Semulia 2013: 9).

These new rituals online of imaging food have both symbolic and instrumental value of marking everyday moments like meal times and staples, but equally veritable feasts and culinary spectacles which celebrate the occasion, providing a means to commemorate and remember while creating a sense of shared and or individual identities. Several authors (e.g. Sahlin, 1974; Lupton. 2003) argue that gift giving is a way of validating social relations. Furthermore, gift giving might not only relate to the giving of physical objects but might also (or perhaps even more so) relate to more symbolic acts and practices and therefore, food image are part of gift giving, the purpose of which is to validate social relations. New rituals online such as imaging food before consumption (or during consumption) have instrumental and symbolic qualities where the invitation to gaze by others authenticates life's experiences while enabling the formation of everyday and special memories offered through the process of transacting the food image. These rituals have their therapeutic function in terms of social sharing and reciprocity, but they are equally intertextual with the wider world of consumerism representing material consumption as a site of desire, meaning making, performance and engagement with capital.

FOOD IN MEDIA AND CONSUMER CULTURE

Throughout history we have been socialised into food imagery whether in art history, food advertising editorials, magazine features, specialised cookbooks or personal photography. Food once transformed as an image or commodity signifies a permanence, defying its perishable and destructible qualities. Imaging provides an ethereality; an ability to transcend time and space and to be accorded different cultural significance by new audiences who consume it, appealing to their senses and sensitivities in different ways. With the invention of mobile photographic equipment, particularly the Kodak camera, food has remained a subject of rites of passages, of events as well as the everyday, marking the moments and routines of life within the domestic and beyond.

With print culture, broadcasting, advertising and branding, food imagery entered a realm of consumer capitalism denoting the construction of desire and its circulation through mass media platforms. The selling and packaging of food to the masses drew on our nostalgic bonds with food while recruiting consumers for advertisers. Food porn in the hands of capital sought to create a consumption community through desire for new offerings on the market. Food advertising came through our TV sets and magazines, offering the ease of assemblage to the homemakers, enticing new audiences while renewing our intrinsic ties with food in domestic settings. The increasing incorporation of leisure readings in newspapers and proliferation of lifestyle and women's magazine also socialised us into accepting stylised food imagery as part of a new consumer culture which packaged fantasy, escapism and romance into everyday fast moving consumer products. Advertising of food took it to new heights pledging desire and enticement through the lens, which could yield pleasure and yearning en masse.

The everyday staples of bread, butter, milk and coffee could be re-fashioned through the co-optation of photography which worked to lure mass audiences to mass production and into the hands of capital. The emergence of mass advertising of consumer products through mass media enabled food imagery to be accepted as part of the consumerist landscape to fashion instant desire like instant coffee. We were socialised into food porn as part of our consumer culture through mass media even before the advent of satellite television, which could assuage niche interests. The increasing tabloidisation of the public sphere and broadcasting also saw a proliferation of cookery shows, food channels and celebrity chefs, making food a ubiquitous subject of human consumption and of decadence and a symbol of high living where the concerns were about offering creativity and variety through food rather than issues of starvation, austerity or famine. With the tele-visualisation and tabloidisation of food, food imagery entered an era of the spectacle where it can be 'groomed' for consumption through the vantage point of the lens but removed from the immediate pleasure of consuming and ingesting food. Food porn online did not emerge from a vacuum – its prominence on the digital platforms today harks back to a wider media and capitalist socialisation which leveraged on our spiritual connection with food as a symbol of culture, survival, sustenance and solidarity.

With increasing globalisation of the world, food is increasingly a part of popular culture and popular imagination. Claude Fischler contends that what we have seen in fast food is not the "menace of Americanization" or a threat to traditional French cuisine, but an essentially benign reflection of the global circulation of culinary cultures. The globalisation of coffee chains and conveyor belt sushi joints symbolises both the increasing diversification of cuisines in cosmopolitan cultures and equally the dominance of standardised offerings through the Mcdonaldization of the globe. In the process, food acquires a popular global currency and can symbolise a multitude of meanings from the McDonaldization of society, the increasing curiosity and acceptance of world cuisines to the exoticisation of the ordinary meal.

Food, UGC, and Prosumerism

With the incorporation of Kodak culture and home photography, food retains a primacy as a subject of photography. With the convergence of technologies in the digital age and the incorporation of the digital photographic tools into mobile telephony the mobile phone becomes an extension of the body and memory, archiving and imaging events and rituals of the everyday. The body embedded with technology such as the smart phone is a space of double articulation in terms of functioning as a repository for memory. Beyond the cognitive ability of the brain to store visual memory and images, mobile technology such as the smart phone facilitates the production of mobile repositories, including cloud computing which can produce and carry images while on the move. Food provides a means to document and memorialise the everyday and the eventful. In the social media economy cultural food production also signifies the production of the self and diarisation of everyday life. New rituals around food consumption including the uploading of the food image before consumption, integrates seamlessly into a UGC economy where content creation and human behaviour fuse together to manifest new social conventions and rituals.

UGC is integrated into many commercial platforms and with the proliferation of social networking sites, image sharing and video archives, UGC has in parts entered a monetised economy while feeding this notion of consumer sovereignty and user empowerment online. This user-centred economy of publishing online through its emphasis on interactivity and online conversations is seen as celebrating a prosumerism, blurring the boundaries between production and consumption. In tandem with this, mobile telephony today enables people to record and publish images while on the move. In this digital economy where people can produce and consume incessantly, the image plays an important role in communication and in enabling connection both in the everyday and in marking the unusual. Web 2.0 celebrates the coexistence of a multitude of forms including images both mobile and static. In expressing everyday flows of life and in establishing co-presence as well as endorsing human communion, images are seen as a vital part of this connectivity. The virtual world yields to our desire to see ourselves in it and equally to look into the lives of others. Food provides a means of intimacy into a private realm while being a symbol of collective consumption.

The prosumer economy online has appropriated food photography as a well-established cultural convention of capture and exchange. This is evident where the Internet is saturated with features to improve techniques of imaging food with a smartphone. Conde Nast Publishers in its Traveler magazine ran a feature in 2014 on 'Food Photography Tips for Instagram and Smartphone,' dispensing technical advice on how to get the right lighting and vantage point while staying true to the protagonist, food. Similar articles have featured in Epicurious.com (2015) and the Guardian which ran a feature entitled, ' How to Photograph Food with your Phone' in 2012. A huge litany of similar articles exist online providing amateurs with tips to mainstream food photography with mobile phones. The Internet craves content and food imagery is a vital part of this economy.

People face the burden as well as the freedom to construct their own identities in postmodernity (Giddens, 1991; Christensen, 2008; Baudrillard, 2002), and new media technologies and the image economy are increasingly implicated in this. Consumption in modern (mass) consumer society can be highly individualistic and even narcissistic. While the sensual pleasures of eating are completely individualised, eating is a highly social activity and regulated by the community (Marshall 2005: 71) and food porn becomes a site of both personal consumption and collective desire. Holt (1995, 1998), refers to the way in which consumers use consumption objects to classify themselves in relation to relevant others. Miller and Edwards (2007) similarly explore online photo-sharing practices with sites such as

Flickr and Facebook in relation to how different types of people manage public and private boundaries in this space. The coalescing of the public and private realms of consumption and notions of space make food porn amenable to multiple iterations. Like the selfie, food is part of this transaction culture and memory creation. What one consumes and experiences is archived and communicated through food. The selfie and the culture of social networking sites are driven through the uploading of content. The commodification of self and food are entwined online. The construction of the self is renewed through the constant engagement in these sites. Food as an everyday object of materiality and as a part of one's personal domain of consumption offers a means to create a personal connection while providing a common theme of interest for others to gaze.

The increasing number of image sharing sites and the communities which have emerged around gazing, curating, tagging, liking and retweeting, and re-blogging images makes food porn a tool of cultural production and interaction online; equally one of technique and aesthetics. The digital economy is made for forms of public and quasi-public sharing, inviting the gaze of the strange and familiar while enabling the self to be consumed and constructed through this image economy. According to a Pew Report in 2012, photos and videos have become a key social currency online (Lee et al. 2012). The rise of social media, especially YouTube and newer services like Pinterest, Instagram, and Tumblr have made curating activities easier because they are organized for easy image and video-sharing. Beyond content creation, the Internet and social networks drive on a circulation economy constantly merging content in unlikely places. Food porn can be part of disparate narratives and conversations online and equally it can convene dedicated niche communities.

Food as a subject of human connection can transcend cultural boundaries and is often considered a product of cultural diplomacy in terms of tourism and national identity. Food images become tools to personify self, communicate intimacy and to connect to a wider audience of similar and disparate interests. Our intimacy with food means it is a site for self-representation but also a means to leave narratives of social history and autobiographies in a transient mortal world. The Internet's virtuality is in many ways is inerasable and enduring while being amenable to wider circulation and search. Our connection to the image binds us to the mortal world in complex ways. Food, then, is a medium and metaphor for this representation and the preservation of the self through the image economy. Digital cultures are undeniably shaped by the culture of the physical world, which reinforces our need to imagine ourselves beyond our situated mortality; the virtual world provides a means to leave traces of your intimate portrayals where you can both avow and disavow ownership to content you produce. The image economy, particularly the intimate images of creation, tap into this need to preserve ourselves beyond our transient world. The ubiquity of new practices and conventions in many ways reassert this, and the imaging of food is no exception; representing both the need to prolong desire and life through the symbolic metaphor of food, recognising it as an ephemeral entity, but seeking to prolong and immortalise it through the image.

CONCLUSION

Amateur food porn online democratised by the smartphone and convergence technologies appropriates many cultural qualities from the food porn crafted by the experts. It relocates desire as something that can be generated through UGC mediating both distance to food porn and its unattainability through ownership and creation of food images. In the process, it provides a mechanism to create social capital and currency online and to produce these to document the everyday and to renew connections with a wider community. Smartphone food porn democratises the production of desire and in doing so taps into representation of self and identity while being intertextual with our consumerist world and consumption cultures. At the heart of virtual life is our quest for self-presentation beyond our mortal existence. The image economy assuages our need to seek immortality through the virtual world. Food then becomes the medium and message.

REFERENCES

Barthes, R. (1972). *'Ornamental Cookery,' Mythologies*. New York: Hill and Wang.

Barthes, R. (1979). Towards a psycosociology of contemporary food consumption. In R. Forster & O. Rarum (Eds.), *Food and drink in history: Selections from the annals economics, societies, civilisations*. Baltimore, MD: John Hopkins University Press. (Original work published 1961)

Baudrillard, J. (2002). The Precession of Simulacra. In G. D. Meenakshi & D. M. Kellner (Eds.), *Media and Cultural Studies: Keyworks* (pp. 521–549). Malden, MA and Oxford: Blackwell Publishers.

Chalfen, R. (1987). *Snapshot Versions of Life*. Bowling Green, OH: Popular Press.

Chamberlain, K. (2004). Food and Health: Expanding the Agenda for Health Psychology. *Journal of Health Psychology*, *9*(4), 467–481. doi:10.1177/1359105304044030 PMID:15231050

Christensen, C. L. (2008). Livsstil som TV-underholdning. *Journal of Media and Communication Research*, *45*, 23–36.

Cockburn, A. (1977, December). Gastro-Porn. *The New York Review of Books*, *8*. Retrieved from www.nybooks.com/articles/8309

De Certeau, M., Giard, L., & Mayol, P. (1998). The Practice of Everyday Life, Volume 2: Living and Cooking. University of Minnesota Press.

Duggan, M. (2013). *Video and Photo Sharing Grow Online*. Pew Research Centre. Retrieved from http://www.pewinternet.org/2013/10/28/photo-and-video-sharing-grow-online/

Durkheim, E. (1976). *The Elementary Forms of Religious Life*. Free Press.

Fischler, C. (1988). Food, Self and Identity. *Social Sciences Information. Information Sur les Sciences Sociales*, *27*(2), 275–292. doi:10.1177/053901888027002005

Foucault, M. (1983). *On the Genealogy of Ethics: An Overview of Work in Progress. In Michel Foucault: Beyond Structuralism and Hermeneutics*. Chicago: University of Chicago Press.

Giddens, A. (1991). *Modernity and Self-Identity*. Stanford, CA: Stanford University Press.

Goffman, E. (1959). *The Presentation of Self in Everyday Life*. Edinburgh, UK: Social Sciences Research Centre.

Goffman, E. (1967). *Interaction Ritual: Essays on Face-to-Face Behaviour*. New Jersey: Transaction Publishers.

Helland, C. (2013). Ritual. In H. Campbell (Ed.), *Digital Religion: Understanding Religious Practice in New Media Worlds*. Routledge.

Hine, C. (2000). *Virtual Ethnography*. Thousand Oaks, CA: Sage. doi:10.4135/9780857020277

Holt, D. B. (1995). How consumers consume: A typology of consumption practices. *The Journal of Consumer Research*, *22*(1), 1–16. doi:10.1086/209431

Holt, D. B. (1998). Does cultural capital structure American consumption. *The Journal of Consumer Research*, *25*(1), 1–25. doi:10.1086/209523

How to Photograph Food with your Phone. (2012, 15 July). *The Guardian*. Retrieved from http://www.theguardian.com/lifeandstyle/2012/jul/15/how-to-photograph-food-smartphone

Ibrahim, Y. (2011). The non-stop capture: The politics of looking in postmodernity. *The Poster*, *1*(2), 167–185. doi:10.1386/post.1.2.167_1

Ibrahim, Y. (2015). Instagramming life: banal imaging and the poetics of the everyday. *Journal of Media Practice*.

Jensen, P. (2008). The International Extent and Elasticity of Lifestyle Television. *Mediekultur*, *45*, 24–45.

Kaufman, F. (2005). Debbie Does Salad: The Food Network at the Frontiers of Pornography. *Harper's*, (October), 55–60.

Kirshenblatt-Gimblett, B. (1999). Playing to the senses, Food as Performance Medium. *Performance Research*, *4*(1), 1–30. doi:10.1080/13528165.1999.10871639

Lee, R., Rainier, J., & Purcell, K. (2012). *Photos and Videos as Social Currency Online*. Pew Research Centre. Retrieved from http://www.pewinternet.org/2012/09/13/photos-and-videos-as-social-currency-online/

Lister, M., & Wells, L. (2001). Seeing Beyond Belief: Cultural Studies as an approach to studying the visual. In Handbook of visual analysis (pp. 61-91). Academic Press.

Lupton, D. (1996). *Food, the Body and the Self*. Thousand Oaks, CA: Sage.

Magee, R. M. (2007). Food Puritanism and Food Pornography: The Gourmet Semiotics of Martha and Nigella. *Americana: The Journal of American Popular Culture, 6*(2). Retrieved from www.american-popularculture.com/journal/articles/ fall_2007/magee.htm

Marshall, D. (2005). Food as ritual, routine or convention. *Consumption Markets & Culture*, *8*(1), 69–85. doi:10.1080/10253860500069042

McBride, A. E. (2010, Winter). "Food porn." Gastronomica. *The Journal of Food and Culture*, *10*(1), 38–46. PMID:21539050

Miller, A. D., & Edwards, W. K. (2007). Give and take: A study of consumer photo-sharing culture and practice.*Proceedings of CHI'07*. San Jose, CA: ACM Press. doi:10.1145/1240624.1240682

Mirzoeff, N. (1999). *An Introduction to Visual Culture*. London: Routledge.

Mitchell, R. D. (Ed.). (2014). *Food Design on the Edge: Proceedings of the International Food Design Conference and Studio 2014*. Otago Polytechnic.

O'Neill, M. (2003). Food Porn. *Columbia Journalism Review*, (September–October), 38–45.

O'Neill, M. (2003). Food porn. *Columbia Journalism Review*, *5*, 38–45.

Ray, K. (2007, Winter). Domesticating cuisine: Food and aesthetics on American television. Gastronomica. *The Journal of Critical Food Studies*, *7*(1), 50–63.

Raymond, W. (1985). *Keywords: A Vocabulary of Culture and Society*. Oxford, UK: Oxford University Press.

Rook, D. (1985). The ritual dimension of consumer behaviour. *Journal of Consumer Behaviour*, *12*(December), 251–264. doi:10.1086/208514

Rousseau, S. (2014). Food "Porn" in Media. In *Encyclopedia of Food and Agricultural Ethics* (pp. 1–8). Springer.

Sahlins, M. (1976). *Culture and Practical Reason*. Chicago, IL: Univ. Chicago Press.

Semulia, J. (2013). *Media and Ritual: Death*. New York: Community and Everyday Life Routledge.

Snapchat: The Ultimate Guide to Mobile Food Photography, From Lighting to Editing. (2015). Retrieved from http://www.epicurious.com/expert-advice/the-ultimate-guide-to-mobile-food-photography-from-lighting-to-editing-article

Sturken, M., & Cartwright, L. (2001). *Practices of Looking: An Introduction to Visual Culture*. Oxford, UK: Oxford University Press.

Turner, V. (1969). *The Ritual Process: Structure and Anti-Structure*. Ithaca, NY: Cornell University Press.

Weiss, A. (2002). *Feast and Folly: Cuisine, Intoxication, and the Poetics of the Sublime Albany*. State University of New York Press.

Wheaton, B. (1983). *Savoring the Past: The French Kitchen and Table from 1300 to 1789 New York*. Simon & Schuster.

Zukin, S., & Maguire, J. (2004). Consumers and Consumption. *Annual Review of Sociology*, *30*(1), 173–197. doi:10.1146/annurev.soc.30.012703.110553

Chapter 10
Developing and Validating the "This Is Why We Can't Have Nice Things Scale": Optimising Political Online Communities for Internet Trolling

Jonathan Bishop
Centre for Research into Online Communities and E-Learning Systems, UK

ABSTRACT

Internet trolling describe the posting of any content on the Internet which is provocative or offensive, which is different from the original meaning online in the 1990s, referring to the posting of messages for humourous effect. Those systems operators (sysops) who run online communities are being targeted because of abuse posted on their platforms. Political discussion groups are some of the most prone to trolling, whether consensual or unwanted. Many such websites ara open for anyone to join, meaning when some members post messages they know are offensive but legal, others might find grossly offensive, meaning these messages could be illegal. This paper develops a questionnaire called the This Is Why We Can't Have Nice Things Scale (TIWWCHNT-20), which aims to help sysops better plan the development of online communities to take account of different users' capacity to be offended, and for users to self-assess whether they will be suited to an online community. The scale is discussed in relation to different Internet posting techniques where different users will act differently.

INTRODUCTION

Internet trolling as a term has changed in meaning through use since the 1990s. Around that time trolling meant posting messages on the Internet in order to provoke a reaction. It has come to mean the posting of provocative or offensive messages more generally (Bishop, 2013a; Bishop, 2014b; Walter, Hourizi, Moncur, & Pitsillides, 2011), but in legal terms it should refer to the posting of messages which are grossly offensive as opposed to simply offensive (Starmer, 2013). The difference between what is

DOI: 10.4018/978-1-5225-1862-4.ch010

offensive and what is not appears to in some cases be driven by the media, meaning people posting offensive messages are falling foul of the criminal justice system as pressure is put on law enforcement authorities to deal with such content

It is now firmly established that cyberspace is not a frontier in its own right but is subject to the jurisdiction of nation states (Bishop, 2011a). Case law has established that what is grossly offensive to one person may not necessarily be grossly offensive to another. The case of DPP v Connolly in the UK for instance found that a person who might send an image of an aborted foetus to pharmacists with a politicial message would not be breaking the law, whereas if they sent the same to an abortion surgeon it would be free speech as the abortion surgeon is unlikely to get grossly offended, but pharmacists unexposed to such images are likely to. In terms of the USA and Canada the cases of Jake Baker and Arthur Gonda respectively has the same outcome which was that by sending abusive messages between one another could not be considered unlawful because they were not intended for a wider audience (Wallace, 1999). In the case of Jake Baker specifically he was found to not have broken US trolling law in the form of the Telecommunications Act 1996 by posting a plot for a rape story to a newslist as it was free speech. This was replicated in the UK with the case of Chambers v DPP, where it was found that a message has to cause apprehension in those receiving it in order for it to be illegal.

Such clear yet complex case law provides a challenge for the systems operators (syspos) who run online communities where the posting of political content is the norm. The chance of someone getting grossly offended when most others in a community are not even offended can create challenges for sysops. Websites like 4chan have tried to deal with this by separating general boards like '/b/' from ones containing hardcore content like '/hc/' so that users know what to expect. However it is difficult for these sysops to plan the design of an online community without knowing which content would be tolerable to which people. This is something this paper hopes to solve.

Politicisation in the Network Society

The term network society is now widely used. The network society is made up of virtual communities and organic communities (Van Dijk, 1999; Van Dijk, 2005). It is almost impossible in today's world to exclude any form of governance over one's life. This has led to online discussion groups and online communities in general to be cesspits for political partisanship where people express opinions on the basis of whether it corresponds with the policies of the political party they support and not their genuine convictions. Equally there are those online discussion groups which are solely dedicated to attacking politicians regardless of their party politics. One might therefore see the world not as a network society per se, but as a collection of network societies in which the social construction each person has received through their senses about the world, is to them the true reality. It is therefore important to understand the political points of views of those who participate in online discussion groups because depending on their point of view and attitudes their participation in an online community may be destined to be successful, or indeed unsuccessful.

The 12 Types of Troller

It is established that there are 12 types of Internet troller that describe many of the types of behaviours online, through clearly defined character theory (Bishop, 2012b; Bishop, 2013b). In addition to this there are four groups of Internet troller in which these can be classified using definitions available in

(Edmonds & Gray, 2002). All of these can be seen in Table 1. Haters include E-Vengers, Iconoclasts and Snerts, who all like to inflame situations for no real benefit to others. Lolcows consist of Big Men, Rippers and Chatroom Bobs, who post messages to to provoke others so that the attention is on them. Bzzzters, namely MHBFY Jennies, Wizards and Flirts like to chat and engage in converstion even if the information or advice they give is inaccurate. Finally Eyeballs are made up of Lurkers, Elders and Trolls, all of which like to watch what others are doing, waiting for their opportune moment to post.

Consider the Flirts and Snerts. These trollers take part in a type of posting called 'snacking' (i.e. intensive posting on specific topics). Both of these types of troller are known to post off-topic, but to what extent something could be considered to be off-topic is often a matter of debate (Wallace, 1999, p.238). One might consider that if an off-topic post results in a flame-war, as Snerts try to achieve if a person of interest to them is the original poster, then as this erodes the discussion it might be considered by sysops and their moderators to be unnecessary and disproportionate (Wallace, 1999).

Table 1. The 12 types of troller and their 4 sub-types

Group type	Troller Character Type (orientation)	Description
Haters (Like to inflame situations for no real benefit to tohers)	E-Venger (Not Criticised)	Driven by 'Vengeance' forces. An E-Venger does trolling in order to trip someone up so that their 'true colours' are revealed.
	Iconoclast (Important)	Driven by 'Destructive' forces. An Iconoclast takes part in trolling to help others discover 'the truth', often by telling them things completely factual, but which may drive them into a state of consternation. They may post links to content that contradicts the worldview of their target.
	Snert (Appreciated)	Driven by 'Anti-social' forces. A Snert takes part in trolling to harm others for their own sick entertainment.
Lolcows Like to provoke others so the attention is on them)	Big Man (Important)	Driven by 'Order' forces. A Big Man does trolling by posting something pleasing to others in order to support their world view.
	Ripper (Not Criticised)	Driven by 'Thanatotic' forces. A Ripper takes part in self-deprecating trolling in order to build a false sense of empathy from others.
	Chatroom Bob (Appreciated)	Driven by 'Existential' forces. A chatroom bob takes part in trolling to gain the trust of other members in order to exploit them.
Bzzzters (Like to chat regardless of accuracy or usefulness of contributions)	MHBFY Jenny (Appreciated)	Driven by 'Forgiveness forces'. A MHBFY Jenny takes part in trolling to help people see the lighter side of life and to help others come to terms with their concerns.
	Wizard (Important)	Driven by 'Creative' forces. A Wizard does trolling through making up and sharing content that they think helps others.
	Flirt (Not Criticised)	Driven by 'Social' forces. A Flirt takes part in trolling to help others be sociable, including through light 'teasing'
Eyeballs (Like to watch what others do for the 'opportune' moment to post a provocative message)	Lurker (Not Criticised)	Driven by 'Surveillance' forces. Lurkers make silent calls by accident, etc., clicking on adverts or 'like' buttons, using 'referrer spoofers', reporting posts, modifying opinion polls or user kudos scores.
	Troll (Appreciated)	Driven by 'Chaos' forces. A Troll takes part in trolling to entertain others, bringing some fun and mischief to an online community.
	Elder (Important)	Driven by 'Escape' forces. An Elder is an outbound member of the community, often engaging in "trolling for newbies", where they wind up the newer members often without questioning from other members.

Consider also MHBFY Jennies (who are empathetic and forgiving) and E-Vengers (who are vengeful). These types of troller often take part in a type of posting called 'mobiling.' Mobiling can be used constructively by trollers to share stories and offer advice (Young & Levine, 2000, p. 13), but it can also be used to provide advice in a non-constructive and deceptive way.

Another set of trollers, Trolls and Big Men, take part in trolling, or 'classical trolling' (Bishop, 2014b) whereby the point of the former's posts is to provide provocative content that is entertaining (Wallace, 1999, p.102; Young & Levine, 2000, p. 275) and the point of the latter's posts is to post messages that assert their point of views which then provokes those posters who either disagree with their point of view, or don't like them per se.

Another type of posting called 'flooding' is often done by users called Chatroom Bobs and Rippers. Flooding can have as its aim to target users through fast, rapid or multiple postings in order to seduce someone to their perspective in the case of the former (Wallace, 1999, p.245), or in the case of the latter to draw attention to how they have been treated unfavourably by others to drown out or bring attention to that point of view (Wallace, 1999, p.238; Young & Levine, 2000).

A further kind of posting is 'spamming.' Whilst this conjures up images of unsolicited emails to either a person or newslist (Wallace, 1999, p.132), the concept extends to the posting of any content in a self-promotional or self-serving way. This can include self-promoting oneself on Wikipedia using a sock puppet account masked with a pseudonym, or using search engine optimisation (SEO) methods to post links to ones content from various providers of free personal homepage creation. Spamming is usually done by Wizards and Iconoclasts.

A final type of participation is 'lurking,' which is traditionally associated with people who do not participate in online communities, except on the periphery, known as Lurkers (Bishop, 2007b; Preece, Nonnecke, & Andrews, 2004). However, it has been extended to those out-bound from the community, known as Elders, who wait for the opportunity to post unconstructively lurking by Elders includes 'trolling for newbies,' where they post messages that go against the grain of the beliefs the new members expect to find in the discussion group. Both these trollers will try to influence the kudos points others may have so that those they disagree with, or who post an idea before they thought of it, are given bad 'karma' (Powazek, 2002, p.132).

THE ROLE OF THE 'THIS IS WHY WE CAN'T HAVE NICE THINGS' SCALE

This section sets out the need for the 'This Is Why We Can't Have Nice Things' Scale (TIWWCHNT-20) in order to help optimise poltical online communities so that their users fit the intended discourses for that website or app. The premise is that if one is offering a website that is anti-politician, trolling is reduced if the members are anti-politician and not pro-politician. Equally, if a website or app is intended for serious debate and discussion of policy then having members who are anti-politician is a recipe for disaster. The 'This Is Why We Can't Have Nice Things' Scale (TIWWCHNT-20) is to help identify which category a particular user is in.

Limitations in the Law and the Need for TIWWCHNT-20

Case law in the UK says that a message is only grossly offensive if the recipient is likely to be offended (DPP v Connolly). Other case law has said if the group to which a message refers is likely to be grossly offended then the message is illegal (DPP v Collins). This poses a challenge for those communities which might want to use the TIWWCHNT-20 scale to attract users who post transgressive or subversive messages that target particular groups, such as on the grounds of race. Whilst the community members might want to ensure that the only members who join are unlikely to be offended within the meaning of DPP v Connolly, they risk posting unlawful messages under DPP v Collins in relation to those who are not in the community whom might be offended.

If one were to look at the legal situation in Great Britain around Internet trolling, it might be possible to see how the TIWWCHNT-20 questionnaire could be used to justify the existences of websites that would offend those for whom they were not intended. A number of precedents have been set on Internet trolling that raises questions about when a website's content should be considered free speech and when it should be considered "*grossly offensive.*"

The case of *DPP v Connolly*, for instance, found that a message is only grossly offensive if the recipients to whom it was targeted would find it to be grossly offensive. A community where users high on Relevant are likely to occupy are likely to offend people who score high on Expression. For instance, on the Urban75.net website, its sysop Mike Slocombe called the London Mayor the T-word because of how the crowd at the London Olympics found him endearing. One might therefore ask whether it would be possible for the police to take action against websites like this if it could be made clear to visitors of the website that there is likely to be a high amount of flame trolling, which some people might find offensive. It might seem a bit much to the reasonable person for websites to be closed simply because others find the content offensive, if that website is dedicated to being offensive, such as the website 'Sickipedia'. Equally, a general website that is open to all persons, might be found to be breaching decency if it is not possible for users to be pre-warned.

Network Politics and TISWCHNT-20

The role of TIWWCHNT-20 in preventing conflict in online discussion groups that discuss politics could be an increasing one for ensuring the effective implementation of 'network politics.' The emerging field of network politics has come about for a number of reasons according to (Solo & Bishop, 2011). Information technology and communication networks have caused many changes in the realm of politics. The newest communication network to have a great impact on politics is the Internet. Recent revolutions in many countries in the Middle East and North Africa have started in large part due to social networking Web sites like Facebook and Twitter. Politicians and candidates use their own Web sites and social networking profiles to get their message out. Equally, the mainstream media no longer have a monopoly on political commentary as anybody can set up a blog or post an article or video online. It is also possible for political activists to network together online.

It can therefore be seen that information and communications technologies, especially the Internet has been a vehicle for social change at all levels. With each technology that enables free speech, humans have a strange way of making it work for the worse aspects of humankind. Whether it is the threatening letter, the abusive phone call, text or tweet, humans are always ready to abuse others. It is therefore imperative that ways are found so that everyone is able to exercise free speech to express their grievances, without harming others in the process.

It is therefore necessary to introduce a concept of 'TISWCHNT Potential.' The acronym TISWWCHNT means, as stated earlier, 'This Is Why We Can't Have Nice Things'. A Website's TISWWCHNT Potential therefore is the extent to which the design and nature of the website is conducive to abusive

Table 2. Overview of how to read results from the This Is Why We Can't Be Nice Scale

Factor	Outcome of High Score	Benefits of more users
Opportunity	Increased TISWCHNT Potential. Flame trolling, unbalanced lurking	Increased content production
Understanding	Reduced TISWCHNT Potential. Reduced flame trolling, increased lurking	Increased content consumption
Relevance	Increased TISWCHNT Potential. Increased flame trolling, increased lurking	Increased posting of flames
Aspiration	Reduced TISWCHNT Potential. Reduced flame trolling, reduced lurking	Increased participation and membership base due to viral marketing
Choice	Reduced TISWCHNT Potential. Reduced flame trolling, reduced lurking	Increased posting of kudos, even if critical
Expression	Moderate TISWCHNT Potential. Unbalanced flame trolling, reduced lurking	Mixed posting of kudos and flames due to increased confidence

forms of posting, such as flame trolling. The outcome of a person's scores on the This Is Why We Can't Have Nice Things Scale (TIWWCHNT-20) could be used to determine which type of online community they would most effectively troll in and which they should use to avoid trolling. The higher their score on a particular factor of the scale, the more suited they are to an online community. Table 2 Overview of how to read results from the This Is Why We Can't Be Nice Scale shows how a high score on a particular part of the scale can help users determine which communities they can avoid the temptation to troll in, and thus have a reduced TWIWWCHNT Potential, as well as those they can most effectively troll in, where their TWIWWCHNT is at its greatest.

The Role of the TIWWCHNT-20 Scale for Choosing a Web-Based Community Platform

Depending on the outcome of a batch of founding users of an online community, the appropriate genre could be chosen to maximise the type of posting that the systems operator (sysop) of that online community wants to achieve. If one considered the 12 types of troller (Bishop, 2008; Bishop, 2012b; Bishop, 2013c) it is possible to see how these different types of user may be reflective of the various types of attitude reflected in the TIWWCHNT-20 scale. Even though it is proven that have then they were members of an online community can be more effective than have been many, the actors not necessarily correspond with the view that an online community should not seek to involve others besides its own members. Social networking services like Facebook are allowing organisations to create pages were they can promote the work they do. Such pages could do far more to increase the membership of an online community in a productive way and also act as a means of recruitment (Bishop, 2010). When people are on Facebook they are unlikely to leave it, but having a page on Facebook allows a dedicated online community to build trust in their brand through cooperating with Facebook, even if it is informally. Cooperative advantage, which refers to avoiding competing with organisations in a market and instead working together for mutual benefit (Bishop, 2012a), can allow a community to grow on a different website one might want to compete with, but instead make use of it to promote one's offerings.

Table 3 presents an amalgamation of established research from the end of the 20th century (Wallace, 1999) and the start of the 21st century (Preece, 2000). The findings are still relevant in the second decade

Table 3. Examples of posting types, their descriptions and associations with online discussion group genres

Pulse type (Post type) Character theory	Description of posting type	Genre to encourage posting type	Genre to discourage posting type	Examples
Social (Snacking) Mostly done by Flirts and Snerts.	Participants who perform snacking offer short bursts of content and consume a lot too. It allows for the posting of 'anecdotal evidence' or other content which is tolerable or acceptable, but also the posting of messages targeting others which cause harm to them in some way that is not necessary or proportionate.	Snacking is more achievable in communities where discussion can flow and where people are looking for sympathetic points of view. Message boards and chat groups are examples.	Snacking is least achievable in communities where people are abused or blocked for going off-topic or digressing from the original post which is asking for an answer and not empathy.	Flirt: "Brighton is a good place to learn to ski. That's where I learned, and I think they offer a special deal for beginners." (Wallace, 1999) Snert: "You are a jerk," "You are stupid" (Hardaker, 2013).
Emotional (Mobiling) Mostly done by MHBFY Jennies and E-Vengers.	Mobiling is where participants use emotions to either become closer to others or make a distance from them. It allows for the posting of passionate opinions and/or resentment of target groups like politicians. The risk is that those affiliated with the target might be offended and start a flame war.	Mobiling is more achievable in communities where communication is fast so that grammatical or others mistakes can be made and picked upon. Examples include Chat Groups, especially where length of posts are limited.	Mobiling is most difficult to achieve in platforms where users can easily correct their mistakes or delete embarrassing posts. Examples include weblogs controlled by the user or message boards with an edit feature.	MHBFY Jenny: "Most newbies will not have the ability to recognize a troll post amid all the good advice posted, or the bad advice that is suggested and then refuted. Leaving bad (troll) advise unrefuted *will* mislead newbies who are diligently trying to educate themselves." (Hardaker, 2013). E-Venger: "Somehow you expect people to be diplomatic to you when you have been trolling us. [...] We only reply to your BS to keep others from thinking that you might be giving them useful advice. [...] you can rest assured that someone is going to call you on it." (Hardaker, 2013).
Cognitive (Trolling) Mostly done by Trolls and Big Men.	Trolling as a more generic pursuit seeks to provoke others into posting a response to a topic, which might be iconoclastic, unpopular or unfashionable. Can involve the posting of satirical or other banter and humour which may be acceptable depending on the website in question.	Trolling is most achievable in communities where it is possible to identify particular interest groups and post alienating or opposing comments. The most effective platforms are those where content is more permanent such as message boards and blogs.	Trolling is least achievable in communities open to a range of materials and where it is easy for sysops to remove confrontational content.	Troll: I love trolling on the horse news groups. It is just plain FUNNY. They have gotten used to my trolls. Any ideas on a good troll for the horse people?" (Hardaker, 2013). Big Man: "bubi: depends what sort of qualifications, experience, intentions, area" (Wallace, 1999)
Physical (Flooding) Mostly done by Chatroom Bobs and Rippers.	Flooding is where participants get heavily involved in posting on a particular topic (often to multiple websites) to further discussion on a topic that might be the subject of censorship because those to which it refers find the 'truth' distasteful or even painful.	Flooding is most achievable in communities where membership is easily achievable and content goes unchecked. Examples include platforms offing blogging and personal homepage hosting.	Flooding its least achievable in communities with strong systems for detecting that users are only posting to SEO existing content or to mass post specific points of view.	Ripper: "Jeny doesn't love me anymore:(" (Preece, 2000). Ripper: "I've had some tough times in my life" (Wallace, 1999) Chatroom Bob: "Are you lonely, solo?" (Wallace, 1999)

continued on following page

Table 3. Continued

Pulse type (Post type) Character theory	Description of posting type	Genre to encourage posting type	Genre to discourage posting type	Examples
Visual (Spamming) Mostly done by Wizards and Iconoclasts.	Spamming, often associated with unsolicited mail, is in general the practices of making available information one has a conflict of interest in so that it is more accessible to others.	Spamming is most achievable in communities which give advice or offer the chance to post their point of view as fact. The partial advice given could actually be to the person's detriment, and is most achievable on Wikis or message boards where pseudonyms are used.	Spamming is least achievable in communities where people have to use their own identities or otherwise strong moderation facilities exist.	Iconoclast: "B, explain to me exactly how I am being a Troll. I am participating in a ng about horses. Thats all. We are discussing a method of horse training that I like and you don't. I have stated from my original post that I was just playing with this method because I was bored. [...] I have not bashed their chosen method of training." (Hardaker, 2013). Wizard: "On many gaming muds, you see server code trying to handle the task of intervening before actual harm is done, and prevent the antisocial activity from occurring (eg, the @player killing siwtch@)" (Wallace, 1999)
Relaxational (Lurking) Mostly done by Lurkers and Elders	Lurking is enacted by those on the periphery of a community. Their judgements for not taking part often relate to a lack of purpose or control. It is essential to build on the skills and knowledge that already exist in the community, for example, by encouraging networks of people who can support each other. Designing the community around allowing people to both see what others are up to, as well as allowing them to have a break from one another can build strong relationships. A 'do not bite the newbies' policy should be enforced.	Lurking is most achievable in communities that have kudos points of other means of secretly influencing the dynamics of online discussions.	Lurking is least achievable in discussion groups where one's actions are transparent and visible to all and where content cannot be accessed by those who do not post.	Lurker: "Since everyone thinks I am a troll, I wont post here anymore. I didn't mean to come across the way I did, and this group doesn't mean anything to me anyway" (Hardaker, 2013). Elder: "What we try to do on uo [Ultima Online] is give tools to the players to help them identify the behaivor THEY don't like, and then to give them tools to easily identify and track repeat offenders." (Wallace, 1999)

of the 21st century, and have been confirmed by recent studies, including research by an acupuncture expert (Hardaker, 2013). Many of these types of posting have been defined since the mid 1990s (Jansen & James, 1995), and Table 3 provides a simple way to understand and differentiate the different kinds in a concise and clear way that older and more contemporary research has failed to do.

The differences between the Snerts and the Flirts, who conduct 'snacking', which would rely on the 'Expression' component of the scale. In the case of the former they will be obnoxious (as they are in real life) and the Flirts will give anecdotes to keep the conversation going. Snacking, which includes 'infosnacking' and 'data-snacking' is the posting and consumption of content in online communities (Jansen, 2002; Jansen & James, 1995). Snerts are more suited to communities where there is a negative attitude to politics and politics, whereas Flirts will fit into most communities – except those where getting to the point and staying on topic are important.

The practice of 'mobiling' is often carried out by MHBFY Jennies and E-Venger, as can be seen from Table 3. In the case of the former these more emotional posts are based on trying to provide empathy and in the case of the latter to 'right wrongs.' In those political online communities where things can become heated it might be common for some posters to have their accounts deleted. This can result in that person becoming an E-Venger and signing up under a new alias to cause havoc (Bishop, 2013b). The longer a person has been in the community often reflects the intensity of their need for vengeance – especially if they earned a lot of kudospoints or had a high post count (Powazek, 2002). In terms of the MHBFY Jenny, as can be seen from Table 3, they will provide help and support to members, including newbies, but this can sometimes be unhelpful or innaccurate. Posters who spread misinformation can be called Bzzzters, and MHBFY Jennies are not the only posters who do this, as Flirts and Wizards can do this as well. Even so, the posts by MHBFY Jennies are often intended to be in good faith and empathetic. Bother these types of users will likely fall into the 'Understanding' component of the TIWWCHNT-20 scale, as MHFBY Jennies want to understand other users, whereas E-Vengers want others to understand them. Someone with a high score on this part of the scale is likely to not engage in flame trolling, but if their comments are not welcomed, they are likely to go back to lurking for a while. Someone with a low score is likely to target those who may lack an understanding of their point of view, which they feel is under-represented or which has been ignored.

The next type of posting – trolling – is more complex than those who rely on grey media such as newspapers might think. Trolling when doen by Trolls (as opposed to 'trolls') is for mischief making and provocation to make others 'laugh out loud' (i.e. 'trolling for the lolz'). Another type of trolling is done by a type of poster called a 'Big Man.' This troller type takes part in trolling to puff themselves up by speaking in an authoritive way to assume the role as expert on a particular topic (Campbell, Fletcher, & Greenhill, 2009). They are often targets of other members of the group, especially Snerts, who often feel the Big Men think they are superior to them, even if they don't.

Flooding is another type of posting online, which is often provoked when an online community deletes content or gives opportunities for content to be created, is the extensive posting of content to a person or website (Jansen, 2002; Jansen & James, 1995). In terms of 'chatroom bobs,' if someone denies a person a right to free speech they will ensure that free speech is widely available (by flooding the Internet). Chatroom bobs can also do a different type of flooding – where they flood a particular user with compliments and other favourable gestures in order to seduce them and take advantage of them (Bishop, 2012c). When flooding is done by another type of troller called a Ripper, it is flooding one or more online communities with 'sob stories' in order to try to get sympathy for whatever they are using to seek attention. Chatroom bobs and Rippers be best recognised through the Opportunity component of the TIWWCHNT-20 scale. The former are more likely to be at the low end of this part of the scale as their posts are only relevant to achieving their own aims regardless of others' interests. The latter are more likely to fit into a high score part of this component as they are likely to flame troll themselves before deciding not to participate.

Spamming is normally thought in terms of sending someone an unwanted email to entice them into buying a product or service, but in terms of online communities it has a broader meaning (Jansen, 2002; Jansen & James, 1995). When Wizards do Spamming it is usualy to share their ideas and generate a lot of content that can be attributed to them. As can be seen from the example in Table 3, a Wizard will also provide help and advice on making use of specific tools in a web-based community so others can enjoy the experiences of creativity they did. In terms of Iconoclasts, their type of Spamming is making other aware of their 'truth' or to challenge the status quo in terms of others' believes, which can be painful to some who would rather not hear it (Bishop, 2013b; Starmer, 2013). Both Wizards and Iconoclasts may fall within the 'Relevance' part of the TIWWCHNT-20 scale. In the case of Wizards (who have a low score) they will try to create content relevant to the community and in the case of Iconoclasts (who have a high score) they will try to remove content they find irrelevant, or which is contrary to their point of view.

Lurking is generally thought of in terms of non-participation and perepherial participation (Bishop, 2007b; Nonnecke & Preece, 2000; Preece et al., 2004). As can be seen from Table 3, it is more complex than that because lurking is not just done by Lurkers who don't post, but also by Elders who have made a lot of contributions. Both of these types of troller look for the opportune moment to post a message. In terms of a Lurker it takes a long time for them to get the confidence to post. Sometimes if they do post and get a bad reaction Lurkers will return to perepherial participation as there is usually something keeping them there (Bishop, 2007b; Preece et al., 2004). Elders know the rules and norms of an online community and can be helping in encouraging Lurkers to become posters (Bishop, 2007b; Kim, 2000). If they are out-bound from the community, however. They can be problemating by posting content to wind up the newer members as a kind of initiation called 'trolling for newbies.' The part of the TIWW-CHNT-20 scale relevant to these trollers is Choice. A low score reflects lurking, where the user thinks by choosing not post they are less likely to be abused or otherwise not have their posts welcomed (Preece et al., 2004). Elders on the other hand are also driven by Choice and a higher score on this part of the scale suggest they will be more likely to flame troll newbies. An overview of these different types of posting, and their connection with the types of discussion group genre are presented in Table 3.

DEVELOPING THE 'THIS IS WHY WE CAN'T HAVE NICE THINGS' SCALE

Tensions in online communities, particularly of a political nature, can have a severe impact on the enjoyment of participating in those online communities (Bishop, 2011c; Bishop, 2013b; Hardaker, 2013). This poses a problem for the systems operators who design and administer online communities can ensure that only the types of poster most suited to their website take part and that they can keep away those who would be offended or otherwise dislike that online community's ethos. There can be no one kind of political online community – some are abusive to politicians and others focus on policy and not personalities. It is therefore important that a scale to assess the suitability of particular users to online communities be developed. Whilst this may be difficult for sysops of online communities to administer adhoc, it is hoped such a scale could help in the planning of online communities and through self-administration by users themselves.

Participants

This research study examined what implications for forms of democratic citizenship and participation that consumption may have on online and media participation. The research covered the ways that people's practices as media consumers were connected (or not) to their practices as citizens. The project involved a telephone survey of over 1000 people, conducted by ICM Research across the United Kingdom that aimed to produce conclusions on the detailed issues about consumption and citizenship (Couldry, Markham,

& Livingstone, 2005). In the end, a total of 1065 observations were made, consisting of people from a variety of backgrounds across the United Kingdom.

In terms of age, 287 of the participants were aged 18-34 (26.9%), 386 aged 35-54 (36.2%), and 344 were aged over 55 (32.3%). In terms of Internet access 295 of the participants (27.7%) had access to the Internet at home, 85 had access to the Internet at work (8%), 47 had access to the Internet somewhere else (4.4%), with 301 not presently having access (28.3%) and 48 of the participants (4.5%) did not respond to this question. In terms of ethnicity, 835 of the participants considered themselves to be British (78.4%) and 13 considered themselves to be Irish (1.2%), with 48 not responding (4.5%) and the remaining 169 (15.9%) being from other ethnic backgrounds.

Measurements

The study administered a set of questions that were derived from analysing the diaries of 37 participants' media consumption as well as initial and subsequent interviews that were conducted with those respondents, and focus group interviews that were conducted with diarists (Couldry et al., 2005). The telephone survey of 1,017 people, was conducted by ICM Research across the United Kingdom that aimed to produce conclusions on the detailed issues about consumption and citizenship raised in Phase One (Couldry et al., 2005).

METHODOLOGY AND METHOD

Factor analysis was the most appropriate method for this dataset, as it is necessary to reduce the data to specific factors, which would hopefully map onto the ecological cognition framework (Bishop, 2007a; Bishop, 2007b). There are three primary analytical techniques for performing a factor analysis; principal components analysis, common factor analysis and Q-method factor analysis. Principal components analysis (PCA), was selected because it yields one of more composite variables that can capture much of the information originally contained in a larger dataset, with the components being weighted as sums of the original sums. It was decided to use the A Priori Criterion and extract six factors from the data as this represented the six processes from stimulus to response in the ecological cognition framework.

Preliminary Analysis

Multi-colinearity was tested by the author before they conducted a factor analysis by measuring the sampling adequacy, using the Kaiser-Meyer-Olkin test. This test compares the magnitudes of the calculated correlation coefficients to the magnitudes of the partial correlation coefficients. The dataset showed individual MSAs of between 0.587 and 0.868 which in the case of the latter is "great" (Field, 2005, p.630). In the case of the latter, 86.8% of the variance of one variable is accounted for by all the others and 58.7% in the case of the former. Taking into account this and the KMO of 0.778 it seemed that there was no reason for concern and that the factor analysis should continue. As well as the overall measure of sampling adequacy, as estimated by the KMO, it is also important to test the sphericity of the data set. The Bartlett test of sphericity examines whether a variance-covariance matrix is proportional to an identity matrix and a dataset is considered suitable for further analysis if the associated probability is less than .05 (Bryde & Pelie, 2006). In the data set it showed a Chi square of 2961.74 and significance of <0.001 making the dataset suitable.

Factor Extraction, Rotation, Description, and Naming

Assessing the loadings of variables on to factor is important in assessing the effectiveness of the factor analysis output. Factor loadings are coefficients that indicate the importance of a variable to a factor. The un-rotated component matrix showed variables loading onto more than one of the factors. Whilst it may have been possible to run the analysis again without restricting it to 6 factors. It seemed more suitable to rotate the data to improve the clarity of the pattern using Quartimax rotation. Loadings under 0.25 were disregarded. As a structure to the data existed, the next stage involved naming and describing the factors and their interrelationships through investigating their loadings using the rotated component matrix.

Opportunity

When someone decides to visit a particular part of a virtual world or take part in an information exchange, they are doing so by giving up the opportunity to do something else, referred to as 'the opportunity cost' (Bishop, 2009). Different generations value certain activities more than others and are more willing to sacrifice certain opportunities over others. This is a core aspect of ecological cognition, where it is stated that users of information systems do not have a hierarchy to their needs that are innate, but have developed cognitions that affect their priorities through exposure to not only their internal environment (i.e. their mind and body), but also their external one (i.e. the world) as suggested by (Bishop, 2007b). Table 2 shows the factor loadings for the 'Opportunity' factor.

It has been argued that the question of fairness across generations should be formulated as a comparison of opportunities available to individuals living at different times (Norton, 1999). From this it is clear to find support for the existence of this factor in understanding the similarities between how different generations use information. The statement, 'You know where to go to find out information that you need' identified in the data is quite relevant to this category as it is known that organisations can be effective when they act on opportunities to transform information into knowledge in order to integrate the wisdom of different generations into the workplace. The statement, 'Sometimes you feel strongly about an issue, but don't know what to do about it' negatively loaded onto this factor, which is appropriate as different age groups approach opportunities in relation to discussing politics differently and it is recommended that organisations manage the communication between them (Hankin, 2005). This could be because actors within an economy are always seeking out opportunities to meet their goals and will narrow their focus within their competencies to achieve those goals (Mantovani, 1996a). It is a clear

Table 4. Factor matrix for 'opportunity'

	Opportunity	Understanding	Relevance	Aspiration	Choice	Expression
1. You know where to go to find out information that you need	.769					
2. Sometimes you feel strongly about an issue, but don't know what to do about it	-.402	.327	.392			

principle of economics that human wants are infinite and resources are scarce, which means that users of virtual worlds will seek out a new opportunity if they lack the resources to take part in their preferred one. For instance, in Second Life where some virtual goods are charged for, the user may go without and instead learn to create them for themselves.

Understanding

The crucial part of responding to an economic opportunity in the environment is an understanding of the stimuli it offers. It has been argued that understanding, particularly of science and faith is spread over many generations, with each adding its own contribution, arising from its own perspective (Polkinghorne, 2000). Table 3 shows the factor loadings for the 'Understanding' factor.

In terms of the factor analysis, the statements, 'It's a regular part of your day to catch up with the news', 'You follow the news to understand what's going on in the world', 'You follow the news to know what other people are talking about' fit well into this factor as it is known that people who follow the news have a greater understanding of their communities and themselves (RW.ERROR - Unable to find reference:514). The statements, 'It's your duty to keep up with what's going on in the world' and 'You have a pretty good understanding of the main issues facing our country' seem relevant to this category as keeping up-to-date with current affairs has been consistent across generations in informing their understanding of the world around them (RW.ERROR - Unable to find reference:515).

Relevance

The relevance of a particular stimulus in the environment to an actor is affected by their ability to consume it (Mantovani, 1996a; Mantovani, 1996b). It can be seen that as a particular user's confidence in a system increases so their consumption of its resources also increase. For instance, in Second Life, as a user becomes aware of how to interact with the system, such as through 'flying' or 'teleporting' then the greater their exposure to different aspects of the system will be and it will become more likely that their inventory will increase as they discover artefacts that are relevant to them. Table 4 shows the factor loadings for the 'Relevance' factor.

Table 5. Factor matrix for 'understanding'

	Opportunity	Understanding	Relevance	Aspiration	Choice	Expression
3. It's a regular part of your day to catch up with the news		.761				
4. You follow the news to understand what's going on in the world		.718				
5. You follow the news to know what other people are talking about		.602				
6. It's your duty to keep up with what's going on in the world		.511		.462		
7. You have a pretty good understanding of the main issues facing our country	0.3	.443				

Table 6. Factor matrix for 'relevanc.'

	Opportunity	Understanding	Relevance	Aspiration	Choice	Expression
8. You often feel that there's too much media, so you need to switch off			.652			.280
9. There's no point in watching the news, because it deals with things you can do nothing about		-.327	.639			
10. It doesn't really matter which party is in power, in the end things go on pretty much the same			.620			
11. People like us have no say in what the government does			.552			-.325
12. Sometimes politics seems so complicated that you can't really understand what's going on	-0.46		.535			

The statements 'You often feel that there's too much media, so you need to switch off' and 'There's no point in watching the news, because it deals with things you can do nothing about' seem fitting to this factor of relevance as people will consume news media if it is relevant to them regardless of whether it is for information or entertainment purposes (Tsfati & Cappella, 2005). The statements, 'It doesn't really matter which party is in power, in the end things go on pretty much the same', and 'People like us have no say in what the government does' are also appropriate as the relevance of government and political parties to a particular household is related to the effect they have on that household's ability to achieve its goals and that all political parties have access to the same instruments for affecting it (Chapman & Palda, 1983). The negatively loaded statement, 'Sometimes politics seems so complicated that you can't really understand what's going on' is also suitable for this factor as individuals are more likely to accept arguments about their democracies if they are simpler and relevant to their lives (Barber, 2003).

Aspiration

People of all generations and within them have different aspirations (Yu & Miller, 2005), although the thing they generally have in common is that they regularly have them (Grikscheit, Cash, & Young, 1993). Table 5 shows the factor loadings for this 'Aspiration' factor.

The two statements in this factor, namely, 'People at work would expect you to know what's going on in the world' and 'Your friends would expect you to know what's going on in the world' seem to fit with the idea that people draw some of their aspirations from those they are in close contact with in the social world. This factor is particularly affected by the principle of 'marginal utility', which is the extent to which the exposure to a particular stimulus leads to demand for a re-exposure or reuptake of that stimulus. It is at this stage that actors become unaware of the externalities of their wants and are driven purely by responding to existing relevant opportunities and going on to create new opportunities, even if this is only to be re-exposed to desirable aspects of the environment.

Table 7. Factor matrix for 'aspiration'

	Opportunity	Understanding	Relevance	Aspiration	Choice	Expression
13. People at work would expect you to know what's going on in the world				.777		
14. Your friends would expect you to know what's going on in the world		.384		.717		

Choice

Different actors will respond differently to the principle of marginal utility and the effect of their judgement on whether to take up another unit of exposure is affected by the universal value of 'choice'. Choice goes beyond the right to choose, as the basis for exercising choice is according to the perceived needs or values of an individual or group of individuals of different generations (Goldring & Shapira, 1993).

While the statements in this factor talk about 'trust', it is apparent from analysing the ecological cognition framework (Bishop, 2007a; Bishop, 2007b) that this factor is more about 'choice' be seen in Table 6. Trust after all is a choice, and the statements represent the different choices individuals take in a democratic society. The statement, 'You trust the government to do what is right' suggests that individuals choose to put their trust in elected representatives, as does the statement, 'You trust politicians to deal with the things that matter'. The statement, 'You trust politicians to tell the truth' is reflective of the choice people make to accept information from these representatives as being accurate. This factor appears to include the reconciliation of internal wants with external costs, or externalities.

Expression

Like the opportunity factor, the expression factor is affected by opportunity cost. While an actor is using a specific product or communicating with a specific actor they may be missing out on the opportunity to do so with somebody else. It has been argued that the need for expressing oneself is evenly distributed across generations, but the means for expression should be expected to vary, as would means for entertainment, and suggests it would be beneficial to map the differences between generations when

Table 8. Factor matrix for 'choice'

	Opportunity	Understanding	Relevance	Aspiration	Choice	Expression
15. You trust the government to do what is right					.823	
16. You trust politicians to deal with the things that matter					.819	
17. You trust politicians to tell the truth					.773	

Table 9. Factor matrix for 'expression'

	Opportunity	Understanding	Relevance	Aspiration	Choice	Expression
18. You can affect things by getting involved in issues you care about						.752
19. You feel that you can influence decisions in your area	.317					.612
20. Politics has little connection with your life	.264		.316	-.265		-0.47

it comes to activities that they carry out (Bolin & Westlund, 2008). The factor loadings for this factor, 'Expression,' are in Table 7.

The statement, 'You can affect things by getting involved in issues you care about' seems appropriate for this factor as increasingly actors are getting involved in political activism as a form of democratic expression (Andersen, 2002). With the mass adoption of Internet technologies and in particular virtual worlds users are exposed evermore to opportunities to express themselves and often to a wider audience that gives them a greater degree of influence. The statement, 'You feel that you can influence decisions in your area' is relevant to this factor as political influence has been linked to the expression of individual identities (Innes & Rendall, 2006). The statement, 'Politics has little connection with your life' if inverted is appropriate as political expression is commonplace and shaped by the social context of the individuals within electoral regions (Agnew, 2014).

VALIDATING THE 'THIS IS WHY WE CAN'T HAVE NICE THINGS SCALE'

The Development of the This Is Why We Can't Have Nice Things Scale (TIWWCHNT-20) needs to be evaluated to ensure its reliability and validity.

Reliability Analysis

According to (Hair, Black, Babin, Anderson, & Tathan, 2006), reliability is an assessment of the degree of consistency between multiple measurements of a variable. They indicate that there are three types of diagnostic measures for determining reliability. The first measure is to consider each separate item, including the item total correlation and the interim correlation. The second type of diagnostic measure is the reliability coefficient that assesses the consistency of the scale with Chronbach's alpha. The third type is to use the reliability measures derived from a confirmatory factor analysis.

To perform the analysis requires selecting one factor at a time and taking into account each of the variables that make up that factor. The Chronbach's alpha for 'Understanding' was 0.689 which is reasonable, and this was not improved by removing variables from the scale. The Chronbach's alpha for 'Relevance' was 0.624 and when items were removed it was significantly reduced, suggesting that the scale is adequate. The Chronbach's alpha for 'Choice' was 0.751 and this was not improved by removing items. The Chronbach's alpha for 'Aspiration' was 0.676 and this was significantly worse when variables were removed, suggesting it is adequate. The Chronbach's alpha for 'Expression' was 0.006, but when 'politics has little connection with your life' was removed it improved to 0.499, suggesting this item should be deleted from the scale. The Chronbach's alpha for 'Opportunity' was -0.254 and this was not improved by removing any variables, suggesting more variables need to be added to make this scale reliable.

Validity Analysis

The dataset used to devise the This Is Why We Can't Have Nice Things Scale (TIWWCHNT-20) was reevaluated to test the reduced variables, making use of those known to be associated with Internet trolling (Bishop, 2014a). Some of these had to be dervived from various pre-collected variables. For instance, whether the participant was a young person not in education, employment or training (NEETs) was computed from a persons age and their employment status. Whether someone was "Intelligence" or more importantly whether they were of above average intelligence or not was based on a combination of age and years of education. This is not a perfect measure of intelligence, but it would have been excessive to have re-interviewed all participants with the variables associated with trolling that have only recently been devised (Bishop, 2014b). The variable Trolling in this case was based on whether or not a person posted to online communities. Whilst this would be a better indicator of whether or not the person was a lurker, this was selected as the most appropriate on the basis that no one would post to an online community unless they were able to elicit a response from others and that all trolling – whether for the lolz or the lulz – is provoking. These variables are presented in Table 10.

Internet Access

The first measure investigated to determine the scale's validity for the digital age was "Internet access." As can be seen from Table 10, the scale as a whole is significant in terms of its ability to differeniate those who have access to the Internet from those who do not ($p=<0.001$). On each element of the scale, however, the significance scores are poorer. The exception is Choice, which might suggest that those with access to the Internet have better access to information so that they can make better judgements on what to believe and what not to.

Trolling

As can be seen from Table 11, the use of the scale for measuring trolling as a global variable – or in this case the propensity to post messages per se – is not effective. This would suggest that on the one hand measuring trolling in terms of posting content to elicit responses might not be a relevant use of the scale, as it is likely that regardless of where people score on the scale that they will engage in trolling, which may even be consensual among users of an online community.

Table 10. T-Test validity analysis results for "Internet access"

Internet Access		N	Mean	t	Sig.
Complete Scale	Yes	710	35.19	4.626	0.000
	No	307	32.86		
Opportunity	Yes	710	3.76	-2.902	0.227
	No	307	4.08		
Understanding	Yes	710	5.70	1.655	0.933
	No	307	5.31		
Relevance	Yes	710	9.97	8.216	0.606
	No	307	7.73		
Aspiration	Yes	710	3.08	-0.304	0.149
	No	307	3.12		
Choice	Yes	710	7.02	1.302	0.001
	No	307	6.75		
Expression	Yes	710	5.65	-1.426	0.042
	No	307	5.86		

Table 11. T-Test validity analysis results for "Internet trolling"

Trolling - Posting		N	Mean	Sig.	t
Complete Scale	Yes	67	34.33	0.726	-0.381
	No	720	34.69		
Opportunity	Yes	67	3.55	0.353	-1.481
	No	720	3.86		
Understanding	Yes	67	4.91	0.206	-0.887
	No	720	5.29		
Relevance	Yes	67	10.61	0.635	1.683
	No	720	9.73		
Aspiration	Yes	67	2.40	0.028	-2.484
	No	720	3.03		
Choice	Yes	67	7.76	0.082	1.898
	No	720	7.01		
Expression	Yes	67	5.10	0.124	-2.474
	No	720	5.77		

NEETs

The role of the scale for measuring whether someone is a NEET – a young person not in education, employment or training – is also not significant. This must be because young people are so diverse that they could fall anywhere on the scale. Simply because someone is not in education, employment or training, it does not mean that will impact of whether they will participate in a political online community in a given way.

"*Intelligent*"

In terms of the test of whether someone is intelligent – crudely measured by whether they have an IQ of 100 or above based on how much their education corresponds to their age – it is also clear that the scale offers no assistance in measuring such differences. Whilst the t-scores for the scale as a whole was high (t=3.008) and for relevance (t=6.542), the significance scores were poor (p=<0.107 and p=<0.355 respective). At most this would suggest that the higher one's intelligence the more important it will be for the media one is consuming to be relevant to one's interests. It would also suggest that to take an active part in the media – including attacking politicians or policy – requires a degree of intellect so that the higher one's intelligence the higher one's score on the scale will be.

Table 12. T-Test validity analysis results for "NEETs"

NEET		N	Mean	t	Sig.
Complete Scale	Yes	94	36.90	3.329	0.993
	No	922	34.24		
Opportunity	Yes	94	4.33	2.947	0.916
	No	922	3.81		
Understanding	Yes	94	7.21	4.838	0.445
	No	922	5.42		
Relevance	Yes	94	9.06	-0.577	0.039
	No	922	9.32		
Aspiration	Yes	94	3.55	2.342	0.057
	No	922	3.04		
Choice	Yes	94	7.10	0.510	0.043
	No	922	6.93		
Expression	Yes	94	5.65	-0.286	0.109
	No	922	5.72		

Table 13. T-Test validity analysis results for "Intelligent"

Intelligent		N	Mean	t	Sig
Complete Scale	Yes	785	34.87	3.008	0.107
	No	231	33.20		
Opportunity	Yes	785	3.81	-1.799	0.212
	No	231	4.03		
Understanding	Yes	785	5.59	0.044	0.196
	No	231	5.58		
Relevance	Yes	785	9.74	6.542	0.354
	No	231	7.77		
Aspiration	Yes	785	3.08	-0.289	0.029
	No	231	3.12		
Choice	Yes	785	6.98	0.723	0.181
	No	231	6.81		
Expression	Yes	785	5.66	-1.362	0.199
	No	231	5.88		

DISCUSSION

The posting of messages on the Internet that are Satirical, or iconoclastic, or rude comment, the expression of unpopular or unfashionable opinion about serious or trivial matters, banter or humour, even if distasteful to some or painful to those subjected to it should and no doubt will continue at their customary level the UK case of DPP v Connolly found. We must therefore accept that after 200,000 years of existence that if the human race has not changed about their acceptance of those who happen to be different from them, they are unlikely to ever change without forcing the evolution of our brains, or more practicably, by changing our environment to promote constructive behaviours over destructive ones. Changing the law so in the words of victims of Internet abuse things "never happens again" is naïve to say the least, especially as most flame trolling offences are illegal in the UK and other countries through dedicated or generic laws on harassment or public order.

This paper has shown that the type of online discussion group genre (i.e. the platform) can have a significant effect on the types of contribution made to them. The paper proposes a scale for predicting the types of contributions a specific troller is likely to post called the 'This Is Why We can't Have Nice Things Scale' (TIWWCHNT-20). Putting the two together the paper has shown how those who control online communities, whom are called sysops (i.e. systems operators), can attract the types of poster they want – whether they have a negative attitude about politics and politics, or whether they want positive and constructive debate.

The paper discussed the different types of post that can be made to an online community and the types of user that are more likely to post that type of message. This can help sysops manage the types of posts they want to encourage members to post while assisting them in ensuring the types of users who are unwelcome in the community can be identified and blocked from access.

ACKNOWLEDGMENT

The author would like to anowledge all those that provided advice and guidance on this paper, in particular Hugh Preston who supervised the factor analysis component of this study, which formed part of the MScEcon in Information Systems at Aberystwyth University (Bishop, 2011b). The author would also like to aknowlege the contributions of (Couldry et al., 2005), who collected the data and made it available for analysis.

REFERENCES

Agnew, J. A. (2014). *From political methodology to geographical social theory? A critical review of-electoral geography, 1960-87*. Developments in Electoral Geography.

Andersen, K. (2002). *Political parties and civil society: Learning from the american case. Democratic Institution Performance: Research and Policy Perspectives* (pp. 15–26). Academic Press.

Barber, B. R. (2003). *Strong democracy: Participatory politics for a new age*. Univ of California Press.

Bishop, J. (2007a). Ecological cognition: A new dynamic for human-computer interaction. In B. Wallace, A. Ross, J. Davies & T. Anderson (Eds.), The mind, the body and the world: Psychology after cognitivism (pp. 327-345). Exeter, UK: Imprint Academic.

Bishop, J. (2007b). Increasing participation in online communities: A framework for human–computer interaction. *Computers in Human Behavior*, *23*(4), 1881–1893. doi:10.1016/j.chb.2005.11.004

Bishop, J. (2008). Increasing capital revenue in social networking communities: Building social and economic relationships through avatars and characters. In C. Romm-Livermore & K. Setzekorn (Eds.), *Social networking communities and eDating services: Concepts and implications* (pp. 60–77). Hershey, PA: IGI Global.

Bishop, J. (2009). Increasing membership in online communities: The five principles of managing virtual club economies.*Proceedings of the 3rd International Conference on Internet Technologies and Applications - ITA09*. Glyndwr University.

Bishop, J. (2010). Increasing the economic sustainability of online communities: An empirical investigation. In M. F. Hindsworth & T. B. Lang (Eds.), *Community participation and empowerment* (p. 349). New York, NY: Nova Science Publishers.

Bishop, J. (2011a). All's WELL that ends WELL: A comparative analysis of the constitutional and administrative frameworks of cyberspace and the united kingdom. In A. Dudley-Sponaugle & J. Braman (Eds.), *Investigating cyber law and cyber ethics: Issues, impacts and practices*. Hershey, PA: IGI Global.

Bishop, J. (2011b). *The equatrics of intergenerational knowledge transformation in techno-cultures: Towards a model for enhancing information management in virtual worlds. Unpublished MScEcon*. Aberystwyth, UK: Aberystwyth University.

Bishop, J. (2011c). Transforming lurkers into posters: The role of the participation continuum.*The Fourth International Conference on Internet Technologies and Applications (ITA'11)*.

Bishop, J. (2012a). Lessons from the emotivate project for increasing take-up of big society and responsible capitalism initiatives. In P. M. Pumilia-Gnarini, E. Favaron, E. Pacetti, J. Bishop, & L. Guerra (Eds.), *Didactic strategies and technologies for education: Incorporating advancements* (pp. 208–217). Hershey, PA: IGI Global. doi:10.4018/978-1-4666-2122-0.ch019

Bishop, J. (2012b). Scope and limitations in the government of wales act 2006 for tackling internet abuses in the form of Flame trolling. *Statute Law Review*, *33*(2), 207–216. doi:10.1093/slr/hms016

Bishop, J. (2012c). Taming the chatroom bob: The role of brain-computer interfaces that manipulate prefrontal cortex optimization for increasing participation of victims of traumatic sex and other abuse online.*Proceedings of the 13th International Conference on Bioinformatics and Computational Biology (BIOCOMP'12).*

Bishop, J. (2013a). The effect of deindividuation of the internet troller on criminal procedure implementation: An interview with a hater. *International Journal of Cyber Criminology*, *7*(1), 28–48.

Bishop, J. (2013b). Increasing capital revenue in social networking communities: Building social and economic relationships through avatars and characters. In J. Bishop (Ed.), *Examining the concepts, issues, and implications of internet trolling* (pp. 44–61). Hershey, PA: IGI Global. doi:10.4018/978-1-4666-2803-8.ch005

Bishop, J. (2013c). The psychology of trolling and lurking: The role of defriending and gamification for increasing participation in online communities using seductive narratives. In J. Bishop (Ed.), *Examining the concepts, issues and implications of internet trolling* (pp. 106–123). Hershey, PA: IGI Global. doi:10.4018/978-1-4666-2803-8.ch009

Bishop, J. (2014a). Digital teens and the antisocial network: Prevalence of troublesome online youth groups and internet trolling in great Britain. *International Journal of E-Politics*, *5*(3), 1–15. doi:10.4018/ijep.2014070101

Bishop, J. (2014b). Representations of trolls in mass media communication: A review of media-texts and moral panics relating to internet trolling. *International Journal of Web Based Communities*, *10*(1), 7–24. doi:10.1504/IJWBC.2014.058384

Bolin, G., & Westlund, O. (2008). Mobile generations: The role of mobile technology in the shaping of swedish media generations. *International Journal of Communication*, *3*, 17.

Bryde, D., & Pelie, D. (2006). The impact of project management practices and project sponsorship on project performance. In M. Khosrow-Pour (Ed.), *Emerging trends and challenges in information technology management* (pp. 122–126). Hershey, PA: IGI Global.

Campbell, J., Fletcher, G., & Greenhill, A. (2009). Conflict and identity shape shifting in an online financial community. *Information Systems Journal*, *19*(5), 461–478. doi:10.1111/j.1365-2575.2008.00301.x

Chapman, R. G., & Palda, K. S. (1983). Electoral turnout in rational voting and consumption perspectives. *The Journal of Consumer Research*, *9*(4), 337–346. doi:10.1086/208928

Couldry, N., Markham, T., & Livingstone, S. (2005). *Media consumption and the future of public connection*. London, UK: London School of Economics and Political Science.

Edmonds, G., & Gray, D. (2002). Internet dictionary. London: Dorling Kindersley Limited.

Field, A. (2005). Discovering statistics using SPSS (introducing statistical methods series) (2nd ed.). Sage Publications Ltd.

Goldring, E. B., & Shapira, R. (1993). Choice, empowerment, and involvement: What satisfies parents? *Educational Evaluation and Policy Analysis, 15*(4), 396–409. doi:10.3102/01623737015004396

Grikscheit, G. M., Cash, H. C., & Young, C. E. (1993). *The handbook of selling: Psychological, managerial, and marketing dynamics*. John Wiley & Sons.

Hair, J. F., Black, W. C., Babin, B. J., Anderson, R. E., & Tathan, R. L. (2006). *Multivariate data analysis*. Upper Saddle River, NJ: Pearson Prentice Hall.

Hankin, H. (2005). *The new workforce: Five sweeping trends that will shape your company's future*. AMACOM Div American Mgmt Assn.

Hardaker, C. (2013). Uh.... not to be nitpicky, but... the past tense of drag is dragged, not drug.": An overview of trolling strategies. *Journal of Language Aggression and Conflict, 1*(1), 57–85. doi:10.1075/jlac.1.1.04har

Innes, S., & Rendall, J. (2006). Women, gender and politics. *Gender in Scottish History Since, 1700*, 43–83.

Jansen, E. (Ed.). (2002). *NetLingo: The internet dictionary*. Ojai, CA: Netlingo Inc.

Jansen, E., & James, V. (Eds.). (1995). *NetLingo: The internet dictionary*. Ojai, CA: Netlingo Inc.

Kim, A. J. (2000). *Community building on the web: Secret strategies for successful online communities*. Berkeley, CA: Peachpit Press.

Mantovani, G. (1996a). *New communication environments: From everyday to virtual*. London: Taylor & Francis.

Mantovani, G. (1996b). Social context in HCI: A new framework for mental models, cooperation, and communication. *Cognitive Science, 20*(2), 237–269. doi:10.1207/s15516709cog2002_3

Nonnecke, B., & Preece, J. (2000). Lurker demographics: Counting the silent. In *Proceedings of the SIGCHI Conference on Human Factors in Computing Systems,* (pp. 73-80). doi:10.1145/332040.332409

Norton, B. (1999). Ecology and opportunity: Intergenerational equity and sustainable options. *Fairness and Futurity: Essays on Environmental Sustainability and Social Justice,* 118-150.

Polkinghorne, J. C. (2000). *Faith, science, and understanding*. Yale University Press.

Powazek, D. M. (2002). *Design for community: The art of connecting real people in virtual places*. Upper Saddle River, NJ: New Riders.

Preece, J. (2000). *Online communities: Designing usability, supporting sociability*. Chichester, UK: John Wiley & Sons.

Preece, J., Nonnecke, B., & Andrews, D. (2004). The top 5 reasons for lurking: Improving community experiences for everyone. *Computers in Human Behavior*, *2*(1), 42.

Solo, A. M. G., & Bishop, J. (2011). *The new field of network politics*. Paper presented at the 2011 International Conference on E-Learning, E-Business, Enterprise Information Systems & E-Government (EEE'11), Las Vegas, NV.

Starmer, K. (2013). *Guidelines on prosecuting cases involving communications sent via social media*. London: Crown Prosecution Service.

Tsfati, Y., & Cappella, J. N. (2005). Why do people watch news they do not trust? the need for cognition as a moderator in the association between news media skepticism and exposure. *Media Psychology*, *7*(3), 251–271. doi:10.1207/S1532785XMEP0703_2

Van Dijk, J. A. G. M. (1999). *The network society: Social aspects of new media* (1st ed.). London: Sage Publications Ltd.

Van Dijk, J. A. G. M. (2005). *The network society: Social aspects of new media* (2nd ed.). London: Sage Publications Ltd.

Wallace, P. M. (1999). *The psychology of the internet*. Cambridge, UK: Cambridge University Press. doi:10.1017/CBO9780511581670

Walter, T., Hourizi, R., Moncur, W., & Pitsillides, S. (2011). Does the internet change how we die and mourn? an overview and analysis. *Omega*, *64*(4), 275–302. doi:10.2190/OM.64.4.a PMID:22530294

Young, M. L., & Levine, J. R. (2000). *Poor richard's building online communities: Create a web community for your business, club, association, or family*. Top Floor Pub.

Yu, H., & Miller, P. (2005). Leadership style: The X generation and baby boomers compared in different cultural contexts. *Leadership and Organization Development Journal*, *26*(1), 35–50. doi:10.1108/01437730510575570

KEY TERMS AND DEFINITIONS

Anonymous: An association of Internet users who take part in 'hacktivism' and often forms of Internet trolling.

Cyberbullying: Bullying that is conducted via the Internet or other public communications network.

E-Politics: Politics enabled via electronic means.

Internet Trolling: The posting of messages on the Internet that are either provocative or offensive.

Troll: A person that does Internet trolling, usually to create gross offence or to act in a way that is indecent, obscene, menacing or threatening. Traditionally it referred to someone who posted provactive messages for humorous effect.

Troller: A person who posts messages to the Internet in order to provoke a response. Anyone who posts a message with the intention of others responding to it is a troller.

APPENDIX: SCALE AND SCORING METHOD

The scale associated with each item is a Likert scale were 1 is "Never Characteristic," 2 is "Rarely Characteristic," 3 is "Sometimes Characteristic," 4 is "Often Characteristic," and 5 is "Always Characteristic." To give the TIWYCHNT-20 score, each value is then added up and the total number of items, namely 20, is then deducted from that number to produce the score. In the case of items 1 to 7, 13 to 15 and 20 the 5-point Likert scale is inverted. The mix in actual item values should avoid perceptions that the scale is biased in the eyes of the participant. The items from 1 to 20 are as follows:

1. You know where to go to find out information that you need.
2. Sometimes you feel strongly about an issue, but don't know what to do about it.
3. It's a regular part of your day to catch up with the news.
4. You follow the news to understand what's going on in the world.
5. You follow the news to know what other people are talking about.
6. It's your duty to keep up with what's going on in the world.
7. You have a pretty good understanding of the main issues facing our country.
8. You often feel that there's too much media, so you need to switch off.
9. There's no point in watching the news, because it deals with things you can do nothing about.
10. It doesn't really matter which party is in power, in the end things go on pretty much the same.
11. People like us have no say in what the government does.
12. Sometimes politics seems so complicated that you can't really understand what's going on.
13. People at work would expect you to know what's going on in the world.
14. Your friends would expect you to know what's going on in the world.
15. You trust the government to do what is right.
16. You trust politicians to deal with the things that matter.
17. You trust politicians to tell the truth.
18. You can affect things by getting involved in issues you care about.
19. You feel that you can influence decisions in your area.
20. Politics has little connection with your life.

Chapter 11
Do Campaigns "Go Negative" on Twitter?

Marija Bekafigo
Northern Arizona University, USA

Allison Clark Pingley
University of South Carolina Upstate, USA

ABSTRACT

The use of negative ads in traditional election campaigns has been well-documented, but we know little about the use of Twitter to "go negative." We content analyze candidate tweets from four different gubernatorial elections in 2011 to understand how candidates are using Twitter. We coded 849 tweets to explain the determinants of "going negative" on Twitter. Our results show that while tweets are overwhelmingly positive, candidates go negative by tweeting about policy. We believe this supports the innovation hypothesis and argue that Twitter is a conducive social media forum for policy-based messages due to its highly partisan nature. However, other determinants of negative campaigning such as competitiveness of the race and campaign funding were consistent with the normalization hypothesis. Our mixed results are consistent with other studies on social media and suggest there is still much to be learned from this tool.

INTRODUCTION

It is undisputed that the Internet has opened many new avenues for candidates and parties to reach voters (Jungherr, 2016). Even though social media sites such as Facebook and Twitter are still relatively new, candidates and parties quickly added the virtually free communication tools to their repertoire to wage campaigns online. As with any new communication tool, an important question to ask is whether campaigns are using the Internet in a novel way or if Internet campaigns are being conducted in the same manner as traditional ones (Druckman, Kifer, & Parkin, 2010; Dulio, Goff, & Thurber, 1999; Johnson, Braima, & Sothirajah, 1999; Xenos & Foot, 2005)? This chapter will examine how candidates are using Twitter, and specifically whether they use it to "go negative."

The normalization thesis (Bimber & Davis, 2003; Margolis & Resnick, 2000) suggests that candidates are simply using social media to amplify messages already being sent through traditional avenues, whereas

DOI: 10.4018/978-1-5225-1862-4.ch011

the innovation thesis (Foot & Schneider, 2002; Johnson et al., 1999) proposes that online messages and campaigns are unique. Internet campaigns are not simply replications of traditional campaigns and therefore scholars must examine how politics are being played out online. We contribute to this puzzle by examining messages on Twitter to determine if campaigns go negative.

Twitter was founded in 2006 and Barack Obama was the first presidential candidate to utilize it for campaign purposes in 2008. By 2016, all the presidential candidates and the majority of lower-level candidates were also campaigning on Twitter. While there is little doubt that the new medium has changed the face of campaigns and challenged the dominance of television (Johnson et al., 1999), we still are trying to understand how and why. Internet campaigns contain higher quality and quantity of information and have an interactive component not possible on television (Corrado & Firestone, 1996), but is the message the same?

This chapter seeks to understand one essential component of the Internet campaign—the message. In particular, we examine campaign rhetoric on Twitter and ask: do candidates go negative? By content analyzing over 800 tweets from four gubernatorial races during the 2011 election cycle, we find competitive races and campaign funds to be determinants of negative campaign messages on Twitter. These findings are in line with the normalization hypothesis and what we would expect to find given the traditional campaign literature. However, we also find candidates go negative by tweeting about policy. We believe this supports the innovation hypothesis and argue that Twitter is a more conducive forum for policy-based messages than television due to its partisan nature (Bekafigo and McBride 2013; Parmalee and Bichard 2012).

This chapter proceeds as follows: First, we examine the traditional media literature on negative campaigns as a baseline for our expectations of the types of messages gubernatorial candidates might be posting on Twitter. Next, we examine the literature on campaigns online and in social media. We position ourselves on the side of the innovation hypothesis and explain why campaigns on Twitter should be different than traditional ones. We then discuss our data, methods, and proposed hypotheses in the third section. Finally, we reveal the determinants of going negative on Twitter. This research is significant because it contributes to the innovation/normalization theory by demonstrating candidates' use of negative campaign messages on Twitter.

Negative Campaigns on Traditional Media

The longest lasting appeals made by candidates are negative (Ansolabehere & Iyengar, 1995; Damore, 2002; Jamieson, 1992; Jerit, 2004; Kaid & Johnston, 1991). Even though most voters claim to dislike negative messages, they are thought to be effective (Martin, 2004). Studies of political messaging have shown that candidates use negative ads because they are memorable and stimulate interest in campaigns (Ansolabehere & Iyengar, 1995; Jamieson, 1992; Jerit, 2004; Kaid & Johnston, 1991; Lau, Sigelman, & Rovner, 2007; Martin, 2004). Following a similar rationale, candidates will post negative tweets on Twitter in order to gain votes.

In traditional campaigns, negative information can be "arousing and attention grabbing" to potential voters (Martin, 2004). Negative campaign messages tend to focus on issues, particularly those that are salient and thought to be "owned" by the opposition party (Damore, 2002; Martin, 2004; Skaperdas & Grofman, 1995). Aside from policy positions, negative messages will also often target candidate's character or personality—for example traits such as competence or trustworthiness (Skaperdas & Grofman, 1995). Based on this literature, tweets are analyzed for negativity, and the mentions of policies and/or personal attributes.

Indeed, most scholarship has focused on the tone of campaign messages as an independent variable seeking to explain its effects on turnout (Gross & Johnson, 2016). Yet, if the goal of campaigns is to garner more votes then we must know if some candidates are more likely to go negative than others. For instance, incumbents are less likely than challengers to go negative mainly because they already have an established voting base (Skaperdas & Grofman, 1995). This encourages incumbents, who are also often frontrunners, to take a more positive approach to campaigning, which is thought to appeal more to undecided voters (Damore, 2002; Skaperdas & Grofman, 1995). However, challengers, who are often trailing in the polls, may go negative in an attempt to undercut the frontrunner's support (Damore, 2002). Competitiveness may also affect the message tone, with negative campaigns more likely to take place in close races (Martin, 2004). To account for these different factors that may affect negativity, we account for incumbency status in our model.

Based on the traditional campaigning literature, we expect candidates will use Twitter to go negative because it is virtually free and has been shown to be an effective technique in traditional campaigns. We also expect challengers to send more negative messages than incumbents, competitive races to be more negative, and for messages to focus on issues and candidate characteristics. Since these expectations are based on traditional campaigns, any findings to support them would also support the normalization hypothesis. However, should we expect candidates to pursue similar strategies on the Internet as they do when utilizing traditional media? Next, we consider the intersection between politics and the Internet to fully inform our hypotheses.

Negative Campaigns on New Media

There is some evidence that candidate discourse present on the Internet reflects the offline political landscape (Druckman et al., 2010; Hong & Nadler, 2012; Tumasjan, Sprenger, Sander, & Welpe, 2010). This is consistent with the normalization hypothesis, which suggests that candidates use the Internet to amplify messages they are already sending through more traditional media (Cornfield, 2004; Foot & Schneider, 2002; Margolis & Resnick, 2000; Ramos-Serrano, Gomez, & Pineda, 2016).

In contrast, the innovation hypothesis suggests that the medium makes a difference and candidates may pursue a more negative strategy online (Schweitzer, 2008). Since voters are more likely to access information consistent with the beliefs they already hold (Hindman, 2005), then visitors to candidates' websites are most likely already supporters. The same rationale could apply to Twitter, with users following candidates who share similar beliefs to their own. If this is the case, then users are less likely to be turned off by negative messages.

Most of what we know about negative (and positive) campaigns on new media comes from an examination of websites. Initially, candidates only posted positive information on their websites (Bimber & Davis, 2003; Corrado & Firestone, 1996; Klotz, 1998; West, 2010). In 2000, candidates' websites blended positive and negative information. However, by 2004, candidates were using their websites to promote themselves positively while negatively attacking their opponent (West, 2010). One of the most apparent changes was the increase in attack ads posted on the candidate's websites. Both George W. Bush and John Kerry "used the Internet to publicize hard-hitting attacks on the opposition" (West, 2010).

Few have examined Twitter campaign messages for their tone. Negative tweets have been shown to be effective mobilization tools for parties (Ceron & d'Adda, 2015). Others have found that congressional and presidential candidates are using Twitter to campaign negatively (Gainous & Wagner, 2014; Evans & Clark 2016; Gross & Johnson, 2016).

Twitter, as a campaign tool, offers candidates several potential advantages which may lend itself more readily to the innovation hypothesis. One advantage is that candidates can use Twitter to speak to voters in a more conversational manner, as opposed to the more formal tone of traditional media (Kruikemeier, 2014; Price, 2012). This may encourage candidates to send different messages than they would through more traditional mediums such as television.

Aside from sending different messages, Twitter may also be a good way for candidates to try out messages (Price, 2012). Depending on how users respond to a tweet – or do not respond at all – candidates can tweak the message to elicit a more positive or negative response before sending it out to a larger audience. Therefore, candidates would not be using Twitter simply to amplify messages as suggested by the normalization hypothesis.

This highlights a third advantage of using Twitter – candidates are able to directly communicate with potential voters without going through the traditional media (Gainous & Wagner, 2014). For example, after Obama's inauguration in 2008, Republicans utilized Twitter a lot as an alternative source of media (Parmalee & Bichard, 2012). Others, too, have found that Republicans have used Twitter to their advantage (Gainous & Wagner, 2014). That being said, even though candidates are able to dictate the initial message sent, they lose most control over it after it is tweeted (Price, 2012). Similar to the effects of traditional media, a message is likely to get distorted the more it is discussed.

A final advantage of Twitter is that it allows candidates to emit information faster than other forms of social and traditional media (Elmer, 2013; Price, 2012; Vergeer, Hermans, & Sams, 2013). Instead of having to compose a press release or response ad when attacked by the opposition, candidates can respond almost instantly. The downside is that the "real time" format of Twitter also means that news gets buried almost as quickly as it is posted. Unless a message is retweeted within the first hour that it is posted, it is unlikely that anyone will see the message (Elmer, 2013). However, messages that are retweeted may reach a large audience. For example in during summer 2010, Senator Jim DeMint had about 38,000 twitter followers, but his tweets were reaching audiences of about 100,000 because of retweeting (Parmalee & Bichard, 2012). The advantages Twitter offers candidates as a campaign tool makes it more likely they would use it to send new messages (innovation hypothesis) instead of simply using it to amplify messages they are already sending using traditional media (normalization hypothesis).

DATA AND METHODS

We use content analysis of campaign messages on the new medium, Twitter, to take up the age-old question of whether candidates go negative. This research also makes a contribution to the normalization/innovation debate by finding that some campaign messages adhere to traditional messaging while others seem to be innovative, thus enhancing our knowledge of old and new campaign tools, alike. It also begins to close the gap in the existing literature on the use of campaign messages as tools on a new medium.

Our primary research questions are: do gubernatorial candidates go negative on Twitter and what factors are determinants of negativity? From these two primary research questions come several sub-research questions: what do negative campaigns look like on Twitter? Are they similar to negativity used in traditional campaigns, such as television, which tend to focus on policies and personal traits? A second sub-research question is do the same factors that lead candidates to go negative using traditional methods hold true on Twitter? In other words, will there be more negativity in competitive races and by challengers, or will different patterns emerge? In order to answer our questions, we conducted content analysis on 849 tweets collected from four gubernatorial races held in 2011 during the thirty days prior to the election.

Twitter was created in 2006 with the intent of users posting primarily status updates called "tweets" in 140 characters or less. It has since evolved into a communications tool for campaigns, politicians, parties, protests, and voters (Larsson & Moe, 2011; Price, 2012; Vergeer et al., 2013). Though most research has examined candidate use of Twitter at the national level, we have no reason to expect gubernatorial candidates would use Twitter differently since scholars have found that gubernatorial elections are tied to presidential politics (Carsey, 2001; Jewell & Olson, 1988). Additionally, a main factor affecting gubernatorial electoral behavior is incumbency (Carsey, 2001; Erikson, Wright, & McIver, 1993; Jewell & Olson, 1988). Therefore, it is expected that gubernatorial candidates would take similar approaches to campaigning.

Each tweet was coded for the overall tone as being positive or negative which is in line with other studies (Druckman et al., 2010). A negative tweet focused on the opponent, whereas a positive tweet centered on the candidate making it (Damore, 2002). Additionally, a tweet was considered negative if it attacked an opponent's issues, personality, or party (Skaperdas & Grofman, 1995). Therefore, a tweet was coded negative if it indicated disapproval of a specific policy, a candidate's opponent, or discussed a negative action. A tweet was considered positive if it focused on the candidate making it, or was a statement of fact. No neutral category was used, so anything non-negative was coded positive. We used logit analysis to model determinants of negative tweeting because our dependent variable is dichotomous (positive=0, negative=1).

Our independent variables are typical of models seeking to explain variations in negative campaigning and are as follows:

- **Policy Tweet, Character Trait, and Call to Action Tweets:** Each tweet was coded for the type of appeal it was making—policy mentions, character traits, and call to action. In a review of the literature, these were noted as the most typical types of messages sent by candidates (Jungherr, 2016), but others did not differentiate between positive and negative tone. Tweets were multiply-coded such that each tweet could contain all three:
    - Policy mentions were typically related to salient issues in the election. For example, Phil Bryant, Mississippi, tweeted, "Each year we struggle to try and fund Medicaid. I propose 1,000 new physicians by 2025 to better serve our state. -PB #msgovdebate #im4phil."
    - Character traits were coded for the mention of a personality/character issue of the candidate posting the tweet, or his opponent. For example, tweets discussing qualities such as leadership, experience, etc., would be considered character traits. For example, Kentucky challenger David Williams tweeted, "@GovSteveBeshear supports Obama for reelection, and supported him in '08. How can he be trusted to stand up for coal? #deepthoughts #kygov." Policy and character trait tweets could be either positive or negative.
    - A third dummy variable was whether each tweet contained a call to action (Pole & Xenos, 2011).

      A call to action was simply asking Twitter users, and likely voters, to do something. For example, registering to vote, watching a debate, donating money, volunteering time, etc. If a tweet contained a call to action, then it was also recorded what that specific action was. Steven

Beshear reminded tweeters to vote, "Only a few hours left! Go vote! #GOTV #cleansweep #kyelect." We include descriptive statistics for this variable below but do not include it in the model because there was no variation. All the call to action tweets were positive tweets.

- **Party ID** *:* We coded Party ID as Democrats=0, Republicans=1. Based on previous studies, there is no reason to expect a difference between the tweeting tones of Democrats and Republicans. For example, others have found congressional Democrats tend to "go negative" on their websites (Druckman et al., 2010), but they argue there was not a reason for the result. Another study found congressional Republicans to tweet more negatively than Democrats (Gainous & Wagner, 2014), another showed Republican governors' tweets were more cohesive than Democratic governors (Yang, Chen, Maity, & Ferrara, 2016), and still another found no party differences (Evans & Clark, 2016). Under different context, we might argue that the out-party has reason to tweet more negatively, but we have no reasons to expect any differences among our sample (Karpf, 2012).
- **Incumbent**: We included a dummy variable for candidate status (0=non-incumbent, 1=incumbent) such that we expect challengers to post more negative tweets due to the low cost. One factor that can affect a candidate's success using social media is length of use – the longer a candidate has been a user, the more contacts he or she is likely to have, and therefore the more people they are likely to reach with their messages (Straus et al., 2016). Therefore, incumbents are likely to be advantaged. For example, during the 2012 election Barack Obama had an online incumbency advantage over Mitt Romney (Price, 2012). Since Obama had been utilizing social media longer, he had more followers so more potential voters received his messages. Therefore, incumbents are likely to benefit more from free media than challengers (Jerit, 2004).
    - In looking at which candidates are most apt to utilize Twitter, it is hypothesized that challengers will use it more than incumbents. Even though some literature indicates that candidates who have been using Twitter longer may be more successful (Price, 2012), other research has shown that Twitter often serves as an alternative media source when traditional media does not provide as much coverage (Parmalee & Bichard, 2012). Still others have found that challengers utilize Twitter more often than incumbents (Evans et al., 2014). Therefore, in their effort to gain more press, Twitter would be a cost effective means of campaigning for challengers.
- **Competitive Race:** We also control for the competitiveness of the race using 60% vote share as the cutoff. As the race becomes more competitive we expect tweets to be more negative than positive in tone (Gross & Johnson, 2016).

RESULTS

Of the 849 tweets, the vast majority – 87.5 percent – were positive. Many of the positive tweets were simple statements of fact – where the candidate would be appearing that day, information about an upcoming debate, and other campaign/election activity (Evans et al., 2014). About 22.6 percent of positive tweets mentioned a policy. For example, a large percentage of the tweets mentioned education. Even fewer of the positive tweets – just 8.5 percent – mentioned a character trait. These tended to focus on the candidate's leadership skills, experience, and abilities to perform well as a governor.

The most common content of positive tweets was a call to action. 28.6 percent of all positive tweets asked followers to do something. Many simply asked that followers tune into a debate or read the latest

Table 1. Various types of Tweets

Positive	87.5%
Negative	12.5%
Policy	29.4%
Character Traits	9.1%
Calls to Action	25.1%

Table 2. Positive and negative Tweets

	Positive Tweets	Negative Tweets
Calls to Action	28.6%	0%
Character Traits	8.5%	13.2%
Policy	22.6%	78.3%

campaign news story (usually including a link to the story). Others asked voters to do something more such as volunteer or donate money. The most common request – which approximately 18.3 percent of positive tweets mentioned – was to register to vote and/or show up to vote on Election Day. One of the key ways candidates used Twitter was to mobilize voters and provide them with Election Day information.

Even though there were more positive tweets, the negative tweets were more revealing. For one, the messages sent were much different. Not surprisingly, none of the negative tweets included a call to action. However, the vast majority – 76.6 percent – mentioned a policy (p=.000). Our finding that more tweets mentioned policies than characteristics is consistent with traditional literature suggesting that gubernatorial campaigns are more policy-oriented (Beyle, 1990; Carsey, 2001; Kone & Winters, 1993). Additionally, it has been found that gubernatorial candidates are strategically structuring their campaigns to accommodate their policy strengths (Carsey, 2001) which our study also confirms. Others have shown that policy oriented tweets are rare (Graham et al., 2013).

There was no systematic relationship indicated between negative tweets and character trait mentions (p=.113). This is not surprising considering that only 13.1 percent of negative tweets mentioned a character trait, however, it does indicate that candidates were more likely to attack their opponents based on their issue positions. Therefore, clear differences existed in the content of positive and negative tweets, with positive tweets focusing more on calls to action and negative tweets more on policy positions.

Aside from tweets differing in terms of content, there was an even larger difference in regards to who was sending the messages. Challengers were much more apt to tweet than incumbents (Evans et al., 2014, Gilmore 2012), with only 11 percent of tweets coming from incumbents. Incumbent governor of West Virginia, Earl Ray Tomblin, only posted one tweet during the election. In two of the other races, there were also noticeable differences. While the incumbent governor of Louisiana, Bobby Jindal, posted 33 tweets, his opponent Tara Hollis posted 234. In the Kentucky race, the incumbent governor Steven Beshear posted 60 tweets compared to his opponent David Williams' 188 tweets. The only exception was the Mississippi gubernatorial race in which Phil Bryant posted 234 tweets and Johnny Dupree posted 72 tweets, however, it was an open seat election so neither candidate was the incumbent.

Non-incumbents and losing candidates were also more likely to post negative tweets. In fact, losing candidates made 91.5 percent of the negative tweets. The difference is just as pronounced when looking at negative tweets by incumbents versus non-incumbents – only one negative tweet was posted by an incumbent candidate.

Logit Results

We estimate the model for our dichotomous dependent variable, negative tweets (0=positive, 1=negative) using logit regression. The model's unit of analysis is the individual tweet. We coded 849 tweets sent by

Table 3. Tweets by candidate

State	Candidate	Total Tweets
Kentucky	Steven Beshear*	60
	David William	188
Louisiana	Bobby Jindal*	33
	Tara Hollis	235
Mississippi	Phil Bryant	234
	Johnny DuPree	72
West Virginia	Bill Maloney	25
	Earl Ray Tomblin*	1

* Indicates an Incumbent Candidate

Table 4. Positive and negative Tweets for incumbency status and electoral success

	Positive Tweets	Negative Tweets
Incumbent	98.9%	1.1%
Non-Incumbent	86.1%	13.9%
Winners	97.3%	2.7%
Losers	81.3%	18.7%

eight gubernatorial candidates 30 days before the 2011 elections. Some of the results are inconsistent with the normalization hypothesis and suggest candidates may be using Twitter as an innovative campaign tool.

We present the determinants of going negative on Twitter in Table 5 and interpret using the odds ratio. Two variables are significant and consistent with the normalization hypothesis—the competitiveness of the race and fundraising. The odds of a tweet being negative were .02 times higher in competitive races. Candidates with more campaign funds were also more likely to go negative. Others, too, have found that negative tones increase in tight races both in television and on the web (Druckman et al., 2010; Lau & Pomper, 2004; Lau & Pomper, 2001; Martin, 2004).

Table 5. Determinants of negative Tweets (logit)

Independent Variables	Odds Ratio
Incumbent	0.524 (0.617)
Competition	0.0225* (0.0443)
Party	274.4* (684.4)
Policy Tweet	14.37*** (3.878)
Character trait Tweet	2.375* (0.923)
Campaign Funds/1000	0.998** (0.000556)
n=849	
Pseudo R-square 0.321	

Standard errors in parentheses.
*p<0.05 **p<0.01 ***p<0.001

CONCLUSION

On the side of the innovation hypothesis, the type of appeal contained in the tweet suggests that a different type of campaign may be waged on Twitter. First, tweets with both character traits and policy mentions are more likely to be negative. Tweets that contained a character trait were two times more likely to have a negative tone. The odds of a policy tweet being negative are 14 times more likely than a policy tweet being positive and the effect is 7 times larger on a policy tweet than a character trait tweet. Of the three types of tweets we coded for the largest percent were policy tweets (29.4%). That is to say gubernatorial candidates mostly posted policy tweets and they tended to be negative.

This differs from traditional campaign messages in several ways. First, on Twitter candidates have more flexibility in terms of what they say. This is partly due to the "Stand By Your Ad" (SBYA) provision that was passed as part of the 2002 Bipartisan Campaign Reform Act. The SBYA provision states that candidates must claim responsibility for their ads, however, the Federal Elections Commission said that the SBYA provision did not apply to campaigns on the Internet (McCullagh, 2004). Therefore, candidates can take a more negative approach online without having to prove the claims they are making as they would in television ads.

A second major difference is that television campaign ads often focus on personal qualities instead of emphasizing a candidate's policy positions (Sanders, 2004; West, 2010). As one study points out, "… political ads find it easier to make appeals where the candidate is a hero (or the opponent is the villain), someone the viewer can relate to and like (or be put off by and dislike) than it is to present a defense of a detailed policy position" (Sanders, 2004, 4). Contrary to the strategy taken in many television ads, our study finds that candidates are more apt to focus on policies when using Twitter. Not only is this finding contrary to our knowledge about traditional television campaigns, but it is also consistent with our knowledge of Twitter and lends evidence to the innovation hypothesis.

Although Twitter is considered a "social" media site, it is not social in the traditional sense where you share pictures and life event stories with friends and family. Twitter allows candidates and politicians to interact with the public, but Twitter users are not the general voting population. This is key to understanding the importance of negative policy tweets being sent.

First, it suggests that candidates may understand who their audience on Twitter is. Others have shown that among Twitter users who are most likely to pay attention to candidates' tweets are strong partisans and likely political activists (Bekafigo & McBride, 2013). Thus candidates' tweets are likely to be seen by those who are already politically engaged and voting, whereas the target of television ads is the general voting population (Goldstein & Strach, 2003;). Moreover, candidates are less likely to make issue appeals than personal appeals on television because it is thought that the voters most concerned with candidates' positions are unlikely to be affected by political ads (Sanders, 2004). Our results demonstrate that gubernatorial candidates' are targeting a nuanced audience by making issue appeals on Twitter, therefore providing some support for the innovation hypothesis.

Second, if candidates' believe they are sending posts to already partisan supporters then it makes sense that they would send negative tweets because negative ads are more effective than positive appeals (Ansolabehere & Iyengar, 1995; Jamieson, 1992; Jerit, 2004; Kaid & Johnston, 1991). Finally, candidates sending policy related tweets is also consistent with our knowledge of political tweeters and may appeal to their policy wonk side (Bekafigo & McBride, 2013).

We also found that Republicans were more likely to send negative tweets. Although we did not expect to find differences between Republican and Democratic tweets, others, too have found differences between Republican and Democratic candidates (Gainous & Wagner, 2014; Yang, Chen, Maity, & Ferrara 2016). Republican candidates may be going negative on Twitter in order to circumvent traditional, if biased media, and control their own messages (Gainous & Wagner, 2014). Twitter is an ideal, and innovative, campaign medium for Republicans to send out a unified party message (Gainous & Wagner, 2014;Yang, Chen, Maity, & Ferrara 2016).

Finally, in traditional television campaigns challengers are more likely to go negative (Lau & Pomper, 2004), but that did not matter for our Twitter campaign. It may be that the cost is so low to tweet and the stakes are not presumed to be that high. Campaigns are still in the beginning stages of understanding the effects of Twitter.

DISCUSSION

How important has Twitter become in election campaigning? Few candidates today would be caught without using social media as a campaign tool to raise funds, garner support, and otherwise communicate with voters. Indeed, all of the gubernatorial candidates in 2012 and all the presidential candidates in 2016 used Twitter to campaign (Bekafigo & Pingley, 2016; Gross & Johnson, 2016). However, neither candidates nor scholars fully understand the implications or effects of campaigning via this new medium, which is likely the reason why our results, like others before us, are mixed (Jungherr, 2016). This is the first study to our knowledge examining negative campaign messages on Twitter by gubernatorial candidates. Therefore, the results are limited to these campaigns. Future research should focus on local and national elections as well as additional gubernatorial races to explain the determinants of negative campaigns on Twitter. Additionally, scholars and candidates alike will want to know if these messages are effective and for whom.

We found that candidates did "go negative" on Twitter, but the majority of tweets sent were positive. Of those positive messages, most called on voters to do something, such as vote or volunteer. Unfortunately, we have no way of knowing whether these calls to action worked. Did these tweets prompt Twitter users to vote or volunteer? Links have been found between online campaign activity and political engagement (Kruikemeier, 2014; Park & Perry, 2008; Wagner & Gainous, 2009), including on Twitter (Ceron & d'Adda, 2015). If positive tweets can have the same effect, they could potentially impact election outcomes.

We also found that gubernatorial candidates went negative on Twitter. In this sense, tried and true negative political campaign messages were sent out on new media. While candidates have adopted the new medium, they may not be embracing its possibilities altogether. On the other hand, we also found that negative messages were uniquely policy-oriented which suggests that candidates view Twitter in terms of targeting a specific audience.

Campaigns are likely at a crossroads between politics as usual and unusual (Xenos & Foot, 2005). On the one hand, some are continuing to use existing, if established, tools and techniques on the new medium even though little is known about their effectiveness. Others are using the new technology to try out new messages. The use of Twitter in elections definitely warrants more study, especially as candidates rely on social media more often to distribute campaign messages.

REFERENCES

Ansolabehere, S., & Iyengar, S. (1995). *Going Negative: How Political Advertising Shrinks and Polarizes the Electorate*. New York: Free Press.

Bekafigo, M. A., & McBride, A. (2013). Who Tweets about Politics? Political Participation of Twitter Users During the 2011 Gubernatorial Elections. *Social Science Computer Review*, *31*(5), 625–643. doi:10.1177/0894439313490405

Bekafigo, M.A. & Pingley A. (2016). *Political Participation on Twitter during the 2012 Gubernatorial Elections.* Unpublished.

Beyle, T. (1990). Costs of Gubernatorial Campaigns! 987-1988. *Comparative State Politics*, *11*(1), 28–33.

Bimber, B., & Davis, R. (2003). *Campaigning Online: The Internet in U.S. Elections*. New York: Oxford University Press.

Carsey, T. (2001). *Campaign Dynamics: The Race for Governor*. Ann Arbor, MI: University of Michigan Press.

Cornfield, M. (2004). *Politics Moves Online*. The Century Foundation.

Corrado, A., & Firestone, C. (1996). *Elections in Cyberspace: Toward a New Era in American Politics*. Washington, DC: The Aspen Institute.

Damore, D. (2002). Candidate Strategy and the Decision to go Negative. *Political Research Quarterly*, *55*(3), 669–686. doi:10.1177/106591290205500309

Druckman, J. N., Kifer, M. J., & Parkin, M. (2010). Timeless Strategy Meets New Medium: Going Negative on Congressional Campaign Web Sites 20022006. *Political Communication*, *27*(1), 88–103. doi:10.1080/10584600903502607

Dulio, D. A., Goff, D. L., & Thurber, J. A. (1999). Untangled Web: Internet Use during the 1998 Election. *PS: Political Science and Politics*, *32*(1), 53–59.

Elmer, G. (2013). Live Research: Twittering an Election Debate. *New Media & Society*, *15*(1), 18–30. doi:10.1177/1461444812457328

Erikson, R. S., Wright, G. C., & McIver, J. P. (1993). Statehouse Democracy: Public Opinion and Policy in the American States. New York: Cambridge.

Evans, H. K., & Clark, J. H. (2016). You Tweet Like a Girl! How Female Candidates Campaign on Twitter. *American Politics Research*, *44*(2), 326–352. doi:10.1177/1532673X15597747

Evans, H. K., Cordova, V., & Sipole, S. (2014). Twitter style: An analysis of how house candidates used Twitter in their 2012 campaigns. *PS: Political Science & Politics*, *47*(2), 454–462.

Foot, K. A., & Schneider, S. M. (2002). Online Action in Campaign 2000: An Exploratory Analysis of the U. S. Political Web Sphere. *Journal of Broadcasting & Electronic Media*, *45*(2), 222–244. doi:10.1207/s15506878jobem4602_4

Gainous, J., & Wagner, K. M. (2014). *Tweeting to Power: The Social Media Revolution in American Politics*. New York: Oxford University Press.

Gilmore, J. (2012). Ditching the pack: Digital media in the 2010 Brazilian congressional campaigns. *New Media & Society*, *14*(4), 617–633. doi:10.1177/1461444811422429

Goldstein, K. M., & Strach, P. (2003). *The Medium and the Message*. Upper Saddle River, NJ: Pearson.

Graham, T., Broersma, M., Hazelhoff, K., & vant Haar, G. (2013). Between broadcasting political messages and interacting with voters: The use of Twitter during the 2010 UK general election campaign. *Information Communication and Society*, *16*(5), 692–716. doi:10.1080/1369118X.2013.785581

Gross, J. H., & Johnson, K. (2016). Strafing, Spats, and Skirmishes: Social Dynamics of Negative Campaigning on Twitter. 9th Annual Political Networks Workshops & Conference. St. Louis, MO: Washington University. Retrieved from http://papers.ssrn.com/sol3/papers.cfm?abstract_id=2799252

Hindman, M. (2005). The Real Lessons of Howard Dean: Reflections of the First Digital Campaign. *Perspectives on Politics*, *3*(1), 121–128. doi:10.1017/S1537592705050115

Hong, S., & Nadler, D. (2012). Which Candidates do the Public Discourse Online in an Election Campaign? The use of Social Media by 2012 Presidential Candidates and its Impact on Candidate Salience. *Government Information Quarterly*, *29*(4), 455–461. doi:10.1016/j.giq.2012.06.004

Jamieson, K. H. (1992). *Dirty Politics: Deception, Distration, and Democracy*. New York: Oxford University Press.

Jerit, J. (2004). Survival of the Fittest: Rhetoric During the Course of an Election Campaign. *Political Psychology*, *25*(4), 563–575. doi:10.1111/j.1467-9221.2004.00387.x

Jewell, M. E., & Olson, D. M. (1988). *Political Parties and Elections in American States*. Chicago: Dorsey Press.

Johnson, R. J., Braima, M. A., & Sothirajah, J. (1999). Doing the Traditional Media Sidestep: Comparing the Effects of the Internet and Other Nontraditional Media with Traditional Media in the 1996 Presidential Campaign. *Journalism & Mass Communication Quarterly*, *76*(1), 99–123. doi:10.1177/107769909907600108

Jungherr, A. (2016). Twitter use in election campaigns: A systematic literature review. *Journal of Information Technology & Politics*, *13*(1), 72–91. doi:10.1080/19331681.2015.1132401

Kaid, L., & Johnston, A. (1991). Negative Versus Positive Television Advertising in U.S. Presidential Campaigns, 19601988. *Journal of Communication*, *41*(3), 53–64. doi:10.1111/j.1460-2466.1991.tb02323.x

Karpf, D. (2012). *The move-on effect*. New York, NY: Oxford University Press. doi:10.1093/acprof:oso/9780199898367.001.0001

Klotz, R. (1998). Virtual Criticism: Negative Advertising on the Internet in the 1996 Senate Races. *Political Communication*, *15*(3), 347–365. doi:10.1080/105846098198939

Kone, S., & Winters, R. (1993). Taxes and Voting: Electoral Redistribution in the American States. *The Journal of Politics*, *63*(2).

Kruikemeier, S. (2014). How Political Candidates Use Twitter and the Impact on Votes. *Computers in Human Behavior, 34*, 131–139. doi:10.1016/j.chb.2014.01.025

Larsson, A. O., & Moe, H. (2011). Studying political microblogging: Twitter users in the 2010 Swedish election campaign. *New Media & Society*. doi:10.1177/1461444811422894

Lau, R. R., & Pomper, G. (2004). *Negative Campaigning: An Analysis of U.S. Senate Elections*. New York: Rowman & Littlefield.

Lau, R. R., & Pomper, G. M. (2001). Negative Campaigning by US Senate Candidates. *Party Politics, 7*(1), 69–87. doi:10.1177/1354068801007001004

Lau, R. R., Sigelman, L., & Rovner, I. B. (2007). The Effects of Negative Political Campaigns: A Meta-Analytic Reassessment. *The Journal of Politics, 69*(4), 1176–1209. doi:10.1111/j.1468-2508.2007.00618.x

Margolis, M., & Resnick, D. (2000). *Politics as usual: the cyberspace "revolution"*. Thousand Oaks, CA: Sage Publications.

Martin, P. (2004). Inside the Black Box of Negative Campaign Effects: Three Reasons Why Negative Campaigns Mobilize. *Political Psychology, 25*(4), 545–562. doi:10.1111/j.1467-9221.2004.00386.x

McCullagh, D. (2004, May 4). Liberal Net Rules Spawn Political Attack Ads. *CNET News*.

Parmalee, J., & Bichard, S. (2012). *Politics and the Twitter Revolution: How Tweets Influence The Relationship Between Political Leaders and the Public*. Lanham, MD: Lexington Books.

Pole, A., & Xenos, M. (2011). *Like, Comments and Retweets: Facebooking and Tweeting on the 2010 Gubernatorial Campaign Trail*. Paper presented at the State Politics and Policy Conference, Hanover, NH. Retrieved from http://www.sppc2011.org/Papers/1_Pole.pdf

Price, T. (2012). A Twitter: A New Political Weathervane. *CQ Researcher, 29*(4), 876–877.

Ramos-Serrano, M., Gómez, J. D. F., & Pineda, A. (2016). Follow the closing of the campaign on streaming': The use of Twitter by Spanish political parties during the 2014 European elections. *New Media & Society*. (forthcoming)

Sanders, A. (2004). Creating Effective Political Ads. In D. Schultz (Ed.), *Lights, Camera, Campaign!* New York: Peter Lang Publishing.

Schweitzer, E. J. (2008). Innovation or Normalization in E-Campaigning. *European Journal of Communication, 23*(4), 449–470. doi:10.1177/0267323108096994

Skaperdas, S., & Grofman, B. (1995). Modeling Negative Campaigning. *The American Political Science Review, 89*(1), 49–61. doi:10.2307/2083074

Straus, J. R., Williams, R. T., Shogan, C. J., & Glassman, M. E. (2016). Congressional Social Media Communications: Evaluating Senate Twitter Usage. *Online Information Review, 40*(5), 643–659. doi:10.1108/OIR-10-2015-0334

Tumasjan, A., Sprenger, T., Sander, P. G., & Welpe, I. (2010). *Predicting Elections with Twitter: What 140 Characters Reveal About Political Sentime.* Paper presented at the 4th International AAAI Conference on Web Blogs and Social Media, Munich, Germany.

Vergeer, M., Hermans, L., & Santms, S. (2013). Online Social Networks and Micro-Blogging in Political Campaigning: The Exploration of a New Campaign Toll and a New Campaign Style. *Party Politics*, *19*(3), 477–501. doi:10.1177/1354068811407580

Wagner, K. M., & Gainous, J. (2009). Electronic Grassroots: Does Online Campaigning Work? *Journal of Legislative Studies*, *15*(4), 502–520. doi:10.1080/13572330903302539

West, D. (2010). *Air wars, 1952-2008.* Washington, DC: CQ Press.

Xenos, M., & Foot, K. A. (2005). Politics as Usual, or Politics Unusual? Position Taking and Dialogue on Campaign Websites in the 2002 US Elections. *Journal of Communication*, *55*(1), 169–185. doi:10.1111/j.1460-2466.2005.tb02665.x

Yang, X., Chen, B. C., Maity, M., & Ferrara, E. (2016). *Social Politics: Agenda Setting and Political Communication on Social Media.* http://arxiv.org/abs/1607.06819v1

Chapter 12
When Citizens in Authoritarian States Use Facebook for Social Ties but Not Political Participation

Wairagala Wakabi
Örebro University, Sweden

ABSTRACT

Numerous researchers have found a correlation between citizens' use of social networking sites (SNS) like Facebook and their likelihood for eParticipation. However, SNS use does not have the same effect on all citizens' political engagement. In authoritarian countries, Facebook offers a platform for citizens to challenge the power of the state, provide alternative narratives and mobilise for political change. This chapter examines how using Facebook affects the participative behaviours of Ugandans and concludes that in low internet use, authoritarian contexts, the Civic Voluntarism Model's postulation of the factors that explain political participation, and the benefits Facebook brings to participation in Western democracies, are upended. Overwhelming detachment from politics, low belief in citizens' online actions influencing change and fear of reprisals for criticising an authoritarian president in power for 30 years, severely dulled the appetite for eParticipation. Hence, Facebook was growing citizens' civic skills but hardly increasing online participation.

INTRODUCTION

Several researchers have over the last two decades sought to establish the causal relationships between digital technologies and political participation. This interest has been fuelled by the belief that the use of Information and Communication Technologies (ICT) can boost the participation of citizens in governance processes. Amidst pessimistic approaches about the future of representative democracy, the role of the Internet in affecting participatory behaviour has become central in political participation debates (Theocharis & Lowe, 2016). But this scholarly interest is not new. Two decades ago, Castells (1996)

DOI: 10.4018/978-1-5225-1862-4.ch012

explained that the internet provides easy access to information and offers a sphere for communication which can enhance political interest and pull citizens into the democratic process. Macintosh and Whyte (2002) observed that over the previous decade there had been a gradual awareness of the need to consider new tools for public engagement that enable a wider audience to contribute to the policy debate and where contributions themselves are both broader and deeper. Besides this interest in the link between ICT and political participation, various studies have investigated whether use of one or the other media increases the proclivity of individuals to participate in civic and political processes. Such research, including that conducted earlier on the popularity of television (for example Cummings et al., 2002), and what was conducted more recently on the internet and social media (Bachmann et al., 2010; Friedl & Vercic 2011; Räsänen, 2008; Tworzecki & Semetko, 2010; Cullen & Sommer, 2011; Bakker & de Vreese, 2011), mostly concluded that there was a correlation between media use and the likelihood for political participation. Many of the studies concluded that there were no universal effects of media use on political engagement across all citizen groups (Holt at al., 2013). Some scholars therefore urge caution when it comes to statements and assumptions about the direction of causality that underlies the relationship between social media use and participation (Theocharis & Lowe, 2016).

Zúñiga et al., (2012) noted that media use related to information acquisition such as TV news and community building (such as online communities) more positively associated with civic participation. On the other hand, use related to entertainment (such as reality shows and online movies) negatively impacted on participation. Meanwhile, in drawing the link between media use and participation, Cullen and Sommer (2011) pointed to the role of ICT as a communications channel and an enabler of online networking; while Gustafsson (2012) identified the proliferating social networking sites (SNS) as a great source for political news and a way of influencing contacts for politically-inclined individuals. However, contemporary research is not wholly in agreement about the effects of using social media on participation nor does it always succinctly explain the link between use of particular media and the resulting likelihood for participation.

This paper investigates the reasoning of Facebook users in Uganda in relation to political content and discussion. It examines how using the social network affects the participative behaviours of individuals that are active in political or interest organizations and those that are not active in organized politics. The paper uses the Civic Voluntarism Model as a frame of analysis.

The research questions of this paper are:

- What effect does the use of Facebook have on the online political participation behaviours of individuals in an authoritarian state?
- What factors are important predictors of online participation among individuals who use Facebook in an authoritarian state?

Notably, most of the research published on this subject discusses developed, democratic countries. Whether in countries such as Uganda with different conditions - low internet penetration, high rates of illiteracy and authoritarian governments - the use of social networks such as Facebook is playing a role in shaping people's proclivity to participate becomes a legitimate subject of inquiry. While the next section provides a contextual background to Uganda, the ones that follow it review literature on the link between the use of social media and political participation in authoritarian regimes.

CONTEXTUAL BACKGROUND TO UGANDA

Access to ICT is low in Uganda, with an internet penetration rate of 39%, while mobile phone teledensity (number of mobile phones per 100 inhabitants) stands at about 59 (UCC, 2016). However, there is multiple cell phone ownership, implying that the actual number of people that use a phone is much less. Facebook is the second most popularly visited website in Uganda after Google.com, while YouTube is the 3rd most visited site. Twitter and Wikipedia are 6th and 9th respectively (SimilarWeb, 2015). Only 16% of the population is connected to the national electricity grid while less than 17% of Ugandans live in urban areas. Up to 19.7% of Uganda's population lives below the poverty line, according to the Uganda Bureau of Statistics. Low literacy rates, high costs of accessing and owning ICT and a lack of usage skills all hamper the use of ICT in Uganda (Wakabi, 2016). Moreover, the use of most ICT, other than for making and receiving calls, is very much pegged to knowledge of the English language. The literacy rate stands at 73%, while gross domestic product per capita is US$ 680, meaning Uganda is a least developed country according to the ranking by the United Nations.

Most users of Facebook, the most popular SNS in Uganda, are in the 18-24 years age group, followed by those in the 25-34 bracket. These two age groups account for 79% of Facebook users in Uganda, and these are mainly young, educated and "wired" individuals who may be opinion leaders in their communities and may be consequential for the future of the country (Grönlund & Wakabi, 2015). Facebook subscribers in Uganda are 66.5% male and 33.5% female (All in One Social, 2013). Relative to other social media such as Instagram and Twitter, Facebook has a longer legacy in Uganda, which partly explains its popularity. Another factor that works in its favour is that subscribers on all the big telecom services providers can use the so-called 'Facebook Zero' which allows a subscriber to access a text-only version of this social network, update their status, read and comment on posts, all for free. The user is only charged if they make downloads, stream audio or video, or upload pictures.

Political space is restricted in Uganda, although the country has been governed under a multi-party system since 2005. President Yoweri Museveni has been in power for the last 30 years, having captured power in 1986 via a guerrilla war. Although he has won elections since 1996, he is accused of stifling political dissent and independent media and has orchestrated a change to the constitution to remove presidential term limits. In February 2016, Museveni got re-elected for another five-year term in a heavily criticised poll. His main challenger was arrested several times during the election week and was placed under house arrest thereafter for 40 days. Thereafter, he was was charged with treason and remanded in the country's maximum security prison (Chullo, 2016; Gaffey, 2016; Baguma, 2016).

Ugandan opposition leaders and journalists are often harassed, arrested and charged in court for criticising government (Amnesty International, 2013; Freedom House, 2015; Chullo, 2016; Mutiga, 2016). Freedom House's Freedom on the Net Report 2015 report ranks Uganda as 'partly free', the same ranking it has had for at least the last four years. Intimidation, threats of violence, and technical attacks against vulnerable groups and marginalised communities, particularly the Lesbian, Gay, Bisexual, Transgender and Intersex (LGBTI) community, are frequent online (Freedom House, 2015). Moreover, according to Freedom House, between June 2014 and May 2015, four individuals were arrested for their alleged involvement with Facebook pages known for critical commentary. In 2013 a cabinet minister announced that the country would establish a social media monitoring center "to weed out those who use it to damage the government and people's reputation". To-date, there is no confirmation that this center exists. In June of 2015, President Museveni ordered security agencies to investigate and arrest persons he said were responsible for inciting ethnic hatred using social media. A week later, one individual was arrested for allegedly defaming the president, the first lady and other government officials through Facebook (Mpuga, 2015). He was charged with making offensive communications against Museveni in contravention of the Computer Misuse Act of 2011. Other individuals were questioned by security agencies over similar allegations. The communications regulator ordered a blockage of access to all social media as the country went to elections on February 18, 2016. The same move was repeated the day before the inauguration of the re-elected President Museveni for his 5th term in office (CIPESA, 2016). In March 2016, Uganda arrested two individuals accused of circulating on social media a picture depicting a 'dead' President Museveni. In 2011, the government ordered service providers to block access to SMS services, Facebook and Twitter in order to deny the opposition an opportunity to mobilize supporters for anti-government protests.

In the last four years, numerous media houses have been forced to close for various periods of time because the government claimed their reporting harmed national security and the public interest. Fears persist of reprisals from the state to those who use ICT to criticise the government and these fears have led to self-censorship by media and ordinary citizens both offline and online (CIPESA, 2014). The ruling party – National Resistance Movement (NRM) – holds a huge majority in parliament, and has been accused of doing little to fight corruption that is rampant in the civil service. Peaceful demonstrations are met with brutal force from security services, and in 2013 Uganda enacted a Public Order Management law that makes spontaneous peaceful demonstration of more than three people a crime, according to Human Rights Watch.

LITERATURE REVIEW

The Internet and Democratic Participation

According to Sanford and Rose (2007), participation can be generally understood as joining in, either in the sense of taking part in some communal discussion or activity, or in the sense of taking some role in decision-making. Participation can take place within the formal political process such as voting, or outside it such as political activism. The eParticipation relates to the online activities of governments, elected representatives, political parties and citizen groups (Kane & Patapan 2004). From a review of various literature and models on online participation or eParticipation (Sæbø et al., 2008; Sanford & Rose 2007; Grönlund 2009; Kalampokis et al., 2008; Grönlund 2011), it emerges that the common features of participation include: Informing, Consulting, Involving, Engagement, Empowerment, and Collaboration. Seeking news and information, joining online networks, political conversations, also constitute eParticipation activities (Tambouris et al., 2007). As such, this paper views a broad range of activities as constituting participation.

Several scholars have researched into the ways in which the internet could enable and motivate participation. Two decades ago, Castells (1996) explained how the internet provided easy access to information and offered a sphere for communication that could enhance political interest and pull citizens into the democratic process. A decade later, Chadwick (2006) observed that the relative anonymity of the online world rendered individuals less accountable for their actions, so they felt empowered to speak up against more powerful actors because they had less fear of punishment. More recently, with the advent and growing popularity of social media, research interest is growing in the use of SNS and its effects on participation (Wakabi, 2016; Kuriyan et al., 2011). The popularity of these sites provides an opportunity to study the characteristics of online social networks at large scale (Mislove (2007). These sites form a network that provides a powerful means of sharing, organising, and finding content and contacts. Gurak and Logie` (2003) similarly argued that activist online groups constituted extensive and easily accessible networks that are central to collective action, as they are able to recruit new members, organise supporters, distribute information about possibilities for engagement, and allow dispersed individuals to effectively plan political action in the real world.

But how exactly the use of SNS such as Facebook affects eParticipation has not been well studied, particularly in parts of the global south. For instance, after reviewing literature on ICT and participation in Africa, Gagliardone et al (2015) concluded that although there was much excitement and optimism about the role of ICT in governance, the evidence of actual impact was thin. They also found that most of the literature exhibited the "simplistic assumption" that ICT will drive democratic development without sufficient consideration of how ICT are actually used by the public. But even in western, democratic countries where eParticipation has a long tradition and has been widely studied, it faces many challenges. These include digital inequalities in the networked society (Effing et al., 2011; Hacker et al., 2009), limited deliberation and politicians' reluctance to embrace new possibilities enabled by eParticipation (Sæbø, 2011; Freschi et al., 2009), and a lack of interest in policy issues and low levels of trust in politicians and in eParticipation endeavours (Lee et al., 2011; Scherer & Wimmer, 2014). In addition, the challenges and opportunities for eParticipation involving non-institutional actors in western countries have not been well studied (Susha & Grönlund, 2012). Mass engagement of citizens in online consultation and decision-making contexts remains an unsatisfied expectation in both developed and developing countries. According to Scherer and Wimmer (2014), to identify and implement measures for increasing trust and minimising distrust in eParticipation endeavours, relevant trust relationships have to be analysed to understand implications of using or not using eParticipation offers. This implies that, even in what appear to be the favourable conditions, eParticipation is not always a straight path to citizen participation or government responsiveness.

The effects of social media use on individuals' participation behaviour also vary. Indeed, in a study conducted in Sweden, Gustafsson (2012) found that using SNS did not affect all users to act in the same way. Whereas respondents active in political organizations tended to view the political side of Facebook as an important new channel for intra-organizational communication, a great source for political news, and a way of influencing contacts, respondents who did not belong to organized political groups tended to hold more sceptical views of the political content. Gustafsson argued that even if not many of the non-organized respondents took active part in political discussions or participatory activities, these passive users were also affected by recruitment attempts, by things they saw that their friends did, and links their friends posted. Distinctly, Bakker and de Vreese (2011) found that using the internet for news was a positive predictor for various forms of participation. Some scholars contend that people with more structurally heterogeneous Facebook networks, who had connections with public political actors through Facebook, and who were exposed to shared political information through Facebook were more likely to participate in political activities (Tang & Lee, 2013).

Other researchers have pointed to uses of SNS that are more related to increased participation. For instance, Räsänen (2008) argued that citizens who followed what happened in their community and kept up-to-date with public affairs tended to be more politically engaged than their peers who did not follow the news. Cullen and Sommer (2011) also concluded that there was a correlation between internet engagement and offline civic engagement, after investigating the impact ICT had as a communications channel and in supporting online networking, on citizens' participation in civic activities. According to Lee and Kim (2012), citizens' eParticipation was less active if they simply searched for information and observed the postings of others, rather than for instance posting their suggestions or replying to others' postings. Zúñiga, et al (2014) found that social media news use has direct effects on offline political participation and indirect effects on offline and online political participation mediated via political expression. In Taiwan, a study found that in addition to active discussion, passive exposure to politically related activities within Facebook networks indirectly contributes to voting and offline participation (Lin, 2016). This study found that the indirect effects of the passive use of Facebook on voting and offline political participation showed that through casual browsing of the information diffused on Facebook and/or active engagement on Facebook, this platform may provide a transitional tool for voters to seek information or become interested in an election. Facebook network size and connections with public political actors have been found to exhibit both direct and indirect effects on participation through Facebook news, expression, and efficacy (Chan, 2016).

While arguing that the positive effects that discussions on social networks have on political behaviours could also be extended to civic participation, Zúñiga and Valenzuela (2011) contended that citizens who reported larger conversational circles—online and offline—tended to engage more in civic life. Klofstad (2009) likewise noted that the growing political science literature on social networks suggested that talking about politics with people in our immediate social environment led us to participate in civic activities. In a study on university students in the U.S., Klofstad found that after engaging in civic talk with a roommate, the average study participant increased participation in voluntary civic organizations by 38%.

In a study in Sweden, Holt et al. (2013) found "substantial support" for the idea that use of social media for political purposes may function as a leveller of political interest and participation between younger and older citizens. Both political interest and offline political participation increased with age. Zúñiga and Valenzuela (ibid.) found that individuals' attitudes could exert a strong effect on their willingness to join and participate in civic activities. They found that when people felt contentment or "life satisfaction", they found a motive to be linked positively to participation in collective activities and civic volunteerism. Successful experiences of civic engagement could lead to higher levels of life satisfaction. Zúñiga and Valenzuela (ibid.) also found that organizational membership and having trust were key ingredients of civic voluntarism, while distrust and cynicism resulted in withdrawal from community affairs. Meanwhile, a study in Finland showed that people's preference for online media contributed to political participation both online and offline (Räsänen, 2008). Likewise, Tworzecki and Semetko (2010) investigated the impact of media use on political knowledge, political participation, and political learning, and concluded that media use had a positive effect on political knowledge and on participation.

Earlier, Weber et al. (2003) contended that participation on the internet exerted a positive influence on political participation, mainly because the internet subsidized the costs of participation. However, Weber and colleagues also noted that while there was debate focusing on the potential of the internet to facilitate social activity, community networks, and political participation, another on-going debate focused on potential social consequences, such as decreased face-to-face social interaction and unequal access to information. Moy and Xenos (2007) similarly observed that scholars had categorized most research on new media effects on civic and political life as either optimistic or pessimistic. While optimists believed new media promoted democracy in a variety of ways (lowering costs of communication, association, and participation), pessimists cautioned that new media would likely not lead to significant changes in political behaviour and may even harm public life.

However, Quintelier (2008) noted that while some researchers had argued that internet use and the accompanying political resources stimulated political participation, there were also fears that intensive internet use was associated with a withdrawal from public life. A study of Young Greek Facebook users, intended to contribute to a better understanding of the causal relationship between digital media and participation, found that maintaining a Facebook account had "clearly negative consequences" on reports of offline and online forms of political and civic participation (Theocharis & Lowe, 2016). These authors argued that a rival theory to the one that sees Facebook as a mobilizing factor for engagement is one that sees it as a demobilizing force whose functions distract the users' attention from politics. It has been argued that nowhere does the influence of the digital explosion appear somehow exaggerated as in the case of Africa, where lack of empirical evidence has seen conclusive statements from policy-makers and commentators about the Internet's potential to shape political processes on the continent (Mutsvairo & Sirks, 2015).

Social Media and Political Participation in Authoritarian Regimes

Authoritarian regimes are often characterised by censorship and repression (Brooker, 2008), as well as by limited pluralism and limited political participation. On the other hand, democratic institutions tend to promote e-Participation than authoritarian regimes and public bodies maintain closer contacts offline and online with citizens relative to those of authoritarian regimes (Jho & Song, 2015; Wakabi, 2016). Authoritarian regimes not only discourage individual participation by greatly increasing the punishments for dissent, "but also control the communicative infrastructure in ways that make it difficult for citizens to coordinate effective collective opposition or to express their dissent in the public sphere" (Tufekci & Wilson, 2012, p.3).

Scholarly interest in understanding the role social media plays in online political processes in authoritarian states has grown considerably following the so-called Arab Spring civilian uprisings in North Africa and Middle East countries, such as Tunisia, Syria, Libya, Yemen, and Egypt. The wave of demonstrations, uprisings, and riots started in Tunisia in December 2010 and spread to other Arab states, and had by February of 2012 forced the rulers of Tunisia, Egypt, Libya, and Yemen out of power (Simpson, 2014). In those 'Arab Spring' uprisings, social media offered safe communication channels for citizens to coordinate collective opposition or to express their dissent (Tufekci & Wilson, 2012; Aman & Jayroe, 2013; Howard et al., 2011); gather and spread information to counter the propaganda and apparatus of the repressive state (Manrique & Mikail, 2011; Allagui, 2014); and reduce transaction costs for protest organisers and present rapid channels for disseminating messages and images (Lynch, 2011). The dominant storyline claims social media played a big role in these uprisings. Because they lower the cost of information acquisition, expose users to unsought political information, and increase the perceived reliability of that information, SNS have the potential to increase political awareness in non-democracies (Reuter & Szakonyi, 2015). Furthermore, SNS and satellite television together also offer powerful tools to protest organisers, reducing transaction costs for organization and presenting rapid and powerful channels for disseminating messages, images, and frames (Lynch, 2011). In countries where there is censorship and citizens lack freedom of expression and action, media and digital communications offer an efficient alternative to counter the apparatus of the repressive state, playing "a strategic role when used for sharing information, seeking support, or tracking funding, or when involved in evaluating risks and advocating for a cause" (Allagui, 2014, p. 3).

In a study of ICT use in uprisings in Egypt, Tunisia, Yemen, and Libya, Aman and Jayroe (2013) determined that digital communications helped protesters to move information around faster and more efficiently than state-controlled media, helping to organize the movements. The protestors were able to record and broadcast pictures and news messages with their mobile phones by uploading them for the world to see and hear. Meanwhile, Howard et al. (2011) found evidence that during the Arab Spring, young, urban, relatively well educated individuals used Facebook, Twitter, and YouTube to put pressure on their governments, used blogs to criticise the governments in Egypt and Tunisia, and utilised Western media sites such as the BBC and CNN to spread "credible information" to their supporters. Based on a survey of 1,200 participants in Egypt's Tahrir Square protests, Tufekci and Wilson (2012) found that social media, particularly Facebook, provided new sources of information the regime could not easily control and were crucial in shaping how citizens made decisions about participating in protests. More than a quarter of the protestors sampled had first heard of the protests on Facebook and, in addition a quarter used Facebook to disseminate pictures and videos they had produced.

Meanwhile, based on a survey of 1,200 participants in Egypt's Tahrir Square protests, Tufekci and Wilson (2012) found that social media, in particular Facebook, provided new sources of information the regime could not easily control and were crucial in shaping how citizens made individual decisions about participating in protests. More than a quarter of the protestors sampled had first heard of the protests on Facebook and, in addition, a quarter used Facebook to disseminate pictures and videos they had produced. The study by Tufekci and Wilson (2012) found that Twitter, along with blogs, was used by protestors to communicate about the demonstrations as they unfolded. The studies by Aman and Jayroe (2013), Howard et al. (2011), Wojcieszak et al. (2013), Manrique and Mikail (2011), Harlow (2012), and Tufekci and Wilson (2012) show that SNS had diminished the repressive state's control over the communicative infrastructure, thus enabling the organising and expression of dissenting opinions.

However, Reuter and Szakonyi (2015) contended that there was no scholarly consensus about the effect of new media on politics in authoritarian regimes, because most scholars tended to view new media as a 'black box' and failed to distinguish between the different ways in which new media are used. They concluded that online social media usage only increases political awareness if the specific social network being used has been politicized to contain political information. Likewise, Lynch (2011) argued that while Arab Spring protestors effectively used social media in their struggles, it was surprisingly difficult to demonstrate rigorously that these new media directly caused any of the outcomes with which they have been associated.

Nonetheless, it has also been argued that the role of Twitter and Facebook in instigating and organisation, or reporting on socio-political change in uprisings in the Middle East and North Africa in 2011 was occasionally overstated (Wojcieszak & Smith, 2013). Based on a survey of 2,800 young, educated, and technologically savvy Iranians, these researchers studied protests that followed the June 2009 presidential elections in Iran and found that politics was not topping the agenda in the new media sphere; social issues were. They argued that the detected patterns "suggest that mobilisation via new media did not continue and/or was not substantial to begin with, and that our sample was more interested in using blogs, text messages, or Twitter to communicate about personal topics, new technologies and work-related affairs than politics" (p.16). They argued that the detected patterns suggested that mobilization via new media did not continue or was not substantial to begin with, and that the sampled individuals were more interested in using blogs, text messages, or Twitter to communicate about personal topics, new technologies and work-related affairs than politics. A study using the uses and gratifications model

– which states that media consumers obtain different gratifications from the usage of the media – names the main reasons Somali youth used Facebook as virtual companionship escape, interpersonal habitual entertainment, and self-description of their country. Others were self-expression, information seeking, and passing time gratifications (Dhaha & Igale, 2013). Although Somalia faces several democracy and governance challenges, political participation is not anywhere among the top uses of Facebook. In Zimbabwe, meanwhile, Mutsvairo and Sirks (2015) found though Facebook had encouraged citizens in authoritarian Zimbabwe to openly discuss and share thoughts, there was no evidence that it had helped facilitate increased democratic participation in the country.

Beyond concerns that the role of SNS may have been overestimated, is the realization that while ICT tools are hailed for their democratizing potential, they can be a double-edged sword. Lynch (2011) contends that ICT tools can strengthen the surveillance and repression capabilities of authoritarian states. Greitens (2013) observes that authoritarian states' approaches to ICT falls in three categories: control (government seeks to limit or curtail citizen access to ICT such as through censorship and filtering); surveillance (the degree to which a regime uses ICT activity and data to monitor the population); and activism (how a regime seeks to actively shape online or social media content in its favor). Similarly, Bryant (2012) argued that while ICT tools can challenge authoritarian rule, the same technology can be used by savvy regimes through filtering and surveillance, censorship, infrastructure control, and propaganda to buttress their own interests.

Ethiopia is an example of such country, as it controls the development of new technologies nationally; "appropriating ICTs to support its ambitious nation-building project, while real or imagined enemies were prevented from developing uses that could challenge it" (Gagliardone, 2014, p.6). Perhaps more than any other country in Africa, Ethiopia regularly blocks websites, undertakes surveillance of websites and social media, and charges journalists over content published offline and online (CIPESA, 2014). However, Laverty (2012) argues that the digital methods of authoritarian regimes in Sub-Saharan Africa are not as well understood or studied as they are in places like Iran or China, but cautions that repression in the offline world will undoubtedly encroach on the digital one, which could result in more overall repression or instability in authoritarian countries. With the strong perception held by many users in Africa, Uganda more specifically, of ongoing monitoring of their online activity, doubts arise as to whether SNS use would raise political participation among citizens.

The Civic Voluntarism Model (CVM) and SNS Use

According to Verba et al. (1995), who advanced the CVM, individuals find the costs of participating low enough, and the benefits high enough, when they are equipped with resources of time, money, and civic skills, have a sense of psychological engagement with politics and current events, and have been recruited by someone in their environment to participate, such as a member of their social network. Verba and colleagues also show that of these factors, resources and engagement are the most important in determining whether the benefits of civic participation outweigh the costs. Social networking sites have various elements that drive down the costs as envisaged by the CVM. The model has, as a result, been applied to studies of SNS use and their effect on individuals' participation behaviour. Gustafsson (2012) argues that whereas resources in themselves would not be affected by using social network sites, a wider repertoire of political activities (such as various forms of online participation) is available compared to, for instance, attending meetings in formal organisations, while lowering the cost of participation by making it more flexible might make participating more attractive. Gustafson (ibid) concluded that SNS might potentially lower the thresholds for participating by introducing new and more flexible forms in which it can be done, but this was not enough for making non-actives ready for participation. Other factors, such as a reluctance to make political views known to friends and other contacts, as well as insecurity concerning the credibility of campaigns, seemed to offset this among several individuals who were not members of organised groups. An extension of the Socio-Economic Status (SES) model, this theory suggests that people become engaged in politics if they have the resources and the time, and if they are asked to participate (Rüdig & Karyotis, 2013). The SES model, itself for long popularly used to explain political behaviour, focuses on the resources of an individual, including their education, occupation, and income, in analysing their political participation. While based on the SES model of participation, civic voluntarism extends the socio-economic model, by for instance conceptualising resources widely to include not only economic and educational resources, but also resources of time (Pattie et al., 2004).

The arguments by Weber (2003), Bachmann et al (2010), Bakker and de Vreese (2011), Tworzecki and Semetko (2010) and others on media use and its impact on participation were similarly expounded by Moy and Xenos (2007), who suggested that behaviour that individuals previously avoided because of cost concerns - such as gathering information, voting, or joining an association - becomes more likely under conditions of low and no-cost communication. Similarly, Moy and Xenos (2007) stated that individuals weighed the costs and benefits associated with taking action; only when costs were low and benefits high did they choose to act. However, cost is not the only issue, as argued by various researchers, notably Verba et al (1995), who advanced the Civic Voluntarism Model. This seems to support the assertion by Bimber (2000) that taking into account differences in user characteristics, political effects of new media use are contingent on individuals' levels of sophistication, motives, and social context. The Civic Voluntarism Model and the belief that using SNS lowers the cost of participation for citizens is a guiding hypothesis for this chapter.

Gustafsson (2012) argues that using SNS might hypothetically influence all three categories of resource imperatives in the Civic Voluntarism Model: time, money, and skills; interest, knowledge, and efficacy; and recruitment procedure.

There are also issues of lack of confidence in the ability of ICT to deliver results while communicating with government and service providers, as reported by Crandall and Mutuku (2011), who found that Kenyan citizens preferred face-to-face interactions for citizen engagement with leaders. Lee and Kim (2012) argued that while it was true that users of SNS who were already active in political or civic networks were more likely to be active eParticipants, they also suggested that people embedded in strong offline social networks were equipped with knowledge about how to initiate, build, and sustain social networks, which enhanced their capability to use eParticipation actively.

METHOD

Six focus groups discussions (FGD) involving 56 individuals were conducted physically in Kampala during January and February 2014. Two focus groups were held for members of political parties, two for members of interest groups, and two for those active in neither political parties nor interest groups. All respondents were users of social networks, since the study was about the effect of the use of SNS on the participation behaviour of its users. Our FGD lasted on average 90 minutes. The respondents were chosen through various methods: Telephone and email contact with political parties and interest groups; contact with participants through their Facebook accounts; and contact with university students. There was then snowball sampling with the contacts who had been identified through these avenues. Snowball sampling uses a small pool of initial informants to nominate other participants who meet the eligibility criteria for a study. Also known as chain referral sampling, snowball sampling is a useful way to pursue the goals of purposive sampling in many situations where there are no lists or other obvious sources for locating members of the population of interest, but it requires that the participants are likely to know others who share the characteristics that make them eligible for inclusion in the study (Morgan, 2008).

As noted by Gustafsson (2012), focus groups are useful when the purpose is not to generalize but to study such motives, experiences and thought processes of individuals as are not obtainable through extensive methods like surveys. Focus groups can also give more in-depth information than individual interviews because the group starts discussing among themselves and then participants remember more – although it is true that sometimes the FGDs run the risk of group-think. Moreover, while focus groups may not on their own be the best tool for eliciting the best qualitative data, they can be gainfully used jointly with other methodologies in a form of triangulation or mixed methodological approach for more quality data (Boateng, 2012).

Using focus groups rather than in-depth interviews (which are often more suitable for respondents to actually show their profile rather than build a reconstruction of their behaviour) was that FGDs allowed for respondents to react to other participants' stories and comparing them to their own experiences (Hundley & Shyles, 2010). The FGDs also enabled for any unclear questions to be clarified and to receive responses to most of the questions posed. However, in a society where citizens fear that expressing certain political opinions could attract reprisals, FGDs can be problematic, as the exploration of SNS use corresponds to an examination of a social behaviour, an attribute to which individuals tend to provide a socially positive image. However, we created trust among respondents, by assuring them of the anonymity of their contributions. This was also enabled because we met face-to-face (rather than through online or phone interviews), and because many respondents were recruited through referrals. Keeping the groups homogeneous (the politically inactive had their own FGDs as did activists and political party members) also aided in creating a conducive atmosphere for frank discussions.

Respondents were asked about their information sharing practices and the main ICT tools and services they used. In order to understand how SNS was affecting individuals' participation habits, we asked, "How is the use of SNS encouraging your participation in the political affairs of your country?" Hindrances to greater eParticipation were explored, through questions such as: "What factors facilitate or constrain your use of ICT for political participation?"; and "Are you free to express your political views freely on social media?" Other questions included: How does Facebook and other social media enable political participation? Do the ties you make on social media, and the activities and conversations you make on Facebook, stimulate participation? What makes you decide whether to be active or silent in online political Facebook groups in which you are a member? What are the effects of using Facebook on your political knowledge, and does any resulting increase in your political knowledge raise your level of eParticipation? The importance of time, money, skills; interest, knowledge, efficiency as motivations for participation was also explored.

In quotes from the FGDs, information about the group to which the quoted respondent belonged is referenced as follows: member of a political party (PP), member of an interest group (IG), and non-member of political party or interest group (NM).

The research questions addressed by this chapter are:

1. What effect does the use of Facebook have on the online political participation behaviours of individuals in an authoritarian state?
2. What factors are important predictors of online participation among individuals who use Facebook in an authoritarian state?

In seeking answers to these questions, participants in the focus groups were asked about their usage of SNS, in particular Facebook, their attitudes towards SNS as a resource for civic and political participation, how they used Facebook as a resource for participation, whether benefits of using the social media network such as acquiring political knowledge translated into increased participation.

RESULTS

Facebook as a Resource for Political Knowledge and Participation

Facebook was promoting access to political knowledge, including through providing access to news and information. Even individuals who did not personally visit news websites or the Facebook pages of news organisations received news and information through links forwarded to them, or viewed comments made on stories by their friends. Discussion forums on Facebook also increased the awareness, debating skills, and information seeking and sharing skills of those on Facebook, whether they were politically inclined or not. According to most FGD participants, by making it easier and more convenient to access news, receive and share information, observe or contribute to discussions, Facebook was helping to grow their civic and informational skills, and ultimately to increase their political knowledge. It was also saving them time and money so as to participate. Sharing news links and forwarding of news articles was widespread, although political news was among the categories least shared. Health, entertainment, and sports news were shared most. As one participant remarked, "I don't send you a link on a topic to which I don't know how you will respond. So I regularly share health news with all my friends and contacts because health is an issue relevant to everyone and it is unlikely that anyone will react negatively to a health story, which is not the same with stories related to politics." Numerous respondents felt Facebook was helping them to gain writing, discussion, and argumentation skills from observing what others posted and fashioning their own arguments along what they considered quality arguments and discussions. Using Facebook gave individuals a high possibility for improved political knowledge regardless of whether these individuals were interested or participating in political related activities. However, whether an individual Facebook user actually got increased political knowledge was largely dependent on variables such as the friends they had and the groups they subscribed to. Political knowledge gained by a person engaged in sports and entertainment groups, or who only shared family-related information with close associates, was lower than that of a person with membership to a political group on Facebook. As such, Facebook was excellent for information acquisition and sharing but did not necessarily stimulate eParticipation.

With regard to the response to political invitation, most respondents who were not already involved with political or activist groups would not accept an invitation to join an online political group. This was due to suspicions about why they were being recruited and fears that joining could compromise their security. A majority of those already involved in activist and political groups would respond positively to an invitation. Recruitment by one's associate, or by an organization that speaks directly to the interests of the individual being invited, was more likely to be responded to positively. Most individuals were more likely to accept an invitation from a civic organization than a political one.

Many Facebook users were taking to using newer social media tools such as Whatsapp, which they considered more private in some ways and which they claimed transmitted messages more instantaneously than Facebook. This was further driving many Ugandan social network users away from the political sphere and into the comfort zones of communicating only with known friends and associates whose telephone numbers they were sure of. In spite of these unfavourable sentiments about Facebook, much was said in its praise, including being platform-independent unlike WhatsApp which requires a user to have a phone, its suggestion of friends to users, enabling a user to reach a wide audience including those who are not his friend, and being more affordable.

Did Political Knowledge and Ease of Use Translate into Participation?

The ties and conversations generated online, the increased political knowledge enabled by the social network, and the ease of exchanging information, contacting leaders and taking part in discussions, were potentially positive predictors for participation. However, they had not in fact led to increased participation among a majority of the respondents. While all these factors could potentially stimulate participation, primarily in individuals who were members of political and civic organisations, other factors trumped this stimulation – notably fear of reprisals, little belief in the ability of ICT to cause change, and irresponsiveness of leaders. Ultimately, most respondents, including members of organised groups, did not become any more politically active as a result of using the social network. This begs the question of why these individuals did not participate even when their political knowledge grew, they had the resources to enable their participation, and also had the time to participate. Below we explore the most prominent reasons:

What Hampered Increased Citizen Participation Online?

Fear of Reprisals

One of the democratizing effects of ICT is that it enables citizens to participate remotely and anonymously with minimal fear of reprisals (Chadwick 2006; Weber et al 2003). In Uganda, for many citizens, social media is a no-go zone politically, precisely because of fear of being traced and attracting reprisal. This fear is rooted in the country's history where commenting negatively on the state carried the assumption of reprimand as well as in a number of recent developments, such as the announcement in March 2013 that the government would form a social media monitoring centre to track anti-state content. It came on the heel of reports in mainstream newspapers that security agencies were seeking to establish the identity of a popular Facebook user who was very critical of government, and revelations by Facebook that Ugandan authorities had asked for the details of Facebook account holders – requests the company turned down (CIPESA 2014). Respondents reported that they regularly practiced self-censorship on Facebook, which had had a chilling effect on their online participation. Several "taboo topics", namely the ones Facebook users thought would attract reprisals from the government, were identified, including the restoration of presidential term limits which were scrapped in 2005 at President Museveni's bidding, the retirement of President Museveni who has been in power for 30 years, whether Museveni's son who has risen swiftly through army ranks will succeed him as the country's president, debate on the tough anti-gay law, deployment of Ugandan forces in conflicts in countries such as Somalia and South Sudan, corruption at high levels of government, and military spending. Some of the statements below from respondents captured the general mood on the fear of reprisals:

- **IG:** It is because of fear of retribution that most people in Uganda who comment online on politics or who are members of political groups online use pseudonyms with scant personal information about them.
- **NM:** There is a fear of retribution for comments on politics. The internet is accessed on our phones [with registered sim cards] so you can be picked [up by security agents].
- **NM:** Many people on Facebook do not use their real names. Even the phone numbers listed are often not their primary contacts but auxiliary numbers which they can throw away. You might say something and they pin you.
- **PP:** Government can tap phones and Facebook. When the issue came up that the government was going to monitor what people say on social media, people stopped commenting on our forums.

Developments offline contributed to citizens' fear of reprisals for online actions. Numerous radio stations have been shut down in recent years, with the two leading independent daily newspapers having been shut down for 12 days during 2013 over a story related to a supposed scheme for the president's son to succeed him as the Ugandan head of state. Opposition leaders and civil society activists have on several occasions been arrested, beaten, incarcerated over peaceful protests (Amnesty International, 2013). A repressive public order management law passed at the end of 2013 prohibits a meeting in a public place by more five people who do not have police authorization, while a February 2014 law (since then nullified by the constitutional court) would hand one a life sentence for "aggravated homosexuality".

Little Belief in Ability of ICT to Cause Change

There was little belief that using Facebook could help cause change. Most respondents knew that many duty bearers had Facebook accounts but said the officials' accounts were largely dormant: the duty bearers rarely posted anything and only a tiny minority ever responded to questions posed to them, or contributed to debates in online forums. Moreover, the Facebook accounts in the names of politicians and other duty bearers were mostly managed by hired individuals whose mandate rarely included engaging in debates or making commitments via social mediums. The duty bearers themselves, it was believed, lacked the skills or the interest to be active on Facebook. As one NM respondent put it, "Responses from leaders would be an incentive for me to participate in political issues. Leaders don't respond so people give up. It's the same way if you are my friend on Facebook and I say hello and you do not respond; I will not bother you again."

Others participants remarked:

- **IG:** Politicians are not consistent in their use of Facebook and once you challenge them on issues to do with their promises to their constituencies or any other pledges, they disappear.
- **NM:** I find it a waste of time if I am not talking directly to the owner of the account.
- **PP:** There is poor accountability on the part of our leaders. They are always running away from us when we raise accountability issues. They don't want to associate with their electorate except during campaign time.

Limited Skills, Time, and Money

According to the study conducted in 2015, data costs are high, with 1 GB of data going for US$12 in a country where 30.7% live on less than US$1.25 a day. The high data costs mean many users, particularly those with limited incomes, prioritize what they do online. Only 18% of Ugandans are connected to electricity, which often forces internet cafés to shut down or mobile phones to be off because their batteries cannot be charged. Furthermore, given that about 49% of the Ugandan users of Facebook were in the 18-24 age group, an age at which many are still in school or otherwise struggling to earn a living, they have limited disposable income to channel into buying data or buying surfing time at an internet café. Many of those using Facebook only used a few basic features. As one participant put it, "Many Facebook users only know how to search for friends and to update their status. They are Facebook tourists not users. They know nothing about hashtags and searching for pages."

Politics Sucks and Facebook is a Social, Not a Political Medium

For some social media users, Facebook is used for socializing not political participation. As one NM respondent put it, "We joined Facebook to communicate with friends; other uses are just coming in." For such users, old habits die hard; they started using Facebook because it satisfied their need and interest in communicating social issues with family and friends. Such individuals – generally those not involved in activist or political groups – may initiate conversations, upload pictures, share stories, and participate in group discussions. However, all this is of a social rather than political nature and it directly serves personal causes and derives personal benefit rather than for the community.

- **NM:** There is little interest in politics. Most people don't want to comment on politics yet as a user you want your Facebook page to be active with users' comments so you go for a topic that will attract comments, that is entertainment or social issues.
- **NM:** I have no hope in political processes. Many things have been promised but not done. Even if I comment what will it change? So I decide not to comment.
- **PP:** Most Facebook users are youths whose main interest is entertainment. Politics is not of interest to them. Even adult users usually use it for entertainment and showing off their children and social lives.

Many respondents reported that they were increasingly taking to using newer social media tools such as Whatsapp, which are considered more private in some ways and which transmit messages more instantaneously relative to Facebook. This was further driving many Ugandan social network users away from the political sphere and into the comfort zones of communicating only with known friends and associates whose telephone numbers they were sure of. Ultimately, this was deepening the political cynicism and apathy.

DISCUSSION

A basic premise of the CVM, and one that is prevalent in the eParticipation literature, holds that access to the internet and other 'resources' such as time, money and civic skills, boosts the proclivity for an individual to participate. Similarly, it is commonly stated in eParticipation theory that there is a link between ICT use and participation, with uses such as news and information seeking, and involvement in community building such as online groups, associated with increased likelihood for an individual to participate. But in the present research, it was found that there were numerous impediments to eParticipation, with the fear of retribution a particularly prominent one. Regarding the use of Facebook and its effect on online participation the ties and conversations generated on Facebook, the increased political knowledge enabled by using this SNS, and the ease of exchanging information, contacting leaders and taking part in discussions, were potentially positive predictors for participation. However, while using Facebook gave individuals a high possibility for improved political knowledge regardless of whether these individuals were interested or participating in political related activities, using the social network had not led to increased participation among a majority of the respondents. There were more engagements among citizens, while interactions between citizens and duty bearers were much less.

The use of ICT had resulted, for the main part, in increased contacts with family, and work relations as opposed to civic and political participation. But as has also been found by previous research (Zúñiga, et al., 2014), social media use for social interaction does not have direct influence in people's political engagement, but rather an indirect effect by means of citizens expressing themselves politically. Where individuals expected to have direct, tangible, personal benefits from using technology, they would be more likely to use it. While many used the internet to read news, place sports bets, announce on Facebook the parties they attended at the weekend, the numbers of those engaging in online civic and political actions were low, particularly for individuals that were not politically inclined. For Ugandan citizens with limited interest in politics, living under an authoritarian regime where critical opinion can attract reprisals, having access to the Internet and civic knowledge rarely translates into eParticipation. These findings are consistent with those in authoritarian Iran (Wojcieszak & Smith, 2013), which showed that most connected citizens were not using the Internet for political processes but to discuss personal topics and work-related affairs. Moreover, majority of Iranian citizens had greater confidence in new media empowering them personally rather than making governmental officials more responsive (Wojcieszak et al., 2012). Besides, in an environment where citizens have no trust in their anonymity and security being assured by the channels of participation, they will be deterred from participating even if they wanted to vent their political frustrations (Wakabi, 2016).

Looking back, what do the results mean for the civic voluntarism model? The internet has been said to subsidize the costs of participation (Weber, et al 2003; Moy and Xenos, 2007). Furthermore, proponents of the positive influence of internet use on participation, like Bakker and de Vreese (2011) and Zúñiga et al (2012), contend that media use related to information acquisition, such as news and online communities, has a positive impact on civic participation. Moreover, as Gustafsson (2012) found out among Swedish respondents active in groups, Facebook was an important channel for intra-organizational communication, a great source for political news, and a way of influencing contacts. From the results of the present research, the use of Facebook no doubt has a great possibility to increase political knowledge. Similarly, it offers a possibility to mobilize support for political causes, recruit members, while also supporting individuals to seek information and to participate in debates at affordable cost and with relative ease. However, the use of Facebook does not necessarily stimulate participation in persons that are not interested in politics, nor does it inevitably raise the level of participation among individuals that are already active in civic or political groups. One of the primary determinants of an individual's participation is the interest they have in politics, but this is often mediated by their ability to participate (i.e. the skills they have to enable them to participate via Facebook), their level of access to Facebook (i.e. resources such as having a smart phone or money to purchase data) and their ability to create time to participate.

This research corroborated the assertion by scholars like Klofstad (2009) that it is when the costs are low and the benefits high that people participate. In the Ugandan context, however, the high cost firstly includes the fees for acquiring an internet enabled device and buying time at an internet café or purchasing data. The cost, in a way which Klofstad, Gustafsson, and proponents of the Civic Voluntarism Model may not have conceived, also includes the possible reprisals that a person believes using Facebook for political purposes can result into: the higher the likelihood and the more severe the reprisals are likely to be, the cost of participating correspondingly goes up and the individual is less likely to participate. This research found that interest in politics was extraordinarily low, partly because of apathy resulting from low belief in the possibility for individuals' actions (mainly online but offline too) to influence change. The specific Ugandan context, with a government in power for 30 years that rigs elections, stifles independent voices by media, the political opposition and citizens, all contributed to making the appetite for participation low and the cost high. But low incomes, high illiteracy rates and the poor spread of the internet also made cost high.

Verba et al (1995) suggested that individuals found costs of participating low enough and the benefits high enough when they were equipped with resources of time, money, and civic skills. Furthermore, added Verba and colleagues, those individuals need to have a sense of psychological engagement with politics and current events and to have been recruited by someone in their social network in order to participate. Besides the overwhelming detachment from politics that we saw among the respondents, even for those individuals that were interested in politics, being members of political parties or other civic organizations, the fear of reprisals and non-engagement by a significant number of Ugandans both citizens and leaders online, dulled these politically-inclined individuals' appetites for online participation. This, in turn, supported assertions by Bimber (2003) that the political effects of new media use are contingent on individuals' levels of sophistication, motives, as well as social context. Interest and cost trump skills possession and all the merits that Facebook enables - including increased political knowledge - as determinants of an individual's participation. Politics lies down the pecking order in a society with high political apathy, non-responsive leaders, a hostile and predominant ruling party in power for three decades, low cost of living ranged against high internet costs, widespread self-censorship and few internet users. In this Ugandan context, many of the benefits that social media including Facebook are believed to bring in Western democratic societies are thus turned on their head.

Ultimately, the Civic Voluntarism Model was not entirely valid in a low income, non-democratic society as it has been shown by Gustafsson (2012) to be in developed democratic countries such as Sweden. Specifically, the determination by Verba and colleagues that resources and engagement are the most important in determining whether the benefits of civic participation outweigh the costs does not seem to hold wholly in as far as it fell short of pinpointing factors such as fear of reprisals and political apathy. However, fears that intensive internet use could lead to a withdrawal from public life (Quintelier 2008) were evident among some of the respondents. People tended to associate with friends and relatives more – i.e. their close social circles as opposed to engaging with civic organizations, political parties or other sorts of online groups whose members they did not personally know or whose interests they did not share. But, as was contended by Tang and Lee (2013), having connections with people such as activists and political representatives via social media would typically result in exposure to a large amount of political information, persuasive messages, or even direct mobilization attempts. Such exposure would have a greater likelihood to stimulate participation compared to connections with one's familial and social circles. It should also be recalled that, as argued by Chan (2016), connections with public political actors exhibit the strongest link between Facebook use and participation. In this context, it could be argued that with most users using Facebook and other social media largely for entertainment, exhibitionism and providing updates to family and friends, Facebook was growing their civic skills but only to a limited extent and for the majority it was not leading to increased online, or offline, political participation.

At one level, it would be expecting too much to be optimistic about eParticipation working in Uganda at the moment – with the low democratic culture, an authoritarian regime, and a citizenry that has low belief in their ability to change the status quo, particularly via ICT. But at another level, it could be legitimately conceivable that because of the limited avenues for offline participation and free expression, citizens would jump into the online world as a platform for unfettered engagement and participation. After all, there is considerable recent research on how citizens in some authoritarian countries have used ICT to circumvent state controls on information and therefore been able to do citizen organising for social and political change. Furthermore, as argued by the equity-fairness theories, groups that feel they cannot get their voices heard through conventional political participation are more likely to vent their frustrations in other types of political participation (Phelps, 2006), which in this case could include the online sphere. This contention by Phelps could have held true in Uganda given the desire by citizens to find alternative (such as online) types of political participation. However, that desire has been upended due to increased government witch-hunt of social media critics, declining civic space in the offline world, higher apathy among citizens, and low trust in the security of ICT tools. On balance, the fears and frustrations that citizens in an authoritarian country have outweigh the benefits of eParticipation. In many instances, these fears are not lived but are based on perceptions or the experiences of others. The sum total of this is that if these fears are not addressed, the great majority of Ugandans, including those with ample access to ICT, and who are aware of the benefits of online participation, will for many years remain out of the fold of eParticipation.

REFERENCES

All in One Social. (2013). *Facebook statistics for Uganda*. Retrieved February 12, 2014, from http://www.allin1social.com/facebook/country_stats/uganda

Allagui, I. (2014). Article. *International Journal of Communication*, *8*, 983–1007.

Aman, M., & Jayroe, T. J. (2013). ICT, Social Media, and the Arab Transition to Democracy: From Venting to Acting. *Digest of Middle East Studies*, *22I*(2), 317–347. doi:10.1111/dome.12024

Amnesty International. (2013). *Uganda: Activists arrested as disturbing crackdown on media continues*. Retrieved October 24, 2014, from http://www.amnesty.org/en/news/uganda-crackdown-newspapers-continues-2013-05-24

Bachmann, I., Kaufhold, K., Lewis, S., & Zúñiga, H. (2010). News Platform Preference: Advancing the Effects of Age and Media Consumption on Political Participation. *International Journal of Internet Science*, *5*(1), 34–47.

Baguma, S. (2016). *Uganda: the presidential election that wasn't?* Retrieved from http://www.afrikareporter.com/uganda-the-presidential-election-that-wasnt/

Bakker, T., & de Vreese, C. (2011). Good News for the Future? Young People, Internet Use, and Political Participation. *Communication Research*, *38*(4), 451–470. doi:10.1177/0093650210381738

Bimber, B. (2000). Measuring the gender gap on the internet. *Social Science Quarterly*, *81*(3), 868–876.

Bryant, E. I. (2012). The Iron Fist vs. the Microchip. *Journal of Strategic Security*, *5*(2), 1–26. doi:10.5038/1944-0472.5.2.1

Castells, M. (1996). The Information Age: Economy, Society and Culture.: Vol. I. *The Rise of the Network Society*. Oxford, UK: Blackwell Publishers.

Chadwick, A. (2006). *Internet Politics: States, Citizens, and New Communications Technologies*. New York: Oxford University Press.

Chan, M. (2016). Social Network Sites and Political Engagement: Exploring the Impact of Facebook Connections and Uses on Political Protest and Participation. *Mass Communication & Society*, *19*(4), 430–451. doi:10.1080/15205436.2016.1161803

Chullo, S. (2016). *Museveni's Flawed Election Victory in Uganda*. Retrieved from http://www.huffingtonpost.com/stan-chu-ilo/musevenis-flawed-election_b_9349490.html

CIPESA. (2014). *State of Internet Freedoms in East Africa*. Retrieved October 25, 2014, from http://www.cipesa.org/?wpfb_dl=76

CIPESA. (2016). *Uganda Again Blocks Social Media to Stifle Anti-Museveni Protests*. Retrieved from http://cipesa.org/2016/05/uganda-again-blocks-social-media-to-stifle-anti-museveni-protests/

Crandall, A., & Mutuku, L. (2011). *MGovernance: Exploratory Survey on Kenyan Service Delivery and Government Interaction*. Retrieved July 12, 2014, from http://ict4dem.dsv.su.se/wp-content/files/iHub_M-Governance_Survey_on_Kenyan_Service_Delivery_and_Government_Interaction.pdf

Cullen, R., & Sommer, L. (2011). Participatory democracy and the value of online community networks: An exploration of online and offline communities engaged in civil society and political activity. *Government Information Quarterly*, *28*(2), 148–154. doi:10.1016/j.giq.2010.04.008

Cummings, J. N., Sproull, L., & Kiesler, S. B. (2002). Beyond hearing: Where the realworld and online support meet. *Group Dynamics*, *6*(1), 78–88. doi:10.1037/1089-2699.6.1.78

Dhaha, I. S. Y., & Igale, A. B. (2013). Facebook Usage among Somali Youth. A Test of Uses and Gratifications Approach. *International Journal of Humanities and Social Science*, *3*(3).

Effing, R., van Hillegersberg, J., & Huibers, T. (2011). Social media and political participation: are Facebook, Twitter and YouTube democratizing our political systems? In *Electronic participation* (pp. 25–35). Springer Berlin Heidelberg. doi:10.1007/978-3-642-23333-3_3

Freedom House. (2013). *Freedom House Condemns Uganda's Restriction of Political Speech*. Retrieved June 15, 2014, from http://freedomhouse.org/article/freedom-house-condemns-ugandas-restriction-political-speech

Freedom House. (2015). *Freedom on The Net 2015 - Uganda*. Retrieved from https://freedomhouse.org/report/freedom-net/2015/uganda

Freschi, A. C., Medaglia, R., & Nørbjerg, J. (2009). A tale of six countries: eParticipation research from an administration and political perspective. In A. Macintosh, & E. Tambouris (Eds.), *Proceedings of 1st international conference on electronic participation, ePart 2009* (pp. 36–45). Berlin: Springer-Verlag. doi:10.1007/978-3-642-03781-8_4

Friedl, J., & Vercic, A. (2011). Media preferences of digital natives internal communication: A pilot study. *Public Relations Review*, *37*(1), 84–86. doi:10.1016/j.pubrev.2010.12.004

Gaffey, C. (2016, June 1). Kizza Besigye blocked from appearing at treason trial. *Newsweek*.

Gagliardone, I. (2014). "A Country in Order": Technopolitics, Nation Building, and the Development of ICT in Ethiopia. *Information Technologies & International Development*, *10*(1), 3–19.

Greitens, S. C. (2013). Authoritarianism Online: What Can We Learn from Internet Data in Nondemocracies? *Political Science & Politics*, *46*(02), 262–270. doi:10.1017/S1049096513000346

Grönlund, Å. (2009). ICT Is Not Participation Is Not Democracy – eParticipation Development Models Revisited. In A. Macintosh & E. Tambouris (Eds.), *Electronic Participation: 1st International Conference, ePart 2009* (pp.12–23). Berlin: Springer Verlag.

Grönlund, Å. (2011). Connecting eGovernment to Real Government - The Failure of the UN eParticipation Index. *Lecture Notes in Computer Science*, *6846*(2011), 26-37. Retrieved June 15, 2014, from http://www.springerlink.com/content/w246q260jt71n557/

Grönlund, Å., & Wakabi, W. (2015). Citizens' use of new media in authoritarian regimes: Case study of Uganda. *The Electronic Journal of Information Systems in Developing Countries*, *67*(1), 1–23.

Gustafsson, N. (2012). The subtle nature of Facebook politics: Swedish social network site users and political participation. *New Media & Society*, *14*(7), 1111–1127. doi:10.1177/1461444812439551

Hacker, K. L., Mason, S. M., & Morgan, E. L. (2009). Digital Disempowerment in a Network Society. *International Journal of Electronic Government Research*, *5*(2), 57–71. doi:10.4018/jegr.2009040104

Harlow, S. (2012). Social Media and Social Movements: Facebook and an Online Guatemalan Justice Movement that Moved Offline. *New Media & Society*, *14*(2), 225–243. doi:10.1177/1461444811410408

Holt, K., Shehata, A., Strömbäck, J., & Ljungberg, E. (2013). Age and the effects of news media attention and social media use on political interest and participation: Do social media function as leveller? *European Journal of Communication*, *28*(1), 19–34. doi:10.1177/0267323112465369

Howard, P. N., Duffy, A., Freelon, D., Hussain, M., Mari, W., & Mazaid, M. (2011). *Opening Closed Regimes: What Was the Role of Social Media During the Arab Spring?* Seattle, WA: Department of Communication, University of Washington.

Hundley, H., & Shyles, L. (2010). US teenagers perceptions and awareness of digital technology: A focus group approach. *New Media & Society*, *12*(3), 417–433. doi:10.1177/1461444809342558

Jho, W., & Song, K. J. (2015). Institutional and technological determinants of civil e-Participation: Solo or duet? *Government Information Quarterly*, *32*(4), 488–495. doi:10.1016/j.giq.2015.09.003

Kalampokis, E., Tambouris, E., & Tarabanis, K. (2008). A Domain Model for eParticipation. *Third International Conference on Internet and Web.*

Kane, J., & Patapan, H. (2004). Challenge and Promise of eDemocracy. *Griffith Review*, *3*(Autumn), 201–207.

Klofstad, C. (2009). Civic Talk and Civic Participation: The Moderating Effect of Individual Predispositions. *American Politics Research*, *37*(5), 856–878. doi:10.1177/1532673X09333960

Laverty, A. R. (2012). *The Missing Connection: ICTs and Democracy in Africa*. UCLA: African Studies 0044.

Lee, D., Loutas, N., Sánchez-Nielsen, E., Mogulkoc, E., & Lacigova, O. (2011). Inform-consult-empower: a three-tiered approach to eParticipation. In Electronic Participation (pp. 121-132). Springer Berlin Heidelberg. doi:10.1007/978-3-642-23333-3_11

Lee, J., & Kim, S. (2012). E-Participation in the Era of Web 2.0: Factors Affecting Citizens' Active E-Participation in Local Governance. In J. R. Gil-Garcia, N. Helbig, & A. Ojo (Eds.), *Proceedings of the 6th International Conference on Theory and Practice of Electronic Governance (ICEGOV)* (pp. 44-47). New York: ACM Press. doi:10.1145/2463728.2463739

Lin, J. (2016). Differential gains in SNSs: Effects of active vs. passive Facebook political participation on offline political participation and voting behavior among first-time and experienced voters. *Asian Journal of Communication*, *26*(3), 278–297. doi:10.1080/01292986.2016.1148184

Lynch, M. (2011). After Egypt: The Limits and Promise of Online Challenges to the Authoritarian Arab State. *Perspectives on Politics*, *9*(2), 301–310. doi:10.1017/S1537592711000910

Macintosh, A., & Whyte, A. (2002). *Analysis and Evaluation of e-consultations*. Retrieved from www.teledemocracy.org

Manrique, M., & Mikail, B. (2011). The Role of New Media and Communication Technologies in Arab Transitions. *FRIDE Policy Briefing No. 106.* Retrieved from http://fride.org/publication/965/the-role-of-new-media-and-communication-technologies-in-arab-transitions

Mislove, A. (2007). Measurement and Analysis of Online Social Networks. *IMC'07.*

Morgan, D. L. (2008). Snowball sampling. In L. M. Given (Ed.), The Sage Encyclopedia of Qualitative Research Methods (vol. 2, pp. 816-817). Thousand Oaks, CA: Sage Publications.

Moy, P., & Xenos, M. (2007). Direct and Differential Effects of the Internet on Political and Civic Engagement. *Journal of Communication*, *54*(7), 704–718.

Mpuga, D. (2015). *Social Media Critic Arrested in Uganda*. Retrieved from http://www.voanews.com/content/social-media-critic-arrested-in-uganda-/2820626.html

Mutiga, M. (2016, March 5). After disputed election, Uganda police target media. *The East African.*

Mutsvairo, B., & Sirks, L. A. (2015). Examining the contribution of social media in reinforcing political participation in Zimbabwe. *Journal of African Media Studies*, *7*(3), 329–344. doi:10.1386/jams.7.3.329_1

Pattie, C., Seyd, P., & Whiteley, P. (2004). *Citizenship in Britain: Values, Participation, and Democracy*. Cambridge University Press. doi:10.1017/CBO9780511490811

Phelps, E. (2006). *Young Adults and Electoral Turnout in Britain: Towards a Generational Model of Political Participation*. Sussex European Institute Working Paper No 92.

Quintelier, E., & Vissers, S. (2008). The Effect of Internet Use on Political Participation: An Analysis of Survey Results for 16-Year-Olds in Belgium. *Social Science Computer Review*, *26*(4), 411–427. doi:10.1177/0894439307312631

Räsänen, P. (2008). The aftermath of the ICT revolution? Media and communication technology preferences in Finland in 1999 and 2004. *New Media & Society*, *10*(2), 225–245. doi:10.1177/1461444807086471

Reuter, O. J., & Szakonyi, D. (2015). Online Social Media and Political Awareness in Authoritarian Regimes. *British Journal of Political Science*, *45*(01), 29–51. doi:10.1017/S0007123413000203

Rüdig, W., & Karyotis, G. (2013, September). Beyond the Usual Suspects? New Participants in Anti-Austerity Protests in Greece. Mobilization. *An International Quarterly*, *18*(3), 313–330.

Sæbø, Ø. (2011). Understanding Twitter use among parliament representatives: A genre analysis. In *Electronic participation* (pp. 1–12). Springer Berlin Heidelberg. doi:10.1007/978-3-642-23333-3_1

Sæbø, Ø., Rose, J., & Flak, L. (2008). The shape of eParticipation: Characterizing an emerging research area. *Government Information Quarterly*, *25*(3), 400–428. doi:10.1016/j.giq.2007.04.007

Scherer, S., & Wimmer, M. A. (2011). Reference framework for E-participation projects. In *Electronic Participation* (pp. 145–156). Springer Berlin Heidelberg. doi:10.1007/978-3-642-23333-3_13

SimilarWeb. (2015). *Top 50 sites in Uganda for all categories*. Retrieved from http://www.similarweb.com/country/uganda

Simpson, J. (2014). *Who are the winners and losers from the Arab Spring?* Retrieved from http://www.bbc.com/news/world-middle-east-30003865

Stroud, N. (2008). Media Use and Political Predispositions: Revisiting the Concept of Selective Exposure. *Political Behavior*, *30*(3), 341–366. doi:10.1007/s11109-007-9050-9

Susha, I., & Grönlund, Å. (2012). eParticipation research: Systematizing the field. *Government Information Quarterly*, *29*(3), 373–382. doi:10.1016/j.giq.2011.11.005

Tambouris, E., Liotas, N., Kaliviotis, D., & Tarabanis, K. (2007). A Framework for Scoping eParticipation. The *Proceedings of the 8th Annual International Digital Government Research Conference*.

Tang, G., & Lee, F. L. (2013). Facebook use and political participation: The impact of exposure to shared political information, connections with public political actors, and network structural heterogeneity. *Social Science Computer Review*.

Theocharis, Y., & Lowe, W. (2016). Does Facebook increase political participation? Evidence from a field experiment. *Information Communication and Society*, *19*(10), 1465–1486. doi:10.1080/1369118X.2015.1119871

Tufekci, Z., & Wilson, C. (2012). Social Media and the Decision to Participate in Political Protest: Observations From Tahrir Square. *Journal of Communication*, *62*(2), 363–379. doi:10.1111/j.1460-2466.2012.01629.x

Tworzecki, T., & Semetko, H. (2010). Media Uses and Effects in New Democracies: The Case of Polands 2005 Parliamentary and Presidential Elections. *The International Journal of Press/Politics*, *15*(2), 155–174. doi:10.1177/1940161209360698

UCC. (2016). *Post, Broadcasting and Telecommunications Market and Industry Report*. Retrieved from http://ucc.co.ug/files/downloads/Q1-Market-Report-for-Jan-March-2016-Mbaga.pdf

Verba, S., Schlozman, K. L., & Brady, H. (1995). *Voice and Equality: Civic Voluntarism in American Politics*. Cambridge, MA: Harvard University Press.

Wakabi, W. (2016). *Motivating eParticipation in Authoritarian Countries* (Doctoral dissertation). Örebro University.

Wakabi, W. & Grönlund, A. (2015). Citizens' use of new media in authoritarian regimes: A case study of Uganda. *Electronic Journal of Information Systems in Developing Countries, 67*(1).

Weber, L., Loumakis, A., & Bergman, J. (2003). Who Participates and Why?: An Analysis of Citizens on the Internet and the Mass Public. *Social Science Computer Review*, *21*(1), 26–42. doi:10.1177/0894439302238969

Wojcieszak, M. (2009). Carrying Online Participation Offline-Mobilization by Radical Online Groups and Politically Dissimilar Offline Ties. *Journal of Communication*, *59*(3), 564–586. doi:10.1111/j.1460-2466.2009.01436.x

Wojcieszak, M., Brouillette, A., & Smith, B. (2013). Outside. In *The Practices and Perceptions of Iranian Diaspora Journalists*. Center for Global Communication Studies, University of Pennsylvania.

Wojcieszak, M., & Smith, B. (2013). Will Politics be Tweeted? New Media Use by Iranian Youth in 2011. *New Media & Society*, *16*(1), 91–109. doi:10.1177/1461444813479594

Zúñiga, G., Molyneux, L., & Zheng, P. (2014). Social Media, Political Expression, and Political Participation: Panel Analysis of Lagged and Concurrent Relationships. *Journal of Communication*, *64*(4), 612–634. doi:10.1111/jcom.12103

Zúñiga, H. G., Jung, N., & Valenzuela, S. (2012). Social Media Use for News and Individuals Social Capital, Civic Engagement and Political Participation. *Journal of Computer-Mediated Communication*, *17*(3), 319–336. doi:10.1111/j.1083-6101.2012.01574.x

Zúñiga, H. G., & Valenzuela, S. (2011). The mediating path to a stronger citizenship: Online and offline networks, weak ties and civic engagement. *Communication Research*, *38*(3), 397–421. doi:10.1177/0093650210384984

Chapter 13
Online Free Expression and Its Gatekeepers

Joanna Kulesza
University of Lodz, Poland

ABSTRACT

This chapter covers the pressing issues of online free expression at the time of global telecommunication services and social media. What once was the domain of the state has become the prerogative of private global companies – it is their terms of service and sense of social responsibility that have replaced local perceptions of morality and set limits to individual personal rights. Whether protecting privacy or defending against defamation, it is the Internet Service Provider who can offer tools far more effective and prompt than any national court and law enforcement agency. And even though the right to free expression is firmly rotted in the global standard of article 19 UDHR, nowhere than online are the differences in its interpretation, originated by history, morality and religion, more palpable. The paper aims to discuss each of the three composite rights of free expression (the right to hold, impart and receive information and ideas) and identify the actual limitations originated by national laws. The author emphasizes states' positive obligation to take active measures aimed at protecting free expression, ensuring that all human rights are "protected, respected and remedied". This obligation makes the interrelationship between national lawmakers and international telecommunication service providers complex as the latter serve as the actual gate keepers of free expression in the information society. The paper covers a discussion on how different countries deal with this challenge through various approaches to ISP liability, including the notice-and-take down procedure as well as content filtering (preventive censorship). The author goes on to criticize those mechanisms as enabling ISPs too much freedom in deciding upon the shape and scope of individuals' right to impart and receive information.

INTRODUCTION

The paper discusses the contemporary perspective of the right to free expression when exercised online with particular regard to the rights and obligations of Internet Service Providers (ISPs). The author briefly recapitulates the origin, definition and interpretation of the three composite rights enshrined in

DOI: 10.4018/978-1-5225-1862-4.ch013

article 19 UDHR: the right to hold, impart and receive information and ideas. She puts emphasis on their limitations legitimately enforced by states. States' duty to protect free expression is than identified as their negative obligation to refrain from infringement as well as a positive one, to guarantee that human rights are "protected, respected and remedied" within national legal systems. Than the role of Internet Service Providers is introduced as the gate keepers of free expression in the information society. Different schemes for national ISP liability mechanisms are presented: the notice-and-take down procedure as well as Internet content filtering (preventive censorship). Kulesza goes on to criticize both mechanisms as enabling ISPs too much freedom in deciding upon the shape and scope of individuals' right to impart and receive information.

FREEDOM OF EXPRESSION: DEFINITION, MEANING, AND ENFORCEMENT

Freedom of expression is deeply rooted in the human rights system – it's one of the fundamental freedoms enshrined in the Universal Declaration of Human Rights (UDHR), adopted as a statement of international consensus on the need to protect certain rights and liberties of individuals against unjustified infringement by state authorities and third parties (United Nations 1948 and 2011, Schauer 1982 and 2004). The wording of its Article 19, phrasing the right to free expression, has been repeated in numerous international treaties and served as a standard of free speech for national courts and international tribunals. Article 19 of the UDHR grants every human the right "freedom of opinion and expression". The very language of the article specifies the three inclusive freedoms that come with the freedom of expression. The "right to freedom of opinion and expression" includes "freedom to hold opinions", as well as the liberty to receive information and (last but not least) to impart it, "regardless of frontiers" (United Nations 1948). Confines for exercising these complementary rights are defined in Article 29 para. 2, which subjects their implementation "to such limitations as are determined by law" and introduced "for the purpose of securing due recognition and respect for the rights and freedoms of others". Restrictions may be set up also in order to meet the "just requirements of morality, public order and the general welfare in a democratic society". The ambiguous wording of the limitative clause results from the "aggressive" compromise of 1948 (Morsnik 1999) and brings numerous interpretative challenges up till today.

The 1948 compromise was possible primarily due to two factors. First, because of the recent horrid remembrances of World War II, driving the world leaders, debating the scope and shape of the Declaration, to emphasize their disaccord with mass human rights violations. The other crucial factor was the non-binding character of the Declaration. When a binding assertion was required, the international community needed almost twenty more years for a suitable form of its stipulations to be successfully introduced into a treaty. The contents of the corresponding Article 19 of the International Covenant on Civil and Political Rights (ICCPR) derive richly from the UDHR original (United Nations 1966). In para. 1 the Article includes a confirmation of the universality of "the right to hold opinions without interference", while putting the human right guarantee into more detail in para. 2. It grants each human the right to "freedom of expression" which – again – includes three complementary liberties: to "seek, receive and impart information and ideas", regardless of frontiers. In the neighboring para. 3 the limitative clauses are repeated, giving state authorities the possibility to set legal boundaries on the exercise of human rights for reasons of national security or public order, to protect public health or morals as well to guarantee the rights of others. Should states decide to introduce such "necessary" limitations, they may do so only through an act of law.

Details of the interpretation of the right have been set by numerous UN bodies. One directly mandated by the UN to enforce Article 19 ICCPR is the Human Rights Council (the successor of the United Nations Commission on Human Rights) (United Nations 2005). This is a inter-governmental body vested with the task of identifying and investigating grave violations of human rights by UN members states. It primarily works through annual reports ("Universal Periodic Review)" of state parties on their implementation of the ICCPR as well as through non-binding guidelines on the interpretation of individual rights. It also issues recommendations directed at states found to be in violation of human rights, following the individual complaint procedure and pursued by a "follow-up procedure" aimed at verifying the implementation of the particular recommendations (United Nations 1966). Its mandate includes the power to submit to the Security Council a request to introduce sanctions against states in grave violations of human rights.

These procedures are subject to criticism, falling along two complimentary lines. The guidelines are regarded as too general for country specific implementation, which complements the lack of state parties' political will to implement them. What is more, the Council often supports countries weak in the implementation of human rights standards, using their national human rights organizations as a cover up for their own violations (Mertus 2009).

In its research and policy shaping activities the Council is supported by the Advisory Committee. The Committee is a group of independent experts providing the Council with "expertise and advice on thematic human rights issues". In 2011 the Committee presented the Council with guidelines on the interpretation of Article 19 ICCPR, as a laying ground for Council guidelines on the particular interpretation of the right of free expression (United Nations 2011). The agreement was reached after two years of intense discussions and consultations with states and civil society. The Committee emphasizes that any limitations to the exercise of the right to free speech may only be introduced through acts of law, where a rule of law is to be understood as "formulated with sufficient precision to enable an individual to regulate his or her conduct accordingly" and "made accessible to the public". Traditional, religious or other such customary law sources are not considered "law" for the purpose of the regulation. A clear guideline for the governments to actively protect the right to impart and receive information by ones within their jurisdiction is enshrined in para. 25, which states that "a law may not confer unfettered discretion for the restriction of freedom of expression on those charged with its execution" (United Nations 2011). This stipulation supports the contents of para. 15, which requires "states to take all necessary steps to foster independence" of new media and ensure individual access thereto. New media are referred to in para. 43 as "operation of websites, blogs or other internet-based, or other information dissemination systems, including (…) internet service providers or search engines". When explaining in what form the limitations foreseen in para. 3 of Article 19 ICCPR may be introduced, the Committee emphasizes, that "the restrictions must be provided by law", may only be introduced on one of the grounds set out in Article 19 and must conform to the strict tests of necessity and proportionality. What is more, when restrictions are applied, that must be done only for the "purposes for which they were prescribed and must be directly related to the specific need on which they are predicated".

The work of the Committee visualizes the right to free expression as a negative obligation of states to refrain from infringing the individual right to have and share information. The Committee does not directly address the issues of limitations put onto the individual right to free expression by private parties nor does it introduce any positive obligations of states to actively protect individuals from such infringements in this very document. It has been doing so however successively since 2004, starting with the Sub-Commission on the Promotion and Protection of Human Rights of the (then) UN Commission on

Human Rights in the form of "Draft Norms on the Responsibilities of Transnational Corporations and Other Business Enterprises with Regard to Human Rights" (United Nations 2003). Referred to as the UN "Protect, Respect and Remedy" Framework for Business and Human Rights the document includes a set of human rights guidelines applicable to non-state parties and was adopted by the Human Rights Council unanimously in 2008 (nicknamed "the Ruggie Report" after the name of the UN Special Representative, tasked with preparing the report serving as the blueprint for the guidelines) (Ruggie, 2006, 2008 and 2011). The "Protect, Respect and Remedy" Framework includes three groups of obligations. The first group covers duties resting upon states, compelling them to protect individuals against human rights abuses by third parties (the obligation to "protect"). This goal ought to be obtained through appropriate policies, law, and adjudication. Crucial to effective protection of human rights is the obligation to show due diligence in assessing human rights risks arising out of corporate responsibility to respect human rights. Through external analysis of human rights threats states are to present their will to effectively respect human rights of individuals within their jurisdiction (meeting the obligation to "respect"). Eventually, states are obliged to provide for effective legal remedies against human rights violations by non-state parties (the obligation to "remedy").

The contents of the right to free expression may therefore be identified in much detail based on the work of the HRC. The crucial problem is its enforcement. For the reasons of cultural differences in interpretation of the guidelines' general language and lack of a suitable, efficient enforcement mechanism there is little chance of an effective enforcement procedure in the near future. As a result no enforceable universal standard for freedom of expression is currently in place. All the work of the UN bodies on the scope and shape of right to free expression may serve as interpretative guidelines. There is however one regional framework that prides itself on effectiveness – the European Convention on Human Rights treaty system. It's functioning envisages the principles defined within the HRC work. Below a closer look at this regional regime, as a practical example of a enforceable consensus, is briefly discussed.

FREEDOM OF EXPRESSION: THE EUROPEAN CONSENSUS

ICCPR derived from Article 19 of the UDHR, however the consensus reached in 1966 was also fueled by negotiations around the first European treaty aimed at protecting human rights, inspired by the success of the UDHR (Bates 2010). Next to the developing trade and industry system of the European Coal and Steel Community, a pan-European legal regime of human rights' protection was being developed. Following successful negotiations, in November 1950 the European Convention for the Protection of Human Rights and Fundamental Freedoms (known as the European Convention on Human Rights; ECHR) was signed, laying the foundations for the work of the Council of Europe (CoE) and the European Court of Human Rights (ECtHR). Deriving from numerous articles of the UDHR, also its stipulations on the freedom of expression resembled those of Article 19 UDHR.

Article 10 ECHR puts the general clauses from Article19 UDHR into more detail. Its wording grants everyone "the right to freedom of expression", including "freedom to hold opinions and to receive and impart information and ideas". Emphasis should be put on the three-element construction of the right, resembling the original Article 19 UDHR scheme, including the right to have, share and access any and all forms of expression. None of those integral freedoms should be infringed through an "interference by public authority". They all ought to be granted to everyone with no discrimination and "regardless of frontiers". A limitative clause in Article 10 para. 2 allows for constraints placed upon the exercise of those freedoms solely when particular conditions are met. Exercise of the freedom of expression may be limited through the introduction of "formalities, conditions, restrictions or penalties" prescribed by law and "necessary in a democratic society" (Arai-Takahashi 2002). The particular reasons, for which the right may be limited are named directly in the text of the convention and have been thoroughly explained in the ECtHR jurisprudence. They include: "the interests of national security, territorial integrity or public safety, for the prevention of disorder or crime, for the protection of health or morals, for the protection of the reputation or rights of others, for preventing the disclosure of information received in confidence, or for maintaining the authority and impartiality of the judiciary".

ECtHR noted on numerous occasions that Article 10 refers to states, and introduces their negative obligation to refrain from interference with the exercise of individual right to free expression, unless particular circumstances, described in Article 10 para. 2 are met. In particular states are obliged to refrain from interfering with the delivery of information or ideas individuals wish to share with others under their jurisdiction. Despite requests, the Court denied the Article 10 clause as a guarantee to access information as such, in particular public information and administrative documents. As the ECtHR noted in Leander v. Sweden: "the right to freedom to receive information basically prohibits a Government from restricting a person from receiving information that others wish or may be willing to impart to him." but at the same time "cannot be construed as imposing on a State, (…) positive obligations to (…) disseminate information of its own motion". The right to receive information may rarely be understood to impose an obligation upon a state to disclose personal information on the individual making a claim for access thereto. Enforcement of such right should be assured primarily through the introduction of "effective and accessible procedure" enabling the applicants to have access to "all relevant and appropriate information" (Council of Europe 2011).

An interesting, recent turn in this line of adjudication seems to be introduced by the 2009 decision in the Társaság a Szabadságjogokért (TASZ) v. Hungary case. The case is of particular interest for these deliberations, as it refers to a "public watchdog" organization, operating primarily on-line. Numerous administrative obstacles introduced by Hungarian authorities were considered in this landmark decision as an infringement of the right to access information, guaranteed by Article 10. Referring to its earlier jurisprudence, the Court observed that "preliminary obstacles created by the authorities in the way of press functions call for the most careful scrutiny". It regards state's duty "not to impede the flow of information sought by the applicant" as an imminent part of its obligations under Article 10 (Council of Europe, 2011).

In its jurisprudence the Court also presented an interpretation of another element constitutive of the freedom of expression as defined in Article 10 – of its universality. In Cox v. Turkey the Court observed that the term "regardless of frontiers" which describes the territorial scope of the right "implies that the Contracting States may only restrict information received from abroad within the confines of the justifications set out in Article 10 § 2" (Council of Europe 2011). They may not therefore exercise outside their territorial jurisdiction any more stringent limitations than those effective within their borders.

ECtHR imposes upon state parties one more obligation under Article 10 freedom of expression guaranties. Until recently positive obligations of states were introduced primarily with regard to privacy protection (Article 8 ECHR) or the right to assembly (Akandji-Kombe 2007). With regard to Article 10 initially states were only under a (negative) obligation to refrain from infringing the right to freedom of expression, while no positive obligation of the states to protect that right from infringement by non-state, private actors was implied. That was the case until 2008, when ECtHR confirmed states' positive obligation to safeguard individuals' possibility to exercise their right to receive and impart information within the limits set in the Convention. In Khurshid Mustafa And Tarzibachi v. Sweden the Court claimed "it cannot remain passive where a national court's interpretation of a legal act, (…) appears unreasonable, arbitrary, discriminatory or, more broadly, inconsistent with the principles underlying the Convention" (European Court of Human Rights 2008). It therefore claimed state parties' obligation to oversee private disputes among individuals within their jurisdictions, in order to safeguard the human rights' guarantees set by the Convention.

Summarizing the European approach the right to freedom of expression may be regarded as states' obligation to guarantee each individual within their jurisdiction the right to hold, receive and impart information regardless of frontiers, unless limitations are introduced within acts of national law when considered necessary in a democratic society. Such limitations may only be exercised by state authorities or entities acting on their behalf. State parties are also under a positive obligation to protect the right from unauthorized infringement by private parties. Safeguarding the execution of those obligations it is the ECtHR that has the authority to hold states responsible for individual breaches of their obligations designated within the convention. The personal complaint procedure proves to be a relatively successful tool in implementing the detailed, European standard of free speech (Bowcott 2012, Greer 2000).

Naturally the European consensus, even though recognized and enforced by numerous states, is not a worldwide paradigm. It thoroughly varies from the U.S. interpretation of the contents of the right to free speech, as based upon the First Amendment and may be set against a comprehensively different cultural background than that of e.g. Asian or African communities. Therefore it may only serve as an example of a possible interpretation of the Article 19 bottom-line universal standard. It is primarily national laws that create the legitimate legal background for the actions of individuals imparting information to various jurisdictions or legal entities, such as communication companies, attempting to render services. In the era of the World Wide Web the challenge of identifying the appropriate application of national legal standards is of particular importance. Below is described the role which telecommunication companies and other Internet Service Providers (ISPs) are obliged to play according to different national laws and regional regulations, as their day-to-day operations leave a lasting mark on the practical significance of Article 19 UDHR and ICCPR.

INTERNET SERVICE PROVIDER: AN ATTEMPTED DEFINITION

"Internet Service Provider" is a term used to describe entities rendering a wide range of services. According to the EU e-commerce directive – a document fundamental to the issue of ISP liability, the term "service provider" is used to describe "any natural or legal person providing an information society service", where the latter are defined in Article 1(2) of Directive 98/34/EC (European Commission 2000). According thereto an "Information Society service" is "any service normally provided for remuneration, at a distance, by electronic means and at the individual request of a recipient of services" (European Commission 2000). This definition was aimed to cover any and all telecommunication companies, offering Internet services, such as providing Internet connectivity to individual users (access providers) or enabling web-hosting services (host providers). The term includes also services consisting of designing and/or hosting websites (to some extent the term covers therefore content providers) (Hoeren 2009). Some authors refer to a fourth category of ISPs, who offer their services through on-line based applications: application-providers (EUROIspa 2008). The phrase covers therefore numerous and diversified groups of entities sharing one joint feature: they provide commercial services enabling Internet access through

IP-assigned devices (be it computers, tablets, "smart-phones" or other "smart" devices, collectively referred to as "the Internet of Things"; IoT) (Weber, Weber 2010). The U.S. Copyright Act offers somewhat similar definition, according to which the term "means a provider of online services or network access, or the operator of facilities therefore" and includes entities "offering the transmission, routing, or providing of connections for digital online communications, between or among points specified by a user, of material of the user's choosing, without modification to the content of the material as sent or received." At the same time numerous national regimes, like acts of e.g. Chinese law contain no legal definition of an ISP or a particular scheme for their liability. Nevertheless – unlike in Europe – those enabling Internet access or hosting digitized data may be held liable for that data (hosted or enabled) based on numerous provisions of statutory law, like regulations on copyright, state secrets or internal security. Guidelines on their liability may be found in "The Interpretation of the Supreme People's Court on Certain Issues Concerning the Application of Laws in the Hearing of Cases Involving Computer Network Copyright Disputes" dated 21 Dec. 2000 (CCH Asia Pte. Ltd. (2005) .The term therefore covers entities such as telecommunications companies, on-line service providers and even every day users (should they be administering or moderating a website enabling others to create content). Their technical capability to disable access to certain data alleged illegal is their only joint feature. Therefore an Internet Service Provider is any entity technically capable of hosting electronic content and disabling access thereto as provided by national laws.

The first challenge ISPs need to face is therefore setting their scope of services against the national definition or understanding of an on-line or telecommunications service provider. Should they meet the criteria set therein, they ought to obey by particular state's limitations on free speech, introduced through acts of national law. Should they act against those regulations they will face civil liability or criminal responsibility within the state where they operate. Should they however go against human rights guarantees, states within which they operate may be held internationally liable. According to the "Protect, Respect and Remedy" Framework any limitations on free speech introduced by non-governmental entities (such as ISPs) or exercised without judicial authorization are against states' international responsibilities. At the same time the national telecommunications regulations usually vest services providers with the power to shape the scope and limits of individual right to receive and impart information, be it through Internet monitoring and filtering mechanisms (preventive censorship of all electronic content originating from acts of law or local ethical standards, primarily business ethics) or notice-and-take down procedures. Thisgives ISPs much power in the information society. The popularity of the global network and its architecture give them the capability to decide what kinds of content may be accessed on-line by the users they render their services to.

ISP LIABILITY: A REGIONAL DICHOTOMY

Regulatory approach to ISP liability falls along two lines. While in Europe and the U.S. state authorities generally do not impose a general obligation onto service providers to monitor the information they provide access to, which they transmit or store, such an obligation is being introduced (explicitly or derived from stipulations of various acts of law) in most Asian and African national regimes (EUROIspa 2008).

Article 15 of the e-commerce Directive provides a good example of a the European general scheme, resembling the U.S. 1996 Digital Millennium Copyright Act (DMCA) notice-and-takedown procedure. The notice-and-takedown procedures generally hold the ISPs free from liability as long as they are unaware of the illegality of the materials they enable access to. Once informed of the illegal character of the data, they are obliged to disable access thereto under the pain of own subsidiary liability. The e-commerce Directive introduces a number of situations, where ISPs might be held liable for on-line content (Articles 12-15). They include providing access to communication networks, transmitting data and hosting information. ISPs are obliged to discontinue enabling access to certain content upon receiving a notification of its illegal character, under the pain of own responsibility. Should an ISP be made aware of a potentially infringing character of the content it enables or hosts and decide not to disable access thereto, they will be the ones facing legal consequences brought about by such content, regardless of the direct responsibility of the individual who had uploaded or created it. ISP liability may therefore result from failing to take down content about the illegal character of which a notice to the ISP was issued. Details of the procedures of issuing such notice and the time periods given to ISP to analyze and execute a decision made upon their contents are left to national legislations, which vary thoroughly (Asbo Baistrocchi 2003, Wood et al 2002). The lack of a detailed notice-and-takedown procedure guidelines within the Directive has been criticized as a threat to human rights, in particular the right to free speech (Asbo Baistrocchi, 2003). Lack of a uniform pan-European procedure allows for much flexibility in the implementation of the Directive, especially since national regulations often include interpretative clauses, which as a result lay upon the ISPs the obligation to decide on their own upon the legality of hosted material. Should an ISP not block access to illegal content of which they are informed, they will be facing liability for the damage that this content might cause. The ISP's decisions on the character of the hosted data and the following decision on (dis)continuing enabling access thereto are of detrimental consequences to the providers, since should they be wrong, they will be facing legal responsibility. This situation brings an undesired chilling effect: ISPs are limiting their own risk of potential lawsuits by blocking the access to any reported content, as potentially exposing them to liability. This makes the ISPs censors of on-line content, deciding upon which content will be imparted to the larger public. The right to free expression of users (in particular their constituent right to impart information) is being restrained based on the decision of a single private law entity, based on a interpretative clause of an act of law. Such practice is clearly contrary to the comments provided by HRC in its 2011 document, where in pt. 25 it states that a limitative clause must be foreseen by law, where "a norm, to be characterized as a "law", must be formulated with sufficient precision to enable an individual to regulate his or her conduct accordingly (…)" (United Nations 2011).What is more, "a law may not confer unfettered discretion for the restriction of freedom of expression on those charged with its execution" (United Nations 2011). A phrase that seems to provide detailed guidelines for ISP liability schemes follows: "Laws must provide sufficient guidance to those charged with their execution to enable them to ascertain what sorts of expression are properly restricted and what sorts are not" (United Nations 2011). Neither the EU notice and takedown procedure, nor the interpretative documents provided for in numerous Asian states meet those guidelines. The current practice may therefore be considered contrary to the interpretations of the contents of the right to free expression provided by both: ECtHR and the HRC, presented above.

The U.S. version of the notice-and-takedown procedure, as enshrined in the DMCA provides clearer guidelines. Although relating to only one category of illegal content (copyright infringing data), the DMCA puts in much detail both: the form of the notice and the mechanism following its issuance (Moore Clayton 2009). The DMCA introduces rigid periods of time for particular phases of the take-down procedure. Regardless its legislative meticulousness it is considered a threat to free expression on-line, primarily due to the national interpretation of international free speech standards (Tian 2009, European Audiovisual Observatory 2004).

Another important matter relating to content liability is the ISP criminal responsibility. This issue is raised with most significance when it comes to copyright infringement, but the criminalization of libel still existent in national legal systems also ought to raise concerns as a possible footpath for ISP subsidiary liability. Numerous national court judgments confirm criminal ISP responsibility for hosted content. They often found ISPs responsible for "contributory copyright infringement" rather than a direct offence, however such a construct may raise questions as instituting a subsidiary criminal liability. Whether the ISP may be regarded as a warrant (entrusted with a particular legal obligation) and therefore criminally liable for its omission seems doubtful in the light of the two issues raised above (the unclear scope of subjects the obligation is addressed to and the contents of the required action designated in an insufficiently detailed manor to bring criminal liability).

Regardless their shortcomings, neither the Directive nor the DMCA oblige the ISP to actively seek information potentially deemed illegal. That is not the case with the majority of national legislative acts and their legally binding interpretations made face ISP rights and duties in Asia and Africa. ISPs' strict criminal responsibility next to direct civil liability for hosting illegal content are a legal standard in numerous countries, mainlyin Asia and the Near East. Open Network Initiative names China, Iran, Uzbekistan, Burma, Vietnam and Turkmenistan as world's top "filtering" countries when it comes to censoring political content (it regards the filtering of political content in those states "extensive") (Deibert 2008). Their national policies include extensive Internet "filtering", obliging ISPs to monitor the content they enable and disable access to all information that might be regarded dangerous to widely defined state interest (Deibert 2008).

Internet filtering is also gaining some popularity in Europe. The recent EU Directive on child pornography provides states with an option to block access to on-line images of adolescent nudity (European Commission 2010). In Europe state-imposed filtering is usually introduced through a court order, obliging a particular national ISP to block access to a certain website the content of which is found contrary to national law (as exercised by Danish, German and numerous other European national courts in their orders against ISPs providing access to e.g. the controversial The Pirate Bay website). This mechanism is questionable with regard to human rights, since it infringes the right to impart and receive information, as confirmed by the recent Organization for Security and Co-operation in Europe (OSCE) report (OSCE 2010). OSCE clearly states, that "Internet access policies, defined by governments, should be in line with the requirements of (…) Article 10 of the European Convention on Human Rights" and defines the very Internet access as a human right (OSCE 2010).

CONCLUSION

The analysis presented above aims to prove that ISP filtering of on-line content, whether following the notice-and-takedown procedure or exercised following a legal or an ethical obligation, is a serious threat to the freedom of expression, as granted by international human rights guarantees. Blocking or disabling access to certain on-line content infringes the individual right to communication, derived from Article 19 ICCPR. Every time when access to information uploaded by a service recipient is disabled, the individual right of that user to impart information is infringed. Article 19 para. 3 ICCPR provides for particular, exceptional circumstances, in which the individual right to free speech may be limited. International jurisprudence and doctrine, including the Committee on Human Rights report recognizes the possibility to introduce limitations onto free speech in those exceptional circumstances through an act of law, exercised by state authorities, in particular the judicature. As expressed explicitly in both: the UN "Protect, Respect and Remedy" Framework for Business and Human Rights and the ECtHR jurisprudence the states are not only under a negative obligation to refrain from limiting free speech, but also under a positive obligation to protect the individual right to free expression from invasions by third parties. Under no circumstances may those invasions be executed by private entities, unless when executing a court order. Therefore, the current scope of ISP rights and obligations must be deemed to wide. Nationals laws authorize them to decide upon the scope of electronic content available on-line. Their individual decisions of disabling access to certain content uploaded by an individual Internet user sets the limits of that user's individual right to free expression. Such practice constitutes a serious threat to the human right expressed in Article 19 UDHR and ought to be replaced with more detailed guidelines for ISPs when they ought to hold liability for content they enable.

REFERENCES

Akandji-Kombe, J.-F. (2007). *Positive obligations under the European Convention on Human Rights; A guide to the implementation of the European Convention on Human Rights; Human rights handbooks, No. 7*. Council of Europe.

Arai-Takahashi, Y. (2002). *The Margin of Appreciation Doctrine and the Principle of Proportionality in the Jurisprudence of the ECHR*. New York: Intersentia.

Asbo Baistrocchi, P. (2003). Liability Of Intermediary Service Providers In The EU Directive On Electronic Commerce. *Computer & High Technology Law Journal*, *19*, 111–130.

Bates, E. (2010). *The Evolution of the European Convention on Human Rights: From Its Inception to the Creation of a Permanent Court of Human Rights*. Oxford University Press.

Council of Europe Research Division. (2011). *Internet: case-law of the European Court of Human Rights*. Available at. http://www.echr.coe.int/ECHR/EN/Header/Case-Law/Case-law+analysis/Research+reports/

Deibert, R. (2008). Access Denied: The Practice and Policy of Global Internet Filtering. MIT Press.

European Commission. (2000). *Directive2000/31/EC of the European Parliament and of the Council of 8 June 2000 on certain legal aspects of information society services, in particular electronic commerce, in the Internal Market (further herein: e-commerce directive)*. Author.

European Commission. (2010). *Proposal for a Directive of the European Parliament and of the Council on combating the sexual abuse, sexual exploitation of children and child pornography, repealing Framework Decision 2004/68/JHA*. Author.

European Court of Human Rights (2008) Khurshid Mustafa et Tarzibachi v. Sweden, (23883/06)

Hoeren, T. (2009). Liability for Online Services in Germany. *German Law Journal, 10,* 561-584.

Mertus, J. (2009). *The United Nations and Human Rights: A Guide for a New Era*. Oxon, UK: Taylor & Francis.

Moore, T., & Clayton, R. (2009). The Impact of Incentives on Notice and Take-down. In E. M. Johnson (Ed.), *Managing Information Risk and the Economics of Security* (pp. 199–223). New York: Springer. doi:10.1007/978-0-387-09762-6_10

Morsink, J. (1999). *The Universal Declaration of Human Rights: Origins, Drafting, and Intent.* University of Pennsylvania Press. doi:10.9783/9780812200416

OSCE. (2010). *Freedom of Expression on the Internet Study of legal provisions and practices related to freedom of expression, the free flow of information and media pluralism on the Internet in OSCE participating states.* Available at: http://www.osce.org/fom/80723

Ruggie, J. (2006). *Interim report of the Special Representative of the Secretary-General on the issue of human rights and transnational corporations and other business enterprises.* UN Doc. E/CN.4/2006/97.

Ruggie, J. (2008). *Protect, Respect and Remedy: a Framework for the Business and Human Rights: Report of the Special Representative of the Secretary-General on the issue of human rights and transnational corporations and other business enterprises, John Ruggie.* UN Doc. E/HRC/8/5.

Ruggie, J. (2011). *Report of the Special Representative of the Secretary-General on the issue of human rights and transnational corporations and other business enterprises, John Ruggie, Guiding Principles on Business and Human Rights: Implementing the United Nations "Protect, Respect and Remedy" Framework.* A/HRC/17/31.

Schauer, F. (1982). *Free Speech: A Philosophical Enquity.* Cambridge, UK: Cambridge University Press.

Schauer, F. (2004). Media Law, Media Content, and American Exceptionalism. In European Audiovisual Observatory, Political Debate and the Role of the Media: The Fragility of Free Speech. European Audiovisual Observatory.

Tian, Y. (2009). *Re-Thinking Intellectual Property: The Political Economy of Copyright Protection in the Digital Era.* Oxon, UK: Taylor & Francis.

United Nations. (1948). *Universal Declaration of Human Rights.* G.A. Res. 217A (III), U.N. Doc. A/810.

United Nations. (1966). International Covenant on Civil and Political Rights (ICCPR), G.A. res. 2200A (XXI), 21 U.N. GAOR Supp. (No. 16) at 52. *U.N. Doc. A, 6316*, 999.

United Nations. (2003). *Social and Economic Council, Sub-Commission on the Promotion and Protection of Human Rights.* E/CN.4/Sub.2/2003/12/Rev.2.

United Nations. (2005). *2005 World Summit Outcome.* GA Res 60/1, 9, UN Doc. A/ RES/60/1.

United Nations. (2011). *Human Rights Committee.* General comment No. 34, Article 19: Freedoms of opinion and expression CCPR/C/GC/34.

Watt, N., & Bowcott, O. (2012). David Cameron calls for reform of European court of human rights. *The Guardian.* Retrieved from http://www.guardian.co.uk/law/2012/jan/25/david-cameron-reform-human-rights

Weber, R. H., & Weber, R. (2010). *Internet of things: legal perspectives*. Berlin: Springer. doi:10.1007/978-3-642-11710-7

Wood, C., Drayson, C., Dye, J., Thomasin, J., McDonell, P., Dillon, M., & Sykes, K. et al. (2002). Great Britain. In G. Spindler & F. Börner (Eds.), *E-commerce law in Europe and the USA* (pp. 246–253). Berlin: Springer. doi:10.1007/978-3-540-24726-5_5

Chapter 14
Exploring the Counting of Ballot Papers Using "Delegated Transferable Vote": Implications for Local and National Elections in the United Kingdom

Jonathan Bishop
Centre for Research into Online Communities and E-Learning Systems, UK

Mark Beech
Centre for Research into Online Communities and E-Learning Systems, UK

ABSTRACT

Delegated transferable voting (DTV) refers to an approach to counting votes in elections that extends non-preferential voting systems like First Past The Post (FPTP) to include a transferable element similar to Single Transferable Voting (STV) but instead of voters indicating who they wish their votes to go to on an individual level they entrust that decision in the candidate they vote for, who could be from a small political party that might otherwise be deemed a "wasted vote" under first-past-the-post systems where the candidate they least want could win by having the most votes but still have less than 50% of the popular vote. This chapter discusses how DTV might work in practice through an auto-ethnographic approach in which the authors play an active part in elections in order to test the approach. The elections contested in the UK included to local council level in the Pontypridd area and national elections to the UK Parliament and Welsh Assembly. The potential impact of DTV on these election and method of campaigning used at some of these elections might have had on the voting outcome are discussed.

INTRODUCTION

It is generally accepted that there is a significant degree of apathy in elections to public office. Two of the reasons often given are that there is "no point in voting" because the same people will get in and that there is no one worth voting for. Whilst the last viewpoint has little merit, because there is little stop-

DOI: 10.4018/978-1-5225-1862-4.ch014

ping those with initiative standing for election, this chapter hopes to address the last point. One of the main reasons why parliamentary constituencies elect someone from the same party time and time again is because the other parties are fragmented in a way that means they will individually not get elected through the first past the post (FPTP) system of election. Suggestions have been made to replace FPTP with more complex methods of voting based on proportional representation (PR), but many of these have been a failure. The authors therefore argue that it is possible through a pluralistic way of thinking to keep the FPTP method while having the benefits of PR through a way of distributing the votes, called 'Delegated Transferable Voting' (DTV). DTV involves losing candidates being able to give their votes to a different candidate they think most represents the views of those who voted for the losing candidate. Delegated transferable voting would mean people could vote how they want to knowing that voting for a candidate from a minor party would not be a wasted vote as it would be given to a party of the choice of the candidate they voted for. This approach would have particular advantage to small political parties, which are often wanted by members of the public but not voted for because of the risk of the alternatives.

President Hollande of France announced several reforms that are supposed to affect Parliament, such as a change of the electoral rules in order to provide a better representation of small political parties, or the total veto of the *cumul des mandats* (Costa, 2013). In Pakistan, politics has actively entered into the corridors of education, such as in colleges and higher education institutions in form of political parties, where small political parties are working (Ahmad, Ali, Iqbal, Ali, & Badshah, 2013). Whilst some researchers have advocated the merits of small political parties, they often restrict analysis to candidates from these three largest parties (Casey, 2013).

BACKGROUND

Government fragmentation, which allows for pluralistic representation of non-partisan interests is an emerging area of discussion. Government fragmentation is useful, as the separation of powers and responsibility is at the core of any democratic system (Gong & Janssen, 2012). Government fragmentation is aggravated by the possibility that small political parties emphasize particularistic interests in their campaigning and legislative activity (Cirone & Urpelainen, 2013).

Thus the strategy of LGBT activists in Mexico has been to launch their own candidates from small political parties while building coalitions with other civil-society groups to pressure the larger parties (England, 2014). In Liberia the small political parties (those with less than 3 per cent of the vote or no representation in the presidential race), and independent candidates, are still prevalent, holding over a third of House seats and half of all Senate seats (Harris & Lewis, 2013). In Latvia, the key actors for the (mostly Russian-speaking) 'non-citizens' have been small political parties and interest groups – in a sense, 'outsiders on the inside', in but not fully of Latvia or the EU in terms of formal citizenship status (Saward, 2013).

Web 2.0 might move on this debate so that within election campaigns, political participation is not limited to voting (Lilleker & Jackson, 2011). In Africa the Internet has become a valuable tool, not only in helping promote pluralism within the media, and support the existence of independent media, but also in promoting participation of different actors in public debates (Salgado, 2012).

Contemporary politics in democratic states have been profoundly transformed by the fragmentation of public agendas, the rise of single issue politics, the impact of the mass media, the decline of political parties and the theatricalization of the political arena (Ezrahi, 2014). Political interest groups widen the political playing field and accelerate established trends such as the growth of direct action and single-issue politics (Brändli, 2014). By concentrating all the attention on 'micro-political' issues, or on short-term single-issue politics, the very real large-scale political structures that govern our everyday lives are disregarded (Mazierska, 2014).

In post-communist countries the medium-sized political parties often decide to join forces to increase their electoral gains, meaning small political parties lost their identity when merging by absorption with larger parties (Gherghina, 2014).In proportional representation (PR) systems, the number of seats won by a political party is proportionate to the number of votes received, which it is argued gives a fair chance to small political parties (Singh, 2013). However, in South Africa questions have been raised about the effectiveness of PR for supporting small political parties (Amtaika, 2013).

It has been argued that tactical voting is an important element of British electoral behaviour, with approximately one sixth of all voters surveyed indicating that they voted tactically at the 2010 general election (Johnston & Pattie, 2011). Tactical voting primarily takes place under single-member district plurality electoral institutions and takes the form of third-party supporters voting for one of the major parties (Kim & Kostadinova, 2011). Analysing tactical voting in the 1987 British elections as many as one in six British voters claimed to have made their decision at least partly on the basis of tactical considerations (Kedar, 2012). In Iceland's 2012 election candidates with a small following were adversely affected by tactical voting but it is unlikely to have had an impact on the outcome of the election (Kristinsson, Indriðason, & Valgarðsson, 2012). There is significant evidence that voters, even those unfamiliar with coalitional government, are drawn to tactical voting and this is particularly influenced by available information (McCuen & Morton, 2010). Although tactical voting attracts a great deal of attention, it is very hard to measure as it requires knowledge of both individuals' voting choices as well as their unobserved preferences (Dupraz, Muller, & Page, 2013).

There are also some forms of strategic behaviour that are specific to multi-winner elections, such as gerrymandering (by the chair) or vote pairing (by the voters) (Lang, Maudet, & Polukarov, 2013). In 2004, the idea of strategic voting was back, but this time most often referred to as "vote pairing," where Web sites were the driving force in this movement (Earl & Kimport, 2011). Previous research on nonpartisan voter engagement has demonstrated that personal contact is highly effective in encouraging voter turnout (LeRoux & Krawczyk, 2012). Anthony Downs' paradox of voting concludes that the benefits of voting are outweighed by the costs (Hargis, 2012). Opposition parties and in particular small political parties complain frequently about the party in power using state resources for its own benefit, thus making the political battle extremely unfair for the opponents, especially the ones that are not represented in parliament (Salgado, 2013).

TOWARDS DELEGATED TRANSFERABLE VOTING

In a simple plurality-based elections, it is possible, and often common, for a candidate to win with much less than 50% of the popular vote. In these circumstances the unsuccessful candidates hold between them over 50% of the vote. A concept of 'Delegated Transferrable Voting' (DTV) is therefore possible. With DTV, after the counting of the votes if no candidate won more than 50% of the popular vote all candidates would be empowered to transfer their votes to another candidate of their choosing within a limited amount of time. This allows people to vote for small political parties or those persons representing single issues without fear of their vote not counting, and thus allows the true wishes of the electorate to be recorded and observed. As discussed earlier, this reduces the impact of Downs paradox as any vote can be pivotal, not just those for 1st of 2nd place.Where there are several candidates with similar manifestos it empowers the electorate to select their preferred candidate knowing that even if they don't win their policy might still be enacted.

DTV encourages horse-trading between candidates and parties, with candidates able to offer their votes in return for policy commitments. The limited amount of time for the candidates to transfer votes would encourage candidates to engage in constructive conversation before the elections, by publicizing these discussions the electorate would have the opportunity to be better informed. DTV would give the unsuccessful candidates the ability to exercise the powers entrusted to them by the electorate, future election results maybe a judgement on how well or popularly they do this. It would enable parties to field more candidates that vacancies giving the public greater choice in that party's candidate selection process.

It could be argued that DTV should, like single transferable voting, involve the candidate with the lowest votes distributing their votes, but this is not necessary. For the reason that DTV is a gentleman's agreement, then the person that gets the most votes decides to give them to the person who came second, then one might argue that should not be prohibited. It may be that all the candidates agree among themselves that for instance the person that came third should be elected, because those with votes to delegate trust them most, then they might feel it would be better to give their votes to the person that came third, rather than to the person that came second.

Different Voting Systems and the Advantages of DTV

If one considers the system of primaries in the US, it ensures that each party has put a dozen or so candidates to the electorate, in order to create a form of choice (Bartels, 1988), and the more candidates in an election, then the more likely the outcome will be different (Wright & Riker, 1989). Over the course of two years and then at the end, there is only two candidates put to the electorate, meaning there is a better chance of one of them getting a majority.

DTV allows for all those candidates to be put to the public at exactly the same time in one election. This would avoid having, for instance, seven candidates for the Republicans having their separate primaries to decide who represent the Republicans. And equally for instance, four candidates from the Democrats would not need to have their separate primaries to decides who represents them, meaning each party could put up four or so candidates to the public and the public to have one simple vote to decide who gets elected. In terms of European systems outside of the United Kingdom, these are usually based on some form of proportional representation, whether "single transferable votes" (STV) or "the party list" (PL). The former involves voters expressing preference through numbering the candidates on the ballot paper, and then these are systematically transferred from the one with the lowest votes to the next person the voters selected. The latter involves people voting for a party who have fielded a number candidates and the more votes that party gets the more of those candidates that are selected. In the case of STV, the improvement of DTV is that it is the candidate a person gives a single preference to that decides who the person voting for them would most want to be elected. In the case of the PL system, parties could field all the candidates on the list at the same time and then share the votes to ensure they get as many of them elected as possible. If there were five vacancies, the people could vote for 5 candidates from the same party, or spread their vote. As DTV is in effect a different way of counting first-past-the-post votes, then people will be able to vote for the candidate they actually want and that candidate would stand a better chance of getting elected, with the voter knowing the candidate they do not want is unlikely to get an advantage from them for not voting for the second worst option, as their candidate might give their votes to them if the worst happened.

DTV would restore trust in the political process, but it would not necessarily be popular with established parties, who might seek to argue that it would promote distrust. In fact, it should be thought that if the voting public have voted for someone to be their MP, then they should trust them enough to make at least one decision on their behalf, namely who would best represent them if they were to lose. So one cannot say the public do not trust the person who they get to share their votes with, when the public have decided they trust them to make laws for the next five years. The advantage DTV therefore is that people are more likely to get a person who is representative of them rather than whoever got the most votes and might not be representative of them, with DTV coming into play only if one of the candidates does not get 50 per cent of the vote.

EMPIRICAL INVESTIGATIONS INTO THE IMPACT OF DELEGATED TRANSFERABLE VOTING

A study was conducted in order to determine the effectiveness of DTV for ensuring the public get their votes distributed to keep out candidates they do not want. To do this an ethnographic study, using both quantitative and qualitative data collection was used. Through the use of numerical observations it is possible to understand the situation more objectively as ethnography is less dependent on what people say they do, have done, or will do, as the observer can discover this for themselves objectively (von Koskull & Strandvik, 2014). Its origins lie in research by sociocultural anthropologists in the first decades of the twentieth century, and particularly in the "participatory observation" method (Levon, 2014). The approach taken by the authors might be seen as unusual for science, because it was seeking to understand a theoretical approach to counting votes, through one of the authors directly participating in elections and by-elections to generate data.

Participants

The two authors were the participants in the election at the same time as being the researchers. Other participants included the other candidates and the voters. The political party that the first author contested the local council elections and General Election in the name of – The Pluralist Party – was a newly established minor party. In the 2016 Welsh Assembly Election the first author contested it as an Independent. The second author contested both the 2015 General Election and the 2016 Welsh Assembly Election in the name of the Official Loony Party (OMRLP). Both the Pluralist Party and the OMRLP could be considered small parties and it would not be inappropriate for the title of "Independent" to be considered the same.

Procedure

The procedure used to collect and analyse the data varied for the local council elections as compared to the national elections, as set out in this section.

Local Council Elections

In terms of votes, these were collected after the election based on the official results. Either the candidates themselves, or a willing member of the party concerned, were asked who they would have given their votes to in the given election. The votes were then distributed accordingly. In terms of data related to the different methods of campaigning the data was collected by the author that took part as a candidate in the elections, as well as making use of the published election date. The interviews with the members of political parties who was asked to say how they would transfer their votes was done after the final election. This was so that the full implications of the transferring of votes would be able to be explained to them. Whilst it was possible in most cases to get the candidate or their agent to say how they would delegate their votes, in some cases due to the nature of politics this was not always possible, so a member of the party was consulted. The reasons given were consistent among all interviewees, namely to "keep Labour out" overall and because they "liked" their preferred candidate.

National Elections

In the case of the UK General Election and Welsh Assembly Elections the approach used was for each of the researchers to indicate through a preferential voting system whom they would prefer their votes to go to. In the case of the Welsh Assembly Election this was used to determine which votes should go to which author on the basis that the more likely a researcher was to give a vote to that party then the more likely that party would be to give their vote to that researcher. This was done because unlike with the local council elections it would not be practical to contact each party or candidate to ask who they would give their votes to under DTV. Table 1 therefore shows the preferential voting for the first author and second author for the 2015 UK General Election and Table 2 shows their preferences for the 2016 Welsh Assembly Election. In the case of Table 1, whilst not all the parties contested the seats that the first and second author contested, the authors gave their preferences for the total combined parties from both seats. In the case of Table 2, as the first author and second author contested the same seat then the parties listed were the same for both.

Table 1. Chosen allocation of delegated transferable votes for the UK General Election in 2015

Party	1st Author	2nd Author
Conservative	5	4
Green	6	**2**
Independent	3	7
Labour Party	7	6
Lib-Dem	4	5
Loony	2	**1**
Pluralist	1	8
UKIP	8	3

Table 2. Chosen allocation of delegated transferable votes for the Welsh Assembly Election in 2016

Party	1st Author	2nd Author
Abolish the Welsh Assembly	11	7
Freedom to Choose	10	5
Independent	1	12
Plaid Cymru	4	11
The Official Monster Raving Loony Party	2	1
UKIP Wales	12	8
Wales Green Party	7	4
Welsh Communist Party	8	3
Welsh Conservatives	5	10
Welsh Labour	3	13
Welsh Liberal Democrats	6	9
Welsh Trade Unionist & Socialist Coalition	9	2
Women's Equality Party	13	5

Results

The results of the study have been presented in terms of the potential impact of DTV on election outcomes, campaigning methods and voting outcomes, as well as considering geo-demographic factors and voting patterns.

Pontypridd Constituency Local Council Elections (2012-2015)

This section looks at how delegated transferable voting might have worked had it been in place for the local council elections and by-elections contested by the first author between 2012 and 2015.

Impact of delegated transferrable voting on election outcomes

It is anticipated that as a result of delegated transferable voting that rotten constituencies, where there is a hegemony as a result of people not being able to agree on a candidate to oust the status quo, will become more democratic. This study took place as a result of four elections being contested by The Pluralist Party fielding the second author after being formally nominated by the first author. Table 3 shows the outcomes of these elections in terms of the votes assigned to each party at the respective election. Those numbers in bold reflect the party that was elected.

As can be seen from Table 3, which does not take account of delegated transferable voting, the Labour Party won two of the elections in the Pontypridd community (i.e. Rhondda, Treforest) in Wales with the independent candidates securing the majority of the votes in the Llantwit Fardre community (i.e. Efail Isaf) and the Llantrisant community (i.e. Beddau), also in Wales. Table 4 on the other hand shows how the votes would have been distributed under delegated transferrable voting.

Table 3. Votes cast at election prior to delegated transferable voting

Election	Lib Dem	Labour	Tory	Plaid	Pluralist	Independent
Efail Isaf	0	131	0	0	33	**253**
Rhondda	137	**220**	25	61	3	111
Treforest	86	**138**	0	33	8	0
Beddau	0	173	0	41	3	**186**
Tynant	0	**207**	0	38	20	**0**

Table 4. Final voting after votes have been transferred

Electoral division	Lib Dem	Labour	Tory	Plaid	Pluralist	Independent
Efail Isaf	0	0	0	0	0	**253**
Rhondda	0	0	0	0	0	**337**
Treforest	0	**138**	0	0	0	0
Beddau	0	0	0	0	0	**230**
Tynant	0	**207**	0	0	0	0

The outcome presented in Table 4 was formed after a number of rounds of redistributing where the candidate with the least votes hypothetically got to transfer their votes to another candidate. The second author who stood for The Pluralist Party decided on all occasions that Plaid Cymru were suitable to give his vote to them – because he trusted the people involved with their campaign. The only exception was in the Efail Isaf election where he would have given the votes to the independent. In the case of all those other parties asked to transfer the reason given was to "keep Labour out," probably because there is a hegemony in the Pontypridd area in relation to the Labour Party.

The United Kingdom General Election in 2015

This section looks at how delegated transferable voting might have worked in the 2015 United Kingdom General Election in which the first author contested on behalf of The Pluralist Party and the second author contested on behalf of the Official Monster Raving Loony Party.

Table 5 shows what would have happened in the UK General Election in the case of the first author's election on the assumption that the other parties agreed with his choice of how to allocate votes. As can be seen in this case, the Green Party, whom are often seen as the 'soft left' with many liking their policies with the exception of those on nuclear power and nuclear deterrents, they benefited from this by going from fourth place to second place. Unintended by the first author, the United Kingdom Independence Party (UKIP) came above the Conservative Party which went from third place to fourth place, even though they were last on their list of preferences. The remaining parties, namely the Liberal Democrats, the Independent and The Pluralist Party maintained their positions of fifth, sixth and seventh respectively. Because the Labour Party got over 50% of the vote from the outset it would not have been possible for DTV to have changed who was elected.

Table 5. Distribution of votes after both authors are eliminated from the election using DTV (Liverpool Walton)

Party	5th DTV	4th DTV	3rd DTV	2nd DTV	1st DTV	Votes Cast	DTV Position	GE Position
Labour Party	31222	31222	31222	31222	31222	31222	1	1
Green Party	7181	3736	1934	1035	979	956	2	4
UK Independence Party	0	3445	3445	3445	3445	3445	3	2
Conservative Party	0	0	1802	1802	1802	1802	4	3
Liberal Democrat	0	0	0	899	899	899	5	5
Independent	0	0	0	0	56	56	6	6
The Pluralist Party	0	0	0	0	0	23	7	7

Table 6. Distribution of votes after both authors are eliminated from the election using DTV (Aldridge & Brownhills)

Party	4th DTV	3rd DTV	2nd DTV	1st DTV	Votes Cast	DTV Position	GE Position
Conservative	20558	20558	20558	20558	20558	1	1
UKIP	18939	10104	8774	7751	7751	2	3
Labour	0	8835	8835	8835	8835	3	2
Lib-Dem	0	0	1330	1330	1330	4	4
Green	0	0	0	1023	826	5	5
Loony	0	0	0	0	197	6	6

Table 6 shows what would have happened in the United Kingdom General Election in the case of the second author's election. The outcome, which might be perceived as disappointing, resulted in only two changes in position with the United Kingdom Independence Party (UKIP) moving from third place to second place and as a result the Labour Party moving from second place to third place. Because the Conservative Party had over 50% of the vote the result would not have changed with DTV, but the outcome might have been politically interesting at the election because it would have put UKIP, which is a party of eurosceptics, only around 1.5k votes behind the Conservatives whom were seen as their nearest rivals.

The Welsh Assembly Elections in 2016

This section looks at how delegated transferable voting might have worked at the 2016 Welsh Assembly Elections in the case of the regional seat of South Wales Central. Both the first author and the second author contested this election, meaning the potential effects of DTV were much easier to measure. In the Welsh Assembly regional seat elections there is a process called "Additional Member" whereby the parties with the most seats are penalised with each round of counting. This was taken into account with the administering of DTV with one seat allocated to the party with the most votes at each DTV round, by taking into account the penalties by having the most seats.

Table 7. Distribution of votes after both authors are eliminated from the election using DTV (South Wales Central)

Party	5th DTV	4th DTV	3rd DTV	2nd DTV	1st DTV	Votes Cast	DTV Position	AM Position
Labour	78366	78366	78366	78366	78366	78366	1	1
Green Party	56306	7949	7949	7949	7949	7949	2	7
Plaid Cymru	48357	48357	48357	48357	48357	48357	3	2
Conservatives	42185	42185	42185	42185	42185	42185	4	3
UKIP	23958	23958	23958	23958	23958	23958	5	4
Liberal Democrats	14875	14875	14875	14875	14875	14875	6	5
Abolish the Welsh Assembly	9163	9163	9163	9163	9163	9163	7	6
OMRLP	0	25134	25134	25134	15971	1096	8	9
Women's Equality Party	0	0	2807	2807	2807	2807	9	8
TUSC	0	0	0	736	736	736	10	10
Independent	0	0	0	0	651	651	11	11
Welsh Communist Party	0	0	0	0	520	520	12	12
Freedom to Choose	0	0	0	0	0	470	13	13

Table 7 shows the outcome in terms of number of votes when each of the two authors were eliminated from the results. As in the General Election, the Greens went into second place compared to their seventh place under the additional member approach. Looking at Table 8, this would have meant they would have got 1 seat in the Welsh Assembly, compared to the 0 they had under Additional Members. The Labour Party, who was first under both systems, would not have got more than the 7 seats they had as a result of the AM system, even with DTV as their votes were unchanged. Under this section Plaid Cymru would have got 1 fewer seats, going from second place to third place and the Conservatives would have got 1 fewer seat, going from third place to fourth place. The Liberal Democrats went from fifth place to sixth place, but would have got an additional seat as can be seen from Table 8. The United Kingdom Independence Party (UKIP) went from fourth place to fifth place under DTV, but would have kept the one seat they had under the AM system.

Campaigning Methods and Voting Outcomes

As can be seen from Table 9 the outcomes of the different elections can be influenced by a number of factors. The variables include the Electorate for a particular electoral division, which is the number of people eligible to vote, as well as the number of Contacts made with electors. Votes is the number of electors who voted for The Pluralist Party. Effort was calculated by dividing the amount invoiced for the election by the costs to the research institute to supply them. The amount invoiced was the election limit for each election, even if it cost the research institute less to produce for instance, which is required by UK tax law. The other variable looked at was 'knol,' which is a unit for measuring the efficiency of the brain. This was computed using a 'detachment' variable representing distance, and an 'interest' representing closeness. In this case the detachment related to how many people voted against the incumbent

Table 8. Difference between number of seats allocated under FPTP+DTV and number allocated under FPTP+AM

Party	DTV Votes	FPTP/DTV Seats	Votes	FPTP/AM Seats	Difference
Welsh Labour	78366	7	78366	7	0
Wales Green Party	56306	1	7949	0	+1
Plaid Cymru	48357	1	48357	2	-1
Welsh Conservatives	42185	1	42185	2	-1
UKIP Wales	23958	1	23958	1	0
Welsh Liberal Democrats	14875	1	14875	0	+1
Abolish the Welsh Assembly	9163	0	9163	0	0
Women's Equality Party	0	0	2807	0	0
The Official Monster Raving Loony Party	0	0	1096	0	0
Welsh Trade Unionist & Socialist Coalition	0	0	736	0	0
Bishop, Jonathan - Independent	0	0	651	0	0
Welsh Communist Party	0	0	520	0	0
Freedom to Choose	0	0	470	0	0

party and in the case of interest this represented how many votes the winning candidate would have gained following delegated transferable voting having taken place. This, as presented in Table 9, involved an independent samples t-test. Whilst this normally requires parametric conditions its simplicity and accuracy is best suited to examining the data.

A number of findings can be seen to be made from the data collected, as shown in Table 9. The area with the highest amount of votes corresponds with the highest amount of effort, by a huge margin. An effort of 2.88 is higher than the others of between 0.01 and 0.10, where the number of votes were between 3 and 8. This clearly shows the success of a campaign is linked to the amount of time and money invested in it. The DVD campaign – which involved the distribution of a video explaining the policies of the second author – was most successful in terms of voting outcomes, but the cost to Crocels was significantly high, giving an effort of 2.88. In terms of the two elections in Pontypridd, namely Beddau and Treforest, it can be seen that the amount of effort and contacts is closely linked with the number of votes – the smaller the effort and contacts then the smaller number of votes. The figures associated

Table 9. Campaigning methods and associated variables for the local council elections (Pluralist Party)

Division	Campaigning Method	Turnout	Contacts	Effort	Votes	knol
Efail Isaf	DVD and Web	417	500	2.88	33	0.51
Rhondda	Letters and Web	557	80	0.08	3	0.58
Treforest	Door to Door and Web	265	19	0.01	8	0.39
Beddau	Newspaper/Online Ads and Web	403	487	0.10	3	0.54
Tynant	Newsletters, Online Ads, Web, Door to Door	265	3,179	0.31	20	0.53

Table 10. Campaigning methods and associated variables for the UK Parliament and Welsh Assembly election

Constituency	Turnout	Online Reach	Online Contacts	Print Contacts	Total Contacts	Votes
Liverpool Walton	38403	26664	1205	206	1411	23
Pontypridd	25331	1991	77	108	185	119
Cardiff North	37329	20124	1272	0	1272	171

with the Beddau election are highly deceiving. Even though the number of contacts were high, these were reflected in the form of the number of people who the Facebook advert was displayed to – there is no guarantee they saw it.

Geo-Demographic Factors and Voting Patterns

It has been established that there are links between whether someone engages in trolling and their NVQ Level, whether their area has a high number of young people who are not in education, employment or training (NEETs) and finally the number of rooms in their house (Bishop, 2014). This section therefore looks at the connection between these and whether a new party's success is linked to them also. It is long thought that NEETs do not vote, but increasingly as dissatisfaction among young people in not being able to reach their potential occurs, so the involvement of young people in the political process is increasing (Sloam, 2013). Whether houses are overcrowded is known to affect voting behaviour (Halleröd & Larsson, 2008). Education is known to affect voting, but often it can reduce voting due to thinking votes are wasted (Dee, 2004), which is something DTV could change. As can be seen from Table 11, there was not a consistent link between the established geo-demographical factors of NEETs, Rooms per House, and NVQ Level (Bishop, 2012).

The turnout figures in Table 11 were not calculated on the basis of the actual number of people eligible to vote at the given election, but the population for those areas as they were at the 2011 census. The reason for this was that the figures would be less disrupted by changes in the number of electors and thus providing for greater reliability in the results across the multiple elections.

In the local elections, a moderate turnout is linked with 3 votes (Rhondda and Beddau) and in another it is linked with a high number of votes, namely 33 for Efail Isaf. In the case of the national elections there was some links between the number of votes and turnout. With the exception of Liverpool Walton there was a direct relationship where the number of votes (119, 171, 197) were proportional to the turnout (31.49%, 42.36%, 51,31%).

As can be seen from Table 11, the number of rooms is on the whole lower where the number of NEETs are on the whole higher. With the exception of Tynant, the areas with the highest NEETs have lower NVQ Levels, which might be expected. The number of votes were high when the number of rooms was also high. In both the local and national elections where number of votes were low, the number of NEETs were high. This may disappoint those who are looking to suggest that young people are less likely to vote, or that the number of people who fell off the electoral register in the 1980s are likely to be associated with low prosperity as a result of that. It is more likely that those who were able to take

Table 11. Geo-demographic factors for local (L) and national (N) electoral divisions

Location	Votes	Turnout (%)	NEETs (%)	Rooms Per House	NVQ Level
Efail Isaf (L)	33	11.76	29	3.16	2.90
Tynant (L)	20	7.53	43	2.79	1.07
Treforest (L)	8	5.61	37	3.16	2.93
Rhondda (L)	3	14.63	53	2.84	2.52
Beddau (L)	3	11.89	48	2.79	2.52
Cardiff North (N)	171	42.36	33	5.17	3.03
Pontypridd (N)	119	31.49	35	5.70	2.77
Liverpool Walton (N)	23	41.80	29	5.07	2.63
Aldridge and Brownhills (N)	197	51.31	29	5.66	2.62

advantage of the reforms since the 1980s in increasing access to education are more likely to be associated with geographies conducive to the learning experience.

DISCUSSION

Increasing engagement in elections to public office is a challenging task for those who truly believe in democracy. Many people are turned off by politics as a result of a lack of trust in politicians who appear to be in it for themselves. An equally problematic issue is the fact that those who get elected are often those who do not have the full confidence of the electorate. That is, they have less than 50% of the vote. This chapter has presented empirical evidence to show the effect that delegated transferable voting (DTV) – a mechanism for allowing losing election candidates to give their votes to a different candidate – has on keeping out the party that least reflects their voter base.

Using the case of a party founded by the authors called The Pluralist Party in the case of the first author and an established party called the Official Monster Raving Loony Party (OMRLP) in the case of the second author, the chapter presented primary data to evaluate the effectiveness of the DTV. In the case of local elections, the chapter found that DTV is more likely to lead to the election of independent candidates over party political ones. Pluralism advocates the election of those who are independent of political party control in order to best represent the people. The election of independent candidates or small parties is a model of pluralism that can achieve this. Other findings of the chapter conclude that a higher number of votes for the Pluralist Party is associated with a higher education level, more rooms in a household, a lower number of people not in education, employment or training, and a lower 'knol,' which is a unit for measuring brain activity. In the case of national elections, the chapter found that parties deemed as moderate, such as the Green Party, were more likely to benefit from votes being transferred to them. In the case of the Welsh Assembly election, where there is a system of allocating seats based on the number of seats already obtained, it found that the main parties were more likely to lose seats and the parties that attract fewer votes but are seen as more worthy of transferred votes.

By looking at election data mixed with geo-demographic data, which found that the number of rooms is on the whole lower where the number of NEETs are on the whole higher, the areas with the highest

NEETs have lower NVQ Levels, and the number of votes were high when the number of rooms was high, conclusions can be drawn about voting patterns for needs, where in both the local and national elections where number of votes were low, the number of NEETs were high. Further research is needed therefore to explore the links between housing and life outcomes. With the bedroom tax in the UK driving some people into inappropriate housing, it might be that adverse consequence; such as fewer people participating in education will be the outcome. Lack of access to appropriate housing in the UK as a result of the bedroom tax might undo all the work that was done by successive governments in the 1980s, 1990s and 2000s to increase economy prosperity of the many and not just the few, making education a less desirable option as opposed to employment.

All in all, this chapter has shown that there are alternative means of electing persons to governmental bodies, which may not need the route and branch reform associated with significant organisational change. Delegated transferable voting may be one way to do this to enable the public to vote both with their heart and head.

IMPLICATIONS AND FUTURE RESEARCH DIRECTIONS

This chapter has looked in depth at a new means of distributing votes, called delegated transferable voting (DTV). The study conducted has shown that DTV can have the effect of preventing the election of candidates who did not secure over 50% of the vote and whom only won by virtue of the vote being fragmented among other candidates. The data collected related to four community elections and it might be that greater investigations into the role DTV can play in elections would result in it becoming a means of ensuring that no vote is a wasted vote – in the sense that a party with less than 50% of the vote, but a higher amount than any other party, is not automatically elected. Future research could look at how to make DTV transparent if implemented, such as how websites like YourNextMP.com could be used so candidates can tell the public who they would give their votes to if they did not win more than 50% of the vote. This chapter has not only made a contribution to theory with regards to looking at DTV as an alternative or add-on to existing voting systems, but it has also made a contribution to research practice. Through making use of auto-ethnographic, yet quantitative, approach to the student, this has shown how anthropology need not be based only on subjective judgements of the research, but can result in the use of quantified data, which can change dependent on those being observed or encountered by the anthropologist.

ACKNOWLEDGMENT

The authors would like to thank all those who provided feedback on earlier versions of this chapter. In particular the second author would like to acknowledge the reasonable adjustments made by the Crocels Community Media Group to enable him to participate in the elections that form part of the chapters's findings. The involvement of former Pontypridd Town councillor Paul Simmonds was helpful in clarifying DTV in a means understandable to those outside political science. Thanks are also due to those from various political parties who helped determine how the votes would likely be delegated if DTV were to be implemented.

REFERENCES

Ahmad, I., Ali, S., Iqbal, S., Ali, F., & Badshah, R. (2013). Problems of government secondary school system in Pakistan: Critical analysis of literature and finding a way forward. *International Journal of Academic Research in Business & Social Sciences, 3*(2).

Amtaika, A. (2013). Limitations of the proportional representation (PR) electoral system in South Africa's local government elections. *Journal of African & Asian Local Government Studies, 2*(4).

Bartels, L. M. (1988). *Presidential primaries and the dynamics of public choice*. Princeton University Press.

Bishop, J. (2011). *The role of the prefrontal cortex in social orientation construction: A pilot study.* Poster Presented to the BPS Welsh Conference on Wellbeing, Wrexham, UK.

Bishop, J. (2012). The antisocial network and 'electronic message faults': Prevalence of troublesome online youth groups and internet trolling in Great Britain. Swansea, UK: The Crocels Press.

Bishop, J. (2014). Digital teens and the antisocial network: Prevalence of troublesome online youth groups and internet trolling in Great Britain. *International Journal of Politics*, *5*(3), 1–15. doi:10.4018/ijep.2014070101

Bishop, J., & Goode, M. M. H. (2014). Towards a subjectively devised parametric user model for analysing and influencing behaviour online using gamification: A review and model. In Gamification for human factors integration: Social, educational, and psychological issues (pp. 80-95). Hershey, PA: IGI Global.

Brändli, M. (2014). *"Politics as usual?" Explaining the use of online communication by political interest groups in Switzerland*. Academic Press.

Casey, K. (2013). *Crossing party lines: The effects of information on redistributive politics*. Academic Press.

Cirone, A. E., & Urpelainen, J. (2013). Political market failure? The effect of government unity on energy technology policy in industrialized democracies. *Technovation*, *33*(10), 333–344. doi:10.1016/j.technovation.2013.06.001

Costa, O. (2013). Conclusion: Challenging the conventional wisdoms about parliamentary representation in France. *Journal of Legislative Studies*, *19*(2), 278–283. doi:10.1080/13572334.2013.787202

Dee, T. S. (2004). Are there civic returns to education? *Journal of Public Economics*, *88*(9), 1697–1720. doi:10.1016/j.jpubeco.2003.11.002

Dupraz, S., Muller, D., & Page, L. (2013). Tactical voting and voter's sophistication in British elections. In Digitally enabled social change: Activism in the internet age. MIT Press.

England, S. (2014). gender and sexuality in Mexico and Brazil intersections of identities, desires, and public policies. *Latin American Perspectives*, *41*(1), 166–171. doi:10.1177/0094582X13512267

Ezrahi, Y. (2014). Ben-David's critique of the sociology of knowledge and his politics of freedom. In The institution of science and the science of institutions (pp. 39-45). Springer.

Gherghina, S. (2014). *The impact of party regulation on membership rates in post-Communist Europe*. Academic Press.

Gong, Y., & Janssen, M. (2012). From policy implementation to business process management: Principles for creating flexibility and agility. *Government Information Quarterly*, *29*, S61–S71. doi:10.1016/j.giq.2011.08.004

Halleröd, B., & Larsson, D. (2008). Poverty, welfare problems and social exclusion. *International Journal of Social Welfare*, *17*(1), 15–25. doi:10.1111/j.1468-2397.2007.00503.x

Hargis, J. E. (2012). The ethics of voting. *The Journal of Politics*, *74*(03), E29. doi:10.1017/S0022381612000230

Harris, D., & Lewis, T. (2013). Liberia in 2011: Still ploughing its own democratic furrow? *Commonwealth and Comparative Politics*, *51*(1), 76–96. doi:10.1080/14662043.2013.752176

Johnston, R., & Pattie, C. (2011). Tactical voting at the 2010 british general election: Rational behaviour in local contexts? *Environment and Planning-Part A*, *43*(6), 1323–1340. doi:10.1068/a43512

Kedar, O. (2012). Voter choice and parliamentary politics: An emerging research agenda. *British Journal of Political Science*, *42*(3), 537–553. doi:10.1017/S0007123411000408

Kim, H., & Kostadinova, T. (2011). Does tactical voting matter? The political impact of tactical voting in Canadian elections. *International Area Studies Review*, *14*(1), 49–72. doi:10.1177/223386591101400103

Kristinsson, G. H., Indriðason, I. H., & Valgarðsson, V. O. (2012). What were the voters thinking? The presidential election in Iceland 2012. *Icelandic Review of Politics & Administration*, *8*(2), 221–244.

Lang, J., Maudet, N., & Polukarov, M. (2013). New results on equilibria in strategic candidacy. In Algorithmic game theory (pp. 13-25). Springer.

Leroux, K., & Krawczyk, K. (2012). Can nonprofit organizations increase voter turnout? Findings from an agency-based voter mobilization experiment. *Nonprofit and Voluntary Sector Quarterly*.

Levon, E. (2014). 10 ethnography and recording interaction. *Research Methods in Linguistics, 195*.

Lilleker, D. G., & Jackson, N. (2011). Political campaigning, elections and the internet: Comparing the US, UK, France and Germany. Routledge.

Mazierska, E. (2014). Introduction: Marking political cinema. *Framework: The Journal of Cinema and Media*, *55*(1), 33–44. doi:10.13110/framework.55.1.0033

Mccuen, B., & Morton, R. B. (2010). Tactical coalition voting and information in the laboratory. *Electoral Studies*, *29*(3), 316–328. doi:10.1016/j.electstud.2010.03.009

Salgado, S. (2012). The web in African countries: Exploring the possible influences of the internet in the democratization processes. *Information Communication and Society*, *15*(9), 1373–1389. doi:10.1080/1369118X.2011.647044

Salgado, S. (2013). Online party politics. *Politics and the Internet in Comparative Context: Views From The Cloud*, *11*, 118.

Saward, M. (2013). The dynamics of European citizenship: Enactment, extension and assertion. *Comparative European Politics*, *11*(1), 49–69. doi:10.1057/cep.2012.2

Singh, M. P. (2013). Elections and electoral systems in constitutional regimes. In Routledge handbook of constitutional law. Routledge.

Sloam, J. (2013). The outraged young: how young Europeans are reshaping the political landscape. *Political Insight*, *4*(1), 4–7. doi:10.1111/2041-9066.12003

Von Koskull, C., & Strandvik, T. (2014). Discovering the unfolding of service innovations. *Journal of Business and Industrial Marketing*, *29*(2), 6–6. doi:10.1108/JBIM-05-2012-0084

Wellard, I. (2014). Starting points and destinations: negotiating factual and fictional pathways: A response to Gilbourne, Jones and Jordan. *Sport Education and Society*, *19*(1), 99–104. doi:10.1080/13573322.2011.633773

Wright, S. G., & Riker, W. H. (1989). Plurality and runoff systems and numbers of candidates. *Public Choice*, *60*(2), 155–175. doi:10.1007/BF00149243

KEY TERMS AND DEFINITIONS

Additional Member System: A form of proportional representation where the parties with the most seats under first past the post are penalised so as to have fewer seats under the system.

Assembly Member: Someone who is elected to the National Assembly for Wales.

Delegated Transferable Voting: A method of counting votes where the candidate with the least votes allocates their votes to the candidate they think those that voted for them would most want to see elected.

First Past the Post: A method of counting votes where the candidate with the most votes is elected, even if they have less than 50% of the vote.

Member of Parliament: Someone who is elected to the House of Commons within the UK Parliament.

Member of the House of Lords: Someone whom becomes a peer of the House of Lords by appointment or election from a pool of hereditary peers.

Proportional Representation: A method of counting votes where the number of seats a party gets its proportionate to the number of votes they get.

UK Parliament: The legislative institution for the United Kingdom made up of Members of Parliament and Members of the House of Lords.

Welsh Assembly: The National Assembly for Wales is the legislative institution in Wales that is made up of Assembly Members who are elected by both first past the post and a form of proportional representation called the Additional Member System.

Chapter 15
Women Can't Win:
Gender Irony and the E-Politics of The Biggest Loser

Michael S. Bruner
Humboldt State University, USA

Karissa Valine
Humboldt State University, USA

Berenice Ceja
Humboldt State University, USA

ABSTRACT

This chapter employs irony as a tool to make clearer the workings of one form of the e-politics of food, namely, the structural food oppression linked to the weight and shape of the female body. The authors argue that the e-politics of the weight and shape of the female body is one of the most important incarnations of the e-politics of food and one of the most vigorously contested. This chapter examines many forms of public discourse and e-politics, from Bing to Tumblr, from Huffington Post to the Mirror (UK), from TV news in Lacrosse, Wisconsin to The Times of India, from the documentary film Killing Us Softly to the book You Are What You Eat, and from WebMD to Twitter, in the end, with a central focus on Rachel Frederickson on the TV show, The Biggest Loser. The critical rhetorical analysis finds some support for the Women Can't Win thesis. Women are in a Catch-22 situation, trapped between fat-shaming and skinny-shaming.

INTRODUCTION

This chapter employs irony as a tool to make clearer the workings of one form of the e-politics of food, namely, the structural food oppression linked to the weight and shape of the female body. The authors argue that the e-politics of the weight and shape of the female body is one of the most important incarnations of the e-politics of food and one of the most vigorously contested. As a window into this realm of the international e-politics of food, the study focuses on Rachel Frederickson, the 2014 winner of the *The Biggest Loser*, an American television reality show that now has several international adaptions.

DOI: 10.4018/978-1-5225-1862-4.ch015

To support the argument that the weight and shape of the female body is an incarnation of the e-politics of food, the analysis points to the broad acceptance of the statement: "You are what you eat." This claim about the food-body relationship may have deep religious roots but, in the modern era, it usually is attributed to Anthelme Brillat-Savarin (1826), Ludwig Andreas Feuerbach (1864), or Victor Lindlahr (1942). Today, *obesity* is one of the dominant themes in the e-politics of food, suggesting that both what and how much one eats are contentious sites in public discourse.

A cartoon attack on Michele Obama, an advocate for healthy school lunches, demonstrates just how contentious this discourse can be. A mocking *Breitbart* cartoon (2011) portrays Michelle Obama devouring hamburgers while saying, "Pass the bacon." Even though this cartoon commits the *ad hominem* fallacy, it reveals the passion underlying the e-politics of food, as well as the gender irony. Michele Obama has been praised for being "fit" and attacked for being "fat." In the shorthand refrain of this essay: Women Can't Win.[1]

The controversy surrounding Rachel Frederickson on *The Biggest Loser* proves the point. *The Biggest Loser* originally was an American television reality show that debuted on NBC October 19, 2004. There now are different variations of *The Biggest Loser* around the world. The show focuses on "obese people competing to win a cash prize by losing the highest percentage of weight relative to their initial weight" (*The Biggest Loser* wiki). The central irony in this reality TV show is contained in the title. In ordinary language, "the biggest loser" is a phrase with derogatory connotations, as it describes a poor example of a human being. However, the TV show transforms the connotation of "loser" into "winner" by reframing the context into that of success in losing weight.

This transformation suggests that only in the context of weight does "loser" move from a derogatory to a complimentary term. However, in an odd form of gender irony, women cannot "win." "Winner" Rachel Frederickson, who began the 2014 show weighing 260 pounds, lost 155 pounds and was then accused of being too thin at the end of the season. According to Dr. Brenda Weber, professor of Gender Studies at Indiana University:

A lot of people feel like it's unfair and inconsistent to say someone is too fat, and now say they're too thin, like there's no place for a person to win ... especially a woman. The obese person and the anorexic person actually trigger very similar kinds of reactions, and it's about these extremes that get written on the body, and they both code as rule- breakers...

The Rachel Frederickson controversy, then, is at the center of this study. But gender irony in the e-politics of food has much broader implications.

This topic is of broader significance due to of the prominent role of food talk in contemporary public discourse (Ferguson, 2014; Frye, 2012; Nestle, 2002/2013; Pollan, 2006, 2009, 2013). One of the best examples of the politics of food can be seen in the national debate over the passage and the subsequent repeal of the so-called "fat tax" in Denmark (Strom, 2012). This case illustrates the complexity of food politics, located as it is at the intersection of nutrition, health, budgets/revenues, business, consumerism, politics, and social policy. Moreover, the tragic toll that structural food oppression takes on women demands attention from those who analyze the e-politics of food.

While the double-bind that women face ("Women Can't Win") is not a novel subject, the use of irony as a tool to help us to understand the e-politics of food breaks some new ground (Hahn, 2015). Kathryn Pauly Morgan (1991) initiated this sort of discussion when she wrote about "The Three Paradoxes of Choice" (p. 35) and the "double pathologizing" (p. 40) faced by women. Female bodies that previously may have been considered "normal" are now stigmatized as "problem areas" (p. 41). A case in point is the recent e-argument over whether Robyn Lawley, named one of the "Rookies of the Year" by the *Sports Illustrated Swimsuit* issue, has a "normal" body or a "plus-side" body (Garcia, Feb. 5, 2015). The point is that it is very difficult today for Robyn Yawley to be Robyn Yawley, due to the policing of what should be an "idealized" body.

The research question that guides this study is:

RQ: To what extent does public discourse in the month after Rachel Frederickson won *The Biggest Loser* (February 2014) tend to confirm the "Women Can't Win" hypothesis, namely, that women are situated in a no-win, double bind with respect to weight and body image ?

This chapter makes two contributions to the analysis of e-politics. First, the study takes *irony* from its usual location in the study of literature and relocates it squarely in the realm of politics. Second, the study's qualitative, critical/rhetorical method, with its goal of increasing understanding and promoting advocacy, supplements the quantitative methods often found in the study of politics. The current analysis of e-politics, then, is nudged closer to critical race and gender studies. The present chapter on the construction of food oppression and the construction of femininity (Cronin, McCarhthy, M., Newcombe, & McCarthy, S., 2014) shines a spotlight on symbolic processes and rhetorical structures in public discourse rather than on traditional political institutions.

The plan of this chapter is to begin with a review of some of the relevant literature, followed by a description of the methodology as "a critical rhetorical approach, which assumes that rhetoric is always politically and ideologically invested" (Shugart, 2011, p. 39). The chapter will then turn to a data analysis of public discouirse in February 2014 concerning Rachel Frederickson. This analysis has two parts: social media posts and 52 articles retrieved from a *Lexis/Nexis* search. The chapter concludes with suggestions about where the use of irony in the analysis of e-politics might lead.

LITERATURE REVIEW

What is E-Politics?

This analysis accepts as a starting point Harold Lasswell's (1936) oft-cited definition of "politics": "Who gets, what, when, how." This definition, with its focus on social processes, is appropriate, because it is broader than a focus on political mechanisms (ballots, elections, voting). Indeed, Lasswell is useful in the present study, because he also connects politics to communication and to the material consequences of discourse. For example, *RandomHistory.com* reports: "The pursuit to become more attractive is a $160 billion-a-year industry that includes weight-loss programs…." The present study investigates the role of e-politics in constructing the assumptions, ideals, and symbols that support this expenditure of resources.

What, then, is e – politics? One of the testimonials for the *International Journal of e-Politics* offers a helpful explanation:

Electronic media is no longer used for information and for interaction, but now is a live media that changes constantly in our lives, thoughts, and beliefs. E-politics quickly replaces the printed media and the public gathering. It changes constantly at a pace and ways unknown to researchers (E. Isaac Mostovicz, Janus Thinking Ltd., USA http://www.igi-global.com/journal/international-journal-politics-ijep/1147).

E-politics refers to the electronic social and communication processes via which politics are conducted. However, even the phrase "electronic media" has become problematic. Where is the line between a paper copy and an online version of, say, *The Washington Post*. Is a tweet still a form of social media if published by *The Huffington Post* online? This chapter will not attempt to answer these evolving questions. However, the data for analysis will be limited to non-print forms of communication, including television, social media, blogs, and online publications.

Structural Food Oppression

Oppression is any "experience of repeated, widespread, systemic injustice" (Deutsch, 2005). Structural food oppression refers to injustices in food systems found within institutionalized expectations, stemming both from society and government regulations (Freeman, 2007). Government policies such as Denmark's controversial "fat tax" (Strom, 2012) and the United States' anti-obesity campaign contribute to the stigmatization of heavy bodies.

Andrea Freeman (2007, 2013), writing about "Food Oppression and the USDA," describes structural food oppression:

This state-sponsored... inequality is obscured by the distinction between public and private spheres of action and is perpetuated by the myth of personal choice, even where a lack of options and resources severely limits the ability to exercise choice. Too often, advocates of 'personal choice' blame [marginalized people] for their own weight issues and health crises, linking these problems to individual moral and cultural failures instead of placing the problems in the broader, historical context of long-entrenched policies and practices.

Concurrently, societal expectations bolster structural food oppression.

By choice this chapter focuses on the "often unconscious assumptions and reactions of well-meaning people in ordinary interactions which are supported by the media and cultural stereotypes..." (Deutsch). Structural food oppression, then, refers to the "unquestioned norms, habits, and symbols" that help to form societal rules about food and body image, as well as the "collective consequences of following those rules" (Deutsch). Women are meant to adhere to specific eating habits if they desire to appear "feminine." If women appear to be overweight, through "fat-shaming," women are expected to "watch their figure." If they appear to be underweight (Cronin, et al., 2014), through "skinny shaming" they are attacked as suffering from an eating disorder. In either instance, the policing of the female body is an essential aspect of structural food oppression. One consequence is that food becomes a vehicle of frustration and shame, rather than something to be enjoyed.

Another consequence of structural food oppression is that it might limit the career paths of women who seek to enter the traditional political arena of elected office. A study by Beth Miller and Jennifer Lundgren (2010) reports that overweight female candidates may face a tougher challenge than "fat" male politicians.

The personal pain resulting from structural food oppression must not be overlooked. Laura Bogart, in her manifesto about wearing a swimsuit one day (31 May 2015), reveals the torment. Starting with being called a "whale" in childhood, women face a lifetime of criticism.

Fat Studies

According to Patty Lou Watkins, writing in the *Journal of Media and Culture*, "The newfound, interdisciplinary field of scholarship known as Fat Studies aims to debunk weight-centric misconceptions by elucidating findings that counter these mainstream suppositions." Advocates of a weight-neutral approach called, "Health at Every Size" (HAES), seek to

....eradicate weight-based discrimination, positioning weight bias as a social justice issue that intersects with oppression based on other areas of difference such as gender, race, and social class, much like Queer Studies.... (Watkins, 2015)

Watkins goes a step further in making the move to advocacy:

What can be done to oppose systemised oppression? What can be learned from the fight for social justice and equality within other arenas? Can research and activism be united to challenge prevailing ideas about fat bodies?

Her views align with the general approach of the current study.

Aimee Bernardette Simpson's work (2015) details the "medicalization" of fat as "obesity." She writes, for example,

Since the 1950s, fatness has been widely regarded as the disease 'obesity'. Sobal argues that this occurred through an extensive process of medicalisation, which can be defined as when non-medical issues and behaviour are redefined and understood as medical problems through the use of medical jargon and medical solutions (Conrad). In particular, fat was portrayed as pathological and requiring medical intervention through "frequent, powerful and persuasive claims that [medicine] should exercise social control over fatness" (Sobal 69). In particular this has been exercised through the widespread implementation of the body mass index [BMI] into healthcare settings, as it is seen as an accessible, practical and affordable measure of 'health' (Ministry of Health). Unlike other markers of health, body weight is highly visible, and thus using it as an overall indicator of health increases surveillance of the self and others within populations. In this way we can see how the medicalisation of fatness works to produce what Bordo refers to as: one of the most powerful normalizing mechanisms of our century, insuring the production of self-monitoring and self-disciplining 'docile bodies' sensitive to any departure from social norms and habituated to self-improvement and self-transformation in the service of these norms (186). Primarily, this is created through a construction of a 'normal' body shape or an 'ideal' weight, which can be specified using the BMI.

Simpson is correct that body weight typically is highly visible, lending itself to quick, often stereotypical judgments. Often fat is seen as a sign of laziness and moral weakness.

Fat Shaming

"Body shaming" includes both "fat shaming" and "skinny shaming." Fat shaming includes the derogatory use of the word "fat," as well as images that focus on the abdomen, buttocks, and thighs of larger women. The vocabulary of fat shaming may include the terms: "cellulite," "double chin," "flabby," "rolls," and "slob." Fat shaming in media and cyberspace inscribes women with shame and blame (Thomson, 2007).

Although Shugart (2011) and Thompson are most interested in the politics of "blame" with respect to obesity, this chapter takes a broader perspective on fat shaming. For the present analysis, two representative fragments from popular culture are presented: "Fat Shaming on the Train" and "Fat Shaming at Bryn Mawr."

Fat Shaming on the Train

This case illustrates a "classic" form of fat shaming – rude and derogatory comments about someone else's body. The face-to-face confrontation was projected into cyberspace (almost 14,000 search results on *Bing*) as a form of e-politics. The target of the comments, Stacy Bias (2015), reports "I Stood Up to a Fat-Shaming Bully on a Train Because I'm Tired of Fighting for the Right to Exist." The comments which triggered her reaction included: "Why should I have to pay [more taxes] because some fat slob is too lazy to get off the couch and take care of themself?" Ms. Bias eventually started to respond, saying first, "Hi! I'm a real live fat person…"

Fat Shaming Scandal at Bryn Mawr

In brief, the scandal erupted when Bryn Mawr College, a well-known all-female school, invited specific students to join a weight-loss class. The invitation was based on Body Mass Index (BMI) data contained in the students' health records. However, it could be noted that the e-controversy (see, for example, *Huffington Post*) over Bryn Mawr's invitation to students took a completely different tack via a decidedly personal outraged tone. Commentators, including some from rival college Swarthmore, reacted with observations about *self-esteem*:

As a recovering fat person, I never needed anyone to point out to me that I was overweight. I was in the morbidly obese category and it wasn't like it was news to me. They certainly didn't have to comb my medical records to clue me in. If I wanted to join a weight loss class, I did. Many times… Thus, Bryn Mawr College decided to call out their supposedly overweight students and put in a position of likely failure. What a great way to build their self-esteem! (McNay, 2015)

This theme often surfaces in discussions of fat shaming. What the analysis reveals is that success and failure; high self-esteem and low self-esteem; and winning and losing often are associated with the weight and shape of the female body, a topic that will be developed below in the analysis of *The Biggest Loser*.

Skinny Shaming

The opposite of fat shaming, of course, is skinny shaming. Skinny shaming is mentioned here because it illustrates the double-bind or the Catch-22 faced by women. A recent example of the e-politics of skinny shaming was a 2014 controversy over a model for *The Gap*. The model was attacked as being "too thin." The e-controversy was especially strong on *Twitter*, where these comments appeared:

In what world do people look like this? Perhaps you could select models who represent regular gals & not a skeleton ghost. (@LittleLadyLH)

Doesn't The Gap feed its models. Seriously she look ill. Please use healthy looking women in your ads next time. (@KJ041912)

The rhetorical analysis suggests that the negative terms "skeleton ghost" and "ill" are used as what Richard Weaver calls "Ultimate Terms/Devil-Terms" - terms which go beyond criticism even to condemnation. Just so, the positive terms "regular gals" and "healthy" are used in an oppositional manner to present a preferred norm.

The response to the skinny-shaming response was just as interesting. One tweet challenged *The Gap* to stand up for the model:

Stand up for this model. There are real women who wear size 0, like me, we don't have an eating disorder. Why is being skinny taboo? (@AlexisBogo)

Another commentator attacked body-shaming:

I get that The GAP uses extremely thin women in some adverts, but body shaming the model (and other naturally small/slight women) is NO. (@HisFeministMama)

Even the husband of the model was moved to respond:

I don't know you IRL, but people say this to my wife all the time and it's just as hurtful as telling a fat person to diet. (@danielralston)

The husband's comment sums up the point that the current study is documenting. Whether critiqued though fat-shaming or skinny-shaming, Women Can't Win.

Irony

In its simplest form, *irony* is a literary device for conveying a meaning that is opposite the literal meaning. Scholars from many disciplines have explored the dynamics of *irony*. Soren Kiekegaard (~1841, 1989, 1992), Kenneth Burke (1962), Wayne Booth (1974), Jeffrey Murray (2002), and others have added to the general understanding. According to Kierkegaard, irony is linked to "the awakening of subjectivity." In turn, Kierkegaard hints, a person must grapple with the paradox of subjectivity linked to external claims of truth. Not only can irony help us to evaluate our own lives, irony also is necessary for a more objective and a more ethical stance on other people.

Kenneth Burke argues that irony provides *perspective,* and that a proper understanding of irony would lead us to abandon a sense of superiority, and move us toward seeing the fundamental kinship between terms. In that vein, the present study points to the critical, reflexive, and deconstructive aspects of irony.

In the focus on gender irony, this study looks for the evidence of a "double bind" or "Catch-22" that is presented to women, especially with regard to their relationship with food, on the one hand, and with regard to the shape and weight of their bodies, on the other hand (LeBesco, 2004).

An Ironic Frame

According to Robert Entman (2003), "framing" suggests to audiences an interpretation of a media or cultural artifact based on the source's decisions regarding selection and emphasis. In other words, a source (such as a news report, a blog, or a TV show) presents only a portion of that which could be portrayed and suggests to the audience how important that slice of life is (or should be) for the audience. Media framing analysis or news framing analysis is a developing area of study (D'Angelo & Kuypers, 2010; Reese, Gandy, & Grant, 2001). Frames now are understood to be interpretive schemes on ways that sources construe reports, so that a report contains within it suggestions on how to interpret the report. These suggestions may be visual, artistic (such as metaphors), or inartistic (such as an implied "if---then" logical connection). Often framing relies upon a story or a narrative that helps the audience to make sense of the report.

One may approach the analysis of framing in two ways. One may try to find audience effects, that is, the impact of framing on audiences. On the other hand, one may focus on the language, images, themes, and frames themselves. This study takes the latter course. The thesis offered by Baldwin Van Gorp also suggests that there might be "culturally embedded frames, likely to have a greater resonance with audiences situated in specific social contexts" (p. 85). Public discourse about "obesity," for example, may contain popular narratives and suggestions on how to interpret the issue (Kim & Willis, 2007; Shugate, 2011).

A FEMINIST LENS: THE BARBIE DOLL MODEL

As irony is brought to bear as a tool in this analysis, one can discern that advertising would lead one to believe the contradiction that a woman is required to be thin, while having large breasts, at the same time. This impossible, false ideal – sometimes exposed as the "The Barbie Doll Model" – was described by *Guest Blogger* (18 April 2012) in these terms:

Barbie has also received criticism for promoting unhealthy body ideals and influencing young girls into believing that the Barbie body is common and attainable and more attractive than their own. This is a troubling thought since, according to a news article in Huffington Post, Barbie's height (if she was a living woman) would be 5'9" tall, with a bust of 39", a waist that is 33", while she would wear a size 3 in shoes. Barbie would then weigh 110 lbs with a BMI of 16.24, which lands her in the BMI range of anorexic.

The impact of this kind of false ideal is potentially so severe that Jean Kilbourne (2012) asserts: "advertising is actually a public health issue."

Thirty years of feminist scholarship in rhetorical criticism has indicated that choices about symbols have consequences (Foss, 1996; Glenn, 1997). With respect to language choices, if a society uses only male terms to convey power and status ("policeman" versus "police officer"), then there are likely to be long-term consequences. With respect to images, the same can be said (Williams, 1994). One also might consult the work of Bormann and colleagues (2001 & 2003), who have produced some significant research on the role of narratives and "fantasies" in shaping group life.

Having reviewed some of the relevant literature, it is time to turn to the Methods section

METHODOLOGY

The method here is a critical rhetorical approach. "Rhetorical" studies are "concerned with how symbols influence perceptions and actions" (Shugart, 2011, p. 39). This method is ideal for studying public discourse in electronic media, including visual rhetoric (Olson, Finnegan & Hope, 2008). "Critical" rhetorical studies focuses on the often covert workings of power, and tends to pursue the demystification of power (McKerrow, 1989). In the application of this method, the analysis is based on "texts" constructed from cultural "fragments" (McGee, 1990; Shugart, 2011, p. 39). Therefore, to provide a traditional illustration, one would not study a "speech" as a text, but the speech as set in a broader array of cultural fragments that, together, could be taken as a "text." With Shugart, the present analysis "combines ideological and thematic analytical techniques" (2011, p. 39). Three of the primary analytical techniques are:

1. To observe the use of irony as a tool for gaining perspective,
2. To apply the notion of "framing" to unearth how sources promote an interpretation of the e-product or e-artifact, and
3. To apply a feminist lens to clarify the privileging of certain forms of hegemony and to demystify the workings of power.

The data for this analysis are drawn from an August 2015 *LexisNexis Academic* search for the phrase "Rachel Frederickson." This search, limited to February 2014 (the month after Rachel Frederickson) won *The Biggest Loser*, unearthed 52 online articles. In addition, the research team created a structured, convenience sample from references to Rachel Frederickson in social media, such as *Twitter* and *Tumblr*.

These materials were analyzed using established Content Analysis methods (Frey, Botan, & Kreps, 2000; Treadwell, 2014), and a critical rhetorical analysis, based on close textual analysis of the headlines and the themes. Themes from the *LexisNexis* search emerged inductively, following the tenets of Grounded Theory (Strauss & Corbin, 1988).

ANALYSIS OF *THE BIGGEST LOSER* (2014)

Part 1: Social Media

The Biggest Loser has been studied from a Business perspective (Ives, 2006), an Obesity/Blame perspective (Shugart, 2011), and a Civic Functions perspective (Ouellette, 2010). While the current study has another mission, it would be wise not to neglect or minimize these other perspectives. For example, the article by Nat Ives on *The Biggest Loser* as a *business* reports that the reality show is a money-making franchise, earning significant amounts of revenue from merchandise as well as over $70 million for ads and $2 million per month from online club memberships. Again, e-politics (in this case, TV images) has material consequences.

What is proposed here is to extend research on *The Biggest Loser* in two ways:

1. By operationalizing irony as a way of understanding the structural nature of oppression and
2. By utilizing a feminist lens on body image to reveal the lose-lose situation in which women are culturally situated.

Rachel Frederickson won the grand prize of $250,000 for losing a remarkable 60% of her body weight during the course of *The Biggest Loser* (2014). Frederickson, 24, and 5"4" in height, started the season weighing 260 pounds. During the finale, she weighed in at 105 pounds.

Immediately following the announcement of Frederickson's win, social media users began criticizing her weight loss and body size. Though the primary goal of the reality weight-loss show is to lose the highest percentage of body weight, viewers were appalled by Frederickson's appearance at the finale. Social media users began labelling her with stigmatizing content such as "too thin," a stark contrast to her "too fat" presence at the beginning of the season.

Many bloggers expressed outrage stemming from her win, claiming that Frederickson was clearly unhealthy and should not be rewarded, but rather should seek help for her "underweight" condition (Tumblr, 2014). Tumblr user *sociallyawkward-jac* (2014) claimed concern for Frederickson's weight loss under body-policing ideals:

I just want her to realize she lost too much weight and she needs to gain a few pounds... She went from one extreme to the next.

This pseudo-concern for Frederickson's well-being was the basis of various unwarranted comments, all of which demonstrated the perpetuation of double standards for the female body. Frederickson had successfully lost the weight which societal principles despised, then was judged for losing it. Blogger Jen Evers (2014) reacted to *The Biggest Loser*'s finale:

Rachel's appearance was shocking. She was thin. And not in an "Oh-my-gosh...look-how-healthy-and-amazing-you-look!" way. But in an "Oh my, what have you done to yourself?" kind of way.

The shock expressed by observers was captured in a tweet by Melanie King and supported with an accompanying photograph of trainers Jillian Michaels and Bob Harper. (https://twitter.com/VGonzee/status/431026731437551616)

@kingmelaniea Looks like we're not the only ones who thought Rachel looked sickly. #BiggestLoser #Backlash

Of course, not all remarks were posted under the guise of health concerns. There were also a plethora of stigmatizing observations about Frederickson's body size. In the commentary section of an article posted on *Mamamia* (2014), users continued to describe her body size as "skeletal," "sickly," and "too skinny." One commenter critiqued:

She's lost too much body fat and it's made her look ten years older. Next she'll be having botox and fillers with her prize money. Very sad and irresponsible.

This commentator not only stigmatized Frederickson's body type, but also critiqued the validity of using her prize money on whatever she wanted. Rather, the commenter made false assumptions and judgments on the future of Frederickson's personal life to further justify the critique. This comment was just one of hundreds describing her body negatively:

She was very, very thin. Too thin in my opinion. (Tumblr, lifeisyourstomiss, 2014).

Way too thin, not fit & healthy! (Twitter, @KatyZembower, 2014).

Furthermore, the Twitter hashtag *#TooThin* was included in *The Biggest Loser* updates.

Social media was ablaze with accusations of the development of an eating disorder. Rather than note *The Biggest Loser's* vigorous exercise routine as a factor of Frederickson's weight loss, viewers chose to place the blame on her apparent "lack of control" (Yoo, 2013, p. 296). Tumblr user *stahp-thinprivilege* (2014) supported this attribution of her success:

It's because she's anorexic and going too far.

In an *ETOnline* article which supports the statement that Rachel Frederickson is "too thin," the author notes the use of the hashtag *#Anorexia* "when referring to her weight loss" (Willis, 2014). Twitter user *@AliAmmerlaan* referred to Frederickson as a "poor skeleton," while user *@JacobWard* called her "the very picture of anorexia" (2014).

A comment on *Tumblr* at *lifeisyourstomiss* (2014) returns to the BMI (medical/scientific) discourse discussed in a previous section:

I almost wish that they had a rule where if you weigh in at an "underweight" BMI at the finale, you're disqualified.

In the last sentence, another irony becomes clear. The very competitiveness of the show itself encourages potentially unhealthy practices, but staff members seemed "shocked" when they saw Frederickson at the finale.

Part 2: *LexisNexis* Search

The earlier articles recovered through the *LexisNexis* search repeated the theme:

"Did 'The Biggest Loser' lose too much?" In fact, Frederickson dropped a higher percentage of body weight than any other contestant in the history of *The Biggest Loser*. The headlines of at least 8 of the 52 articles (~15 per cent) used terms such as "uproar," "stirs debate," "sparks debate," and "touches a nerve."

Another theme that emerged was a "skinny" theme, found in headline language such as "too thin," "skinny," "loses too much weight," unhealthy," and "gone too far." This type of language appeared in at least 11 of the 52 articles (~20 per cent). Did Frederickson have an eating disorder? There is reason for concern, stated Jennifer Thomas, the co-director of the Eating Disorders Clinical and Research Program at Massachusetts General Hospital (Conlin, 9 February 2014). Another commentator, Jillian Lampert of the Emily Program, a nationally recognized eating disorder treatment program, said that Frederickson is below the normal BMI range, but "I think it's a very interesting reflection of our society that we're obsessed with weight loss and then we get mad when someone does it too much" (Gustafson, 4 February 2014). Lampert's statement supports the "Women Can't Win" thesis featured in the present study.

At least one article in the *LexisNexis* search focused on the discomfort of viewers (Li, 6 February 2014). *The New York Post* listed a series of quotations containing negative evaluations, such as:

"Biggest Loser Should Be Ashamed"

"I don't think I've ever been this uncomfortable watching the finale."

"Rachel just looks sickly. She shouldn't be able to win."

"Does a contestant have to drop dead on the scale before #TheBiggestLoser

addresses how dangerous this spectacle is?"

"If someone was doing something like this to a prisoner, they'd be in violation of some Geneva convention."

Meanwhile, a commentator on *EW.com* wrote, "This made me so sad. Rachel looked beautiful at 150 pounds. I expected her to end up in the 120s. The girl who came out last night looked frail and sick, not like an athlete." Many comments on Frederickson's *Facebook* page urged her to get medical help. But what about Frederickson's reaction?

The *LexisNexis* search revealed two articles that reported Frederickson's view of herself. At the end of Jennifer Conlin's article in *The New York Times* (9 February 2014), Frederickson is given one line: "I've never felt this great, and it's very exciting." A longer biographical piece in the Minneapolis *Star Tribune* (Ward, 4 February 2014) contains a number of quotations from the winner of *The Biggest Loser* (2014) on the eve of the finale. Frederickson is quoted as saying: "Not only have I gotten my health back, I feel alive and energetic." Frederickson credits the show with giving her "my relationship with my dad back." A final quotation at the end of the article is very upbeat: "I truly won already. I'm in charge of my life. I'm ready to take control. I've gotten my life back. I'm not going to let anybody or anything take that away." There it is in the words of the winner: I am a winner.

CONCLUSION

Tumblr is a microblogging platform and social networking website that is extremely relevant for this chapter on the e-politics of food and the female body. It claims to have over 200 million bloggers, a large audience by any standard. A rant posted by user *dear-melinda-count-me-in* captures the frustration of "bigger" women:

I'm sick of "curvy girls" being portrayed as flat-stomached, wide-hipped girls, while people say things like "yes, love bigger girls? love curves! fat is beautiful too!" Most "fat" girls don't have bodies like that; there are stretchmarks and cellulite and rolls and those all go unnoticed making actual big girls feel pretty shitty.

What *dear-melinda-count-me-in* is describing is the perfect Catch-22, defined by *The Free Dictionary* as: "A situation in which a desired outcome or solution is impossible to attain because of a set of inherently contradictory rules or conditions." Earlier in the chapter the authors noted that fat-shaming and skinny-shaming place contradictory and impossible demands upon women. Now the analysis reveals that "large" is praised but is *disguised* as "thin." Again, Women Can't Win.

The introduction to this chapter promised to break some new ground by using irony as a tool to make clearer the workings of one form of the e-politics of food, namely, the structural food oppression linked to the weight and shape of the female body. The authors have argued and documented that the e-politics of the weight and shape of the female body is one of the most important incarnations of the e-politics of food and one of the most vigorously contested. As a window into this realm of the international e-politics of food, many forms of public discourse and e-politics were examined, with a focus on the case study of Rachel Frederickson. The critical rhetorical analysis has found some support for the Women Can't Win thesis.

However, the authors are faced with an obligation to go beyond analysis to positive suggestions. In conclusion, then, two recommendations are offered. As with most studies, this study has accomplished something but left much undone or incomplete. Therefore, scholars and practitioners must continue to demystify the workings of power in the international e-politics of food/female body. For example, Lisa Tillmann (2014) has produced a documentary, the *Weight Problem: Cultural Narratives of Fat and "Obesity,"* that might contribute to this project and that motivate the ongoing work of others. One also could take note of the new field of "Solution Photojournalism" that calls for journalists to give aid and direction via visual media (Nwankpa, 2014).

The final recommendation to help alleviate the gender irony contained in the impossible demands upon the female body is to advocate for *Body Positivity*. *Huffington Post* included a story on Body-Positive Movements, especially for teenage girls, in its February 3, 2015 online edition. The story by Roxie Jane Hunt featured the e-politics of *The Free Your Pits Movement*:

Young people all over the world proudly posted their colored armpit hair pics on Facebook and Instagram, posing in solidarity with those who stand for freedom of choice, body positivity, personal expression, and a new international standard of beauty.

One might smile at this particular form of advocacy by adolescents. Nevertheless, it serves as a clear model for the future of e-politics. If social media can lead to government reform, e-politics also can serve as a way to replace the Catch-22 of current female body ideals with positive alternatives.

REFERENCES

Ammerlaan, A. (2014, February 5). *Twitter*. Retrieved from https://twitter.com/aliammerlaan/status/431257179430338560

Anderson, J., & Bresnahan, M. (2013). Communicating stigma about body size. *Health Communication*, *28*(6), 603–615. doi:10.1080/10410236.2012.706792 PMID:22928811

Arndt, A., & Jaeschke, W. (Eds.). (2000). Materialismus und Spiritualismus: Philosophie und Wissenschaften nach 1848. Hamburg, Germany: Meiner.

Benzmiller, H. (2013). The cyber-samaritans: Exploring criminal liability for the 'innocent' bystanders of cyberbullying. *Northwestern University Law Review*, *107*(2), 927–962.

Bias, S. (2015). *I stood up to a fat-shaming bully on a train because I'm tired of fighting for the right to exist*. Retrieved from http://www.xojane.com/issues/fat-shaming-train-bully

Biesecker, B. (2007). No time for mourning: The rhetorical production of the melancholic citizen-subject in the war of terror. *Philosophy & Rhetoric*, *40*(1), 147–169. doi:10.1353/par.2007.0009

Blair, C., Brown, J., & Baxter, L. (1999). Disciplining the feminine. In Contemporary rhetorical theory (pp. 563-590). New York, NY: The Guilford Press.

Blogger, G. (2012, April 18). *The impossible trend: Look like Barbie*. Retrieved from http://www.thef-word.org.uk/blog/2012/04/the_impossible_

Body Mass Index (BMI). (n.d.). *WebMD*. Retrieved from http://webmd.com/men/weight-loss-bmi

Bogart, L. (2015, May 31). I will wear a swimsuit one day: Manifesto of a righteous fat-ass. *Salon.com*. Retrieved from http://salon.com/2015/06/01/I_will_wear_a_swimsuit_one_day

Booth, W. (1974). *A rhetoric of irony*. Chicago, IL: University of Chicago Press.

Bormann, E. G., Cragan, J. F., & Shields, D. C. (2001). Three decades of developing, grounding, and using Symbolic Convergence Theory (SCT). In W. Gudykunst (Ed.), *Communication Yearbook 25* (pp. 271–313). Yahweh, NJ: Lawrence Earlbaum. doi:10.1080/23808985.2001.11679006

Bormann, E. G., Cragan, J. F., & Shields, D. C. (2003). Defending Symbolic Convergence Theory from an imaginary Gunn. *The Quarterly Journal of Speech*, *89*(4), 366–372. doi:10.1080/0033563032000160990

Brillat-Savarin, A. (1826). *Physiologie du gout, ou meditations de gastronomie transcendante*. Paris, France: Feydeau.

Burke, K. (n.d.). A grammar of motives. Berkeley, CA: University of California Press.

Cleveland, A. (2014, February 5). *Twitter*. Retrieved February 10, 2015, from https://twitter.com/BrunetteWife/status/431074346409279488

Conlin, J. (2014, February 9). A big reveal touches a nerve. *The New York Times*.

Cronin, J., McCarthy, M., Newcombe, M., & McCarthy, S. (2014). Paradox, performance and food: Managing difference in the construction of femininity. *Consumption Markets & Culture*, *17*(4), 367–391. doi:10.1080/10253866.2013.872548

dear-melinda-count-me-in. (n.d.). *Tumblr*. Retrieved from: http://www.tumblr.com/search/body+image+rant+

Deutsch, M. (2005, March). The nature and origins of oppression. *Beyond Intractability*. Retrieved from http://beyondintractability.org/essay/nature-origins-oppression

Duvall, S. (2011). *Top 10 Countries Celebrating Female Obesity*. Retrieved from http://www.toptenz.net/top-10-countries-celebrating-female-obesity.php

Entman, R. (2007). Framing bias: Media in the distribution of power. *Journal of Communication, 57*(1), 163–173. doi:10.1111/j.1460-2466.2006.00336.x

Evers, J. (2014, February 5). Biggest loser finale: what happened to Rachel? *Me, Myself, and Jen.* Retrieved from http://www.memyselfandjen.com/life-and-kids/biggest-loser-finale-happened-rachel/

1. fallin-4-u. (2014, February 6). Retrieved from: http://1fallin-4-u.tumblr.com/post/75867793189

Fallon, P., Katzman, M., & Wooley, S. (Eds.). (1996). *Feminist perspectives on eating disorders.* New York, NY: Guilford Press.

familydrivenfate. (2014, February 5). *Tumblr.* Retrieved from http://familydrivenfate.tumblr.com/post75660799176/

Ferguson, P. P. (2014). *Word of mouth: What we talk about when we talk about food.* Berkeley, CA: University of California Press, California Studies in Food and Culture.

Festl, R., & Quandt, T. (2013). Social relations and cyberbullying: The influence of individual and structural attributes on victimization and perpetration via the internet. *Human Communication Research, 39*(1), 101–126. doi:10.1111/j.1468-2958.2012.01442.x

forever-one-twenty. (2014, February 5). *Tumblr.* Retrieved from http://forever-one-twenty.tumblr.com/post/75697273079/

Foss, S. (1996). *Rhetorical criticism: Exploration and practice* (2nd ed.). Prospects Heights, IL: Waveland Press.

Freeman, A. (2007). Fast food: Oppression through poor nutrition. *California Law Review, 95*(6), 2221-2259. Retrieved from: http://scholarship/law.berkeley.edu/californialawreview/vol95/iss6/8

Freeman, A. (2013). The unbearable whiteness of milk: Food oppression and the USDA. *Irvine Law Review, 3*(4). Retrieved from http://scholarship.lawuci.edu/ucilr/vol3/iss4/16

Frye, J. (Ed.). (2012). *The rhetoric of food.* New York, NY: Routledge.

Fuller, B. (2014, June 26). Jillian Michaels quits 'biggest loser' over too skinny Rachel Frederickson. *Hollywood Life.* Retrieved from http://hollywoodlife.com/2014/06/26/jillian-michaels-quits-biggest-loser-reason-rachel-fredrikson/

Garcia, L. (Feb. 5, 2015). Robyn Lawley, model with normal body, graces *Sports Illustrated's Swim Issue.* Retrieved from https://www.yahoo.com/style/model-with-normal-body-graces-sports-illustrated-110196422508.html

Glenn, C. (1997). *Rhetoric retold: Regendering the tradition from antiquity through the Renaissance.* Carbondale, IL: Southern Illinois University Press.

Granger, G. (2014, April 4). *Twitter.* Retrieved from https://twitter.com/NewSlenderUByVi/status/452106129594916865

Gustafson, A. C. (2014, February 4). Stillwater native's 'Biggest Loser' weight loss stirs debate. *St. Paul Pioneer Press.*

Hahn, L. K. (2015). Irony and food politics. *Communication and Critical Cultural Studies*. doi:10.1080/14791420.2015.1014185

Hunt, R. J. (February 3, 2015). *Why our daughters need more body-positive movements*. Retrieved from http://www.huffingtonpost.com/roxie-jane-hunt/why-our-daughters-need-more-body-positive-movements_b_6592076.html

icywinterstorm. (2014, February 6). *Tumblr.* Retrieved from http://icywinterstorm.tumblr.com/post/756632534211/

imdreamingyourdreams. (2014, February 5). *Tumblr.* Retrieved from http://imdreamingyourdreams.tumblr.com/post/75696839972/

Ives, N. (2006). Loser' Wins. *Advertising Age, 77*(10).

jiffytiffy. (2014, February 6). *Tumblr.* Retrieved from http://jiffytiffy.tumblr.com/post/75725874828/

Kilbourne, J. (1979/2010). *Killing us softly: Advertising's image of women*. Cambridge Documentaries.

Kilbourne, J. (2012). *Women's bodies in advertising*. Retrieved from http://www.ourbodiesourselves.org/health-info/womens-bodies-in-advertising/

Kim, S., & Willis, L. (2007). Talking about obesity: News framing of who is responsible for causing and fixing the problem. *Journal of Health Communication, 12*(4), 359–376. doi:10.1080/10810730701326051 PMID:17558788

Kuebler, M., Muennig, P., Pelleg, D., Puhl, R. M., & Yom-Tov, E. (2013). When overweight is the normal weight: An examination of obesity using a social media internet database. *Plus ONE, 8*(9), 1–8. doi:10.1371/journal.pone.0073479 PMID:24058478

Lasswell, H. (1936). *Politics: Who gets, what, when, how*. New York, NY: Whittlesey House.

LeBesco, K. (2004). *Revolting bodies? The struggle to redefine fat identity*. Amherst, MA: University of Massachusetts Press.

Li, D. K. (2014). It's too little too soon! Critics fear "Loser" health. *The New York Post.*

lifeisyourstomiss. (2014, February 5). *Tumblr.* Retrieved from http://lifeisyourstomiss/tumble.com/post/75696998240/

lillythelegend. (2014, February 5). *Tumblr.* Retrieved from http://lillythelegend.com/2014/02/05/biggest-loser-winner-too-skinny/

Lindlahr, V. (1942). *You are what you eat: How to win and keep health with diet*. New York, NY: National Nutrition Society.

Livingston, J. (2012). *Jennifer Livingston responds to viewer letter about her weight*. Retrieved from www.news8000.com/news/Jennifer-Livingston-responds.../16832410

lunalovebad. (2014, February 5). *Tumblr.* Retrieved from http://lunalovebad.tumblr.com/post/75796841935

Marrow, D. (2014, February 13). *Tumblr*. Retrieved from http://spiel-it.tumblr.com/post/76557966735

McGee, M. C. (1990). Text, comntext, and the fragmentation n of cobntemporary culture. *Western Journal of Speech Communication*, *54*(3), 274–289. doi:10.1080/10570319009374343

McKerrow, R. (1989). Critical rhetoric: Theory and praxis. *Communication Monographs*, *56*(2), 91–111. doi:10.1080/03637758909390253

McNay, D. (2015, February 10). The fat shaming scandal at Bryn Mawr. *Huffington Post*. Retrieved from http://www.huffingtonpost.com/don-mcnay/the-fat-shaming-scandal_b_6654676.html

Miller, B., & Lundgren, J. (2010, April). An experimental study on the role of weight bias in candidate evaluation. *Obesity (Silver Spring, Md.)*, *4*(18), 712–718. doi:10.1038/oby.2009.492 PMID:20111025

Morgan, K. P. (1991). Women and the knife: Cosmetic surgery and the colonization of womens bodies. *Hypatia: Feminism and the Body*, *6*(3), 25–53. doi:10.1111/j.1527-2001.1991.tb00254.x

Murray, J. W. (2002). Dialogue of motives. *Philosophy & Rhetoric*, *35*(1), 22–49. doi:10.1353/par.2002.0004

Nestle, M. (2002/2013). *Food politics: How the food industry influences nutrition and health*. Berkeley, CA: University of California Press, California Studies in Food and Culture.

Nunez, D. (2014, April 3). *Twitter*. Retrieved Febr 10, 2015, from https://twitter.com/dpn5/status/451737726363385856

Nwankpa, N. (2014). An advocacy for "Solution Photojournalism" in disaster situations. *Journal of Communication and Media Research*, *6*(2), 21–29.

Olson, L., Finnegan, C., & Hope, D. (Eds.). (2008). *Visual rhetoric*. Thousand Oaks, CA: Sage Publications.

Oulette, L. (2010). Reality TV gives back: On the civic functions of reality entertainment. *Journal of Popular Film & Television*, *38*(2), 66–71. doi:10.1080/01956051.2010.483347

Pollan, M. (2006). *The omnivore's dilemma: A natural history of four meals*. New York, NY: Penguin.

Pollan, M. (2008). *In defense of food: An eater's manifesto*. New York, NY: Penguin.

Pollan, M. (2013). *Cooked: A natural history of transformation*. New York, NY: Penguin.

rundreamlive. (2014, February 6). *Tumblr*. Retrieved from http://rundreamlive.tumblr.com/post/75835484002/

Shahid, A. (n.d.). Andrew Breitbart posts cartoon of fat First Lady. *The New York Daily News*. Retrieved from: http://www.nydailynews.com/news/politics/andrew-breitbart-website-posts-cartoon-fat-lady-mocking-anti-obesity-campaign-article-1.136361

Shari. (2014, February 5). Did the 'biggest loser' winner rachel frederickson lose too much weight? *Have U Heard*. Retrieved February 10, 2015, from http://haveuheard.net/2014/02/biggest-loser-winner-rachel-fredricksons-lost-weight/

Shugart, H. A. (2011). Shifting the Balance: The contemporary narrative of obesity. *Health Communication, 26*(1), 37-47. doi: 10.1080/10410236.2011.527620

Simpson, A. B. (2015). At what cost?: Problematising the achievement of 'Health' through thinness – The case of Bariatric Surgery. *M/C Journal: Journal of Media and Culture*, (18), 3. Retrieved from http://journal.media-culture.org.au/index.php/mcjournal/article/viewArticle/970

sociallyawkward-jac. (2014, February 5). *Tumblr.* Retrieved from http://sociallyawkward-jac.tumblr.com/post/75745541663

stahp-thinprivilege. (2014, February 5). Retrieved from http://stahp-thinprivilege.tumblr.com/post/76017096719

Strauss, A., & Corbin, J. (1988). Grounded theory methodology. In N. K. Denzin & Y. Lincoln (Eds.), *Strategies of Qualitative Inquiry* (pp. 158–183). Newbury Park, CA: SAGE.

Strom, S. (November 12, 2012). 'Fat tax' in Denmark is repealed after criticism. *New York times.com.* Retrieved February 27, 2015, from http://www.nytimes.com/2012/11/13/ business/global/fat-tax-in-denmark-is-repealed-after-criticism.html?_r=0

sweethappiness. (2014, February 6). *Tumblr.* Retrieved from http://sweethappiness.tumblr.com/post/75809262441/

Takeda, A. (2014, April 3). Rachel frederickson, 'biggest loser' winner, gains 20 pounds. *US Magazine.* Retrieved from http://www.usmagazine.com/celebrity-rachel-frederickson-biggest-loser-winner-gains-20-pounds-im-at-my-perfect-weight-201434

The Biggest Loser. (n.d.a). Retrieved from http://en.wikipedia.org/wiki/The_Biggest_Loser

The Biggest Loser. (n.d.b). Retrieved from http://www.biggestloser.com/

The Biggest Loser. (n.d.c). Retrieved from http://www.nbc.com/the-biggest-loser

thepursuittobecomemoreattractive. (n.d.). *Factoh.* Retrieved from http://factoh.com/the-pursuit-to-become-more-attractive-is-a-160-billion-a-year-global-industry

Thompson, D. (2007). *Spectacular decapitations: The body politics of shaming fat with personal responsibility.* Paper presented at the annual meeting of the National Communication Association. Retrieved from http://web.b.ebscohost.com/ehost/pdfviewer/pdfviewer?vid=6&sid=3dc64fe6-b6be-49bd-b970-f6241eef710c%40sessionmgr113&hid=109

Tillman, L. M. (2014). *Weight problem: Cultural narratives of fat and "obesity".* Retrieved from http://www.imdb.com/title/tt3787894/?ref_=nm_flmg_dr_1

Van Gorp, B. (2010). Strategies to take subjectivity out of framing analysis. In Doing news framing analysis: Empirical and theoretical perspectives (pp. 84-109). New York, NY: Routledge.

Ward, J. (2014, February 4). Stillwater native has toned her body and rebuilt her life. *Minneapolis Star Tribune.*

Ward, J. (2014, February 5). *Twitter.* Retrieved from https://twitter.com/_jacobward_/statuses/431083808134139904

Watkins, P. L. (2015). Fat Studies 101: Learning to have your cake and eat it too. *M/C Journal: Journal of Media and Culture,* (18), 3. Retrieved from http://journal.media-culture.org.au/index.php/mcjournal/article/viewArticle/968

Web, M. D. (n.d.). *Body Mass Index (BMI), according to WebMD*. Retrieved from http://www.webmd.com/men/weight-loss-bmi)

Weber, B. (2014, February 6). Critics call The Biggest Loser irresponsible. *Here and Now*. Retrieved from http://hereandnow.wbur.org/2014/02/06/biggest-loser-rachel

Wegge, D., Vandebosch, H., & Eggermont, S. (2014). Who bullies whom online: A social network analysis of cyberbullying in a school context. *Communications, 39*(4), 415–433. doi:10.1515/commun-2014-0019

Williams, M. (1994). A reconceptualization of women's protest rhetoric: Women's quilts as rhetorical forms. *Women's. Studies in Communications, 17*, 2–44.

Willis, J. (2014, February 5). Biggest loser scandal! Is the winner too thin? *Entertainment Tonight.* Retrieved from http://www.etonline.com/dailyfirst/143214_Biggest_Loser_Scandal_Rachel_Frederickson_Deemed_Too_Thin_By_Audiences/

Yoo, J. H. (2013). No clear winner: Effects of the biggest loser on the stigmatization of obese persons. *Health Communication, 28*(3), 294–303. doi:10.1080/10410236.2012.684143 PMID:22742588

Zembower, K. (2014, February 6). *Twitter*. Retrieved from https://twitter.com/KatyZembower/status/431549411039408129

ENDNOTES

1 While this chapter focuses on gender irony and the e-politics of the female body, some of the same processes may be at work in the case of the e-politics of the male body. For example, "six pack abs" are celebrated in public discourse as a model for men of all ages: 1) Aaron Schock, a youthful United States Congressman, showed off his six pack abs on the cover of *Men's Health Magazine* (May, 2011); and 2) *The Daily Mail* (London) reported that actor Dennis Quaid, age 57, revealed a six-pack that would be the envy of many men half his age (November 1, 2011). Six pack abs have gone international, according to *The Times of India* (November 14, 2011), which reported that Bollywood star "Himesh Reshammiya aspires to get six pack abs just like Salman Khan."

Chapter 16
Critical Issues on Gender Equality and ICTs in Latin America

Aimée Vega Montiel
UNAM CEIICH, Mexico

ABSTRACT

In the context of the new media environment, several social, political and economic divides are being produced. As the effects of those changes are not neutral, because of gender inequality, the status of women's human rights in the digital age are precarious. To what extent does the new media environment promote women's human and communication rights or contribute to sustaining the oppression of women in society? Based on the feminist political economy perspective, the aim of this paper is to analyze some of the critical issues on gender equality and ICTs in Latin America.[1]

INTRODUCTION

The Beijing Platform for Action (1995) drew attention to the importance of communication and information technologies to encourage gender equality and women's human rights. The Strategic Objective J1 emphasized the urgency to increase participation and access of women to expression and decision-making in and through the media, as well as in the call that women and girls should be empowered by enhancing their skills, knowledge and access to information technologies.

In 2003, the WSIS Declaration of Principles and Plan for Action, stressed specifically the importance of ICTs in reaching that goal:

We affirm that development of ICT provides enormous opportunities for women, who should be an integral part of, and key actors in, the Information Society. We are committed to ensuring that the Information Society enables women's empowerment and their full participation on the basis of equality in all spheres of society and in all decision-making processes. To his end, we should mainstream a gender equality perspective and use ICT as a tool to that end (WSIS, 2003).

DOI: 10.4018/978-1-5225-1862-4.ch016

However, in the context of the new media environment several social, political and economic divides are being produced. As the effects of those changes are not neutral, because of the gendered division of power, the status of women's human rights in the digital age - particularly, their human right to communicate - are precarious.

At this point though the question is: To what extent does the new media environment promote women's human and communication rights or contribute to sustaining the oppression of women in society in Latin America?

Feminist Political Economy Perspective

According to the feminist political economy perspective, capitalism is not the only process of class relations. As patriarchy is the first social construct, class is not generically neutral. For this reason, the capitalist structure does not have the same implications for men than for women, then both patriarchy and capitalism reproduce together social injustices (Riordan, 2002: 7).

With this base, ICTs –the driving force of the digital communication- are not a 'natural' effect of the development of society, but a product of hegemonic interests who seek to gain maximum benefit from these technologies; which bases its benefits in the exploitation of the labour force (Martin, 2002: 54). ICTs neither exist in a 'neutral' way. As they are produced by the gendered structures of power, the ICTs represent the male culture.

Then communication and information technologies are playing a double role. On one hand, they constitute a key element for social, political and economic women's empowerment, as they could help to reduce poverty, illiteracy, gender-based violence and social segregation. On the other hand, they are also exacerbating gender and class inequalities (Martin, 2002: 54).

In addition, given that women are involved in capitalism as workers, but also as consumers, their interests are largely in the hands of communication and information industries (Martin, 2002: 57). ICTs are responding to the stereotyped association of both women and men to patriarchal identities –women as commodified bodies and sexual objects for the male consumption and men as subjects of power (Byerly, 2002; Ross, 2012: 112). As result, most of the contents that circulate in the digital environment, reproduce sexist stereotypes that prevail in traditional media and that discriminate women.

Then ideology plays a central role in the support of the androcentric power that dominates the communication and information industries. "Those with the ownership and control of the media industries also have the power to silence and render invisible women's voice, ideas, experiences, problems, and achievements" (Gallagher, 1980, in Byerly, 2002: 136). But these industries can generate significant transformations if they ensure that women are able to reach these areas.

However, although in the age of digital communication media are structured by the dominant paradigm of patriarchal capitalism that serves to ensure "a male-ordered and global system of social and economic control" (Ross, 2002: 113), women have been able to expand their communicative resources, in order to reach their human right to communicate.

In this paper we will review the central dimensions of this problem and will focus the attention in the Latin American region: women's access to and use of ICTs, their access to decision making positions, their incorporation into the labour market of the ICTs and their working conditions in less qualified positions, the lack of State intervention to regulate these systems with a gender mainstreaming, the lack of policies to eliminate gender inequality in access to ICTs and the domination of sexist stereotypes in the contents, as well as the use of these technologies for sex trafficking. This analysis does not fail to recognize the potential of ICTs for the development of women.

Digital Gender Divide

The concept of digital divide has been useful to raise awareness of the inequalities in resources and skills necessary to access the benefits of communication in the digital age. Factors such as poverty, illiteracy, language barriers and computer illiteracy, constitute some of the major obstacles, especially in developing countries (UN, 2005).

The ICT Development Index (IDI)[2] shows that in 2011 the Republic of Korea headed the IDI, followed by Sweden, Denmark, Iceland, Finland, Netherlands, Luxembourg, UK and Switzerland. This index establishes that countries in the first 30 places are those with more income, which shows the relationship between income and development levels. The gap between developed and developing countries is three times higher in developed countries. Europe is the only region in the world where the digital divide is being reduced (ITU, 2012).

In relation to access to ICT's, the NRI 2011 shows that in developing countries there are 81 mobile telephony subscriptions per 100 population, while in developed nations there are 111 per 100. There are 8.8 mobile broadband subscriptions per 100 population in developing countries and 64.8 per 100 population in developed -this is the sector with the highest growth (ITU, 2012). Percentage of households with a computer is 77.7% in developed countries and 22.2% in developing countries.

If we look at the Internet dimension, the digital divide grows wider. Most of the world population are not online: 4.6 billion people do not access to the Internet (two thirds of the total population). There are 2.4 billion Internet users. 77.3% of individuals in developed countries use the Internet, while in developing countries they are 25% (ITU, 2012).

Access by region shows the next tendencies:

- North America has 274 million users (79% penetration)
- Oceania/Australia has 24 million users (68% penetration)
- Europe has 519 million users (61% penetration)
- Latin America & the Caribbean have 255 million users (43% penetration)
- Middle East has 90 million users (40% penetration)
- Asia has 1.1 billion users (28% penetration) (Intel & Dalberg Global Development Advisors, 2012).

The digital divide is also evident in the domain of the English as the language of the Internet. In 2002, 75% of the Internet pages were in English, 3% in Spanish and 1% in Portuguese (UN, 2002).

This divide is deepened by the cost of technology. Although the cost is being reduced mainly in the area of fixed telephony, the cost of services of the ICTs are still very high in developing countries. The highest prices are registered in Africa, followed by Asia-Pacific, the Arab States and the Americas. Europe is the region with the cheapest ICTs services around the world (ITU, 2012).

If we adopt the feminist perspective, we will see that the costs of the digital divide are not the same for men than for women. In the words of Abdul Waheed Khan, the gender divide is "one of the most significant inequalities to be amplified by the digital revolution, and cuts across all social and income groups. Through the world women face serious challenges that are not only economic but social as well as cultural obstacles that limit or prevent their access to, set of, and benefits from ICT's"(Primo, 2003: 5).

According to Nancy Hafking (2003), since technologies are not gender-neutral as they impact on women and men differently, among the most important indicators to analyse these differences are:

1. ICTs access and use,
2. Content,
3. Employment,
4. Education,
5. Gender ICTs policy,
6. Participation in ICTs industry decision making and
7. Differential impact of information technology on women and men.

However, the availability of official data about these indicators is very low, mainly in developing countries, where most of governments are not documenting the gender divide, and "without data, there is no visibility; without visibility, there is no priority" (Hafking, 2003: 1). This is the case in Latin America and the Caribbean, Africa and Middle East, where data are precarious. In North America, the data point mainly to access. The European Union is the one that has probably done more efforts to build data. Among Asian countries, Korea is a good exception - this government is reporting quantitative and qualitative data of access to and use of ICTs, such as rates of Internet usage by sex and age, purposes of usage, frequency of Internet usage, and so on (Hafking, 2003).

Some available data about general indicators have been produced by international agencies –UN, UN Women, UNESCO, ITU, OECD-, by scholars and by national and regional NGOs. These analyses document primarily access to Internet, but very few about other tools. Finally, data come too from market firms -Nielsen, Media Matrix/Jupiter Communications-, for commercial purposes. But as warns Nancy Hafking (2003), some of these data are questionable, even among private firms[3].

Access and Use

Women are minority in the number of users of ICTs in both developed and developing countries. In most of the OECD countries, men access is at least 5% greater than women (OECD, 2007).

In contexts with a lack of resources, access and use of ICTs are very limited. It is important to emphasize that, behind the numbers of the digital age, there are conditions of poverty, marginalisation and violence of gender which determine the use women make of technologies.

In developing countries, there are 300 million less women than men as mobile phone suscribers (Global System of Mobil Communications Operator Organisation, 2010)

27% of men in developing countries access to the Internet, while only 21% of women do it. This results in 600 million women online in developing countries -200 million less than men. The gender gap is 23%. According to Intel & Dalberg Global Development Advisors (2012), comparing these data with that reported in 2009, 69% of women in USA had access to the Internet, while 68% of men had. This means women in USA access opportunities to the Internet are more than three times than women in developing countries (Intel & Dalberg Global Development Advisors, 2012).

By region, we can see that, of the total population:

- In Latin America the access of women to the Internet is 36%, men is 40%, resulting in a gender gap (weighted) of 10%
- In Europe and Central Asia, 35% of users are women, 49% are men and there is a gender gap (weighted) of 29%
- In East Asia/Pacific, 29% of users are women, 37% are men and a there is a gender gap (weighted) of 20%
- In South Asia, women are 8% of users, men are 11% and there is a gender gap (weighted) of 33%
- In the Middle East and North Africa, 18% of users are women, 28% are men and there is a gender gap (weighted) of 34%
- In Sub Saharan Africa, 9% of women access to the Internet, 16% of men do it, resulting in a gender gap (weighted) of 43% (Intel & Dalberg Global Development Advisors, 2012).

According to CEPAL (2014), Internet access at home has increased in some Latin American countries during last years. Argentina, Chile, Costa Rica and Uruguay have the highest percentages of connectivity, with least gender divide. In opposite, Bolivia, Ecuador, El Salvador and Honduras have the lower rates within the region (see Table 1).

Although we must recognise the number of users has increased in recent years, it is important to point out that differences grow depending on education. Argentina, Brazil, Chile, Colombia, Costa Rica and Uruguay have the highest percentages of access to Internet among students –between 80% and 90% (CEPAL, 2014).

Table 1. Internet access at home in Latin American countries

	Women	Men
Argentina	46.1%	46.9%
Costa Rica	51.6%	50.7%
Brazil	40.0%	38.7%
Chile	44.7%	45.2%
Uruguay	47.9%	48.0%
Colombia	34.5%	33.1%
Mexico	25.8%	25.7%
Panama	24.7%	22.6%
Paraguay	25.5%	23.4%
Peru	18.7%	18.3%
Bolivia	5.5%	5.8%
Ecuador	6.7%	6.6%
El Salvador	8.7%	7.9%
Honduras	8.9%	7.5%

Source: CEPAL, 2014.

Differences in the use of technology are also linked to the social construction of gender and to cultural norms related to variables of age, ethnicity, class, and education. These tendencies prevail in all regions of the world, including Latin America:

- Women access to Internet decreases dramatically in rural towns around the region. This places these women at the lowest level of the gender divide. Constrains include poverty, social norms, infrastructure, lack of education and geographical location;
- The use of Internet is limited by gender norms: women are not familiar with ICTs since childhood, while men are formed in online environments;
- While women identify themselves as users, men do it as producers of content[4];
- While for men the Internet is a tool for work and leisure, for women it is for work, leisure and consumption of services related to the needs of the family (health, education, food, care, travel, etc.);
- In countries such as Mexico, women without formal education, are not familiar with the Internet (CEPAL, 2014; Intel & Dalberg Global Development Advisors, 2012; EC, 2009; OECD, 2007; UN, 2005; Primo, 2003).

It is important to recognise these uses also promote changes towards gender equality. In Colombia and Mexico, the Association for Progressive Communications has improved the program "End violence: Women's rights and safety online". "S.O.S Women" gives support and attention to women victims of violence of gender in Guatemala. In Spain the program "Hola Fabiola" offers ICTs training programs to Latin American women. Another example is the potential use of the Internet for networking feminist scholars and activists within the region (CEPAL, 2014).

Education and Training

One of the greatest challenges in the digital age is to ensure that the ICTs have a positive impact on education. However, as it operates at the structural level, patriarchy has prevented the benefits of ICTs to reach women and men equally. A fact that reflects the structural nature of the patriarchy, reveals that two-thirds of the illiterate people in the world are women. It makes difficult digital literacy among women (Hafking, 2003).

In this area, there is also a lack of disaggregated data by sex. Among the studies that have analysed the educational dimension of ICTs with a gender perspective, is *ICTs and Gender*, published by the OECD in 2007. According to this organisation, only 1.9% of students of computing in 28 OECD countries, were women. This number includes countries such as USA, United Kingdom, Italy, Turkey, Poland and Switzerland.

The CEPAL reports that 39% of women engineering students in Latin America change of career because of the prevalence of gender discrimination (CEPAL, 2014).

At the level of research, women are between 25% and 35% of researchers in the areas related to ICTs in most countries of the OECD. This data reveals a very important progress, because 20 years ago this was not the case, which shows the speed of this change and the power of the ICTs as a driving force of the advancement of women in the field of research.

According to the CEPAL, the rates in Latin America are dramatically higher than in other regions: women are 46% of researchers in these areas. However, gender divide is evident per country: in Mexico, men reach 31% of research positions while women are 16%; in Brazil, men are 38% and women 25%; in Argentina, men reach 55% and women 28% (CEPAL, 2014). To face this challenge, L'Oréal Foundation together with UNESCO launched the program "Woman and Science" to award senior and young scholars in these areas (CEPAL, 2014).

The reasons for of the limited access of women to these fields, are associated to their gender condition: domestic responsibilities associated to maternity and marriage, and fewer opportunities to work as scholars in research institutes (CEPAL, 2014).

In terms of digital literacy, the percentage of women that do not have basic computer skills (39%), it is equally high as the percentage of men (34%). The gender divide is wide again in the level of computer skills: 15% of women have high level computer skills, compared to 29% of men (OECD, 2007). There are not data available in Latin America.

However, literacy is much more than having knowledge to operate digital tools. It has to do with having skills to face the challenges of being overwhelmed by the amount of information (Picard, 2011). Literacy in the digital age is related to people developing capabilities to use information and contents to produce creatively.

In this regard, successful projects on gender, literacy and ICTs in Latin America show these tools can operate to favour the advancement of women and girls in society. Examples are: BiblioRedes (Chile), "Género y TIC: Igualdad y equidad en la E-dominicana" (República Dominicana) (CEPAL, 2014).

Contents

The Internet is the platform used by most women and feminist groups to disseminate their contents. Radio and television stations as PuntoGenero (Mexico) is a good example of this. Under the title "Protecting Women's Rights: Internet content from a Gender Perspective", the Association for Progressive Communication (APC) promotes training workshops for women to produce their Internet sites.

However, for the reasons explained, women have few opportunities to access training programs through which they can learn how to produce content.

From the perspective of the feminist political economy, the digitalization is a project of the patriarchal capitalism, so the same problems already existing in traditional media, related to concentration and content production, have been transferred to this scenario. This explains why relevant Internet content for women -health, e-government services, safe online communities-, is not a general tendency in Latin American countries.

It explains too that one of the most dramatic expressions of patriarchy in ICTs contents, is the wide dissemination of violence of gender. The UN Broadband Commission launched in 2015 the report "Cyber Violence Against Women and Girls". This document demonstrates that 73% of women and girls online have been exposed to some form of cyber violence.

ICTs open a new window to the promotion of violence against women and girls. Violence online and offline feed into each other. *Hacking* -the use of technology to gain illegal access to systems to acquire personal information; *impersonation* -the use of technology to assume the identity of the victim or someone else to shame the victim; *surveillance* -the use of technology to stalk and monitor victim's activities; *harassment* -the use of technology to continuously contact the victim; *recruitment* –the use of technology to attract potential victims; and *malicious distribution* –the use of technology to distribute defamatory materials related to the victim, are the most commonly associated forms to cyber violence.

Based on this report, the UN Braodband Commission urges governments and industry to improve policies and laws to better protect the growing number of women and girls who are victims of online threats. In particular, it proposes three wide actions:

1. Prevent VAWG through change in societal attitudes & norms, what includes changing norms, training, learning and community development and justice and security/police to integrate Cyber VAWG concerns into all criminal and cyber-security training
2. Oversight and monitoring to minimise risks for women and girls. It calls industry to maintain responsible Internet infrastructure and customer care practices. As well, the development of technical solutions and the promotion of due diligence and duty to report abuse
3. To develop laws, regulations and governance mechanisms; to encourage courts and legal system to enforce compliance and punitive consequences for perpetrators; and promotion of consultations on a cyber civil rights agenda (UN Broadband Commission for Digital Development Working Group on Broadband and Gender, 2015).

In Mexico, the cyberviolence has been at the core of public debates in the early months of 2016. At least ten young women denounced, through social networks, that have been harassed by men in public spaces. These women have exhibited the agressors. In response, they have been victims of both sexual and death threats from Facebook and Twitter users.

A very powerful response came from young women in this country. Through the hashtagh *My First Harassment*, 100 thousand of women told her first experience as victims of sexual violence. Results speake for themselves: 8 is the average age for Mexican women to live their first experience as victims of sexual violence; 38% of agressors were male family members; 47% of aggressions occured in public spaces.

Another central problem worsened by the tools of digital communication, is the circulation of pornography. Videogames is another dimension of the problem. Some of the most popular show assaults on women, rape, prostitution and murder.

Linked to pornography, is the sexual trafficking of women, girls and boys that has been enhanced through the Internet. Some of the authors call it as "virtual traffic", and points out the implications of the Internet and other ICTs in sex trafficking (Maltzahn, 2006). Sex trafficking operates mainly in countries with a lack of Internet regulation and policy (UN, 2003). This is, in developing countries such as most in Latin America, where there is a high percentage of poor women, what shows that social class places women in situations of greater vulnerability.

In this way, the lack of opportunities for women to become content producers, are countered by the wide dissemination of sexist representations that promote gender-based violence and that have been multiplied with the diversification of channels in the digital age.

Employment

The labour market of the digital communication is causing new gender inequalities and it is creating both a horizontal and vertical segregation. The majority of women only access to the less-skilled/payed positions, such as word-processing and data entry. As the work positions get higher in the hierarchical scale, we find less women in decision-making positions.

According to UN, women are 9% of mid to upper-level information technology jobs, 28.5% computer programs and 26.9% system analysts. Data entry workers are 85% (UN, 2005). In Argentina, there is one woman per three men working in this sector. In Costa Rica, women are between 7% and 17% of workers (CEPAL, 2014).

Women are misrepresented in all decision-making structures, including policy and regulatory bodies and related institutions, ministry and boards of private companies, at the national, regional and global levels. According to the report "Gender Issues in the Information Society" (Primo, 2003):

- In 2001, in 18 countries in Europe, only 9% of the high-level positions and 9% of regulatory bodies of the telecommunications sector, were represented by women
- In 2001, in the United States women occupied 13% of the executive positions of telecommunications companies
- In 2001, there were women ministers of communication and/or telecommunications in only three countries in the world: Mali, South Africa and Colombia
- In 1999, among 19 countries analysed by the ITU, 12 did not include any women in their regulatory agencies
- Costa Rica seems to be an exception in Latin America: women are 13% of managers in this sector (CEPAL, 2014).

What are the consequences of having few women participating in the decision-making positions? First, there is potential that is not used by the sector of the ICTs. Second, gender stereotypes that prevail in this area, may not be deleted unless the access of a significant number of women in this level is ensured. Third, policies and laws will remain without incorporating a gender perspective, which will result in little innovative regulations (EC, 2009).

Another problem related to employment, is the recruitment of women in call centres and teleworking. With the increasing of the trade of banking services, information and entertainment, the demand of workers has been transferred from developed to developing countries. In these countries, women are employed by a lower salary and without the guarantee of labour rights. In addition, when it comes to a work that is performed from home, women have to combine it with domestic responsibilities, which reinforces the sexual division of labour (UN, 2005). According to the CEPAL, in six Latin American countries, women are 71% of workers in call centers (CEPAL, 2014), and Jamaica and Barbados are considered Free Trade Zones, where workers do not enjoy labour rights (Primo, 2003).

However, we must recognise that even though those are jobs with lower security conditions, call centres and teleworking have become important sources of paid work for women in developing countries, what shows another contradiction of the digital age.

Additionally, ICTs firms in Latin America have promoted specific policies to increase the recruitment of women: women are 34% of workers at HP Costa Rica 43% at Oracle Colombia; and 50% at Accenture Argentina. Microsoft Costa Rica counts on 25% of women in decision-making positions (CEPAL, 2014).

Public and Political Participation

One of the key dimensions of ICTs and gender equality, is the use of these technologies for transparency and accountability purposes, both linked to the fulfilment of women's right to information. However, most laws and policies do not assume gender equality principles. This is the case of Mexico, where the General Law of Transparency and Access to Public Information represents a good opportunity for feminist NGOs, scholars and activists to access to official data. However, as this law does not promote gender equality, it is difficult for these groups to have on this regulation a useful skill for the fulfilment of women's citizenship and human rights.

Another potentiality of ICTs, is they open new possibilities for women to be heard at global level. Women all around, are creating blogs, websites and using social networks for political participation purposes. Recent examples in Latin America, are feminist groups in Mexico, Argentina and Uruguay to widely call for public demonstrations against violence of gender.

A third dimension linked to public and political participation, is that related to the visibility of human and civil rights of LGBT communities. Definitely, Internet has helped to expand the visibility of sexual diversity groups and their networking. Paradoxically, risks of being victims of violence of gender, have increased as expressions of homophoby, combined with anonymity, allows attackers to freely discriminate.

Regulation and Policy

All the problems listed previously, are associated with an almost non-existent gender dimension in the ICTs regulations and policies in the region. Most Latin American governments are producing policies for the new communication environment. However, these plans do not adopt a gender perspective that shortens the gender gaps.

As a consequence of the Summit of Information Society, CEPAL improved the Action Plan for the Information Society, eLAC, with the objective to support digital strategies in Latin American countries. Programs such as Argentina Conectada and Conectar Igualdad (Argentina), Programa Nacional de Banda Ancha (Brazil), Programa Enlaces y Chile Compra (Chile), Estrategia Nacional para la Sociedad de la Informaci6n (República Dominicana) and Plan Ceibal (Uruguay), give priority to both the increasing of infrastructure in telecommunications and access. Most recent initiatives include broadband access, ICTs literacy ("Habilidades digitales para todos", Mexico) and Internet governance. However, there is a lack of gender mainstreaming in these programs (CEPAL, 2014).

More recently, countries such as Mexico and Argentina have adopted new regulations that are considered 'avant-garde', but they do not assume the principles promoted by the Beijing Platform for Action (1995).

The CEPAL launched a working group on gender and broadband access with the purpose to promote digital inclusion of women in the region, digital literacy among women and girls, development of apps for women, training for women workers and online protection for women and girls.

According to this organization, digital agendas must go ahead promoting access and digital inclusion, but to guarantee the promotion of gender mainstreaming in all areas: literacy, use, training, access, science and technology and employment (CEPAL, 2014).

CONCLUSION

In this paper we have seen how ICTs are increasing gender divides in Latin America and proved that the effects of the digital divide are worse in women and girls.

The digital divide is evident in all the levels we have reviewed: access and use of the Internet and other ICTs, education and training, contents, employment, decision-making, regulation and policy.

The causes of the gender divide are directly linked to the patriarchal capitalism that has increased the unfavorable conditions of women in the fields of education, employment, health and income. Thus, as long as these problems are not solved, technology and universal access won't solve by themselves social divides.

For this, it is needed a holistic perspective in the design of policies and programs that guarantee women's and girls' right to communicate. Actions include:

- To increase women's access to financial and technological resources to develop fully in the digital age
- The development of digital and information literacy programs with a gender perspective
- To promote the enrolment of women in careers related to science and technology.
- Promote equal opportunities for women in ICTs and technology companies, at both levels: training and labour opportunities
- Provide incentives for women to develop their own business, through e-commerce platforms
- Promote access of women to decision-making positions
- To promote the increasing of contents produced by women and NGOs, with the guarantee to be disseminated through the ICTs
- Finally, gender issues need to be addressed in all dimensions of the digital agenda. This is because all the dimensions that are currently discussed about digitalization, affect women and girls. For this, all the points listed above, are related to regulation, law and policy. Gender mainstreaming in those instruments, would guarantee the address of specific gender needs.

REFERENCES

Bilbao-Osorio, B., Dutta, D., & Lanvin, B. (Eds.). (2013). Global Information Technology Report 2013. Growth and Jobs in a Hyperconnected World. Geneva: INSEAD/WEF. Available at http://www3.weforum.org/docs/WEF_GITR_Report_2013.pdf

Blazquez, N. (2008). *El retorno de las brujas*. CEIICH UNAM.

Byerly, C. (2002). Gender and the Political Economy of Newsmaking: A Case Study of Human Rights Coverage. In Sex & Money, Feminism and Political Economy in the Media. University of Minnesota Press.

Castaño, C. (2005). *Las mujeres y las tecnologías de la información. Internet y la trama de nustra vida*. Madrid: Alianza Editorial.

CEPAL (2014). *El nuevo paradigma productivo y tecnológico. La necesidad de políticas para la autonomía económica de las mujeres*. CEPAL.

EC. (2010). *Women and ICT Status Report 2009*. Lisbon: European Commision.

Feminist Peace Network. (2006). *Pornography Revenue Statistics*. Available at: http://www.feministpeacenetwork.org/2010/10/20/pornography-the-obscene-statistics/

Gallagher, M. (1980). *Unequal Opportunities: The Case of Women and the Media*. Paris: UNESCO.

GSMA. (2010). *Women & Mobile: A Global Opportunity – A Study on the Mobile Phone Gender Gap in Low and Middle-income Countries*. GSM Association.

Hafkin, N. (2003). *Some thoughts on gender and telecommunications/ICT statistics and indicators.* Available at: http://www.itu.int/ITU-D/pdf/5196-007-en.pdf

Hafkin, N., & Huyer, S. (2007). Women and Gender in ICT Statistics and Indicators for Development. *Information Technologies& International Development*, *4*(2), 25–41. Available at: http://www.itu.int/ITU-D/pdf/5196-007-en.pdf

Intel & Dalberg Global Development Advisors. (2012). *Women and the Web. Bridging the Internet gap and creating new global opportunities in low and middle-income countries.* Available at: http://dalberg.com/documents/Women_Web.pdf

ITU. (2012). *Measuring the Information Society 2012.* Available at: http://www.itu.int/en/ITU-D/Statistics/Documents/publications/mis2012/MIS2012_without_Annex_4.pdf

Maltzahn, K. (2006). *Digital Dangers. Information and Communication Technologies and Trafficking Women.* Available at: http://www.genderit.org/sites/default/upload/digital_dangers_EN_1.pdf

Martin, M. (2002). An Unsuitable Technology for a Woman? Communication as Circulation. In Sex & Money, Feminism and Political Economy in the Media. University of Minnesota Press.

Martin, S. (2002). The Political Economy of Women's Employment in the Information Sector. In Sex & Money, Feminism and Political Economy in the Media. University of Minnesota Press.

OECD. (2007). *ICTs and Gender.* doi:10.1787/231011217663

Picard, R. (2011). *Digitization and Media Business Models.* Open Society Foundations. Available at: http://www.opensocietyfoundations.org/sites/default/files/digitization-media-business-models-20110721.pdf

Primo, N. (2005). Gender Issues in the Information Society. Paris: UNESCO. Available at http://portal.unesco.org/ci/en/file_download.php/250561f24133814c18284feedc30bb5egender_issues.pdf

Riordan, E. (2002). Intersections and New Directions: On Feminism and Political Economy. In Sex & Money, Feminism and Political Economy in the Media. University of Minnesota Press.

Ross, K. (2002). Selling Women (Down the River): Gendered Relations and the Political Economy of Broadcast News. In Sex & Money, Feminism and Political Economy in the Media. University of Minnesota Press.

Simard, C., Davies, A., Gilmartin, S., Schiebinger, C., & Whitney, T. (n.d.). *Climbing the Technical Ladder: obstacles and solutions for mied-level women in technology.* Stanford University, Clyman Institute for Gender Research, Anita Borg Institute for Women and Technology. Available at: http://anitaborg.org/files/Climbing_the_Technical_Ladder_Exec_Summary.pdf

UN. (1995). *Beijing Declaration and Platform for Action.* The Fourth World Conference on Women. Available at: http://www.un.org/womenwatch/daw/beijing/pdf/BDPfA%20E.pdf

UN. (2005). *Women 2000 and beyond. Gender equality and empowerment of women through ICT.* Available at: http://www.un.org/womenwatch/daw/public/w2000-09.05-ict-e.pdf

UN Broadband Commission for Digital Development Working Group on Broadband and Gender. (2015). *Cyber Violence Against Women and Girls. A World-Wide Wake-Up Call.* Author.

World Bank. (n.d.). *Indicators for Monitoring Gender and ICT*. Available at: http://web.worldbank.org/WBSITE/EXTERNAL/TOPICS/EXTGENDER/EXTICTTOOLKIT/0,contentMDK:20272986~menuPK:562601~pagePK:64168445~piPK:64168309~theSitePK:542820,00.html

WSIS. (2003). *Building the Information Society: a global challenge on the new Millennium*. WSIS. Available at: http://www.itu.int/wsis/docs/geneva/official/dop.html

ENDNOTES

1. This article emerges from an ongoing research 'Gender, Power and Communication. The influence of women in decision-making processes in media industries', financed by the PAPIIT-UNAM Program (IN300214).
2. This index is composed by 11 indicators and its objective is to monitor the progress in the field of ICTs and measure the gap. It has three sub-indices: access, use, and skills (ITU, 2012).
3. An example is the recent report from Google about Internet access in India. The company reports that 40% of Internet users are women: (http://articles.timesofindia.indiatimes.com/2013-06-20/computing/40092965_1_hair-care-four-women-skin-care, access August 1, 2013). In constrast, the CISCO Institute reports that women are only 23% of Internet users in that country (http://www.hrindiaonline.com/printContent.php?MpoQSrPnM=MjE=&flag=2, Access: August 1, 2013).
4. According to OECD's classification, the differentiated aptitudes of ICTs users classify them as *ICT specialists, advanced users and basic users*. Women are around 60% of basic users, 25% of advanced users and between 10% and 20% of ICT specialists (OECD, 2007). According to the OECD, the reason why women participation is lower in the more specialised levels is because of the male dominance in this area.

Chapter 17
Food Photography, Pixelated Produce, and Cameraless Images:
A Photographic Journey from Farmville to Kheti Badi

Aileen Blaney
Srishti Institute of Art, Design, and Technology, India

ABSTRACT

In today's screen saturated culture, perceptions of food are overwhelmingly formed by images circulated via the internet and mobile. The Facebook game FarmVille is the subject of Kheti Badi (Shah, 2015), a photographic artwork reflexively engaging with the contemporary scenario of 'post-photography'. The work comprises not of photographs taken with a traditional camera but of screenshots of a farm and its holdings as displayed in Farmville; the highly compressed jpegs cropped and resized to the point of destabilizing visual coherence are depictions not of pastoral landscapes but of computer vision and the programmable character of photography. While photography remains an instrument for recording material realities, its power extends toward feeding back into the very processes through which science and technology modify food production. This chapter explores how Kheti Badi, through a series of hyper artificial and un-photographic images, shows the constructed nature of both what we put our hands on in the supermarket and see in advertising's dreamscapes.

INTRODUCTION

I believe that we have lost the ability to see and be moved by images. Nothing moves us anymore, nothing has any meaning – Alfredo Jarr

DOI: 10.4018/978-1-5225-1862-4.ch017

Kheti Badi is a photographic artwork produced from screenshots taken of an online game called FarmVille. Chinar Shah began making Kheti Badi at the height of the game's popularity, choosing to pixelate the already pixelated screenshots, a strategy of representation that would exaggerate what she terms the images' 'synthetic' and 'cartoon' appearance. This article sets out to explore the significance of Kheti Badi within a contemporary context of photography that is changing as fast as the digital technologies that have become its tools. The concept of post photography, alluded to time and again in discussions of contemporary photographic culture, encapsulates in many respects the focus of my investigation; this same category is apparent for example in the subheading – 'photogr@phy after photography' – of a collection of essays titled 'Pandora's Camera', written by the Catalan visual artist, writer and curator Joan Fontcuberta. Alluded to in Fontcuberta's catch-phrase and captured in Kheti Badi are those significant shifts in photography that cannot be reduced to changes in the materiality of the image – from grain to pixel – or in the photographic apparatus – the existence of a digital sensor where there was once light sensitive paper – but that, and more crucially, are a function of its waning intimacy with documentary as compared to that of its analogue forerunner. Expectations that photography maintain the indexical bond with its subject matter and adhere to the conventions of realism are in contemporary times less determining, freeing photographers to make arguments about reality not necessarily in its likeness but with the urgency of rehabilitating vision. The documentary image has served us well, and will continue to do so. What is becoming increasingly clear however is that the speed with which photographs are being taken, displayed and consumed across various digital platforms such as Facebook, Instagram and Snapchat is leading not to more types of images but rather to a high degree of sameness and a visuality dominated by clichéd and generic images. Kheti Badi belongs to a politically engaged domain of photographic practice that shares with documentary its commitment to the social world but that seeks new and creative ways to critically frame social reality. The set of images comprising this work cannot be properly understood without reference to the historical and national contexts to which they are contiguous. The discussion of Kheti Badi in this article therefore is located at the intersections between histories of photography,

Figure 1. [Untitled]
(© [2015], [Chinar Shah], Used with permission.).

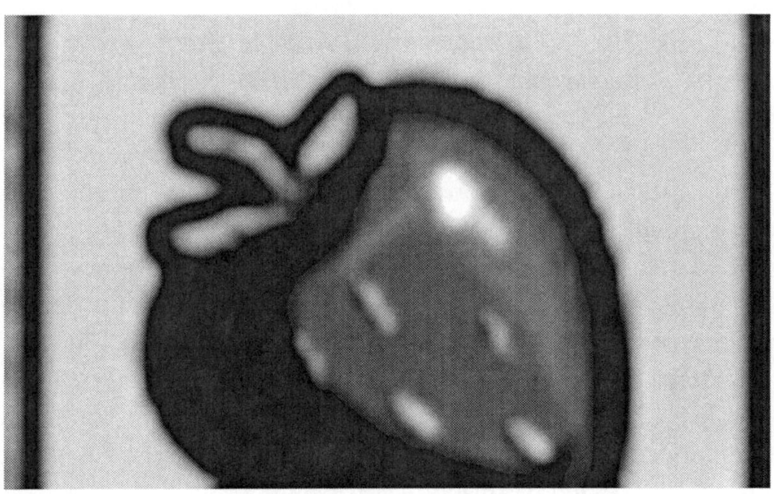

the spectacularization of food in the multinational food industry and elsewhere in visual culture, and the realities of the lives of people farming the land in India.

Chinar Shah remembers sitting in class in what must have been second standard when she learned for the first time that India was an agriculture-based economy. This news came to young Chinar as a surprise for she had never set foot on a farm. Neither was she aware of the importance of farming to the approximated 53% of the population who, according to the Census of India 2011, made all or a substantial part of their livelihood from the land (Sainath, 2013). All these years later, Shah is planting seeds, growing crops, and raising farm animals and livestock on virtual plots of land in an online game called FarmVille. The measure with which the invitation of the game's developer Zygna to 'take a nostalgic journey into the countryside' has resonated worldwide is evident in the 38,404,103 likes garnered by its Facebook fan page (Farmville Facebook Page, 2015). However, the notional transposition of farming and animal husbandry to a virtual environment has attracted much criticism too: Time magazine named it among the '50 worst inventions' of 2010 for being predicated on a 'series of mindless chores on a digital farm' (Fletcher, 2010). In its editorial a little over a year after the game launched, and by which time 61,411,787 Facebook users worldwide were playing FarmVille, The New York Times (2010) cautioned readers that 'what is being farmed isn't only the virtual crops. It's also the users' social connections, their attention, and, ultimately, their credit cards' (p. A18). These millions of people worldwide who had begun transitioning freely and easily between social networking and gaming became for these voices in journalism a metaphor for the ease with which global capitalism in the age of networked cultures can profit from the individual's affective ties to food and nostalgia for farming. Meantime, in the heyday of Shah's virtual farm, Shah's virtual farm, and at the height of strawberry season, she was known to rush home, to rush home, go online and harvest her berries before they spoiled.

'I was a farmer online and a photographer on the land' – this ironic self-declaration of Shah's contrasts with the indispensible nature of photography to on the ground agricultural research conducted by the 'plant explorers' who traversed Asia's farmlands at the height of colonialism. By the early 20th century, it had supplanted drawing as their preferred tool of documentation and record keeping:

The team of senior plant explorer Palemon Howard Dorsett, who had begun working for the U.S. Department of Agriculture in 1909, and William Joseph Morse, his junior associate, sent approximately nine thousand plant accessions from the Far East to Washington D.C., of which some 4,500 were soybean specimens, including microbe-resistant strains. Other products of the Expedition included pressed herbarium species, insect specimens, native publications, soybean food products, bamboo items, motion picture film, and over three thousand photographs from Japan, Korea, and Manchurian China. (Alvarez, 2007, p. 30)

It was photography's association with notions of objectivity, truth, and the archive that enabled it to become of crucial importance to those 'agents [who] formed a cadre of remarkable explorers who pushed at the frontiers of botanical science and changed forever what we buy at our markets, plant in our gardens, and cook for our meals.' (Alvarez, 2007. p. 28) While avowedly beguiled by their intrepid ways and the eccentricities of their reputations, and not ignorant of the fact that 'as any food historian knows, the global economy is nothing new; foodstuffs have, from the earliest times, been transported afar' (Goldstein & Du Puis, 2007, iv), Alvarez goes on to point out that 'the collective imperative of their actions and ideas reflects a period of colonial transformation and a geopolitical vision of a new world hierarchy. This was the beginning of the major metamorphosis of global agriculture' (Alvarez,

2007, p. 33). While, obviously enough, photography was not singularly responsible for this reordering, as a key technology of knowledge, it played an important role in the classification and appropriation of plant species for economic exploitation, setting in train an enduring relationship with global agriculture.

By the postwar period, the documentary uses to which photography was being applied were flourishing. Historian of photography John Tagg looks back on what he perceived as an ''ideological conception of the photograph as a direct and 'natural' cast of reality'' as being ''there from the very beginning'' (Tagg, 1993, p. 41). He identifies the expediency to the state of construing photography as a neutral record of reality and part of a documentary tradition anchored in notions of transparency and truth: 'Understanding the role of photography in the documentary practices of these [state] institutions means retracing the history of a far from self-evident set of beliefs and assertions about the nature and status of the photograph, and of signification generally, which were articulated into a wider range of techniques and procedures for extracting and evaluating 'truth' in discourse' (ibid., pp. 60-61). For Tagg, from the second half of the nineteenth century onwards, it was not the power of photography but that of newly formed institutions of the state in the US, Britain and France – the foci of his study – that were capable of producing evidence and 'truth' out of images. In other words, a photograph alone could not prove anything since the 'power it [the camera] wields is never its own' (ibid., p. 64). All the more reason that photography would see no abeyance in its importance to government, science, industry and the emerging field of advertising in the first half of the twentieth century. Writing in 1953, president of the Royal Photographic Society in Great Britain describes how:

In addition to its uses in military reconnaissance and mapping, aerial photography is being used for forestry and geological survey, for traffic surveys in busy cities, to determine the location of oil pipe lines, electrical transmission lines and cross-country highways, to measure the areas of crops in farming country, to study soil erosion, to count seals and shoals of fish, to determine underwater features and a variety of other purposes. (Wratten, 1953, p. 271)

Albeit a biased proponent of photography by virtue of the position he occupied in the Royal Photographic Society, Wratten's belief that photography, in aerial and other forms, was 'one of the most important tools in modern scientific, technical and business progress' (Wratten, 1953, p. 271) is corroborated in other later accounts pertaining to the same period (Berger, 1980; Burgin, 1982; Tagg, 1988). By the late seventies, Susan Sontag had published a book theorizing photography, which would go on to become a seminal text, in which she sees the same tendencies that are under discussion in the way the professions were at this point in time instrumentalizing photography:

Photographs are valued because they give information. They tell one what there is; they make an inventory. To spies, meteorologists, coroners, archaeologists, and other information professionals, their value is inestimable (Sontag, 2005, p. 16).

Significantly however, in the very same paragraph, she goes on to make the point that 'in the situations in which most people use photographs, their value as information is of the same order as fiction' (Sontag, 2005), introducing the paradox, and by now widely accepted notion, of photography's effectiveness at constructing personal and family histories in the aim of telling oneself pleasing stories and, at the same time, as proof incontrovertible enough to convince others of such fictions.

In more contemporary times, with its transformation into a predominantly digital medium, the capacities of photography have exceeded the efficiency with which it served science and industry, during an analogue period, as an instrument to record, investigate and classify; the global trade in picture perfect licensed digital imagery and marketing strategies operating at the different strata of a multinational food industry possess the bandwidth to redefine the appearance of food, reconstituting global perceptions and expectations of agricultural commodities. Nowhere is this more apparent than in the expectations consumers bring with them when they visit their local green grocer: the expectation is for the blemish-free skin of apples, vegetables that match mentally ingrained colour charts, and neither bananas that are too big nor blueberries too small. For some time now, photography has ceased to operate as a mechanism for capturing something that is already out there, a development seen by Fontcuberta in terms of a reversal: 'Applying the indexical interpretation, we used to think that some kind of referent was embedded in the photograph, but now we have to think the contrary: something of the photograph is embedded in the referent.' (Fontcuberta, 2014, p. 26) By the time food finds its way from the farm to the fork, it has already been refracted through images in advertising and the by now proliferating sites of 'food porn' everywhere around us. 'Food has travelled far from the soil and into the world of visual pleasures' – a statement made by Shah – resonates strongly with the degree to which Kheti Badi explores the role of photography under discussion, of not simply imaging food but imagining it for a consumer gaze. Like food, images of food circulate globally, Like food, images of food circulate across borders, and with visual communicators and designers in different parts of the world having instant access to common pools of licensed photography, they too are generic and globalized commodities. Stock photographs from agencies such as Getty Images, the world's largest, and Shutterstock – the 'global marketplace for imagery' with a stock of 48,852,739 images – can be purchased online at any time from anywhere. In our current global community's visual culture, the chocolate brownie lightly dusted with icing sugar decorating a dessert menu in London's Covent Garden is liable to be identically matched in a restaurant in one of Delhi's shopping malls.

''We are clearly in a 'Post Documentary' photographic world now'' (2010) are the words of photographer Paul Graham at the first MOMA photography forum in 2010. It's no coincidence then that the images we find in Shah's work are of photographs taken neither with a conventional camera, nor in physical space. In their place are screenshots of the isometric graphics and illustrations that portray a farm and its holdings as featured in FarmVille, and which in the process proves quintessential in its demonstration of how 'the computer has overtaken the camera in importance, and the lens has become incidental to the capturing of an image' (Fontcuberta, 2014, pp. 10-11). Digital photography now occupies some common ground with painting – when it is considered the extent to which images are being made as much as taken, with the hand of the photographer having the creative freedom to move and alter pixels in contrast to the limitations imposed by the relative fixity of the photochemical film grain imposed by the relative fixity of the photochemical film grain. However, in spite of this and the by now widespread awareness that photographs have always been liable to undergo changes in postproduction that would bring multiple fictional elements into the frame, they continue to be read as reliable representations of 'the real'. In recognition of this, Fontcuberta points out how even though 'The digital image no longer shares the essential functions of a photography committed to authenticating experience, [...] its tremendous impact is still based on simulating membership of a pre-digital photographic culture, even though that culture has fallen into abeyance' (Fontcuberta, 2014, p. 61). Notwithstanding the out-datedness of the father of photography Louis Daguerre's comparison of photography in 1839 to 'a chemical and physical process which gives nature the ability to reproduce herself', the camera nevertheless has retained some of its archaic power to seduce spectators into feeling that what they are seeing is at a level of documentary evidence interchangeable with what was placed in front of the camera when the image was taken.

Kheti Badi, by contrast, a child of Graham's 'post-documentary' times, purposefully refuses the viewer any such illusion in making the images themselves into reflexive representations of the crude processes of image capture and postproduction out of which they spring. For example, highly compressed jpeg files are in this instance cropped and resized to the point at which vision is completely destabilized – in these blown-up images and blurred out text, it is image distortion above all else that we see. In making visible these effects, even if they are produced out of screenshots from an anyway unrealistic online game, attention is drawn to the digital processes that have deviated Cartier Bresson's 'defining moment' from the second the shutter button is released to when the image is remade in applications such as Photoshop; the picture that can tell a thousand words can also tell a thousand lies. But however much the food industry has found in photography a machine with which to dream, this work uses the machine's same tools to show the constructed nature of what we see in advertising's visual campaigns and what, subsequently, we get to put our hands on in the supermarket. With analogue photography owing its invention to science, and having been applied extensively in this context, it is hardly surprising then that its digital descendent plays such a crucial if radically different role in food science and industry today.

The same photogenic imperative motivating changes to the DNA of images in food advertising is at work in the scientific laboratories where genetic modifications are made to the DNA of seeds. In the period since 1994 when genetically modified (GM) tomatoes became the first GM food to be introduced to US consumers – ironically, today, nowhere in the world are genetically engineered tomatoes available for sale – consumers, by and large, have become accustomed to the manmade character of organic produce. The jpeg images in Shah's work, pixelated almost to breaking point, pose as metaphors for the changes introduced into the natural world by science and technology. It is almost as though the images very molecules break apart and reform, an analogy perhaps for the reorganization of food genomes by now everywhere around us. The photographer in this case uses the precise editing tools that are the bulwarks of digital photography to as it were break into images captured, using her computer's built in camera, from the online game. There is a further irony in the work: in accentuating the ugliness of these images, by making their pixels show and breaking every rule of framing and composition, photography's hyper-aestheticisation of food elsewhere finds its way into the focal plane. Walter Benjamin famously viewed the film image as an 'orchid in the land of technology' (Benjamin, 1968, p. 233) and this photographic series indirectly refers to the brilliance with which photography has used its apparatuses to reinvent the 'natural' beauty of fruit, vegetables and grain.

The very fact of farmlands being represented in an online environment combined with the magnificently large fan following the game earned among Indians at the height of its popularity stands in ironic and stark contrast with traditional perceptions of the land that continue to prevail in rural parts of India: 'Festivals held before sowing season as well as harvest festivals, celebrated in the fields, symbolize people's intimacy with nature. For the farmer, the field is the mother; worshipping the field is a sign of gratitude toward the earth, which, as mother, feeds the millions of life forms that are her children.' (Shiva, 2000, p. 8) Moreover, despite the rapid changes to lifestyle and working arrangements overtaking urban India today, harvest festivals, celebrated at various times of the year, are enthusiastically celebrated by city dwellers in their overwhelming majority. Makara Sankranti, the most popular – also known, according to region, as Pongal, Uttarayana, Khichdi, Shishur Saenkraat and Maghi – is a national holiday on which dishes such as pongal, a sweet rice preparation, and other dessert-like delicacies, many of which have sesame (due to its historical importance as a source of oil) as a base ingredient, are prepared. For some,

Figure 2. [Untitled]
(© [2015], [Chinar Shah], Used with permission.).

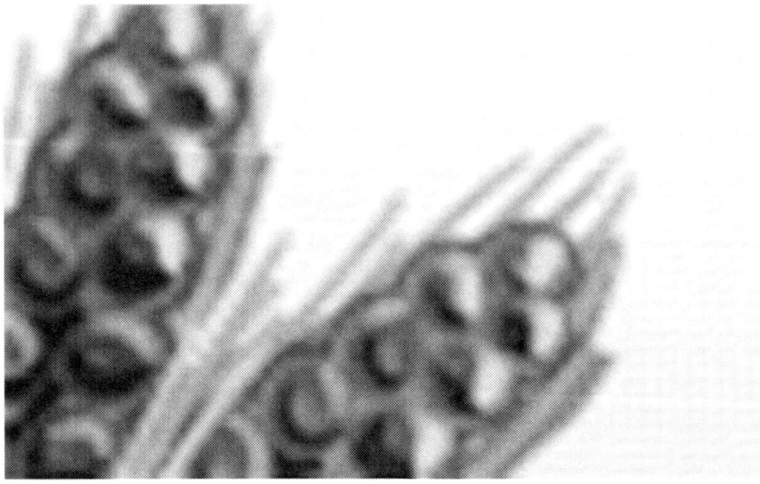

such festivals revolve simply around the enjoyment of eating good food, which anyway is the traditional mode of acknowledging harvest, while others, despite being urbanized and living in cities, partake in rituals that might involve the parading of cows decorated with bells and flower garlands, an opportunity for a community to express its gratitude its gratitude to the animals for their role in farming and the harvest. The ironies of these celebrations taking place in urban settings provides one of the contexts in which this work can be understood, opening up as it does questions that include the complex relationship of India's rapidly growing middle class to agriculture, what they have come in recent years to expect of food plants and inequalities that exist between food producers and consumers in the subcontinent.

'Farmers disappear in death and food disappears in genetics' are the words of the artist in her stark summing up of the growing number of fruit, vegetable and grain species sanctioned for genetic engineer-

Figure 3. [Untitled]
(© [2015], [Chinar Shah], Used with permission.).

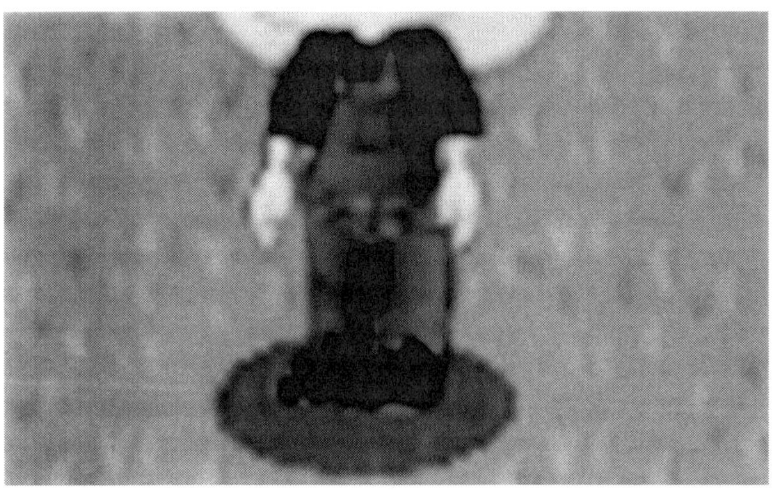

ing by governments worldwide, while the reference to disappearance in death alludes in all probability to the phenomenon of farmer suicides in India where in 2009 for example it has been estimated that every 30 minutes a farmer took their own life (Centre for Human Rights and Global Justice, 2011). In Maharashtra, the state with the highest recorded rates, for every day in the last ten years, there have been 10 farmers who have killed themselves (Sainath, 2014). In the writings of many of the most well known commentators on the subject of farmer suicides (Sainath; Shiva and Jalees: 2009; Nagaraj, 2008), the prohibitively high cost of GM seeds, distribution of which is overwhelmingly controlled by a U.S. based agri-business sector, the unavailability of bank credit to small farmers, and the consequent indebtedness to money-lenders are identified as the key contributing factors. This is a viewpoint corroborated in a report conducted by the International Food Policy Research Institute which is otherwise reluctant to pinpoint a hierarchy in the set of causes discussed: 'there is no single explanation or even consistent explanations across reported cases. However, one leading factor seems to connect several causes particularly related to agriculture: the heavy indebtedness of farm households, particularly in the suicide-prone states.' (Guillaume P., Gruère Purvi Mehta-Bhatt & Debdatta Sengupta., 2008, p. 25). In analogous fashion, a document produced by the UN puts the figure of farmers who committed suicide that were financially indebted at 86.5%. The disappearance of farmers from the land is reflected in how micro news reports of their deaths that rarely occupy more than an inch of column space quickly and silently dissolve into the media's past tense. Given the gravity of hardship why then don't farmers in India protest against inadequate financial supports, the failures of agricultural policies to date, and the urgency of transforming farming into a viable occupation?

In a similar respect, why are their voices set at such a low volume in the various media outlets? But perhaps it is worth looking at this question from an alternative angle by taking into account that as crucial as it is for farmers to have a voice, without access to a space in which to be listened, there can be no agency. More than three decades ago Gayatri Spivak argued that the question of 'Who should speak?' is less critical than that of 'who will listen?' (Spivak in Couldry, 2009, p. 579). Without listeners any

Figure 4. [Untiled]
(© [2015], [Chinar Shah], Used with permission.).

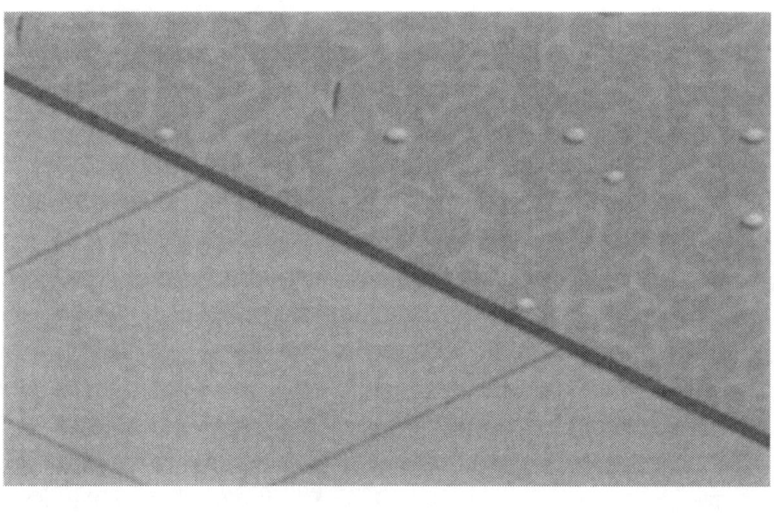

recognition of a person's right to speak and acknowledgement of what they are saying is foreclosed. Nick Couldry's viewpoint on the politics of voice is instructive in this regard. He comments that:

... it is through the process of listening that the value of voice is mutually registered between us. The adjustments we make in order to listen better to others turn precisely on finding better ways of taking account of the complexities, the processual subtleties, of voice.' (Couldry, 2009, p. 580)

Moblising a concept of recognition derived from the work of the German social theorist Axel Honneth [2007], he goes on to call attention to how the web promises more than it delivers in this regard: 'An ''interactive'' website is worth nothing, unless someone is listening to the process of interaction, and as a result some impacts ensue.' (Couldry, 2009, p. 581) If impactful protest remains elusive for those who farm for a living in India, its online 'farmers' who rallied in great numbers to protest the absence of the Indian flag on FarmVille, a feature that would allow them to geo-mark the location of their online farms, had a position from which they could speak and a space in which to interact and be listened to. Consequent to an online protest joined by more than 20,000 Facebook users, the San Francisco based games developer Zygna answered the Indian flag supporters' patriotic demand by adding the tricolour to its menu of flags, which included those of the U.S. and the U.K., alongside Australia, New Zealand, the Philippines together with a number of European and South American countries.

However, this former absence of the Indian flag is not replicated in a lack of images in circulation that represent India, predominantly via stock photos using the visual tropes of landscape and people in traditional Indian clothing. At this point in history, I would argue that India does not need any more beautiful images. The world has seen and seen again its dignified rural people in images of women balancing great loads on the crown of their heads, of turbaned men, of yet more women at work – colourful forms bent double in green fields. These are the images at the head of a Google search engine's queue, that are spread across magazine features, illustrate newspaper articles, and that, also, are the dominant visual register of the People's Archive of Rural India (PARI), an online resource of still photos, video, audio and text archiving 'the world's most diverse and complex countryside.'[1] Still in its early years, the archive is interspersed throughout with images but includes to date 4 albums dedicated solely to photography: the 'Weavers of Walahjapet', in which weavers young and old are seen operating the family business loom by hand; the 'Koilawallahs of Godda', in which wiry men push bicycles over-laden with enormous lumpy packages of waste coal across great distances; images of rice paddies being sown by a rudimentary looking rice transplanter operated by a male driver, and by hand in what appears to be an exclusively female oriented task; and, finally, 'Faces' – a compendium, alphabetized by district, of multigenerational portraits in close-up. All united in belonging to a tradition of social documentary photography, but also for their quality of déjà-vu – the already seen – for it is difficult not to see in these images what the likes of Getty and Shutterstock have not already shown us.

The Chilean born visual artist Alfredo Jaar has with arresting force explored the politics of images vis-à-vis race and culture in his work. In specific instances of his artistic practice, notably those in which he looks at how documentary images in the U.S. media have been mobilised to visually construct Africa, which gets portrayed as an amorphous continent, there is much that is relevant to this discussion's identification of how visual clichés can operate to inscribe a particular kind of worldview. 'Searching For Africa in Life' (1996) is a photographic installation comprising five light box illuminated vertical panels onto which Jaar assembled 2,158 covers of Life Magazine published between its creation in 1936 and 1996 when it ceased publication. On inspection of these covers, with the prompt of the work's title, viewers will discover that there are a mere 5 covers dedicated to Africa, none of which show anything of the continent outside of its wildlife and poverty. For Jaar however the poverty is to be found in the visuality of a Western media that continues to recycle photojournalism's stereotypes, photojournalism's visual stereotypes, and that from his point of view perniciously erase 'a vast continent's cultural richness and racial diversity' (Jarr, 2014). From the beginning, Life Magazine, credited with being the publication responsible for inventing photojournalism, would boast to its subscribers that through it they would be enabled to see and understand the world through photographs. In a much quoted mission statement, its founder Henry Luce (2007) described what Life set out to achieve: 'To see life; to see the world; to eyewitness great events; … to see things thousands of miles away, … to see and to take pleasure in seeing; to see and be amazed; to see and be instructed ...'. Jaar's work would suggest that what it revealed was not of this world but rather a uniquely 'First World' perception of the world shaped by its own self-interest and a mission serving spectacle and not information. In another photo-based work 'From Time to Time' (1996), he adopts a similar approach of using magazine covers to problematise a type of visual culture being perpetuated through photojournalism. In this case, nine covers taken from Time Magazine are arranged in three rows such that each set of images reflects the themes alluded to in his previous project: wildlife, hunger and disease. The abundance of such images make invisible Africa's many and varied urban landscapes, the diversity of its people, the vibrancy of arts and culture, in short everything that does not fall within the categories to which it has been reduced by a myopic U.S. media with global reach.

To return to PARI, it must be said that it is doing venerable work and its archives are not the problem. However it exists in the context of a politics of global information and a visual culture in which images depicting the very complexities to which it refers, such as the thorny contradictions of the centrality and marginalization of rural India and its farmers, are absent. The trope of the Indian pastoral, perpetuated across its albums of weavers and rice paddies and so forth, cannot communicate these contemporary and layered realities. In the current field of the visible, in PARI and other online media spaces, what unfolds on and the issues that are folded into the fields worked by farmers are not being visualized. Judith Butler, in a discussion pertaining to photojournalism, makes a distinction between the field of 'representability' and 'representation'; she argues that 'we cannot understand this field of representability simply by examining its explicit contents, since it is constituted fundamentally by what is cast out and maintained outside the frame within which representations appear' (Butler, 2007, p. 952). What I'm referring to as the Indian pastoral frames how we see India's rural population, their labour and day-to-day activities, and, as a result, crucial factors responsible for these daily realities are kept out of sight and mind. This frame of the Indian pastoral is used and reused at the expense of other frameworks of seeing; arguably, Kheti Badi's visual language provides one such alternative framework, opening up a familiar topic to new ways of seeing.

In a manner of thinking analogous to that of Butler, describing Michel Foucault's 'art of seeing', John Rajchman sees as inseparable from Foucault's work as philosopher and historian the art of 'trying to see what is unthought in our seeing, and to open as yet unseen ways of seeing' (Rajchman, 1988, p. 96). He goes on to point out that:

Foucault's hypothesis was that there exists a sort of ''positive unconscious'' of vision which determines not what is seen, but what can be seen. His idea is that not all ways of visualizing or rendering visible are possible at once. A period only lets somethings be seen and not others. It ''illuminates'' somethings and so casts others in the shade. (Rajchman, 1988)

Kheti Badi can be seen as doing this as yet unseen historical work in a 'territory of the visual [that] spans knowledge, art, ethics and politics' (Rajchman, 1988: 88). The content of the images we find here, and the mode of their production are firmly rooted in the realm of Rajchman's 'as yet unseen ways of seeing' (ibid., p. 92) As earlier stated, at this point in time in India, a glut of highly aesthetic images depicting the dignity in suffering of the Indian agricultural worker is not sufficient to the task of helping us see what is happening on the land; what, as mentioned previously, is needed is a new kind of visual vocabulary, one with the semantic force to cauterise nostalgia and write over the images that repeat on a loop.

At the same time as images of Indian farmlands and labour are everywhere in a global digital environment, farmer suicides and other forms of suffering connected to the land and rural life have remained *obscene* – in the sense of the term deriving from the Latin *obscaena* or Greek *ob skene* meaning off-stage. And this, despite their being frequently reported in newspaper dailies. P. Sainath makes a satirical swipe at at the manner in whcih these deaths are reported in the Indian media in the Indian media in creating the 'fictional' headline: 'Farmer commits suicide, Adani gets the loan' (Sainath, 2015) – the Adani Group is a Gujarat based industrial conglomerate headed by Gautam Adani who occupies eleventh place in a list of India's wealthiest people (Economic Times, 2014). But reading does not belong to the same order as seeing, for as is demonstrated in the Sainath quote the readers eyes move quickly across the surface of words without necessarily seeing what lies behind them. This is a perspective echoed in Sontag's insight that in spite of in-depth journalistic reporting, before the advent of photography and its mass circulation, the world did not and could not know of the graphic horrors of war:

The Spanish Civil War (1936-39) was the first war to be witnessed ("covered") in the modern sense: by a corps of professional photographers at the lines of military engagement and in the towns under bombardment … Ever since, battles and massacres filmed as they unfold have been a routine ingredient of the ceaseless flow of domestic, small-screen entertainment. … The understanding of war among people who have not experienced war is now chiefly a product of the impact of these images. (Sontag, 2003. pp. 32-3)

While the Sontag citation here serves the function of alluding to a type of knowing that is bound up with seeing, because the issue of farmer suicides pushes at the ethical limits of photographic representation, the question of whether or not and how to use photography in this context is a moot one. There is the barbarity of showing at one end of the spectrum and the indifference bred from what is unseen at the other. Notwithstanding the double bind in question, I would argue that via a critical visual language, Kheti Badi can be seen as answering the demand cultural theorist W.J.T. Mitchell makes of scholarship, and in this he includes visual and not simply text based forms of knowledge production, when he says 'what we need is a critique of visual culture that is alert to the power of images for good and evil and that is capable of discriminating the variety and historical specificity of their uses' (Mitchell, 1994, pp. 2-3). In inimitable fashion, this work produces imagery that is alert to the dilemmas any representation of death and discontent linked to agriculture and farming in India poses. In what it shows, and the technological creativity with which it performs this action, it neither extracts from suffering a type of spectacularization nor aestheticizes the qualities of the pastoral so readily associated with the land.

In Kheti Badi, what is on display are those elements that are currently redefining the medium of photography, and how these are in turn implicated in some of the changes taking place at the level of farming and agricultural practices in India, which themselves are global in scope. These screenshots in the guise of photographs take full advantage of the status of the photograph as a digital object to reflect on the politics of the image in its relationship to global markets and agriculture, and the flows of capital that interconnect these domains. By compressing the bite-sized images, attention is being drawn to the irrevocable extent to which relationships to food and farming are digitally interfaced. What is at stake, it is suggested, is not simply what gets lost in digital translation but how the very materiality of food and perceptions of farming are being reconfigured through digital photography – bringing to mind, and it is worth reiterating once more, Fontcuberta's insight that in contemporary times 'something of the photograph is embedded in the referent' (Fontcuberta, 2014, p. 26). In its effort to make visible the extent to which digital technologies are shaping perceptions of food and farming related issues, Kheti Badi supplants the Indian pastoral with a new pictorial.

REFERENCES

Alfredo Jarr's searching for Africa in life unveiled at The New School [Blog post]. (2014). Retrieved 13 February, 2015, from http://blogs.newschool.edu/news/2014/12/alfredo-jaars-searching-for-africa-in-life-unveiled-at-the-new-school/#.VN9udYvfM20

Alvarez, R. R. (2007). The march of empire: Mangos, avocados, and the politics of transfer. *Gastronomica: The Journal of Food and Culture, 7*(3), 28-33.

Benjamin, W. (1968). *Illuminations* (H. Zohn, Trans.). New York: Schocken Books.

Berger, J. (1980). *About looking*. New York: Pantheon Books.

Burgin, V. (1982). *Thinking photography*. London: Macmillan. doi:10.1007/978-1-349-16716-6

Butler, J. (2007). Torture and the ethics of photography. *Environment and Planning. D, Society & Space, 25*(6), 951–966. doi:10.1068/d2506jb

Center for Human Rights and Global Justice. (2011). *Every thirty minutes: Farmer suicides, human rights, and the agrarian crisis in India*. New York: NYU School of Law.

Couldry, N. (2009). Rethinking the politics of voice. *Continuum (Perth), 23*(4), 579–582. doi:10.1080/10304310903026594

Down on the social farm [Editorial]. (2010, August 14). *The New York Times*, p. A18.

Fletcher, D. (2010, May 27). Worst inventions: FarmVille. *Time Magazine*. Retrieved 10 February, 2015, from http://content.time.com

Fontcuberta, J. (2014). *Pandora's camera: Photogr@phy after photography*. London: MACK.

Goldstein, D., & Du Puis, M. (2007). Gastronomica. *The Journal of Food and Culture, 7*(3), iii–v.

Graham, P. (2010). *The Unreasonable Apple* [Blog post]. Retrieved 1 June, 2015, from http://www.paulgrahamarchive.com

Gruère, G. P., Mehta-Bhatt, P., & Sengupta, D. (2008). *Bt Cotton and farmer suicides in India: Reviewing the evidence, IRPRI discussion paper*. Retrieved May 30, 2015, from http://www.ifpri.org/sites/default/files/publications/ifpridp00808.pdf

Honneth, A. (2007). *Disrespect: The normative foundations of critical theory*. Cambridge, UK: Polity Press.

Luce, H. (2007). *History of life magazine. History as it happened blog*. Retrieved 13 February, 2015, from https://historyasithappened.wordpress.com/2007/10/15/7/

Mitchell, W. J. T. (1995). *Picture theory: Essays on verbal and visual representation*. Chicago: University of Chicago Press.

Page, F. F. (n.d.). Retrieved 21 February, 2015, from https://www.facebook.com/FarmVille

People's Archive of Rural India (PARI). (n.d.). Retrieved 10 February, 2015, from http://www.ruralindiaonline.org/about/

Rajchman, J. (1988). Foucault's art of seeing. *October, 44*, 88-117.

Reporter, S. (2009, October 9). Facebook farmers want India flag. *BBC News*. Retrieved from http://news.bbc.co.uk

Reporter, S. (2014, September 25). Forbes India rich list: Mukesh Ambani tops again, Gautam Adani moves up. *Economic Times*. Retrieved from http://articles.economictimes.indiatimes.com

Sainath, P. (2014). *Maharashtra crosses 60,00 farm suicides*. Retrieved 11 February, 2015, from http://psainath.org/maharashtra-crosses-60000-farm-suicides/

Sainath, P. (2013, May 2). Over 2000 fewer farmers every day. *The Hindu*. Retrieved, 20 February, 2015, from http://www.thehindu.com/opinion/columns/sainath/over-2000-fewer-farmers-every-day/article4674190.ece

Sainath, P. (2015, January 15). *Farmer commits suicide, Adani gets the loan. Happy Pongal.* Retrieved 7 February, 2015 from http://psainath.org/farmer-commits-suicide-adani-gets-the-loan/

Shah, C., & Blaney, A. (2015, January 1). Farming pixels. *The Forager Magazine*. Retrieved 24 February, 2015, from http://www.theforagermagazine.com

Shiva, V. (2000). *Stolen harvest: The hyjacking of the global food supply*. Cambridge, MA: South End Press.

Shiva, V., & Kunwar, J. (2009). *Farmers suicides in India*. New Delhi: Research Foundation for Science, Technology and Ecology.

Wratten, I. D. (1953). A century of photography. *Journal of the Royal Society of Arts, 101*(4894), 259–271.

Chapter 18
eLearning Political Strategies:
A Four Act Play

Celia Romm-Livermore
Wayne State University, USA

Mahesh Raisinghani
Texas Woman's University, USA

Pierluigi Rippa
University of Napoli Federico II, Italy

ABSTRACT

The starting point for this paper is the eLearning Political Strategies (ELPoS) model. The model is based on two dimensions: 1) the direction of the political strategy (upward or downward), and 2) the scope of the political strategy (individual or group based). The interaction between the above dimensions defines four different types of eLearning political strategies, which result in different political outcomes. The model is accompanied with one case study that is divided into four parts ("acts"). Each of the acts provides an example of one of the four strategies in the model. The discussion and conclusions sections integrate the findings from the case study, outline the rules that govern the application of political strategies in the context of eLearning, and list some of the theoretical and practical implications from a better understating of the politics of eLearning.

POLITICS AND eLEARNING

Cross (2004) is considered the person who coined the term eLearning. Since then, a range of definitions have been offered for this term. The first type of definitions focus on the fact that eLearning is based on the Internet. For example, Rosenberg (2001, p. 5) defines eLearning as: "the use of internet technologies to deliver a broad array of solutions that enhance knowledge and performance, Rossett and Sheldon (2001) defines eLearning as: "Web-based training (WBT)", and Adrich (2004, p. 240) defines eLearning as: "a broad combination of processes, content, and infrastructure to use computers and networks to scale and/or improve one or more significant parts of a learning value chain, including management and delivery".

DOI: 10.4018/978-1-5225-1862-4.ch018

Other definitions of eLearning are so general that they include just about all interactions and experiences in organizations. For example, Manville (2003, p. 50) defines eLearning as: "Not only Internet-published courseware, but also the tools for managing, modularizing and handling: different kinds of content and learning objects (including both electronic and non-electronic forms, and even traditional classroom instruction), just-in-time and asynchronous learning, such as virtual labs, virtual classrooms and collaborative work spaces, simulations, document repositories and publishing programs, tools for prescribing learning, managing development pathways and goals and handling e-commerce and financial transactions related to learning, and the utilities and capabilities for supporting informal learning, mentoring, communities of practice and other non-training interventions". In other words, according to Manville, eLearning includes just about everything that happens in the corporate world except training.

For the purpose of this paper, we define eLearning as both electronically based and related to teaching and learning. However, this does not mean that we restrict eLearning to activities that occur in a classroom (even an on-line classroom) or that we consider eLearning a process that takes place during the delivery of content. Thus, activities that occur between students, instructors, and administrators, within an organization that engages in eLearning (such as a university) that involve electronic means and are related to the teaching and learning process would meet our definition of eLearning.

There are a number of central themes in the literature on eLearning that are directly related to our study. First, is the discussion of factors that predict attitudes to eLearning. Previous research lists many factors as affecting attitudes to eLearning, including: age: gender, personality, and computer experience (e.g., Miller & Varma, 1994; Taylor & Todd, 1995; Sanchez et al., 2006). Thus, the literature shows that users who are young, male, with a higher risk tolerance and more experience with computers, are more inclined to have positive views of eLearning than users who do not meet these criteria.

The effectiveness of eLearning programs has attracted much research as well. Studies focusing on this issue identified three sets of factors that impact the effectiveness of eLearning programs:

1. Technology factors (Masie, 2001; Brown, 2002);
2. Psychological factors (Henning, 2003); and
3. Organizational factors (Guest, 1998; Herriot et al., 1998; Martin et al.,1998; Capelli, 1998; Martin and Beaumont, 2003).

Applying the above framework, Mital (2011) found that learner perceptions of the characteristics of learning technology can explain acceptance behavior, particularly in relation to the inclination to adopt eLearning technologies. Learner perceptions also explain the effectiveness of utilizing eLearning technologies in the long term. Most importantly, according to Mital (2011), acceptance behavior correlates with learner's expectations of the technology in terms of the suitability of the learning to the task, the applicability of the technology to the learner's needs, and the availability of the right incentives to motivate learners to use the technology.

To the best of our knowledge and with the exception of a few studies (Romm-Livermore et al.2014a; Romm-Livermore et al., 2014b), the politics of eLearning has not been investigated much to date. Given this, we start this section of the literature review by defining the concept of organizational politics and then exploring its possible manifestations in the eLearning environment.

Building on the body of literature on organization politics, Drory and Romm (1991) created a conceptual framework or a "map" of the range of behaviors that should be considered political. Their framework considers organizational politics as a combination of three types of elements:

1. Necessary elements (e.g., "influence attempts" and "informal means"),
2. Defining elements (e.g., whether the actor is an individual or a group and whether the political behavior is directed upward, downward or laterally), and
3. Circumstantial elements (e.g., "the existence of a state of conflict", "working against one's organization", "power attainment", and "concealment of motive").

Based on this conceptualization, Romm (1999) outlined nine different styles of political behavior in virtual communities, depending on the number of actors involved in the political behavior and the direction of the political behavior. This conceptualization was applied to a range of empirical studies that explored the manifestations of politics in a range of computer mediated environments, including: industrial relations (Pliskin et al, 1997), gender relations (Romm and Pliskin, 1997), group dynamics (Romm & Pliskin, 1998), group development (Pliskin and Romm, 1997), and leadership (Romm & Pliskin, 1999).

Applied to this paper, there are a number of conclusions that can be drawn from the research reviewed in the previous sections.

Who is likely to behave politically in the eLearning environment? The research that we reviewed in the previous sections supports the assertion that the power that individuals have within a community (social capital), and the role that individuals play as members of the community impact their ability to act politically. Thus, more powerful members of the eLearning community (teachers, team leaders) would be more inclined to play a political role than other members of the community.

How are actors likely to behave politically in the eLearning environment? The research that we reviewed in the previous sections outlines a large number of strategies that political actors are likely to employ, including: influencing other members, exerting control over other members, resolving conflicts between members, etc. The research also suggests other attributes of political behavior such as the number of actors involved (either as initiators or objects of the political behavior) and the direction of the political act (downward, lateral, upward).

Why is it important to understand the political behavior of actors in the eLearning environment? Here too the literature in the previous sections provides some answers. If the interactivity of the eLearning environment has big impact on the effectiveness of the learning experience, then understanding the interactions between teachers and learners during the process of eLearning is necessary for improving the quality of eLearning.

As power and politics are present in most human interactions, particularly in groups, we have to assume that they are present in the eLearning environment too and we have to assume also that understanding this facet of eLearning is bound to promote the effectiveness of eLearning. In the following sections we explore how political issues manifest in the eLearning environment and discuss the theoretical and practical implications from this phenomenon.

THE eLEARNING POLITICAL STRATEGIES MODEL

The eLearning Political Strategies (ELPoS) model is based on several sources, including the definition of organizational politics, as "influence attempts" offered by Drory and Romm (1991), and the political strategies model proposed by Romm (1999).

The following sections in this manuscript explain the origins of the model and its major assumptions.

1. **Political Behavior in the eLearning Context Involves "Influence Attempts":** In line with the Drory and Romm (1991) political behavior framework, the ELPos model defines political behavior as "influence attempts". This implies that sets of behaviors or strategies such as "convincing", "selling", "negotiating", "manipulating", "coercing", etc are seen as political strategies.
2. **eLearning Political Strategies are Affected by the Identity of the Initiator of the Political Activity:** In line with the Romm (1999) political strategies model, the ELPoS model assumes that the identity of the initiator of the political activity (whether an individual or a group) will affect the type of political E-Learning strategy utilized.
3. **E-Learning Political Strategies are Affected by the Direction of the Political Strategy and Moderated by Demographic and Situational Variables**: In line with the Romm (1999) political strategies model, the ELPoS model assumes that political strategies are shaped by their direction (whether upward or downward).
4. **E-Learning Political Strategies are Moderated by Demographic and Situational Variables**: In line with the literature on E-Learning (Miller & Varma,1994; Taylor & Todd, 1995; Sanchez et al.,2006 and others) the ELPoS model assumes that demographic variables (e.g., age, gender, ethnicity, experience, etc.) and situational variables (specific events within or outside the classroom) will affect the E-Learning strategies utilized by actors.

Figure 1 shows the major variables in the model and the relationships between them. As indicated in the figure, the ELPoS model consists of three sets of variables. The Independent or "causing" variables are Identity (of the political actor) and Direction (of the political strategy). The political strategy is seen as the independent or "outcome" of the interaction between the Independent variables. The demographic variables (gender, ethnicity, age, experience and situation) are seen as moderating the relationship between the Independent and Dependent variables. Note that not all the variables and the relationships in the model are explored in this paper. As the research that this paper presents is based on a case study methodology, its focus is the Independent variables only, namely, the Identity of the political actor (one individual versus a group) and the Direction of the political strategy (downward or upward). Table 1 below shows the interaction between the two variables and the four types of eLearning political strategies that can result from this interaction.

Table 1. Acts as examples of political behavior in each cell of the model

	Individual	Group
Downward	**Act One** – The Students demand that marks for one presentation be invalidated	**Act Three** – The students demand that marks for two presentations and final assignment be invalidated
Upward	**Act Two** – The students demand that marks for two presentations be invalidated	**Act Four** – The students demand that the marks for all assessment tasks other than the exams be invalidated

Figure 1.

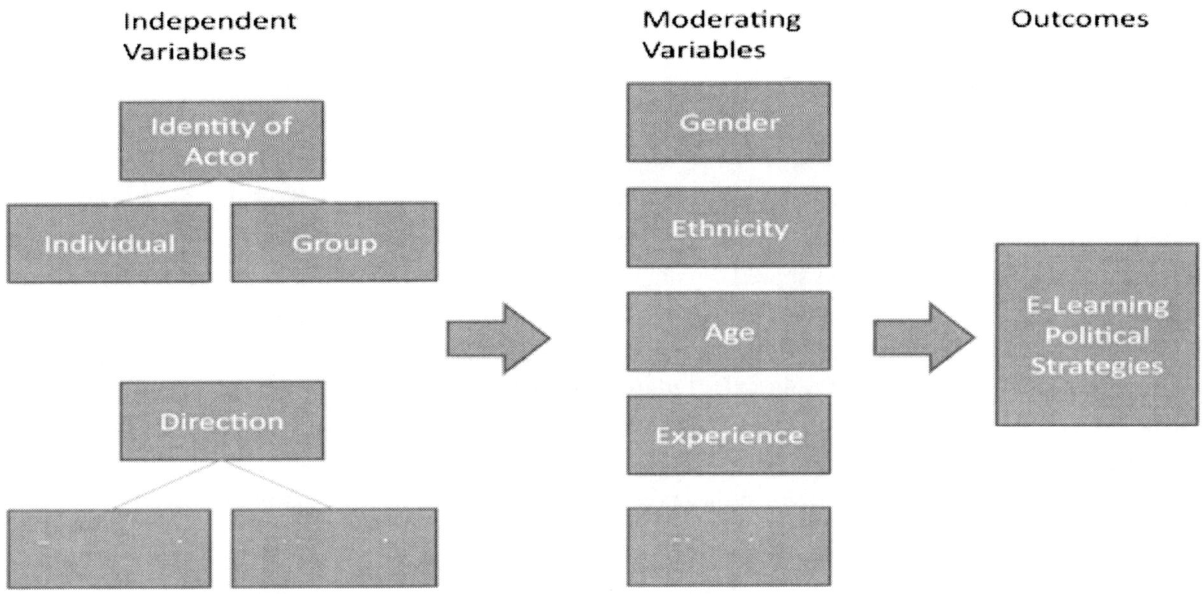

RESEARCH METHODOLOGY

The objective of this study was to develop rather than test hypotheses. As such, this research should be seen as fitting the categories of "exploratory", "inductive", and "qualitative". In line with this methodological philosophy, the main source of data for the study was open-ended, un-structured, in-depth interviews.

The Interviews

Twenty interviews were conducted. The interviews were held with instructors from a number of universities who indicated in preliminary conversations that they experienced incidents at work that fit our definition of politics during eLearning. The interviews focused on the interviewees' experience with the politics of eLearning and started with an exploratory discussion in which would-be interviewees were asked to identify an incident that involved politics within an eLearning context. Once the interviewee identified an incident that could be described as political, the rest of the interview focused on that one incident.

The interviews followed the chronological order of the events that formed the incident, with special emphasis on who initiated the political acts, who was the object of these acts, how the acts were executed, who benefited from the political acts, and how they impacted the eLearning community as a whole.

The Interviewees

Potential interviewees were identified by one of the authors through her professional network. Preliminary conversations with the potential interviewees determined their suitability and once found suitable, arrangements were made with them as to the time and place of the interview. Most interviews were held on-line through Skype. However, some interviews took place face-to-face or by phone. No interviews were held on the premises of any of the universities that employed the interviewees to protect the interviewees' privacy.

THE FOUR ACT PLAY

The discussion in the following sections uses one major case study ("Play") divided into four parts ("Acts") to demonstrate the major tenets of the model. The case study is based on one of the interviews undertaken. Other than the information shared during the interview, the description in the following sections is also based on e-mail messages forwarded by the interviewee as background information on the case.

This particular case was selected as the basis for this paper because given its length and complexity; it demonstrates the range of political strategies outlined in the model. The case is not intended to "prove" the model but to demonstrate its major components and provide examples of how the model can manifest in an eLearning environment. To help the reader, the four acts of the case study are presented first in terms of how they fit the cells in the model (Table 1) and then each act is discussed in terms of its fitness with the model.

BACKGROUND

The events of the case took place in a class of over 70 students in a university in the US. The course, Introduction to Management of Information Systems, is a mandatory course for all students in the School of Business. The majority of the students taking it are from disciplines other than Information Systems, including, Finance, Accounting, Marketing and Management.

The professor teaching the course (henceforth referred to as "the professor"), a relative new- comer to the US from a non-English speaking country in Asia, has been teaching for over twenty years. However, at the time that this case started, his experience in teaching in the US spanned just five years. He was appointed as an untenured Associate Professor several years earlier, and he was expecting to obtain tenure by the end of the school year.

During the semester in which the case took place, the professor was teaching two sections of the same course, one section was defined as "on-line" and the other was defined as "face-to-face". The professor was using the "concurrent" model for teaching the two sections, namely, the lectures in the face-to-face section were recorded and made available to both classes. When several lectures were canceled in the face-to-face class because of the professor's ill health, he had them recorded at home. This occurred during the few weeks when the professor was unable to teach face-to-face.

In both classes students did some of the work in teams. Each team was led by a "leader" and several of the assignments were to be undertaken by the teams. Even though one of the classes was defined as "face-to-face", some activities in it took place on-line. Thus, the exams and many of the group interactions were on-line and most communication among the students and between the students and the professor took place on-line too. In this sense, the face-to-face class, where all of the case events took place, was in reality a "hybrid" class.

Table 2 below shows the distribution of assessment tasks in the class that is the focus of this article. Note, as the case events started on the very last week of the semester, the early assignment was marked more than a month earlier.

Table 2. Assessment tasks

Assessment Components	Weight	Basis
7. Early assignment	15%	Group
8. Presentation 1	5%	Group
9. Presentation 2	5%	Group
10. Final assignment	20%	Group
11. Mid-term multiple choice exam	25%	Individual
12. Final multiple choice exam	30%	Individual

ACT ONE: THE STUDENTS DEMAND THAT MARKS FOR ONE PRESENTATION BE INVALIDATED

The case started at the end of the last week of the semester when John Smith (a fictitious name used for privacy of the individual), the leader of team 3, sent the message below to the professor, requesting that the mark for the in-class presentation for his team (5% of the overall mark for the course) be changed because the procedure (marking by the other teams) was "unfair". Indeed, John's team was marked by the other teams at the bottom of the class.

Excerpt from Message from John

Professor, I don't usually write to complain about marks but this time I feel I have to. My team is devastated by the mark that we got from the other teams in the class. Marking us at the bottom of the class is highly unfair. We invested much work and time in our presentation and we did not deserve to get as low a mark as we did. This whole idea of letting teams mark each other is bad. Other professors are not doing this and we are not paying tuition to the university to be marked by students. You should be marking us – not the other students.

Following the receipt of the above message, the professor checked into the marks of the members of team 3, finding that not just John but all other members of his team appeared to have cheated on the mid-term exam. Thus, while the students in all other teams in the class had different marks on the exam, all the members of John's team got 100% on the multiple choice exam. Given the size of John's team (ten members), the professor was convinced that the only way they could have all earned these marks was by somehow managing to obtain a copy of the exam and the correct answers.

The professor decided not to take any action on what appeared to be cheating on the mid-term exam because he did not feel that he had strong enough evidence to prove it and was worried that accusing the students for cheating could affect his tenure prospects. At the same time, he decided not to change John's team's marks. To make sure that John and his team understood the rationale for his decision, the professor sent the message below to John.

Excerpt from a Message from the Professor to John

Hi John, I am sorry that you and your team are disappointed with the mark that you received from the other teams for your in-class presentation. Still, the principle of team evaluation is widely practiced in industry and in academe. It is considered the most reliable form of performance appraisal. Your peers know best what is required to accomplish a task and are better able to assess whether you did a good job than anyone else. Also, the use of peer evaluation was shared with the class at the very beginning of the semester and is in the syllabus. For this reason, I cannot change the rules of the game at this time.

Analysis

John's message to the professor at the beginning of the case is an example of an individual upward political manipulation. John's message is individual because it was initiated by him alone. It is upward because he was attempting to manipulate the professor. It is an example of political manipulation because it was intended to influence and change the professor's behavior into modifying the marking of one of the class presentations, and as the exchange took place within an eLearning environment, it can be seen as an example of eLearning political behavior. As such, John's behavior during the first Act meets the criteria of the first cell in the model.

ACT TWO: THE STUDENTS DEMAND THAT MARKS FOR TWO PRESENTATIONS BE INVALIDATED

Once his request to have his team's mark changed was denied, John approached the Chair of the department with the same request. The Chair forwarded John's message to the professor advising that by now, he, the Chair, received similar messages from all members of John's team. They all insisted that team evaluation was "unfair" and demanded that all marks resulting from the team evaluations should be modified.

When the professor explained to the Chair that the students were informed of the marking procedures at the beginning of the semester and that it was mentioned in the syllabus (a legal document that all parties were bound by), the Chair explained that using students to mark each other was not a common practice in the School and should not have been undertaken. In any case, the Chair, repeated, the students were very upset and something had to be done about it.

After further discussions between the professor and the Chair through e-mail, the professor decided to comply with the Chair's demand and he re-marked the teams by himself. He informed the Chair of his decision, shared the criteria for the marking with the students, and sent a detailed e-mail message to each team informing the team of how his marking criteria were applied to their presentation. As it happened, the new marks were very similar to the marks that the teams gave each other and team 3 ended again with the lowest mark in the class.

Analysis

The insistence of the Chair that the students' presentations had to be re-marked by the professor is an example of an individual downward political manipulation. It is seen as individual because it was undertaken by the Chair alone. It is seen as downward because the target was the professor, a subordinate of the Chair. The intention of the messages from the Chair was to change the behavior of the professor, which makes it political, and the exchanges on e-mail between the professor and the Chair took place within the context of an eLearning environment. Thus, the behavior of the Chair during the second Act can be seen as an example of the attributes of the second cell in the model.

ACT THREE: THE STUDENTS DEMAND THAT MARKS FOR TWO PRESENTATIONS AND FINAL ASSIGNMENT BE INVALIDATED (30%)

As the semester was drawing to a close, the class took the final exam and submitted the final research reports. Checking the final exams, the professor became aware that the cheating has now spread to the whole class. In fact, while during the mid-term exam just ten members of the class (the members of team 3) obtained 100% on the exam, now, in the final exam, 55 students out of the 70 in the class received 100% on the 40 multiple choice questions of the exam. This, the professor concluded, could only be the result of the members of team 3 sharing the link to the exam correct answers with the other students in the class.

Given the scope of the cheating on the end of term exam, the professor decided to share his suspicions with management. While waiting to hear if any action was to be taken about the cheating, the professor attended to the marking of the research assignments, which were also team based. Given the cheating on the final exam, the professor decided to be very strict with the marking of the assignments. This resulted in all the teams in the class receiving lower than usual marks for the assignments, including the members of team 3.

Once all assignments were marked and the final grades published, the professor received the message below from John Smith, the leader of Team 3. This time, John insisted that the marks for all group assignments should be scaled up because they were too low.

Excerpt from Message from John to the Professor

Professor, I am very upset about my mark in this course. I wrote to you previously about our in class presentation and the fact that it was marked by the other teams. I am happy that you fixed this problem. Now I am concerned that our mark for the final assignment is even more unfair. How can we get a mark as low as 6 out of 10 for an assignment that we put so much work into? This is highly unfair and we demand that you scale the marks up.

Within minutes after receiving the above message, the professor received two more messages from members of team 3 (see below).

Excerpt from Message from Jane Cook (Fictitious Name), a Member of John's Team

Professor, I just saw the message from our leader, John Smith, and I want you to know that I agree with every word in his message. I am so disappointed with my mark in the course. I worked so hard this semester and I expected a much higher result, particularly given how well I did on the mid-term and end of term exam. I received 100% on both exams, and, yet, because of the marks for the presentations and the final assignment, I will be getting a B for the course. This is very unfair and very disappointing.

Excerpt from Message from Jennifer Sand (Fictitious Name), a Member of Another Team in the Class, Requesting the Same

Professor, I cannot understand how after getting 100% on both the mid-term and the end of term exams, I will end up with A- on the course. I saw the message from John Smith and I agree that you should scale up the marks for the final assignment. It is simply unfair that I should not get an A for the course. Your marking is flawed and the only way to fix it is to scale the marks.

A few hours after receiving these messages, the professor heard from his Chair that both the Chair and the Dean were being flooded with copies of the e-mail messages that he received. The messages demanded that all group based marks in the class be scaled up. To keep the professor updated on all developments, the Chair started forwarded the messages to the professor as he was receiving them. In all instances, all identifying information about the senders was removed. The Chair confirmed that most of the messages came from members of team 3. However, as the flood of messages continued, some messages came from members of other teams in the class, as well as, from students in the other class that the professor was teaching. The demand from all the students was the same – all group marks had to be scaled up because the students felt they adversely affected their final grades.

Reading the messages forwarded to him by the Chair, the professor maintained that there was no need to change the marks for the last assignment because in contrast to the marks for the presentation, which were initially based on students evaluating each other (and have been "corrected"), the assignment marks were never undertaken by the students. The professor maintained that his criteria for marking the assignments were sound and that there was no need to change them and reminded management that the students cheated on the two exams and should not be rewarded for it by scaling up their assignment marks.

Analysis

The behavior of the students in this act is an example of a group upward political manipulation because the students' e-mail messages were a group activity, targeting the management of the school. The e-mail messages can be seen as political because their intent was to change the behavior of the members of the management team, and, consequently, the behavior of the professor. As the exchanges took place on e-mail and within the context of an eLearning environment, they can be seen as examples of eLearning political activities. Thus, the behavior of the students during the third Act can be seen as an example of attributes of the third cell in the model.

ACT FOUR: THE STUDENTS DEMAND THAT THE MARKS FOR ALL ASSESSMENT TASKS OTHER THAN THE EXAMS BE INVALIDATED

The last act in this saga started when the professor was sent an e-mail message by the Chair informing him that the flood of e-mail messages from the students did not involve only demands for scaling up of the marks for the research assignment, but addressed every aspect of the professor's teaching of the two classes throughout the whole semester. According to the students, the lectures did not contain any valuable content and the professor missed lectures for no reason. See below examples of some of the messages forwarded to the professor by the Chair at this stage, with all identifying information removed:

Excerpt from a Message Attacking the Content of the Professor's Lectures

I am writing to you because I am very disappointed with the course. The professor did not teach us anything in the lectures. In fact, given what he said in the lectures, I don't understand why you even hired him. He knows nothing about information technology and should not be teaching in a university in the US. He should be sent back where he came from.

Excerpt from a Message Attacking the Marking of Students' Work

I can't understand how the professor can get away with using students to mark each other. He is too lazy to do the job that he was hired to do, namely, to mark us. Also, his criteria stink. To think that he reduced our mark because, according to him, our presentation was lacking in originality, is infuriating. Since when is originality a basis for marking? My marks on the mid-term and end of term exams were very high and I deserve an A in the course. If I don't get it, I want my money back.

Excerpt from a Message Attacking the Professor's Taping of Lectures

This professor is a disgrace. He cancelled most of the lectures this semester and then had the lectures recorded on his computer so we could watch them on-line. I did not sign up to take this course as an on-line course and changing the course into an on-line course without ever teaching is a disgrace. I consulted on this matter with a friend who is a lawyer and he advised me that I can sue the university for this. Had I known that the course would be an on-line course, I would never take it. I want compensation for your false advertising and I want my money back.

As the professor did, indeed, miss three lectures because of ill-health and had the lectures recorded and sent to the students, the students complained that this constituted a conversion of the course from a face-to-face to an-line course. This, they insisted, went against the "promise" made to them when they registered that the course was going to be face-to-face. This, they claimed, was grounds for suing the University for breach of contract or false advertising. The only remedy, they claimed, was to give them their money back.

As all messages from the students to the Dean were being forwarded by the Chair to the professor, the professor tried, at least initially, to refute the accusations hurled at him. He told the Chair that he only missed three lectures and not the whole semester and that the students did not complain about any aspect of the course, including the quality of his teaching up until the very last week of the semester when they were concerned, primarily, with their marks. The Chair did not respond to the professor's explanations.

As the barrage of messages from the students continued, the Dean decided to invite the representatives of the students to a meeting in his office. As relayed by the Chair to the professor, during the meeting, the students stated that if getting their money back for the course was not an option (the Dean explained that this was not an option), then the least the university could do for them was to invalidate all the marks that the professor gave them other than the marks for the two exams. This meant that they were demanding the invalidation of 40% of the assessment tasks for the course. The marks for the exams, the students insisted, should remain unchanged despite the professor's claim that many of the students cheated on both exams.

Following the meeting in the Dean's office, the professor was forced to scale the marks for the class by invalidating all assessment tasks and giving the students their exam marks. This resulted in all the members of team 3 getting A's as final grades for the course. It also resulted in no action being taken about the cheating on both exams.

As for the professor, by the end of the school year the professor's application for tenure was denied, his contract with the university was discontinued, and he was forced to seek employment in another university.

Analysis

The behavior of the Chair and the Dean in this act of the case was an example of a group downward political manipulation because the initiative came from the members of the School's management team (the Deans, the Chair, and the other members of the School top administrative team), the manipulation was directed downward because the target was the professor, a subordinate of this group of actors. It was political because the intention was to change the professor's behavior and it took place on-line and in the context of eLearning. Thus, the behavior of the Chair and the Dean during the fourth Act can be seen as an example of the attributes of the fourth cell in the model.

DISCUSSION AND CONCLUSION

The goal of this paper was to present the ELPoS model and use the case study methodology to demonstrate how it can manifest in an eLearning environment. Even though the findings are not generalizable since one case study cannot be used to draw conclusions about the whole area of eLearning, the discussion in the previous sections suggests a number of interesting findings:

1. **The Personal Attributes and Number of Political Actors Make a Difference:** The different parts of the case study demonstrate that a political manipulation undertaken by one student is likely to be less effective than a political action undertaken by a group of students, and a political action undertaken by one professor is likely to be less effective than one taken by a group of professors and/or by a group of members of the management team. A group of students working with management is more effective politically than a group of students acting alone.
2. **Downward Political Manipulation is More Effective than Upward Political Manipulation:** The various parts of the case demonstrate that invariably all upward political manipulation (undertaken by either the students or the professor) were less effective in changing behavior than the downward political manipulations undertaken by either the Chair (against the professor) or by the Chair and the Dean (also against the professor). By definition, acting politically in a downward direction is likely to result in a victory to the actor no matter who the actors are and how many of them are involved in the political manipulation.

3. **Breaking the Law Tips the Scale in Favor of Those Who Expose It:** In the last act of the case, when the students used the excuse that canceling some of the lectures by the professor and turning them into "on-line teaching" was a breach of the contract with them because they were promised a face-to-face and not an on-line class, management felt obligated to side with the students. Faced with a possible legal action and a demand to give money back to the students, management chose to force the professor to not only change all assessment procedures after the fact (the elimination of peer evaluation and group based marks) but to actually impose new grades, giving just about every student in the class an A. The professor was forced to comply for the exact same reason. Threatened with legal action by the students, both the professor and the management of the school chose to acquiesce rather than stand up to the students.

The most important contribution of this research to the body of knowledge on eLearning is the ELPoS model, which establishes the central role of politics in eLearning. The case study in the previous sections outlines a few examples of the unique political strategies outlined by the model. Each one of the four parts of the case could not have happened if the class was not an eLearning/hybrid class in lieu of a face-to-face class. The case data in the previous sections also has important implications for practitioners:

1. **Class Design:** The design of the eLearning class has far reaching political implications. For example, using a synchronous class design where students and teacher interact with each other on-line but in real time would give the more politically astute students a chance to express themselves politically in class, while conducting the class asynchronously would push the political maneuvering to e-mail, or into the students' groups.
2. **The Behavior of the Professor:** The behavior of the professor has far reaching implications to the political dynamics of the eLearning class than is usually appreciated. The case study in the previous sections contains several examples on how the behavior of the professor made the students escalate their attack on him. The teacher's behavior vis-à-vis the student leaders can either empower or dis-empower them politically, and the behavior of the professor when conflict erupts can empower or dis-empower students. Thus, an awareness of the political underpinnings of the class dynamics is a must if eLearning is to be effective.
3. **The Political Aspects of eLearning Occur in and Out of the "Class":** As the different parts of the case study in the previous sections demonstrate much of what can be defined as "political" happens outside of the formal eLearning class. Political manipulations may involve officials at all levels of the university, as well as, other professors or students. As the eLearning class can take place anywhere anytime, so can the political maneuvering that accompanies it. Even though some politicking can take place in a synchronous "in-class" environment, most of the political activities in the eLearning environment take place outside of the class.

More research is required to establish whether the patterns that this research revealed are generalizable to larger samples of eLearning case studies. Behavioral studies are necessary to discern the building blocks of political behavior in various eLearning setting, and experimental research may help uncover the underlying rationale for the political strategies that are undertaken by actors and the practical implications that can be derived from them.

REFERENCES

Adrich, C. (2004). *Simulations and the Future of Learning*. San Francisco: Pfeiffer.

Brown, K. G. (2002). *Influence of job characteristics and perceived learning support on e-learning activity*. Paper presented at the Seventeenth Annual Meeting of the Society of Industrial and Organizational Psychology, Toronto, Canada.

Cappelli, P. (1998). *The New Deal at Work: Managing the Market-driven Workforce*. Boston: Harvard University School Press.

Cross, J. (2004). An Informal History of eLearning. *On the Horizon*, *12*(3), 103–110. doi:10.1108/10748120410555340

Drory, A., & Romm, C. T. (1991). The definition of organizational politics: A review. *Human Relations*, *43*(11), 1133–1154. doi:10.1177/001872679004301106

Guest, D. E. (1998). Is the psychological contract worth taking seriously? *Journal of Organizational Behavior*, *19*(S1), 649–664. doi:10.1002/(SICI)1099-1379(1998)19:1+<649::AID-JOB970>3.0.CO;2-T

Henning, E. (2003). I click, therefore I am (not): Is cognition distributed or is it contained in borderless e-learning programs? *International Journal of Training and Development*, *7*(4), 303–316. doi:10.1046/j.1360-3736.2003.00188.x

Herriot, P., Hirsch, W., & Reilly, P. (1998). *Trust and Transition: Managing Today's Employment Relationship*. Chichester, UK: John Wiley.

Manville, B. (2003, May). Organizing Enterprise-Wide eLearning and Human Capital Management. *Chief Learning Officer*, 50-55.

Martin, G., & Beaumont, P. B. (2003). *What's in a Name? Building the Relationship between Branding and People Management*. Wimbledon, UK: Chartered Institute of Personnel and Development.

Martin, G., Beaumont, P. B., & Staines, H. (1998). Determinants of Management Development–Evidence from Scotland. *The International Journal of Organizational Analysis*, *6*(2), 132–145. doi:10.1108/eb028881

Masie, E. (2001). *If we build it, will they come?* Retrieved insert 02/04/2014, from http://www.astd.org/virtual_community/ research/pdf/844-6110pdf.pdf

Miller, F., & Varma, N. (1994). The Effects of Psychosocial Factors on Indian Childrens Attitudes toward Computers. *Journal of Educational Computing Research*, *10*(3), 223–238. doi:10.2190/BMT6-WPJY-FXAR-VU06

Mital, M. (2011). Does Technology Uptake Convert to Effectiveness: Re-Evaluating E-Learning Effectiveness. In E. M. W. Ng, N. Karacapilidis, & M. R. Raisinghani (Eds.), *Evaluating the Impact of Technology on Learning, Teaching, and Designing Curriculum: Emerging Trends*. Hershey, PA: IGI Global.

Pliskin, N., & Romm, C. T. (1997). The Impact of E-mail on the Evolution of a Virtual Community During a Strike. *Information & Management*, *32*(5), 245–254. doi:10.1016/S0378-7206(97)00027-X

Pliskin, N., Romm, C. T., & Markey, R. (1997). E-mail as a weapon in an industrial dispute. *New Technology, Work and Employment*, *12*(1), 3–12. doi:10.1111/1468-005X.00018

Romm, C. T. (1999). *Virtual Politicking*. Cresskill, NJ: Hampton Press.

Romm, C. T., & Pliskin, N. (1997). Battle of the sexes on e-mail- or is it? *The Information Society*, *13*(3), 207–225. doi:10.1080/019722497129106

Romm, C. T., & Pliskin, N. (1998). Electronic mail as a coalition-building information technology. *ACM Transactions on Information Systems*, *16*(1), 82–100. doi:10.1145/267954.267958

Romm, C. T. & Pliskin, N. (1999). The role of charismatic leadership in diffusion and implementation of e-mail. *The Journal of Management Development*, *17*(1), 273-290.

Romm-Livermore, C. Raisinghani, M. S. & Rippa, P (2014a). The Politics of eLearning: A Theoretical Model. *International Journal of E-Politics*.

Romm-Livermore, C., Raisinghani, M. S., & Rippa, P. (2014b). eLearning as a Political Arena. In eLearning as a Socio Cultural System – A Multidimensional Analysi. IGI Global.

Rosenberg, M. J. (2001). *E-Learning. Strategies for Delivering Knowledge in the Digital Age*. Columbus, OH: McGraw Hill.

Rossett, A., & Sheldon, K. (2001). *Beyond The Podium: Delivering Training and Performance to a Digital World*. San Francisco: Jossey-Bass/Pfeiffer.

Sanchez, R. J., Bauer, T. N., & Paronto, M. E. (2006). Peer-Mentoring Freshmen: Implications for Satisfaction, Commitment, and Retention to Graduation. *Academy of Management Learning & Education*, *5*(1), 25–37. doi:10.5465/AMLE.2006.20388382

Taylor, S., & Todd, P. (1995). Assessing IT Uptake: The Role of Prior Experience. *Management Information Systems Quarterly*, *19*(4), 561–570. doi:10.2307/249633

Compilation of References

Bilbao-Osorio, B., Dutta, D., & Lanvin, B. (Eds.). (2013). Global Information Technology Report 2013. Growth and Jobs in a Hyperconnected World. Geneva: INSEAD/WEF. Available at http://www3.weforum.org/docs/WEF_GITR_Report_2013.pdf

1. fallin-4-u. (2014, February 6). Retrieved from: http://1fallin-4-u.tumblr.com/post/75867793189

Aaker, J., & Smith, A. (2010). *The dragonfly effect: Quick, effective, and powerful ways to use social media to drive social change*. San Francisco, CA: Jossey-Bass.

Abramowitz, A. L., & Saunders, K. L. (2008). Is polarization a myth? *The Journal of Politics*, *70*(2), 542–555. doi:10.1017/S0022381608080493

Adams, T. (2014, February 16). Jack Monroe — Loathed by the Daily Mail, loved by almost everyone else. *Observer Food Monthly*. Retrieved from http://www.theguardian.com/lifeandstyle/2014/feb/16/jack-monroe-cook-girl-called-jack-interview

Adi, A., Erickson, K., & Lilleker, D. G. (2014). Elite Tweets: Analyzing the Twitter Communication Patterns of Labour Party Peers in the House of Lords. *Policy & Internet*, *6*(1), 1–27. doi:10.1002/1944-2866.POI350

Adrich, C. (2004). Simulations and the Future of Learning (p. 240). San Francisco: Pfeiffer. Retrieved from http://www.amazon.com/Simulations-FutureLearning-Innovative-Revolutionary/dp/0787969621/bigdogsbowlofbis

Adrich, C. (2004). *Simulations and the Future of Learning*. San Francisco: Pfeiffer.

Aftonbladet. (2013). *No, we did not claim that LCHF is necessarily the best diet* [my translation]. Retrieved February 2, 2015, from http://www.aftonbladet.se/debatt/article17631151.ab

Agatston, A. (2003). *The South Beach Diet*. London: Headline.

Agnew, J. A. (2014). *From political methodology to geographical social theory? A critical review ofelectoral geography, 1960-87*. Developments in Electoral Geography.

Ahmad, I., Ali, S., Iqbal, S., Ali, F., & Badshah, R. (2013). Problems of government secondary school system in Pakistan: Critical analysis of literature and finding a way forward. *International Journal of Academic Research in Business & Social Sciences, 3*(2).

Aichholzer, G. (2016). Citizen Participation in Climate Governance. In G. Aichholzer, H. Kubicek, & L. Torres (Eds.), *Evaluating e-Participation. Frameworks, Practice, Evidence* (pp. 47–62). London: Springer. doi:10.1007/978-3-319-25403-6_3

Akandji-Kombe, J.-F. (2007). *Positive obligations under the European Convention on Human Rights; A guide to the implementation of the European Convention on Human Rights; Human rights handbooks, No. 7*. Council of Europe.

Aldrich, J. H., Gibson, R. K., Cantijoch, M., & Konitzer, T. (2015). Getting out the vote in the social media era: Are digital tools changing the extent, nature and impact of party contacting in elections? *Party Politics*, *22*(2), 165–178. doi:10.1177/1354068815605304

Aleman-Meza, B., Nagarajan, M., Ding, L., Sheth, A., Arpinar, I. B., Joshi, A., & Finin, T. (2008). Scalable semantic analytics on social networks for addressing the problem of conflict of interest detection. *ACM Trans. Web, 2*(1), 1–29. Retrieved from http://portal.acm.org/citation.cfm?id=1135777.1135838#

Alexander, A., & Aouragh, M. (2011). The Egyptian Experience:Sense and Nonsense of the Internet Revolution. *International Journal of Communication*, (5): 1344–1358.

Alfredo Jarr's searching for Africa in life unveiled at The New School [Blog post]. (2014). Retrieved 13 February, 2015, from http://blogs.newschool.edu/news/2014/12/alfredo-jaars-searching-for-africa-in-life-unveiled-at-the-new-school/#.VN9udYvfM20

All in One Social. (2013). *Facebook statistics for Uganda*. Retrieved February 12, 2014, from http://www.allin1social.com/facebook/country_stats/uganda

Allagui, I. (2014). Article. *International Journal of Communication, 8*, 983–1007.

All-Party Parliamentary Inquiry. (2014). *Feeding Britain*. http://doi.org/<ALIGNMENT.qj></ALIGNMENT>10.1136/bmj.1.4348.621-a

Altman, A. (2014, February 19). No-budget recipes. *The New Yorker*. Retrieved from http://www.newyorker.com/culture/culture-desk/no-budget-recipes

Alvarez, R. R. (2007). The march of empire: Mangos, avocados, and the politics of transfer. *Gastronomica: The Journal of Food and Culture, 7*(3), 28-33.

Aman, M., & Jayroe, T. J. (2013). ICT, Social Media, and the Arab Transition to Democracy: From Venting to Acting. *Digest of Middle East Studies*, *22I*(2), 317–347. doi:10.1111/dome.12024

AMIPCI. (2016). *12º Estudio sobre los Hábitos de los Usuarios de Internet en México 2016.* Asociación Mexicana de Internet. Retrieved from https://www.amipci.org.mx/images/Estudio_Habitosdel_Usuario_2016.pdf

Ammerlaan, A. (2014, February 5). *Twitter*. Retrieved from https://twitter.com/aliammerlaan/status/431257179430338560

Amnesty International. (2013). *Uganda: Activists arrested as disturbing crackdown on media continues*. Retrieved October 24, 2014, from http://www.amnesty.org/en/news/uganda-crackdown-newspapers-continues-2013-05-24

Amtaika, A. (2013). Limitations of the proportional representation (PR) electoral system in South Africa's local government elections. *Journal of African & Asian Local Government Studies, 2*(4).

Andersen, K., & Medaglia, R. (2009). *The Use of Facebook in National Election Campaigns: Politics as Usual?* Springer Berlin / Heidelberg. Retrieved from http://www.springerlink.com/content/b74507487472jv24/abstract/

Andersen, K. (2002). *Political parties and civil society: Learning from the american case. Democratic Institution Performance: Research and Policy Perspectives* (pp. 15–26). Academic Press.

Anderson, L. (2011, May/June). Demystifying the Arab Spring. *Foreign Affairs*. Retrieved from http://www.foreignaffairs.com/articles/67693/lisa-anderson/demystifying-the-arab-spring

Anderson, M. (2015, October 29). Technology device ownership: 2015. *Pew Research Center Internet, Science & Tech*. Retrieved from http://www.pewinternet.org/2015/10/29/technology-device-ownership-2015/

Anderson, A. A., Brossard, D., Scheufele, D. A., Xenos, M. A., & Ladwig, P. (2014). The nasty effect: Online incivility and risk perceptions of emerging technologies. *Journal of Computer-Mediated Communication*, *19*(3), 373–387. doi:10.1111/jcc4.12009

Anderson, B. (1991). *Imagined communities: reflections on the origins and spread of nationalism*. London: Verson.

Anderson, J., & Bresnahan, M. (2013). Communicating stigma about body size. *Health Communication*, *28*(6), 603–615. doi:10.1080/10410236.2012.706792 PMID:22928811

Ansolabehere, S., & Iyengar, S. (1995). *Going Negative: How Political Advertising Shrinks and Polarizes the Electorate*. New York: Free Press.

Appadurai, A. (1988). How to make a national cuisine: Cookbooks in contemporary India. *Comparative Studies in Society and History*, *30*(1), 3–24. doi:10.1017/S0010417500015024

Applebaum, Y. (2016, April 7). Why Donald Trump voters are civically disengaged—a fact that may cost him the nomination. *The Atlantic*. Retrieved May 16, 2016, from http://www.theatlantic.com/politics/archive/2016/04/voting-alone/477270/

Arai-Takahashi, Y. (2002). *The Margin of Appreciation Doctrine and the Principle of Proportionality in the Jurisprudence of the ECHR*. New York: Intersentia.

Aristegui, C. (2012, March 15). *Metodología de monitoreo político en redes sociales - Aristegui Noticias*. Retrieved July 5, 2014, from http://aristeguinoticias.com/1503/post-elecciones/metodologia-de-monitoreo-politico-de-redes-sociales/

Arndt, A., & Jaeschke, W. (Eds.). (2000). Materialismus und Spiritualismus: Philosophie und Wissenschaften nach 1848. Hamburg, Germany: Meiner.

Arnstein, S. R. (1969). A ladder of citizen participation. *Journal of the American Planning Association*, *35*(4), 216–224.

Asbo Baistrocchi, P. (2003). Liability Of Intermediary Service Providers In The EU Directive On Electronic Commerce. *Computer & High Technology Law Journal*, *19*, 111–130.

Ashton, J. R., Middleton, J., & Lang, T. (2014). Open letter to Prime Minister David Cameron on food poverty in the UK. *Lancet*, *383*(9929), 1631. doi:10.1016/S0140-6736(14)60536-5 PMID:24794817

Atkins, C. R. (1972). Dr. Atkins' Diet Revolution: The High Calorie Way to Stay Thin Forever. D. McKay Co.

Ayers, & Maccaughey. (2003). *Cyberactivism: Online Activism in Theory and Practice* (1st ed.). New York: Routledge. Retrieved from http://www.powells.com/biblio/61-9780415943208-1

Bachmann, I., Kaufhold, K., Lewis, S., & Zúñiga, H. (2010). News Platform Preference: Advancing the Effects of Age and Media Consumption on Political Participation. *International Journal of Internet Science*, *5*(1), 34–47.

Baguma, S. (2016). *Uganda: the presidential election that wasn't?* Retrieved from http://www.afrikareporter.com/uganda-the-presidential-election-that-wasnt/

Bakker, T., & de Vreese, C. (2011). Good News for the Future? Young People, Internet Use, and Political Participation. *Communication Research*, *38*(4), 451–470. doi:10.1177/0093650210381738

Baldwin-Philippi, J. (2013). Constructing Skeptical Citizens: How Campaign Microsites Foster New Ways of Engaging Political Information and Understanding Citizenship. *Journal of Information Technology & Politics*, *10*(3), 245–260. doi:10.1080/19331681.2013.771295

Bannister, F., & Wilson, D. (2011). O(ver)-Government? Emerging technology, citizen autonomy and the regulatory state. *Information Polity*, *16*(1), 63–79.

Banting, W. (1863). *Letter on Corpulence, Addressed to the public*. London: Harrison and Sons.

Barber, B. (1984). *Strong Democracy. Participatory Politics for a New Age*. Los Angeles, CA: University of California Press.

Barber, B. R. (2003). *Strong democracy: Participatory politics for a new age*. Univ of California Press.

Bartels, L. M. (1988). *Presidential primaries and the dynamics of public choice*. Princeton University Press.

Barthes, R. (1972). *'Ornamental Cookery,' Mythologies*. New York: Hill and Wang.

Barthes, R. (1979). Towards a psycosociology of contemporary food consumption. In R. Forster & O. Rarum (Eds.), *Food and drink in history: Selections from the annals economics, societies, civilisations*. Baltimore, MD: John Hopkins University Press. (Original work published 1961)

Barzilai-Nahon, K., & Neumann, S. (2005). *Bounded in cyberspace: An empirical model of self-regulation in virtual communities*. Paper presented at the 38th Annual Hawaii International Conference on System Sciences (HICSS), Hawaii, HI. doi:10.1109/HICSS.2005.124

Bates, E. (2010). *The Evolution of the European Convention on Human Rights: From Its Inception to the Creation of a Permanent Court of Human Rights*. Oxford University Press.

Bates, T. (2001). Gramsci and the theory of hegemony. *Journal of the History of Ideas*, *36*(2), 351–366. doi:10.2307/2708933

Baudrillard, J. (2002). The Precession of Simulacra. In G. D. Meenakshi & D. M. Kellner (Eds.), *Media and Cultural Studies: Keyworks* (pp. 521–549). Malden, MA and Oxford: Blackwell Publishers.

Bazerman, C. (1988). *Shaping Written Knowledge: The Genre and Activity of the Experimental Article in Science*. Madison, WI: University of Wisconsin Press.

BBC News. (2013, September 10). *Michael Gove "insulted" food bank users, says Labour*. Retrieved from http://www.bbc.co.uk/news/uk-politics-24042446

BBC News. (2014, August 11). *Food poverty in Scotland "not acceptable" says Sturgeon*. Retrieved from http://www.bbc.co.uk/news/uk-scotland-scotland-politics-28731402

Bekafigo, M.A. & Pingley A. (2016). *Political Participation on Twitter during the 2012 Gubernatorial Elections*. Unpublished.

Bekafigo, M. A., & McBride, A. (2013). Who Tweets about Politics? Political Participation of Twitter Users During the 2011 Gubernatorial Elections. *Social Science Computer Review*, *31*(5), 625–643. doi:10.1177/0894439313490405

Belleflamme, P., Lambert, T., & Schwienbacher, A. (2014). Crowdfunding: Tapping the Right Crowd. *Journal of Business Venturing*, *29*(5), 585–609. doi:10.1016/j.jbusvent.2013.07.003

Benjamin, W. (1968). *Illuminations* (H. Zohn, Trans.). New York: Schocken Books.

Benkler, Y. (2006). *The wealth of networks: How social production transforms markets and freedom*. New Haven, CT: Yale University Press.

Bennett, J., Strange, N., Kerr, P., & Medrado, A. (2012). *Multiplatforming public service broadcasting: The economic and cultural role of UK digital and TV independents*. London: Royal Holloway and University of London. Retrieved from http://eprints.bournemouth.ac.uk/21021/1/bennett-strange-kerr-medrado-2012-multiplatforming-psb-industry-report.pdf

Bennett, W. L., Wells, C., & Freelon, D. (2011). Communicating civic engagement: Contrasting models of citizenship in the youth web sphere. *Journal of Communication*, *61*(5), 835–856. doi:10.1111/j.1460-2466.2011.01588.x

Bennhold, K. (2014, January 14). From hunger to fame, with a shoestring budget: Jack Monroe has become Britain's austerity celebrity. *New York Times (Europe)*. Retrieved from http://www.nytimes.com/2014/01/15/world/europe/jack-monroe-has-become-britains-austerity-celebrity.html?_r=0

Benzmiller, H. (2013). The cyber-samaritans: Exploring criminal liability for the 'innocent' bystanders of cyberbullying. *Northwestern University Law Review*, *107*(2), 927–962.

Bercow, J. (2014). *Why the future of democracy is digital*. Retrieved from http://www.theguardian.com/public-leaders-network/2014/jun/16/john-bercow-digital-democracy-parliamentutm_content=buffera4aaf&utm_medium=social&utm_source=facebook.com&utm_campaign=buffer

Berger, J. (1980). *About looking*. New York: Pantheon Books.

Best, S. J., Krueger, B. S., & Ladewig, J. (2007). The Effect of Risk Perceptions on Online Political Participatory Decisions. *Journal of Information Technology & Politics*, *4*(1), 5–17. doi:10.1300/J516v04n01_02

Best, S., & Krueger, B. S. (2005). Analyzing the representativeness of Internet political participation. *Political Behavior*, *27*(2), 183–216. doi:10.1007/s11109-005-3242-y

Beyle, T. (1990). Costs of Gubernatorial Campaigns! 987-1988. *Comparative State Politics*, *11*(1), 28–33.

Bias, S. (2015). *I stood up to a fat-shaming bully on a train because I'm tired of fighting for the right to exist*. Retrieved from http://www.xojane.com/issues/fat-shaming-train-bully

Biesecker, B. (2007). No time for mourning: The rhetorical production of the melancholic citizen-subject in the war of terror. *Philosophy & Rhetoric*, *40*(1), 147–169. doi:10.1353/par.2007.0009

Bimber, B. (1998). The Internet and Political Transformation: Populism, Community, and Accelerated Pluralism. *Polity*, *31*(1), 133–160. doi:10.2307/3235370

Bimber, B. (1999). The Internet and Citizen Communication With Government: Does the Medium Matter? *Political Communication*, *16*(4), 409–428. doi:10.1080/105846099198569

Bimber, B. (2000). Measuring the gender gap on the internet. *Social Science Quarterly*, *81*(3), 868–876.

Bimber, B., & Copeland, L. (2013). Digital Media and Traditional Political Participation Over Time in the U.S. *Journal of Information Technology & Politics*, *10*(2), 125–137. doi:10.1080/19331681.2013.769925

Bimber, B., & Davis, R. (2003). *Campaigning Online: The Internet in U.S. Elections*. New York: Oxford University Press.

Bimber, B., Stohl, C., & Flanagin, A. J. (2009). Technological Change and the Shifting Nature of Political Organization. In A. Chadwick & P. N. Howard (Eds.), *Routledge Handbook of Internet Politics* (pp. 72–85). London: Routledge.

Bishop, J. (2007a). Ecological cognition: A new dynamic for human-computer interaction. In B. Wallace, A. Ross, J. Davies & T. Anderson (Eds.), The mind, the body and the world: Psychology after cognitivism (pp. 327-345). Exeter, UK: Imprint Academic.

Bishop, J. (2011). *The role of the prefrontal cortex in social orientation construction: A pilot study*. Poster Presented to the BPS Welsh Conference on Wellbeing, Wrexham, UK.

Bishop, J. (2012). The antisocial network and 'electronic message faults': Prevalence of troublesome online youth groups and internet trolling in Great Britain. Swansea, UK: The Crocels Press.

Bishop, J., & Goode, M. M. H. (2014). Towards a subjectively devised parametric user model for analysing and influencing behaviour online using gamification: A review and model. In Gamification for human factors integration: Social, educational, and psychological issues (pp. 80-95). Hershey, PA: IGI Global.

Bishop, J. (2007b). Increasing participation in online communities: A framework for human–computer interaction. *Computers in Human Behavior*, *23*(4), 1881–1893. doi:10.1016/j.chb.2005.11.004

Bishop, J. (2008). Increasing capital revenue in social networking communities: Building social and economic relationships through avatars and characters. In C. Romm-Livermore & K. Setzekorn (Eds.), *Social networking communities and eDating services: Concepts and implications* (pp. 60–77). Hershey, PA: IGI Global.

Bishop, J. (2009). Increasing membership in online communities: The five principles of managing virtual club economies. *Proceedings of the 3rd International Conference on Internet Technologies and Applications - ITA09*. Glyndwr University.

Bishop, J. (2010). Increasing the economic sustainability of online communities: An empirical investigation. In M. F. Hindsworth & T. B. Lang (Eds.), *Community participation and empowerment* (p. 349). New York, NY: Nova Science Publishers.

Bishop, J. (2011a). All's WELL that ends WELL: A comparative analysis of the constitutional and administrative frameworks of cyberspace and the united kingdom. In A. Dudley-Sponaugle & J. Braman (Eds.), *Investigating cyber law and cyber ethics: Issues, impacts and practices*. Hershey, PA: IGI Global.

Bishop, J. (2011b). *The equatrics of intergenerational knowledge transformation in techno-cultures: Towards a model for enhancing information management in virtual worlds. Unpublished MScEcon*. Aberystwyth, UK: Aberystwyth University.

Bishop, J. (2011c). Transforming lurkers into posters: The role of the participation continuum.*The Fourth International Conference on Internet Technologies and Applications (ITA'11)*.

Bishop, J. (2012a). Lessons from the emotivate project for increasing take-up of big society and responsible capitalism initiatives. In P. M. Pumilia-Gnarini, E. Favaron, E. Pacetti, J. Bishop, & L. Guerra (Eds.), *Didactic strategies and technologies for education: Incorporating advancements* (pp. 208–217). Hershey, PA: IGI Global. doi:10.4018/978-1-4666-2122-0.ch019

Bishop, J. (2012b). Scope and limitations in the government of wales act 2006 for tackling internet abuses in the form of Flame trolling. *Statute Law Review*, *33*(2), 207–216. doi:10.1093/slr/hms016

Bishop, J. (2012c). Taming the chatroom bob: The role of brain-computer interfaces that manipulate prefrontal cortex optimization for increasing participation of victims of traumatic sex and other abuse online.*Proceedings of the 13th International Conference on Bioinformatics and Computational Biology (BIOCOMP'12)*.

Bishop, J. (2013a). The effect of deindividuation of the internet troller on criminal procedure implementation: An interview with a hater. *International Journal of Cyber Criminology*, *7*(1), 28–48.

Bishop, J. (2013b). Increasing capital revenue in social networking communities: Building social and economic relationships through avatars and characters. In J. Bishop (Ed.), *Examining the concepts, issues, and implications of internet trolling* (pp. 44–61). Hershey, PA: IGI Global. doi:10.4018/978-1-4666-2803-8.ch005

Bishop, J. (2013c). The psychology of trolling and lurking: The role of defriending and gamification for increasing participation in online communities using seductive narratives. In J. Bishop (Ed.), *Examining the concepts, issues and implications of internet trolling* (pp. 106–123). Hershey, PA: IGI Global. doi:10.4018/978-1-4666-2803-8.ch009

Bishop, J. (2014a). Digital teens and the antisocial network: Prevalence of troublesome online youth groups and internet trolling in great Britain. *International Journal of E-Politics*, *5*(3), 1–15. doi:10.4018/ijep.2014070101

Bishop, J. (2014b). Representations of trolls in mass media communication: A review of media-texts and moral panics relating to internet trolling. *International Journal of Web Based Communities*, *10*(1), 7–24. doi:10.1504/IJWBC.2014.058384

Blair, C., Brown, J., & Baxter, L. (1999). Disciplining the feminine. In Contemporary rhetorical theory (pp. 563-590). New York, NY: The Guilford Press.

Blake, H. (2011, February 28). Hugh Fearnley-Whittingstall wins his Fish Fight: Discarding dead fish may be banned. *The Telegraph*. Retrieved from http://www.telegraph.co.uk/news/worldnews/europe/8350443/Hugh-Fearnley-Whittingstall-wins-his-Fish-Fight-discarding-dead-fish-may-be-banned.html

Blazquez, N. (2008). *El retorno de las brujas*. CEIICH UNAM.

Block, E. (2013). A culturalist approach to the concept of the mediatization of politics: The age of media hegemony. *Communication Theory*, *23*(3), 259–278. doi:10.1111/comt.12016

Blogger, G. (2012, April 18). *The impossible trend: Look like Barbie*. Retrieved from http://www.thefword.org.uk/blog/2012/04/the_impossible_

Blyth, M. (2013a). Austerity as ideology: A reply to my critics. *Comparative European Politics*, *11*(6), 737–751. doi:10.1057/cep.2013.25

Blyth, M. (2013b). The austerity delusion: Why a bad idea won over the West. *Foreign Affairs*, (May/June): 1–11.

Bode, L. (2012). Facebooking It to the Polls: A Study in Online Social Networking and Political Behavior. *Journal of Information Technology & Politics*, *9*(4), 352–369. doi:10.1080/19331681.2012.709045

Bodomo, A. (2011). Strategies for Enhancing and Evaluating Interactivity in Web-Based Learning and Teaching. In Evaluating the Impact of Technology on Learning, Teaching, and Designing Curriculum: Emerging Trends. Hershey, PA: IGI Global.

Body Mass Index (BMI). (n.d.). *WebMD*. Retrieved from http://webmd.com/men/weight-loss-bmi

Bogart, L. (2015, May 31). I will wear a swimsuit one day: Manifesto of a righteous fat-ass. *Salon.com*. Retrieved from http://salon.com/2015/06/01/I_will_wear_a_swimsuit_one_day

Bokus. (2015). *Bestseller list - Medical literature* [my translation]. Retrieved February 5, 2015, from www.bokus.com/topplistor/medicin

Bolin, G., & Westlund, O. (2008). Mobile generations: The role of mobile technology in the shaping of swedish media generations. *International Journal of Communication*, *3*, 17.

Bonchek, M. S. (1995). *Grassroots in Cyberspace: Using Computer Networks to Facilitate Political Participation*. Presented at the Midwest Political Science Association, 53rd Annual Meeting, Chicago, IL.

Bonetta, L. (2007). Scientists Enter the Blogosphere. *Cell*, *129*(3), 443–445. doi:10.1016/j.cell.2007.04.032 PMID:17482534

Bonsu, S. K., & Darmody, A. (2008). Co-creating Second Life: Market-Consumer Cooperation in Contemporary Economy. *Journal of Macromarketing*, *24*(4), 355–368. doi:10.1177/0276146708325396

Booth, W. (1974). *A rhetoric of irony*. Chicago, IL: University of Chicago Press.

Bormann, E. G., Cragan, J. F., & Shields, D. C. (2001). Three decades of developing, grounding, and using Symbolic Convergence Theory (SCT). In W. Gudykunst (Ed.), *Communication Yearbook 25* (pp. 271–313). Yahweh, NJ: Lawrence Earlbaum. doi:10.1080/23808985.2001.11679006

Bormann, E. G., Cragan, J. F., & Shields, D. C. (2003). Defending Symbolic Convergence Theory from an imaginary Gunn. *The Quarterly Journal of Speech*, *89*(4), 366–372. doi:10.1080/0033563032000160990

Boulianne, S. (2009). Does Internet Use Affect Engagement? A Meta-Analysis of Research. *Political Communication*, *26*(2), 193–211. doi:10.1080/10584600902854363

boyd, D. (2010). Social network sites as networked publics: Affordances, dynaicms, and implications. In Z. Papacharissi (Ed.), *Networked self: Identity, community, and culture on social network sites* (pp. 39-58). New York, NY: Routledge.

Boynton, B. (2009). Going Viral: The Dynamics of Attention. In S. Shulman & M. Xenos (Eds.), 1st Annual Journal of Information Technology & Politics Conference, YouTube and the 2008 Election Cycle in the United States (pp. 11–39). University of Massachusetts.

Bradham, D. (2013). Crowdsourcing: A model for leveraging online communities. In A. Delwiche & J. Henderson (Eds.), *The participatory culture handbook* (pp. 120–129). New York, NY: Routledge.

Brändli, M. (2014). *"Politics as usual?" Explaining the use of online communication by political interest groups in Switzerland*. Academic Press.

Braun, V., & Clarke, V. (2006). Using thematic analysis in psychology. *Qualitative Research in Psychology*, *3*(2), 77–101. doi:10.1191/1478088706qp063oa

Bravo, L. (n.d.). Fish labels debunked. *Channel 4*. Retrieved from http://www.channel4.com/programmes/hughs-fish-fight/articles/all/fish-labels-debunked

Breuer, A. (2012). *The Role of Social Media in Mobilizing Political Protest*. Bonn: D.I.E.

Brillat-Savarin, A. (1826). *Physiologie du gout, ou meditations de gastronomie transcendante*. Paris, France: Feydeau.

Brough, M. M., & Shresthova, S. (2012). Fandom meets activism: Rethinking civic and political participation. *Transformative Works and Cultures*, *10*. doi:10.3983/twc.2012.0303

Brown, K. G. (2002). *Influence of job characteristics and perceived learning support on e-learning activity*. Paper presented at the Seventeenth Annual Meeting of the Society of Industrial and Organizational Psychology, Toronto, Canada.

Brown, K. G. (2002). *Influence of job characteristics and perceived learning support on eLearning activity*. Paper presented in seventeenth Annual Meeting of the Society of Industrial and Organizational Psychology, Toronto, Canada.

Brunel, O., & Pichon, P.-E. (2004). Food-related risk-reduction strategies: Purchasing and consumption processes. *Journal of Consumer Behaviour*, *3*(4), 360–374. doi:10.1002/cb.148

Bryant, E. I. (2012). The Iron Fist vs. the Microchip. *Journal of Strategic Security*, *5*(2), 1–26. doi:10.5038/1944-0472.5.2.1

Bryde, D., & Pelie, D. (2006). The impact of project management practices and project sponsorship on project performance. In M. Khosrow-Pour (Ed.), *Emerging trends and challenges in information technology management* (pp. 122–126). Hershey, PA: IGI Global.

Bucchi, M. (1998). *Science and the Media: Alternative routes in scientific communication*. London: Routledge. doi:10.4324/9780203263839

Buckels, E. F., Trapnell, P. D., & Paulhaus, D. L. (2014). Trolls just want to have fun. *Personality and Individual Differences*, *67*, 97–102. doi:10.1016/j.paid.2014.01.016

Burgin, V. (1982). *Thinking photography*. London: Macmillan. doi:10.1007/978-1-349-16716-6

Burke, K. (n.d.). A grammar of motives. Berkeley, CA: University of California Press.

Butler, P. (2013, July 23). Jack Monroe: The face of modern poverty. *The Guardian*. Retrieved from http://www.theguardian.com/society/2013/jul/23/jack-monroe-face-modern-poverty

Butler, J. (2007). Torture and the ethics of photography. *Environment and Planning. D, Society & Space*, *25*(6), 951–966. doi:10.1068/d2506jb

Byerly, C. (2002). Gender and the Political Economy of Newsmaking: A Case Study of Human Rights Coverage. In Sex & Money, Feminism and Political Economy in the Media. University of Minnesota Press.

Cai, D. A., & Fink, E. L. (2002). Conflict style differences between individualists and collectivists. *Communication Monographs*, *69*(1), 67–87. doi:10.1080/03637750216536

Campbell, J., Fletcher, G., & Greenhill, A. (2009). Conflict and identity shape shifting in an online financial community. *Information Systems Journal*, *19*(5), 461–478. doi:10.1111/j.1365-2575.2008.00301.x

Campbell, S. W. (2013). Mobile media and communication: A new field, or just a new journal? *Mobile Media & Communication*, *1*(1), 8–13. doi:10.1177/2050157912459495

Caplan, P. (2016). Big society or broken society? *Anthropology Today*, *32*(1), 5–9. doi:10.1111/1467-8322.12223

Cappella, J. N., & Jamieson, K. H. (1997). *Spiral of cynicism*. New York: Oxford University Press.

Cappelli, P. (1998). *The New Deal at Work: Managing the Market-driven Workforce*. Boston: Harvard University School Press.

Caraher, M., & Cavacchi, A. (2014). Old crises on new plates or old plates for a new crises? Food banks and food insecurity. *British Food Journal*, *116*(9), 1426–1445.

Caraher, M., & Coveney, J. (2016). Food poverty and insecurity: The poor in a world of global austerity. In M. Caraher & J. Coveney (Eds.), *Food poverty and insecurity: International food inequalities* (pp. 1–8). Heidelberg, Germany: Springer. doi:10.1007/978-3-319-23859-3_1

Carpentier, N., & Dahlgren, P. (2014). The social relevance of participatory theory. In G. Patriarche, H. Bilandzic, N. Carpentier, C. Ponte, K. C. Schrøder, & F. Zeller (Eds.), Building bridges: Pathways to a greater societal significance for audience research (pp. 37–52). Brussels, Belgium: COST Action ISO906.

Carpentier, N. (2011). *Media and participation: A site of ideological–democratic struggle*. Bristol, UK: Intellect.

Carpentier, N. (2015). Differentiating between access, interaction and participation. *Conjunctions: Transdisciplinary Journal of Cultural Participation*, 2(2), 7–28. doi:10.7146/tjcp.v2i2.22915

Carpentier, N. (2016). Beyond the ladder of participation: An analytical toolkit for the critical analysis of participatory media processes. *Javnost. The Public*, *23*(1), 70–88.

Carsey, T. (2001). *Campaign Dynamics: The Race for Governor*. Ann Arbor, MI: University of Michigan Press.

Casey, K. (2013). *Crossing party lines: The effects of information on redistributive politics*. Academic Press.

Castaño, C. (2005). *Las mujeres y las tecnologías de la información. Internet y la trama de nustra vida*. Madrid: Alianza Editorial.

Castells, M., & Díaz, M. H. (2009). *Comunicación y Poder*. Madrid, España: Alianza Editorial.

Castells, M. (1996). The Information Age: Economy, Society and Culture.: Vol. I. *The Rise of the Network Society*. Oxford, UK: Blackwell Publishers.

Castells, M. (2007). Communication, power and counter-power in the network society. *International Journal of Communication, 1*, 238–266.

Cederholm, T., & Rothenberg, E. (2016). Krypskytte mot vetenskapen äventyrar folkhälsosatsningar[Sniper attacks against science jeopardize public health investments]. *Lakartidningen, 113*(16).

Center for Human Rights and Global Justice. (2011). *Every thirty minutes: Farmer suicides, human rights, and the agrarian crisis in India*. New York: NYU School of Law.

CEPAL (2014). *El nuevo paradigma productivo y tecnológico. La necesidad de políticas para la autonomía económica de las mujeres*. CEPAL.

Chadwick, A. (2006). *Internet Politics: States, Citizens, and New Communications Technologies*. New York: Oxford University Press.

Chakrabortty, A. (2015, February 3). Britain's epidemic of private despair makes this an economic crisis like no other. There is no public spectacle to observe. But behind closed doors an everyday wretchedness blights lives. *The Guardian*. Retrieved from http://www.theguardian.com/commentisfree/2015/feb/03/britain-economic-crisis-public

Chalfen, R. (1987). *Snapshot Versions of Life*. Bowling Green, OH: Popular Press.

Chamberlain, K. (2004). Food and Health: Expanding the Agenda for Health Psychology. *Journal of Health Psychology, 9*(4), 467–481. doi:10.1177/1359105304044030 PMID:15231050

Chan, M. (2016). Social Network Sites and Political Engagement: Exploring the Impact of Facebook Connections and Uses on Political Protest and Participation. *Mass Communication & Society, 19*(4), 430–451. doi:10.1080/15205436.2016.1161803

Channel 4. (n.d.a). *Campaign results*. Retrieved from http://www.channel4.com/programmes/the-great-british-property-scandal/articles/all/campaign-results

Channel 4. (n.d.b). *The Great British Property Scandal*. Retrieved from http://www.channel4.com/programmes/the-great-british-property-scandal

Chapman, R. G., & Palda, K. S. (1983). Electoral turnout in rational voting and consumption perspectives. *The Journal of Consumer Research, 9*(4), 337–346. doi:10.1086/208928

Chase, E., & Bantebya-Kyomuhendo, G. (2014). *Poverty and shame: Global experiences*. Oxford, UK: Oxford University Press.

Chivers, T. (2014, March 2). Hugh's Fish Fight, Channel 4, review. *The Telegraph*. Retrieved from http://www.telegraph.co.uk/culture/tvandradio/tv-and-radio-reviews/10669329/Hughs-Fish-Fight-Channel-4-review.html

Chozik, A. (2016, May). Hillary Clinton targets republicans turned off by Donald Trump. *New York Times*. Retrieved May 9, 2016, from http://www.nytimes.com/2016/05/07/us/politics/hillary-clinton-republican-party.html

Christensen, C. L. (2008). Livsstil som TV-underholdning. *Journal of Media and Communication Research, 45*, 23–36.

Chullo, S. (2016). *Museveni's Flawed Election Victory in Uganda*. Retrieved from http://www.huffingtonpost.com/stan-chu-ilo/musevenis-flawed-election_b_9349490.html

CIPESA. (2014). *State of Internet Freedoms in East Africa*. Retrieved October 25, 2014, from http://www.cipesa.org/?wpfb_dl=76

CIPESA. (2016). *Uganda Again Blocks Social Media to Stifle Anti-Museveni Protests*. Retrieved from http://cipesa.org/2016/05/uganda-again-blocks-social-media-to-stifle-anti-museveni-protests/

Cirone, A. E., & Urpelainen, J. (2013). Political market failure? The effect of government unity on energy technology policy in industrialized democracies. *Technovation*, *33*(10), 333–344. doi:10.1016/j.technovation.2013.06.001

Clarke, H., Sanders, D., Stewart, M., & Whiteley, P. (2004). Theories and Models of Turnout. In Political Choice in Britain. Oxford, UK: Oxford University Press.

Clarke, J., Gewirtz, S., & McLaughlin, E. (2000). Reinventing the welfare state. In *New managerialism, new welfare* (pp. 1–26). London, UK: Sage. Retrieved from https://books.google.co.uk/books?hl=en&lr=&id=1nLeXq_V4HQC&oi=fnd&pg=PA1&dq=(reinventing+the+welfare+state)&ots=l4cFFd7Frg&sig=doEzKzgxZFXnKBieZQMAwpc80fQ#v=onepage&q=(reinventing the welfare state)&f=false

Clay, X. (2013, March 4). My 49p lunch with a girl called Jack. *The Telegraph*. Retrieved from http://www.telegraph.co.uk/foodanddrink/9900773/My-49p-lunch-with-a-girl-called-Jack.html

Cleaver, H. (1998). The Zapatista Effect: The Internet and the Rise of an Alternative Political Fabric. *Journal of International Affairs*, *51*(2), 621–640.

Clery, L., & Lee, L. (2013, April). Public attitudes to poverty and welfare 1983–2011. *Joseph Rowntree Foundation Report*. Retrieved from http://www.natcen.ac.uk/our-research/research/public-attitudes-to-poverty-and-welfare-1983-2011/

Cleveland, A. (2014, February 5). *Twitter*. Retrieved February 10, 2015, from https://twitter.com/BrunetteWife/status/431074346409279488

Cockburn, A. (1977, December). Gastro-Porn. *The New York Review of Books*, *8*. Retrieved from www.nybooks.com/articles/8309

Coe, K., Kenski, K., & Rains, S. A. (2014). Online and uncivil? Patterns and determinants of incivility in newspaper website comments. *Journal of Communication*, *64*(4), 659–679. doi:10.1111/jcom.12104

Cohen, C., Kahne, J., Bowyer, B., Middaugh, E., & Rogowski, J. (2012). *Participatory politics: New media and youth political action*. Oakland, CA: Mills College School of Education.

Coleman, S. (2005). Direct Representation. Towards A Conversational Democracy. London: The Institute for Public Policy Research (IPPR).

Coleman, S., & Firmstone, J. (2014a). *Contested Meanings of Public Engagement: Exploring Discourse and Practice within a British City Council*. Media, Culture and Society.

Coleman, S., & Blumer, J. (2001). *Realising Democracy Online: A civic commons in cyberspace*. London: IPPR.

Coleman, S., & Firmstone, J. (2014b). *Public engagement in local government: The voice and influence of citizens in online communicative spaces*. London: *IPPR*.

Coleman, S., & Gotze, J. (2001). *Bowling together: Online Public Engagement in Policy Deliberation*. London: Hansard Society.

Conlin, J. (2014, February 9). A big reveal touches a nerve. *The New York Times*.

Conrad, C. (1991). Communication in conflict: Style-strategy relationships. *Communication Monographs*, *58*(2), 135–151. doi:10.1080/03637759109376219

Conroy, M., Feezell, J. T., & Guerrero, M. (2012). Facebook and political engagement: A study of online political group membership and offline political engagement. *Computers in Human Behavior*, *28*(5), 1535–1546. doi:10.1016/j.chb.2012.03.012

Cornfield, M. (2004). *Politics Moves Online*. The Century Foundation.

Corrado, A., & Firestone, C. (1996). *Elections in Cyberspace: Toward a New Era in American Politics*. Washington, DC: The Aspen Institute.

Costa, O. (2013). Conclusion: Challenging the conventional wisdoms about parliamentary representation in France. *Journal of Legislative Studies*, *19*(2), 278–283. doi:10.1080/13572334.2013.787202

Couldry, N. (2009). Rethinking the politics of voice. *Continuum (Perth)*, *23*(4), 579–582. doi:10.1080/10304310903026594

Couldry, N., Markham, T., & Livingstone, S. (2005). *Media consumption and the future of public connection*. London, UK: London School of Economics and Political Science.

Council of Europe Research Division. (2011). *Internet: case-law of the European Court of Human Rights*. Available at. http://www.echr.coe.int/ECHR/EN/Header/Case-Law/Case-law+analysis/Research+reports/

Counihan, C., & Van Esterik, P. (2013). *Food and Culture: A Reader* (Vol. 3). New York: Routledge.

Craig, S. C. (1979). Efficacy, trust, and political behavior. *American Politics Research*, *7*(2), 225–239. doi:10.1177/1532673X7900700207

Craig, S. C., Niemi, R. G., & Silver, G. E. (1990). Political efficacy and trust: A report on the NES pilot study items. *Political Behavior*, *12*(3), 289–314. doi:10.1007/BF00992337

Crandall, A., & Mutuku, L. (2011). *MGovernance: Exploratory Survey on Kenyan Service Delivery and Government Interaction*. Retrieved July 12, 2014, from http://ict4dem.dsv.su.se/wp-content/files/iHub_M-Governance_Survey_on_Kenyan_Service_Delivery_and_Government_Interaction.pdf

Craven, N. (2013, February 16). Horsemeat scandal: We eat as many ready meals as the rest of Europe combined—Britain's passion for the cheapest food. *Financial Mail on Sunday*. Retrieved from http://www.dailymail.co.uk/money/news/article-2279664/Chilling-truth-horsemeat-scandal-ALL-blame.html#ixzz2Lf4RYofE

Crawford, R. (1980). Healthism and the medicalization of everyday life. *International Journal of Health Services*, *10*(3), 365–388. doi:10.2190/3H2H-3XJN-3KAY-G9NY PMID:7419309

Criado, J., Martínez-Fuentes, G., & Silván, A. (2012). Social Media for Political Campaigning. The Use of Twitter by Spanish Mayors in 2011 Local Elections. In C. G. Reddick & S. K. Aikins (Eds.), *Web 2.0 Technologies and Democratic Governance* (Vol. 1, pp. 219–232). Springer New York. doi:10.1007/978-1-4614-1448-3_14

Cronin, J., McCarthy, M., Newcombe, M., & McCarthy, S. (2014). Paradox, performance and food: Managing difference in the construction of femininity. *Consumption Markets & Culture*, *17*(4), 367–391. doi:10.1080/10253866.2013.872548

Cross, J. (2004). An Informal History of eLearning. *On the Horizon, 12*(3), 103-110.

Cross, J. (2004). An Informal History of eLearning. *On the Horizon*, *12*(3), 103–110. doi:10.1108/10748120410555340

Cullen, R., & Sommer, L. (2011). Participatory democracy and the value of online community networks: An exploration of online and offline communities engaged in civil society and political activity. *Government Information Quarterly*, *28*(2), 148–154. doi:10.1016/j.giq.2010.04.008

Cummings, J. N., Sproull, L., & Kiesler, S. B. (2002). Beyond hearing: Where the realworld and online support meet. *Group Dynamics*, *6*(1), 78–88. doi:10.1037/1089-2699.6.1.78

Cwiertka, J. K. (2006). *Modern Japanese cuisine: food, power and national identity*. London: Reaktion Books.

Dahlgren, P. (2013). Do social media enhance democratic participation? – The importance and difficulty of being realistic. Policy Paper No. 4/2013. Academic Press.

Dahlgren, P. (2009). *Media and Political Engagement: Citizens, Communication and Democracy*. Cambridge: Cambridge University Press.

Dahlqvist, A. (2014). Mai-Lis Hellenius: Sedentary disease [my translation]. *Dr Dahlqvist's blog concerning food and health*. Retrieved January 18, 2015, from http://annikadahlqvist.com/2014/07/06/mai-lis-hellenius-sittsjukan/

Dahlqvist, A. (2015). About Dr Annika Dahlqvist [my translation]. *Dr Annika Dahlqvist's weblog about food and health*. Retrieved January 21, 2015, from http://annikadahlqvist.com/om-dr-annika-dahlqvist/

Dalisay, F. (2012). The spiral of silence and conflict avoidance: Examining antecedents of opinion expression concerning the U.S. military buildup in the Pacific Island of Guam. *Communication Quarterly*, *60*(4), 481–503. doi:10.1080/01463373.2012.704567

Dalrymple, K. E., & Scheufele, D. A. (2007). Finally Informing the Electorate? How the Internet Got People Thinking about Presidential Politics in 2004. *The Harvard International Journal of Press/Politics*, *12*(3), 96–111. doi:10.1177/1081180X07302881

Daly, T. M., Lee, J. A., Soutar, G. N., & Rasmi, S. (2010). Conflict-handling style measurement: A best-worst scaling application. *The International Journal of Conflict Management*, *21*(3), 281–308. doi:10.1108/10444061011063180

Damore, D. (2002). Candidate Strategy and the Decision to go Negative. *Political Research Quarterly*, *55*(3), 669–686. doi:10.1177/106591290205500309

Dang-Xuan, L., Stieglitz, S., Wladarsch, J., & Neuberger, C. (2013). An Investigation of Influentials and the Role of Sentiment in Political Communication on Twitter During Election Periods. *Information Communication and Society*, *16*(5), 795–825. doi:10.1080/1369118X.2013.783608

Davis, J. K. (2003). Self-Experimentation. *Accountability in Research*, *10*(3), 175–187. doi:10.1080/714906095 PMID:14979319

Davison, C., Smith, G. D., & Frankel, S. (1991). Lay epidemiology and the prevention paradox: The implications of coronary candidacy for health education. *Sociology of Health & Illness*, *13*(1), 1–19. doi:10.1111/1467-9566.ep11340301

Davis, R. (1999). *The web of politics: The Internet's impact on the American political system*. New York: Oxford University.

Davis, R. (2005). *Politics online: Blogs, chatrooms, and discussion groups in American democracy*. New York: Routledge.

De Brun, A., McCarthy, M., McKenzie, K., & McGloin, A. (2014). Weight stigma and narrative resistance evident in online discussions of obesity. *Appetite*, *72*, 73–81. doi:10.1016/j.appet.2013.09.022 PMID:24096083

De Certeau, M., Giard, L., & Mayol, P. (1998). The Practice of Everyday Life, Volume 2: Living and Cooking. University of Minnesota Press.

de Zúñiga, H. G., Bachmann, I., Hsu, S.-H., & Brundidge, J. (2013). Expressive Versus Consumptive Blog Use: Implications for Interpersonal Discussion and Political Participation. *International Journal of Communication*, *7*(0), 22.

Deans, J. (2013, August 27). Jamie Oliver bemoans chips, cheese and giant TVs of modern-day poverty. *The Guardian*. Retrieved from http://www.theguardian.com/lifeandstyle/2013/aug/27/jamie-oliver-chips-cheese-modern-day-poverty

dear-melinda-count-me-in. (n.d.). *Tumblr.* Retrieved from: http://www.tumblr.com/search/body+image+rant+

Dee, T. S. (2004). Are there civic returns to education? *Journal of Public Economics*, *88*(9), 1697–1720. doi:10.1016/j.jpubeco.2003.11.002

Deibert, R. (2008). Access Denied: The Practice and Policy of Global Internet Filtering. MIT Press.

Denveater. (2009). The virtual roundtable: Food blogging as citizen journalism. *World Literature Today, 83*(1), 42–46.

Department for Environment, Food & Rural Affairs. (2016). *UK fishermen see next phase of the discard ban take effect* [Press release]. Retrieved from https://www.gov.uk/government/news/uk-fishermen-see-next-phase-of-the-discard-ban-take-effect

Deutsch, M. (2005, March). The nature and origins of oppression. *Beyond Intractability.* Retrieved from http://beyondintractability.org/essay/nature-origins-oppression

Dhaha, I. S. Y., & Igale, A. B. (2013). Facebook Usage among Somali Youth. A Test of Uses and Gratifications Approach. *International Journal of Humanities and Social Science*, *3*(3).

Diet Fund. (2014a). *About the diet fund* [my translation]. Retrieved January 27, 2015, from http://www.kostfonden.se/om-kostfonden/

Diet Fund. (2014b). *Our vision: more people should lead a healthier life* [my translation]. Retrieved January 3, 2015, from http://www.kostfonden.se/var-vision-fler-manniskor-ska-leva-ett-friskare-liv/

Dimitrova, D. V., & Bystrom, D. (2013). The Effects of Social Media on Political Participation and Candidate Image Evaluations in the 2012 Iowa Caucuses. *The American Behavioral Scientist*, *57*(11), 1568–1583. doi:10.1177/0002764213489011

Dimitrova, D. V., Shehata, A., Strömbäck, J., & Nord, L. W. (2014). The Effects of Digital Media on Political Knowledge and Participation in Election Campaigns Evidence From Panel Data. *Communication Research*, *41*(1), 95–118. doi:10.1177/0093650211426004

DN. (2013). *The popular high fat diets are a threat to public health* [my translation]. Retrieved January 8, 2015, from http://www.dn.se/debatt/de-populara-fettdieterna-ar-ett-hot-mot-folkhalsan/

Doctor, D. (2008). *The National Board of Health and Welfare approves of low carb diet* [my translation]. Retrieved January 18, 2015, from http://www.kostdoktorn.se/socialstyrelsen-godkanner-lagkolhydratskost

Doctor, D. (2012). *Food revolution: consume real food and eat your way to a better health* [my translation]. Retrieved February 4, 2015, from https://www.youtube.com/watch?v=9Hy737EuL-o

Doctor, D. (2013). *We who want to close down the National food agency* [my translation]. Retrieved January 12, 2015, from http://www.kostdoktorn.se/vi-som-vill-avveckla-livsmedelsverket

Doctor, D. (2014a). *My blood values after eight years of following the LCHF diet* [my translation]. Retrieved January 17, 2015, from http://www.kostdoktorn.se/mina-halsovarden-efter-atta-ar-pa-lchf

Doctor, D. (2014b). *Overall, I Now Have a Completely New Life.* Retrieved February 3, 2015, from http://www.dietdoctor.com/overall-now-completely-new-life

Doctor, D. (2015a). *About Diet Doctor.* Retrieved January 2, 2015, from http://www.dietdoctor.com/about

Doctor, D. (2015b). *The Launch of the Amazing LCHF Conference*. Retrieved February 27, 2015, from http://www.dietdoctor.com/the-launch-of-the-lchf-conference

Doctor, D. (2015c). *Reliable health products* [my translation]. Retrieved January 23, 2015, from http://www.kostdoktorn.se/rekommenderade-halsoprodukter

Douglas, M. (2003). *Food in the social order: Studies of food and festivities in three American communities*. London, UK: Routledge.

Dowler, E., & Lambie-Mumford, H. (2015a). How can households eat in austerity? Challenges for social policy in the UK. *Social Policy and Society*, *14*(3), 417–428. doi:10.1017/S1474746415000032

Dowler, E., & Lambie-Mumford, H. (2015b). Introduction: Hunger, food and social policy in austerity. *Social Policy and Society*, *14*(3), 411–415. doi:10.1017/S1474746415000159

Dowler, E., & OConnor, D. (2012). Rights-based approaches to addressing food poverty. *Social Science & Medicine*, *74*(1), 44–71. doi:10.1016/j.socscimed.2011.08.036 PMID:22000764

Down on the social farm [Editorial]. (2010, August 14). *The New York Times*, p. A18.

Downing, E., Kennedy, S., & Fell, M. (2014). *Food banks and food poverty*. London, UK: House of Commons. Retrieved from http://www.parliament.uk/briefing-papers/SN06657/food-banks-and-food-poverty

Doyle, J. (2012). New media and democratisation. *Irish Studies in International Affairs*, *23*, 1-4. doi:10.3318/ISIA.2012.23.1

Drory, A., & Romm, C. T. (1991). The definition of organizational politics: A review. *Human Relations*, *43*(11), 1133–1154. doi:10.1177/001872679004301106

Drucker, P. (2000). *Need to Know: Integrating e- Learning with High Velocity Value Chains*. A Delphi Group White Paper.

Druckman, J. N., Kifer, M. J., & Parkin, M. (2010). Timeless Strategy Meets New Medium: Going Negative on Congressional Campaign Web Sites 20022006. *Political Communication*, *27*(1), 88–103. doi:10.1080/10584600903502607

Dubois, E., & Gaffney, D. (2014). The Multiple Facets of Influence: Identifying Political Influentials and Opinion Leaders on Twitter. *The American Behavioral Scientist*, *58*(10), 1260–1277. doi:10.1177/0002764214527088

Duggan, M. (2013). *Video and Photo Sharing Grow Online*. Pew Research Centre. Retrieved from http://www.pewinternet.org/2013/10/28/photo-and-video-sharing-grow-online/

Dulio, D. A., Goff, D. L., & Thurber, J. A. (1999). Untangled Web: Internet Use during the 1998 Election. *PS: Political Science and Politics*, *32*(1), 53–59.

Dunne, K. (2009). Cross cutting discussion: A form of online discussion discovered within local political online forums. *Information Polity*, *14*, 219.

Dupraz, S., Muller, D., & Page, L. (2013). Tactical voting and voter's sophistication in British elections. In Digitally enabled social change: Activism in the internet age. MIT Press.

Durkheim, E. (1976). *The Elementary Forms of Religious Life*. Free Press.

Dutton, W. H., & Peltu, M. (2007). Reconfiguring Government-Public Engagements: Enhancing the Communicative Power of Citizens 2007. Oxford Internet Institute.

Duvall, S. (2011). *Top 10 Countries Celebrating Female Obesity*. Retrieved from http://www.toptenz.net/top-10-countries-celebrating-female-obesity.php

EC. (2010). *Women and ICT Status Report 2009*. Lisbon: European Commision.

Eckler, P., Worsowicz, G., & Rayburn, J. W. (2010). Social Media and Health Care: An Overview. *PM & R*, *2*(11), 1046–1050. doi:10.1016/j.pmrj.2010.09.005 PMID:21093840

Edelman Trust Barometer. (2012). Retrieved 12 April, 2015, from http://trust.edelman.com/trust-download/global-results/

Edmonds, G., & Gray, D. (2002). Internet dictionary. London: Dorling Kindersley Limited.

Effing, R., Hillegersberg, J. van, & Huibers, T. W. C. (2013). *Social Media Participation and Local Politics: A Case Study*. Enschede Council in the Netherlands.

Effing, R., van Hillegersberg, J., & Huibers, T. (2011). *Social Media and Political Participation: Are Facebook, Twitter and YouTube Democratizing Our Political Systems?* Springer Berlin / Heidelberg. Retrieved from http://www.springerlink.com/content/yg70206q2p648001/abstract/

Effing, R., Hillegersberg, J., & Huibers, T. W. C. (2012). Measuring the Effects of Social Media Participation on Political Party Communities. In C. G. Reddick & S. K. Aikins (Eds.), *Web 2.0 Technologies and Democratic Governance* (Vol. 1, pp. 201–217). Springer New York. doi:10.1007/978-1-4614-1448-3_13

Effing, R., van Hillegersberg, J., & Huibers, T. (2011). Social media and political participation: are Facebook, Twitter and YouTube democratizing our political systems? In *Electronic participation* (pp. 25–35). Springer Berlin Heidelberg. doi:10.1007/978-3-642-23333-3_3

Electoral Commission. (2004). *An Audit of Democratic Engagement*. London: Electoral Commission / Hansard Society.

Elgot, J. (2014, December 9). Feeding Britain: Poor people don't know how to cook, says Tory Baroness Jenkin. *Huffington Post (UK)*. Retrieved from http://www.huffingtonpost.co.uk/2014/12/08/feeding-britain-tory-cook_n_6287454.html

Ellison, N., & Hardey, M. (2014). Social media and local government: Citizenship, consumption and democracy. *Local Government Studies*, *40*(1), 21–40. doi:10.1080/03003930.2013.799066

Elmer, G. (2013). Live Research: Twittering an Election Debate. *New Media & Society*, *15*(1), 18–30. doi:10.1177/1461444812457328

Eltantawy, N., & Wiest, J. (2011). Social Media in the Egyptian Revolution:Reconsidering Resource Mobilization Theory. *International Journal of Communication*, (5): 1207–1224,

Embiricos, G. (2015, February 10). 20 of the world's top chefs are gathering for a cause: To save the oceans. *Food Republic*. Retrieved from http://www.foodrepublic.com/2015/02/10/20-worlds-top-chefs-are-gathering-cause-save-ocean

England, S. (2014). gender and sexuality in Mexico and Brazil intersections of identities, desires, and public policies. *Latin American Perspectives*, *41*(1), 166–171. doi:10.1177/0094582X13512267

Entman, R. (2007). Framing bias: Media in the distribution of power. *Journal of Communication*, *57*(1), 163–173. doi:10.1111/j.1460-2466.2006.00336.x

Erikson, R. S., Wright, G. C., & McIver, J. P. (1993). Statehouse Democracy: Public Opinion and Policy in the American States. New York: Cambridge.

Eriksson, N. (2009). *Stupidly fat? The Doctor's solution to disease stirs debate* [my translation]. Retrieved February 1, 2015, from http://www.aftonbladet.se/nyheter/svininfluensan/article11978275.ab

European Commission. (2000). *Directive2000/31/EC of the European Parliament and of the Council of 8 June 2000 on certain legal aspects of information society services, in particular electronic commerce, in the Internal Market (further herein: e-commerce directive)*. Author.

European Commission. (2010). *Proposal for a Directive of the European Parliament and of the Council on combating the sexual abuse, sexual exploitation of children and child pornography, repealing Framework Decision 2004/68/JHA*. Author.

European Court of Human Rights (2008) Khurshid Mustafa et Tarzibachi v. Sweden, (23883/06)

Evans, H. K., & Clark, J. H. (2016). You Tweet Like a Girl! How Female Candidates Campaign on Twitter. *American Politics Research*, *44*(2), 326–352. doi:10.1177/1532673X15597747

Evans, H. K., Cordova, V., & Sipole, S. (2014). Twitter style: An analysis of how house candidates used Twitter in their 2012 campaigns. *PS: Political Science & Politics*, *47*(2), 454–462.

Evans, H. K., & Ulbig, S. (2012). Social Butterflies and Politics: Exploring the Link between Sociability and Political Engagement, Online and Off. *Journal of Information Technology &amp. Politics*, *9*(4), 402–414. doi:10.1080/19331681.2012.691039

Evers, J. (2014, February 5). Biggest loser finale: what happened to Rachel? *Me, Myself, and Jen*. Retrieved from http://www.memyselfandjen.com/life-and-kids/biggest-loser-finale-happened-rachel/

Expressen. (2014). *Mats Lindgren, 61: LCHF cured me* [my translation]. Retrieved 8 February, 2015, from http://www.expressen.se/halsoliv/halsovikt/mats-lindgren-61-lchf-gjorde-mig-frisk/

Ezrahi, Y. (2014). Ben-David's critique of the sociology of knowledge and his politics of freedom. In The institution of science and the science of institutions (pp. 39-45). Springer.

Fallon, P., Katzman, M., & Wooley, S. (Eds.). (1996). *Feminist perspectives on eating disorders*. New York, NY: Guilford Press.

familydrivenfate. (2014, February 5). *Tumblr*. Retrieved from http://familydrivenfate.tumblr.com/post75660799176/

Farrell, H. (2012). The Consequences of the Internet for Politics. *Annual Review of Political Science*, *15*(1), 35–52. doi:10.1146/annurev-polisci-030810-110815

Feminist Peace Network. (2006). *Pornography Revenue Statistics*. Available at: http://www.feministpeacenetwork.org/2010/10/20/pornography-the-obscene-statistics/

Ferguson, P. P. (2014). *Word of mouth: What we talk about when we talk about food*. Berkeley, CA: University of California Press, California Studies in Food and Culture.

Fernandez-Poncela, A.-M. (2015). Ayotzinapa, Protestas, Solidaridades y movimientos juveniles en México. *Sapiens Research*, *5*(2), 61–65.

Fernholm, A. (2012). *A sweeter blood: consequences on our health of living with a century of sugar* [my translation]. Stockholm: Natur & kultur.

Fernholm, A. (2015). Om Ann Fernholm [About Ann Fernholm]. *A sweeter life* [my translation]. Retrieved January 24, 2015, from http://ettsotareblod.se/ann-fernholm/

Festl, R., & Quandt, T. (2013). Social relations and cyberbullying: The influence of individual and structural attributes on victimization and perpetration via the internet. *Human Communication Research*, *39*(1), 101–126. doi:10.1111/j.1468-2958.2012.01442.x

Field, A. (2005). Discovering statistics using SPSS (introducing statistical methods series) (2nd ed.). Sage Publications Ltd.

Field, F. (2011, October 3). The welfare state—Never ending reform. *BBC*. Retrieved from http://www.bbc.co.uk/history/british/modern/field_01.shtml

File, T. (2014). *Young-adult voting: An analysis of presidential elections, 1964–2012*. U.S. Department of Commerce. Retrieved from http://www.census.gov/prod/2014pubs/p20-573.pdf

Fischler, C. (1988). Food, self and identity. *Social Sciences Information. Information Sur les Sciences Sociales*, *27*(2), 275–292. doi:10.1177/053901888027002005

Fish Fight campaign launch in Poland. (2012, March 15). *The Fisheries Secretariat*. Retrieved from http://www.fishsec.org/2012/03/15/fish-fight-campaign-launch-in-poland/

Fish Fight included in app store rewind 2011. (2011, December 20). *Clusta*. Retrieved from http://www.clusta.com/blog/fish-fight-included-in-app-store-rewind-2011

Fish Fight. (2014). Retrieved from http://www.fishfight.net/

Fish for the Future. (2013). Retrieve from https://fishforthefutureeu.wordpress.com/

Fiske, J. (1992). British cultural studies and television. In R. C. Allen (Ed.), *Channels of discourse, reassembled: Television and contemporary criticism* (pp. 214–246). Chapel Hill, NC: University of North Carolina Press.

Fletcher, D. (2010, May 27). Worst inventions: FarmVille. *Time Magazine*. Retrieved 10 February, 2015, from http://content.time.com

Fontcuberta, J. (2014). *Pandora's camera: Photogr@phy after photography*. London: MACK.

Foot, K. A., & Schneider, S. M. (2002). Online Action in Campaign 2000: An Exploratory Analysis of the U. S. Political Web Sphere. *Journal of Broadcasting & Electronic Media*, *45*(2), 222–244. doi:10.1207/s15506878jobem4602_4

forever-one-twenty. (2014, February 5). *Tumblr*. Retrieved from http://forever-one-twenty.tumblr.com/post/75697273079/

Forgette, R., & Morris, J. S. (2006). High-conflict television news and public opinion. *Political Research Quarterly*, *59*(3), 447–456. doi:10.1177/106591290605900312

Foss, S. (1996). *Rhetorical criticism: Exploration and practice* (2nd ed.). Prospects Heights, IL: Waveland Press.

Foucault, M. (1978). *The History of sexuality* (Vol. 1). New York: Pantheon Books.

Foucault, M. (1983). *On the Genealogy of Ethics: An Overview of Work in Progress. In Michel Foucault: Beyond Structuralism and Hermeneutics*. Chicago: University of Chicago Press.

Foucault, M. (1997). Ethics: Essential works of Michel Foucault 1954-1984. Penguin.

Foucault, M. (2000). Power. The Essential Works of Michel Foucault, 1954-1984. Penguin.

Fox, R. L., & Ramos, J. (2012). iPolitics: Citizens, elections, and governing in the new media era. New York: Cambridge University Press.

Francoli, M. (2014). Exploring the concept of "social media campaign.". In J. Bishop (Ed.), *Transforming politics and policy in the digital age* (pp. 133–144). Hershey, PA: IGI Global. doi:10.4018/978-1-4666-6038-0.ch009

Freedom House. (2013). *Freedom House Condemns Uganda's Restriction of Political Speech*. Retrieved June 15, 2014, from http://freedomhouse.org/article/freedom-house-condemns-ugandas-restriction-political-speech

Freedom House. (2015). *Freedom on The Net 2015 - Uganda*. Retrieved from https://freedomhouse.org/report/freedom-net/2015/uganda

Freeman, A. (2007). Fast food: Oppression through poor nutrition. *California Law Review, 95*(6), 2221-2259. Retrieved from: http://scholarship/law.berkeley.edu/californialawreview/vol95/iss6/8

Freeman, A. (2013). The unbearable whiteness of milk: Food oppression and the USDA. *Irvine Law Review, 3*(4). Retrieved from http://scholarship.lawuci.edu/ucilr/vol3/iss4/16

Freeman, B., & Chapman, S. (2008). Gone viral? Heard the buzz? A guide for public health practitioners and researchers on how Web 2.0 can subvert advertising restrictions and spread health information. *J Epidemiol Commun H, 62*(9), 778–782. doi:10.1136/jech.2008.073759 PMID:18701726

Freschi, A. C., Medaglia, R., & Nørbjerg, J. (2009). A tale of six countries: eParticipation research from an administration and political perspective. In A. Macintosh, & E. Tambouris (Eds.), *Proceedings of 1st international conference on electronic participation, ePart 2009* (pp. 36–45). Berlin: Springer-Verlag. doi:10.1007/978-3-642-03781-8_4

Friedl, J., & Vercic, A. (2011). Media preferences of digital natives internal communication: A pilot study. *Public Relations Review, 37*(1), 84–86. doi:10.1016/j.pubrev.2010.12.004

Friend, C. (2015). *Social contract theory. The Internet encyclopedia of philosophy: A peer-reviewed academic resource.* Retrieved from http://www.iep.utm.edu/soc-cont/#SH2c

Frye, J. (Ed.). (2012). *The rhetoric of food*. New York, NY: Routledge.

Fuller, B. (2014, June 26). Jillian Michaels quits 'biggest loser' over too skinny Rachel Frederickson. *Hollywood Life*. Retrieved from http://hollywoodlife.com/2014/06/26/jillian-michaels-quits-biggest-loser-reason-rachel-fredrikson/

Gaffey, C. (2016, June 1). Kizza Besigye blocked from appearing at treason trial. *Newsweek*.

Gagliardone, I. (2014). "A Country in Order": Technopolitics, Nation Building, and the Development of ICT in Ethiopia. *Information Technologies & International Development, 10*(1), 3–19.

Gainous, J., & Wagner, K. M. (2013). *Tweeting to Power: The Social Media Revolution in American Politics*. Oxford University Press. doi:10.1093/acprof:oso/9780199965076.001.0001

Gallagher, M. (1980). *Unequal Opportunities: The Case of Women and the Media*. Paris: UNESCO.

Galliers, R. F. L., & Myers, M. A. D. (2002). Choosing Appropriate Information Systems Research Methodologies. In M. D. Myers & D. Avison (Eds.), Qualitative Research in Information Systems (pp. 13–16). SAGE Publications. doi:10.4135/9781849209687.n2

Gambarato, R. R. & Alzamora, G. (2012). Transmedia storytelling initiatives in Brazilian media. *Medien Journal – Zeitschrift für Kommunikationskultur, 4*, 51–62.

Gambarato, R. R. (2013). Transmedia project design: Theoretical and analytical considerations. *Baltic Screen Media Review, 1*, 80–100.

Gambarato, R. R. (2014). Transmedia storytelling in analysis: The case of Final Punishment. *Journal of Print and Media Technology Research, 3*(2), 95–106.

Garcia, L. (Feb. 5, 2015). Robyn Lawley, model with normal body, graces *Sports Illustrated's Swim Issue*. Retrieved from https://www.yahoo.com/style/model-with-normal-body-graces-sports-illustrated-110196422508.html

Garrido, M., & Halavais, A. (2003). Mapping networks of support for the Zapatista movement: applying social-network analysis to study contemporary social movements. In M. Mccaughey & M. D. Ayers (Eds.), *Cyberactivism: online activism in theory and practice* (pp. 165–184). New York: Routledge.

Gayo-Avello, and Takis Metaxas Panagiotis. (2011). Limits of Electoral Predictions Using Twitter. *Proceedings from the Fifth International AAAI Conference on Weblogs and Social Media*. Retrieved from http://www.aaai.org/ocs/index.php/ICWSM/ICWSM11/paper/view/2862

Gayo-Avello, D., & Panagiotis, T. M. (2011). *Limits of Electoral Predictions Using Twitter*. Presented at the Fifth International AAAI Conference on Weblogs and Social Media, Barcelona, España. Retrieved from http://www.aaai.org/ocs/index.php/ICWSM/ICWSM11/paper/view/2862

Gerbaudo, P. (2012). *Tweets and the Streets. Social Media & Contemporary Action*. London: Pluto Press.

Gerstenfeld, P. B., Grant, D. R., & Chiang, C.-P. (2003). Hate Online: A Content Analysis of Extremist Internet Sites. *Analyses of Social Issues and Public Policy (ASAP)*, *3*(1), 29–44. doi:10.1111/j.1530-2415.2003.00013.x

Gherghina, S. (2014). *The impact of party regulation on membership rates in post-Communist Europe*. Academic Press.

Gibson, R., Lusoli, W., & Ward, S. (2002). UK political participation. The public response. A survey of citizens' political activity via the internet. Salford: ESRC.

Gibson, R., Lusoli, W., & Ward, S. (2003). Online Participation and mobilisation in Britain: Hype, Hope and reality. *Parliamentary Affairs*, *56*(4), 652–668. doi:10.1093/pa/gsg108

Giddens, A. (1990). *The consequences of modernity*. Cambridge, UK: Polity Press.

Giddens, A. (1991). *Modernity and Self-Identity*. Stanford, CA: Stanford University Press.

Gil de Zúñiga, H., Copeland, L., & Bimber, B. (2014). Political consumerism: Civic engagement and the social media connection. *New Media & Society*, *16*(3), 488–506. doi:10.1177/1461444813487960

Gil de Zúñiga, H., Puig-I-Abril, E., & Rojas, H. (2009). Weblogs traditional sources online & political participation: An assessment of how the Internet is changing the political environment. *New Media & Society*, *11*(4), 553–574. doi:10.1177/1461444809102960

Gil de Zúñiga, H., Veenstra, A., Vraga, E., & Shah, D. (2010). Digital democracy: Reimagining pathways to political participation. *Journal of Information Technology & Politics*, *7*(1), 36–51. doi:10.1080/19331680903316742

Gilad, L., Erhardt, G., Mike, A., Devin, G., & Ian, P. (2011). The Arab Spring| The Revolutions Were Tweeted: Information Flows during the 2011 Tunisian and Egyptian Revolutions. *International Journal of Communication*, *5*. Retrieved from http://www.ijoc.org/ojs/index.php/ijoc/article/viewArticle/1246

Gilmore, J. (2012). Ditching the pack: Digital media in the 2010 Brazilian congressional campaigns. *New Media & Society*, *14*(4), 617–633. doi:10.1177/1461444811422429

Glenn, C. (1997). *Rhetoric retold: Regendering the tradition from antiquity through the Renaissance*. Carbondale, IL: Southern Illinois University Press.

Godwin, R. (2013). Austerity's poster girl Jack Monroe, and a storm over her very middle class recipe for kale pesto. *Evening Standard*. Retrieved from http://www.standard.co.uk/lifestyle/london-life/austeritys-poster-girl-jack-monroe-and-a-storm-over-her-very-middle-class-recipe-for-kale-pesto-8932248.html

Goffman, E. (1959). *The Presentation of Self in Everyday Life*. Edinburgh, UK: Social Sciences Research Centre.

Goffman, E. (1967). *Interaction Ritual: Essays on Face-to-Face Behaviour*. New Jersey: Transaction Publishers.

Golding, S. (2009). *Change: It's what's for dinner: 'Food, Inc.' takes on agribusiness*. International Documentary Association. Retrieved from http://www.documentary.org/content/change-its-whats-dinner-food-inc-takes-agribusiness

Goldring, E. B., & Shapira, R. (1993). Choice, empowerment, and involvement: What satisfies parents? *Educational Evaluation and Policy Analysis*, *15*(4), 396–409. doi:10.3102/01623737015004396

Goldstein, D., & Du Puis, M. (2007). Gastronomica. *The Journal of Food and Culture*, *7*(3), iii–v.

Goldstein, K. M., & Strach, P. (2003). *The Medium and the Message*. Upper Saddle River, NJ: Pearson.

Gong, Y., & Janssen, M. (2012). From policy implementation to business process management: Principles for creating flexibility and agility. *Government Information Quarterly*, *29*, S61–S71. doi:10.1016/j.giq.2011.08.004

Gonzalez-Bailon, S. (2014). Online Social Networks and Bottom-up Politics. In H. Dutton & M. Graham (Eds.), *Society and the internet: How Networks of Information and Communication are Changing Our Lives* (p. 209). Oxford, UK: Oxford University Press. doi:10.1093/acprof:oso/9780199661992.003.0014

Google Inc. (2015). *Google trends*. Retrieved February 8, 2015, from http://www.google.se/trends/

Google. (2008). *Google Technology*. Retrieved from http://www.google.com/technology/

Goos, K., Beckert, B., & Lindner, R. (2016). Electronic, Internet-Based Voting. In R. Lindner, G. Aichholzer, & L. Hennen (Eds.), *Electronic Democracy in Europe. Prospects and Challenges of E-Publics, E-Participation and E-Voting* (pp. 135–184). London: Springer.

Gottschall, J. (2013). *The storytelling animal: How stories make us human*. New York, NY: Houghton Mifflin Harcourt.

GP. (2012). *Real meals are best for the health* [my translation]. Retrieved January 8, 2015, from http://www.gp.se/nyheter/debatt/1.901957-riktig-mat-ar-bast-for-halsan

Graham, P. (2010). *The Unreasonable Apple* [Blog post]. Retrieved 1 June, 2015, from http://www.paulgrahamarchive.com

Graham, T., Broersma, M., Hazelhoff, K., & vant Haar, G. (2013). Between broadcasting political messages and interacting with voters: The use of Twitter during the 2010 UK general election campaign. *Information Communication and Society*, *16*(5), 692–716. doi:10.1080/1369118X.2013.785581

Granger, G. (2014, April 4). *Twitter*. Retrieved from https://twitter.com/NewSlenderUByVi/status/452106129594916865

Gray, J. A. (1999). Postmodern medicine. *Lancet*, *354*(9189), 1550–1553. doi:10.1016/S0140-6736(98)08482-7 PMID:10551517

Gregory, J., & Miller, S. (2000). Science. In *Public: Communication, Culture, And Credibility*. Cambridge, MA: Perseus Publishing.

Greitens, S. C. (2013). Authoritarianism Online: What Can We Learn from Internet Data in Nondemocracies? *Political Science & Politics*, *46*(02), 262–270. doi:10.1017/S1049096513000346

Grikscheit, G. M., Cash, H. C., & Young, C. E. (1993). *The handbook of selling: Psychological, managerial, and marketing dynamics*. John Wiley & Sons.

Grönlund, Å. (2009). ICT Is Not Participation Is Not Democracy – eParticipation Development Models Revisited. In A. Macintosh & E. Tambouris (Eds.), *Electronic Participation: 1st International Conference, ePart 2009* (pp.12–23). Berlin: Springer Verlag.

Grönlund, Å. (2011). Connecting eGovernment to Real Government - The Failure of the UN eParticipation Index. *Lecture Notes in Computer Science*, *6846*(2011), 26-37. Retrieved June 15, 2014, from http://www.springerlink.com/content/w246q260jt71n557/

Grönlund, Å., & Wakabi, W. (2015). Citizens' use of new media in authoritarian regimes: Case study of Uganda. *The Electronic Journal of Information Systems in Developing Countries*, *67*(1), 1–23.

Gross, J. H., & Johnson, K. (2016). Strafing, Spats, and Skirmishes: Social Dynamics of Negative Campaigning on Twitter. 9th Annual Political Networks Workshops & Conference. St. Louis, MO: Washington University. Retrieved from http://papers.ssrn.com/sol3/papers.cfm?abstract_id=2799252

Gruère, G. P., Mehta-Bhatt, P., & Sengupta, D. (2008). *Bt Cotton and farmer suicides in India: Reviewing the evidence, IRPRI discussion paper*. Retrieved May 30, 2015, from http://www.ifpri.org/sites/default/files/publications/ifpridp00808.pdf

Gruzd, A., & Roy, J. (2014). Investigating Political Polarization on Twitter: A Canadian Perspective. *Policy & Internet*, *6*(1), 28–45. doi:10.1002/1944-2866.POI354

GSMA. (2010). *Women & Mobile: A Global Opportunity – A Study on the Mobile Phone Gender Gap in Low and Middle-income Countries*. GSM Association.

Guest, D. E. (1998). Is the psychological contract worth taking seriously? *Journal of Organizational Behavior*, *19*(S1), 649–664. doi:10.1002/(SICI)1099-1379(1998)19:1+<649::AID-JOB970>3.0.CO;2-T

Gunnarsson, A., & Elam, M. (2012). Food Fight! The Swedish Low-Carb/High Fat (LCHF) Movement and the Turning of Science Popularisation Against the Scientists. *Science as Culture*, *21*(3), 315–334. doi:10.1080/09505431.2011.632000

Gustafson, A. C. (2014, February 4). Stillwater native's 'Biggest Loser' weight loss stirs debate. *St. Paul Pioneer Press*.

Gustafsson, N. (2012). The subtle nature of Facebook politics: Swedish social network site users and political participation. *New Media & Society*, *14*(7), 1111–1127. doi:10.1177/1461444812439551

Habermas, T., & Kober, C. (2014). Autobiographical reasoning is constitutive for narrative identity: The role of the life story for personal continuity. In K. McLean & M. Syed (Eds.), *The Oxford handbook of identity development* (p. 149). Oxford, UK: Oxford University Press. doi:10.1093/oxfordhb/9780199936564.013.010

Hacker, K. L., Mason, S. M., & Morgan, E. L. (2009). Digital Disempowerment in a Network Society. *International Journal of Electronic Government Research*, *5*(2), 57–71. doi:10.4018/jegr.2009040104

Hafkin, N. (2003). *Some thoughts on gender and telecommunications/ICT statistics and indicators*. Available at: http://www.itu.int/ITU-D/pdf/5196-007-en.pdf

Hafkin, N., & Huyer, S. (2007). Women and Gender in ICT Statistics and Indicators for Development. *Information Technologies& International Development*, *4*(2), 25–41. Available at: http://www.itu.int/ITU-D/pdf/5196-007-en.pdf

Hahn, L. K. (2015). Irony and food politics. *Communication and Critical Cultural Studies*. doi:10.1080/14791420.2015.1014185

Hair, J. F., Black, W. C., Babin, B. J., Anderson, R. E., & Tathan, R. L. (2006). *Multivariate data analysis*. Upper Saddle River, NJ: Pearson Prentice Hall.

Halleröd, B., & Larsson, D. (2008). Poverty, welfare problems and social exclusion. *International Journal of Social Welfare*, *17*(1), 15–25. doi:10.1111/j.1468-2397.2007.00503.x

Hamnett, C. (2014). Shrinking the welfare state: The structure, geography and impact of British government benefit cuts. *Transactions of the Institute of British Geographers*, *39*(4), 490–503. doi:10.1111/tran.12049

Hancox, D. (2014, January 10). Amplified activism: Transmedia storytelling and social change. *The Writing Platform*. Retrieved from http://www.thewritingplatform.com/2014/01/amplified-activism-transmedia-storytelling-and-social-change/

Hankin, H. (2005). *The new workforce: Five sweeping trends that will shape your company's future*. AMACOM Div American Mgmt Assn.

Hansard Society. (2011). *Connecting Citizens to Parliament*. London: Hansard Society.

Hardaker, C. (2013). Uh.... not to be nitpicky, but... the past tense of drag is dragged, not drug.": An overview of trolling strategies. *Journal of Language Aggression and Conflict*, *1*(1), 57–85. doi:10.1075/jlac.1.1.04har

Harfoush, R. (2009). *Yes We Did! An inside look at how social media built the Obama brand* (1st ed.). New Riders Press.

Hargis, J. E. (2012). The ethics of voting. *The Journal of Politics*, *74*(03), E29. doi:10.1017/S0022381612000230

Hargittai, E., & Shaw, A. (2013). Digitally savvy citizenship: The role of Internet skills and engagement in young adults political participation around the 2008 presidential election. *Journal of Broadcasting & Electronic Media*, *57*(2), 115–134. doi:10.1080/08838151.2013.787079

Harlow, S. (2012). Social Media and Social Movements: Facebook and an Online Guatemalan Justice Movement that Moved Offline. *New Media & Society*, *14*(2), 225–243. doi:10.1177/1461444811410408

Harris, D., & Lewis, T. (2013). Liberia in 2011: Still ploughing its own democratic furrow? *Commonwealth and Comparative Politics*, *51*(1), 76–96. doi:10.1080/14662043.2013.752176

Harrison, L., Reinecke, K., & Chang, R. (2015). Infographic aesthetics: Designing for the first impression. In *Proceedings of the SIGCHI Conference on Human Factors in Computing Systems* (pp. 1187–1190). New York, NY: ACM. doi:10.1145/2702123.2702545

Hartley-Parkinson, R. (2014, February 4). Benefits row live: Jack Monroe hits back at Edwina Currie in open letter after "revolting" TV debate attack. *Mirror*. Retrieved from http://www.mirror.co.uk/news/uk-news/benefits-row-live-jack-monroe-3111253

Harvard Institute of Politics. (2014, August 29). *Survey of young Americans' attitudes toward politics and public service* (25th ed.). Retrieved from http://www.iop.harvard.edu/Spring-2014-HarvardIOP-Survey

Harvey, F. (2013a, February 6). MEPs vote to ban discards in historic reform of fishing policy. *The Guardian*. Retrieved from http://www.theguardian.com/environment/2013/feb/06/meps-back-fishing-policy-reform

Harvey, F. (2013b, February 14). Fish Fight renews campaign to protect the seabed. *The Guardian*. Retrieved from http://www.theguardian.com/environment/2013/feb/14/fish-fight-campaign-marine-life

Hayes, A. F. (2013). *Introduction to mediation, moderation, and conditional process analysis: A regression-based approach*. New York: Guilford Press.

Hayes, A. F., Scheufele, D. A., & Huge, M. E. (2006). Nonparticipation as self-censorship: Publicly observable political activity in a polarized opinion climate. *Political Behavior*, *28*(3), 259–283. doi:10.1007/s11109-006-9008-3

Helland, C. (2013). Ritual. In H. Campbell (Ed.), *Digital Religion: Understanding Religious Practice in New Media Worlds*. Routledge.

Henning, E. (2003). I click, therefore I am (not): Is cognition distributed or is it contained in borderless eLearning programs? *International Journal of Training and Development*, *7*(4), 303–316. doi:10.1046/j.1360-3736.2003.00188.x

Herbst, S. (2010). *Rude democracy: Civility and incivility in American politics*. Philadelphia, PA: Temple University Press.

Herriot, P., Hirsch, W., & Reilly, P. (1998). *Trust and Transition: Managing Today's Employment Relationship*. Chichester, UK: John Wiley.

Hessel, V. (2015). Conferences are scientific market places. *Green Processing and Synthesis*, *4*(1), 1–2. doi:10.1515/gps-2014-0106

Hilgartner, S. (1990). The Dominant View of Popularization: Conceptual Problems, Political Uses. *Social Studies of Science*, *20*(3), 519–539. doi:10.1177/030631290020003006

Himelboim, I., Lariscy, R. W., Tinkham, S. F., & Sweetser, K. D. (2012). Social Media and Online Political Communication: The Role of Interpersonal Informational Trust and Openness. *Journal of Broadcasting & Electronic Media*, *56*(1), 92–115. doi:10.1080/08838151.2011.648682

Hindman, M. (2005). The Real Lessons of Howard Dean: Reflections of the First Digital Campaign. *Perspectives on Politics*, *3*(1), 121–128. doi:10.1017/S1537592705050115

Hine, C. (2000). *Virtual Ethnography*. Thousand Oaks, CA: Sage. doi:10.4135/9780857020277

Hinsliffe, G. (2014, February 14). No sneering. Talking for other people is allowed. *The Times*. Retrieved from http://www.thetimes.co.uk/tto/opinion/columnists/article4005134.ece

Hmielowski, J. D., Hutchens, M. J., & Cicchirillo, V. J. (2014). Living in an age of online incivility: Examining the conditional indirect effects of online discussion on political flaming. *Information Communication and Society*, *17*(10), 1196–1211. doi:10.1080/1369118X.2014.899609

Hoeren, T. (2009). Liability for Online Services in Germany. *German Law Journal, 10,* 561-584.

Hollows, J., & Jones, S. (2010). At least hes doing something: Moral entrepreneurship and individual responsibility in Jamies Ministry of Food. *European Journal of Cultural Studies*, *13*(3), 307–322. doi:10.1177/1367549410363197

Holmberg, C., Chaplin, E. J., Hillman, T., & Berg, C. (2016). Adolescents presentation of food in social media: An explorative study. *Appetite*, *99*, 121–129. doi:10.1016/j.appet.2016.01.009 PMID:26792765

Holt, D. B. (1995). How consumers consume: A typology of consumption practices. *The Journal of Consumer Research*, *22*(1), 1–16. doi:10.1086/209431

Holt, D. B. (1998). Does cultural capital structure American consumption. *The Journal of Consumer Research*, *25*(1), 1–25. doi:10.1086/209523

Holt, K., Shehata, A., Strömbäck, J., & Ljungberg, E. (2013). Age and the effects of news media attention and social media use on political interest and participation: Do social media function as leveller? *European Journal of Communication*, *28*(1), 19–34. doi:10.1177/0267323112465369

Hong, S., & Nadler, D. (2012). Which Candidates do the Public Discourse Online in an Election Campaign? The use of Social Media by 2012 Presidential Candidates and its Impact on Candidate Salience. *Government Information Quarterly*, *29*(4), 455–461. doi:10.1016/j.giq.2012.06.004

Honneth, A. (2007). *Disrespect: The normative foundations of critical theory*. Cambridge, UK: Polity Press.

How to Photograph Food with your Phone. (2012, 15 July). *The Guardian*. Retrieved from http://www.theguardian.com/lifeandstyle/2012/jul/15/how-to-photograph-food-smartphone

Howard, P., Hussain, M., Mari, W., Mazaid, M., Freelon, D., & Duffy, A. (2011). Opening Closed Regimes: What Was the Role of Social Media During the Arab Spring? The Project on Information Technology and Political Islam, University of Washington.

Howard, P. N., Duffy, A., Freelon, D., Hussain, M., Mari, W., & Mazaid, M. (2011). *Opening Closed Regimes: What Was the Role of Social Media During the Arab Spring?* Seattle, WA: Department of Communication, University of Washington.

Hugh's Fish Fight shortlisted again. (2012, February 21). *KEO films*. Retrieved from http://www.keofilms.com/news/hughs-fish-fight-shortlisted-again/

Hugh's Fish Fight. (n.d.). In *Facebook* [Page type]. Retrieved from https://www.facebook.com/hughsfishfight

Hugh's Fish Fight: Join the Fish Fight. (2010, November 17). Retrieved from http://www.youtube.com/watch?v=L2fZcmjbqpA

Hundley, H., & Shyles, L. (2010). US teenagers perceptions and awareness of digital technology: A focus group approach. *New Media & Society*, *12*(3), 417–433. doi:10.1177/1461444809342558

Hunt, R. J. (February 3, 2015). *Why our daughters need more body-positive movements*. Retrieved from http://www.huffingtonpost.com/roxie-jane-hunt/why-our-daughters-need-more-body-positive-movements_b_6592076.html

Huovila, J., & Saikkonen, S. (2015). Establishing credibility, constructing understanding: The epistemic struggle over healthy eating in the Finnish dietetic blogosphere. *Health*. doi:10.1177/1363459315595849 PMID:26220062

Ibrahim, Y. (2009). Social Networking Sites (SNS) and the 'Narcissistic Turn'. In Collaborative Technologies and Applications for Interactive Information Design: Emerging Trends in User Experiences. Academic Press.

Ibrahim, Y. (2015). Instagramming life: banal imaging and the poetics of the everyday. *Journal of Media Practice*.

Ibrahim, Y. (2015). Instagramming life: Banal imaging and the poetics of the everyday. *Journal of Media Practice*.

Ibrahim, Y. (2008a). The New Risk Communities: Social Networking Sites and Risk. *International Journal of Media and Cultural Politics*, *4*(2), 245–253. doi:10.1386/macp.4.2.245_3

Ibrahim, Y. (2008b). The Co-opted Body and Counter-Surveillance: The Body as Data and Surveillance. *International Journal of the Humanities*, *5*(12), 1–8.

Ibrahim, Y. (2010). The regulation of gaze and capture: New media and the image economy. *International Journal of Technoethics*, 40–63.

Ibrahim, Y. (2011). The non-stop capture: The politics of looking in postmodernity. *The Poster*, *1*(2), 167–185. doi:10.1386/post.1.2.167_1

Ibrahim, Y. (2012). The Politics of Watching: Visuality and the New Media Economy. *International Journal of E-Politics*, *3*(1), 1–11. doi:10.4018/jep.2012010101

Ibrahim, Y. (2015). Instagramming life: Banal imaging and the poetics of the everyday. *Journal of Media Practice*, *16*(1), 42–54. doi:10.1080/14682753.2015.1015800

icywinterstorm. (2014, February 6). *Tumblr.* Retrieved from http://icywinterstorm.tumblr.com/post/75663253421l/

imdreamingyourdreams. (2014, February 5). *Tumblr.* Retrieved from http://imdreamingyourdreams.tumblr.com/post/75696839972/

INEGI. (2016). *Encuesta Nacional sobre Disponibilidad y Uso de Tecnologías de la Información en los Hogares (ENDUTIH) 2015*. Instituto Nacional de Estadística y Geografía. Retrieved from http://www3.inegi.org.mx/sistemas/tabuladosbasicos/tabniveles.aspx?c=33734

Innes, S., & Rendall, J. (2006). Women, gender and politics. *Gender in Scottish History Since*, *1700*, 43–83.

Intel & Dalberg Global Development Advisors. (2012). *Women and the Web. Bridging the Internet gap and creating new global opportunities in low and middle-income countries*. Available at: http://dalberg.com/documents/Women_Web.pdf

ITU. (2012). *Measuring the Information Society 2012*. Available at: http://www.itu.int/en/ITU-D/Statistics/Documents/publications/mis2012/MIS2012_without_Annex_4.pdf

Ives, N. (2006). Loser' Wins. *Advertising Age, 77*(10).

Jaffe, A. (2016, May 7). Trump slams Hillary Clinton as 'nasty, mean enabler,' of husband's affairs. *NBC News*. Retrieved May 9, 2016, from http://www.nbcnews.com/politics/2016-election/trump-slams-hillary-clinton-nasty-mean-enabler-husband-s-affairs-n569791

Jamieson, K. H. (1992). *Dirty politics: Deception, distraction, and democracy*. New York: Oxford University Press.

Jamieson, K. H. (1992). *Dirty Politics: Deception, Distration, and Democracy*. New York: Oxford University Press.

Jamieson, K. H., & Cappella, J. N. (2009). *Echo chamber: Rush Limbaugh and the conservative media establishment*. New York, NY: Oxford University Press.

Jansen, E. (Ed.). (2002). *NetLingo: The internet dictionary*. Ojai, CA: Netlingo Inc.

Järvelä, K., Mäkelä, J., & Piiroinen, S. (2006). Consumers everyday food choice strategies in Finland. *International Journal of Consumer Studies, 30*(4), 309–317. doi:10.1111/j.1470-6431.2006.00516.x

Jauho, M. (2016). The social construction of competence: Conceptions of science and expertise among proponents of the low-carbohydrate high-fat diet in Finland. *Public Understanding of Science (Bristol, England), 25*(3), 332–345. doi:10.1177/0963662514558167 PMID:25415233

Jenkins, H. (2003, January 15). Transmedia storytelling. *Technology Review*. Retrieved from http://www.technologyreview.com/news/401760/transmedia-storytelling/

Jenkins, H. (2006). *Convergence culture: Where old and new media collide*. New York, NY: New York University Press.

Jenkins, H. (2008). *Convergence Culture: Where Old and New Media Collide*. New York: NYU Press.

Jenkins, H., & Deuze, M. (2008). Editorial: Convergence culture. *Convergence (London), 14*(D), 5–12. doi:10.1177/1354856507084415

Jenkins, H., Ford, S., & Green, G. (2013). *Spreadable Media: Creating Value and Meaning in a Networked Culture*. New York: NYU Press.

Jenkins, H., Ford, S., & Green, J. (2013). *Spreadable media: Creating value and meaning in a networked culture*. New York, NY: New York University Press.

Jenkins, H., Ito, M., & Boyd, D. (2015). *Participatory culture in a networked era: A conversation on youth, learning, commerce, and politics*. Malden, MA: Polity Press.

Jensen J. (2003). Public Spheres on the Internet: Anarchic or Government-Sponsored – A Comparison. *Scandinavian Political Studies, 26*(4).

Jensen, M. (2014). *Social Media and Australian Local Government*. Canberra: ANZSIG / ACELG.

Jensen, P. (2008). The International Extent and Elasticity of Lifestyle Television. *Mediekultur, 45*, 24–45.

Jerit, J. (2004). Survival of the Fittest: Rhetoric During the Course of an Election Campaign. *Political Psychology, 25*(4), 563–575. doi:10.1111/j.1467-9221.2004.00387.x

Jewell, M. E., & Olson, D. M. (1988). *Political Parties and Elections in American States*. Chicago: Dorsey Press.

Jho, W., & Song, K. J. (2015). Institutional and technological determinants of civil e-Participation: Solo or duet? *Government Information Quarterly*, *32*(4), 488–495. doi:10.1016/j.giq.2015.09.003

jiffytiffy. (2014, February 6). *Tumblr.* Retrieved from http://jiffytiffy.tumblr.com/post/75725874828/

Johansson, I., Nilsson, L., Stegmayr, B., Boman, K., Hallmans, G., & Winkvist, A. (2012). Associations among 25-year trends in diet, cholesterol and BMI from 140,000 observations in men and women in Northern Sweden. *Nutrition Journal*, *11*(1), 40. doi:10.1186/1475-2891-11-40 PMID:22686621

Johnson, S. (2011, March 1). Fishermen attack "superficial TV" discards ban. *The Telegraph*. Retrieved from http://www.telegraph.co.uk/news/uknews/scotland/8354266/Fishermen-attack-superficial-TV-discards-ban.html

Johnson, R. J., Braima, M. A., & Sothirajah, J. (1999). Doing the Traditional Media Sidestep: Comparing the Effects of the Internet and Other Nontraditional Media with Traditional Media in the 1996 Presidential Campaign. *Journalism & Mass Communication Quarterly*, *76*(1), 99–123. doi:10.1177/107769909907600108

Johnston, R., & Pattie, C. (2011). Tactical voting at the 2010 british general election: Rational behaviour in local contexts? *Environment and Planning-Part A*, *43*(6), 1323–1340. doi:10.1068/a43512

Jolly, M. (2011). Life writing as intimate publics. *Biography*, *34*(1), v–xi. doi:10.1353/bio.2011.0007

Jon, B. A. (1998). New Media, New Politics? From Satellite Television to the Internet in the Arab World. The Washington Institute.

Jones, S. (1999). Studying the Net: Intricacies and Issues. In Doing Internet Research -Critical Issues and Methods for Examining the Net. Thousand Oaks, CA: Sage Publications.

Jo, Y. N. (2013). Psycho-social dimensions of poverty: When poverty becomes shameful. *Critical Social Policy*, *33*(3), 514–531. doi:10.1177/0261018313479008

Juarez, G. (2011). *Se dicta auto de formal prisión a los dos "tuiteros" veracruzanos*. Alt1040. Retrieved from http://alt1040.com/2011/09/alarmasocial-dictan-auto-de-formal-prision-a-dos-tuiteros-veracruzanos

Jungherr, A. (2015). *Twitter as Political Communication Space: Publics, Prominent Users, and Politicians*. Springer International Publishing; doi:10.1007/978-3-319-20319-5_4

Jungherr, A. (2016). Twitter use in election campaigns: A systematic literature review. *Journal of Information Technology & Politics*, *13*(1), 72–91. doi:10.1080/19331681.2015.1132401

Jungherr, A., Jürgens, P., & Schoen, H. (2011). Why the Pirate Party Won the German Election of 2009 or The Trouble With Predictions: A Response to Tumasjan, A., Sprenger, T. O., Sander, P. G., & Welpe, I. M. "Predicting Elections With Twitter: What 140 Characters Reveal About Political Sentiment". *Social Science Computer Review*. doi:10.1177/0894439311404119

Jung, N., Kim, Y., & Gil de Zúñiga, H. (2011). The mediating role of knowledge and efficacy in the effects of communication on political participation. *Mass Communication & Society*, *14*(4), 407–430. doi:10.1080/15205436.2010.496135

Kagan, R. A. (1991). Adversarial legalism and American government. *Journal of Policy Analysis and Management*, *10*(3), 369–406. doi:10.2307/3325322

Kaid, L., & Johnston, A. (1991). Negative Versus Positive Television Advertising in U.S. Presidential Campaigns, 19601988. *Journal of Communication*, *41*(3), 53–64. doi:10.1111/j.1460-2466.1991.tb02323.x

Kalampokis, E., Tambouris, E., & Tarabanis, K. (2008). A Domain Model for eParticipation. *Third International Conference on Internet and Web.*

Kane, J., & Patapan, H. (2004). Challenge and Promise of eDemocracy. *Griffith Review*, *3*(Autumn), 201–207.

Kaplan, M. D. (2012). *The Philosophy of Food*. University of California Press.

Karlsen, R. (2013). Obamas Online Success and European Party Organizations: Adoption and Adaptation of U.S. Online Practices in the Norwegian Labor Party. *Journal of Information Technology & Politics*, *10*(2), 158–170. doi:10.1080/19331681.2012.749822

Karpf, D. (2012). *The move-on effect*. New York, NY: Oxford University Press. doi:10.1093/acprof:oso/9780199898367.001.0001

Kata, A. (2012). Anti-vaccine activists, Web 2.0, and the postmodern paradigm – An overview of tactics and tropes used online by the anti-vaccination movement. *Vaccine*, *30*(25), 3778–3789. doi:10.1016/j.vaccine.2011.11.112 PMID:22172504

Katz, J. E., Barris, M., & Jain, A. (2013). *The Social Media President: Barack Obama and the Politics of Digital Engagement*. Palgrave Macmillan. doi:10.1057/9781137378354

Kaufman, F. (2005). Debbie Does Salad: The Food Network at the Frontiers of Pornography. *Harper's*, (October), 55–60.

Kavanaugh, A. L., Sheetz, S. D., Sandoval-Almazan, R., Tedesco, J. C., & Fox, E. A. (2014, November 23). Media Use During Conflicts: Information Seeking Gratifications & Efficacy During 2012 Mexican Elections. *Proceedings of the 15th Annual International Conference on Digital Government Research (Dg.o 2014).* http://doi.org/ doi:10.1145/2612733.2612738

Kavanaugh, A., Seungwon, Y., & Fox, E. (2011). *Between a Rock and a Cell Phone: Social Media Use during Mass Protests in Iran, Tunisia and Egypt* (No. 1149). Virginia Tech. Retrieved from http://eprints.cs.vt.edu/archive/00001149/

Kedar, O. (2012). Voter choice and parliamentary politics: An emerging research agenda. *British Journal of Political Science*, *42*(3), 537–553. doi:10.1017/S0007123411000408

Keen, A. (2007). *The cult of the amateur: How today's Internet is killing our culture* (1st ed.). New York: Doubleday.

Khamis, S., & Vaughn, K. (2012). We Are All Khaled Said: The potentials and limitations of cyberactivism in triggering public mobilization and promoting political change. *Journal of Arab & Muslim Media Research*, *4*(2-3), 145–163. doi:10.1386/jammr.4.2-3.145_1

Kilbourne, J. (2012). *Women's bodies in advertising*. Retrieved from http://www.ourbodiesourselves.org/health-info/womens-bodies-in-advertising/

Kilbourne, J. (1979/2010). *Killing us softly: Advertising's image of women*. Cambridge Documentaries.

Kim, A. J. (2000). *Community building on the web: Secret strategies for successful online communities*. Berkeley, CA: Peachpit Press.

Kim, H., & Kostadinova, T. (2011). Does tactical voting matter? The political impact of tactical voting in Canadian elections. *International Area Studies Review*, *14*(1), 49–72. doi:10.1177/223386591101400103

Kim, S., & Willis, L. (2007). Talking about obesity: News framing of who is responsible for causing and fixing the problem. *Journal of Health Communication*, *12*(4), 359–376. doi:10.1080/10810730701326051 PMID:17558788

Kiousis, S., & Dimitrova, D. V. (2006). Differential impact of Web site content: Exploring the influence of source (public relations versus news), modality, and participation on college students perceptions. *Public Relations Review*, *32*(2), 177–179. doi:10.1016/j.pubrev.2006.02.013

Kirshenblatt-Gimblett, B. (1999). Playing to the senses, Food as Performance Medium. *Performance Research*, *4*(1), 1–30. doi:10.1080/13528165.1999.10871639

Kjaernes, U. (2003). Food and nutrition policies of Nordic countries: How have they been developed and what evidence substantiates the development of these policies? *The Proceedings of the Nutrition Society*, *62*(2), 563–570. doi:10.1079/PNS2003269 PMID:14506905

Kligler-Vilenchik, N., McVeigh-Schultz, J., Weitbrecht, C., & Tokuhama, C. (2012). Experiencing fan activism: Understanding the power of fan activist organizations through members' narratives. *Transformative Works and Cultures*, *10*. doi:10.3983/twc.2012.0322

Klofstad, C. (2009). Civic Talk and Civic Participation: The Moderating Effect of Individual Predispositions. *American Politics Research*, *37*(5), 856–878. doi:10.1177/1532673X09333960

Klotz, R. (1998). Virtual Criticism: Negative Advertising on the Internet in the 1996 Senate Races. *Political Communication*, *15*(3), 347–365. doi:10.1080/105846098198939

Knight, C. (2011). If Youre Not Allowed to Have Rice, What Do You Have with Your Curry?: Nostalgia and Tradition in Low-Carbohydrate Diet Discourse and Practice. *Sociological Research Online*, *16*(2), 8. doi:10.5153/sro.2342

Knight, C. (2015). We Can't Go Back a Hundred Million Years. *Food, Culture & Society*, *18*(3), 441–461. doi:10.1080/15528014.2015.1043107

Kone, S., & Winters, R. (1993). Taxes and Voting: Electoral Redistribution in the American States. *The Journal of Politics*, *63*(2).

Kristinsson, G. H., Indriðason, I. H., & Valgarðsson, V. O. (2012). What were the voters thinking? The presidential election in Iceland 2012. *Icelandic Review of Politics & Administration*, *8*(2), 221–244.

Kruikemeier, S. (2014). How political candidates use Twitter and the impact on votes. *Computers in Human Behavior*, *34*, 131–139. doi:10.1016/j.chb.2014.01.025

Kuebler, M., Muennig, P., Pelleg, D., Puhl, R. M., & Yom-Tov, E. (2013). When overweight is the normal weight: An examination of obesity using a social media internet database. *Plus ONE*, *8*(9), 1–8. doi:10.1371/journal.pone.0073479 PMID:24058478

Kushin, M. J. (2009). How young adults and social media are challenging traditional perspectives of civic life. *Rocky Mountain Communication Review*, *6*, 26–31.

Kushin, M. J., & Yamamoto, M. (2010). Did social media really matter? College students use of online media and political decision making in the 2008 election. *Mass Communication & Society*, *13*(5), 608–630. doi:10.1080/15205436.2010.516863

Lambie-Mumford, H., Crossley, D., & Jensen, E. (2014). *Household food security in the UK: A review of food aid final report*. Retrieved from https://www.gov.uk/government/uploads/system/uploads/attachment_data/file/283071/household-food-security-uk-140219.pdf

Lambie-Mumford, H., & Dowler, E. (2014). Rising use of food aid in the United Kingdom. *British Food Journal*, *116*(9), 1418–1425. doi:10.1108/BFJ-06-2014-0207

Lampe, C., Zube, P., Lee, J., Park, C.-H., & Johnston, E. (2014). Crowdsourcing civility: A natural experiment examining the effects of distributed moderation in online forums. *Government Information Quarterly*, *31*, 317-326. http://dx/doi.org/10.1016/j.giq.2013.11.005

Lang, J., Maudet, N., & Polukarov, M. (2013). New results on equilibria in strategic candidacy. In Algorithmic game theory (pp. 13-25). Springer.

Lang, T., & Heasman, M. (2004). *Food Wars: The Global Battle for Mouths, Minds and Markets*. London: Earthscan Publications.

Lansley, S., & Mack, J. (2015). *Breadline Britain: The rise of mass poverty*. London: Oneworld Publications.

Larsson, A. O., & Moe, H. (2011). Studying political microblogging: Twitter users in the 2010 Swedish election campaign. *New Media & Society*. doi:10.1177/1461444811422894

Lassen, D. S., & Brown, A. R. (2011). Twitter The Electoral Connection? *Social Science Computer Review*, *29*(4), 419–436. doi:10.1177/0894439310382749

Lasswell, H. (1936). *Politics: Who gets, what, when, how*. New York, NY: Whittlesey House.

Latour, B. (1987). *Science in Action: How to Follow Scientists and Engineers through Society*. Milton Keynes, UK: Open University Press.

Laugharne, R. (1999). Evidence-based medicine, user involvement and the post-modern paradigm. *Psychiatric Bulletin*, *23*(11), 641–643. doi:10.1192/pb.23.11.641

Lau, R. R., & Pomper, G. (2004). *Negative Campaigning: An Analysis of U.S. Senate Elections*. New York: Rowman & Littlefield.

Lau, R. R., & Pomper, G. M. (2001). Negative Campaigning by US Senate Candidates. *Party Politics*, *7*(1), 69–87. doi:10.1177/1354068801007001004

Lau, R. R., Sigelman, L., & Rovner, I. B. (2007). The Effects of Negative Political Campaigns: A Meta-Analytic Reassessment. *The Journal of Politics*, *69*(4), 1176–1209. doi:10.1111/j.1468-2508.2007.00618.x

Laverty, A. R. (2012). *The Missing Connection: ICTs and Democracy in Africa*. UCLA: African Studies 0044.

LeBesco, K. (2004). *Revolting bodies? The struggle to redefine fat identity*. Amherst, MA: University of Massachusetts Press.

LeBesco, K., & Naccarato, P. (2008). *Edible ideologies: Representing food and meaning*. New York: State University of New York.

Lee, D., Loutas, N., Sánchez-Nielsen, E., Mogulkoc, E., & Lacigova, O. (2011). Inform-consult-empower: a three-tiered approach to eParticipation. In Electronic Participation (pp. 121-132). Springer Berlin Heidelberg. doi:10.1007/978-3-642-23333-3_11

Lee, R., Rainier, J., & Purcell, K. (2012). *Photos and Videos as Social Currency Online*. Pew Research Centre. Retrieved from http://www.pewinternet.org/2012/09/13/photos-and-videos-as-social-currency-online/

Lee, J., & Kim, S. (2012). E-Participation in the Era of Web 2.0: Factors Affecting Citizens' Active E-Participation in Local Governance. In J. R. Gil-Garcia, N. Helbig, & A. Ojo (Eds.), *Proceedings of the 6th International Conference on Theory and Practice of Electronic Governance (ICEGOV)* (pp. 44-47). New York: ACM Press. doi:10.1145/2463728.2463739

Lee, J., & Myers, T. A. (2016). Can social media change your mind? SNS use, cross-cutting exposure and discussion, and political view change. *Social Media Studies*, *2*, 87–97. doi:10.15340/2147336622992

Lénárt-Cheng, H., & Walker, D. (2011). Recent trends in using life stories for social and political activism. *Biography*, *34*(1), 141–179. doi:10.1353/bio.2011.0005

Lenhart, A., Smith, A., Anderson, M., Duggan, M., & Perrin, A. (2015). *Teens, Technology and Friendships: Video Games, Social Media and Mobile Phones Play an Integral Role in How Teens Meet and Interact With Friends*. Retrieved August 10, 2015, from http://www.pewinternet.org/files/2015/08/Teens-and-Friendships-FINAL2.pdf

Leroux, K., & Krawczyk, K. (2012). Can nonprofit organizations increase voter turnout? Findings from an agency-based voter mobilization experiment. *Nonprofit and Voluntary Sector Quarterly*.

Levon, E. (2014). 10 ethnography and recording interaction. *Research Methods in Linguistics, 195*.

Lewenstein, B. V. (1995). From Fax to Facts: Communication in the Cold Fusion Saga. *Social Studies of Science*, *25*(3), 403–436. doi:10.1177/030631295025003001

Li, D. K. (2014). It's too little too soon! Critics fear "Loser" health. *The New York Post*.

Lieb, C. W. (1929). The effects on human beings of a twelve months exclusive meat diet: Based on intensive clinical and laboratory studies on two arctic explorers living under average conditions in a new york climate. *Journal of the American Medical Association*, *93*(1), 20–22. doi:10.1001/jama.1929.02710010026005

lifeisyourstomiss. (2014, February 5). *Tumblr*. Retrieved from http://lifeisyourstomiss/tumble.com/post/75696998240/

Lilleker, D. G., & Jackson, N. (2011). Political campaigning, elections and the internet: Comparing the US, UK, France and Germany. Routledge.

lillythelegend. (2014, February 5). *Tumblr*. Retrieved from http://lillythelegend.com/2014/02/05/biggest-loser-winner-too-skinny/

Lim, L. L. (2009). The influences of harmony motives and implicit beliefs on conflict styles of the collectivist. *International Journal of Psychology*, *44*(6), 401–409. doi:10.1080/00207590802512765 PMID:22029658

Lindlahr, V. (1942). *You are what you eat: How to win and keep health with diet*. New York, NY: National Nutrition Society.

Lin, J. (2016). Differential gains in SNSs: Effects of active vs. passive Facebook political participation on offline political participation and voting behavior among first-time and experienced voters. *Asian Journal of Communication*, *26*(3), 278–297. doi:10.1080/01292986.2016.1148184

Lister, M., & Wells, L. (2001). Seeing Beyond Belief: Cultural Studies as an approach to studying the visual. In Handbook of visual analysis (pp. 61-91). Academic Press.

Littlejohn, R. (2013, November 8). Ah, Pesto! These poverty poster girls of Welfare Britain want the gravy too ... without having to pay for it. *Daily Mail*. Retrieved from http://www.dailymail.co.uk/debate/article-2482111/RICHARD-LITTLEJOHN-Ah-Pesto-Meet-poverty-poster-girls.html

Livingston, J. (2012). *Jennifer Livingston responds to viewer letter about her weight*. Retrieved from www.news8000.com/news/Jennifer-Livingston-responds.../16832410

Loader, B. D., & Mercea, D. (2012). *Social Media and Democracy: Innovations in Participatory Politics*. London: Routledge.

Lowndes, L. P., & Stoker, G. (2006). Diagnosing and remedying the failings of official participation schemes: the CLEAR framework. Social Policy and Society, 5(2), 281-91.

Lowndes, L. P., & Stoker, G. (2001). Trends in Public Participation: Part 2 – Citizens Perspectives. *Public Administration*, *79*(2), 445–455. doi:10.1111/1467-9299.00264

Luce, H. (2007). *History of life magazine. History as it happened blog*. Retrieved 13 February, 2015, from https://historyasithappened.wordpress.com/2007/10/15/7/

lunalovebad. (2014, February 5). *Tumblr.* Retrieved from http://lunalovebad.tumblr.com/post/75796841935

Lupton, D. (1996). *Food, the Body and the Self.* Thousand Oaks, CA: Sage.

Lynch, M. (2011). After Egypt: The Limits and Promise of Online Challenges to the Authoritarian Arab State. *Perspectives on Politics*, *9*(2), 301–310. doi:10.1017/S1537592711000910

Maas, A. (2012). Living storytelling as an impetus for organizational change: Towards connective observing and writing. *Narrative Works: Issues, Investigations, and Interventions*, *2*(1), 150–169.

Macintosh, A., & Whyte, A. (2002). *Analysis and Evaluation of e-consultations*. Retrieved from www.teledemocracy.org

Macintosh, A., Malina, A., & Farrell, S. (2002). Digital Democracy through Electronic Petitioning. In W. J. McIver & A. K. Elmagarmid (Eds.), *Advances in Digital Government. Technology, Human Factors, and Policy* (pp. 137–148). Norwell, MA: Kluwer Academic Publishers. doi:10.1007/0-306-47374-7_8

Mackenzie, W. (2011, August 4). Hug brings his Fish Fight for one last round. *Greenpeace*. Retrieved from http://www.greenpeace.org.uk/blog/oceans/hugh-fearnley-whittingstall-brings-back-fish-fight-one-last-round-20110804

Magee, R. M. (2007). Food Puritanism and Food Pornography: The Gourmet Semiotics of Martha and Nigella. *Americana: The Journal of American Popular Culture, 6*(2). Retrieved from www.americanpopularculture.com/journal/articles/fall_2007/magee.htm

Makłowicz, R. (2012). *Ryba za Burta!* [Fish Overboard!]. Retrieved from http://www.maklowicz.pl/o-mnie/robert-maklowicz/akcje

Maltzahn, K. (2006). *Digital Dangers. Information and Communication Technologies and Trafficking Women*. Available at: http://www.genderit.org/sites/default/upload/digital_dangers_EN_1.pdf

Mälzer, T. (2012). *Tims Fish Fight*. Retrieved from http://www.tim-maelzer.info/tag/wwwfishfightde/

Mann, J., McLean, R., Skeaff, M., & Morenga, L. T. (2014). Low carbohydrate diets: Going against the grain. *Lancet, 384*(9953), 1479–1480. doi:10.1016/S0140-6736(14)61413-6 PMID:25390561

Mann, J., & Nye, E. R. (2009). Fad diets in Sweden, of all places. *Lancet*, *374*(9692), 767–769. doi:10.1016/S0140-6736(09)61575-0 PMID:19733769

Manrique, M., & Mikail, B. (2011). The Role of New Media and Communication Technologies in Arab Transitions. *FRIDE Policy Briefing No. 106.* Retrieved from http://fride.org/publication/965/the-role-of-new-media-and-communication-technologies-in-arab-transitions

Mantovani, G. (1996a). *New communication environments: From everyday to virtual.* London: Taylor & Francis.

Mantovani, G. (1996b). Social context in HCI: A new framework for mental models, cooperation, and communication. *Cognitive Science*, *20*(2), 237–269. doi:10.1207/s15516709cog2002_3

Manville, B. (2003). *Organizing Enterprise-Wide eLearning and Human Capital Management.* Chief Learning Officer.

Manville, B. (2003, May). Organizing Enterprise-Wide eLearning and Human Capital Management. *Chief Learning Officer*, 50-55.

Margolis, M., & Resnick, D. (2000). *Politics as usual: the cyberspace "revolution"*. Thousand Oaks, CA: Sage Publications.

Margolis, M., & Resnick, D. (2000). *Politics as Usual: The Cyberspace Revolution*. London: Sage.

Markwood, R., & Johnstone, S. (1994). *New Pathways to a degree: Technology opens the college*. Boulder, CO: Western Cooperative for Educational Telecommunications, Western Interstate Commission for Higher Education.

Marrow, D. (2014, February 13). *Tumblr*. Retrieved from http://spiel-it.tumblr.com/post/76557966735

Marshall, D. (2005). Food as ritual, routine or convention. *Consumption Markets & Culture*, *8*(1), 69–85. doi:10.1080/10253860500069042

Martin, M. (2002). An Unsuitable Technology for a Woman? Communication as Circulation. In Sex & Money, Feminism and Political Economy in the Media. University of Minnesota Press.

Martin, R. (2011). *Sweden battles national butter shortage*. Retrieved January 17, 2015, from www.thelocal.se/20110928/36412

Martin, S. (2002). The Political Economy of Women's Employment in the Information Sector. In Sex & Money, Feminism and Political Economy in the Media. University of Minnesota Press.

Martin, E. (1998). Anthropology and the Cultural Study of Science. *Science, Technology & Human Values*, *23*(1), 24–44. doi:10.1177/016224399802300102

Martinez, R. (2011). *Liberan a cibernautas acusados de terrorismo y sabotaje*. Proceso.

Martin, G., & Beaumont, P. B. (2003). *What's in a Name? Building the Relationship between Branding and People Management*. Wimbledon, UK: Chartered Institute of Personnel and Development.

Martin, G., Beaumont, P. B., & Staines, H. (1998). Determinants of Management Development–Evidence from Scotland. *The International Journal of Organizational Analysis*, *6*(2), 132–145. doi:10.1108/eb028881

Martin, J. A. (2015). Mobile news use and participation in elections: A bridge for the democratic divide? *Mobile Media & Communication*, *3*(2), 230–249. doi:10.1177/2050157914550664

Martin, P. (2004). Inside the Black Box of Negative Campaign Effects: Three Reasons Why Negative Campaigns Mobilize. *Political Psychology*, *25*(4), 545–562. doi:10.1111/j.1467-9221.2004.00386.x

Mashable. (2012). *Politics Transformed: The High Tech Battle for Your Vote*. Mashable, Inc.

Masie, E. (2001). *If we build it, will they come?* Retrieved from http://www.astd.org/virtual_community/ research/pdf/844-6110pdf.pdf

Masie, E. (2001). *If we build it, will they come?* Retrieved insert 02/04/2014, from http://www.astd.org/virtual_community/ research/pdf/844-6110pdf.pdf

Matz, D. C., & Wood, W. (2005). Cognitive dissonance in groups: The consequences of disagreement. *Journal of Personality and Social Psychology*, *88*(1), 22–37. doi:10.1037/0022-3514.88.1.22 PMID:15631572

Mazierska, E. (2014). Introduction: Marking political cinema. *Framework: The Journal of Cinema and Media*, *55*(1), 33–44. doi:10.13110/framework.55.1.0033

McBride, A. E. (2010, Winter). "Food porn." Gastronomica. *The Journal of Food and Culture*, *10*(1), 38–46. PMID:21539050

McClurg, S. (2006). Political disagreement in context: The conditional effect of neighborhood context, disagreement and political talk on electoral participation. *Political Behavior*, *28*(4), 349–366. doi:10.1007/s11109-006-9015-4

Mccuen, B., & Morton, R. B. (2010). Tactical coalition voting and information in the laboratory. *Electoral Studies*, *29*(3), 316–328. doi:10.1016/j.electstud.2010.03.009

McCullagh, D. (2004, May 4). Liberal Net Rules Spawn Political Attack Ads. *CNET News*.

McGee, M. C. (1990). Text, comntext, and the fragmentation n of cobntemporary culture. *Western Journal of Speech Communication*, *54*(3), 274–289. doi:10.1080/10570319009374343

McKerrow, R. (1989). Critical rhetoric: Theory and praxis. *Communication Monographs*, *56*(2), 91–111. doi:10.1080/03637758909390253

McLean, J., & Maalsen, S. (2015). *From# destroythejoint to far reaching digital activism: Feminist revitalisation stemming from social media and reaching beyond*. Civic Media Project.

Mcleod, J. M., Scheufele, D., & Moy, P. (1999). Community, communication, and participation: The role of mass media and interpersonal discussion in local political participation. *Political Communication*, *16*(3), 315–336. doi:10.1080/105846099198659

McNay, D. (2015, February 10). The fat shaming scandal at Bryn Mawr. *Huffington Post*. Retrieved from http://www.huffingtonpost.com/don-mcnay/the-fat-shaming-scandal_b_6654676.html

Mertus, J. (2009). *The United Nations and Human Rights: A Guide for a New Era*. Oxon, UK: Taylor & Francis.

Milenio. (2012, May 14). *Responden en video 131 alumnos de la Ibero: "No somos acarreados"*. Retrieved June 2, 2012, from http://www.milenio.com/cdb/doc/noticias2011/1db22ab7d4f97d7491d79e46da38c215

Miller, A. D., & Edwards, W. K. (2007). Give and take: A study of consumer photo-sharing culture and practice.*Proceedings of CHI'07*. San Jose, CA: ACM Press. doi:10.1145/1240624.1240682

Miller, B., & Lundgren, J. (2010, April). An experimental study on the role of weight bias in candidate evaluation. *Obesity (Silver Spring, Md.)*, *4*(18), 712–718. doi:10.1038/oby.2009.492 PMID:20111025

Miller, F., & Varma, N. (1994). The Effects of Psychosocial Factors on Indian Childrens Attitudes toward Computers. *Journal of Educational Computing Research*, *10*(3), 223–238. doi:10.2190/BMT6-WPJY-FXAR-VU06

Milner, J. (2010, April 20). Documentary review: Food, Inc. *My Literary Quest*. Retrieved from https://myliteraryquest.wordpress.com/2010/04/20/documentary-review-food-inc/

Mirzoeff, N. (1999). *An Introduction to Visual Culture*. London: Routledge.

Mislove, A. (2007). Measurement and Analysis of Online Social Networks. *IMC'07*.

Mital, M. (2011). Does Technology Uptake Convert to Effectiveness: Re-Evaluating ELearning Effectiveness. In E. M. W. Ng, N. Karacapilidis, & M. R. Raisinghani (Eds.), *Evaluating the Impact of Technology on Learning, Teaching, and Designing Curriculum: Emerging Trends*. Hershey, PA: IGI Global.

Mital, M. (2011). Does Technology Uptake Convert to Effectiveness: Re-Evaluating E-Learning Effectiveness. In E. M. W. Ng, N. Karacapilidis, & M. R. Raisinghani (Eds.), *Evaluating the Impact of Technology on Learning, Teaching, and Designing Curriculum: Emerging Trends*. Hershey, PA: IGI Global.

Mitchell, R. D. (Ed.). (2014). *Food Design on the Edge: Proceedings of the International Food Design Conference and Studio 2014*. Otago Polytechnic.

Mitchell, W. J. T. (1995). *Picture theory: Essays on verbal and visual representation*. Chicago: University of Chicago Press.

Moeller, J., de Vreese, C., Esser, F., & Kunz, R. (2014). Pathway to political participation: The influence of online and offline news media on internal efficacy and turnout of first-time voters. *The American Behavioral Scientist*, *58*(5), 689–700. doi:10.1177/0002764213515220

Moeng, B. (2004). *IBM tackles learning in the workplace*. Retrieved from http://www.itweb.co.za/sections/business/2004/0411081222.asp?A=BED&S=Business%20Education%20and%20Training&O=FPIN

Monroe, J. (2012, July 30). *Hunger hurts* [Blog post]. Retrieved from http://agirlcalledjack.com/2012/07/30/hunger-hurts/

Monroe, J. (2013a, January 31). Chef for less. *Echo and Gazette (Southend)*. Retrieved from http://agirlcalledjack.com/2013/01/31/taste-echo-gazette-31st-jan/

Monroe, J. (2013b, February 2). *Courgette & Mint Fritters* [Blog post]. Retrieved from http://agirlcalledjack.com/2013/02/02/quick-courgette-mint-fritters-18p/

Monroe, J. (2013c, July 20). How blogging about £10 a week food shop helped me cope with life. *The Guardian*. Retrieved from http://www.theguardian.com/lifeandstyle/2013/jul/20/10-pound-food-shop-blog

Monroe, J. (2013d, September 10). The government are feckless, neglectful and abusive. *HuffPost (UK)*. Retrieved from http://www.huffingtonpost.co.uk/jack-monroe/government-are-feckless-neglectful-abusive_b_3900933.html

Monroe, J. (2013e, September 18). Austerity bites: You can starve on benefits in this country. *The Guardian*. Retrieved from https://www.theguardian.com/society/2013/sep/18/jack-monroe-starve-benefits-england

Monroe, J. (2013f, October 16). Food banks are testimony to the Tories' massacre of hope and dignity. *The Guardian*. Retrieved from http://www.theguardian.com/society/2013/oct/16/food-banks-tories-policies

Monroe, J. (2013g, October 16). *We need an inquiry into food banks: My column in today's Guardian* [Blog post]. Retrieved from http://agirlcalledjack.com/2013/10/16/we-need-an-inquiry-into-food-banks-my-column-in-todays-guardian/

Monroe, J. (2013h, October 29). Some British people can't afford to heat their food. Aren't we ashamed? *The Guardian. Comment Is Free* [Blog post]. Retrieved from http://www.theguardian.com/commentisfree/2013/oct/29/british-cant-afford-heat-food-big-six-energy-jack-monroe

Monroe, J. (2013i, November 1). Dear Richard Littlejohn—Here's some polish for that turd. *HuffPost (UK)*. Retrieved from http://www.huffingtonpost.co.uk/jack-monroe/richard-littlejohn-polish-for-that-turd_b_4191747.html

Monroe, J. (2013j, November 19). MPs' bedroom tax hypocrisy—a sensible solution, at last. *The Guardian*. Retrieved from http://www.theguardian.com/society/2013/nov/19/mps-bedroom-tax-hypocrisy-block-of-flats

Monroe, J. (2013k, December 3). We went hungry in world' s seventh-richest nation—It has to stop. *Mirror*. Retrieved from http://www.mirror.co.uk/news/real-life-stories/jack-monroe-food-poverty-went-2877510

Monroe, J. (2014, February 18). *Poverty can happen to anyone* [Blog post]. Retrieved from http://agirlcalledjack.com/2014/02/18/poverty-can-happen-to-anyone-guardian-column-feb-2013/

Monroe, J. (2015a, February 19). *I can't even answer my own front door* [Blog post]. Retrieved from http://agirlcalledjack.com/2015/02/19/i-cant-even-open-my-own-front-door/

Monroe, J. (2015b, April 27). *Live below the line: My £5 shop, crying in the supermarket, and the dreaded mushy peas* [Blog post]. Retrieved from http://agirlcalledjack.com/2015/04/27/live-below-the-line-my-5-shop-crying-in-the-supermarket-and-the-dreaded-mushy-peas/

Moore, A., & Stilgoe, J. (2009). Experts and Anecdotes: The Role of Anecdotal Evidence in Public Scientific Controversies. *Science, Technology & Human Values*, *34*(5), 654–677. doi:10.1177/0162243908329382

Moore, T., & Clayton, R. (2009). The Impact of Incentives on Notice and Take-down. In E. M. Johnson (Ed.), *Managing Information Risk and the Economics of Security* (pp. 199–223). New York: Springer. doi:10.1007/978-0-387-09762-6_10

Morgan, D. L. (2008). Snowball sampling. In L. M. Given (Ed.), The Sage Encyclopedia of Qualitative Research Methods (vol. 2, pp. 816-817). Thousand Oaks, CA: Sage Publications.

Morgan, K. P. (1991). Women and the knife: Cosmetic surgery and the colonization of womens bodies. *Hypatia: Feminism and the Body*, *6*(3), 25–53. doi:10.1111/j.1527-2001.1991.tb00254.x

Morozov, E. (2011). Whither Internet Control? *Journal of Democracy*, *22*(2), 62–74. doi:10.1353/jod.2011.0022

Morris, N. (2013, July 2). Demand for food banks has nothing to do with benefits squeeze, says Work Minister Lord Freud. *The Independent*. Retrieved from http://www.independent.co.uk/news/uk/politics/demand-for-food-banks-has-nothing-to-do-with-benefits-squeeze-says-work-minister-lord-freud-8684005.html

Morse, F. (2013, October 3). Tory MP Paul Maynard suggests food banks could become a "habit" for people in poverty. *The Independent*. Retrieved from http://www.independent.co.uk/news/uk/tory-mp-paul-maynard-suggests-food-banks-could-become-a-habit-for-people-in-poverty-8855762.html

Morsink, J. (1999). *The Universal Declaration of Human Rights: Origins, Drafting, and Intent*. University of Pennsylvania Press. doi:10.9783/9780812200416

Mossberger, K., Tolbert, C., & Stansbury, M. (2003). *Virtual Inequality - Beyond the Digital Divide*. Washington, DC: Georgetown University Press.

Moy, P., & Xenos, M. (2007). Direct and Differential Effects of the Internet on Political and Civic Engagement. *Journal of Communication*, *54*(7), 704–718.

Mpuga, D. (2015). *Social Media Critic Arrested in Uganda*. Retrieved from http://www.voanews.com/content/social-media-critic-arrested-in-uganda-/2820626.html

Murray, J. W. (2002). Dialogue of motives. *Philosophy & Rhetoric*, *35*(1), 22–49. doi:10.1353/par.2002.0004

Mutiga, M. (2016, March 5). After disputed election, Uganda police target media. *The East African*.

Mutsvairo, B., & Sirks, L. A. (2015). Examining the contribution of social media in reinforcing political participation in Zimbabwe. *Journal of African Media Studies*, *7*(3), 329–344. doi:10.1386/jams.7.3.329_1

Mutz, D. (2006). *Hearing the other side: Deliberative versus participatory democracy*. Cambridge, MA: Cambridge University Press. doi:10.1017/CBO9780511617201

Mutz, D. C. (2002). The consequences of cross-cutting networks for political participation. *American Journal of Political Science*, *46*(4), 838–855. doi:10.2307/3088437

Mutz, D. C. (2015). *In-your-face politics: The consequences of uncivil media*. Princeton, NJ: Princeton University Press. doi:10.1515/9781400865871

Mutz, D. C., & Reeves, B. (2005). The new videomalaise: Effects of televised incivility on political trust. *The American Political Science Review*, *99*(01), 1–16. doi:10.1017/S0003055405051452

Myers, G. (2003). Discourse Studies of Scientific Popularization: Questioning the Boundaries. *Discourse Studies*, *5*(2), 265–279. doi:10.1177/1461445603005002006

Nahon, K., & Hemsley, J. (2011). Democracy.com: A Tale of Political Blogs and Content. In *Proceedings of the 44th Annual Hawaii International Conference on System Sciences (HICSS 2011)* (pp. 1–10). Kauai, HI: IEEE Computer Society Conference Publishing Services. doi:10.1109/HICSS.2011.140

Nanì, A. (2013). *Crossmedia practices for the enhancement of civic engagement* (Unpublished master's thesis). Tallinn University Baltic Film and Media School, Tallinn, Estonia.

Nardi, B., Schiano, D., Gumbrecht, M., & Swartz, L. (2004). Why we blog. *Communications of the ACM*, *47*(12), 41–46. doi:10.1145/1035134.1035163

Närlid, M. (2008). The National Board of Health and Welfare exonerate Annika Dahlqvist, but does not address the dietary recommendations [my translation]. *Journal of the Swedish Medical Association* [my translation]. Retrieved February 9, 2015, from http://www.lakartidningen.se/OldWebArticlePdf/8/8643/LKT0804s191_193.pdf

Närvänen, E., Kartastenpää, E., & Kuusela, H. (2013). Online lifestyle consumption community dynamics: A practice-based analysis. *Journal of Consumer Behaviour*, *12*(5), 358–369. doi:10.1002/cb.1433

Nelson, N. (2012, January 25). 'Food, Inc.' fans helped changed national school lunch policy. *Take Part*. Retrieved from http://www.takepart.com/article/2012/01/25/lunch-looking-new-federal-guidelines-mandate-more-fruits-and-veggies-school-kids

Nestle, M. (2002/2013). *Food politics: How the food industry influences nutrition and health*. Berkeley, CA: University of California Press, California Studies in Food and Culture.

NFA. (2011). *Annual report - 2010* [my translation]. Retrieved January 8, 2015, from http://tinyurl.com/ldlx2lx

NFA. (2013a). *Annual report - 2012* [my translation]. Retrieved January 8, 2015, from http://tinyurl.com/k7d3la4

NFA. (2013b). *Good school meals: Guidelines for primary schools, secondary schools and youth recreation centres*. Retrieved January 8, 2015, from http://tinyurl.com/lue3maa

Niemi, R. G., Craig, S. C., & Mattei, F. (1991). Measuring internal political efficacy in the 1988 National Election Study. *The American Political Science Review*, *85*(4), 1407. doi:10.2307/1963953

Noakes, T. (2014). *The Noakes Foundation*. Retrieved February 26, 2015, from http://thenoakesfoundation.org/

Nonnecke, B., & Preece, J. (2000). Lurker demographics: Counting the silent. In *Proceedings of the SIGCHI Conference on Human Factors in Computing Systems,* (pp. 73-80). doi:10.1145/332040.332409

Nordic Council of Ministers. (2014). *Nordic Nutrition Recommendations 2012* (5th ed.). Author.

Norman, C. (2012). Social media and health promotion. *Global Health Promotion and Education*, *19*(4), 3–6. doi:10.1177/1757975912464593 PMID:24803437

Norris, P. (2001). *Digital Divide. Civic Engagement, Information Poverty, and the Internet Worldwide*. Cambridge, UK: Cambridge University Press. doi:10.1017/CBO9781139164887

Norton, B. (1999). Ecology and opportunity: Intergenerational equity and sustainable options. *Fairness and Futurity: Essays on Environmental Sustainability and Social Justice,* 118-150.

Norton, S. (2015, January 20). How a Girl Called Jack revolutionised budget cooking. *The Independent*. Retrieved from http://www.independent.co.uk/life-style/health-and-families/features/a-girl-called-jack-how-jack-monroe-revolutionised-budget-cooking-9989853.html?origin=internalSearch

Nunez, D. (2014, April 3). *Twitter*. Retrieved Febr 10, 2015, from https://twitter.com/dpn5/status/451737726363385856

Nwankpa, N. (2014). An advocacy for "Solution Photojournalism" in disaster situations. *Journal of Communication and Media Research*, *6*(2), 21–29.

O'Connell, R., Knight, A., & Brannen, J. (2015). Food austerity from an historical perspective. *Discover Society*, (16). Retrieved from http://discoversociety.org/2015/01/03/food-austerity-from-an-historical-perspective-making-sense-of-1950s-mass-observation-data-in-the-contemporary-era/

O'Neill, M. (2003). Food Porn. *Columbia Journalism Review*, (September–October), 38–45.

O'Neill, M. (2003). Food porn. *Columbia Journalism Review*, *5*, 38–45.

OECD. (2007). *ICTs and Gender.* doi:10.1787/231011217663

Oetzel, J. G. (1998). The effects of self-construals and ethnicity on self-reported conflict styles. *Communication Reports*, *11*(2), 133–144. doi:10.1080/08934219809367695

Old Mutual Health Convention. (2015). *The Old Mutual Health Convention 2015 Cape Town*. Retrieved February 19, 2015, from https://www.youtube.com/watch?v=x4XgqJjfLqs

Olson, L., Finnegan, C., & Hope, D. (Eds.). (2008). *Visual rhetoric*. Thousand Oaks, CA: Sage Publications.

OSCE. (2010). *Freedom of Expression on the Internet Study of legal provisions and practices related to freedom of expression, the free flow of information and media pluralism on the Internet in OSCE participating states*. Available at: http://www.osce.org/fom/80723

Oulette, L. (2010). Reality TV gives back: On the civic functions of reality entertainment. *Journal of Popular Film & Television*, *38*(2), 66–71. doi:10.1080/01956051.2010.483347

Oxfam, U. K. (2012). *The perfect storm: Economic stagnation, the rising cost of living, public spending cuts and the impact on UK poverty*. Retrieved from http://policy-practice.oxfam.org.uk/publications/the-perfect-storm-economic-stagnation-the-rising-cost-of-living-public-spending-228591

Padgett, T. (2012, July 2). How Enrique Peña Nieto Won Himself and His Party the Mexican Presidency. *Time*. Retrieved from http://world.time.com/2012/07/02/mexico-election-how-enrique-pena-nieto-won-himself-and-his-party-the-presidency/

Page, F. F. (n.d.). Retrieved 21 February, 2015, from https://www.facebook.com/FarmVille

Papacharissi, A. Z. (2010). *A Private Sphere: Democracy in a Digital Age*. Malden, MA: Polity.

Papacharissi, Z. (2004). Democracy online: Civility, politeness, and the democratic potential of online political discussion groups. *New Media & Society*, *6*(2), 259–283. doi:10.1177/1461444804041444

Papacharissi, Z. (2009). The Virtual Sphere 2.0: The Internet, the Public Sphere and Beyond. In *Routledge Handbook of Internet Politics* (pp. 230–245). London: Routledge.

Papaloi & Gouscos. (2012). An Overview of E-Parliament Services: Designing for Citizen Awareness and Participation. In E-Parliament and ICT Based Legislation: Concept, Experiences and Lessons. IGI Global.

Papaloi, A., Staiou, E.-R., & Gouscos, D. (2012). Blending social media with parliamentary websites: just a trend, or a promising approach to eparticipation? In C. Reddick & S. Aikins (Eds.), *Web 2.0 Technologies and Democratic Governance: Political, Policy and Management Implications*. Springer. doi:10.1007/978-1-4614-1448-3_17

Park, C. S. (2013). Does Twitter Motivate Involvement in Politics? Tweeting, Opinion Leadership, and Political Engagement. *Computers in Human Behavior, 29*(4). doi:.10.1016/j.chb.2013.01.044

Parkinson, J. R. (2012). *Democracy and public space: The physical sites of democratic performance*. Oxford, UK: Oxford University Press. doi:10.1093/acprof:osobl/9780199214563.001.0001

Parmalee, J., & Bichard, S. (2012). *Politics and the Twitter Revolution: How Tweets Influence The Relationship Between Political Leaders and the Public*. Lanham, MD: Lexington Books.

Pateman, C. (1970). *Participation and Democratic Theory*. Cambridge, UK: Cambridge University Press. doi:10.1017/CBO9780511720444

Pattie, C., Seyd, P., & Whiteley, P. (2004). *Citizenship in Britain: Values, Participation, and Democracy*. Cambridge University Press. doi:10.1017/CBO9780511490811

Pellizzoni, L. (2003). Knowledge, Uncertainty and the Transformation of the Public Sphere. *European Journal of Social Theory*, *6*(3), 327–355. doi:10.1177/13684310030063004

People's Archive of Rural India (PARI). (n.d.). Retrieved 10 February, 2015, from http://www.ruralindiaonline.org/about/

Perry, J., Williams, M., Sefton, T., & Haddad, M. (2014, November). *Emergency use only: Understanding and reducing the use of food banks in the UK*. Child Poverty Action Group, the Church of England, Oxfam and the Trussell Trust. Retrieved from http://www.cpag.org.uk/sites/default/files/FoodbankReport_web.pdf

Peters, R. (2011, January 11). Quiz: do you know your sea fish? *The Guardian*. Retrieved from http://www.theguardian.com/lifeandstyle/quiz/2011/jan/11/sea-fish-quiz

Phelps, E. (2006). *Young Adults and Electoral Turnout in Britain: Towards a Generational Model of Political Participation*. Sussex European Institute Working Paper No 92.

Picard, R. (2011). *Digitization and Media Business Models*. Open Society Foundations. Available at: http://www.opensocietyfoundations.org/sites/default/files/digitization-media-business-models-20110721.pdf

Pliskin, N., & Romm, C. T. (1997). The impact of e-mail on the evolution of a virtual community during a strike. *Information & Management*, *32*(5), 245–254. doi:10.1016/S0378-7206(97)00027-X

Pliskin, N., Romm, C. T., & Markey, R. (1997). E-mail as a weapon in an industrial dispute. *New Technology, Work and Employment*, *12*(1), 3–12. doi:10.1111/1468-005X.00018

Pole, A., & Xenos, M. (2011). *Like, Comments and Retweets: Facebooking and Tweeting on the 2010 Gubernatorial Campaign Trail*. Paper presented at the State Politics and Policy Conference, Hanover, NH. Retrieved from http://www.sppc2011.org/Papers/1_Pole.pdf

Polkinghorne, J. C. (2000). *Faith, science, and understanding*. Yale University Press.

Pollan, M. (2006). *The omnivore's dilemma: A natural history of four meals*. New York, NY: Penguin.

Pollan, M. (2008). *In defense of food: An eater's manifesto*. New York, NY: Penguin.

Pollan, M. (2013). *Cooked: A natural history of transformation*. New York, NY: Penguin.

Poppendieck, J. (1998). *Sweet charity: Emergency food and the end of entitlement*. Harmondsworth, UK: Viking Penguin.

Powazek, D. M. (2002). *Design for community: The art of connecting real people in virtual places*. Upper Saddle River, NJ: New Riders.

Pratchett, L. (2006). Making local e-democracy work? In M. Virapatirin & T. Peixoto (Eds.), *e-AGORA, Le Livre Blanc de la e-démocratie locale: Réflexions et Perspectives* (pp. 319–331). Paris: Ville d'Issy-les-Moulineaux.

Pratchett, L., Wingfield, M., & Karakaya-Polat, R. (2005). *Barriers to e-Democracy: Local government experiences and responses*. London: Local e-Democracy National Project.

Pratten, R. (2011). *Getting started in transmedia storytelling: A practical guide for beginners*. Seattle, WA: CreateSpace.

Preece, J. (2000). *Online communities: Designing usability, supporting sociability*. Chichester, UK: John Wiley & Sons.

Preece, J., Nonnecke, B., & Andrews, D. (2004). The top 5 reasons for lurking: Improving community experiences for everyone. *Computers in Human Behavior*, *2*(1), 42.

Price, T. (2012). A Twitter: A New Political Weathervane. *CQ Researcher*, *29*(4), 876–877.

Primo, N. (2005). Gender Issues in the Information Society. Paris: UNESCO. Available at http://portal.unesco.org/ci/en/file_download.php/250561f24133814c18284feedc30bb5egender_issues.pdf

Purdam, K., & Garratt, E. A. (2015). Hungry? Food insecurity, social stigma and embarrassment in the UK. *Sociology*, 1–17. doi:10.1177/0038038515594092

Purves, L. (2013, February 18). Do stop shuddering you poncey gourmands. *The Times*. Retrieved from http://www.thetimes.co.uk/tto/opinion/columnists/libbypurves/article3691099.ece

Putnam, L. L., & Poole, S. M. (1987). Conflict and negotiation. In F. M. Jablin, L. L. Putnam, K. H. Roberts, & L. W. Porter (Eds.), Handbook of organizational communication: An interdisciplinary perspective (pp. 549-599). Thousand Oaks, CA: Sage.

Quintelier, E., & Vissers, S. (2008). The Effect of Internet Use on Political Participation: An Analysis of Survey Results for 16-Year-Olds in Belgium. *Social Science Computer Review*, *26*(4), 411–427. doi:10.1177/0894439307312631

Rahim, M. A. (1983). A measure of styles of handling interpersonal conflict. *Academy of Management Journal*, *26*(2), 368–376. doi:10.2307/255985 PMID:10263067

Rainie, L., Smith, A., Schlozman, K. L., Brady, H., & Verba, S. (2012). Social media and political engagement. *Pew Internet & American Life Project*. Retrieved from http://pewinternet.org/~/media//Files/Reports/2012/PIP_SocialMediaAndPoliticalEngagement_PDF.pdf

Rajchman, J. (1988). Foucault's art of seeing. *October, 44*, 88-117.

Ramos-Serrano, M., Gómez, J. D, F., & Pineda, A. (2016). Follow the closing of the campaign on streaming': The use of Twitter by Spanish political parties during the 2014 European elections. *New Media & Society*. (forthcoming)

Räsänen, P. (2008). The aftermath of the ICT revolution? Media and communication technology preferences in Finland in 1999 and 2004. *New Media & Society*, *10*(2), 225–245. doi:10.1177/1461444807086471

Ray, K. (2007, Winter). Domesticating cuisine: Food and aesthetics on American television. Gastronomica. *The Journal of Critical Food Studies*, *7*(1), 50–63.

Raymond, W. (1985). *Keywords: A Vocabulary of Culture and Society*. Oxford, UK: Oxford University Press.

Real Meal Revolution. (2015). *The Real Meal Revolution*. Retrieved February 14, 2015, from http://realmealrevolution.com/

Reporter, S. (2009, October 9). Facebook farmers want India flag. *BBC News*. Retrieved from http://news.bbc.co.uk

Reporter, S. (2014, September 25). Forbes India rich list: Mukesh Ambani tops again, Gautam Adani moves up. *Economic Times*. Retrieved from http://articles.economictimes.indiatimes.com

Retriever. (2015). Retrieved January 3, 2015, from http://www.retriever-info.com/en/category/news-archive/

Reuter, O. J., & Szakonyi, D. (2015). Online Social Media and Political Awareness in Authoritarian Regimes. *British Journal of Political Science*, *45*(01), 29–51. doi:10.1017/S0007123413000203

Rhue, L., & Sundararajan, A. (2014). Digital access, political networks and the diffusion of democracy. *Social Networks*, *36*, 40–53. doi:10.1016/j.socnet.2012.06.007

Richardson, C. (2012, July 23). River Cottage's Hugh Fearnley-Whittingstall is coming to town. *Mercury*. Retrieved from http://www.thewestonmercury.co.uk/what-s-on/latest-films-reviews/river_cottage_s_hugh_fearnley_whittingstall_is_coming_to_town_1_1455913

Riches, G., & Silvasti, T. (2014). Hunger in the rich world: Food aid and right to food perspectives. In G. Riches (Ed.), *First world hunger* (pp. 1–14). Basingstoke, UK: Palgrave Macmillan. doi:10.1057/9781137298737_1

Riley, T., & Riley, C. (2003). International Tracking Survey Report '03 Number Five. *Egovernance to E-Democracy: Examining the Evolution.* Ottawa, Canada: Commonwealth Centre for E-Governance, Prepared under the auspices of the Commonwealth Secretariat And Co-sponsored Telecommunications and Informatics Program, Public Works and Government Services Canada.

Riordan, E. (2002). Intersections and New Directions: On Feminism and Political Economy. In Sex & Money, Feminism and Political Economy in the Media. University of Minnesota Press.

Roberts, C. (2013, February 15). Why Hugh Fearnley-Whittingstall's Fish Fight is still necessary. *The Guardian*. Retrieved from http://www.theguardian.com/commentisfree/2013/feb/15/hugh-fearnley-whittingstall-fish-fight-necessary

Robertson, Douglas, Maruyama, & Chen. (2012). Political Dialog Evolution in a Social Network. In *Proceedings of the 13th Annual International Conference on Digital Government Research* (pp. 40–48). ACM.

Robertson, S. P., Vatrapu, R. K., & Medina, R. (2009). The social life of social networks: Facebook linkage patterns in the 2008 U.S. presidential election. In *Proceedings of the 10th Annual International Conference on Digital Government Research: Social Networks: Making Connections between Citizens, Data and Government (dg.o 2009)* (pp. 6–15). Puebla, Mexico: Digital Government Society of North America.

Robertson, S. P., Vatrapu, R. K., & Medina, R. (2010). Off the wall political discourse: Facebook use in the 2008 U.S. presidential election. *Information Polity*, *15*(1), 11–31. doi:10.3233/IP-2010-0196

Romm, C. T. & Pliskin, N. (1999). The role of charismatic leadership in diffusion and implementation of e-mail. *The Journal of Management Development*, *17*(1), 273-290.

Romm, C. T., & Pliskin, N. (1999). The role of charismatic leadership in diffusion and implementation of e-mail. *The Journal of Management Development*, *17*(1), 273-290.

Romm, C. T. (1999). *Virtual Politicking*. Cresskill, NJ: Hampton Press.

Romm, C. T., & Pliskin, N. (1997a). Toward a virtual politicking model. *Communications of the ACM*, *40*(11), 95–102. doi:10.1145/265684.265696

Romm, C. T., & Pliskin, N. (1997b). Battle of the sexes on e-mail- or is it? *The Information Society*, *13*(3), 207–225. doi:10.1080/019722497129106

Romm, C. T., & Pliskin, N. (1998). Electronic mail as a coalition-building information technology. *ACM Transactions on Information Systems*, *16*(1), 82–100. doi:10.1145/267954.267958

Romm-Livermore, C. Raisinghani, M. S. & Rippa, P (2014a). The Politics of eLearning: A Theoretical Model. *International Journal of E-Politics.*

Romm-Livermore, C., Raisinghani, M. S., & Rippa, P. (2014b). eLearning as a Political Arena. In eLearning as a Socio Cultural System – A Multidimensional Analysi. IGI Global.

Romm-Livermore, C. (2012). *E-politics and organizational implications of the internet: Power, influence, and social change*. Hershey, PA: IGI Global. doi:10.4018/978-1-4666-0966-2

Romm-Livermore, C., & Rippa, P. (2010). The Politics of Implementing ERP – A Cross-Cultural Comparison. In *Proceedings of the Tenth Global Information Technology Management World Conference (GITM).*

Ronson, D., & Caraher, M. (2016). Food banks: Big society or shunting yards? Successful failures. In M. Caraher & J. Coveney (Eds.), *Food poverty and insecurity: International food inequalities* (pp. 79–88). Heidelberg, Germany: Springer. doi:10.1007/978-3-319-23859-3_8

Rook, D. (1985). The ritual dimension of consumer behaviour. *Journal of Consumer Behaviour, 12*(December), 251–264. doi:10.1086/208514

Rosenberg, M. (2001). *eLearning: Strategies for Delivering Knowledge in the Digital Age.* Retrieved from http://www.amazon.com/ELearning-Strategies-Delivering-Knowledge-Digital/dp/0071362681/bigdogsbowlofbis

Rosenberg, M. J. (2001). *E-Learning. Strategies for Delivering Knowledge in the Digital Age.* Columbus, OH: McGraw Hill.

Rösner, L., Winter, S., & Krämer, N. C. (2016). Dangerous minds? Effects of uncivil online comments on aggressive cognitions, emotions, and behavior. *Computers in Human Behavior, 58*, 461–470. doi:10.1016/j.chb.2016.01.022

Ross, K. (2002). Selling Women (Down the River): Gendered Relations and the Political Economy of Broadcast News. In Sex & Money, Feminism and Political Economy in the Media. University of Minnesota Press.

Rossett, A., & Sheldon, K. (2001). *Beyond The Podium: Delivering Training and Performance to a Digital World.* Retrieved from http://www.amazon.com/exec/obidos/tg/detail/-/0787955264/bigdogsbowlofbis

Rossett, A., & Sheldon, K. (2001). *Beyond The Podium: Delivering Training and Performance to a Digital World.* San Francisco: Jossey-Bass/Pfeiffer.

Rousseau, S. (2012). *Food and Social Media: You Are What You Tweet.* Lanham, MD: AltaMira Press.

Rousseau, S. (2014). Food "Porn" in Media. In *Encyclopedia of Food and Agricultural Ethics* (pp. 1–8). Springer.

Roussopoulos, R., & Benello, G. (2005). Components of New Society: Introduction. In R. Roussopoulos & G. Benello (Eds.), *Participatory Democracy - Prospects for Democratizing Democracy* (2nd ed.; pp. 3–11). Montreal: Black Rose Books.

Rowe, I. (2015). Civility 2.0: A comparative analysis of incivility in online political discussion. *Information Communication and Society, 18*(2), 121–138. doi:10.1080/1369118X.2014.940365

Rüdig, W., & Karyotis, G. (2013, September). Beyond the Usual Suspects? New Participants in Anti-Austerity Protests in Greece. Mobilization. *An International Quarterly, 18*(3), 313–330.

Ruggie, J. (2006). *Interim report of the Special Representative of the Secretary-General on the issue of human rights and transnational corporations and other business enterprises.* UN Doc. E/CN.4/2006/97.

Ruggie, J. (2008). *Protect, Respect and Remedy: a Framework for the Business and Human Rights: Report of the Special Representative of the Secretary-General on the issue of human rights and transnational corporations and other business enterprises, John Ruggie.* UN Doc. E/HRC/8/5.

Ruggie, J. (2011). *Report of the Special Representative of the Secretary-General on the issue of human rights and transnational corporations and other business enterprises, John Ruggie, Guiding Principles on Business and Human Rights: Implementing the United Nations "Protect, Respect and Remedy" Framework*. A/HRC/17/31.

rundreamlive. (2014, February 6). *Tumblr.* Retrieved from http://rundreamlive.tumblr.com/post/75835484002/

Sæbø, Ø. (2011). Understanding Twitter use among parliament representatives: A genre analysis. In *Electronic participation* (pp. 1–12). Springer Berlin Heidelberg. doi:10.1007/978-3-642-23333-3_1

Sæbø, Ø., Rose, J., & Flak, L. (2008). The shape of eParticipation: Characterizing an emerging research area. *Government Information Quarterly*, *25*(3), 400–428. doi:10.1016/j.giq.2007.04.007

Sahlins, M. (1976). *Culture and Practical Reason*. Chicago, IL: Univ. Chicago Press.

Sainath, P. (2013, May 2). Over 2000 fewer farmers every day. *The Hindu*. Retrieved, 20 February, 2015, from http://www.thehindu.com/opinion/columns/sainath/over-2000-fewer-farmers-every-day/article4674190.ece

Sainath, P. (2014). *Maharashtra crosses 60,00 farm suicides*. Retrieved 11 February, 2015, from http://psainath.org/maharashtra-crosses-60000-farm-suicides/

Sainath, P. (2015, January 15). *Farmer commits suicide, Adani gets the loan. Happy Pongal.* Retrieved 7 February, 2015 from http://psainath.org/farmer-commits-suicide-adani-gets-the-loan/

Salgado, S. (2012). The web in African countries: Exploring the possible influences of the internet in the democratization processes. *Information Communication and Society*, *15*(9), 1373–1389. doi:10.1080/1369118X.2011.647044

Salgado, S. (2013). Online party politics. *Politics and the Internet in Comparative Context: Views From The Cloud*, *11*, 118.

Sanchez, R. J., Bauer, T. N., & Paronto, M. E. (2006). Peer-Mentoring Freshmen: Implications for Satisfaction, Commitment, and Retention to Graduation. *Academy of Management Learning & Education*, *5*(1), 25–37. doi:10.5465/AMLE.2006.20388382

Sanders, A. (2004). Creating Effective Political Ads. In D. Schultz (Ed.), *Lights, Camera, Campaign!* New York: Peter Lang Publishing.

Sandoval-Almazan, R., & Gil-Garcia, R. (2013). Cyberactivism through Social Media: Twitter, YouTube, and the Mexican Political Movement "I'm Number 132". In *Proceedings of the 46th Annual Hawaii International Conference on System Sciences* (Vol. 1, pp. 1704–1713). Manoa, HI: IEEE. Retrieved from http://www.cide.edu/publicaciones/status/dts/DTAP%20273.pdf

Sandoval-Almazan, R., & Gil-Garcia, J. R. (2012). Government–Citizen Interactions Using Web 2.0 Tools: The Case of Twitter in Mexico. In C. G. Reddick & S. K. Aikins (Eds.), *Web 2.0 Technologies and Democratic Governance* (Vol. 1, pp. 233–248). Springer New York. doi:10.1007/978-1-4614-1448-3_15

Saward, M. (2013). The dynamics of European citizenship: Enactment, extension and assertion. *Comparative European Politics*, *11*(1), 49–69. doi:10.1057/cep.2012.2

Schauer, F. (2004). Media Law, Media Content, and American Exceptionalism. In European Audiovisual Observatory, Political Debate and the Role of the Media: The Fragility of Free Speech. European Audiovisual Observatory.

Schauer, F. (1982). *Free Speech: A Philosophical Enquity*. Cambridge, UK: Cambridge University Press.

Scherer, S., & Wimmer, M. A. (2011). Reference framework for E-participation projects. In *Electronic Participation* (pp. 145–156). Springer Berlin Heidelberg. doi:10.1007/978-3-642-23333-3_13

SCHTA. (2010). *Food when you have Diabetes: A systematic literature review* [my translation]. Retrieved January 19, 2015, from http://www.sbu.se/contentassets/923855c431bc4f668746920cfb49d590/mat_vid_diabetes_fulltext.pdf

Schweitzer, E. J. (2008). Innovation or Normalization in E-Campaigning. *European Journal of Communication*, *23*(4), 449–470. doi:10.1177/0267323108096994

Scientific Journalists. (2015). *The scientific journalists* [my translation]. Retrieved January 8, 2015, from http://www.vetenskapsjournalisterna.se/index.php?page=english

Scottish National Party (SNP). (2015). *Stronger for Scotland: Election Manifesto*. Retrieved from http://votesnp.com/docs/manifesto.pdf

Sedgwick, M. (2013, May 30). What is it like to rely on food banks? *BBC News Magazine*. Retrieved from http://www.bbc.co.uk/news/uk-22715458

Selby, J. (2014, November 25). Sarah Vine criticizes lesbian mother Jack Monroe. *The Independent*. Retrieved from http://www.independent.co.uk/news/people/sarah-vine-on-jack-monroe-being-a-lesbian-mother-if-she-was-unsure-about-her-sexuality-she-should-have-taken-greater-precautions-9882054.html?origin=internalSearch

Semetko, H. A. (2004). Media, public opinion, and political action. In J. Downing (Ed.), *Handbook of media studies* (pp. 351–374). Thousand Oaks, CA: Sage. doi:10.4135/9781412976077.n18

Semulia, J. (2013). *Media and Ritual: Death*. New York: Community and Everyday Life Routledge.

Sen, A. (1983). Poor, relatively speaking. *Oxford Economic Papers*, *35*(2), 153–169.

Setälä, V., & Väliverronen, E. (2014). Fighting Fat: The Role of Field Experts in Mediating Science and Biological Citizenship. *Science as Culture*, *23*(4), 517–536. doi:10.1080/09505431.2014.905526

Shah, C., & Blaney, A. (2015, January 1). Farming pixels. *The Forager Magazine*. Retrieved 24 February, 2015, from http://www.theforagermagazine.com

Shah, D. V., McLeod, J. M., & Lee, N. (2016). Conversation is the soul of democracy: Expression effects, communication mediation, and digital media. *Communication and the Public*, *26*(1), 12–18. doi:10.1177/2057047316628310

Shahid, A. (n.d.). Andrew Breitbart posts cartoon of fat First Lady. *The New York Daily News*. Retrieved from: http://www.nydailynews.com/news/politics/andrew-breitbart-website-posts-cartoon-fat-lady-mocking-anti-obesity-campaign-article-1.136361

Shapin, S. (Ed.). (2007). *Expertise, common sense, and the Atkins diet*. Toronto, Canada: University of Toronto Press. doi:10.3138/9781442684720-012

Shari. (2014, February 5). Did the 'biggest loser' winner rachel frederickson lose too much weight? *Have U Heard*. Retrieved February 10, 2015, from http://haveuheard.net/2014/02/biggest-loser-winner-rachel-fredricksons-lost-weight/

Shehata, A., Ekström, M., & Olsson, T. (2015). Developing Self-Actualizing and Dutiful Citizens Testing the AC-DC Model Using Panel Data Among Adolescents. *Communication Research*, 0093650215619988.

Shepherd, A., Sanders, C., Doyle, M., & Shaw, J. (2015). Using social media for support and feedback by mental health service users: Thematic analysis of a twitter conversation. *BMC Psychiatry*, *15*(1), 29. doi:10.1186/s12888-015-0408-y PMID:25881089

Shih, T., & Fan, X. (2008). Comparing response rates from web and mail surveys: A meta-analysis. *Field Methods*, *20*(3), 249–271. doi:10.1177/1525822X08317085

Shiva, V. (2000). *Stolen harvest: The hyjacking of the global food supply*. Cambridge, MA: South End Press.

Shiva, V., & Kunwar, J. (2009). *Farmers suicides in India*. New Delhi: Research Foundation for Science, Technology and Ecology.

Shugart, H. A. (2011). Shifting the Balance: The contemporary narrative of obesity. *Health Communication, 26*(1), 37-47. doi: 10.1080/10410236.2011.527620

Simard, C., Davies, A., Gilmartin, S., Schiebinger, C., & Whitney, T. (n.d.). *Climbing the Technical Ladder: obstacles and solutions for mied-level women in technology*. Stanford University, Clyman Institute for Gender Research, Anita Borg Institute for Women and Technology. Available at: http://anitaborg.org/files/Climbing_the_Technical_Ladder_Exec_Summary.pdf

SimilarWeb. (2015). *Top 50 sites in Uganda for all categories*. Retrieved from http://www.similarweb.com/country/uganda

Simpson, A. B. (2015). At what cost?: Problematising the achievement of 'Health' through thinness – The case of Bariatric Surgery. *M/C Journal: Journal of Media and Culture*, (18), 3. Retrieved from http://journal.media-culture.org.au/index.php/mcjournal/article/viewArticle/970

Simpson, J. (2014). *Who are the winners and losers from the Arab Spring?* Retrieved from http://www.bbc.com/news/world-middle-east-30003865

Singh, M. P. (2013). Elections and electoral systems in constitutional regimes. In Routledge handbook of constitutional law. Routledge.

Skaperdas, S., & Grofman, B. (1995). Modeling Negative Campaigning. *The American Political Science Review, 89*(1), 49–61. doi:10.2307/2083074

Slater, T. (2014, February 7). "Recessionista" Jack Monroe is a hero of the thrift-obsessed middle classes, not the poor. *Spiked*. Retrieved from http://www.spiked-online.com/newsite/article/jack-monroe-pleb-lite-for-guardianistas/14622

Sloam, J. (2013). The outraged young: how young Europeans are reshaping the political landscape. *Political Insight, 4*(1), 4–7. doi:10.1111/2041-9066.12003

Small, T. A. (2011). What the hashtag? A content analysis of Canadian politics on Twitter. *Information Communication and Society, 14*(6), 872–895. doi:10.1080/1369118X.2011.554572

Smith, A. (2014). Cell phones, social media and campaign 2014. *Pew Internet & American Life Project*. Retrieved from http://www.pewinternet.org/2014/11/03/cell-phones-social-media-and-campaign-2014/

Smith, A. (2015, April 1). U.S. smartphone use in 2015. *Pew Research Center Internet, Science & Tech*. Retrieved from http://www.pewinternet.org/2015/04/01/us-smartphone-use-in-2015/

Smith, A., & Duggan, M. (2012a). Online political videos and campaign 2012. *Pew Internet & American Life Project*. Retrieved from http://pewinternet.org/Reports/2012/Election-2012-Video.aspx

Smith, A., & Duggan, M. (2012b). Presidential campaign donations in the digital age. *Pew Internet & American Life Project*. Retrieved from http://pewinternet.org/~/media//Files/Reports/2012/PIP_State_of_the_2012_race_donations.pdf

Smith, A., & Duggan, M. (2012c). The state of the 2012 election – Mobile politics. *Pew Internet & American Life Project*. Retrieved from http://pewinternet.org/Reports/2012/Election-2012-Mobile.aspx

Smith, C. (2016). *By the numbers: 170 + Amazing Twitter Statistics*. Retrieved from http://tinyurl.com/mbkv9t6

Snapchat: The Ultimate Guide to Mobile Food Photography, From Lighting to Editing. (2015). Retrieved from http://www.epicurious.com/expert-advice/the-ultimate-guide-to-mobile-food-photography-from-lighting-to-editing-article

Sobieraj, S., & Berry, J. M. (2011). From incivility to outrage: Political discourse in blogs, talk radio, and cable news. *Political Communication*, *28*(1), 19–41. doi:10.1080/10584609.2010.542360

sociallyawkward-jac. (2014, February 5). *Tumblr.* Retrieved from http://sociallyawkward-jac.tumblr.com/post/75745541663

Solo, A. M. G., & Bishop, J. (2011). *The new field of network politics*. Paper presented at the 2011 International Conference on E-Learning, E-Business, Enterprise Information Systems & E-Government (EEE'11), Las Vegas, NV.

Stahl, A. B. (2013). *Lchf less militant* [my translation]. Retrieved February 12, 2015, from http://www.svd.se/mat-och-vin/lchf-mindre-militant_8053806.svd

stahp-thinprivilege. (2014, February 5). Retrieved from http://stahp-thinprivilege.tumblr.com/post/76017096719

Starmer, K. (2013). *Guidelines on prosecuting cases involving communications sent via social media.* London: Crown Prosecution Service.

Stepanova, E. (2011). *The Role of Information Communication Technologies in the "Arab Spring".* PONARS Eurasia Policy Memo No. 159.

Straus, J. R., Williams, R. T., Shogan, C. J., & Glassman, M. E. (2016). Congressional Social Media Communications: Evaluating Senate Twitter Usage. *Online Information Review*, *40*(5), 643–659. doi:10.1108/OIR-10-2015-0334

Strauss, A., & Corbin, J. (1988). Grounded theory methodology. In N. K. Denzin & Y. Lincoln (Eds.), *Strategies of Qualitative Inquiry* (pp. 158–183). Newbury Park, CA: SAGE.

Strom, S. (November 12, 2012). 'Fat tax' in Denmark is repealed after criticism. *New York times.com.* Retrieved February 27, 2015, from http://www.nytimes.com/2012/11/13/ business/global/fat-tax-in-denmark-is-repealed-after-criticism.html?_r=0

Stroud, N. (2008). Media Use and Political Predispositions: Revisiting the Concept of Selective Exposure. *Political Behavior*, *30*(3), 341–366. doi:10.1007/s11109-007-9050-9

Sturken, M., & Cartwright, L. (2001). *Practices of Looking: An Introduction to Visual Culture.* Oxford, UK: Oxford University Press.

Su, N. M., Wang, Y., & Mark, G. (2005). *Politics as usual in the blogosphere.* Paper presented at the 4th International Workshop on Social Intelligence Design (SID).

Suler, J. (2004). The online disinhibition effect. *Cyberpsychology & Behavior*, *7*(3), 321–326. doi:10.1089/1094931041291295 PMID:15257832

Susha, I., & Grönlund, Å. (2012). eParticipation research: Systematizing the field. *Government Information Quarterly*, *29*(3), 373–382. doi:10.1016/j.giq.2011.11.005

Swamynathan, G., Wilson, C., Boe, B., Almeroth, K., & Zhao, B. Y. (2008). Do social networks improve e-commerce?: a study on social marketplaces. In *Proceedings of the first workshop on Online social networks* (pp. 1–6). Seattle, WA: ACM. doi:10.1145/1397735.1397737

sweethappiness. (2014, February 6). *Tumblr.* Retrieved from http://sweethappiness.tumblr.com/post/75809262441/

Syndicut. (n.d.). *The Great British Property Scandal.* Retrieved from http://www.syndicut.com/Posts/Channel-4/Great-British-Property-Scandal

Take Part. (n.d.). *Food, Inc.* Retrieved from http://www.takepart.com/foodinc/

Takeda, A. (2014, April 3). Rachel frederickson, 'biggest loser' winner, gains 20 pounds. *US Magazine.* Retrieved from http://www.usmagazine.com/celebrity-rachel-frederickson-biggest-loser-winner-gains-20-pounds-im-at-my-perfect-weight-201434

Tambouris, E., Liotas, N., Kaliviotis, D., & Tarabanis, K. (2007). A Framework for Scoping eParticipation. The *Proceedings of the 8th Annual International Digital Government Research Conference.*

Tang, G., & Lee, F. L. (2013). Facebook use and political participation: The impact of exposure to shared political information, connections with public political actors, and network structural heterogeneity. *Social Science Computer Review.*

Tang, G., & Lee, F. L. F. (2013). Facebook Use and Political Participation: The Impact of Exposure to Shared Political Information, Connections With Public Political Actors, and Network Structural Heterogeneity. *Social Science Computer Review*, *31*(6), 763–773. doi:10.1177/0894439313490625

Taylor, S., & Todd, P. (1995). Assessing IT Uptake: The Role of Prior Experience. *Management Information Systems Quarterly*, *19*(4), 561–570. doi:10.2307/249633

Terranova, T. (2000). Free Labour: Producing Culture for the Digital Economy. *Social Text*, *18*(2), 33–58. doi:10.1215/01642472-18-2_63-33

The Biggest Loser. (n.d.a). Retrieved from http://en.wikipedia.org/wiki/The_Biggest_Loser

The Biggest Loser. (n.d.b). Retrieved from http://www.biggestloser.com/

The Biggest Loser. (n.d.c). Retrieved from http://www.nbc.com/the-biggest-loser

The Economist. (2012). Mexico election diary: The students are revolting. *The Economist.* Retrieved from http://www.economist.com/blogs/americasview/2012/05/mexico-election-diary

The National Board of Health and Welfare. (2013). *The National Public Health Report 2013* [my translation]. Retrieved January 9, 2015, from http://www.socialstyrelsen.se/Lists/Artikelkatalog/Attachments/19032/2013-3-26.pdf

Theocharis, Y., & Lowe, W. (2015). Does Facebook Increase Political Participation? Evidence from a Field Experiment. *Information Communication and Society*, *4462*(March). doi:10.1080/1369118X.2015.1119871

thepursuittobecomemoreattractive. (n.d.). *Factoh.* Retrieved from http://factoh.com/the-pursuit-to-become-more-attractive-is-a-160-billion-a-year-global-industry

Thompson, D. (2007). *Spectacular decapitations: The body politics of shaming fat with personal responsibility.* Paper presented at the annual meeting of the National Communication Association. Retrieved from http://web.b.ebscohost.com/ehost/pdfviewer/pdfviewer?vid=6&sid=3dc64fe6-b6be-49bd-b970-f6241eef710c%40sessionmgr113&hid=109

Thompson, C. J. (2005). Consumer Risk Perceptions in a Community of Reflexive Doubt. *The Journal of Consumer Research*, *32*(2), 235–248. doi:10.1086/432233

Thompson, H. (2013). Austerity as ideology: The bait and switch of the banking crisis. *Comparative European Politics*, *11*(6), 729–736. doi:10.1057/cep.2013.24

Tian, Y. (2009). *Re-Thinking Intellectual Property: The Political Economy of Copyright Protection in the Digital Era.* Oxon, UK: Taylor & Francis.

Tichenor, P., Donohue, G. A., & Olien, C. N. (1980). *Community conflict and the press.* Thousand Oaks, CA: Sage.

Tillman, L. M. (2014). *Weight problem: Cultural narratives of fat and "obesity"*. Retrieved from http://www.imdb.com/title/tt3787894/?ref_=nm_flmg_dr_1

Ting-Toomey, S. (1994). Managing interpersonal conflict effectively. In L. Samovar & R. Porter (Eds.), *Intercultural communication: A reader* (7th ed.; pp. 360–372). Belmont, CA: Wadsworth.

Ting-Toomey, S., Yee-Jung, K. K., Shapiro, R. B., Garcia, W., Wright, T. J., & Oetzel, J. G. (2000). Ethnic/cultural identity salience and conflict styles in four US ethnic groups. *International Journal of Intercultural Relations*, *24*(1), 47–81. doi:10.1016/S0147-1767(99)00023-1

Tolbert, C. J., & Mcneal, R. S. (2003). Unraveling the Effects of the Internet on Political Participation? *Political Research Quarterly*, *56*(2), 175–185. doi:10.1177/106591290305600206

Toledo-Bastos, M., Galdini-Raimundo, R. L., & Travitzki, R. (2013). Gatekeeping Twitter: Message diffusion in political hashtags. *Media Culture & Society*, *35*(2), 260–270. doi:10.1177/0163443712467594

Towner, T. L., & Muñoz, C. L. (2016). Baby Boom or Bust?: The New Media Effect on Political Participation. *Journal of Political Marketing* (forthcoming).

Towner, T. (2013). All political participation is socially networked? New media and the 2012 election. *Social Science Computer Review*, *31*(5), 527–541. doi:10.1177/0894439313489656

Towner, T. L. (2012). Campaigns and Elections in a Web 2.0 World: Uses, Effects, and Implications for Democracy. In C. G. Reddick & S. K. Aikins (Eds.), *Web 2.0 Technologies and Democratic Governance* (Vol. 1, pp. 185–199). Springer New York. doi:10.1007/978-1-4614-1448-3_12

Towner, T. L., & Dulio, D. A. (2011). An experiment of campaign effects during the YouTube election. *New Media & Society*, *13*(4), 626–644. doi:10.1177/1461444810377917

Tremayne, M. (2007a). *Blogging, citizenship and the future of media*. London, UK: Routledge.

Tremayne, M. (2007b). Introduction: Examining the blog–media relationship. In *Blogging, citizenship and the future of media*. London, UK: Routledge.

Tsfati, Y., & Cappella, J. N. (2005). Why do people watch news they do not trust? the need for cognition as a moderator in the association between news media skepticism and exposure. *Media Psychology*, *7*(3), 251–271. doi:10.1207/S1532785XMEP0703_2

Tufekci, Z., & Wilson, C. (2012). Social Media and the Decision to Participate in Political Protest: Observations From Tahrir Square. *Journal of Communication*, *62*(2), 363–379. doi:10.1111/j.1460-2466.2012.01629.x

Tumasjan, A., Sprenger, T., Sander, P. G., & Welpe, I. (2010). *Predicting Elections with Twitter: What 140 Characters Reveal About Political Sentime*. Paper presented at the 4th International AAAI Conference on Web Blogs and Social Media, Munich, Germany.

Tumasjan, A., Sprenger, T. O., Sandner, P. G., & Welpe, I. M. (2011a). Election Forecasts With Twitter. *Social Science Computer Review*, *29*(4), 402–418. doi:10.1177/0894439310386557

Turner, V. (1969). *The Ritual Process: Structure and Anti-Structure*. Ithaca, NY: Cornell University Press.

Tusa, F. (2009). How Social Media Can Shape a Protest Movement: The Cases of Egypt in 2011 and Iran in 2009. *Arab Media and Society, 17*.

Twingly. (2015). *The Blog portal* [my translation]. Retrieved January 3, 2015, from http://www.bloggportalen.se/BlogPortal/view/Home

Tworzecki, T., & Semetko, H. (2010). Media Uses and Effects in New Democracies: The Case of Polands 2005 Parliamentary and Presidential Elections. *The International Journal of Press/Politics*, *15*(2), 155–174. doi:10.1177/1940161209360698

UCC. (2016). *Post, Broadcasting and Telecommunications Market and Industry Report.* Retrieved from http://ucc.co.ug/files/downloads/Q1-Market-Report-for-Jan-March-2016-Mbaga.pdf

Ulbig, S. G., & Funk, C. L. (1999). Conflict avoidance and political participation. *Political Behavior*, *21*(3), 265–282. doi:10.1023/A:1022087617514

UN Broadband Commission for Digital Development Working Group on Broadband and Gender. (2015). *Cyber Violence Against Women and Girls. A World-Wide Wake-Up Call.* Author.

UN. (1995). *Beijing Declaration and Platform for Action.* The Fourth World Conference on Women. Available at: http://www.un.org/womenwatch/daw/beijing/pdf/BDPfA%20E.pdf

UN. (2005). *Women 2000 and beyond. Gender equality and empowerment of women through ICT.* Available at: http://www.un.org/womenwatch/daw/public/w2000-09.05-ict-e.pdf

United Nations. (1948). *Universal Declaration of Human Rights.* G.A. Res. 217A (III), U.N. Doc. A/810.

United Nations. (1966). International Covenant on Civil and Political Rights (ICCPR), G.A. res. 2200A (XXI), 21 U.N. GAOR Supp. (No. 16) at 52. *U.N. Doc. A*, *6316*, 999.

United Nations. (2003). *Social and Economic Council, Sub-Commission on the Promotion and Protection of Human Rights.* E/CN.4/Sub.2/2003/12/Rev.2.

United Nations. (2005). *2005 World Summit Outcome.* GA Res 60/1, 9, UN Doc. A/ RES/60/1.

United Nations. (2011). *Human Rights Committee.* General comment No. 34, Article 19: Freedoms of opinion and expression CCPR/C/GC/34.

Vaccari, C., & Nielsen, R. K. (2013). What Drives Politicians Online Popularity? An Analysis of the 2010 U.S. Midterm Elections. *Journal of Information Technology & Politics*, *10*(2), 208–222. doi:10.1080/19331681.2012.758072

Van Dijk, J. A. G. M. (1999). *The network society: Social aspects of new media* (1st ed.). London: Sage Publications Ltd.

Van Gorp, B. (2010). Strategies to take subjectivity out of framing analysis. In Doing news framing analysis: Empirical and theoretical perspectives (pp. 84-109). New York, NY: Routledge.

Vargo, C. J., & Hopp, T. (in press). Socioeconomic status, social capital, and partisan polarity as predictors of political incivility on Twitter: A congressional district-level analysis. *Social Science Computer Review*. doi:10.1177/0894439315602858

Vaughn, J. S. (2015). *Controlling the Message: New Media in American Political Campaigns.* NYU Press.

Verba, S., Schlozman, K. L., & Brady, H. (1995). *Voice and Equality: Civic Voluntarism in American Politics.* Cambridge, MA: Harvard University Press.

Verba, S., Schlozman, K. L., & Brady, H. E. (1995). *Voice and equality: Civic voluntarism in American politics.* Cambridge, MA: Harvard University Press.

Vergeer, M., Hermans, L., & Santms, S. (2013). Online Social Networks and Micro-Blogging in Political Campaigning: The Exploration of a New Campaign Toll and a New Campaign Style. *Party Politics*, *19*(3), 477–501. doi:10.1177/1354068811407580

Vernon, J. (2009). *Hunger: A modern history.* Cambridge, MA: Harvard University Press; doi:10.1080/03071020902778634

Villamil, J. (2012, May 22). Televisa y la Primavera Mexicana. *Homozapping*. Retrieved from http://homozapping.com.mx/2012/05/televisa-y-la-primavera-mexicana/

Von Koskull, C., & Strandvik, T. (2014). Discovering the unfolding of service innovations. *Journal of Business and Industrial Marketing*, *29*(2), 6–6. doi:10.1108/JBIM-05-2012-0084

von Stackelberg, P., & Jones, R. E. (2014). Tales of our tomorrows: Transmedia storytelling and communicating about the future. *Journal of Futures Studies*, *18*(3), 57–76.

Vraga, E. K., Thorson, K., Kligler-Vilenchik, N., & Gee, E. (2015). How individual sensitivities to disagreement shape youth political expression on Facebook. *Computers in Human Behavior*, *45*, 281–289. doi:10.1016/j.chb.2014.12.025

Wagner, K. M., & Gainous, J. (2009). Electronic Grassroots: Does Online Campaigning Work? *Journal of Legislative Studies*, *15*(4), 502–520. doi:10.1080/13572330903302539

Wakabi, W. & Grönlund, A. (2015). Citizens' use of new media in authoritarian regimes: A case study of Uganda. *Electronic Journal of Information Systems in Developing Countries*, *67*(1).

Wakabi, W. (2016). *Motivating eParticipation in Authoritarian Countries* (Doctoral dissertation). Örebro University.

Walker, R. (2014). *The shame of poverty*. Oxford, UK: Oxford University Press. doi:10.1093/acprof:oso/9780199684823.001.0001

Wallace, P. M. (1999). *The psychology of the internet*. Cambridge, UK: Cambridge University Press. doi:10.1017/CBO9780511581670

Wallsten, K. (2008). Political Blogs: Transmission Belts, Soapboxes, Mobilizers, or Conversation Starters? *Journal of Information Technology & Politics*, *4*(3), 19–40. doi:10.1080/19331680801915033

Wallsten, K. (2010). Yes We Can: How Online Viewership, Blog Discussion, Campaign Statements, and Mainstream Media Coverage Produced a Viral Video Phenomenon. *Journal of Information Technology & Politics*, *7*(2-3), 163–181. doi:10.1080/19331681003749030

Walter, T., Hourizi, R., Moncur, W., & Pitsillides, S. (2011). Does the internet change how we die and mourn? an overview and analysis. *Omega*, *64*(4), 275–302. doi:10.2190/OM.64.4.a PMID:22530294

Wansink, B., Tal, A., & Brumberg, A. (2014). Ingredient-based food fears and avoidance: Antecedents and antidotes. *Food Quality and Preference*, *38*(0), 40–48. doi:10.1016/j.foodqual.2014.05.015

Ward, J. (2014, February 4). Stillwater native has toned her body and rebuilt her life. *Minneapolis Star Tribune*.

Ward, J. (2014, February 5). *Twitter*. Retrieved from https://twitter.com/_jacobward_/statuses/431083808134139904

Watkins, P. L. (2015). Fat Studies 101: Learning to have your cake and eat it too. *M/C Journal: Journal of Media and Culture*, (18), 3. Retrieved from http://journal.media-culture.org.au/index.php/mcjournal/article/viewArticle/968

Watt, N., & Bowcott, O. (2012). David Cameron calls for reform of European court of human rights. *The Guardian*. Retrieved from http://www.guardian.co.uk/law/2012/jan/25/david-cameron-reform-human-rights

Web, M. D. (n.d.). *Body Mass Index (BMI), according to WebMD*. Retrieved from http://www.webmd.com/men/weight-loss-bmi)

Weber, B. (2014, February 6). Critics call The Biggest Loser irresponsible. *Here and Now*. Retrieved from http://hereandnow.wbur.org/2014/02/06/biggest-loser-rachel

Weber, L., Loumakis, A., & Bergman, J. (2003). Who Participates and Why?: An Analysis of Citizens on the Internet and the Mass Public. *Social Science Computer Review*, *21*(1), 26–42. doi:10.1177/0894439302238969

Weber, R. H., & Weber, R. (2010). *Internet of things: legal perspectives*. Berlin: Springer. doi:10.1007/978-3-642-11710-7

Wegge, D., Vandebosch, H., & Eggermont, S. (2014). Who bullies whom online: A social network analysis of cyberbullying in a school context. *Communications*, *39*(4), 415–433. doi:10.1515/commun-2014-0019

Weiss, A. (2002). *Feast and Folly: Cuisine, Intoxication, and the Poetics of the Sublime Albany*. State University of New York Press.

Wellard, I. (2014). Starting points and destinations: negotiating factual and fictional pathways: A response to Gilbourne, Jones and Jordan. *Sport Education and Society*, *19*(1), 99–104. doi:10.1080/13573322.2011.633773

Wells, R., & Caraher, M. (2014). UK print media coverage of the food bank phenomenon: From food welfare to food charity? *British Food Journal*, *116*(9), 1426–1445. doi:10.1108/BFJ-03-2014-0123

West, D. (2010). *Air wars, 1952-2008*. Washington, DC: CQ Press.

Wheaton, B. (1983). *Savoring the Past: The French Kitchen and Table from 1300 to 1789 New York*. Simon & Schuster.

Widdowson, E. M. (1993). Self-Experimentation in Nutrition Research. *Nutrition Research Reviews*, *6*(01), 1–17. doi:10.1079/NRR19930004 PMID:19094300

Williams, R. (1974) Television: Technology and Cultural Form. London: Fontana. doi:10.4324/9780203426647

Williams, Z. (2013, January 9). Skivers v strivers: The argument that pollutes people's minds. *The Guardian. Comment Is Free* [Blog post]. Retrieved from http://www.theguardian.com/politics/2013/jan/09/skivers-v-strivers-argument-pollutes

Williams, M. (1994). A reconceptualization of women's protest rhetoric: Women's quilts as rhetorical forms. *Women's. Studies in Communications*, *17*, 2–44.

Willis, J. (2014, February 5). Biggest loser scandal! Is the winner too thin? *Entertainment Tonight*. Retrieved from http://www.etonline.com/dailyfirst/143214_Biggest_Loser_Scandal_Rachel_Frederickson_Deemed_Too_Thin_By_Audiences/

Wilson, M., & Corey, K. (2012). The Role of ICT In the Arab Spring. *Networks and Communication Studies*, *26*(3-4), 343-356.

Wilson, K., & Keelan, J. (2009). Coping with public health 2.0. *CMAJ: Canadian Medical Association Journal*, *180*(10), 1080–1080. doi:10.1503/cmaj.090696 PMID:19433834

Winbladh, L. F. (2011). *LCHF: A fat food philosophy* [my translation]. Retrieved February 13, 2015, from http://www.sydsvenskan.se/mat--dryck/lchf-en-fet-matfilosofi/

WIP. (2013). *Estudio 2013 de hábitos y percepciones de los mexicanos sobre Internet y diversas tecnologías asociadas*. World Internet Project. Retrieved from http://www.wip.mx/estudios_wip.html

Wofford, J. (2012). User-generated content. *New Media & Society*, *14*(7), 1236–1239. doi:10.1177/1461444812453563

Wojcieszak, M. (2009). Carrying online participation offline: Mobilization by radical online groups and politically dissimilar offline ties. *Journal of Communication*, *59*(3), 564–586. doi:10.1111/j.1460-2466.2009.01436.x

Wojcieszak, M., Brouillette, A., & Smith, B. (2013). Outside. In *The Practices and Perceptions of Iranian Diaspora Journalists*. Center for Global Communication Studies, University of Pennsylvania.

Wojcieszak, M., & Smith, B. (2013). Will Politics be Tweeted? New Media Use by Iranian Youth in 2011. *New Media & Society*, *16*(1), 91–109. doi:10.1177/1461444813479594

Wood, C., Drayson, C., Dye, J., Thomasin, J., McDonell, P., Dillon, M., & Sykes, K. et al. (2002). Great Britain. In G. Spindler & F. Börner (Eds.), *E-commerce law in Europe and the USA* (pp. 246–253). Berlin: Springer. doi:10.1007/978-3-540-24726-5_5

World Bank. (n.d.). *Indicators for Monitoring Gender and ICT*. Available at: http://web.worldbank.org/WBSITE/EXTERNAL/TOPICS/EXTGENDER/EXTICTTOOLKIT/0,contentMDK:20272986~menuPK:562601~pagePK:64168445~piPK:64168309~theSitePK:542820,00.html

Wratten, I. D. (1953). A century of photography. *Journal of the Royal Society of Arts*, *101*(4894), 259–271.

Wren, A. (2013, July 7). The rise and rise of austerity blogs. *The Guardian*. Retrieved from http://www.theguardian.com/media/shortcuts/2013/jul/07/rise-and-rise-of-austerity-blog#comments

Wright, S. (2012). Politics as Usual? Revolution, normalization and a new agenda for online deliberation. *New Media & Society*, *14*(2), 244–261. doi:10.1177/1461444811410679

Wright, S. G., & Riker, W. H. (1989). Plurality and runoff systems and numbers of candidates. *Public Choice*, *60*(2), 155–175. doi:10.1007/BF00149243

WSIS. (2003). *Building the Information Society: a global challenge on the new Millennium.* WSIS. Available at: http://www.itu.int/wsis/docs/geneva/official/dop.html

Xenos, M., & Foot, K. A. (2005). Politics as Usual, or Politics Unusual? Position Taking and Dialogue on Campaign Websites in the 2002 US Elections. *Journal of Communication*, *55*(1), 169–185. doi:10.1111/j.1460-2466.2005.tb02665.x

Xenos, M., Vromen, A., & Loader, B. D. (2014). The great equalizer? Patterns of social media use and youth political engagement in three advanced democracies. *Information Communication and Society*, *17*(2), 151–167. doi:10.1080/1369118X.2013.871318

Yamamoto, M., & Kushin, M. J. (2014). More harm than good? Online media use and political disaffection among college students in the 2008 election. *Journal of Computer-Mediated Communication*, *19*(3), 430–445. doi:10.1111/jcc4.12046

Yamamoto, M., Kushin, M. J., & Dalisay, F. (2015). Social media and mobiles as political mobilization forces for young adults: Examining the moderating role of online political expression in political participation. *New Media & Society*, *17*(6), 880–898. doi:10.1177/1461444813518390

Yang, H., & DeHart, J. L. (2016). Social media use and online political participation among college students during the US election 2012. *Social Media + Society*, *2*, 1-18. doi:10.1177/2056305115623802

Yang, X., Chen, B. C., Maity, M., & Ferrara, E. (2016). *Social Politics: Agenda Setting and Political Communication on Social Media*. http://arxiv.org/abs/1607.06819v1

Yoo, J. H. (2013). No clear winner: Effects of the biggest loser on the stigmatization of obese persons. *Health Communication*, *28*(3), 294–303. doi:10.1080/10410236.2012.684143 PMID:22742588

Young, M. L., & Levine, J. R. (2000). *Poor richard's building online communities: Create a web community for your business, club, association, or family*. Top Floor Pub.

Yu, H., & Miller, P. (2005). Leadership style: The X generation and baby boomers compared in different cultural contexts. *Leadership and Organization Development Journal*, *26*(1), 35–50. doi:10.1108/01437730510575570

Zeiser, A. (2015). *Transmedia marketing: From film and TV to games and digital media*. Burlington, MA: Focal Press.

Zembower, K. (2014, February 6). *Twitter*. Retrieved from https://twitter.com/KatyZembower/status/431549411039408129

Zukin, S., & Maguire, J. (2004). Consumers and Consumption. *Annual Review of Sociology*, *30*(1), 173–197. doi:10.1146/annurev.soc.30.012703.110553

Zúñiga, G., Molyneux, L., & Zheng, P. (2014). Social Media, Political Expression, and Political Participation: Panel Analysis of Lagged and Concurrent Relationships. *Journal of Communication*, *64*(4), 612–634. doi:10.1111/jcom.12103

Zúñiga, H. G., Jung, N., & Valenzuela, S. (2012). Social Media Use for News and Individuals Social Capital, Civic Engagement and Political Participation. *Journal of Computer-Mediated Communication*, *17*(3), 319–336. doi:10.1111/j.1083-6101.2012.01574.x

Zúñiga, H. G., & Valenzuela, S. (2011). The mediating path to a stronger citizenship: Online and offline networks, weak ties and civic engagement. *Communication Research*, *38*(3), 397–421. doi:10.1177/0093650210384984

About the Contributors

Yasmin Ibrahim a Reader in International Business and Communications at Queen Mary, University of London. She researches on new media technologies exploring the cultural dimensions and social implications in the appropriation of ICTs in different contexts and has written on a diverse range of issues which affect humanity and society through our everyday interactions. Her forthcoming book on The Politics of Gaze; Image Capture and Consumption on Digital Media with Intellect examines human vulnerabilities in the digital age when the body embedded with mobile technologies is burdened through new forms of subjectivity where it becomes part data and part content. Beyond new media and digital technologies she writes on political communication and political mobilisation from cultural perspectives. Her other research interests include globalization, migration, Islam, visual culture and memory studies. She is a visiting professor at MYRA School of Business in Mysore, India

***

Mark Beech, full-time student, part-time teacher and sometime unemployed career politician. He is known to be something of a wordpress mangler and a camera wrangler. He is also a radio ham, a collector of uranium glassware, quite a slow runner, and a connoisseur of fine ales.

Marija Bekafigo is a political scientist at Northern Arizona University. Her publications can be found in Social Science History, Social Science Computer Review, and Comparative Political Studies.

Jonathan Bishop is an information technology executive, researcher and writer. He founded the Centre for Research into Online Communities and E-Learning Systems in 2005, now part of the Crocels Community Media Group. Jonathan's research and development work generally falls within human-computer interaction. He has over 75 publications in this area, including on Internet trolling, cyber-stalking, gamification, cyberlaw, multimedia forensics, Classroom 2.0 and Digital Teens. In addition to his BSc(Hons) in Multimedia Studies and various postgraduate degrees, including in law, economics and computing, Jonathan serves in local government as a councillor, and has been a school governor and contested numerous elections, including to the UK Parliament and Welsh Assembly. He is a fellow of BCS, CILIP, the InstAM, the RAI, the RSS and the RSA, senior member of IEEE and a member of the IMarEST with MarTech. Jonathan has won prizes for his literary skills and been a finalist in national and local competitions for his environmental, community and equality work, which often form part of action research studies. In his spare time Jonathan enjoys listening to music, swimming and chess.

Aileen Blaney is Faculty at Srishti Institute of Art, Design and Technology, India, where she is Course Leader in the MA in Screen Studies. She has published in the areas of film and photography studies, and is co-editor of Photography in India: from Archives to Contemporary Practice (2017).

Michael S. Bruner earned his Ph.D. in Rhetoric and Communication from the University of Pittsburgh. His current research is on public discourse about food issues. He is co-editor of The Rhetoric of Food (Routledge, 2012) and a contributor to the new SAGE Encyclopedia of Food Issues. His recent journal articles have appeared in M/C Journal and Communication and Critical/Cultural Studies.

Berenice Ceja is an alumna of Humboldt State University, currently working in Southern California. As a Research Fellow her expertise is in Feminism and Social Media.

Francis Dalisay (PhD, Washington State University) is an Assistant Professor at the Communication and Fine Arts program of the College of Liberal Arts and Social Sciences at the University of Guam. His research interests include international and intercultural communication issues in the Pacific Islands.

Kerill Dunne is an unaffiliated, independent researcher. He received his PhD from the University of Surrey in 2008. His PhD examined the ability of online forums to reverse political disengagement. His primary areas of research are E-Democracy and E-Participation.

Christopher Holmberg is a PhD candidate in Food and Nutrition at the University of Gothenburg, with a focus on online food communication utilizing an epidemiological and health promotion perspective. Mr. Holmberg has an interdisciplinary background with an MSc in Public administration, and he is also a registered psychiatric-mental health nurse (PMHN). Christopher has worked as a ward manager overseeing an acute psychiatric ward, and was previously a consultant for the World Health Organization department of Mental Health Policy and Service Development. Christopher is also a former research fellow at the National Center of Neurology and Psychiatry (NCNP) in Japan and is a member of Japan Society for the promotion of Science (JSPS), the European Association for the Study of Obesity (EASO), and International Society of Behavioral Nutrition and Physical Activity (ISBNPA).

Anita Howarth is a senior lecturer at Brunel University and researches on politics, communication and social issues. Her research focus is media interventions in policy and her concern is to investigate how and why the media legitimize or challenge, resist or disrupt policy. She has published on food poverty and food banks, migration and refugees as well as environmental and health risks.

Joanna Kulesza, PhD, is a professor of international law and Internet governance at the University of Lodz, Poland and an expert on human rights online for the Council of Europe and European Commission, most recently working in Ukraine and Moldova. She is also an expert for the Sino-European Cybersecurity Dialogue (SECD) and serves as Membership Committee Chair for the Global Internet Governance Academic Network (GigaNet). Her most recent publication on "Due Diligence in International Law" (BRILL 2016) follows five other monographs and over 50 peer-reviewed papers on international law and Internet governance. She has been a visiting professor with the Oxford Internet Institute, Oslo University, Justus-Liebig-Universität Gießen, and Westfälische Wilhelms Universität Münster. Kulesza was also a visiting researcher with the University of Cambridge and Ludwig-Maximilians-Universität München as well as a scholar of the Robert Bosch Stiftung, Polish Ministry of Foreign Affairs and the Foundation for Polish Science. She often engages with various NGOs working on cybersecurity and human rights.

Matthew J. Kushin (Ph.D Washington State University) is an Associate Professor in the Department of Communication at Shepherd University. His research focuses on social media, politics, and civic life.

Sergei Medvedev is a PhD candidate in Media Studies at Dublin Institute of Technology, Ireland. He authored peer-reviewed articles and book chapters on Transmedia Storytelling in Politics and Advertising. His research interests are in the areas of Transmedia Storytelling, E-Politics, Digital Advertising and Science Promotion.

Allison Pingley got her Ph.D. from the University of Florida and is an associate professor of political science at University of South Carolina Upstate. Her focus is on American politics, and specifically U.S. campaigns and elections, voting behavior, and media and politics.

Mahesh S. Raisinghani is currently a Professor in the Executive MBA program at the TWU School of Management. Dr. Raisinghani was awarded the 2016 Fulbright Award, the 2015 Distinction in Distance Education award, the 2008 Excellence in Research & Scholarship award and the 2007 G. Ann Uhlir Endowed Fellowship in Higher Education Administration. He has edited eight books and he has published over hundred manuscripts in peer reviewed journals, conferences, and book series and has consulted for a variety of public and private organizations on IT management and applications. Dr. Raisinghani serves as the Editor in Chief of the International Journal of Web based Learning and Teaching Technologies; on the board of Global IT Management Association; and as an advisory board member of the World Affairs Council. He is included in the millennium edition of Who's Who in the World, Who's Who among Professionals, Who's Who among America's Teachers and Who's Who in Information Technology.

Renira Rampazzo Gambarato is Assistant Professor in the Faculty of Communications, Media and Design at the National Research University Higher School of Economics, in Moscow, Russia. Her Postdoctorate in Film Studies is from Concordia University, Canada and she holds a PhD in Communication and Semiotics from Pontifical Catholic University of São Paulo, Brazil; a MA in Communication and Semiotics also from Pontifical Catholic University of São Paulo and a BA in Industrial Design from São Paulo State University, Brazil.

Pierlugi Rippa is Assistant Professor in the School of Managerial Engineering at Federico II University of Naples, Italy. He received his PhD in Business Management at the Engineering Faculty of the Federico II. He spent a period as Visiting Researcher at California State University, Chico, USA and at Wayne State University, Michigan. His research interests include information system management, ERP systems, Knowledge Management Systems, Innovation. He is author of papers published in international journals and presented at international conferences, and he received two awards for best paper in two different international conferences. He has been president for 2014 of the Global Information and Technology Management Association.

Celia Romm-Livermore was Professor at Wayne State University (retired from May, 2016) and Founder of the International Journal of E-Politics (IJEP). She published seven books: "Virtual Politicking" (1999), "Electronic Commerce: A Global Perspective" (1998), "Doing Business on the Internet" (1999), "Self-Service on the Internet" (2008), "Social Networking Communities and eDating Services" (2008), "Gender and Social Computing: Interactions, Differences and Relationships" (2011), and "E-Politics and Organizational Implications of the Internet: Power, Influence and Social Change" (2012), and over 200 journal articles, book chapters, and conference papers. Her research was published in The Harvard Business Review, Communications of the ACM, Information & Management, Transactions on Information Systems and other peer-reviewed scholarly journals.

Rodrigo Sandoval-Almazan is Professor of the Political and Social Sciences School of the Autonomous University of the State of Mexico (UAEM) in Toluca, México. He has been professor of the Graduate School of Public Administration (EGAP) and Business Administration (EGADE) of the Institute of Technology and Superior Studies of Monterrey(ITESM), Campus Estado de Mexico He is a member of the National Researchers System Level 2 . He has authored or coauthored more than 40 research papers. In 2013 he won the 2nd Latin American Award for Public Administration (INAP). Former Editor of the Academic Journal RECAI (Journal of Studies on Accounting, Management and Informatics) 2011-2014 sponsored by the UAEM. Dr. Sandoval Almazan is a member of NovaGob and some editorial boards e-government journals. His research interests include e-government, public innovation, information technology organizations, social networks in government and digital divide.

Karissa Valine is an alumna of Humboldt State University, currently working in the Seattle area. As a Research Fellow, her expertise is on Gender and Communication.

Aimée Vega Montiel is a Researcher at the National Autnomous University of Mexico, Center for Interdisciplinary Research in Sciences and Humanities. She is an expert on Gender, Media and ICTs.

Wairagala Wakabi is a long-time a practitioner in the field of ICT4D in East Africa, and completed his PhD in informatics at Örebro University. Wakabi's research interests include ICT and citizen participation in Africa, the use of new media in authoritarian regimes, securing ICT use for at-risk communities, and open governance. He works with the Collaboration on International ICT Policy for East and Southern Africa (CIPESA, www.cipesa.org) which is based in Kampala, Uganda.

Masahiro Yamamoto (PhD, Washington State University) is an assistant professor in the Department of Communication at the University at Albany, State University of New York. His research interests include communication in community contexts, civic and political participation, and social media.

Index

T

U

V

W

Y

CPSIA information can be obtained
at www.ICGtesting.com
Printed in the USA
BVOW02*2259141216
470833BV00005B/29/P

9 781522 518624